Selling Ancestry

Selling Ancestry

Family Directories and the Commodification of Genealogy in Eighteenth-Century Britain

STÉPHANE JETTOT

OXFORD
UNIVERSITY PRESS

Great Clarendon Street, Oxford, OX2 6DP,
United Kingdom

Oxford University Press is a department of the University of Oxford.
It furthers the University's objective of excellence in research, scholarship,
and education by publishing worldwide. Oxford is a registered trade mark of
Oxford University Press in the UK and in certain other countries

© Stéphane Jettot 2023

The moral rights of the author have been asserted

All rights reserved. No part of this publication may be reproduced, stored in
a retrieval system, or transmitted, in any form or by any means, without the
prior permission in writing of Oxford University Press, or as expressly permitted
by law, by licence or under terms agreed with the appropriate reprographics
rights organization. Enquiries concerning reproduction outside the scope of the
above should be sent to the Rights Department, Oxford University Press, at the
address above

You must not circulate this work in any other form
and you must impose this same condition on any acquirer

Published in the United States of America by Oxford University Press
198 Madison Avenue, New York, NY 10016, United States of America

British Library Cataloguing in Publication Data
Data available

Library of Congress Control Number: 2023936134

ISBN 978–0–19–286596–0

DOI: 10.1093/oso/9780192865960.001.0001

Printed and bound in the UK by
Clays Ltd, Elcograf S.p.A.

Links to third party websites are provided by Oxford in good faith and
for information only. Oxford disclaims any responsibility for the materials
contained in any third party website referenced in this work.

Acknowledgements

This book took six years in its making, during the tumultuous period of 2016–22, which is all too familiar to the reader. In this bewildering context, it was crucial to benefit from the support of well-established institutions: the French scientific institute (CNRS) and Sorbonne University, which allowed me to spend two years at the Maison Française in Oxford. I acknowledge with gratitude the generous assistance offered by François-Joseph Ruggiu and Perry Gauci: both have been a tremendous source of assistance and advice throughout these years. While the former initiated me in the importance of genealogical sources, the latter became my guide and cultural broker in Oxford academic life. Both patiently went through my chapters with enthusiastic and salient criticisms. I also wish to thank Denis Crouzet and Cyril Grange, the successive directors of my highly accommodating research unit (Centre Roland Mousnier).

I greatly benefited from my experience as visiting fellow at Lincoln College and from the stimulating environment of the Oxford Graduate seminar (1680–1850). I am also most grateful for the feedback offered by the convenors of the Long 18th Century Seminar (IHR), in particular Arthur Burns, Margot Finn, Amanda Goodrich, Sally Holloway, and Tim Hitchcock. For two decades, the Franco-British seminar hosted by Sorbonne University led to countless scientific exchanges from both sides of the Channel and to many publications. I am also deeply indebted to many archivists and staff at the Bodleian Library, the British Library, and the College of Arms, in particular Lynsey Darby and Clive Cheesman, who gave me access to an underrated collection of precious manuscripts. This monograph owes much to the exciting scholarship developed by Roberto Bizzocchi, Rosemary Sweet, and Daniel Woolf. My work is informed by the constructive remarks formulated by the examiners of my 'HDR' (French accreditation to supervise research), Lucien Bély, Fabrice Bensimon, Emmanuelle Chapron, Edmond Dziembowski, Liliane Hilaire-Perez, and François-Joseph Ruggiu. Their expertise and encouragement were crucial in my decision to publish this monograph. I am much indebted to Nigel Ramsay for his willingness to go through the first draft of the book. Many colleagues also consented to read my chapters meticulously: Joanna Innes, Sandrine Parageau, Julian Pooley, Allan Potofsky, Béatrice Robic, Anna Schaffner. Elizabeth Rowley, and Stéphanie Slockyj offered valuable assistance.

Moreover, many friends and colleagues kindly helped me in my research with references and inspiring comments. I would like to thank in particular Volker Bauer, Giles Bergel, Caroline Callard, Richard Cust, Emmanuelle de Champs,

Jean-François Dunyach, Robin Eagles, Markman Ellis, Henry French, Markus Friedrich, Claire Gheeraert-Graffeuille, Ann Hughes, Mark Knights, Gijs Kruijtzer, David Parrott, Valérie Piétri, James Raven, Isabelle Robin, Hamish Scott, Richard Sharpe, Jon Stobart, Rosemary Sweet, Naomi Tadmor, Simon Teuscher, Ted Valance, Daniel R. Woolf, Susan E. Whyman. The criticisms and detailed comments offered by the Oxford University Press reviewers were encouraging and invaluable. I am very grateful to Stephanie Ireland, Cathryn Steele, and her colleagues for their interest and patient support in publishing this book.

Finally, a special tribute to Marie, Juliette, Oscar, and Elliot.

Contents

List of tables, maps, genealogical tables, and illustrations	ix
Abbreviations	xi
Introduction	1
1. 'The milk of human kindness'	2
2. Defining the subject and its periodization	5
3. Ancestry and genealogy: a brief state of the field	9
4. Method and sources	16

PART I. A WIDE RANGE OF DIRECTORIES AND THEIR READERS

1. A Format for Every Use	23
1. Pocket guidebooks for aspiring gentlemen	25
2. Genealogical histories in octavo	42
3. 'Ornamental for the library': monumental folios and quartos	55
2. The Many Ways of Reading and Selling	71
1. Exploring readers' mindsets	73
2. Editorial strategies and copyrights	85
3. Genealogies and social shaming	97
Conclusion to part I	113

PART II. THE PUBLISHERS AND THEIR CUSTOMERS

3. Hundreds of Customers: Looking for Some Common Patterns	119
1. Wotton and the threat of 'displeasing accounts'	119
2. The Bethams and the making of the first British *Baronetage*	131
3. Burke's *Commoners*: 'A picture of England to future times as the Doomsday book is to us of England'	148
4. Family Ties and Publishers' Enquiries	168
1. The 'fountain-head' and the publishers	172
2. Women in the publishing process	189
3. Family feuds and legal claims	203
Conclusion to part II	225

viii CONTENTS

PART III. COMPILERS AND THE MAKING OF CREDIBLE NARRATIVES

5. The Protagonists of a 'Shoddy Industry'	233
1. 'At the risk of some booksellers' and 'unfortunate authors'	234
2. Servile authors and senior ministers	242
3. Impersonators and forged identities	255
6. The Keys to a Rewarding Posterity	266
1. Antiquaries and their prescriptive authority	268
2. Family devotion and reputation	287
3. Conflicts with the customers and their rewarding potential	296
Conclusion to part III	303
Conclusion	306

Appendices

Appendix 1. List of *Peerages* and *Baronetages* (1700–1835)	315
Appendix 2. The copyright of Collins's *Peerage* (1755–1768)	331
Appendix 3. Thomas Wotton's correspondents (1727–1740)	333
Appendix 4. William Betham's correspondents (1803–1805)	342
Appendix 5. John Burke's correspondents (1828)	345
Bibliography	365
Index	383

List of tables, maps, genealogical tables, and illustrations

Tables

1.1	Family compilations and their formats	23
2.1	A parody of mottoes	109
4.1	Wotton's untitled correspondents	174
4.2	Transmission of baronetcies among Wotton's correspondents	188

Maps

3.1	Wotton's correspondents	130
3.2	Betham's correspondents	139
3.3	Burke's correspondents	162

Genealogical tables

4.1	The Lloyds of Welcombe, according to William Horton Lloyd *Commoners* (1833) vol. 1, 244)	169
4.2	The illegitimate Julia Eliza Twisleton	211
4.3	Bethell Codrington, Bethell Walrond, and their kin	223
6.1	The Wotton–Abney family in Burke's *Commoners*	294

Illustrations

1.1	N. Salmon, *Short Views of the families of the present English Nobility* (1759) © The British Library Board, digitized by the Google Books project Digital Store 1474.aa.11	29
1.2	*The Pocket Peerage of Great Britain* (1778) © Bodleian Library, G.Pamph. 1315 (1)	31
1.3	William Kingdom, *The Peerage Charts, the Baronetage Charts* (1821) © The British Library Board, Tab.1337.c. (3.)	34
1.4	*The Master-Key to the Rich Ladies Treasury* (1742) © Bodleian Library, 24752 d.9	36
1.5	*Collins's Peerage*, frontispiece (1710). © Bodleian Library, 8vo M 51 Jur.	48
1.6	*A complete history of the English Peerage* (1763). © National Library of Scotland, AB. 8.90.2	63

X   LIST OF TABLES, MAPS, GENEALOGICAL TABLES, AND ILLUSTRATIONS

1.7 *A complete history of the English Peerage* (1763).   64
© National Library of Scotland, AB. 8.90.2

1.8 *Baronagium Genealogicum*. Frontispiece (1764).   66
© National Library of Scotland, A. 34a. 12–16

3.1 Reorganizing a family tree: the Hoghtons (Lancashire) (Betham, *Baronetage,*
vol. 1, 41)   134
© All Souls College Library, 4:SR.39.*c*.3/1

3.2 From pedigree to horizontal kinship: Sir Henry Etherington (Betham,
Baronetage, vol. 4, 11)   142
© All Souls College Library 4:SR.39.*c*.3/4

4.1 The complaint of Vandeput Drury (Betham, *Baronetage*, vol. 3, 205)   215
© All Souls College Library 4:SR.39.*c*.3/3

5.1 George Allan. Engraving by T. A. Dean after a painting by T. L. Busby.   254
© Durham County Record Office, D/XD 124/1

5.2 Sir William Dugdale (1656). Etching by Wenceslaus Hollar. Used as
frontispiece to Dugdale, *The History of St Paul's Cathedral in London* (1658).   255
© The Metropolitan Museum of Art, 2017.320.1

Abbreviations

BC	Burke's *Commoners*
BL Add.	British Library, Additional Manuscript
BM	British Museum
BNF MSS	Bibliothèque Nationale de France (Département des Manuscrits)
Bod. Lib.	Bodleian Library
CA	College of Arms
CC	Court of Chancery
CCI	Centre Culturel Irlandais (Paris)
CKA	Centre for Kentish Archives
CSP	Calendar of State Papers
EHR	*English Historical Review*
ERO	Essex Record Office
ERYA	East Riding of Yorkshire Archives
ESRO	East Sussex RO
GA	Gloucestershire Archives
GM	*Gentleman's Magazine*
NA	National Archives (Kew)
NPG	National Portrait Gallery
NRO	Norfolk Record Office
ODNB	*Oxford Dictionary of National Biography*
SHC	Surrey History Centre
YAS	Yorkshire Archaeological and Historical Society

Introduction

> Those gentle historians dip their pens in nothing but the milk of human kindness. They seek no further for merit than the preamble of a patent, or the inscription of a tomb. With them every man created a Peer is first a hero ready-made [...]. They, who alive, were laughed at or pitied by all their acquaintance, make as good a figure as the best of them in the pages of Guillim, Edmondson and Collins.[1]

In *A Letter to a noble Lord* (1796), Edmund Burke commented on the 'gentle historians' and the many family directories that were published in London at that time. He was referring to compilers such as John Guillim (*A Display of Heraldry*, 1610 and later editions), Arthur Collins, whose *Peerages* had been printed throughout the eighteenth century (thirteen editions in total), and Joseph Edmondson, who sold a luxurious folio entitled *The Baronagium Genealogicum* (1764) and *A Companion to the Peerage of Great Britain and Ireland* (1776). They were mostly indexers, journalists, heralds like Edmondson, or self-proclaimed 'authors' like Collins. Their publications typically listed all the names, deeds, pedigrees, alliances, and descendants of all living peers (*Peerages*), baronets (*Baronetages*), and later from 1830 the gentry that were related to the family. Some took the form of lists, charts, or lengthy family trees, while others contained anecdotes and narratives.

Between the *Baronage*, published in 1675 by William Dugdale, and the serial directories of John Debrett and John Burke in the 1820s and 1830s, numerous ancestry-related texts were launched, ranging from inaccessible heavy folios to a very diversified range of directories. As such works grew in number, they came to be sold in different formats and prices and circulated throughout Britain and its colonies. Their purpose was to satisfy dynastic pride, to provide a variety of information on titled families (names, connections, and locations), or to fulfil historical and antiquarian interests. Hence, these publications met the many needs of titled families as well as of those of the urban middling sort. Family members were often actively involved in the making of these directories, by sending personal details to the publishers or by writing long letters on pedigrees and

---

[1] *A Letter from the Right Honourable Edmund Burke to A Noble Lord on the attacks made upon him and his pension, in the House of Lords, by the Duke of Bedford and the Earl of Lauderdale* (London, 1796), 40. See also the French translation, *Lettre de Mr Burke à un noble Lord* (London, 1796).

Selling Ancestry: Family Directories and the Commodification of Genealogy in Eighteenth-Century Britain. Stéphane Jettot, Oxford University Press. © Stéphane Jettot 2023. DOI: 10.1093/oso/9780192865960.003.0001

2 SELLING ANCESTRY

various historical anecdotes. At first financed by subscriptions, these texts came in time to draw the interest of larger groups of London booksellers, who shared copyrights of increasing value. In 1725 Collins's *Peerage* was estimated at just £21, whereas in 1857 Henry Colburn sold John Burke's *Peerage and Baronetage* for the hefty sum of £4,900.[2] In the nineteenth century, hundreds of thousands of individuals claimed to be connected to ancient families. However, we still do not know much about these peculiar directories, their production processes, their place in the wider book market, and the extent of their circulation among the public. Far from being politically neutral, these publications raised many questions regarding their legitimacy and their reliability at a time of rapid social change. Were they expected to celebrate the exclusiveness of a 'natural' nobility or the deeds and merits of an inclusive aristocracy? Contemporary pamphlets and novels abounded with allusions to these texts. Precisely because they were so familiar to the public, they were mostly only mentioned in passing and so their wider significance is open to debate.

1. 'The milk of human kindness'

Burke's quotation fully illustrates this point. Borrowed from *Macbeth*, the expression 'the milk of human kindness' can either refer to a compassionate impulse or designate excessive sentimentalism.[3] The sarcastic tone applied by Burke suggests that it was used in a derogatory manner. The quotation was much later interpreted as conveying a sense of 'squeamishness', a 'lady-like fear of hurting people's feelings by telling the truth', and heralds and biographers were compared to writers who dipped their pen in 'honey-water, essence of violets, or parfait amour'.[4] Burke's pamphlet was a targeted swipe at Lords Bedford and Lauderdale, his personal enemies, who attacked him for having accepted a pension from Pitt. Burke, in turn, accused them of deceiving themselves by thinking that their families came from time immemorial and he reminded them that their ancestors owed their prominence to the dissolution of the monasteries and the generosity of Henry VIII. Similar criticisms had been made before, notably in 1719 by Richard Steele against several Lords such as Sunderland or Stanhope. During the dispute

---

[2] On Collins's copyrights, see the catalogue for the sale of William Taylor's copies at the Queen's Head Tavern in Pater-Noster-Row, on Thursday, 3 Feb. 1725. Longman trade sales (1718–68), BL, Sale Catalogues, C170. aa.1. On Colburn, see John Gough, *The Herald and Genealogist*, vol. 3 (London, 1866), 359.

[3] 'I fear thy nature: It is too full o' th' milk of human kindness To catch the nearest way'. Shakespeare, *Macbeth*, in Stanley Wells et al. (eds), *The Oxford Shakespeare: The Complete Works*, 2nd edn (Oxford, 2005), I, v, 15–17; James Adair in his pamphlet against slavery used the expression in a positive way, meaning empathy. James Adair, *Unanswerable arguments against the abolition of the slave Trade* (London, 1790), 45.

[4] From a reviewer of a *New Navy List* published by Joseph Allen (1846) in *The Spectator*, vol. 20 (1847), 882.

INTRODUCTION 3

regarding the Peerage Bill, he insisted on the primacy of politics over blood in the attribution of titles and declared that 'the milk such nobles are nursed up with, is hatred and contempt for every human creature but those of their imaginary dignity'.[5] If in the early modern Europe, blood and milk were often considered as vehicles of innate virtues, Steele was only hinting at the complacent education received by some noble children. If the negative meaning of the 'milk of human kindness' was pretty straightforward, the wider implication of Burke's criticism had been amply commented on and led to conflicting interpretations.

One response, formulated by radical writers, relates more generally to the vexing resilience of an aristocratic culture to which the many amateur historians and family history compilers contributed. William Cobbett quoted Burke to direct his attack on some other magnates who had been unfairly celebrated despite having engaged in corrupt activities in the East India Company.[6] After the Great Reform Act, William Carpenter, the London publisher of the *Political Magazine*, added to the list of 'gentle historians' other compilers such as John Debrett and John Burke, for their 'servile, if not sordid adulation' for the titled families.[7] Another radical journalist claimed that the strength of aristocratic prejudices protected these compilers from public scrutiny, and he deplored the devastating effect of their publications: 'the sons of painters and cotton-spinners declare themselves ready to defend the aristocracy to the death'.[8] Under the spell of these directories, many individuals were led to ignore their own family history, sacrificing the memory of their close and worthy ancestors to an aristocratic chimera: 'Men are to be found capable of drawing a sponge over whole generations of their kindred for an apparent increase of proximity to their pedigrees,' whereas 'we should have equal reason for honouring our own ancestors, however plebeian'.[9]

Burke's quotation has also been interpreted in a different way. 'Gentle historians' such as Arthur Collins or Joseph Edmondson, were accused of debasing noble values, by indiscriminately blending old families with newcomers. In his *Biographical Peerage of the British Empire*, Sir Egerton Brydges claimed that his work would be 'very different from former compilers of Peerages; of whom Burke speaks with so much elegance and just humour!'[10] He made sure that 'the families of true celebrity will be at once distinguished from those who are obscure' as the

---

[5] Richard Steele, *The Plebeian: By a Member of the House of Commons* (London, 1719), 8. *The Plebeian* was later republished by John Nichols in 1789.

[6] Cobbett mentioned the case of Lord Seymour 'who lived till the year 1708 and being an ancestor of dukes of Somerset his memory is honoured with a very encomiastic display by Collins of his incorruptible, inflexible consistency, disinterested patriotism and numerous other virtues. Thus it is, as Mr Burke says, "These gentle historians" etc.', *Cobbett's Complete Collection of State Trial*, vol. 8 (London, 1810), 131.

[7] *Peerage for the People* (London, 1837), 7.

[8] *The London and Westminster Review*, vol. 27 (July 1837), 102.   [9] Ibid., 102.

[10] Brydges, *A Biographical Peerage of the Empire of Great Britain* (London, 1808), preface, 1.

4   SELLING ANCESTRY

pen of the historian 'is guided by sounder test of fame; or less equivocal marks of infamy'.[11] In a later review of John Burke's compilation, Brydges complained that the 'new purchasers, who call themselves gentlemen, have come into their places, they are of a new class, [...] sprung from tailors and pawnbrokers, Jews, jobbers, and contractors, from public peculators and adventurous upstarts'.[12] In the Tory *Quarterly Review*, Burke's quotation was re-used in order to call for more 'personal encouragement and pecuniary resources' to help to produce respected family compilations. The absence of 'any attractive family history' risked undermining the position of the elite and depriving their heirs of constructive and stimulating examples.[13]

There is a third interpretation which moves away from debates around the survival or the debasement of noble ideals. If one defines the context of Burke's *Letter* more precisely, it appears that he was aiming not at the compilers as such but rather at the readers who were conceited enough to take their tales at face value. Burke's comment can be fitted into the growing literature on reading and its dangers which followed the rapid expansion of the book market in the Romantic period.[14] Histories of reading have warned us against the temptation of singling out one interpretation of a book at the expense of others. If he was condemning the way in which Bedford and Lauderdale used to read these compilations, Burke was not an enemy of genealogies as such. In a rather utilitarian line of argument, he had formerly stressed the need of fables and myth for the creation of social distinctions against the levelling principles of the French republicans.[15] Fictions about heroes and the deeds of ancestors were not simply to be dismissed if they served a wider social purpose that went beyond narrow, self-centred family pride. But if complacent and gullible aristocrats started believing in their own family myth, they would be likely to end up like their French counterparts. Burke's views may be compared to Francisco de Goya's aquatint *Asta su abuelo* (1799), reproduced as the frontispiece. Number 39 in the *asnerias* series, the illustration depicts 'a poor animal turned crazy by genealogists and royal heralds'.[16] The caricature can be seen either as a condemnation of the resilient influence of aristocratic culture or as a critique of its abasement through the selling of donkeys' genealogies. Donkeys, as well as foolish aristocrats, embodied in Spain the emerging

---

[11]   Ibid., 2.

[12]   [Sir Egerton Brydges], 'Ancient Country Gentlemen of England', *Fraser's Magazine*, vol. 7 (June 1833), 645.

[13]   *The London Quarterly Review*, vol. 72 (1843), 90.

[14]   See William St Clair, *The Reading Nation in the Romantic Period* (Cambridge, 2004), 131; Abigail Williams, *The Social Life of Books: Reading Together in the Eighteenth-Century Home* (New Haven, 2017), 256–7.

[15]   'The government of a civil society always involved this kind of trade-off, which created distinctions in order to serve the goals of justice and the common welfare,' Richard Bourke, *Empire and Revolution: The Political Life of Edmund Burke* (Princeton, 2015), 716.

[16]   'A este pobre animal lo volvieron loco los genealogistas y reyes de Armas'. The latter comment is found on the copy preserved in the Prado (no. G02127).

INTRODUCTION 5

urban elite. Some are portrayed as vain lawyers or clueless doctors.[17] Alternatively, Goya may have been alluding to the rather strange and fantastic effect these serial compilations might have had on some customers. They were deluded into seeing themselves as fashionable and worthy stallions from a long and worthy line, while to the spectator they appear as they truly are.[18] In the late eighteenth century, there were widespread European debates about the need to better accommodate the memories of noble families to the requirements of more inclusive national narratives. Linda Colley has demonstrated that in Britain the landed class had to reinvent its sense of honour to 'convince others—and itself—of its right to rule and its ability to rule'.[19] Similar views were expressed in Germany by August Wilhelm Rehberg in his *Essai sur la noblesse allemande* (1803).[20] A failure to do so would bring about, at best, comical creatures such as Goya's ass, or, at worst, bloodthirsty monsters, such as the French Jacobins.

2. Defining the subject and its periodization

For all its ambiguity and its richness, Burke's quotation offers a good starting point for considering the significance of family directories in the long eighteenth-century Britain.

Eager to distance themselves from antiquarians and genealogists, historians have for long regarded these publications with much circumspection. Augustus Freeman condemned them in the strongest terms in the *Contemporary Review* (1877).[21] As a positivist historian, he was keen to distinguish his archival expertise from amateur work. While he understood the need for families to rehearse and present their own stories, the publishers who profited from them deserved to be blamed. Their dubious compilations contrasted with more reliable undertakings, such as *The Great Landowner* by John Bateman (1883): a vast and systematic enquiry which was conducted through correspondence with all the most affluent families.[22] It was only when the herald G. E. Cokayne carried out more critical editions of the

---

[17] John Dowling, 'Burros and Brays in Eighteenth-Century Spanish Literature and Art', *Hispanic Journal*, vol. 4, no. 1 (1982): 7–21 at 15.

[18] On Goya and lunacy, see Peter K. Klein, 'Insanity and the Sublime: Aesthetics and Theories of Mental Illness in Goya's Yard with Lunatics and Related Works', *Journal of the Warburg and Courtauld Institutes*, vol. 61 (1998): 198–252.

[19] Linda Colley, *Britons: Forging the Nation 1707–1837* (New Haven, 1992), 193.

[20] Martin Wrede, 'De la haute noblesse à la semi-noblesse: formes d'existence nobiliaires en Europe au XVIIIe siècle', in Nicolas Le Roux and Martin Wrede (eds), *Noblesse oblige: identités et engagements aristocratiques à l'époque moderne* (Rennes, 2017), 47–71.

[21] For his rant against Bernard Burke: Edward Augustus Freeman, 'Pedigrees and Pedigree-Makers', *Contemporary Review*, vol. 30 (1877): 12.

[22] Barbara English, 'Bateman Revisited: The Great Landowners of Great Britain', in Didier Lancien, Monique de Saint Martin, and Pierre Bourdieu (eds), *Anciennes et nouvelles aristocraties de 1880 à nos jours* (Paris, 2007), 75–90.

6 SELLING ANCESTRY

Peerage (1887–98) and *The Baronetage* (1900) that these guides were viewed with less suspicion. As a result, for many decades, historians who have worked on demography and social and family history have privileged Cokayne's editions over previous compilations. John V. Beckett in his attempt to 'count the aristocracy' relied on Cokayne's directories as opposed to the 'contemporary listings of doubtful accuracy'.[23] In most historical studies of the period, these compilations are primarily used as part of a wider argument about British society and are not considered objects worthy of detailed consideration in their own right.

Paul Langford mentioned a few important directories such as Joseph Edmonson's *A Companion to the Peerage* (1776) which listed noble women who 'retained their title on mariage', Colemans' *A Satirical Peerage* (1782), and the last edition of *Collins's Peerage* (1812): 'one of the ways in which the virtues of the nobility were trumpeted to a mass audience'.[24] He also named the 'crank' William Playfair who, after his personal experience of the French Revolution, attempted to demonstrate that 'the peerage exemplified virtue, learning, invention out of all proportion to its numerical strength'.[25] David Cannadine has referred to the growing significance of 'consolidated systematic guides to the titled and leisured class' which were conducted on a British and imperial scale.[26] Dror Wahrman has alluded to 'the inventor-cum-publicist William Playfair' and his *British Family Antiquity* (1809), as well as Sir Egerton Brydges and the re-edition of Collins's *Peerage of England* (1812): both illustrated 'the quest for a new image of praise-worthy aristocracy' against the 'middle-class idioms'.[27] Should these compilations be seen primarily as a loyalist and circumstantial response to revolutionary events or rather as an already well-established commodity?

To provide a satisfactory answer, one should take a long view and consider the commercial ancestry behind the emergence of Burke's and Debrett's directories. Richard Cust has rightly argued in favour of a major gap between 'the great age of material celebration of lineage' of the sixteenth and seventeenth centuries and 'the gothic revival of the late eighteenth and early nineteenth century' which was defined by 'a very different set of preoccupations'.[28] Daniel Woolf has contended

---

[23] *The Aristocracy in England, 1660–1914* (Oxford, 1986), 483; John Cannon, *Aristocratic Century: The Peerage of Eighteenth-Century England* (Cambridge, 1984).

[24] Paul Langford, *Public Life and the Propertied Englishman, 1689–1789* (Oxford, 1991), 517, 541, 567.

[25] Ibid., 580.

[26] David Cannadine, *The Decline and Fall of the British Aristocracy* (New Haven, 1990), 13.

[27] Dror Wahrman, *Imagining the Middle Class: The Political Representation of Class in Britain, c.1780–1840* (Cambridge, 1995), 165; on Playfair, see Jean-François Dunyach, *The Enlightenments of William Playfair: Invention, Politics and Patronage in the Time of the French Revolution* (Princeton, 2024 forthcoming).

[28] Richard Cust, 'The Material Culture of Lineage in Late Tudor and Early Stuart England', in Catherine Richardson, Tara Hamling, and David R. M. Gaimster (eds), *The Routledge Handbook of Material Culture in Early Modern Europe* (London, 2017), 271; Nigel Ramsay (ed.), *Heralds and Heraldry in Shakespeare's England* (Donington, 2014).

INTRODUCTION 7

that after the late sevententh century, 'genealogical knowledge more generally had increased in value as a species of cultural currency' and therefore became 'erratic, undisciplined, or shallow'.[29] Hence the eighteenth century is seen either as the end of a former lineage culture or as predating the age of Burke's and Debrett's directories.[30] However, from 1700 to 1840, it appears that ancestry was at the centre of important entrepreneurial activity. Publishers labelled their directories with a whole range of titles: *Compendium*, *List*, *Companion*, *Synopsis*, *Account*, *View*, *Dictionary*, *Biography*, *History*, *Register*. In the many library and auction catalogues of the period, they were classified in different categories such as 'References', 'Dictionaries', 'Heraldry', 'Miscellanies', 'Antiquaries'.[31] In 1830, compilers such as William Perry defined his activity as an 'art, or science or branch of literature'.[32] Directories were also categorized as being part of the 'nomenclators, which constitute the useful part of the modern library'.[33] Their lack of clear generic boundaries might be considered an epistemological weakness, but it was also indicative of a process of redefinition which took place in the cultures and representations of ancestry.

This book attempts to provide a missing link between the seventeenth and the nineteenth centuries and by doing so questions the narrow definition which is too often attributed to ancestry. These compilations not only were perceived as registers of pedigrees but were endowed with transformative effects on the whole of society, whether nefarious or positive. They not only reflected profound changes within the social elites but contributed to making them acceptable and even legitimate. Such undertaking, which relied on considerable correspondence networks, continued to reflect important currents in knowledge creation and politics, in ways which have not previously been documented.

This book starts with the ending of heraldic visitations by the College of Arms, which was mainly caused by the violence of partisan struggle in 1688 and not by a declining interest in genealogy.[34] Unlike the heraldic visitations, the first

---

[29] Daniel R. Woolf, *The Social Circulation of the Past: English Historical Culture, 1500–1730* (Oxford, 2003), 113–15; see also Mervyn James about the 'proneness to present honour, virtue and nobility as detachable from their anchorage in pedigree and descent', *English Politics and the Concept of Honour, 1485–1642*, Past and Present Supplements (Oxford, 1978), 59.

[30] David Allan also wondered about the Scots and what they 'were doing between the celebrated historical productions of the sixteenth-century Renaissance and the "historical age" confidently detected by David Hume in the Third quarter of the eighteenth'. David Allan, '"What's in a Name?": Pedigree and Propaganda in Seventeenth-Century Scotland', in Edward J. Cowan and Richard J. Finlay (eds), *Scottish History: The Power of the Past* (Edinburgh, 2002), 147–67, at 149.

[31] See, for example, in London the catalogues of John Noble's circulating libraries in 1746 and of William Bent, *The London Catalogue of Books in all Languages* (1773).

[32] *The Gentleman's Magazine*, vol. 100, part 2 (1830), 410.

[33] 'A guide to the new-english tongue must have as great a sale as the British Peerage, Baronetage, Register of Races, List of the Houses, and other such like nomenclators, which constitute the useful part of the modern library', *World*, no. 102, 12 Dec. 1754.

[34] 'Visitations were abandoned after 1688, but reputedly because it was thought the Tory gentry would ignore William III's commission', Michael John Sayer, 'English Nobility: The Gentry, the Heralds, and the Continental Context' (Norfolk Heraldry Society, 1979), 14. Anthony Wagner laid

8 SELLING ANCESTRY

directories published between 1709 and 1715 had the advantage of being printed in London and circulated throughout Britain. Families were able to make their ancestors more widely known than through mere registration at the College of Arms. They contributed to modify the way their past was expressed and conveyed to a wider public. At the other end of the period, the Great Reform Act can be understood as an important shift in the redefinition of the national elite. The significance of this pivotal event was warmly celebrated by John Burke. He saw his cheaper dictionaries as a contribution to a decisive political change and to the strengthening of a new inclusive elite, whose openness would be demonstrated by 'a family history such as perhaps the annals of no other country could produce', which included 100,000 individuals.[35] Hence, it will be proved that the nature and scale of these directories changed over time, becoming more commercialized and broader in scope.

This research has been inspired by a variety of studies conducted on continental Europe. From the late Middle Ages to the early modern period, lists of nobility in Italy fulfilled distinct tasks. They had been used either to denounce unworthy *magnati*, to vindicate the independence of ancient and 'natural' nobles, or to coalesce old and recent families distinguished by the prince. In the latter case, these lists were later turned into 'golden books of nobility' which were 'transcribed on precious materials, and decorated with the finest illuminations'.[36] In the late seventeenth century, in most capitals, a distinctive trend could be observed with the decline of luxurious volumes and the rise of cheaper compilations, which were consumer driven and linked to urban growth and to a much higher circulation of prints.[37] In the German Empire, the *Special Genealogien* dealing with the territorial ruling houses were gradually replaced by the spread of *Staatskalenders*, which provided an annual list of office-holders. This shift did not lead to the irrelevance of genealogies, nor the rejection of birth over merit. Family directories were instead reconfigured to uphold the legitimacy of a renewed social elite but potentially could be used to 'criticize court life and the monarchical regime'.[38] In France, it has been argued that before the abolition of the nobility, genealogical

---

the blame on the Whigs. Commenting on the 'breakdown in heraldic authority', he accused the Whig grandees of having 'little interest in the strict regulation of a privilege—that of bearing arms—which they and the poorest gentry shared', *English Genealogy* (London, 1972), 117.

[35] *The Times*, 23 Jan. 1829. Simultaneously, William Berry launched a serie of 'County Genealogies', starting with Kent and Sussex.

[36] Federico Del Tredici, '"My desire would be to list them all": Lists of Nobility in the Cities of Central and Northern Italy (Late Middle Ages–Early Modern Period)', *Quaderni storici, Rivista quadrimestrale*, vol. 1 (2020): 139–58 at 149.

[37] Dorit Raines, *L'invention du mythe aristocratique: l'image de soi du patriciat vénitien au temps de la Sérénissime* (Venice, 2006).

[38] Volker Bauer, 'The Scope, Readership and Economy of Printed Genealogies in Early Modern Germany: "Special Genealogien" vs. "Universal Genealogien"', in Stéphane Jettot and Marie Lezowski (eds), *The Genealogical Enterprise: Social Practices and Collective Imagination in Europe (15th–20th Century)* (Brussels, 2016), 287–301.

INTRODUCTION 9

practices were kept closely under the administration of the state and the official 'généalogistes du roi' in the *Cabinet des Titres*, where all the pedigrees were registered. However, the royal monopoly on genealogies may have been overestimated, as it was challenged by various commercial undertakings in many cities and provinces.[39] In Paris, the *Grand dictionnaire de la noblesse* by Louis Moréri, for example, went through eight editions between 1698 and 1725. It played a significant role in ennobling actors and literary authors and functioned as a 'laboratory' where new social ideals were put to the test.[40] Moréri's *Dictionnaire* was part of the redefinition of the notion of credit and reputation. As genealogies became part of a commercialized knowledge on an unprecedented scale, the ability of the 'ancien régime' to discuss and reinterpret the noble values of birth and lineage should not be underestimated.[41]

3. Ancestry and genealogy: a brief state of the field

Beyond the specific subject of family directories, it is worth mentioning at least three recurrent themes in the existing research on ancestry and genealogy.

A first category of publications deals with the importance of representations and objects in the establishment of social hierarchies. It is only relatively recently that historians have been urged by sociologists such as Pierre Bourdieu to become more 'agnostic' and to pay more credit to the beliefs and assumptions of the individuals.[42] Far from being impartial judges retrospectively assessing the objective tenets of hierarchies, they ought better to record contemporary representations. In France, ethnologists such as Françoise Zonabend have carried out some collective enquiries with several social and cultural historians, such as André Burguière and Christiane Klapisch-Zuber, and these have led to the rehabilitation of genealogies as proper objects of scientific enquiry.[43] Moving away from the

---

[39] William Doyle has insisted on 'the pitiless and incorruptible scrutiny of the king's *juges d'armes* or his genealogist, Chérin', *Aristocracy and its Enemies in the Age of Revolution* (Oxford, 2009), 10; for a less centralized perspective on French genealogical practices, see Valérie Piétri, 'Les nobiliaires provinciaux et l'enjeu des enealogies collectives en France', in Olivier Rouchon (ed.), *L'opération généalogique: cultures et pratiques européennes, Xve–XVIIIe siècles* (Rennes, 2014), 213–43.

[40] Jean-Luc Chappey, *Ordres et désordres biographiques. Dictionnaires, listes de noms, réputation, des Lumières à Wikipédia* (Seyssel, 2013), 102. See also for the egalitarian effects of the 'the great chain of buying': Colin Jones, 'The Great Chain of Buying: Medical Advertisement, the Bourgeois Public Sphere, and the Origins of the French Revolution', *American Historical Review*, vol. 101, no. 1 (1996): 13–40 at 14.

[41] For a recent overview see Stéphane Jettot and J.-P. Zuniga (eds), *Genealogy and Social Status in the Enlightenment* (Liverpool, 2021).

[42] Pierre Bourdieu, 'La noblesse: capital social et capital symbolique', in Lancien et al. (eds), *Anciennes et nouvelles aristocraties de 1880*, 333.

[43] 'La culture généalogique', *Annales: économies, sociétés, civilisations*, vol. 46, no. 4 (1991): 761–847; Germain Butaud and Valérie Piétri, *Les enjeux de la généalogie (XIIe–XVIIIe siècle): pouvoir et identité* (Paris, 2006).

'factual criteria' such as acreages, positions, or wealth, social historians and demographers have increasingly been interested in the way in which individuals and communities portrayed themselves through their own narratives. Defining who was a gentleman and who was not no longer presented as a positivist process.[44] While Saint-Simon may have objected to the Rohans' fictitious ancestry, he 'nonetheless felt obliged to devote an entire chapter of his memoirs to "stories concerning the house of Rohan"'.[45] Eighteenth and nineteenth-century elites have been reconsidered by various historians, who have stressed the need to take more fully into account the strength of the 'symbolic and social imaginary'.[46] Social identities were defined not only by 'objective criteria' but by literary representations as well as judgements exchanged on a daily basis. In a rather agnostic way, Paul Langford contended that 'measuring public awareness of the distinctiveness of titles is an impossible task'.[47] There were, he added, a wide range of human emotions, whether it be anger, anxiety, happiness, or obsequiousness, which could be used as reliable indicators of the significance of rank and status within British society.

Furthermore, he rightly stressed 'the impact of commercialism on aristocratic manners', on the way they were understood by the titled families as well as the public in general.[48] Part of the symbolic capital was indeed firmly rooted in a larger material culture and in consumption habits. Social distinction and a sense of rootedness are reverberated through words, texts, clothes, images, and many other artefacts, whose potency relied on their ability to interact with each other. Family directories should not simply be perceived in isolation as historical discourses but as 'potent things', as portable objects of consumption, which interacted with other commodities such as letters, gravestones, linens, furniture, carriages, libraries, engravings, and portraits.[49] As well as moving beyond the distinction between truth and fiction, many historians invite us to reconsider binary oppositions such as exclusivity and inclusivity, tradition and modernity, birth and merit. In a seminal work, Neil McKendrick demonstrated that the marketing strategies of Boulton and Wedgwood relied on a complex interplay between exclusivity and inclusiveness, between aristocratic patronage and the

---

[44] Cyril Grange, *Gens du Bottin Mondain, 1903–1987: y être, c'est en être* (Paris, 1996); Robert Descimon and Élie Haddad (eds), *Épreuves de noblesse: les expériences nobiliaires de la haute robe parisienne (XVIe–XVIIIe siècle)* (Paris, 2010).

[45] 'Setting practical realities and familial myths alongside each other [...] allows us to see some of the otherwise-hidden mechanisms of social advancement in the Old regime,' Jonathan Dewald, *Status, Power, and Identity in Early Modern France: The Rohan Family, 1550–1715* (University Park, Pa, 2015), 4, 13.

[46] Among many references, see in particular Sarah Mazah, *The Myth of the French Bourgeoisie: An Essay on the Social Imaginary, 1750–1850* (Cambridge, Mass., 2003).

[47] *Public Life*, 521.   [48] Ibid., 579.

[49] On objects and social practices, see Gianenrico Bernasconi, *Objets portatifs au Siècle des Lumières* (Paris, 2015); Stephanie Downes, Sally Holloway, and Sarah Randles (eds), *Feeling Things: Objects and Emotions Through History* (Oxford, 2018).

wider public, while John H. Plumb wisely reminded us that 'the minds of men can carry contradictory ideas, even contradictory hopes, with consummate ease. The acceptance of modernity does not imply the rejection of all tradition.'[50] By the same token, gender boundaries have been amply revisited. In the last two decades, we have a better understanding of the considerable involvement of women in the material culture of ancestry: 'women contributed significantly to the gentry house's genealogical decoration, sometimes on a grand scale by commissioning, guiding, and even designing a building's architecture and interior decorative'.[51] From a geographical perspective, recent researches have been dedicated to the many overlaps existing in the consumption patterns of elite families, whether they resided in their country estates or in their London lodgings. The role of aristocratic suppliers is now better documented in the local communities as well as in the capital.[52] Similarly, family directories played a significant part in creating cohesion and distinction both on a local and national scale. They fit into the 'urban cultural service' which helped thousands of visiting landowners to navigate their way in the metropolis, 'away from their county networks, surrounded by a sea of strange faces'.[53] James Raven demonstrated that a London cartel of powerful 'book trade entrepreneurs' provided a large gamut of publications, which 'became prominent exemplars of the new decencies adorning the homes of propertied men and women'.[54]

A second theme deals with the relevance of genealogies beyond their function of establishing social status. Differences regarding the content and format of genealogies could be accounted for by divergent rationales, such as specific family expectations and religious and political agendas. Researching the peers' demographic behaviour, Thomas Hollingsworth reflected on the *Peerages* and their unreliable use of data. Moving away from passing a moral argument, he pondered the fact that these compilations catered to distinct family needs. Collins's first *Peerage* in 1709 mainly dealt with 'the character and achievement of former members of the family but generally omitted dates of birth of Peers' sons and

---

[50] Neil McKendrick, John Brewer, and J. H. Plumb (eds), *The Birth of a Consumer Society: The Commercialization of Eighteenth-Century England* (Bloomington, Ind., 1982), 71–5 and 316; on material culture and social capital, see Bruno Blondé, Natacha Coquery, Jon Stobart, and Ilja Van Damme (eds), *Fashioning Old and New: Changing Consumer Patterns in Europe (1650–1900)* (Turnhout, 2009).

[51] Marie H. Loughlin, *Early Modern Women Writers Engendering Descent: Mary Sidney Herbert, Mary Sidney Wroth, and their Genealogical Cultures* (London, 2022), 10; Daniel R. Woolf, 'A Feminine Past? Gender, Genre, and Historical Knowledge in England, 1500–1800', *American Historical Review*, vol. 102 (1997): 645–79; Susan D. Amussen, 'The Contradictions of Patriarchy in Early Modern England', *Gender & History*, vol. 30, no. 2 (2018): 343–53.

[52] Jon Stobart and Mark Rothery, *Consumption and the Country House* (Oxford, 2016).

[53] Peter Clark and R. A. Houston, 'Culture and Leisure, 1700–1840', in Peter Clark (ed.), *The Cambridge Urban History of Britain*, vol. 2 (Cambridge, 2000), 575–615 at 592.

[54] James Raven, 'Production', in Peter Garside and Karen O'Brien (eds), *The Oxford History of the Novel in English*, vol. 2: *English and British Fiction, 1750–1820* (Oxford, 2015), 26.

12 SELLING ANCESTRY

sometimes even of peers'.[55] Conversely, he noted that the *Peerage* (1827) published by the Innes sisters was more likely to include the families of younger sons. Hollingsworth pointed out the necessity to better contextualize these *Peerages* in order to understand their internal rationale, leaving aside the question of their reliability. Collins's pedigrees were shaped by the need to provide eminent ancestors for the new peers created after 1688, whereas the Inneses' *Peerage* was aimed at supplying data on close kinship for the extended family.

Hence, genealogies are to be seen as ego-documents, texts that offered insights into the strength and nuances of different 'family cultures'.[56] In each family, individuals are shaped by multigenerational layers of norms and behaviours, which greatly differ within a comparable social group. Naming practices, marriage strategies, and godparenthood are often used as reliable clues of idiosyncratic patterns through several generations. Families and their close or their extended circles of relations did not fit into clear-cut social distinctions and their behavioural differences regarding ancestry led to many possible explanations. Often of an unequal status, both close and remote relations exchanged letters about their ancestors, thereby maintaining solidarity and emotional bonds.[57] Such exchanges were not intended to be merely recreational or limited to a narrow private circle. Learning about and/or identifying with one's ancestors was a way to socialize and to develop a wider interest in history and politics. Genealogical artefacts transmitted their owner's perspective on religion and political issues. In the early modern period, dynastic and heraldic imagery was part and parcel of an intense domestic piety among the 'godly' gentry and the middling sort.[58] For some families, genealogies were often instrumental in providing partisan and confessional identities to their children. Kate Redford has demonstrated that far from conveying a so-called modern intimacy, eighteenth-century family portraits fit into the partisan struggles between Whigs, Tories, and Jacobites.[59] In the urban sphere, political debates and identities, too, were shaped by invocation of the

---

[55] Thomas H. Hollingsworth, 'The Demography of the British Peerage', *Supplement to Population Studies*, vol. 18, no. 2 (1964): 73–6.

[56] François-Joseph Ruggiu, Vincent Gourdon, and Céline Alexandre, 'Les cultures familiales dans la France de la fin du XVIIe siècle au début du XIXe siècle', *Ohm: Obradoiro de Historia Moderna*, vol. 31 (2022): 1–34.

[57] See, for example, Henry R. French, 'The "Remembered Family" and Dynastic Senses of Identity Among the English Gentry c. 1600–1800', *Historical Research*, vol. 92, no. 257 (2019): 229–46; Imogen Peck, "Of no sort of use"?: Manuscripts, Memory, and the Family Archive in Eighteenth Century England', *Cultural and Social History*, vol. 20, no. 2 (2023): 183–204.

[58] See Alexandra Walsham, *Generations: Age, Ancestry, and Memory in the English Reformations* (Oxford, 2023); Tara Hamling, *Decorating the 'Godly' Household: Religious Art in Post-Reformation Britain* (New Haven, 2010), 219–73; on the culture of civic loyalty as well the 'moral and ethical stance' apparent in the Kay panels of 1567, see Robert Tittler, 'Social Aspiration and the Malleability of Portraiture in Post-Reformation England: The Kaye Panels of Woodsome, Yorkshire, c. 1567', *Northern History*, vol. 52, no. 2 (2015): 182–99 at 195.

[59] Kate Retford, 'Sensibility and Genealogy in the Eighteenth Century Family Portrait: The Collection at Kedleston Hall', *The Historical Journal*, vol. 46, no. 3 (2003): 533–60 at 548.

family past. The latter gave a sense of purpose to Jansenist craftsmen in Paris who were actively engaged in the struggle against the absolute monarchy. What was at play was not a quest for prominent ancestors but rather the display of close alliances and the strength of their local standing. Horizontal bonds between neighbouring families were more significant than the antiquity of their lineages.[60] In eighteenth-century London, outsiders hoping to make their way into public life used their ancestry to reinforce their trustworthiness. This 'dynastic sensibility' was demonstrated for example by William Beckford's seal in 1739, which corresponded to the arms of his grandfather, William Beckford of Mincing Lane, 'a connection which would simultaneously gain him status within both the City and a wider social orbit'.[61] Family directories were also closely linked to the reconfiguration of urban histories, which are now understood as instrumental in the expression of civic values in the Enlightenment and the Industrial Revolution. The deeds of urban dynasties were included in larger narratives which appealed to the upper middle sorts and which incorporated archaeology, philology, numismatics, documentary, and natural history.[62] Antiquarians and authors of urban and county histories, though often derided, 'were important actors in that explosion of print and ideas, that thirst for knowledge and understanding which some have called the British Enlightenment'.[63] More generally, interest in the descent of ruling families was linked to larger projects related to local and national history.[64] In many ways, genealogy, after being artificially disconnected from other historical texts, is now seen as a more casual and multifaceted relation to the past.

A third theme relates to the circulation of genealogical knowledge across geographic areas and its complex reception, which involves many changes in meanings and usages. The 'social circulation of the past' has been dealt with convincingly by Daniel Woolf. But far from being restricted to one nation, genealogies provided ways of reasoning, of ordering facts and memories which crossed from one country to another. In the early modern age, textual communities in Europe shared the same interest in dynasties, heraldry, and its complex jargon. Several studies have demonstrated the existence of a 'republic' of eminent

---

[60] N. Lyon-Caen and Mathieu Marraud, 'Multiplicité et unité communautaire à Paris: appartenances professionnelles et carrières civiques, xviie–xviii^{e}siècles', *Histoire urbaine*, vol. 40, no. 2 (2014): 19–35.

[61] Perry Gauci, *William Beckford: First Prime Minister of the London Empire* (New Haven, 2015), 54.

[62] Rosemary Sweet, *The Writing of Urban Histories in Eighteenth-Century England* (Oxford, 1997); Helen Berry and Jeremy Gregory, *Creating and Consuming Culture in North-East England, 1660–1830* (London, 2019); Huw Pryce, *Writing Welsh History: From the Early Middle Ages to the Twenty-First Century* (Oxford, 2022); Nicholas Canny, *Imagining Ireland's Pasts: Early Modern Ireland through the Centuries* (Oxford, 2021).

[63] Rosemary Sweet, *The Discovery of the Past in Eighteenth Century Britain* (London, 2004), 3.

[64] There is a considerable scholarship on this subject; see in particular for the early modern period: Roberto Bizzochi, *Généalogies fabuleuses: inventer et faire croire dans l'Europe moderne* (Paris, 2010) (first published, Bologna, 1995); Hilary J. Bernstein, 'Genealogical History and Local History: André Duchesne and the History of France', in Bernstein, *Historical Communities: Cities, Erudition, and National Identity in Early Modern France* (Leiden, Boston, 2021), 235–75.

14 SELLING ANCESTRY

genealogists which was animated through the exchange of correspondence and manuscripts.[65]

In France as in the British Isles, there is plenty of evidence which makes the case for the intense circulation of knowledge and practices. French 'nobiliaire' were influential in the production of the first English reference book. The catalogue of names and titles written by Robert Glover and compiled by his nephew Thomas Milles, the 'Catalogue of Honour' (1610), was inspired by Claude Paradin's *Alliances genealogiques* (1561). Edward Chamberlayn's *Angliæ Notitia, or The Present State of England* (1669) was an adaptation of *L'Estat Nouveau de la France* (Paris, 1661). William Dugdale, too, in the preface of his *Baronage*, acknowledged his debt to André Duchesne and *his Histoire généalogique des maisons de Guines, d'Ardres, de Gand, et de Coucy* (1631). In the late seventeenth century, Huguenots who settled on the British Isles contributed to the transfer of antiquarian methods. In many ways, British directories copied or responded to French 'nobiliaires' and vice versa. Jacobite exiles crafted pedigrees which stood uneasily between English and French norms.[66] British *Peerages* were introduced as 'nobiliaire', thus enabling comparisons with their French counterparts, like Lodge's *Irish Peerage*, which was translated and sold in Paris in 1779.[67]

It was only during the French Revolution that a common genealogical culture was temporarily ripped apart. The antiquary James Dallaway referred to 'the total abolition of titular dignities which throw a melancholy grace over the detail of honours, which have been so rudely torn from their native branches'[68]. Using the metaphor of a tree, he depicted the British Isles and France as having shared the same roots since the Norman conquest. However, in the post-revolutionary time, right across Europe genealogies were beginning to be shaped by a national agenda. In Italy, the compilation of the 'famous Italian families', *Famiglie Celebri Italiane* (1819), undertaken by the patrician Pompeo Litta Biumi (1781–1851), could be seen as a reaction to the French invasion and the promotion of republican values.

---

[65] Jean Boutier (ed.), *Étienne Baluze (1630–1718): erudition et pouvoirs dans l'Europe Classique* (Limoges, 2008). On the 'archival turn' among European historians, see Markus Friedrich, *Die Geburt des Archivs: Eine Wissensgeschichte* (Munich, 2013); Alexandra Walsham, 'The Social History of the Archive: Record-Keeping in Early Modern Europe', *Past & Present*, vol. 230, no. 1 (2016), 9–48; Liesbeth Corens, *Confessional Mobility and English Catholics in Counter-Reformation Europe* (Oxford, 2019).

[66] Stéphane Jettot, 'Les vaincus des guerres civiles: exil et réinvention de soi dans la gentry jacobite irlandaise (xviiᵉ–xviiiᵉ siècle)', in Emmanuel Dupraz and Claire Gheeraert-Graffeuille (dir.), *La guerre civile: représentations, idéalisations, identifications* (Rouen, 2014), 77–94.

[67] 'Monsieur Collins nous a donné une nouvelle édition corrigée et augmentée de son nobiliaire d'Angleterre: *The Peerage of England*', in *Bibliothèque raisonnée des ouvrages des savans de l'Europe* (June 1741), 469. *Pairie d'Irlande, Ou histoire généalogique de la noblesse actuelle de ce royaume; Par M. Lodge, député teneur des archives de la tour de Bermingham* (Paris, 1779).

[68] James Dallaway, *Inquiries into the origin and progress of the science of Heraldry in England* (London, 1793), 364.

INTRODUCTION   15

In Britain, the production of William Playfair's *British Family Antiquity* in 1807 was an explicit challenge to the enlightened ethos and the French Revolution.[69]

In the European colonies, various artefacts such as bibles, family trees, or almanacs were moved across the Atlantic and reconfigured to better suit local expectations. Like the Britons at home, American colonists were encouraged by the state to take part in the celebration of the Hanoverian dynasty. Such interest was not only state generated, however, as both elite and non-elite communities 'asserted familial connections to achieve credit, inherit property, or argue for their freedom from slavery'.[70] Comparisons between the French and the British colonies is also helpful. Whereas the French nobility benefited from a firm legal framework on both sides of the Atlantic, certain cultural aspects of the British gentility generated much anxiety among the colonial elites. Reference books such as *Peerages* and *Baronetages* were useful for any gentleman in the British colonies eager to 'assess his own status or to gain insight into the status of his neighbours or prospective marriage partners'.[71] In Spanish America, colonial society embraced the enlightened values of merit and professional skills promoted by the administration, even though colour remained a key criterion in the prevailing social hierarchies.[72] During the American Revolution, there was a 'contemporary nervousness about the contingency and unreliability of identities'.[73] The colonial elite which were so keen to attach its families to British imperial gentility redirected their genealogical impulse towards a more republican mindset. Richard Smith, a representative in the Continental Congress in 1774–6 and brother to the New Jersey historian Samuel Smith, defended the 'important role of genealogy in shaping American historical identities in the early Republic'.[74] A few decades later, New Jersey's landed elite and the upper middle classes started to collaborate on collective and inclusive compilations such as *The Genealogical Register of the First Settlers of New England* by John Farmer (1829).[75]

---

[69] Cinzia Cremonini, 'Les "généalogies crédibles" de Pompeo Litta, entre tradition et innovation' and Jean- François Dunyach, 'Le British Family Antiquity de William Playfair (1809–1811), une entreprise généalogique', in Jettot and Lezowski (eds), *The Genealogical Enterprise*, 303–39.

[70] Karin Wulf, 'Bible, King and Common Law: Genealogical Literacies and Family History Practices in British America', *Early American Studies: An Interdisciplinary Journal*, vol. 10, no. 3 (2012), 470; see also her forthcoming book *Lineage: Genealogy and the Power of Connection in Early America* (Oxford, 2023).

[71] François-Joseph Ruggiu, 'Extraction, Wealth and Industry: The Ideas of Noblesse and of Gentility in the English and French Atlantics (17th–18th Centuries)', *History of European Ideas*, vol. 34, no. 4 (2008), 451.

[72] Arnaud Exbalin and Brigitte Marin (ed.), 'Polices urbaines recomposées—Les *alcaldes de barrio* dans les territoires hispaniques, XVIIIe–XIXe siècle', *Nuevo mundo mundos nuevos* (2017). <http://nuevomundo.revues.org/70742>.

[73] Dror Wahrman, 'The English Problem of Identity in the American Revolution', *American Historical Review*, vol. 106, no. 4 (2001): 1236–62 at 1259.

[74] Mark Towsey, *Reading History in Britain and America, c.1750–c.1840* (Cambridge, 2019), 216.

[75] On the new genealogical 'regime' after the American Revolution, see François Weil, *Family Trees: A History of Genealogy in America* (Cambridge, Mass., 2013); Francesca Morgan, 'A Noble Pursuit? Bourgeois America's Uses of Lineage', in Sven Beckert and Julia B. Rosenbaum (eds), *The American Bourgeoisie: Distinction and Identity in the Nineteenth Century* (New York, 2010), 135–51.

16 SELLING ANCESTRY

4. Method and sources

Critically engaging with this rich field of existing research, this book is organized in three parts. The first part covers the significance of *Peerages* and *Baronetages* in the history of books and readership in the long eighteenth century. It explores their financing, their marketing, and the various ways of reading them. As in many subjects related to the history of the book, the scarcity of materials left by London booksellers presents a significant challenge. However, using the considerable printed sources accessible in the British libraries or in digital collections, many references have been gathered in order to create a list of all the *Peerages* and *Baronetages* with their authors, publishers, prices, and formats.[76] These criteria shaped the meaning of these prints in many ways. The authors' prefaces provide many clues as to the general uses the public was expected to make of the directories. The latter were instrumental in identifying the growing number of names and connections which circulated in the larger public spheres in the provinces, in London, and in the colonies. As such, they were employed as portable gateways to navigate and to be seen in many circles. Some of these compilations were also used as didactic tools in order to make historical know-ledge more accessible. Some others were clearly designed as rare and expensive status objects aimed at distinguishing wealthy families and collectors from the middle classes, although we will see this functional approach does not do justice to the unpredictable ways in which readers were consuming these publications. For instance, printed genealogies, especially after 1760, could be instrumentalized to sustain radical ideas.

The second part focuses more precisely on families' expectations as expressed in their hundreds of letters to the publishers. This unique source-base has enabled us to gather much evidence about their status, their residence, their occupations, and their political inclinations. Of these directories, families were simultaneously the subjects, the main readership, and the co-authors. While genealogical guides were published in London, they relied on a constant flow of information from the counties to the centre. And reciprocally, their local standing was reinforced by these national directories. This interconnectedness between provincial circles and the London market place will be a guiding principle. Letter-writing has been recognized as an important tool in the creation of virtual sociability among the elite, but it was also an essential tool in the publishing business. The commercial success and growing spread of these publications relied on a new relationship between ancestry and the 'public'. In the early modern period, most families were

---

[76] Appendix 1. *The English Short Title Catalogue, Eighteenth-Century Collections Online, The Waterloo Directory, 17th and 18th Century Nichols Newspapers Collection, Nichols Archive Project, The John Johnson Collection, British Library Newspapers, The Times Digital Archive, The British Newspaper Archive, The History of Parliament, The UCL Legacy of Slave Ownership, The Clergy of the Church of England Database 1540–1835.*

more likely to deny any involvement in the crafting of their pedigree, and were keen to hide their participation. The credibility of their claims was better established if certified by an authority outside the family circle.[77] In the eighteenth century, publishers were more likely to stress the engagement of the 'public', understood as co-authors as well as informed consumers. As a consequence, the heralds and their expertise came to be challenged by elite amateur knowledge networks in the counties.

The importance of ancestry within hundreds of households has been explored through case studies of three compilations, published in 1727–41, 1801–5, and 1832–8.[78] Far from being neutral, these directories were defined by distinct expectations and historical references and reflected the political claims and self-justifications of different parts of the social elite. Even, if many correspondents were guided by the defence of their honour and status, one should resist a narrow utilitarian approach.[79] Individuals are motivated by unconscious impulses which cannot be easily reconstructed. Many families also genuinely believed that their participation fitted into a wider enlightened scheme. They saw their involvement and, in particular, the disclosure of their archives as an act of generosity and as a duty to inform and educate the public about certain periods in British history.

These letters also illuminate our understanding of how family values were negotiated and adapted to the clients' needs. They give a more nuanced picture than the prescriptive literature on patriarchy and lineage. Although their contributions were rarely acknowledged, many women were at the centre stage of the publication process, either as the main correspondents or else as providers of data to their husbands or sons.

The third and final part of this study considers the making of these compilations and the problem of their credibility. As in other periods, notions of truth and untruth were closely related to a social context. As compilers were mostly from a modest background, they had to struggle to defend the reliability of their works. There are countless derogatory comments among polite circles or in literary magazines about these 'unworthy hacks' and 'servile' and 'mercenary' authors. Some were even chastised during public trials and condemned as fraudsters or impersonators. Despite such negative publicity, most of these guides were commercially viable and sometimes highly successful. Even if many compilers remained obscure, a few managed to tap into the genealogical resources that they had gathered in order to improve their own social status as well as increase their

---

[77] Olivier Poncet, 'Cercles savants et pratiques généalogiques en France (fin XVIe siècle–milieu du XVIIe siècle)', in Rouchon (ed.), *L'opération généalogique*, 112.

[78] Appendix 3: Thomas Wotton's correspondents (1727–40); Appendix 4: William Betham's correspondents (1803–05); Appendix 5: John Burke's correspondents (1828).

[79] On the relation between archival practices and social status, see the stimulating introduction by Joseph Morsel, in Laurent Vissière and Philippe Contamine (eds), *Défendre ses droits, construire sa mémoire: les chartiers seigneuriaux, XIIIe–XXIe siècle* (Paris, 2010), 10–17.

literary reputation. A few obtained a benevolent treatment from such institutions as the College of Arms, the Royal Society, and various local antiquarian circles. These were instrumental in establishing the credibility of the compilations. Regarding their customers, publishers had a vested interest in maintaining a collaborative and harmonious relationship. However, when conflicts arose, whether these were engineered or not, a few compilers were crafty enough to fashion themselves as honest brokers beset by bullying clients.

PART I

A WIDE RANGE OF DIRECTORIES AND THEIR READERS

In the eighteenth century, the British book market was dominated by a tightly knit group of London booksellers. The key to their success was their ability to keep for themselves most copyrights, thus preserving considerable margins on their largely overpriced books (for the most part, novels, and dictionaries).[1] The legal case of *Donaldson v Becket*, brought by a Scottish bookseller in 1774 against his London competitors, might have led to the decline of the London book trade monopoly and to the growth of many cheaper and abridged editions.[2] While ready to recognize the long-term significance of this particular case, some historians have also argued that, with respect to bookselling practices, the continuity was remarkable down to the 1820s.[3] A greater need for capital and less profitable margins had reinforced the position of certain powerful firms, such as Longmans, Murray, and Colburn-Bentley. On average, retail prices per volume were estimated at 2 shillings in 1750 but registered a sharp increase in 1810 to about 6 shillings.[4] Ranging in price from 1 shilling to as much as several pounds, the cost of family directories such as the *Peerages* and the *Baronetages* kept them beyond the reach of most Britons. Even though they could be consulted in coffee houses and in the emerging circulating libraries, they were not objects of ordinary consumption.[5] Nonetheless, there is still room for interpretation as to what their intended readership would have been. Were they simply used by titled families in a self-absorbed exercise of admiration, or were they of any practical use to outsiders? The rationales behind acts of reading are indeed hard to retrieve and have justly been described as

---

[1] James Raven, *Publishing Business in Eighteenth-Century England* (Woodbridge, 2014), 201–5.

[2] See William St Clair, *The Reading Nation in the Romantic Period* (Cambridge, 2004), in particular chapter 6, 'The Explosion of Reading', 103–20.

[3] Raven, *Publishing Business*, 326.

[4] Ibid., 302; J. E. Elliot, 'The Cost of Reading in Eighteenth-Century Britain: Auction Sale Catalogues and the Cheap Literature Hypothesis', *English Literary History*, vol. 77, no. 2 (2010): 353–84.

[5] The annual income for a minor tradesman did not exceed £40 and a plain shirt would cost at least 12 shillings (prices collected from trade bills in the Fitzwilliam Museum collection for the years 1764–86).

20 SELLING ANCESTRY

'a bewildering, labyrinthine, common and yet personal process of reconstruction'.[6] Publishers and compilers themselves were hardly explicit in setting out their intended target. In prefaces, they rarely referred to their customers' precise needs, merely alluding to the undefined needs of the 'public'. The aim was to avoid being too exclusive so as not to discourage potential buyers. Publishers were reluctant to endow their publications with an overly practical design which would have reduced their social cachet. In his first *Peerage*, in 1709, Arthur Collins wrote: 'I shall not say anything of the usefulness of this work, as thinking it sufficient to answer for itself'.[7] In 1766 Edward Kimber argued that the utility of his work was so obvious that it did not require any explanation, adding that the book could be used 'on various occasions [. . .] it is well known how necessary it is for the man of business and the Gentleman, to be acquainted with the matters laid before'.[8] In a similarly vague tone, William Smith claimed that his alphabetical directories in 1778 'will show their utility in many instances'.[9] In 1790 George and Catherine Kearsley, the booksellers and proprietors of an annual *Complete Peerage*, were no more specific when they saw their publication as destined to 'add to the comfort, or increase the pleasures of social life'.[10] In 1813, the antiquary Thomas Dudley Fosbrooke was even more ambitious and described his *Biographical Peerage* as 'the best support to General History' by exposing 'ancient family documents' which, 'by the light thrown upon the manners and customs of particular ages, become most interesting indeed'.[11] In 1832, John Burke's *Genealogical and Heraldic History of the Commoners* was designed to cater to a 'large share of interest attached to such an object, both for the parties themselves and for all connected with them, by the ties either of alliance, friendship, neighbourhood, patronage or political constituency'.[12] Burke mentioned many social circles, from kinship to political life, but we are left in the dark as to how exactly his compilation was to be used in each of them. Furthermore, few archives survive of the leading London booksellers, thus compromising any further attempts to recover their practical functions.

There is much evidence that, depending on price and format, these compilations were intended for different categories of readers. The first chapter will be dedicated to a raw typology based on three main formats: pocket-size, octavo, and quarto-to-folio. Through the categorization of book history, we will deal with

---

[6] Alberto Manguel, *A History of Reading* (London, 1996), 39; Ian Jackson, 'Approaches to the History of Readers and Reading in Eighteenth-Century Britain', *The Historical Journal*, vol. 47, no. 4 (2004): 1041–54.

[7] *The Peerage of England* (London, 1709), preface, ii.

[8] *The Peerage of England, A complete view* (London, 21 July 1766), i.

[9] *The Pocket Peerage of Great Britain* (London, 1778), preface, ii.

[10] *The Complete Peerage* (London, 1790), preface, ii.

[11] *Prospectus of A Biographical Peerage, upon a plan of General Reading, Instruction and Entertainment.* Rachael Fanny Dashwood papers, NA, TS 11/289.

[12] 'Important works published for Henry Colburn', *The Quarterly Literary Advertiser* (Jan. 1832), 2.

three different reading practices. Different formats did correspond to different social needs and thus different social groups: some compilations could be read in passing, as pocketbooks for aspiring gentlemen, while others in octavo were advertised as reserved to a narrower public, titled families and their descendants who would benefit from more detailed narratives. Finally, we will consider the gilded luxury volumes in quarto and folio for wealthier collectors.

In the second chapter, the initial typology set out above will be somewhat blurred. As became readily apparent from perusing customers' letters to the publishers, readers regularly mobilized different formats in different contexts. Most pocketbooks were not kept safely in libraries and were unlikely to be preserved. Hence, most fell into oblivion and were eclipsed by the expensive folio, which as luxury items generated many derogatory comments. The literary trope of the isolated old gentlemen and his precious directory came into existence.[13] However, this well-known figure did not account for all readers' experiences. The latter were indeed multifaceted and could not be broken down into rigid social identities. Furthermore, it will be demonstrated that the same content could be sold through different formats. Only a small number of London booksellers owned the majority of copyrights. They were able to sell the same product in a variety of formats and prices, leading to a considerable porosity between these compilations. It should be noted too, that for various editorial reasons, some titles had nothing to do with the actual content of the book, notably when the publishers followed some anti-aristocratic agenda. Under the pretence of being 'historical' or didactic, such publications fed a more critical view of the titled families.

---

[13] See the incipit in Jane Austen, *Persuasion* (Oxford, 2004), 9.

1

A Format for Every Use

In his *History of the Worthies of England* (1662), Thomas Fuller assimilated different qualities of papers to different social status: 'There are almost as many severall kinds of papers as conditions of Persons between the Emperor and Beggar, imperial, Royal.'[1] Similarly, reflecting on rank and precedence in the publishing business, Joseph Addison wrote in 1712, that 'the Author of a *Folio*, in all companies and conversations, sets himself above the Author of a Quarto; the Author of a Quarto above the Author of an Octavo and so on, by a graduall descent and subordination to an Author in *Twenty Fours*'.[2] Though meant as a jest, Addison alluded to the hierarchical differences which pervaded every corner of the social fabric, even in the literary world. Applied to these compilations, this tripartite distinction is justified. The commodification of the family past was influenced by the stratification of the book market which has been explored in various studies. In her work on urban histories, Rosemary Sweet noticed that they had become recognized as a genre in their own right: 'their commercial viability marked them off from county histories, as did their subject-matter and intended readership'.[3] The folio county histories which had prospered since the early modern period were clearly different in scope and in price from the hundreds of local histories which mirrored the specialization of the eighteenth-century towns. These directories reflected this same fragmentation. From their descriptive list in the first appendix, we have sorted the titles into three categories of formats (Table 1.1).

Table 1.1 Family compilations and their formats

	Pocket	Octavo	Quarto-folio
1700–20	2	9	1
1721–40	6	3	2
1741–60	3	3	1
1761–80	11	14	7
1781–1800	12	5	4
1801–1820	13	2	4
1821–1840	17	10	3
Total (132)	64	46	22

[1] David McKitterick, *The Invention of Rare Books: Private Interest and Public Memory, 1600–1840* (Cambridge, 2018), 73.

[2] *The Spectator*, no. 529 (6 Nov. 1712).   [3] Sweet, *The Writing of Urban Histories*, 35.

Selling Ancestry: Family Directories and the Commodification of Genealogy in Eighteenth-Century Britain. Stéphane Jettot, Oxford University Press. © Stéphane Jettot 2023. DOI: 10.1093/oso/9780192865960.003.0002

24 SELLING ANCESTRY

At first produced in small numbers, pocketbooks came to represent the vast majority of our database, especially after 1780 when they were updated annually. After 1774, following the verdict overturning booksellers' claims of perpetual copyright, the book market started to make accessible cheaper publications, priced between 1 and 3 shillings. The cost pressures on booksellers as well as increasing competition led them to favour smaller formats. These were cheaper as they required fewer sheets of paper which could be cut into many more pages. Their print run was considerable and could be compared to those of *The Polite repository or Pocket Companion*, published from 1790 onwards, which exceeded 7,000 copies annually.[4] We can safely assume that the sudden increase of hereditary titles after 1784, boosted in the 1790s by the wars against the French Republic and during the Napoleonic Empire, played an essential part.[5] The sudden elevation of many families into the peerage and the baronetage had far-reaching consequences. The promotion of one individual rippled through many social circles outside his immediate kinship. Many individuals in search of patronage needed to stay up to date with the latest creations and comprehend the specific networks linked to each new title. This quantitative change brought about more qualitative effects. It created a renewed appetite for the landed ethos, heraldry, and genteel values which any aspiring gentleman could only ignore at his own peril.

With regard to octavos, we know from some surviving publishers' ledgers that their print run was much lower than the pocket publications, ranging around 1,000 issues.[6] Many of them were advertised as 'genealogical history' and aimed at providing more speculative discourses. Sold usually for over 6 shillings, they were advertised as providing not only a descriptive list of titled families but also some historical and biographical background. Genealogy was increasingly seen as problematic by most well-established historians; enlightenment values did not sit easily with family ancestry. Hence in long prefaces, the compilers went to great lengths to justify their projects, thus engaging with the usual criticisms voiced by enlightened historians. Two emblematic titles will be viewed in detail: Arthur Collins's *Peerage of England, or an Historical Account of the Present Nobility* (1709–68) and Egerton Brydges's *Biographical Peerage of the Empire* (1808).

Finally, we will consider the rarer, luxury editions published in several volumes, which reached the eye-watering price of £90 for Playfair's *British Family Antiquity* (1809). Customers' expectations in this case were of a different nature as far as the

---

[4] Nigel Temple, 'Humphry Repton, Illustrator, and William Peacock's "Polite Repository," 1790–1811', *Garden History*, vol. 16, no. 2 (1988): 161–73 at 161.

[5] M. McCahill and E. Wasson, 'The New Peerage: Recruitment to the House of Lords, 1704–1847', *The Historical Journal*, vol. 46, no. 1 (2003): 1–38.

[6] 1,000 copies of Collins's *Peerage* were printed in 1735 and in 1769. K. I. D. Maslen and J. Lancaster, *The Bowyer Ledgers: The Printing Accounts of William Bowyer, Father and Son* (New York, 1991), ref. no. 2918, no. 3783, no. 4838.

value of the object was concerned, in that it resided mostly in the quality of the engravings, the paper, and the binding.

1. Pocket guidebooks for aspiring gentlemen

From the Restoration onwards, a close relationship between urban growth and the circulation of pocket directories and reference books is established by historians.[7] They were used to provide a range of customers, including lawyers, merchants, and travellers, with useful reference materials, such as tables of interest and of fees, road maps, and accounts of weights and measures. They were part of a booming market of services and products which catered to the needs of the emerging middling sort. They were connected to the production of legal documents, receipts, administrative forms, and papers related to the processes of exchange, identification and registration.[8] Some reference books were intended specifically for ladies whose pockets, carried around the waist, contained all the accessories required in their social life.[9] Whether equipped with or without extra blank pages, they were applied to record family or personal events and useful information such as recipes and business records. How then did family directories fit into this broad category?

A shift away from the tedious and long pedigrees

Just as with other reference books, family directories were not intended to be read from A to Z but rather to be skimmed through so that specific data could be mined. They were both administrative and genealogical publications insofar as they supplied synoptic lists of titled individuals with a brief account of their public offices and dignities, ancestors, and descent. Similar registers were sold all over Europe as the modern states and the urban space grew in size.[10] The wider circulation of the social elites, both in their own country, in Europe, and even in

---

[7] On the importance of trade directories, see Perry Gauci, *The Politics of Trade: The Overseas Merchant in State and Society, 1660–1720* (Oxford, 2003), 28; P. J. Corfield, "Giving directions to the town': The Early Town Directories', *Urban History Yearbook*, vol. 11 (1984): 22–35; C. W. F. Goss (ed.), *The London Directories 1677–1855* (London, 1932); J. E. Norton (ed.), *Guide to the National and Provincial Directories of England and Wales, Excluding London, Published before 1856* (London, 1950); Stephen Colclough, 'Pocket Books and Portable Writing: The Pocket Memorandum Book in Eighteenth-Century England and Wales', *The Yearbook of English Studies*, vol. 45 (2015): 159–77.

[8] Raven, *Publishing Business*, 8.

[9] Jennie Batchelor, 'Fashion and Frugality: Eighteenth-Century Pocket Books for Women', *Studies in Eighteenth-Century Culture*, vol. 32, no. 1 (2003): 1–18; Barbara Burman and Ariane Fennetaux, *The Pocket: A Hidden History of Women's Lives* (New Haven, 2019).

[10] On the relation between state and identification in France, see Denis Vincent and Vincent Milliot, 'Police et identification dans la France des Lumières', *Genèses*, vol. 54, no. 1 (2004): 4–27.

26   SELLING ANCESTRY

the colonies, required better means of identification. On the continent, annual guidebooks offered lists of royal dynasties, noble families, and officials. Whether it be in France with François-Alexandre Aubert de la Chesnaye des Bois (*Calendrier des Princes et de la principale noblesse*, 1762) or the Habsburg Empire with *The Almanach de Gotha* (1786), most European 'Staatskalenders' provided comparable data. Justifying the alphabetical order of his dictionary, Aubert de la Chesnaye admitted that it led to the levelling up of ranks within nobility but retorted that it corresponded to the mere taste of the 'public'.[11] He published a directory of merchants in France as well as of all the species in the animal world.[12] Some *Staatskalenders* were used by statisticians to develop a comparative approach between the European states. August Wilhelm Schlözer (1735–1809), a teacher at the university of Göttingen, possessed a collection of *Staatskalenders* from all over Europe which has enabled a research programme based on the statistical exploitation of their lists of office-holders.[13] Apart from their portability and price, their prime selling point was to give an up-to-date snapshot of the titled families. Comparisons with the almanacs were often made, although Robert Dodd in his 1846 edition contended that 'an old almanach is by no means so useless as an old Peerage'.[14]

This practical function impacted on the way kinship was formally displayed. Most of the data were presented through a list of names, columns, and alphabetical tables which could be viewed at a single glance.[15] The first long-lasting publication was *The British Compendium,* sold for 5 shillings by Francis Nichols and which ran to twelve editions between 1718 and 1761, including separate editions for Irish and Scottish families. For each name, Nichols featured the title-holders, their most ancient ancestors, parents, and descendants. It was first sold in 1718 by several booksellers scattered all over London, and notably Thomas Griffiths at the London Gazette near Charing Cross. Griffiths provided the latest information, which was inserted at the last minute either at the end or in the

---

[11] 'L'ordre alphabétique m'a paru le plus convenable. C'est l'extrait de mon dictionnaire généalogique, dressé pour ceux qui n'aiment qu'à connaître les vivans, & qui se soucient peu de parcourir des degrés souvent secs et arides [...]. Le goût du public depuis plusieurs années se déclare pour les dictionnaires: c'est ce qui m'a déterminé; & le Lecteur éclairé, au milieu de cette espece de mélange de Rois, de Princes, de Grands & de Nobles, reconnoitra toujours dans un ordre si simple & si ordinaire tout chacun pour ce qu'il est.' *Calendrier des Princes* (Paris, 1762), vi.

[12] *Almanach des corps des marchands et des communautés du royaume* (Paris, 1753); *Dictionnaire raisonné universel des animaux, ou le règne animal, consistant en quadrupèdes, cétacés, oiseaux, reptiles, poissons, insectes* (Paris, 1759).

[13] Volker Bauer, 'Herrschaftsordnung, Datenordnung, Suchoptionen. Recherchemöglichkeiten in Staatskalendern und Staatshandbüchern des 18. Jahrhunderts', in Thomas Brandstetter, Thomas Hübel, and Anton Tantner (eds), *Vor Google: Eine Mediengeschichte der Such-maschine im analogen Zeitalter* (Bielefeld, 2012): 85–108.

[14] *The Peerage, Baronetage and Knightage of Great Britain and Ireland* (London, 1846), ii.

[15] 'Reference books were also at the forefront of innovations in finding devices to facilitate rapid retrieval of information,' Ann Blair, 'Managing Information', in James Raven (ed.), *The Oxford Illustrated History of the Book* (Oxford, 2020), 179.

beginning of the book.[16] Nichols's *Compendium* could be seen as a by-product of the numerous gazettes and newsletters which appeared after 1695. In the second edition of his *Compendium* (16mo), Nichols stressed the novelty of his work, 'I am very sensible, that a work of this nature, in which so many different persons, families, &c. are more or less concerned, must expose the Author to a variety of censures [...]. For though every reader will have his own sentiment, yet they may allow me to say, (and that without vanity) that none has ever done the like upon this subject, so perfect and instructive, and so small a compass; for brevity being the most excellent help to the Memory, I have therefore avoided tedious impertinences, which many books are swell'd with.'[17] His *Compendium* became a brand shared by many more booksellers such as Arthur Bettesworth in Paternoster Row and later John Klapton, and the sale of copyright raised up to £121 in January 1759.[18] They were later joined by Andrew Millar, who traded in the Strand for more than forty years. Bookseller to the Society for the Encouragement of Learning, he was the publisher of 2,000 books between 1728 and 1768.[19]

A similar product was sold from 1751 onward by William Owen at Homer's Head near Temple Bar (Fleet Street) and George Woodfall at the King's Arms (Charing Cross) for 1 shilling, along with free land-tax and window-tax receipts.[20] Under the title *Short View of the Families of the Present Nobility*, the directory had been composed by the antiquary Nathaniel Salmon.[21] Owen invested in many reference books on fairs, travel, and road maps, as well as gazettes such as the *St James's Chronicle*. Similarly, Woodfall invested in several newspapers: *The General Evening Post* and *The London Chronicle*. As previously, the complementarity of functions between gazettes and family compilations was confirmed. Salmon would gather most of his data from his publishers' gazettes in order to produce an abridged account of the present peers, 'their marriages, issue, and immediate ancestors; the posts of honour and profit they hold in the government' and 'their near relations, as was consistent with my design'd Brevity, that it might fall into every Hand'.[22] He was the first compiler to start with a description of the actual title-holder and to add further elements on his ancestors. Such a presentation will become the norm in most directories. Another selling point was that

---

[16] 'Preferments, birth and marriages, which have happen'd since this Book was in the press, that could not be inserted in their proper place', *The British Compendium* (London, 1718), 199.

[17] *The British Compendium*, vol. 2 (London, 1725), vi.

[18] Original Assignments of Copyrights of Books and other Literary Agreements between various Publishers (1703–1810). BL, Add. MS 38728, fol. 10.

[19] James Raven, *The Business of Books: Booksellers and the English Book Trade 1450–1850* (New Haven, 2011), 159.

[20] *Books printed for and sold by W. Owen at Homer's Head, near Temple-Bar, in Fleet-Street* (London, 1755).

[21] W. Raymond Powell, 'Salmon, Nathanael (1675–1742), antiquary', *ODNB*. Retrieved 23 Dec. 2019, from <https://doi-org.janus.bis-sorbonne.fr/10.1093/ref:odnb/24555>.

[22] *Short Views of the families of the present English Nobility* (London, 1750), i.

28 SELLING ANCESTRY

Salmon had devised an index which provided a bird's-eye view of all the peerage, thus allowing a rapid skimming of the notices (Illus. 1.1).[23]

Gazettes would then be used to puff up the compilations. In 1759 *The London Chronicle* informed the readers of the combined re-edition of all the *Short Views* for the English, Irish, and Scottish nobility, at 3 shillings each, for a bound copy.[24]

After 1760 the amount of pocket directories grew more rapidly, in parallel with the increase in numbers of parliamentary journals such as *The Debates and Proceedings of the British House of Commons* by John Almon. Almon had been selling a yearly *Royal Kalendar* with all the arms of the peers for 1 shilling and the *Military Register* for 2 shillings. The indexer and journalist Edward Kimber published a series of seven pocket compilations between 1766 and 1769 for Almon and the other members of the powerful London consortium ('conger'). Kimber drew most of his inspiration from Nichols's *Compendium*. It is very likely that his London publishers acquired the copyright after Nichols's death, although we do not have any evidence to substantiate this claim. In one advert, the *Complete Peerage of The Three Kingdoms* was sold for 2 shillings with the *Royal Kalendar*, as they were intended to be read together.[25] The family compilation would give some genealogical depth on the latest persons promoted by George III. The London consortium that Almon was part of invested in the *Monthly Review*, which delivered favourable reviews of their compilations. Kimber's pocket publications were favourably compared with heavy folios such as Robert Douglas's *Peerage* (1764), which was criticized for all its 'disadvantages of prolixity and a large price' and its many mistakes.[26]

Two years later, the *Monthly Review* dedicated several articles to the promotion of Almon's directories (*The New Irish Peerage*, *The New Baronetage*, *The Pocket British Peerage*, *The Extinct Peerage*, and the *Pocket Herald*). His *Pocket Herald* was advertised as 'the cheapest complete peerage ever printed in this kingdom'.[27] It was reviewed as 'a useful pocket companion for such readers as chuse to become acquainted with the various connections and alliances of the present representatives of all our noble families'.[28] About his *Irish Peerage* and 'its manifest superiority', the reviewer made sure to defend his credibility by pointing to a few mistakes which were attributed to the printer's giddiness in transcribing manuscripts: 'we must suppose him to have been blind not to have seen the difference, in the manuscript betwixt Richmond and Rutland'.[29] The mention of a few scattered minor issues was part of the strategy applied by the publishers to convince the reader of its general reliability.

---

[23] See also a comparable product published by Cave & Robinson, *Tabulae Illustres* (London, 1744).
[24] *London Chronicle*, 1 May 1759, issue 365.
[25] *London Evening Post*, 14 Nov. 1767, issue 6246.
[26] *Monthly Review*, vol. 36 (June 1767), 479.
[27] *A new catalogue of books and pamphlets, printed for John Almon* (London, 1770), 5.
[28] *Monthly Review*, vol. 40 (Jan. 1769), 175.   [29] Ibid.

I N D E X.

Containing the Dates of the reſpective Creations, and the Pages referred to.

	Dukes.	Barons.	Viſc.	Earls	Marq	Dukes.	Eldeſt Sons.	Page
1	Norfolk ——	1472		1483		1483	Earl of Surrey ——	1
2	Somerſet ——	1536				1547	Baron Seymour ——	3
3	Cleveland ——	1670		1670		1670	Earl of Chicheſter —	4
4	Richmond ——	1675		1675		1675	Earl of March ——	6
5	Grafton — ——	1675		1675		1675	Earl of Euſton ——	8
6	Beaufort — ——	1461		1513	1642	1682	Marquis of Worceſter	9
7	St. Albans ——	1676		1676		1683	Earl of Burford ——	11
8	Bolton — ——	1538		1549	1551	1689	Marq. of Wincheſter	13
9	Leeds, S. V. ——	1673	1673	1674	1689	1694	Marq. of Carmarthen	14
10	Bedford —— ——	1538		1549	1694	1694	Marquis of Taviſtock	16
11	Devonſhire ——	1605		1618	1694	1694	Marq. of Hartington	18
12	Marlborough ——	1685		1689	1702	1702	Marquis of Blandford	20
13	Rutland — ——	1295		1525	1703	1703	Marquis of Granby	25
14	Dover, S. D. ——	1708			1708	1708	Marquis of Beverly	27

3

Illus. 1.1 N. Salmon, *Short Views of the families of the present English Nobility* (1759)

30   SELLING ANCESTRY

When directories from other competitors were reviewed, they did not get the same benevolent treatment. *The New Peerage* published by Davis & Owen in 1769 was severely judged for its 'obvious' errors such as announcing premature deaths.[30] The reviewer was outraged by the fact that the Dowager Countess Fitzwilliam was said to have died in 1759 while she was still living until very recently. He mentioned its title, which was the same as the one devised by Almon: 'we cannot subscribe to the propriety of its title, *The New Peerage,* as it appears in reality to be little more than a new edition of Salmon's *Short View* of the families'.[31] Customers were warned not to be fooled by the 'new' label affixed to an old formula. In reprisal, Almon's *Extinct Peerage* was savaged in the *Critical Review*. It allegedly lacked the most fundamental sources of authority such as Sir William Segar's *Book of Honor and Arms* (1590): 'as Segar is the dictator of English genealogy, we cannot expect to see any extinct peerage of England complete, without marking his treatie'.[32] The reviewer was contrasting Almon's cheap and unreliable book to the putatively respectable source provided by an Elizabethan herald.

In 1778, William Smith printed a *Pocket Peerage* for 2 shillings, adding on the frontispiece that he 'sells stationary ware, and all other manufactures by commission; and cleans Pictures by ingredients which cannot hurt the painting. He also sells the Jesuits balsam for the cure of green wounds, and a well experienced sear cloth for the cure of old ones.'[33] His *Peerage* was part of a miscellaneous list of products which could be useful to a wide range of customers. Some readers would condemn these adverts as being contrary to the dignity of titled families. The 'bibliomaniac', Sir Thomas Phillipps, later complained about the incongruous blend between polite publications and medical advertisement: 'Nothing is more disgusting than to find mixed up with literary food such ingredients as these "Ornamental hair at Ross & Sons!", "a certain cure for all corns & Bunions!", "Distortion of the spine".'[34]

Furthermore, William Smith claimed to offer in his *Pocket Peerage* 'a concise view, thereof to help the memory and to discover individuals en passant, by alphabetical directories'.[35] Encounters with social superiors were often unexpected, and so, to facilitate an instant check, Smith separated in series of columns, titles, family names, and mottoes with some initials: E for English and Earl, I for Irish, and so on (Illus. 1.2).

In the late eighteenth century, the sudden rise in the creation of titles proved the commercial viability of these pocket calendars. They were sold by a few

---

[30] *Monthly Review*, vol. 41 (Dec. 1769), 239.   [31] Ibid.

[32] *Critical Review*, vol. 27 (Oct. 1769), 288.

[33] See also his advert in the *St James's Chronicle*, 21 Nov. 1778, issue 2760.

[34] Sir Thomas Phillipps to the Revd Hartshorn, Bod. Lib. MS Phillipps-Robinson, c. 224, fol. 14, Jan. 1839.

[35] *The Pocket Peerage of Great Britain*, preface.

PEERAGE DIRECTORY.

C.

Candide et conftanter,	Coventry,	E E	Coventry
Candor dat viribus alas,	Belvidere,	I E	Rochfort
Caffis tutiffima virtus,	{ Cholmondeley, E E { Cholmondeley, I V		Cholmon- dely
Cavendo tutus,	Devonfhire,	E D	Cavendifh
Caufe caufed it,	Elphingfton,	S B	Elphingfton
Che fara fara,	Bedford,	E D	Ruffel
Clarior e tenebris,	Miltown,	I E	Leefon
Cœlum non animum,	Waldegrave,	E E	Waldgrave
Comme je fus,	{ Dudley and { Ward,	E V	Ward
Commit thy work to God,	Caithnefs,	S E	Sinclair
Confido,	Kilmarnock	S E	Boyd
Confido conquiefco,	Dyfart,	S E	Tollemache
Confequitur quodcun- que petit,	} Beƈtive,	I E	Taylor
Confilio et animis,	Lauderdale,	S E	Maitland
Conftantia et virtute,	Amherft,	E B	Amherft
Cor unum, via una,	Exeter,	E E	Cecil
Courage fans peur,	Gage,	I V	Gage
Craignez honte,	Portland,	E D	Bentinck
Crede Byron,	Byron,	E B	Byron
Crefcit fub pondere virtus,	{ Denbigh, { Defmond,	E E I E	Fielding
Crom a boo,	{ Leinfter, { Leinfter,	I D E V	Fitzgerald
Cruci dum fpiro fido,	Netterville,	I V	Netterville

B 2   Data

Illus. 1.2 *The Pocket Peerage of Great Britain* (1778)
© Bodleian Library, G.Pamph. 1315 (1)

32 SELLING ANCESTRY

booksellers, notably John Debrett (John Almon's successor in Piccadilly), John Stockdale, George Kersley, and John Fielding. Debrett, who had been apprenticed to Robert Davis, the co-publisher of *The Short View of the Families*, went to work for Almon for the edition of the *New Peerage*. He then merged the two directories into one issue in 1784 and launched with William Clarke the *Peerage Directory* (Debrett & Clarke, 1790–1) at the selling cost of just 1 shilling. The bookseller John George Kearsley and his wife invested in the smallest format (18mo) but were mostly copying the standards initiated by Nichols in 1717 in his *Compendium*.

The most inventive graphical representation was later conceived by William Kingdom in 1821 under the title *The Peerage Chart, the Baronetage Chart*. For 5 shillings, his *Peerage Chart* is 'printed upon a sheet drawing paper, and embellished with the Coronets of the Several Orders of Nobility, tastefully coloured', 'exhibiting at one view, much interesting information, and forming, upon the whole, a complete Peerage in Miniature'.[36] He published a large sheet, embellished with a few coloured engravings, which could be folded in one's pocket for 5 shillings, in a neat case for 8 shillings, or on canvas and rollers for 10 shillings. His alphabetical charts included a few decisive elements which can be read in a few seconds: the name of the current title-holder, the date of creation, number in descent, age of the present baronet or peer, his marital status, number of children and the origins of his title (army, legal, wealth) as well as the century of the first supposed paternal ancestor (Illus. 1.3).

The most interesting innovation was the indication of the means used by the family to obtain the title. William Kingdom did not bother to account for the deeds of the baronets and the peers by providing elaborate narratives. In a quantitative manner, each family whether old or recent was attributed the same amount of space in the chart. In a descriptive and straightforward manner, it pointed to the fact that most families owed their rise to being courtiers, professional (legal, civic), military, or even through 'the influence of their wealth'. According to Kingdom's chart, most families gained their title from their money. Furthermore, the origins of these families, however remote and prestigious, were clearly separated from the conditions in which they obtained their titles. Kingdom's charts may have been inspired by the synoptic biographical and historical charts published by Joseph Priestley in 1769 with their horizontal and vertical distribution of dates and names.[37] Vertically, the reader was able to look at all the empires in the world and horizontally to follow their evolution through each century. As they indicated a breakthrough in the history of chronographic representation, Priestley's charts had been very influential and were later applied in many pedagogical publications in the late eighteenth and early nineteenth

[36] W. Kingdom, *The Peerage Chart for 1821* (London, 1821–3).
[37] On Priestley, see Daniel Rosenberg and Anthony Grafton, *Cartographies of Times: A Visual History of the Timeline* (Princeton, 2010), 119–27.

centuries. C. V. Lavoisne's *New Genealogical, Historical and Chronological Atlas* (1807) was based upon similar principles. Unlike a complex family tree, Kingdom's charts did not require much effort to comprehend and were designed to give an instantaneous view of the recent and ancient British peers in 1821. As in the historical charts, the need to condense many family data in a cheap and pocket format led to a remarkable creativity in terms of graphic representations. Publishers such as William Smith or William Kingdom were breaking away from the old-fashioned and self-centred family tree. Their books could be seen either as a debased form of genealogical culture or as useful guides into the London scene for a wider readership. A similar point could be made about the publication by William Robson of a London directory which included the residences of most merchants, manufacturers as well as 'fifteen thousand of the nobility and gentry'.[38]

Making one's way into social venues

From the last example, one can easily see why these calendars were accused of debasing the very essence of nobility. Some contemporaries suspected them of being little more than a tool for preying on available heiresses. In his study on aristocratic marriage in Ireland, A. P. W. Malcomson mentioned a fake guide to Irish heiresses: *The Irish Register or a List of Duchess Dowagers, Countesses, Widows Ladies and Misses of Large Fortune* (1742).[39] A similar theme could be seen in other publications, notably *The Master-Key to the Rich Ladies Treasury or the Widower and Batchelor's Directory* (1742) (Illus. 1.4).[40]

This satirical vein was further explored in *Harris's list; or, Cupid's London directory* (1757–95) displayed as a polite guide for the 'Man of pleasure' to prostitutes. These were unfounded accusations. These publications expressed either the anxieties caused by the threat of some impersonators and rakes in the great metropolis or a more radical agenda by pointing out the debasement of the old families which could be bought off. In the peerage, most unions remained endogamous. In fact, the idea of an open English aristocracy has been much contested by historians. John Beckett has reminded us that, in the eighteenth century, '81 dukes contracted 102 marriages, of which 53 were with the daughters

---

[38] *Robson's London directory, street key, classification of trades, and royal court guide and peerage* (London, 1842).

[39] A. P. W. Malcomson, *The Pursuit of the Heiress: Aristocratic Marriage in Ireland, 1750–1820* (Belfast, 1982), 26.

[40] 'Now could any Method have been found more expedient to remove these stumbling blocks in the road to Fortune and Matrimony than the following?—In the first column, Gentlemen—you have the Title or Name of the Lady;—in the second her Place of Abode;—in the third, her reputed Fortune,—and in the fourth, you will find her Fortunes in the Stocks, as rated in the respective Companies Lists', *The Master-Key*, preface, iv.

Illus. 1.3 William Kingdom, *The Peerage Charts, the Baronetage Charts* (1821)
© The British Library Board, Tab.1337.c. (3.)

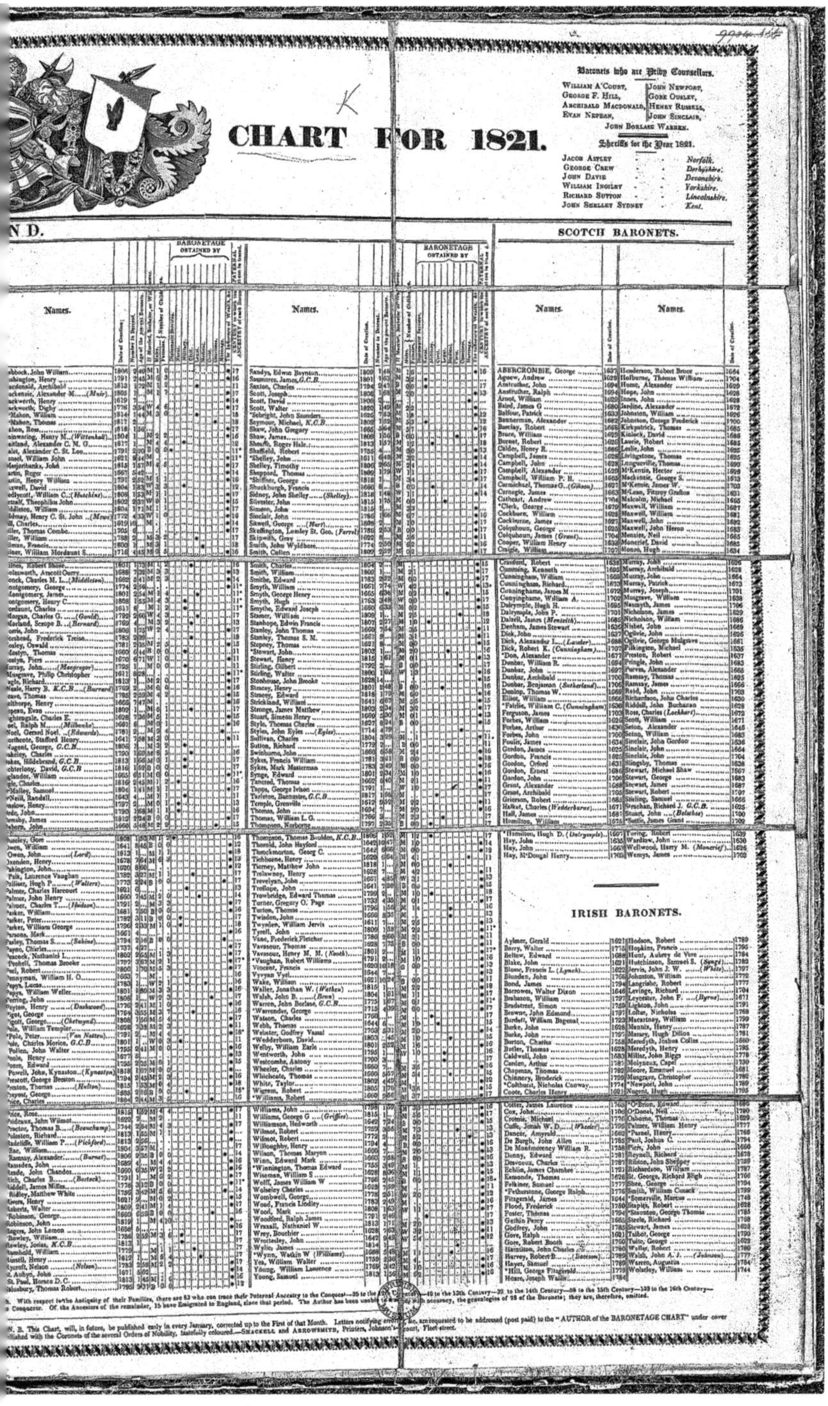
CHART FOR 1821.
Baronets who are Privy Counsellors.
William A'Court,
George F. Hill,
Archibald Macdonald,
Evan Nepean,
John Newport,
Gore Ouseley,
Henry Russell,
John Sinclair,
John Borlase Warren.
Sheriffs for the Year 1821.
Jacob Astley - - - Norfolk.
George Crew - - - Derbyshire.
John Davie - - - Devonshire.
William Ingilby - - - Yorkshire.
Richard Sutton - - - Lincolnshire.
John Shelley Sydney - - - Kent.
N D.
SCOTCH BARONETS.
BARONETAGE OBTAINED BY
Names.
IRISH BARONETS.

36 SELLING ANCESTRY

A

MASTER-KEY

TO THE

RICH LADIES TREASURY.

Duchefs Dowagers.

Titles.	Places of Abode.	Reputed Fortunes.	In the Stocks.
Duchefs . of			
A THOLE	- -	40,000	
Buckingham	*St.* James's Park	60,000	
Gordon	Pall-Mall -	50,000	
Hamilton -	Pall-Mall -	50,0c0	
Kendal *and* Munfter	Grofvenor-Square	80,000	4000. S. S. 2000. E. I.
Kent -	*St.* James's Square	50,000	
Manchefter -	Dover Street	40,000	
Marlborough	Pall-Mall -	Millions	4000. B. -
Norfolk -	Arlington Street	50,000	
Rutland -	Grofvenor Square	40,000	
Rutland -	Chelfea -	40,000	
Wharton -	Soho - -	30,000	

Marchionefs Dowagers.

Marchionefs of			
Annandale -	Pall-mall -	40,000	1000 S.S.
Blandford -	Grofvenor-fquare	40,000	
Montandre -	Brook-ftreet, -	60,000	4000 B. 2000 E. I.

A 2

Countefs

Illus. 1.4 *The Master-Key to the Rich Ladies Treasury* (1742).
© Bodleian Library, 24752 d.9

of peers (including 12 with the daughters of other dukes) and 49 with commoners. Of the latter only five lacked a gentle background.'[41] Legal settlements often

---

[41] J. V. Beckett, *The Aristocracy in England, 1660–1914* (New York and London, 1989), 104; on the stable rate of endogamous marriages, see David Thomas, 'The Social Origins of Marriage Partners of the British Peerage in the Eighteenth and Nineteenth Centuries', *Population Studies*, vol. 26, no. 1 (1972): 99–111.

prevented exogamic unions by stipulating that a portion would not be payable unless younger children married with the consent of their parents. The decline in mortality among titled families after 1740 was of less benefit to outside suitors than it was to collateral male heirs. With respect to landed gentry, the alliances were more widespread, notably with the aldermen, 'la crème de la crème of the London bourgeoisie', or the mercantile elite in Parliament.[42] These eminent merchants were able to fit into the polite norms of the landed gentry without denying their own civic and professional values. In terms of matrimonial strategy, the utility of these directories should not be overestimated. Courtship was a complex process which required access to well-guarded venues and the complicity of various intermediaries during the London Season. Rumours about available heiresses circulated within limited circles.[43]

If not to significantly increase the chance of marrying into the titled families, these compilations could still be used by anyone in search of patronage and protections. The economic and social relevance of sponsorship has been explored in many studies and has been crucial in understanding the links and, in some cases, the porousness between the upper and middle sort. Nobles and titled families in general were key brokers in the distribution of public positions in the state departments and counties. Thomas Wotton, who published *Baronetages* in 1727 and 1740, was the owner of Edward Chamberlain's *Present State of the British Court*, which gave the detailed Civil List offices along with their occupants and salaries.[44]

Furthermore, pocket family directories could be cross-referenced with other books such as court almanacs and travel books. All these guides served as tools in order to navigate in larger and more complex networks within and without the metropolis, in Britain and even into the colonial world.

To improve one's social position, one should be able to move as effortlessly as possible in different venues through the appropriation of spaces and practices. Although the 'urban Renaissance' enabled places of sociability to become more accessible, this did not mean that they were open to anyone. Peter Borsay has underlined a fundamental tension in the urban scene: 'The promotion of sociability sits rather uneasily alongside that other great preoccupation of urban culture, the pursuit of status. Whereas one sought to unify society, the other encouraged fragmentation. The two motives cannot be easily harmonized; nor should they be.'[45]

London booksellers provided crucial resources for anyone willing to learn his way into the complex and changing social venues. Their tight-knit network of

---

[42] Nicholas Rogers, 'Money, Land and Lineage: The Big Bourgeoisie of Hanoverian London', *Social History*, vol. 4, no. 3 (1979): 537–54 at 438.

[43] On the functioning of the 'marriage market', the importance of the London seasons and the presentations at court after 1760, see Kimberly Schutte, *Women, Rank and Marriage in the British Aristocracy, 1485–2000: An Open Elite?* (Basingstoke, 2014), 92–4.

[44] Bod. Lib., MS Don. c. 66, fol. 17.

[45] Peter Borsay, *The Urban Renaissance: Culture and Society in the Provincial Town 1660–1770* (Oxford, 1989), 278.

38   SELLING ANCESTRY

shops enabled them to play the role of gatekeepers into many circles of sociability between the City and West End. Booksellers were clearly identified through their address, thus contributing to their reputation and the trust they could gain from their customers: 'the ability of booksellers to remain within a particular neighbourhood, irrespective of changing needs for space, proved a valuable feature in the changing city'.[46] Close to many coffee houses and situated in the busiest streets, their premises served as an intense place of polite sociability. Their commercial appeal lies in the fact that the shops were located near prominent City venues such as the Inns of Court, St Paul's Cathedral, the Court of Chancery, and the Exchange. Not coincidentally, of course, these three venues were where family directories were sold, particularly, in the three main spaces of Fleet Street, Paternoster Row, and the West End.

In content, many of these publications could be best described as a cross-over between almanacs and town directories. John Fielding supplied his *New Pocket Peerage* (1782) with a London guide plan and an index listing the public and private buildings of London, a metropolis where 'merchants here are as rich as Noblemen'.[47] He stressed the difficulty of finding one's way in a city of about one million, and indicated where to locate the Chancery Court, the Excise Office, and the College of Arms.

On a smaller scale, these compilations dispensed some guidance outside the metropolis, especially for those travelling outside their local circles and who were deprived of the social networks enjoyed by the landed elites. One key element provided by Nichols's *Compendium* was the systematic location of family seats, with their distance from the nearest county town and from the City of London. At the beginning of the nineteenth century, with the strengthening of the imperial governance in India and the British Isles, most compilations included most colonial elites from the army and administration. One of the most successful was the pocket *Annual Peerage and Baronetage of the British Empire* (1827–9) published and sold by Simon Saunders and Edward John Otley. They were the owners of several American almanacs and relied on the Innes sisters (Anna, Eliza, and Maria) for an annual update. The sisters had previously worked as indexers for John Nichols's *Gentleman's Magazine* where, predictably, an enthusiastic account of their compilation was issued.[48] The sisters, celebrated for 'their unwearied perseverance and diligent enquiries, had been able to insert in it the names of three thousand members of the families of the nobility' which had not been linked before.[49] In their preface, the Innes sisters claimed to have found the best nomenclature to represent the kinship of what they called the 'higher class'. Discarding the family tree, they alleged to be inspired by the 'Almanac de Gotha' with its long listing of family names arranged in order of precedence. Its tabular

---

[46] Raven, *Business of Books*, 155.   [47] *New Pocket Peerage* (London, 1782), preface, i.
[48] Innes papers, ESRO, Gil/4/134; CKA, U1475; U1500.   [49] *GM*, vol. 151 (Jan. 1832), 60.

form enabled the reader to skim through hundreds of names very quickly as all the lines without issue were suppressed.[50]

A veneer of polite culture

Quite apart from locating the social elite, these compilations provided some guidance on how to identify its members, to address them in the correct manner, and to hold a polite conversation. With regard to recognition, the use of coats of arms was still essential. In Nichols's *Compendium*, the reader could find a didactic explanation of the notion of 'Honour in general', a description of the several degrees of gentry, and their precedents, as well as the antiquity and usefulness of arms. Nichols proposed a method to recognize the peers' arms, 'as commonly borne on their coaches'.[51] There were in London several hundred carriages equipped with armorial display.[52] Along with the peers' coats in woodcut, he inserted the basic symbols in heraldry to distinguish the family houses. It was probably with his *Compendium* that William Upcott, a bookseller's assistant in Pall Mall, managed to identify some coats of arms, which he noted in his diary: 'I took up my little volume of Heraldry and already can take up a pep from a chevron.'[53] Learning about coats of arms was part and parcel of a wider antiquarian culture in which Upcott would later excel by cataloguing the Evelyn library. The aim followed by the printer Samuel Kent in publishing his *Grammar of heraldry: or, Gentleman's vade mecum* (1716, 1718, 1720, 1724) was more ambiguous. While offering his readers an introduction to the rules of blazoning, he provided his sponsors with the unique opportunity to have their coats of arms printed next to those of all the peers and baronets. Among his 150 blazoned subscribers were many middle-sort customers such as James Austin of Southwark ('inventor of the Persian Ink-Powder'), John Cluer (Printer in Bow-Churchyard), Roger Grant (Oculist), John Hoo (Serjeant-at-Law), the diarist Narcissus Luttrell, Francis Pie (Herald-Painter), Joseph Sewel (Customs collector, Chester), John Slany of Worcestershire (Woollen-Draper), and Mr Smith (Vintner in Cheapside). In his preface, Kent justified his method by his willingness to print a dictionary 'not too cumbersome for the pocket' and to prioritize the needs of the 'Majority', adding that 'what I have done is advantageous to the Buyer. [...] My

---

[50] The Innes sisters later worked with John Gough Nichols, the editor of the *GM*.

[51] Nichols, *British Compendium*, iv.

[52] 'In the London excise division, in 1766, 527 titled carriage owners were listed from the Dissenting brewing magnate and City knight Sir Benjamin Truman at the bottom, up to the owner of five carriages in St James, King George [...]. They constituted one in ten of all London carriage owners.' Paul Langford, *Public Life and the Propertied Englishman*, 522.

[53] William Upcott, [*Diary 1803–1807*], <http://www.open.ac.uk/Arts/reading/UK/record_details. php?id=5920>, accessed 28 Nov. 2019.

40 SELLING ANCESTRY

little Grammar of 6sh. is on a Level with the Voluminous Gwillim of 35s.'[54] For the subscribers, Kent's dictionary may have satisfied a claim to gentility or a way to advertise their trade.[55] To gratify the upper end of the market, Kent later published a new edition of John Guillim, *The British Banner Display'd* in two volumes (1726-28).

Similarly, the heraldic engraver Hugh Clark publicized his *Short and Easy Introduction to Heraldry* (3 shillings) as a useful tool 'to instruct a few private Persons, who, by its short and easy Method, soon gained a knowledge of the Science'.[56] His *Introduction* in 1775 attracted a much wider pool of subscribers well into the urban middle sort: 'Of Clark's 217 subscribers all but three lived in London or its environs, only three were titled, and a significant proportion lived in, or close to, Soho', and this 'appears to be the first book on heraldry compiled specifically for middle-class readers with little or no knowledge of the subject'.[57] In 1790, *The Peerage Directory* was advertised as a useful tool 'in order to assist in pointing out the arms (blazoned, a Carriage, or otherwise) of any individual Nobleman'.[58]

Apart from offering a crash course into the exclusive art of heraldry, these compilations provided only a few brief historical references. As well as fanciful pedigrees, tedious family narratives had been scrapped for being inimical to polite conversation. John Constable warned against the scourge of several categories of bores, notably the pedant who 'takes you into a long pedigree of some Greek, or Hebrew Origin' and the genealogists, as 'you can never stop them, till they are got to the Conquest at least' and the herald 'with his Lions Rampant and Couchant'.[59] He further added that 'the Ancientness of a Man's Family seldom fails to be a ridiculous, and fulsome subject in his own mouth'.[60] However, by the same token, for the middle sort, mocking someone for his vanity was not acceptable: 'it generally betrays an Envy and Pride, to be ready at ridiculing, or undervaluing the Advantage of an antient Pedigree'.[61] Envious and resentful dispositions were to be found among newcomers: 'the pretended and proud contempt of such a Descent, is often observable in Men, who by some tolerable natural Parts, have risen to very easy or rich circumstances'.[62] Constable was condemning two unpolite behaviours which revolved around excessive praise or disdain. A well-born gentleman would have the good sense not to talk about his family and a

---

[54] Samuel Kent, *Grammar of Heraldry* (London, 1718), preface, vi, ix; see also his less successful *Grammar of Heraldry, or a catalogue of the Nobility of Scotland and Ireland* (London, 1716, 3s.).

[55] On artisans and advertising almanacs in Paris see Nicolas Lemas, 'Les "pages jaunes" du bâtiment au XVIIIe siècle: sur une source méconnue de l'histoire du bâtiment parisien', *Histoire urbaine*, 2005/1 (no. 12), 175–82.

[56] *Short and Easy Introduction to Heraldry* (London, 1775), preface, ii.

[57] Colin Lee, 'Hugh Clark (1745–1822), heraldic engraver', *ODNB*, retrieved 5 June 2020, from <https://doi-org.janus.bis-sorbonne.fr/10.1093/ref:odnb/62418>.

[58] *The Peerage Directory* (London, 1790), preface.

[59] John Constable, *The Conversation of Gentlemen* (London, 1738), 138, 174.   [60] Ibid., 198.

[61] Ibid.   [62] Ibid., 199.

modest upstart would avoid poking fun at pedigrees. Genealogies excited contrary passion (vanity or envy) which were incompatible with mundane and social interactions. Hence some basic knowledge of history was required to better make sense of a family's eminence. Along with his short view of the titled families, Thomas Salmon published *The Chronological Historian* (1723) which was then sold after his death under the title *Chronology; or, the historian's vade-mecum with the dates affixed. Also the dates of the creation of all the peerage* (18mo). Fourteen editions appeared between 1769 and 1802.

Finally, William Kingdom published *The Charts* as well as *The Secretary's Assistant* and both were aimed to be used in a complementary way: applicants for patronage were counselled to learn about the various and most correct modes of addressing and conclusion when writing letters to persons of every degree of rank. They were hailed in various magazines as works which 'will prove highly useful to young correspondents and even afford information to those whose occupations or connections require their occasional correspondence with persons of superior ranks'.[63] William Kingdom advised the readers on how to address titled families, important members of public companies (banks, insurance companies, East India House), as well as principal officers and commissioners in governmental departments. Similarly, Dod's *Peerage* (1842) was praised especially for its practical utility. In *The Monthly Magazine*, the reviewers underlined its simplicity in explaining 'the complex and little-known system called "precedence" and for its usefulness it is comparable to a manual for grown up horsemen; for it teaches those who enter good society late in life, the means of escaping a great deal of ridicule'.[64] The priority again was not to justify the social eminence of titled families but rather to avoid embarrassment in ignoring some simple rules of precedence.

For all its practicality, such pocket literature generated some hostile comments. The Innes sisters recognized that family compilations have too often been described as a 'dry and laborious work', merely 'a barren catalogue of names and dates'.[65] A reviewer of the *Historic Peerage of England* by Sir Nicholas Harris Nicolas viewed it as 'a necessary companion to the student of English history' as opposed to the 'one of the common Peerages which lies on the tables of Tyburnia to tell who is the wife and what the age of the Last Whig nobleman appointed to the government of a colony'.[66] The journalist saw the flourishing of 'common Peerage' as the unmistakable sign of the abasement of aristocratic values, as Tyburnia referred to one of the prominent places of public execution near Marylebone.[67]

---

[63] *The Literary Gazette*, vol. 6, no. 279 (25 May 1822), 333; *Literary Chronicle*, no. 112 (7 July 1821), 422.

[64] *Monthly Magazine* (Aug. 1842), 161.   [65] *The Annual Peerage* (London, 1827), i.

[66] *The Quarterly Review*, vol. 103 (Jan. 1858), 28.

[67] T. F. T. Baker, Diane K. Bolton, and Patricia E. C. Croot, 'Paddington: Tyburnia', in C. R. Elrington (ed.), *Victoria County History: Middlesex*, vol. 9 (London, 1989), 190.

42   SELLING ANCESTRY

2. Genealogical histories in octavo

As we have seen, some genealogists wished to be perceived as respected authors and endeavoured to distinguish their work from pocket compilations. They generally preferred an octavo format, and the selling price ranged from 6 to 10 shillings. But they faced an uphill battle in presenting their work as truly historical. It is little wonder that their compilations were often preceded by a long preface aimed at vindicating the seriousness of their methods and sources. They were also keenly aware of the general suspicion towards any form of genealogical history.

The fate of a dubious source of knowledge

The Enlightenment has been studied as a key period in the definition of a 'modern' and secular history. The growth of a more conjectural and critical approach had led to the demise of a genealogical way of thinking.[68] As early as the late seventeenth century, the French theologian Jean-Baptiste Massillon contended that the most widespread historical errors were tales about noble blood and vain genealogies.[69] In the same way in the late eighteenth century, Edward Gibbon set new standards in scholarship, by celebrating 'our calmer judgment which rather tends to moderate than to suppress the pride of an ancient and worthy race'.[70] He dismissed William Dugdale for what he saw as an excessive reverence towards family fictions. If the Courtenays, earls of Devon, had previously been keen to uphold fanciful ancestors, Gibbon was relieved to witness that in his day and age, 'the rational pride of the family now refuses to accept this imaginary founder'.[71] The new critical methods applied by Gibbon had been welcomed by the public since his *History of the Decline and Fall of the Roman Empire* rose to £4,000 in copyright value (1776), an amount which would have dwarfed any copyright of *Peerages*.[72] Along with innovative historians, criticisms against genealogists were echoed in many literary gazettes. In the *Miscellanea Critica* (1768), a reviewer found that 'the business of pedigree and family history is usually so very dry and frequently so uninteresting, as not to suit the general taste'.[73] In the *English Review* (1785), another complained about the last *Peerage* published by Barak Longmate:

---

[68] Mark S. Phillips, *Society and Sentiment: Genres of Historical Writing in Britain 1740–1820* (Princeton, 2010); Chantal Grell, *L'histoire entre érudition et philosophie: étude sur la connaissance historique au siècle des Lumières* (Paris, 1993).

[69] 'La noblesse du sang et la vanité des généalogies est de toutes les erreurs, la plus généralement établie', Article 'Généalogie' by Jacques M. de Tupigny in Charles Samaran, *L'histoire et ses méthodes* (Paris, 1961), 726.

[70] H. H. Milman, *The Life of Edward Gibbon* (Paris, 1840), 2.

[71] Edward Gibbon, *The History of the Decline and Fall of the Roman Empire* (London, 1788), 217.

[72] David Fielding and Shef Rogers, 'Copyright Payments in Eighteenth-Century Britain, 1701–1800', *Economics Discussion Papers*, no. 1506 (2015), 3–44 at 12.

[73] *Miscellanea Critica*, vol. 1 (1768), 444.

'Longmate and his master do not vary widely. Their diction is harsh, dry and unornamented and they are perfect strangers even to the idea of speculation.'[74]

Today, however, the opposition between history and genealogy is taken with a grain of salt. Mark Salber Phillips, in his discussion of the differences between history and antiquarianism, has argued that: 'though new doctrines may be formulated, the more substantial change lies in the reconfiguration of existing elements in relation to the whole'.[75] For their lack of conceptualization, their tedious accumulation of lineages, genealogies may have been relegated to an auxiliary status, a minor branch of knowledge, but they still retained some historical value for the general public. Over the long eighteenth century, parallel historical practices colluded with each other. One need not think in terms of 'paradigm shifts' but in a cumulative manner, recognizing that 'new ways of engaging with the past have emerged side by side with older ones and coexist, or even interact, with them, so that pre-modern and modern ways of practising memory can exist side by side'.[76] As we have seen, the same literary gazettes could be simultaneously critical and eulogistic about family directories, depending on their authors and publishers. Several enlightened historians still demonstrated a keen interest in genealogies. From 1698 onwards, Leibniz carried out detailed research on the House of Guelph in order to document the Hanoverian rights to the British throne. His dynastic enquiries had far-reaching implications 'regarding history, imperial law and interest-driven politics'.[77] Voltaire, who aimed to write a universal history of mankind in his *Essai sur les Mœurs*, could not deny the Eurocentric and genealogical perspective of his project. Genealogy is guided by a 'presentist' relation which Voltaire and his readership had with their own history.[78] Some major contradictions among enlightened historians could not be easily dismissed. An oft-cited quotation from Voltaire, namely that heraldry was 'the science of fools with long memories', is nowhere to be found in his work.[79] Edward Gibbon's autobiography provides 'a slightly quizzical, equivocal description of the lineage of his own family'.[80] While he stated that he knew nothing about his ancestors since in his childhood 'genealogy was never a topic of conversation',

---

[74] *The English Review*, vol. 6 (5 Jan. 1785), 43.

[75] Mark Salber Phillips, 'Reconsiderations on History and Antiquarianism: Arnaldo Momigliano and the Historiography of Eighteenth-Century Britain', *Journal of the History of Ideas*, vol. 57, no. 2 (1996): 297–316 at 305.

[76] Judith Pollman, *Memory in Early Modern Europe, 1500–1800* (Oxford, 2017), 72.

[77] Friedrich Beiderbeck, 'Leibniz's Political Vision for Europe', in Maria Rosa Antognazza (ed.), *The Oxford Handbook of Leibniz* (Oxford, 2018), 678.

[78] Antoine Lilti, 'La civilisation est-elle européenne? Écrire l'histoire de l'Europe au XVIIIe siècle', in Antoine Lilti and Céline Spector (eds), *Penser l'Europe au XVIIIe siècle: commerce, civilisation, empire* (Oxford, 2014), 139–66.

[79] *Notes and Queries*, no. 63 (11 Jan. 1851), 31.

[80] Quoted by Henry French, '"Sighing for Past Greatness"? Dynastic Senses of Family Identity in England c.1650–1800', in Stephane Jettot and Jean-Paul Zuniga (eds), *Genealogy and Social Status in the Enlightenment* (Liverpool, 2021), 99–123.

44 SELLING ANCESTRY

he then went on to admit that a great-great-uncle had been a seventeenth-century herald and that he was descended from Kentish esquires of the fifteenth century.

A few compilers sought to address the criticisms formulated by well-established historians by trying to make a case for a reconfigured genealogical history. Among several names, we will consider the emblematic cases of Arthur Collins and Sir Egerton Brydges. Both had been keen to distinguish their publications from the pocket directories. Collins's *Peerages* were to be used by 'our young Nobility and Gentry' and for their improvement: 'tis no small happiness for anyone to be descended from a brave and worthy stock, as it naturally leads him into an enquiry of what figure his ancestors have made in their several ages'.[81] This was a conventional argument often made by antiquaries, such as Sir Robert Atkins in his county history of Gloucestershire (1711).[82] Brydges desired to distance himself from the makers of 'common pocket Peerages' which could be read 'like a red-book or a Parish-register and which provided information of a very low order'.[83] Moreover, while recognizing their debt towards respected historians such as Burnet, Hume, or Clarendon, neither Collins nor Brydges spared their criticisms. They wished to be acknowledged as polite historians, above the fray of partisan battles. Their ability to avoid any unpleasant remarks about the Whigs or the Tories laid the commercial appeal of their compilation.

In his 1709 preface, Collins refused to comment on the reign of James II: 'what is memorable of him, his succession to the throne and unfortunate misguided reign, we leave to history as not being properly the business of this present work'.[84] Similarly, about William III and Mary he stated that 'their history is referr'd to, having no issue for us to speak of in this place'.[85] Deploring the polarized historical discourses on the later Stuarts, Collins tried to conceive an inclusive narrative acceptable to any peer. Brydges perceived himself as a continuator of Collins's work, by re-editing his compilation in 1812. In the preface, he introduced his predecessor as a 'biographer and historian'.[86] Brydges saw the most prominent historians as being too engaged in political bickering and regretted that Clarendon's and Burnet's pens had been so 'dipped in the venom of party'.[87] The duty of the 'general historian' was to record the 'private connections of his heroes, which often give a clue to their public conduct and characters'.[88] However, while both authors aimed at composing consensual narratives based on biographies and genealogies, their historical views were strikingly different.

---

[81] Arthur Collins, *English Peerage* (London, 1735), preface. See also a positive assessment of Collins's *Peerage* in *Directions for a proper choice of authors to form a library, which may both improve and entertain the mind, and be of real use in the conduct of life. Intended for Those Readers who are only acquainted with the English Language* (London, 1766), 17.

[82] 'That a Genealogical History of Families has its peculiar use, it stimulates and excites the brave to imitate the generous actions of their ancestors, and it shames the debauched and reprobate, both in the eyes of others and in their own breasts, when they consider how they have degenerated', *The Ancient and Present State of Gloucestershire* (London, 1712, re-ed. 1974), xxv.

[83] Egerton Brydges, *A Biographical Peerage* (London, 1808), preface, iii.

[84] *The English Peerage* (1709), 28.   [85] Ibid.   [86] Ibid. preface, i.   [87] Ibid., iv.

[88] Ibid., iv.

Collins and his polite account of the 'Modern families'

At the end in his life, Collins reflected on his various publications and considered that his most important contribution was to have established an 'account of all the Modern families'.[89] He started to serialize his *Historical Peerage* with his business partner Abel Roper, the owner of the thrice-weekly newspaper *Post Boy* and whose uncle published in 1675 the monumental *Baronage* by Dugdale. Unlike the *Baronage*, which had been an expensive folio, Collins's *Peerage* was a serial edition (1709–19) printed in octavo at 6 shillings each. By 'modern', Collins meant that he had set himself the task to celebrate the families who had recently come to prominence. Most of his notices are dedicated to the early modern period and for the Middle Ages, he relied on 'the substance of Sir William Dugdale's Baronage'.[90] Arguing in favour of political nobility, Collins was implicitly hostile to the 1719 Peerage Bill, which if successful, would have limited the prerogative of the Crown. The antiquity of lineages was second to personal achievements: 'great and worthy actions were ever the footsteps to attain honour and preferment'.[91]

His publication coincided with a surge in the creation of peers. Between 1689 and 1718 no less than eighty titles had been granted, more than double the rate of increase over the previous thirty years (1660–89). Thirty new peers were made under Anne and twenty by George I up to the Peerage Bill. Collins duly included all the peers created by Ann and George even though he could not provide the same account for each family. Some were dealt with in less than a page, while others benefited from dozens of pages. On the newly created Lord Bathurst in 1712, whose origins in Sussex were much later established in the pre-Norman period, Collins remained vague: 'a very ancient family, in the county of Kent as appears from the antiquities of that county and other records, was possess'd of estates in several parts of it'.[92] Lord Bingley's ancestors were not even mentioned, in contrast to his eminent activities in Parliament for the City of York and as under-treasurer of the Exchequer.[93] About Lord Masham, elevated by Harley, Collins simply stated that his family was 'anciently seated in the North parts of England, where they were of good account' without being more specific.[94] Collins's celebration of modern families may have been influenced by the continental debate on the Ancients and the Moderns. His partner in trade, Abel Boyer, was working with him for the *Post Boy* as a translator of French newsletters. An exiled Huguenot, Boyer had been a significant broker between France and England and was hired at first as a tutor to the young Allen Bathurst.[95] In his

---

[89] *The English Peerage*, supplement to vol. 4 (London, 1750), viii.

[90] *The English Peerage* (London, 1709), preface, i.   [91] Ibid.

[92] *The English Peerage* (London, 1716), 275. Compare with the Bernard Burke's *Genealogical and Heraldic Dictionary*: 'The Bathursts are stated to have come into England in the time of the Saxons, from a place called batters in the duchy of Luneburg' (London, 1878), 84.

[93] *The English Peerage* (London, 1716), 177.   [94] Ibid., 268.

[95] See also *The Compleat French master 1694 and A Geographical and Historical Description of those Parts of Europe* (London, 1698).

46   SELLING ANCESTRY

Characters of the Virtues and Vices of the Age (1695) dedicated to his pupil, Boyer composed an alphabetical digest of many quotations from French and English authors such as Saint-Évremond and La Bruyère. Collins may have been inspired by an article on nobility and gentility which stated that:

> The great mistake of most noblemen is that they look upon their nobility as a character given them by Nature. The more ancient that nobility is, which we derive from our ancestors, the more suspicious and uncertain it is and therefore the less valuable [...]. The spring of honour is yet fresh in the son's veins and kept up by the example of the father, but the further it runs from the fountain, the weaker and drier it grows. [...] Fortune has turn'd all things topsie-turvy, in a long story of revolutions. But it matters not whence we come but what we are; nor is it any more to our honour, the glory of our predecessors, than it is to their shame, the wickedness of their posterity.[96]

Far from restricting themselves to the domain of learning and poetry, the French 'moderns' had magnified the power of Louis XIV and his ability to find among his subjects the most virtuous men and to elevate them to nobility.[97] The glory of the 'siècle de Louis Le Grand' was not grounded on the ancient origins of his nobles, but on their contemporary deeds. Collins's historical perspective fits precisely into the view that modern families should not blush from their recent background. Transferred into England, the 'Querelle des Anciens et des Modernes' did not reflect a partisan agenda. As a Modern, Boyer had first been recruited by Bishop Burnet and then worked for Roper, who was rather on the Tory side. It has been demonstrated that in the 'battle of the books', Whig authors such as William Temple could defend the Ancients. Collins's Modern views were also echoed in the *Spectator* by Addison:

> It has been usual to remind Persons of Rank, on great Occasions in Life, of their Race and Quality, and to what Expectations they were born; that by considering what is worthy of them, they may be withdrawn from mean Pursuits, and encouraged to laudable Undertakings. This is turning Nobility into a Principle of Virtue, and making it productive of Merit.[98]

Through his serial *Peerages*, Collins was composing a progressive and optimistic narrative which celebrated the heroes of his times. In order to do so, he worked to

---

[96] Graham Gibbs, 'Boyer, Abel (1667?–1729), lexicographer and journalist', *ODNB*, 2008. Retrieved 26 Dec. 2019, from <https://doi-org.janus.bis-sorbonne.fr/10.1093/ref:odnb/3122>.

[97] Levent Yilmaz, *Le temps moderne: variations sur les Anciens et les contemporains* (Paris, 2004); Joseph M. Levine, *The Battle of the Books: History and Literature in the Augustan Age* (Ithaca, NY, 1991).

[98] *The Spectator*, 15 Nov. (1712), 537.

establish a common ground between the Whigs and the Tories in a consensual vindication of liberty and Protestantism.[99] Collins dealt with the period from the Glorious Revolution to the Act of Union while omitting its most contentious elements. He duplicated the totality of the Act of Settlement, which was depicted as the product of bipartisan effort.[100] He then went on to demonstrate that the Treaty of Union had been essential 'for preserving the Protestant succession'.[101] This smooth transition from the Stuarts to the Hanoverians is celebrated on the first page by a rough engraving displaying a dynastic tree from James I to George of Hanover (Illus. 1.5).

In this floral structure, the subversive nature of the Glorious Revolution was obliterated, continuity was triumphing over change. In the centre stage, the medallion of James, the first British monarch, was hanging at the bottom of the tree and above that of Queen Anne, which was prolonged by the branches of the peers and the five coronets.

Collins devoted himself to a balanced biographical account of eminent Whig and Tory peers. The Whig Devonshire 'having with an heroick spirit stood the brunt of King James's reign, [. . .] was upon the happy revolution that follow'd (in which he had also a large share) constituted Lord High Steward'.[102] The Tory James Butler was described as among the first nobles who supported William III. His role in the repression of the Monmouth rebellion was omitted, unlike his deeds in many battlefields (Ireland, Flanders, Spain) during the Nine Years War and the War of the Spanish Succession. He should be seen as 'a lively example of the valour and gallantry of his two great ancestors'.[103]

The consistency of his non-partisan approach was illustrated in the later editions (1735, 1740, 1756) and notably in the case of the Seymours. The speaker Sir Edward Seymour had been one of the favourite targets of the Whig historians. A collateral of the first duke of Somerset, Seymour imposed himself at the main leader in the Tory party between 1679 to 1707. Gilbert Burnet had inserted in his history a severe portrait of the 'haughty' Seymour, which in turn generated a counter-attack from Thomas Salmon, who strongly contested that Seymour had been 'the most assuming Speaker that ever that House had'.[104] In 1740, Nicolas Tindal, the translator and the continuator of Rapin's *History of England*, went on to expose a series of damaging anecdotes on the Seymours. He described how Francis Seymour, the fifth duke of Somerset, had been found shot dead in a

---

[99] Mark Knights pointed out that both Tory and Whig histories shared many commonalities, notably the idea of progress. On Herbert Butterfield, he demonstrated that 'his criticisms of the Whig methodology of history might equally be applied to the Tory methodology', in 'The Tory Interpretation of History in the Rage of Parties', Paulina Kewes (ed.), *The Uses of History in Early Modern England* (San Marino, Calif., 2006), 355.

[100] *Peerage of England* (London, 1709), 35.   [101] Ibid., 36.   [102] Ibid., 85.

[103] Ibid., 61.

[104] Thomas Salmon, *An Impartial Examination of Bishop Burnet's History of His Own Times* (London, 1724), 724.

48 SELLING ANCESTRY

Illus. 1.5 *Collins's Peerage*, frontispiece (1710).
© Bodleian Library, 8vo M 51 Jur.

A FORMAT FOR EVERY USE   49

Genoese inn by a jealous husband. Narratives of the Grand Tour and its many dangers were crucial in the celebration of elite masculine identities.[105] In this case, however, this unfortunate and ridiculous death in a tavern was intended to bring shame to the whole family. As for Sir Edward Seymour, he was accused of having opportunistically rallied to the cause of William III in the hope of the 'great expectations from the new settlement [...] as they could have no sense of civil and religious liberty, no real concern for its interest either at home or abroad'.[106] Tindal accused Edward Seymour of mean treachery when in 1692 he requested the arrest of the republican Edmund Ludlow in order to steal his estate. In comparison to these hostile accounts, Collins's narratives remained entirely neutral until his death in 1760. Concerning Francis Seymour's Grand Tour, Collins laid the blame on the French Gentlemen who were travelling with him and who had provoked the jealous Genoese husband. Edward Seymour was presented as an enemy of James II, who never forgave him for refusing to attend the Pope's Nuncio.[107]

However, after Collins's death, his *Peerage*'s copyright was bought by a larger group of London booksellers who outsourced most of the editing to unknown hacks. Hence, the new edition in 1768 was compiled without any supervision. The first volume contained a violent attack against the Whig historians and their 'malevolence' towards the Seymours.[108] The unidentified compiler mentioned various insulting passages in Tindal's history. For all his vanity and misdeeds, Edward Seymour would have been deserted by all his friends and servants in his last years. In 1708, he would have met 'an old female beggar of the maddish tribe' who broke into his house: 'finding the great man thus alone, she reproached him for all his cruelty and oppressions, threatened, terrified and handled him in a manner, the effects of which soon put an end to a life'.[109] In so publicly settling scores with a Whig historiography, the anonymous writer generated a strong reaction from many readers, forcing the publishers to issue an apology:

> The whole account of Sir Edward teems with inconsistencies and is dictated by a virulent spirit of party which must be ascribed to the editor employed in preparing the first part of this work, as Mr. Collins in his last edition, talks in a very different strain.[110]

The discrepancies observed in the directory before and after Collins's death demonstrated that he was not simply compiling data. Despite denials by protagonists, political and historical agenda could be seen in his *Peerages* from 1709 to 1760.

---

[105] 'Rather than avoiding this danger, the culture of eighteenth-century British elite was to proactively embrace and use it as a tool in the formation of elite masculinity.' Sarah Goldsmith, *Masculinity and Danger on the Eighteenth-Century Grand Tour* (London, 2020), 210.

[106] Nicholas Tindal, *The History of England. Written in French by Mr Rapin de Thoyras. Continued from the revolution to the accession of King George II*, vol. 3 (London, 1744), 509.

[107] *Peerage*, vol. 1 (1741), 53.   [108] Ibid., vol. 1 (1768), 177.   [109] Ibid., 178.

[110] Ibid., vol. 1, Additions and corrections, 2.

50 SELLING ANCESTRY

Brydges's history of honourable and unworthy peers

In 1812, Brydges had set himself the task of reviving Collins's *Peerage*, a task which commanded broad support among the London booksellers. Among them was William Otridge, owner of a stock of books containing 50,000 volumes. The Paynes, father and son, were 'Booksellers Extraordinary' to the Prince Regent and to the University of Oxford.[111] They had been involved in the last 1778 and 1784 editions. Composed at the beginning of the nineteenth century, Brydges's historical *Peerages* were to be markedly different from those compiled by Collins. His directories reflected a very different historical consciousness and a loyalist culture which thrived after the revolutionary wars.[112] He could not ignore the powerful challenges mounted by the reformist movements after 1760. The term 'aristocracy' had been reinterpreted by radicals and reformers in a derogatory and larger meaning: 'linguistic usage of "aristocracy" veered increasingly towards the negative and this highlights a shift in public perception about those who governed'.[113] Unlike Collins, who celebrated the peerage as a group, Brydges wrote first, in 1808, a more critical and discriminate compilation. We have seen in the introduction how he started his preface with a long quotation from Burke on the dangers of proud aristocrats who would take obliging genealogists at face value. In these unpredictable times, Brydges agreed with Burke that one could not afford to be too complacent with one's inherited peerage. Therefore, he launched himself in a genealogy of 124 peers who deserved, for better or for worse, to obtain a place 'in the pages of general history', from the Saxon to the present time.[114]

His aim was to provoke a rupture with directories 'in which the good and the bad, the high and low are recorded with such indiscriminate honours [...]. There the upstart of yesterday has a longer pedigree than the Nevilles, the Cliffords and the Talbots, and a fellow who got his money out of a shop by fraud and extortion and bought his Peerage with a portion of his disgraceful spoils, makes a greater figure than a Somers.'[115] His method was to avoid the 'tiresome minutiae of genealogy', retaining a selection of a few families in order to stir the Lords to their sense of political and social responsibility.[116] Their weakness and deeds should be used to provide a more inclusive narrative of the past. He wished to

---

[111] P. A. H. Brown, *London Publishers and Printers, c.1800–1870* (London, 1982), 146–7; David Fallon, '"Stuffd up with books": The Bookshops and Business of Thomas Payne and Son, 1740–1831', *History of Retailing and Consumption*, vol. 5, no. 3 (2019): 228–45.

[112] Thomas P. Schofield, 'Conservative Political Thought in Britain in Response to the French Revolution', *The Historical Journal*, vol. 29, no. 3 (1986): 601–22; Colin Jones and Dror Wahrman (eds), *The Age of Cultural Revolution: Britain and France, 1750–1820* (Berkeley, 2002); Emma Vincent Macleod. *A War of Ideas: British Attitudes to the Wars Against Revolutionary France, 1792–1802* (Aldershot, 1998).

[113] Amanda Goodrich, 'Understanding a Language of "Aristocracy", 1700–1850', *The Historical Journal*, vol. 56, no. 2 (2013): 369–98, at 377.

[114] *The Biographical Peerage*, preface, ii.   [115] *GM*, vol. 76 (Aug. 1806), 692.

[116] *Biographical Peerage*, preface, i.

celebrate the historical importance of certain 'names which were a kind of passport beyond the narrow boundaries, and the microscopic eyes of the mere genealogist'.[117]

Unsurprisingly, among the prime heroic figures were the Pitts. 'When a man, like the late Lord Chatham, blazes forth in society, all thoughts or pedigree are eclipsed and forgotten' and his son was depicted as 'the most undaunted minister this country, or perhaps any other, ever experienced' and a safe pair of hands against 'the threatened mania of the French revolution'.[118] The celebration of Burke was closely linked to that of Pitt. Burke's rallying of Pitt was a proof of political integrity.[119] The Pitts' deeds as well as Burke's aura demonstrated that merit and genius preceded distinctions, a principle which is often repeated by Brydges.

He selected some heroic peers in various categories. Military excellence was incarnated by Earl Nelson: 'never was a name, in the British annals, surrounded with such glory' even though he was modestly introduced as the son of an obscure Norfolk rector.[120] Industrial entrepreneurs such as Francis and the third duke of Bridgewater were also celebrated: 'the national work of this ingenious noble will preserve his name as long as the history of his country remains: he was the great projector of inland navigation (while) passing his useful days without personal splendour or luxuries'.[121] Among the scientists, George Parker, second earl of Macclesfield, as president of the Royal Society and renowned astronomer, deserved much praise.[122] His successes were all the more remarkable, Brydges added, in that his father had been impeached in 1725 on the grounds of corruption and was then imprisoned in the Tower of London. Against any biological determinism, the failure of the elders did not compromise the chances of their descendants. This argument was advanced by Mark Noble in his *Lives of the English Regicides* (1798), quoted extensively by Brydges. Noble's compilation was aimed at distinguishing English regicides from French Jacobins. About Cromwell, Noble noted that 'he must be always recorded as a wicked man but not like Robespierre: he can never be called a monster, which that most infamous of wretches ever must; like the tiger he seemed pleased with slaughter [...] there is no analogy between the English and French usurpers: one had not a single requisite for a great prince, the other was deficient in scarce any one to make him a most exalted monarch'.[123] Unlike the *damnatio memoriae* which took place during the Restoration, Noble went on to demonstrate that most of the regicides were from a genteel background. But it did not follow that their descendants were to be blamed for their ancestors' crimes. In their criticism of aristocrats, some

---

[117] Ibid., vol. 1, 332.   [118] Ibid., vol. 1, 290–3.
[119] J. J. Sack, 'The Memory of Burke and the Memory of Pitt: English Conservatism Confronts Its Past', *The Historical Journal*, vol. 30, no. 3 (1987): 623–40.
[120] *A Biographical Peerage*, vol. 1, 387.   [121] Ibid., 141.   [122] Ibid., 231.
[123] Ibid., 161.

52 SELLING ANCESTRY

radicals had been quick to use genealogical arguments to establish that stains and corruption could be transmitted from one generation to another. Burke referred to the use of family compilations by the Jacobins to hunt down and persecute the nobility and its race.[124] Noble's as well as Brydges's dictionaries could be seen as a counter-argument against the most common aspersions against nobles.

But if circumstances so required, Brydges did not shy away from denouncing some peers. In the gallery of villains, Brydges condemned in the strongest terms radical politicians accused of threatening the social order. He mentioned the scandalous Wilkes, 'that demagogue's celebrity', and Charles Fox's unacceptable behaviour as he had 'pleaded for, and too much supported, the excesses of the French revolution'.[125] He noted that some nobles, despite their privileges and excellent education, did not do much for Britain. On Richard Grosvenor, the son of a man deprived of 'any lustre' and whose wealth had enabled him to secure a peerage in 1784, he commented that he 'was better known in the annals of gallantry at Newmarket, than anywhere else; and it must be confessed, that peerages appear of little value, as long as it is observed that they can be obtained by such qualifications'.[126]

While praising Pitt the younger, Brydges was implicitly critical of his generous distribution of titles and honours. One gets the sense in reading his *Peerages* that the balance between the worthy and the vile peers was about to tip on the wrong side. In his autobiography, Brydges recalled his bitter and personal experience of the revolutionary times: 'I have seen society turned topsy-turvy since those days—not merely by the contagion of the French Revolution, for it began in England [...] it began with Pitt's first parliament in 1784.'[127] Unlike Collins, Brydges saw with great concern the inflation of honours after 1784.

Another distinctive feature was his taste for the material and tangible proofs of the past. Brydges described in great detail the main seats of the eminent families and their estates and insisted on their relevance for the whole nation. In the late eighteenth century, architecture and domesticity had been used to 'reduce the historical distance' with the past and to create a narrative more palatable to the whole nation.[128] Landscape and some prominent buildings were much valued as

---

[124] 'After destroying all other genealogies and family distinctions, they invent a sort of pedigree of crimes. It is not very just to chastise men for the offences of their natural ancestors: but to take the fiction of ancestry in a corporate succession, as a ground for punishing men who have no relation to guilty acts, except in names and general descriptions, is a sort of refinement in injustice belonging- to the philosophy of this enlightened age.' E. Burke, *Reflections on the revolution in France* (London, 1910), 137.

[125] *A Biographical Peerage*, vol. 1, 319 and vol. 2, 162.   [126] Ibid., vol. 1, 320–1.

[127] *The Autobiography, Times, Opinions, and Contemporaries of Sir Egerton Brydges, Bart. K.T. (Per legem terrae) Baron Chandos of Sudeley*, vol. 1 (London, 1831), 196.

[128] Marilyn Butler, *Romantics, Rebels and Reactionaries: English Literature and Its Background 1760–1830* (Oxford, 1982), 37, 180–1; Peter Mandler, '"In the olden time": Romantic History and English National Identity, 1820–1850', in L. Brockliss and D. Eastwood (eds), *A Union of Multiple Identities* (Manchester, 1997), 78–92.

they conveyed the notion of a more accessible past. As with many other writers, Brydges was strongly influenced by the Gothic revival so prevalent at that time: 'towards the end of the century [...] the category of Gothic was increasingly invoked as part of the urgent project to re-imagine national identity' against the dangerous rantings of enlightened historians.[129] Clouded with mystery, the medieval time was reinvented as a much more inclusive period. In the 'old times' the elite and the population were not set apart, they were living in a more organic society where every man knew his place and fulfilled his duty.[130]

Unlike Collins, who mostly ignored the medieval roots of the Hanoverians, Brydges mentioned the quarrels of the Guelphs and Ghibellines and even earlier 'the venerable tree, which has since overshadowed Germany and Britain, was planted in the Italian soil'.[131] Brydges went on to describe with much detail Arundel Castle in Sussex, which had been repaired in a 'kind of Gothic style'.[132] He proceeded similarly with the depiction of Chatsworth and Hardwick Hall.[133] As for Blenheim, he presented the edifice as 'the gift of national gratitude, a palace of uncommon splendour, and, in point of ornamented grounds, perhaps the most beautiful in Europe'.[134] Of Lord Orford, he recounted that 'no man had a purer taste in building than Earl Henry' and he illustrated his new Lodge in Windsor Park. Brydges was keen to demonstrate that Orford's private interest had not prevented him from promoting and overlooking, for the utility and honour of the country, the construction of Westminster Bridge.[135] He commented on the Harleys, who had suffered the destruction of their castle of Brampton in 1643 and who later amassed a considerable collection of books and manuscripts 'which now forms the principal treasure of the British Museum'.[136] Similarly, he added the Cowpers and their family castle of Hertford 'now made use of for the East India College'.[137]

The description of the aristocratic seats as part of a wider national heritage was later pursued in his re-edition of Collins's *Peerage* in 1812. He portrayed them as 'national treasures' insofar as they were the repository of an ancient time: 'The Stafford, Carlisle and Grosvenor collections of pictures, the Spencer, Marlborough, Devonshire, Bridgwater and Pembroke libraries are national treasures, becoming a people who are contending for the empire of the world'.[138] Private though accessible places were converted into national places of memory. It fit into a new sensibility against the revolutionary politics of the 1790s. Against the abstract notions of the Enlightenment, the comforting taste for stately houses and

[129] James Watt, *Contesting the Gothic: Fiction, Genre and Cultural Conflict, 1764–1832* (Cambridge, 1999), 46–7.
[130] Rosemary Sweet, 'Antiquarian Transformations in Historical Scholarship', in Elaine Chalus and Perry Gauci (eds), *Revisiting the Polite and Commercial People: Essays in Georgian Politics, Society and Culture in Honour of Professor Paul Langford* (Oxford, 2019), 167.
[131] *A Biographical Peerage*, vol. 1, 2.   [132] Ibid., vol. 1, 73.   [133] Ibid., 87.
[134] Ibid., 89.   [135] Ibid., 144.   [136] Ibid., 208.   [137] Ibid., 225.
[138] Brydges, *Collins's Peerage*, x.

54   SELLING ANCESTRY

their supposed openness was a definite feature of the period. Destructions and ruins were seen as worrying signs of forthcoming social upheavals. Ancient republican families were not spared by the egalitarian passions which engulfed Britain. When the regicide Robert Wallop, earl of Portsmouth, 'fell into universal contempt' at the Restoration and died in the Tower in 1667, his houses at Hurstbourne Park, near Andover, burnt down to the ground the same year. When his brother was later made Baron Wallop in 1720, the family house was rebuilt. But during the French Revolution, their Irish property, the Castle of Enniscorthy, was devastated in 1798.[139]

Alternatively, modern architectures were looked at unfavourably. As early as December 1789, David Wells of Burbach, Leicestershire, writing as 'Observator' in the *Gentleman's Magazine*, conflated two separate places within the property of a single country magnate called Sir Edward Littleton in Penkridge (Staffordshire). At Tildesley Park, a new habitation was 'in the style of modern taste, quite plain on the outside and rather deficient in the usual graces of architecture' and the old Pillaton Hall 'which is about to be destroyed and which still conveys the grandeur and generosity of the old time'.[140] The remains of the ancient mansion, about to be destroyed, still conveyed the traces of a well-balanced social order, when prestigious lineage went hand in hand with a sense of hospitality: 'the lengthened oaken table, having carried many a load of substantial food [...] the arched stone chimney, where logs of solid oak have cheerfully blazed [...] are all standing marks of convivial mirth and good old cheer'.[141] Similarly, he condemned the Grosvenor family for their newly built Eaton Hall near Chester, which was built upon an 'immense scale', a sign of regrettable excess leading to the destruction of ancient county houses.[142] The opposition between the modern, luxurious seat and the medieval hospitable mansion was a well-established theme and amply developed by Brydges. Unlike Collins, modernity was no longer celebrated as a positive phenomenon. He rather conveyed the sense of a nostalgic and remote past as opposed to the uncertainties of the present. Rosemary Sweet has alluded to the role of 'images of age-old hospitality conjured up in the great halls of baronial mansions [...] in sustaining the nineteenth-century ideal of Merry England'.[143] In his effort to neutralize popular radicalism, Brydges set himself the task of legitimizing the peerage by a moral assessment of its members and by composing a more palatable history based on the emerging notion of heritage.

---

[139] *Biographical Peerage*, vol. 1, 251.
[140] *GM*, vol. 59 (Dec. 1789), 1078. Wells is identified by Emily Lorraine de Montluzin in her online publication, *Attributions of Authorship in the Gentleman's Magazine, 1731–1868: An Electronic Union List* available at <https://bsuva.org/bsuva/gm2/>, accessed 12 June 2020.
[141] *GM*, vol. 59 (Dec. 1789), 1078.   [142] *A Biographical Peerage*, vol. 1, 321.
[143] Sweet, 'Antiquarian Transformations in Historical Scholarship', in Chalus and Gauci (eds), *Revisiting the Polite and Commercial People*, 167.

Although, Collins and Brydges belonged to very different periods, they both shared many characteristics; notably their ambition to be seen as authors and their insistence on biographies. Both were prompt to adapt their publication to the general taste of the public and to bring forward distinct sets of arguments to justify the historical value of their compilations. They also used their directories as a conduit to express conciliatory views which can be accepted both by the old and new elites.

3. 'Ornamental for the library': monumental folios and quartos

In the preface to his *English Peerage* in 1790, Charles Catton argued that it was necessary to 'raise the appearance of the book to some proportion with the dignity of the subject', and so 'a particular paper was manufactured and types were cast on purpose for the present work, the object having been, to render the whole ornamental to the library, and honourable to the state of arts and printing in England'.[144] Catton was one of the founding members of the Royal Academy in 1768 and master of the Worshipful Company of Painter Stainers in 1784. Along with portraits, he would paint arms on carriages and on various kinds of furniture such as chairs, tables, and clocks. Nicknamed the 'prince of coach makers', Catton was competing against the three London companies owned by John Hatchett, John Wright, and Philip Godsal.[145] In his *Peerage*, the engraving for the book-plates was carried out by James Heath and Francis Chesham, the latter already well known for his topographical views and painted coats of arms. They desired to celebrate both the prestige of the peers and the skill of their craft. Their work was to be completed with hand-coloured engraved plates which could be bound into the volume or in larger formats to be displayed at home. Catton described his volumes as 'works of compilation' without any pretence to historical originality.[146] Their work was published for John Robinson (Paternoster Row) for the hefty sum of 3 guineas each. Like many other genealogists, Catton and his publisher Robinson tried to attract consumers from the highest ranks of society. Their selling point was to insist on the material value of the directory and its prominent place in a library, which had become both a social and a living space. Genealogical practices had been transformed by the rise of a luxury market, although this aspect has been little studied.[147]

---

[144] *The English Peerage* (London, 1790), vi–vii.

[145] James Ayre, *Art, Artisans and Apprentices: Apprentice Painters & Sculptors in the Early Modern Tradition* (London, 2014), 220–2.

[146] *The English Peerage*, ii.

[147] Maxine Berg chooses rather to study the impact of global commerce on new consumer cultures in her *Luxury and Pleasure in Eighteenth-Century Britain* (Oxford, 2007).

56 SELLING ANCESTRY

Indeed, with regard to material culture, the eighteenth century witnessed a shift in the representation of ancestry. Family estates were no longer saturated with coats of arms displayed on mantelpiece and window-panes. Nor were funeral monuments adorned with complex heraldic devices. This is not to say that the material traces of a lineage culture disappeared altogether. In a recent study, Kate Redford has demonstrated the role of family portraits in preserving a sense of dynastic identity at Kedleston Hall, seat of Lord Scarsdale.[148] By the same token, coats of arms were still displayed indoors on large wooden frames. The trade card of Christopher Gibson, upholsterer at St Paul, represents these items on sale in his shop.[149] If London tradesmen held a key position in the commodification of ancestry, in terms of books or portraits, many landed families relied on their local suppliers for a range of dynastic insignia which could be seen in their country houses.[150]

In the wider material culture surrounding ancestry, the genealogical impulse found in the library its appropriate place. The acquisition of expensive folios and their display were a common occurrence. In 1650 very few country houses had libraries and even fewer had them incorporated into their design, but by the late eighteenth century, a house without a library was almost unthinkable as the latter had become one of the 'central living rooms'.[151] The long galleries were now lined with lower shelves showing off the golden spines of folios and quartos. Abigail Williams rightly argued that 'the sales in book-related furniture and accessories' was related to 'a new culture of book display' which was so prevalent in the second half of the eighteenth century.[152] Expensive mahogany bookcases were crafted by Thomas Chippendale and the Society of Upholsterers and painted by Charles Catton and other artisans. Library furniture (chairs, sofas, tables), as well as county maps and busts were luxury commodities which interacted with these large family compilations. In the inventory of Colworth House (Bedfordshire), a 'Valuable and Costly Library Table' was bought by the politician William Lee Antonie (1764–1815): the table was wide enough to carry large folios and equipped 'with four drawers cover'd with best Spanish Leather Carved and Gilt in Spanish Wood' as well as ten 'handsome Library Chairs'.[153]

---

[148] Kate Retford, 'Sensibility and Genealogy in the Eighteenth Century Family Portrait: The Collection at Kedleston Hall', *The Historical Journal*, vol. 46, no. 3 (2003): 533–60.

[149] See in particular, Ashley Sims, '"Selling Consumption": An Examination of Eighteenth-Century English Trade Cards', *Shift*, vol. 5 (2012): 1–22.

[150] On this nuanced dichotomy in the geographies of supply and on the shopping patterns of the Newdigates, the Leighs, and the Drydens, see Jon Stobart and Mark Rothery, *Consumption and the Country House* (Oxford, 2016), 230–40.

[151] Mark Girouard, *Life in the English Country House: A Social and Architectural History* (London, 1978), 108. Christopher Christie, *The British Country House in the Eighteenth Century* (Manchester, 2000).

[152] Abigail Williams, *The Social Life of Books: Reading Together in the Eighteenth-Century Home* (New Haven, 2017), 51.

[153] James Collett-White (ed.), *Inventories of Bedfordshire Country Houses, 1714–1830* (Bedford, 1995), 54.

A FORMAT FOR EVERY USE   57

Furthermore, owners of sizeable volumes were adding their bookplates with their distinctive armorial styles, which kept changing throughout the century: 'a plain shield of squarish proportions, surmounted by a crest and helm, is surrounded by amply mantling' was then replaced by 'the Jacobean style', inspired by the carving of wood and distinguished by the presence of a scallop-shell, and so on.[154] A single bookplate was more expensive than three pocketbooks. Newspapers abounded with adverts from engravers such as William Stephens, who charged 12 shillings for a copper engraving with its 'natural-looking flowers and foliage'.[155] A printer and bookseller from Newcastle Upon Tyne, Joseph Barber, suggested as a remedy against theft to paste on the inside cover of each book 'the owner's name, coat of arms and place of abode'.[156] The rise of luxury taste in the book market is well illustrated by the sharp increase in the number of London engravers: from 63 in 1763 to over 200 in 1802.[157]

To account for the growth of luxury publications, one could assume that many rich customers were to turn to expensive artefacts as 'instruments of social and cultural assertiveness'.[158] For some families, the dignity of ancient ancestors could not be supported by a pocket format but required rather a quarto or folio edition with a personalized binding. As status symbols, they materially embodied the social significance of their owner. *Peerages* and *Baronetages* in this sense could be turned into family treasures. The collecting of expensive volumes not only was a statement but was linked to memory and ways of reassessing the past, as 'books mutate in the values that are set on them in each generation'.[159] We should therefore pay attention to the context in which these monumental volumes were created. Through various examples, we will consider both the material aspect of these luxury items as well as their political significations.

Some early British monuments

Subscription was the most common device used to produce these volumes. It enabled publishers to secure down payments or promises to purchase the book before its publication. This ensured that its production and distribution costs were covered before it went to press. In exchange, subscribers would purchase the volume at a discounted price.[160] Subscriptions gained momentum during the Restoration. The new edition of Camden's *Britannia* by Richard Blome in 1673

---

[154] David Pearson, *Provenance Research in Book History* (London, 1994), 6; see also his useful catalogue of bookplates and named owners of libraries online: <https://bookowners.online>.

[155] Brian North Lee, *Bookplate Collections in Britain: Past and Present* (Apsley, 1991), 64.

[156] Joseph Barber, *The Arms of Northumberland Gentry* (Newcastle, 1743), i; see also his printed crests of the members of the municipal Corporation (1742), BM, Cc,5.4.c.

[157] Raven, *The Business of Books*, 137.   [158] Ibid., 372.

[159] McKitterick, *The Invention of Rare Books*, 65.   [160] Raven, *The Business of Books*, 105.

58   SELLING ANCESTRY

listed about 800 subscribers.[161] Similarly, Dugdale's *Baronage* was supported by a large network within the landed elite. Dugdale took much interest in the growing bibliophilia and even advised Lord Hatton in Kirby Hall on his project of purpose-built country house libraries.[162]

His *Baronage*—a luxury folio in two volumes—was clearly a political statement. In his preface, he indicated that the project of his compilation came into fruition during the Civil War: 'I had not any thoughts of attempting this Work, here made publick, until (by God Almighties disposal) attending the late King Charles the First (of Blessed Memory) in his Garrison at Oxford [...]. I had both leisure and opportunity of perusing many excellent Historical Manuscripts preserved in the famous Bodleian Library.'[163] His book was dedicated to the king and all the nobility who suffered during the last revolution. It relied on the fiction that all the nobles had been zealously attached to the king, thus omitting the role of many noble republicans such as Lord Herbert of Cherbury. Dugdale's initiative was intended to celebrate the restoration of the established religion and the rightful monarch. In this sense, it could be compared to John Foxe's monumental *Book of Martyrs* published a century before.[164] Foxe had relocated the traumatizing history of the Protestant martyrs in the remote medieval history of the Church of England. The execution of Protestants gained further weight by being situated in an earlier period when courageous English clerks had defended their Church from dubious 'Roman' practices. The novelty of the breakdown with Rome was dissimulated by a pluri-secular narrative which was both inclusive and heroic. Similarly, Dugdale attenuated the subversive nature of the last revolution by inserting it in a larger narrative, from the Middle Ages to the Restoration. Some very wealthy nobles still invested directly in the compilation of their own pedigrees. Among them was the earl of Peterborough, who patronized in 1685 the publication of *The Succinct Genealogies of the Noble and Ancient Houses*. Twenty-four copies were printed, and one was purchased for the King's Library for the considerable sum of £15.[165] In England, after 1685, these initiatives became less frequent, in contrast to Scotland and Ireland where luxury directories came to fruition in the first half of the eighteenth century.

Four years after the Act of Union, in 1711, George Crawfurd advertised his project publicly to create 'Monuments of honour and antiquity'.[166] Subscribers

---

[161] Sarah Mendyk, 'Richard Blome', *ODNB*, 2004, Retrieved 6 Jan. 2020, from <https://doi-org.janus.bis-sorbonne.fr/10.1093/ref:odnb/2662>.

[162] John Preston Neale, *Views of the Seats of Noblemen and Gentlemen*, vol. 3 (London, 1826), n.p.

[163] William Hamper (ed.), *The Life, Diary and Correspondence of Sir William Dugdale* (London, 1827), 494.

[164] Alexandra Walsham, *The Reformation of the Landscape: Religion, Identity, and Memory in Early Modern Britain and Ireland* (Oxford, 2011).

[165] Thomas Moule, *Bibliotheca Heraldica Magnæ Britanniæ* (London, 1822), 230.

[166] *Proposal for printing a baronage or a genealogical and historical account of all the noble families of Scotland* (Edinburgh, 1711).

were invited to send their participation to David Freebairn in Edinburgh and to Andrew Millar in London. The large folio was five years in the making. It opens with an alphabetical list of the 230 subscribers, including forty Scottish Lords and many professionals (lawyers, merchants, doctors, etc.) and officers. Twenty-three subscribers bore the name of Crawfurd: some belonged to the nobility, such as Patrick Crawfurd, viscount of Garnock, and others to the middle sorts: several merchants from Glasgow (Matthew and Henry Crawfurd). While George Crawfurd complained of the 'loose' and unreliable genealogical collections gathered by Sir James Balfour, Lord Lyon King of Arms in the reign of Charles I, he was particularly grateful to the University of Glasgow and several of its professors, notably Alexander Dunlop, Gershom Carmichael, and Andrew Ross.[167] Crawfurd's initiative was aimed mainly at celebrating the Scottish peers involved in the Treaty of Union, notably the marquess of Montrose, Lord Privy Seal for Scotland since 1707, and the earl of Marchmont, who 'us'd his utmost endeavours to have it brought about as the only means he thought could secure religion and establish a firm and lasting peace betwixt the two nations'.[168] This initiative fits into the cultural rapprochement between the Scots and the English peers although David Alan insisted on the distinctiveness of Scottish historians which saw history 'as a succession of specifically dynastic achievements' whereas 'their English counterparts [...] frequently expressed the struggle for English liberty in terms of the institutional histories of law and parliament'.[169]

In 1733, a similar project was launched by another Scottish gentleman, David Scott. Dismissing Crawfurd's compilation, Scott found it deprived of any biographical depth which enabled the readers to understand 'behaviours in every action mention'd in the general history'.[170] Again, as for Crawfurd, this Anglo-Scottish operation was conducted from a coffee house in London, where the author would be collecting sums of money. A folio of 150 sheets printed on fine royal paper, his work was advertised by Scott as 'a natural history, Peerage and Baronetage of Scotland' which would include a geographic description of all the shires and cities, as well as engravings of seats, maps, and plates of arms.[171] Subscribers were required to pay half a guinea before the publication and half a guinea when the book was delivered. A remaining prospectus bears some comments from Scott, namely that 680 families had already subscribed to the work, among them the distinguished 'Honble William Trumbull Esq of East-Hampstead' having given already 1 guinea. He was referring to the son of Sir William

---

[167] *Peerage of Scotland* (Edinburgh, 1716), vii.   [168] Ibid., 317.

[169] Allan, '"What's in a Name?": Pedigree and Propaganda in Seventeenth-Century Scotland', 151; Colin Kidd, *British Identities before Nationalism: Ethnicity and Nationhood in the Atlantic World, 1600–1800* (Cambridge, 1999), 132–3.

[170] *Proposals for printing by subscription, a Natural History, Peerage, and Baronetage of Scotland. Being a necessary Supplement to the History of that Nation* (Edinburgh, 1733).

[171] Ibid.

60 SELLING ANCESTRY

Trumbull (1639–1716), a long-serving diplomat for James II and William III and Secretary of State in 1695–7. His father had left a diary in which he claimed to descend from Scottish ascendants:

> As to my family I have never troubled myself to search for a long pedigree, being of opinion that no man's dead ancestors can support his credit, if he himself does not keep it by some merit of his own. However, we may derive from a very antient Family & name in Scotland, ennobled at first by an act of valour (yt time & just originall of all honours), as may be seen in Hector Boetius & Holingshead.[172]

By subscribing to this expensive book, William Trumbull's son, out of filial piety, desired to celebrate his father's deeds and fulfil his wishes to be linked to a Scottish dynasty. In Ireland, Aaron Crowley, who presented himself as 'herald painter of Dublin', produced in 1725 a *Peerage* in folio dedicated to the Lord Lieutenant, Lord Carteret. In his preface, he inserted an exchange of letters between him and Robert Dale of the College of Arms. The aim was to discredit William Hawkins, the Ulster King of Arms, condemned for being unable to 'contribute much for making the work entirely perfect' and even to be 'averse' to the initiative.[173] Like Charles Catton, Crowley was a craftsman whose reliability in genealogical matters was open to question. He therefore presented his writing as being the result of a close collaboration between him and Dale since 1699. Again, the publisher insisted on the connection between Dublin and London against his local enemy. Crowley advertised his prowess for all the nobles and gentlemen in need of escutcheons and hatchments and all other coats of arms and pedigrees for coaches and rooms as well as coffins and inscriptions 'for men, women and Children, as they are in London, at reasonable rates'.[174] A curious poem also celebrated the skills of Crowley:

> The Art and knowledge that adorns his Name,
> Made Envy strive to crush his growing fame
> But still his Judgment and prov'd skill prevail'd
> And envy of her vile designs has fail'd
> But this new work, *HIBERNIA's PEERAGE nam'd*
> Like Gold refin'd shall always be esteem'd.[175]

In the first part, Crowley designed some elaborate floral patterns which illustrate a detailed account of the symbols attached to flowers and trees used in heraldic art.

---

[172] Oxford, All Souls College, MS 317, fol. 1. [173] *Peerage of Ireland* (Dublin, 1725), preface.
[174] Ibid.   [175] Ibid.

A FORMAT FOR EVERY USE   61

Scattered initiatives of this sort contrasted with the more ambitious projects which took place in London at the accession of George III.

Luxury folios and the accession of George III

In the 1760s several monumental *Peerages* were published and were aimed at reinforcing public loyalism. In 1762, William Guthrie released his *Complete history of English Peerage* (£2. 16s.), followed by Joseph Edmondson, *Baronagium Genealogicum* (£25. 5s.), Sir Robert Douglas and his *Scottish Peerage* (£1. 16s.) and Alexander Jacob, *Complete English Peerage* (£5). Far from being a mere coincidence, these initiatives were designed to reinvigorate a dynastic culture centred around the celebration of the royal prerogative and coincided with the creation of sixteen new peerages.[176]

In his *Proposals for printing by subscription a complete history of English Peerage*, Guthrie claimed to have created a new sort of genealogical history. He contended that his book 'may serve as a supplement to all the general histories of England [...] supported with characters and reflections to which this species of writing has always been a stranger'.[177] The publication was to be illustrated with elegant copper-plates ('handsomely finished') by skilled engravers such as Charles Grignion and Barak Longmate, both of whom had worked for the *Gentleman's Magazine*. His venture was supported by many booksellers. Some operated in London, but the majority were located outside London, notably in Salisbury, Bath, Bristol, Tunbridge Wells, Oxford, Cambridge, York, Edinburgh, Dublin, and The Hague. The two volumes contained the pedigrees of the royal family and of twelve peers. Again, the luxury profile of the edition was in itself a political statement. The celebration of George III and his family could not be achieved through the publication of mere shilling pocket family guides.

The second luxurious compilation was directed by Joseph Edmondson (*Baronagium Genealogicum: or the pedigrees of the English peers*), financed by subscription under royal patronage. Edmondson was coach-painter to Queen Charlotte and rose to a herald's position in 1764.[178] As Guthrie's *Peerage*, the *Baronagium* was presented to the public as a grandiose project in folio which contained the king's and the lords' family trees on imperial paper. Copper plates were made by Francisco Bartolozzi, who had just been appointed engraver to the

---

[176] There was a strong correlation between the edition of large folios and the aspiration for a stronger government. On this subject, see Isabelle Olivero: 'Les grands formats paraissent privilégiés dans les périodes où les structurent du savoir et du pouvoir se hiérarchisent et se rigidifient comme sous la Restauration', *Les trois révolutions du livre de poche* (Paris, 2022), 74.

[177] *Proposals for printing by subscription a complete history of English Peerage* (London, 1762).

[178] Adrian Ailes, 'Edmondson, Joseph (bap. 1732, d. 1786)', *ODNB*, 2008. Retrieved 27 May 2020, from <https://doi-org.janus.bis-sorbonne.fr/10.1093/ref:odnb/8491>.

62 SELLING ANCESTRY

king. Both publications in 1762 and 1763 were dedicated to the king, 'the fountain of honour', and his family (the dukes of Cornwall, Cumberland, and York, as well as the prince of Wales). George III was represented in Guthrie's preface with his regalia and parliamentary robes. It seems likely that Guthrie and Edmondson were collaborating together. Their lists of subscribers included the same individuals: the royal family, ninety-eight peers, two booksellers, Mr Edwards and Mr Walter (six copies), All Souls College, and Gray's Inn. Their compilations could be used in a complementary manner. Guthrie provided historical narrative, while Edmondson published mostly pedigrees. Although in a different style, they dealt with similar subjects, namely the celebration of the royal peace inside and outside Britain, and the mystical virtue of a British king.

Against Pitt's bellicose views, both publications celebrated the peace treaty with the French and the many British victories. The latter were linked to the restoration of the royal prerogative over his subjects. The defeat of the French went hand in hand with the humbling of some fractious magnates and the strengthening of the royal prerogative over Parliament. George III was justified in his attempt to rein in parliamentary opposition and free himself from some unruly advisers such as Pitt and other Whig ministers. The king would later be able to rely on his elder son George, duke of Cornwall, born in August 1762, who was celebrated by Guthrie as a 'child of the public', the one who would always stand 'foremost in the opposition to dangerous and unconstitutional measures'.[179] An engraving depicted the royal couple in a state of adoration in front of their newly born child. This very Catholic scene of adoration is rendered more acceptable to Protestant norms by the insertion of mythical figures, Zeus and Diana, holding the child (Illus. 1.6).

In the background to this nativity scene, a well-ordered crowd in London gathered to raise the British flag, in contrast with the riots which took place during the Excise Crisis of 1733. The monarchs and their family were the only ones able to rise above the factional struggle and to impose peace and justice on their subjects. Alluding to George II and his son Frederick, Guthrie deplored the domestic troubles which had prevented them from ruling as they wished. Implicitly, Walpole and some other ministers were accused of having weakened the royal prerogative, whereas the prince of Wales had 'comported himself with just regret and duty to his Majesty's person and authority'.[180] Only a king restored to his former prerogative would be able to give a voice to the people outside Parliament, to re-establish trust in the monarchy and to defend the commercial interests of London, 'the great emporium of commerce'.[181] Guthrie borrowed many of his ideas from Bolingbroke, including his notion of a 'patriot king'.[182]

---

[179] *A complete history*, xii.　　[180] *A complete history*, vol. 1, 30.　　[181] Ibid.

[182] Max Skjönsberg, 'Lord Bolingbroke's Theory of Party and Opposition', *The Historical Journal*, vol. 59, no. 4 (2016): 947–73. Christine Gerrard, *The Patriot Opposition to Walpole: Politics, Poetry, and National Myth, 1725–1742* (Oxford, 1994).

Illus. 1.6 *A complete history of the English Peerage* (1763).
© National Library of Scotland, AB. 8.90.2

Furthermore, his *Peerage* was aimed at countering the anti-Caledonian feelings which rocketed after the nomination of Lord Bute as the prime favourite. The campaign of libels against him was driven by an old fear of a disproportionate Scottish influence. Some prominent Scots, such as the eminent publisher William Strahan, felt the need to Anglicize their names.[183] Guthrie insisted on the celebration of British heroes, whether Whig or Tory, English or Scottish. In an implicit parallel with Bute, he depicted Marlborough as a champion of the royal prerogative and of the British cause, praising his importance as an astute favourite to the queen: 'who appeared to be herself so little of a party-woman, that she inclined to the opinion of the earl of Marlborough'.[184] The queen's affection enabled him to give the full measure of his talents. Narrating Marlborough's glorious victories against the French, Guthrie described the pillar at Blenheim which conveyed 'the sense which the British nation had of his transcendent merit' and shall stand 'as long the British name and language last'.[185] Along with Marlborough, he celebrated some moderate Whigs for their involvement in the

---

[183] John Brewer, 'The Misfortunes of Lord Bute: A Case-Study in Eighteenth-Century Political Argument and Public Opinion', *The Historical Journal*, vol. 16, no. 1 (1973): 3–43 at 19.
[184] *A complete history*, vol. 1, 165.   [185] Ibid., 366.

Act of Union: 'we must not forget, that by the indefatigable efforts of the Whig ministry in England, the Scotch parliament before the union, settled the crown in the same line'.[186] Guthrie also defended the memory of some Tories such as Sir Edward Seymour, who like Marlborough, was instrumental in the establishment of 'the Protestant religion and personal liberty'.[187] Alluding to his 'lineal descent' from the first duke of Somerset, Guthrie added that Seymour was 'the first patriot who obtained for Englishmen the just and precise knowledge of that freedom, which constitutes their birth-right. The treatment his character has met with from history, is a flagrant instance, that nothing can be sacred from the sting of party.'[188] Sir Edward Seymour and the first duke of Somerset were depicted as leading the allegory of liberty in front of Britannia (Illus. 1.7).

Finally, both Guthrie's and Edmondson's *Peerages* insisted on the crucial role played by the College of Arms. Guthrie praised the support provided by the king's heralds in his compilation and claimed that all arms had been blazoned in the 'Heralds-Office'. Edmondson was the first herald since Dugdale to commit to

Illus. 1.7 *A complete history of the English Peerage* (1763).
© National Library of Scotland, AB. 8.90.2

---

[186] Ibid., 14.   [187] Ibid., 172.   [188] Ibid., 173.

A FORMAT FOR EVERY USE   65

the publishing of a *Peerage*. He is depicted in the first volume kneeling in front of the king, dedicatee of the whole work (Illus. 1.8).

As the natural chain of being was being restored, the king appeared both as the ultimate arbiter in the distribution of honours and as the guardian of the validity of the pedigree. George III had exhibited a singular interest in the details of peerage creation and in the increasing number of abeyant baronies. He had been keen to regain his control of the peerage and at first showed a clear intention to limit its expansion.[189] Despite many requests for peerages, the elections of 1768 and 1774 were not followed by any such promotion. The short-term value of these creations was made obvious to the reader and was seen as weakening the royal prerogative. Guthrie deplored the 'backwardness of the House of Peers' in 1712, and notably the Whigs, who had forced Queen Anne and her ministers to the 'desperate expedient of creating twelve peers in one day'.[190] Whig oligarchs were described as the enemy of the kingdom's hierarchical structure.

And so in both compilations, the king and his College of Arms appeared as the keeper of the nobility against the corrosive effect of partisan spirit in Parliament. In their monumental folios, Guthrie and Edmondson celebrated the restoration of a well-ordered sequence of ranks and degrees in human society, at the top of which were God and king. Such longing for a well-ordained social hierarchy was supported by even more prominent literary figures, such as Samuel Johnson who defended the existence of 'fixed, invariable, external rules of distinction of rank, which create no jealousy, as they are allowed to be accidental'.[191] If social pre-eminence is not necessarily a sign of merit, it must be respected. While expressing middle rank values, Johnson did not hide his concern for social order in the chaotic and anonymous metropolis. 'Jealousy' and resentment were as destructive as pride and entitlement.

The publication of Guthrie's *Peerage* was met with mixed responses. Unsurprisingly, it was hailed by Smollett in the *Critical Review*: 'This Work denominated a history, to distinguish it as we suppose from the jejune, skeleton, undertakings of this kind' and Guthrie was compared to Dugdale, 'the principal dealer in the walk of antiquity'.[192] Bute's enemies were less enthusiastic. John Almon, who was at the centre of the country Whig opposition to the Scottish favourite, was certainly less impressed. In the spring of 1763, he published *The Review of Lord Bute's Administration*. Dedicated to Lord Cavendish, duke of

---

[189] 'The dominant impression that emerges from the king's handling of such requests is that political considerations were normally subordinate to social ones, especially the suitability of a prospective peer in terms of family and estate', William C. Lowe, 'George III, Peerage Creations and Politics, 1760–1784', *The Historical Journal*, vol. 35, no. 3 (1992): 587–609 at 592.

[190] *A complete history*, vol. 1, 455.

[191] Quoted by Penelope J. Corfield, 'Class by Name and Number in Eighteenth-Century England', *History*, vol. 72 (1987), 40.

[192] Tobias George Smollett (ed.), *The Critical review, or, Annals of literature*, vol. 18 (London, 1764), 161.

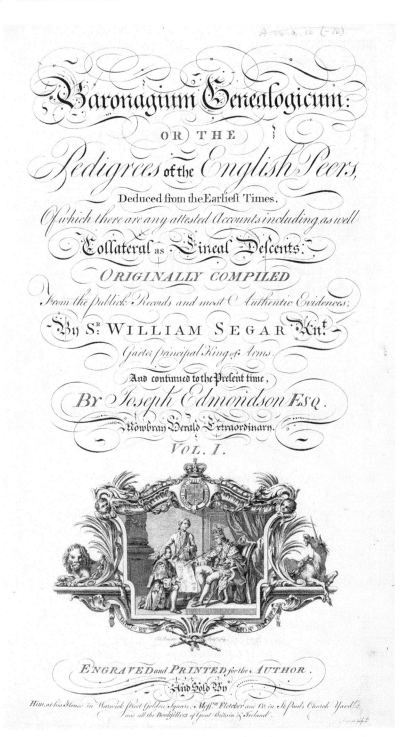

Illus. 1.8 *Baronagium Genealogicum.* Frontispiece (1764).
© National Library of Scotland, A. 34a. 12–16

Devonshire, *The Review* started with a quotation from Guthrie's *Peerage*, namely: 'the title of favourite, let him be ever so deserving, has always been odious in England'.[193] He was referring to the long passage in which Guthrie celebrated the success of Marlborough and the unjust criticism that even the worthiest favourites had received from the opposition. Guthrie implied that Bute, as Marlborough, was to be judged more favourably by posterity than by his ungrateful contemporaries. Almon invited his readers to consider what he thought to be a more relevant parallel, that between Walpole and Bute. A chart opposed the two favourites: Walpole had obtained his peerage after many decades of services while Bute had been elevated by George III before achieving anything:

Sir Robert Walpole's rewards	The Earl of Bute's rewards
An English peerage *after* his services.	An English peerage *before* his services.
Richmond Park.	Richmond Park.
The Garter.	The Garter.
A great place in the Exchequer for his son.	A great place in the Exchequer for his son.
Ample provision for his brother and immediate dependants.	Ample provision for his brother and immediate dependants.[194]

Furthermore, Almon's dedication to Lord Cavendish could be interpreted as a vindication of this family against the many insinuations interspersed by Guthrie in his compilation. The latter implied that Cavendish draped himself as a main figure of the uncorrupted parliamentary opposition while most of his ancestors had been astute courtiers. He recalled that during the reign of Henry VIII, William Cavendish 'stood in a high degree of favour and intimacy with the Cardinal Wolsey' and 'received vast additions to his fortune from the Crown; particularly several lands and manors belonging to dissolved Priories and Abbeys'.[195] Under James II, William Cavendish, the first duke of Devonshire, is described as a refined courtier with an excessive sense of honour. Guthrie reminded the reader that Devonshire was sent to prison and fined £30,000, not for the defence of high Protestant ideals but for a squalid dispute with Doctor Nicholas Culpepper. Against the order of the king, Devonshire had led the seemingly insolent doctor 'by the nose out of the room and chastised him with his cane'.[196]

As the Whig authors chose Sir Edward Seymour as the prime target for his supposed haughtiness, Guthrie counter-attacked by providing the portrait of an even more conceited magnate. Cavendish was described as a 'rational Christian, in every sense of the word, but that which is adopted by madmen and enthusiasts'.[197]

---

[193] John Almon, *Review of Lord Bute's Administration* (London, 1763), i.   [194] Ibid., 114.
[195] *A complete history*, vol. 1, 303.   [196] Ibid., 326.   [197] Ibid., 346.

68   SELLING ANCESTRY

Guthrie's initiative had not been ignored by the Whig and the perfidious attack hidden among long narratives was not lost on his readers.

Bibliomania in revolutionary times

The late eighteenth century is characterized by a reinforced bibliomania, which had been facilitated by the growth of cheaper editions in the 1780s and much later by the introduction of the steam press and stereotype printing. Hence, seasoned book collectors wished to distinguish themselves from the flood of cheap formats. It may well be, too, that some events during the French Revolution, notably the destruction of noble documents, triggered a defensive attachment in favour of expensive family treasures.[198] This could be best characterized by the publication of highly expensive compilations. In 1793, the engraver Robert Pollard sold a *Peerage* for £1. 11s. per volume in quarto (*The Peerage of Great Britain*). Each volume was limited to the history of fifteen families along with ten engravings of their castles, their portraits, and coats of arms. They were to be printed in royal quarto by the press of William Bulmer (1757–1830) and revised by an officer of the College of Arms. This undertaking, it seems, was not successful as only one volume was actually published. Similarly, the most expensive directory of the period was a complete commercial failure. The nine volumes of *British Family Antiquity* were sold by William Playfair for £90. Although he managed to obtain royal patronage, his production costs were such that he was bankrupted even before selling his volumes on the market.[199] Like most entrepreneurs who launched themselves in the making of luxury directories, Playfair came from the world of craftsmen.[200] In his appeal for subscribers, he aimed 'to convert the history of our illustrious nobility into a barrier against such unprincipled innovation'.[201] He informed the readers of his intimate knowledge of France and of his witnessing the destruction of the noble order.[202] The extravagant price of his collection was due not only to the number of volumes but also to the many coloured engravings. Playfair indeed attempted to demonstrate the importance of birth and of ancestors through logarithmic graphs and charts, hence divesting 'the pedigree out of its antiquated form'.[203]

---

[198] Albert Soboul, 'De la pratique des terriers au brûlement des titres féodaux', *Annales historiques de la Révolution française*, vol. 36 (1964): 149–58.

[199] J. F. Dunyach, 'Le British Family Antiquity de William Playfair (1809–1811), une entreprise généalogique', in Jettot and Lezowski (eds), *The Genealogical Enterprise*, 319–39.

[200] He was first apprenticed at the Houston Mill near East Linton. Ian Spence, 'Playfair, William (1759–1823)', *ODNB*, 2004. Retrieved 10 Apr. 2020, from <https://doi-org.janus.bis-sorbonne.fr/10.1093/ref:odnb/22370>.

[201] *A fair and candid address to the nobility and baronets of the United Kingdom* (London, 1809), 10.

[202] 'Amongst many strange exhibitions of a levelling spirit, that I was witness to in France, one was the burning the records belonging to all the nobility in that Kingdom, which took place by order of the legislative assembly', ibid., 95.

[203] Ibid., 91.

A FORMAT FOR EVERY USE 69

Apart from these last monumental initiatives which did not sell well, a more significant trend was the growth of bibliographic catalogues intended to guide wealthy collectors in their acquisitions. Expensive books were changing hands rapidly and their values increased considerably in the late eighteenth century.[204] The first catalogues appeared in Italy and France and soon became a common occurrence in Britain. The *Bibliographia Parisina* (1643), by Jacob de Saint-Charles and dedicated to Gabriel Naudé, became a stepping stone in the introduction of the bibliographic practices to Britain. In his *Traicté des plus belles bibliothèques* (1644), Saint-Charles transcribed many Italian, English, and German titles.[205] His European outlook increased its influence throughout the continent. The presence of many English collectors in Paris during the English civil war and its aftermath was instrumental in the growing success of bibliophilia in England. A catalogue in Latin was published in 1674 by the gentleman-antiquary Thomas Gore: *Catalogus in Certa Capita*. In the late eighteenth century, extensive and specialized catalogues became available. Some were enumerating all the genealogical works which had been issued between 1674 and 1800. Written in English, they provided some guidance into an unprecedented number of references. Unlike Gore's catalogue, the late eighteenth-century publications contained many detailed descriptions and commentaries on those works as well as biographical notes on the publishers. The main catalogues were made successively by James Dallaway in 1793 (*Inquiries into the origin and progress of the science of heraldry*), Thomas Moule in 1822 (*Bibliotheca Heraldica Magnae Britanniae*), and the herald Charles George Young in 1827 (*Catalogue of Works on the Peerage and the Baronetage of England, Scotland and Ireland*). They were destined to demonstrate the formation of a 'genealogical science' accessible to the social elite and made with the latter's contribution. The publication of Dallaway's *Inquiries* led to an enthusiastic review in the high conservative *British Critic*, which insisted on the common heraldic culture, initially in France and England, and their late separation. In a stark contrast to the situation in France, the journalist quoted Dallaway at length about the English Civil War, which had allowed the survival of genealogical practices thanks to the ambiguous behaviour of Cromwell and the fact that among royalist families, 'many of remote ancestry had nothing to transmit to their successors but the satisfaction of innate nobleness'.[206]

Some publishers of these bibliographical catalogues had been involved in the sale of family directories. This was the case with the Lowndes family, prominent London booksellers who invested in the various editions of Collins's *Peerage*

---

[204] Archer Taylor, *Book Catalogues: Their Varieties and Uses* (Winchester, 2nd edn, 1986).

[205] Ian Maclean, 'Louis Jacob de Saint-Charles and the Development of Specialist Bibliography', in *Learning and the Market Place: Essay in the History of the Early Modern Book* (Leiden, Boston, 2009), 403; Henri-Jean Martin, *Livre, pouvoirs et société à Paris au XVIIe siècle, 1598–1701* (Geneva, 3rd edn, 1999).

[206] *The British Critic and Quarterly Theological Review*, vol. 4 (1794), 232.

70   SELLING ANCESTRY

(1766, 1768, 1778, 1784, 1812). Thomas Lowndes's circulating library consisted of over 10,000 volumes. They also imposed themselves as specialist retailers in expensive second-hand compilations. Lowndes's catalogue of books for the year 1794 advertised a copy of Dugdale's *Baronage* for £5. He later sold a copy, old gilt Russia, bordered with gold on the sides, for £10. Later, the Lowndeses published two influential reference books: *Bibliotheca Britannica* (1824) and *The Bibliographer's manual of English literature* (1834). Similarly, Thomas Payne and Henry Foss in Pall Mall advertised in 1819 a copy of Brydges's *Peerage* (calf gilt) for 8 guineas or in Russia extra with marbled leaves for 9; a Douglas's *Peerage* (neat in Russia) for 3 guineas and its new edition by Wood in 1813 for £4. 10s. Pocket directories with woodcuts had little value. Kimber's *Peerage* would be offered for only 2s.[207]

Despite similar titles, the *Peerages* and *Baronetages* which were sold in eighteenth-century Britain came in many formats and prices, thus accounting for the increasingly fragmented state of the book market. Though their publishers were reluctant to define their precise functions, one could assume that they were initially intended for distinct readers and users. Some major differences existed between the practical content of pocket compilations, the more speculative historical directories, and the monumental editions. Some were used as registers, others as historical guidelines or expensive luxury items to be admired in private libraries.

They also sustained different political mindsets. The pocket versions were immune to the celebration of ancient lineage and mainly provided up-to-date practical data. Meanwhile, the octavo historical compilations and larger formats were aimed at celebrating the virtues of titled families. While their authors had political axes to grind, their perspectives were very different: from the celebration of modern families to the gothic reactionary universe of the post-revolutionary period. These ideological aspects should not be overestimated. Many publishers, even the more radical booksellers such as John Almon, eschewed partisan agendas in favour of pure profit. Almon launched himself into a scathing attack against the Tories and Guthrie's *Peerage* while at the same time failing to notice that, in his own edition of Collins's *Peerage*, several articles were also directed at the Whigs. Like many other prominent London booksellers, Almon distributed a vast range of publications, aimed at distinct audiences and fulfilling different agendas. He was either unable or unwilling to impose strict controls over his large portfolio. Therefore, in the second chapter, we will reconsider our tripartite definition with a more critical view, as it ignores the many overlaps between these publications and creates the risk of singling out social expectations.

---

[207] *A catalogue of books now selling*, vol. 7 (London, 1819), 247.

2
The Many Ways of Reading and Selling

In her diary Gertrude Savile commented sarcastically on an evening that her brother Sir George Savile and his wife passed in London between supper at 5 and 11 p.m. She observed how the couple spent 'most of the time compareing the Pedigree of the Saviles (in a book of the Baronets lately come out), with the account Brother sent to be inserted'.[1] The book she was referring to was *The English Baronets* published by Thomas Wotton in 1727. What they were actually doing for six hours, perusing this directory, is somewhat of a riddle. How were they reading it? Were they reading the book aloud or turning the pages in silence? Were they reading it in isolation or alongside gazettes or heavier county histories? Indeed, these compilations could be read in many ways.

In Savile's case, a further clue appeared in the preface. Wotton explained to his readers that whenever a baronet was elevated to the peerage, his previous distinctions were 'swallow'd up in higher Titles' and as a consequence, the author chose not to deal with collateral branches.[2] However, he mentioned several exceptions including Savile's, whose baronetcy had been reversed to a younger branch. One could imagine why Gertrude's brother had been so eager to collaborate with Wotton and spend so much time perusing his work. As the only son of a rector, the new Sir George Savile inherited the title in 1701 from William Savile, second marquess of Halifax, a distant cousin in the senior line of the first baronet.[3] He may have enjoyed seeing his name linked to many prominent families and famous ancestors, from the 'Savelli', Roman 'consuls before and after the time of our Saviour', to some nobles in Anjou as well as to the learned Sir Henry Savile in the Elizabethan period and the 'Trimmer' Baron Halifax.[4] Savile would not be wrong in believing that the whole of English history could be read through his 'own' article. His name completed a continuous patrilineal dynasty which overshadowed the legal struggles and resentment raised by succession. By contrast, Wotton's *Baronetage* merely mentioned that Gertrude was 'yet unmarried'.[5] One might well understand that while Sir George Savile and his wife were so absorbed in the

---

[1] Gertrude Savile, 29 Dec. 1727, in Alan Saville (ed.), *Secret Comment: The Diaries of Gertrude Savile, 1721–1757* (Nottingham, 1997), 87.
[2] *The English Baronets*, vii.
[3] On the Savile Baronets, see Andrew Hanham, 'Savile, Sir George, seventh baronet (bap. 1678, d. 1743), landowner and politician', *ODNB*, 2003. Retrieved 21 Jan. 2020 from <https://doi-org.janus.bis-sorbonne.fr/10.1093/ref:odnb/93366>.
[4] *The English Baronets*, vol. 1, 60–3.   [5] Ibid., 63.

Selling Ancestry: Family Directories and the Commodification of Genealogy in Eighteenth-Century Britain. Stéphane Jettot, Oxford University Press. © Stéphane Jettot 2023. DOI: 10.1093/oso/9780192865960.003.0003

72 SELLING ANCESTRY

complex niceties of the Savile branches, his sister was less impressed as she did not benefit much from this change of fortune. Her diary conveys her bitterness for being under the despotic authority of her brother and for her financial dependence.

The quotation demonstrates that, as well as a folio or an octavo, a duodecimo directory could be intensely scrutinized by a baronet in his library. As a Fellow of the Royal Society, Savile may have been interested in the historical aspect of the compilation, composed of three volumes of more than 600 pages: hardly a synoptic pocketbook. In the case of Wotton's *Baronetage*, the format was misleading. A duodecimo could be read not only in passing but in a more detailed way for hours on end. For some moralists, it could be regarded as a salutary family ritual. John Brown complained about the 'man of fashion' who would have little regard for the importance of 'family devotion, which concluded the guiltless evening entertainments of his ancestry'.[6] The distinction between a utilitarian or a polite reader appears fraught with difficulty. In many ways, reader expectations and appropriations could not be easily predicted.

To better explore this theme, we will first consider various reading experiences described in certain novels. Gertrude Savile, as an angry 'self-pitying eighteenth-century spinster', jealous of her brother, provides 'a veritable antidote to the cloying heroines of contemporary fiction'.[7] This comment is worth mentioning as it points out the problematic nature of novels for social historians.[8] With respect to these compilations, one should interpret with great caution the novels in which family directories are mentioned. Paul Langford rightly stated that 'a *Complete Peerage* drawn from the pages of contemporary fiction would be an impressive tome, far outweighing its factual counterpart'.[9] Whether in the case of Austen's *Persuasion* or in Thackeray's *Vanity Fair*, we will see that both related to the same caricatural figure, namely solitary old patriarchs in their libraries. While these fictitious characters are worth considering in their complexity, we should also look into the correspondence between publishers and their customers. An underlying tension existed between the taste for expensive compilations which reflected the family honour and practical needs related to their constant perambulations between estates and cities. Many polite customers condemned the publication of heavy compilations as cumbersome and even useless.

Secondly, with few exceptions such as John Debrett and later Henry Colburn, who created their own brand in the 1810s and 1820s, most of the family compilations, whether small or large, cheap or expensive, were owned by tight-knit

---

[6] *An Estimate of the Manners and Principles of the Times*, vol. 1 (London, 1758), 54.

[7] Elaine Chalus, 'Shorter Notice. Secret Comment: The *Diaries of Gertrude Savile*', *The English Historical Review*, vol. 114, no. 456 (1999): 451–2.

[8] For a stimulating essay on the subject, see Judith Lyon-Caen, *La griffe du temps: ce que l'histoire peut dire de la littérature* (Paris, 2019).

[9] *Public Life and the Propertied Englishman*, 522.

THE MANY WAYS OF READING AND SELLING   73

groups of the most prominent London booksellers such as Knapton, Cadell, Longman, Almon, Nichols, and the Lowndeses. Their dominant position enabled them to provide many different versions of the same content. Through their shops, circulating libraries, or gazettes, they were in a position to make these prints accessible to many individuals which otherwise would have been beyond their purchasing power.

Finally, the genealogical enquiries generated by these publications unearthed many unsavoury stories which were likewise read with pleasure and interest. Correspondence between publishers and their customers abounds with many derogatory comments and gossip. Some readers used the margins of their directories to compose their own critical accounts. In the 1770s and 1780s in particular, a few compilations went so far as to exploit the rich satirical vein of the bashing of nobles. Even if they bear a conventional title, they followed a more radical and subversive agenda, raising various debates on the definition of nobility.

1. Exploring readers' mindsets

Old gentlemen and their 'precious'

As a highly symbolic venue, libraries feature in many stunning events invented by novelists such as murder, breath-taking revelations, or joyful reconciliation. In the dramatic plot, reading practices had even some worrying consequences and some books are endowed with a malign influence. It would be hard not to mention, in *Persuasion*, Sir Walter Elliot laying his *Baronetage* on the table of his library opened at his own article. Labelled as the 'book of the book', his compilation appeared as the quintessential family treasure for a self-centred landlord. His 'two handsome duodecimo pages' corresponded to the 1808 edition of Debrett sold for the hefty sum of £1. 13s.[10] Unlike Sir George Savile and his wife, who were reading their directory together, Elliot consumed his alone. Jane Austen described how the compilation strengthened the baronet in his vain patriarchal attitude and his hopeless self-delusion. It would be tempting to oppose this kind of reading to that of the almanacs and pocketbooks which were linked to the practical bustle of urban politeness. His daughter Anne is displayed reading the *Navy List* which recorded the 'honours earned and merited and denotes the active and effective'.[11] Navy almanacs were resources for the young, eager to embrace the urban life and

---

[10] Jane Austen, *Persuasion*, ed. James Kinsley (Oxford, 2004), 9, 12.

[11] Sandy Byrne, *Jane Austen's Possessions and Dispossessions: The Significance of Objects* (London, 2014), 155. See also Deidre Shauna Lynch in her preface to the 2004 edition: 'While her family has cultivated their obliviousness to history, with the result that after two decades of war the names of admirals still mean nothing to them, Ann had had the chronicles of public life—history's raw material—all to herself', *Persuasion*, xxii.

74 SELLING ANCESTRY

who were seeking the latest war news in trying times. As for Elizabeth, the eldest daughter, she expressed much resentment toward the *Baronetage*, an emotion which could be compared to that felt by Gertrude Savile. Like her, Elizabeth 'made the book an evil; and more than once, when her father had left it open on the table near her, had she closed it, with averted eyes, and pushed it away'.[12] Elliot's silent reading contrasted with Savile and his wife reading together. The same dramatic function is assigned to the Peerage in *Vanity Fair*, though the social context was somewhat different. Old Osborne belonged to the ascending London middle sort and wanted to emulate his superiors. To satisfy this passion that was the object of ridicule, he kept a copy of the *Peerage* next to a 'great scarlet Bible and Prayer-Book' in his study where 'no member of the household, child or domestic, ever enter [...] without a certain terror'.[13] His Peerage was described as the 'great red bible', 'a pompous book [...] shining all over with gold' kept safely in his bookcase.[14] In Osborne's mind, 'The Peerage replaces the Bible as the ultimate parental text, laying claim to ownership of a particular family line.'[15] His behaviour was contrasted to that of the old baronet Sir Crawley, who was introduced as the least likely man to have a *Baronetage* in his pocket, although he was later described as consulting Louis Pierre d'Hozier's armorial to convince himself of the 'high breeding' of his governess, whom he hoped to marry.[16] Whether it be Elliot, Osborne, or Crawley, the intrigues revolved around old men in their library using directories as a tool to enforce their patriarchal agenda on the younger generation. From these extracts, we would be right in assuming that these compilations were instrumental in the imposition of the fathers' wishes on their children's matrimonial choices.

A similar point could be made about lesser-known fiction. In 1798, Mary Ann Hanway in *Ellinor: Or, The World as it is*, described the old duke of Southernwood's pursuit of the youthful Ellinor. Again, he was mocked by her friend Lady John, who reminded him that he would soon 'be gathered to [his] noble progenitors, as that Doomsday Book of youthful love and young desires, y'ecleped Collins's Peerage'.[17] In his 1771 drama (*The Man of the Family. A Sentimental Comedy*), Charles Jenner displayed a similar generational conflict between the young Charles and his 'poor father' who urged him to study Collins's *Peerage* in order to 'trace your own extraction, and contemplate on the importance and antiquity of your descent'.[18] To which the son replied that he had

---

[12] *Persuasion*, 12.   [13] William Makepeace Thackeray, *Vanity Fair* (London, 1993), 215.
[14] Ibid., 217.
[15] Melissa S. Jenkins, *Fatherhood, Authority, and British Reading Culture, 1831–1907* (London, 2016), 82.
[16] Thackeray, *Vanity Fair*, 81.
[17] Mary Ann Hanway, *Ellinor: Or, The World as it is*, vol. 3 (London, 1798), 23.
[18] *The Man of the Family* (London, 1771), 3.

THE MANY WAYS OF READING AND SELLING   75

little faith in 'this foible of family-pride' and hoped to acquire some merit, 'without depending absolutely upon that of my great-great grandfather'.[19]

These literary commonplaces could be linked to the taste of a middle-class novel-reading public which gained the upper hand during the age of revolutions and imperial wars in the late eighteenth century.[20] Such passages are crucial in the dramatic structure of these novels and allude to genealogical obsessions and the tyrannical patriarchy which were familiar to contemporaries. That said, interpretations of these extracts are problematic and still much discussed among historians and literary scholars. Contemporary novels did not simply reflect the triumph of individualistic and idealistic values, nor condone the impractical desires of some protagonists. Some critics have argued that in *Persuasion*, the *Baronetage* or the *Navy List* were merely two sides of the same coin and conveyed an equal 'respect for rank and tradition'.[21] Jane Austen was familiar with genealogical guides as her elder brother, Edward Austen Knight, owned in his library at Chawton House three copies of *Debrett's Baronetage* (1802, 1804, 1806) and two *Pocket Peerages*.[22] One copy—*The New Baronetage of England* (1804)—has been heavily annotated at the entry for his wife's family, the Bridges of Goodnestone.[23] Far from being on the wane, interest in lineage and rank was still a prevailing feature among Austen's contemporaries. Ruth Perry rightly pointed out that 'one cannot extrapolate from fiction to historical reality [...]. Fiction must thus be understood variously as compensatory, nostalgic, wishful, consoling.'[24]

In another passage from *Vanity Fair*, Thackeray wrote that the Osborne daughters shared the same curiosity and 'conned over the peerage, and talked about the nobility'.[25] Expensive compilations were not only the preserve of patriarchal values. In his previous novel, *The Placid Man*, Charles Jenner described Miss Clayton, a young woman in the breakfast room, reading 'Collins's Peerage, which together with the Court Kalendar, always lay in the window'.[26] She was congratulated by her father for her taste: 'I love to see young women usefully employed. You will find there many of your illustrious ancestors,

---

[19] Ibid.   [20] Robert Miles, *Romantic Misfit* (London, 2008), 149.

[21] Janine Barchas, *Matters of Fact in Jane Austen: History, Location, and Celebrity* (Baltimore, 2012), 253.

[22] <https://chawtonhouse.org/the-library/the-knight-collection> (bay 1, col. 1, sh. 2).

[23] On the marginalia left by Edward Austen or Elizabeth Bridges, see Gillian Dow and Katie Hasley, 'Jane Austen's Reading: The Chawton Years', *Jane Austen Society of North America*, vol. 30, no. 2 (2010). Retrieved 17 Apr. 2022 from <https://jasna.org/persuasions/on-line/vol30no2/dow-halsey.html>.

[24] Ruth Perry, ' "All in the Family": Consanguinity, Marriage, and Property', in Peter Garside and Karen O'Brien (eds), *English and British Fiction, 1750–1820: The Oxford History of the Novel in English*, vol. 2 (Oxford, 2015), 409.

[25] 'Becky and Briggs and Mrs Bute's daughters all, for their differing reasons, pore over Burke's *Peerage*, a repeated object of veneration', Kate Flint, 'Women, Men and the Reading of *Vanity Fair*', in James Raven, Helen Small, and Naomi Tadmor (eds), *The Practice and Representation of Reading in England* (Cambridge, 1996), 254.

[26] *The Placid Man: Or, Memoirs of Sir Charles Beville*, vol. 2 (London, 1773), 121.

76 SELLING ANCESTRY

which by the help of the table I have drawn up at the end, you may trace with their collaterals down to your grand-mother.'[27] Another counter-example can be found in the preface of *Annual Peerage* (1827). The publishers, the Innes sisters, claimed that they 'even in the season of youth and gaiety, surrounded by the enjoyments of social life, and the blessing of the paternal roof, have passed many hours of high gratification in extended investigation'.[28]

Admittedly, one should not presume too much from these scattered extracts. Though alluding to familiar practices, novelists' ambitions far exceeded this task. As such, their novels offer some exciting perspectives for historians, though one should not jump to the conclusion that Elliot or Osborne, these peculiar readers, actually existed. The literary trope of the old man in his library was not necessarily indicative of a social reality, as many novels romanticized the experience of reading, endowing it with moral significance. Another element which makes the interpretation of these passages problematic is the uneven survival of family compilations. One recent study on eighteenth-century copy-rights alluded to this issue: 'reference works, probably the genre most frequently commissioned by booksellers, and thus most likely to have involved a contact and a payment to the author or compiler, are regretfully underrepresented'.[29] Most pocket versions, despite larger print runs, were prone to disappear and became 'invisible'.[30] They were expected to be destroyed or recycled as scrap paper for other uses.

Hence there is a risk of bestowing undue significance on the expensive editions which have been preserved up to now in public and private collections. Furthermore, as luxury products for the happy few, they were more likely to attract unfavourable and sarcastic comments from novelists. These extracts, to be rightly interpreted, should be situated in the wider derogatory discourses on luxury and new money. In other circumstances, the reading of these directories could be seen from a religious perspective. In his *Memoirs*, the Newcastle merchant Ambrose Barnes referred to his cousin Sir James Clavering, who claimed to spend every Sunday closeted in his library 'within doors', reading Dugdale's expensive *Baronage*.[31] This could be perceived as another case of open middling sort versus lineage-obsessed landed elite. In fact, this extract rather deals with

---

[27] Ibid.   [28] *The Annual peerage of the British Empire* (1727), ii.

[29] David Fielding and Shef Rogers, *Copyright Payments in Eighteenth-Century Britain, 1707–1800* (Otago, 2015), 8.

[30] On this notion of invisibility, see Margaret J. M. Ezell, 'Invisible Books', in Laura Runge and Pat Rogers (eds), *Producing the Eighteenth-Century Book: Writers and Publishers in England, 1650–1800* (Newark, NJ, 2009), 53–4.

[31] 'I hope I shall be saved for I never make visits on Sundayes, but keep within doors, and read Dugdale's Baronage of England,' *Memoirs of the life of Mr Ambrose Barnes, Late Merchant and Sometime Alderman of Newcastle Upon Tyne* (Gateshead, 1866), 52. Quoted by F.-J. Ruggiu, 'The Urban Gentry in England, 1660–1780: A French Approach', *Historical Research*, vol. 74, no. 185 (2001): 249–70 at 263.

THE MANY WAYS OF READING AND SELLING 77

divergences in confessional practices between a god-fearing Barnes and a less Protestant baronet whose son took part in the 1715 Jacobite rising.[32]

It is quite clear that the reading of these compilations was widespread and attracted a wide range of comments even if it is essential to closely contextualize them.

Another interesting observation one may gain from these sources is related to their practical uses. Considering their cost, expensive directories should be devoid of any scribbles and kept intact in a library case. In fact they were often heavily commented on and updated in the margins.[33] Marginalia express emotions shared by the reader, but they could be intended for a third party or for posterity. The lonely Sir Walter Elliot had used his own copy as a notebook, 'improving it by adding for the information of himself and his family, these words, after the date of Mary's birth—married. Dec. 16, 1810, and by inserting most accurately the day of the month on which he had lost his wife'.[34] When George Osborne refused to comply with his father's directions the latter, who used to note 'according to custom, [...] recorded on the fly leaf, and in his large clerk-like hand, the dates of his marriage and wife's death' and the births and christenings of his children, 'carefully obliterated George's name from the page'.[35] Other annotators can be moved by kindness, respect, or by the impulse to redress an unfair account of the family past. In the Irish Cultural Centre in Paris, a copy of the second edition of Lodge's *Peerage* (1789) is enriched with many notes by its owner, Trophim-Gérard Lally-Tollendal (1751–1830) in his later years.[36] As the legitimized son of an illustrious Jacobite, he set himself the task of rewriting the notice dedicated to his family. He branched his family to the Viscounts of Dillon, through Sir Lucas Dillon, high sheriff of the county of Mayo during the Restoration. He noted that Lucas's sister-in-law was Mary Moor, who would have married 'Isaac O'Mullally or Lally Chief and styled Baron of Tully-Mullally, alias Tully-na-hally, father to James Lally and grand-father to Thomas Lally'.[37] He then added that the Lallys had been persecuted and deprived of the estates for their adherence to James II and

---

[32] 'What is underlined here is a spiritual as opposed to a social, difference between the two cousins', Ibid.

[33] 'Annotation combines—synthesizes, I should say—the functions of reading and writing. This fact in itself heightens the natural tension between author and reader by making the reader a rival of the author, under conditions that give the reader considerable power.' H. J. Jackson, *Marginalia: Readers Writing in Books* (New Haven, 2002), 90; David Allan, *Commonplace Books and Reading in Georgian England* (Cambridge, 2010).

[34] *Persuasion*, 9.   [35] *Vanity Fair*, 217.

[36] John Lodge, *The Peerage of Ireland*, vol. 1 (London, 1789) (Irish Cultural Centre, CCI, B 674). I am very grateful to Emmanuelle Chapron for her assistance in discovering this copy. For the crucial significance of the Irish College and its library after 1688 for the exiled community, see her detailed study in 'Les bibliothèques des séminaires et collèges britanniques à Paris, de l'Ancien Régime à l'Empire', *Bibliothèque de l'École des Chartes*, tome 169, 2011, pp. 567–96.

[37] Notes by Trophim-Gérard Lally-Tollendal, p. 193.

78   SELLING ANCESTRY

his father was 'this illustrious and unfortunate general *Thomas Arthur*, count de *Lally*'.[38] In an impulsive manner, Trophim-Gérard twice underlined his father's name and title. With his marginalia, he was keen not only to link his dynasty to one of the most prestigious Irish lineages but also to commemorate the suffering of his family in Ireland in 1689 and in France. Lodge had only mentioned that a 'Brigadier General Lally, Colonel of an Irish regiment in the French service, was wounded at the battle of Fontenoy'.[39] His son was keen to enrich this partial account by adding that his father was the famous general who played a key role in the Jacobite invasion of 1745 and who was executed for treason after the defeat of Pondicherry in 1761. Despite a long legal battle, Trophim-Gérard failed to obtain from the Council of State in 1783 a statement according to which Thomas Lally was not guilty of the crime of high treason.[40] In 1787, he commissioned a painting of himself unveiling the bust of his father, a portrait which was publicly exposed as a testimony against absolutism when he became a deputy to the Estates-General.[41] His marginalia were not only an act of private devotion. They fit into a campaign at vindicating the memory of his father and later at celebrating the deeds of the Franco-Irish nobility in a revolutionary context.

Copies left by many readers confirmed that such practices were not confined to commenting on one's family. James Ker, on his Burke's *Dictionary of the Peerage*, wrote next to the entry dedicated to the marquess of Salisbury: 'Dowager—84 rides every morning all seasons in Kings Ride Pimlico' or on Viscount Ancon, 'the Earl of Lichfield = Whig Earl'.[42] Similarly, John Dawson, an officer of the London Excise and the son of a Leeds textile worker, collected 879 books between 1710 and 1762. In his 'catalogue of my books', which ranged from books in folio to pocket size, he possessed a copy of *Collins's Peerage* in which he left many annotations about various individuals.[43] Somehow, these directories were used as notebooks or diaries by filling them with various extracts from gazettes or memories from personal encounters.

Finally, marginalia were part and parcel of antiquarian practices. This was in effect a continuation of what the compilers used to do in the making of their volumes. To complete his *Baronage*, Dugdale worked daily on an almanac to 'record snippets

---

[38] Ibid.   [39] Ibid.

[40] *Mémoire produit au conseil d'État du roi par Trophim-Gérard, comte de Lally-Tolendal* (Paris, 1778).

[41] Jean-Baptiste-Claude Robin, *Trophime-Gérard, comte de Lally-Tollendal, dévoilant le buste de son père*. Vizille-Versailles, Musée de la Révolution française de Vizille et Edition Art Lys, 2005.

[42] On James Ker, see The Reading Experience Database: <http://www.open.ac.uk/Arts/RED/index.html>.

[43] On John Dawson, see Stephen Colclough, *Consuming Texts: Readers and Reading Communities, 1695–1870* (Basingstoke, 2007): 75–6; Stephen Colclough, '"The Catalogue of My Books": The Library of John Dawson (1692–1765), "Exciseman and Staymaker", c.1739', *Publishing History*, vol. 47 (2000): 45–66 at 57.

THE MANY WAYS OF READING AND SELLING   79

of information that could later be retrieved to provide material for a narrative'.[44] In Wales, the almanacs, published by Thomas Jones from 1689 to 1712, provided Edward Lhuyd with ballads, legends, and 'astrological prognostications', as well as 'a wide variety of other material, some of it historical in nature'.[45] In Germany, the imposing volumes by Jacob Wilhelm Imhoff, on the noble genealogies of the Holy Roman Empire (*Notitia Procerum Sancti Romani Germani Imperii*, 1684) relied on a 'wide range of ephemeral printed texts', legal documents, funeral sermons, and so on.[46] Hence, even the most expensive folios were heavily annotated. These handsome volumes could be used as status symbols for wealthy book collectors though they had a practical value similar to that of pocket directories. It would be misleading therefore to assume a clear-cut distinction between the two. Scribbling practices came to blur the difference between notebooks and luxury editions. Many book owners saw themselves as semi-antiquarians and rarely viewed their collections as untouchable objects. In the book auction catalogues, the market value of a directory partly depended on its formal quality or its rarity but most of all on the reputation of the previous owner. Horace Walpole and the Reverend Samuel Parr left many manuscript notes on their Collins's editions.[47] Signatures and marginalia from eminent authors or antiquarians served to drive up prices, whether they were in a pocket directory or folio. In the *Catalogus Bibliothecae Harleianae* (1743), a copy of Collins's far exceeded its initial selling price as it had been interspersed with notes by Edward Harley, earl of Oxford.[48] Francis Hargrave, the eminent lawyer involved in the 'Somersett's case', left many notes on the margins of Collins's *Peerage* and Wotton's *Baronetage*.[49] Similarly the sale of the James West Library in 1773 generated much public attention and raised almost £3,000.[50] West acquired many books from the most respectable antiquaries, notably Peter Le Neve and his annotated copy of Dugdale's *Baronage* which sold for 13 guineas, a sum higher than many other well-preserved copies. Part of the stock was bought by Richard Gough, not for its material value but for its marginalia.

---

[44] Stephen K. Roberts, '"Ordering and Methodizing": *William Dugdale* in Restoration England', in Christopher Dyer and Catherine Richardson (eds), *William Dugdale, Historian, 1605–1686: His Life, His Writings and His County* (Woodbridge, 2007), 79; see, for example, the copy of Dugdale's *Baronage* in the British Library, (fJ/00086).

[45] Huw Pryce, *Writing Welsh History: From the Early Middle Ages to the Twenty-First Century* (Oxford, 2022), 184.

[46] Markus Friedrich, 'How an Early Modern Genealogist Got his Information', in Eickmeyer, Friedrich, and Bauer (eds), *Genealogical Knowledge in the Making*, 73.

[47] *Bibliotheca Parrianna. A catalogue of the library of the late Reverend and learned Samuel Parr, curate of Hatton* (London, 1827), 398; see also Horace Walpole's annotated 1714 *Peerage* (GRT 249, Yale). Alexander Lindsay, *Index of English Literary Manuscripts*, vol. 3, part 2 (London, 1997), 236.

[48] Thomas Osborne, *Catalogus bibliothecae Harleianae* (London, 1743), 822.

[49] R. C. Alston, *Books with Manuscript: A Short Title Catalogue of Books with Manuscript Notes in the British Library* (London, 1994), 124, 617.

[50] William Noblett, 'The Sale of James West's Library in 1773', in John Hinks and Matthew Day (eds), *Compositor to Collector: Essays on Book Trade History* (London and New Castle, Del., 2012), 291.

80 SELLING ANCESTRY

Gentlemen and their pocketbooks: 'Either to explain or illustrate?'

In a letter to John Burke, Alexander Barnewall, an Irish gentleman, pointed out the dilemma faced by most titled families.[51] Many were frustrated by the fact that compilers failed to combine a practical purpose with a pleasing layout. Barnewall was referring to Debrett's pocket directories, which he accused of ignoring the order of creation, whereas in 'polite company of Peers and Baronets, there is a proper etiquette on precedency which must depend upon date of patents'.[52] The alphabetical order threatened to level the complex and indispensable order of precedence. Debrett's plates were seen as 'intolerably bad' and the engraving of the arms 'miserably deficient'.[53] Some elite readers mistook the genealogical history in pocketbook form to be an early form of democratic 'yellow pages'. They feared to become partially assimilated in the popular imagination to more humble social groups. Barnewall hoped Burke, 'taking the field as the competitors of Debrett' would be able to reconcile clarity and dignity. In order to challenge the domination of what he scornfully referred to as 'the Debrett's and Co', he advised him to feature a general and alphabetical index so that it would have all the appearance of a dictionary, without disrupting the displaying of families by order of precedence. An index would allow expansion of the book to include collaterals: 'that could be done without very materially adding to the size of your projected work'.[54] He later suggested the creation of an appendix of all the names in five columns (surnames, title, date of creation, heir apparent, heir presumptive) which would enable the reader 'to have as much information of each individual family exhibited at one view as possible'.[55] Hence he was suggesting that the two types of directories should be merged into one formula.

A Scottish customer expressed a similar requirement. Richard Broun, the elder son of Sir James Broun of Colstoun Park (Dumfriesshire) contended that 'the general & only repository of the genealogy, chronology, heraldry, biography of a great nation Nobility should be splendid in form, & constructed for the restauration of posterity'.[56] However, Burke should help his readers by providing tools to better search and to establish the connections between distinct families scattered all over Britain. Burke has inserted 'the accts of families not in alphabetical order as to their names, but titles'.[57] Ideally, 'an individual of my own name desirous to see an account of all the ennobled families of Brown has to seek up on three different places, for the houses of Sligo, Kenmar and Kilmaine and in as many more for their armorial bearings' and 'to have all the alliances under his eyes, at a single glance'.[58] Among Burke's correspondents, Broun, who called himself 'eighth baronet of Scotland and Nova Scotia', was somehow an oddity.

---

[51] 7 Nov. 1828, Barnewall to Burke, CA, BC, vol. 58, n.p.   [52] Ibid.   [53] Ibid.
[54] Ibid.   [55] 17 Nov. 1828, ibid.   [56] Sept. 1829, Broun to Burke, CA, BC, vol. 58, n.p.
[57] Ibid. Broun to Burke, 18 Feb. 1828, CA, BC, vol. 58, n.p.   [58] Ibid.

THE MANY WAYS OF READING AND SELLING 81

He had sent him already a dozen letters about his 'British stock' and about the fact that 'his name could be traced through all the variety of Bruno, de Bron, de Brun, le Brien, Bruun, Bruyn, Brunne, Brune, Bruine, Bruen, Broun, Broune, Brown, Browne'.[59] Presented as a 'pamphleteer and fraudster' by his biographer, Broun belonged to the world of 'schemers' as he was later involved in diverse dubious projects such as 'the Anglo-Canadian Company', the 'British–American Association for Emigration and Colonization', and the Committee of the Baronetage for Privileges.[60]

Publishers' correspondence provides considerable insight into readers' expectations. Far from being passive consumers of what they read, they were not shy of making various concrete proposals. To explain or to illustrate: such requirements, by Barnewall's or Broun's own admission, were indeed hard to reconcile. Keen to accommodate the desires of his customers, Burke came up in the third and fourth editions of his *General and Heraldic Dictionary* with a hybrid formula: 'enumerating, in almost all instances, the individual members of the immediate past [...], in deducing the pedigrees from the remotest period instead of limiting the research to the personage first dignified by an hereditary title of honour; and in comprehending the Baronets of Ireland, and (Scotland, or) Nova Scotia'.[61] By doing so, Burke claimed that he would be able to include at least 1,800 families and more than 100,000 dates and names.

Earlier compilations had raised similar remarks from the public. In 1725, the Yorkshire landowner Sir Roger Beckwith of Aldborough had criticized the choice of a small format by Wotton in his soon to be released *Baronetage*. Even before publication, he warned Wotton that 'if you do not print your book in a larger vol. than the last [one] I think you will have a little sale for it'.[62] His argument was that the previous edition by Arthur Collins in 1720 had been successfully sold as an octavo: 'Collins's baronetage contains the number first design'd by King James and is at present in many hands so that if your book were a continuation in the same size I think it would sell better.'[63] He urged that Wotton should not disappoint the public's expectations by downsizing Collins's edition. A former mayor of Leeds and briefly Yorkshire high sheriff (1706–7), Beckwith desired to see his family and his neighbours depicted in a more monumental edition. He insisted on sending Wotton his illuminated coat of arms in vellum, allegedly as recorded by Dugdale in his 1666 visitation. After his death, the title went to his

---

[59] Ibid.; interestingly, a similar point could be found on the current family website: 'Any persons bearing the name Broun, Brown, Browne, De Broun, Le Broun, Le Brun, De Brun or in any of its various forms and spellings, including the spouse or descendant of such person is eligible for membership'. <http://www.broun.com/clan%20association.html>.

[60] Anita McConnell, 'Sir Richard Broun, eighth baronet (1801–1858), pamphleteer and fraudster', *ODNB*, 2004. Retrieved 23 Dec. 2019, from <https://doi-org.janus.bis-sorbonne.fr/10.1093/ref:odnb/3595>.

[61] John Burke, *General and Heraldic Dictionary* (London, 1832), vii.

[62] 18 July 1725, BL, Add. MS 24120, fol. 46.   [63] Ibid.

82   SELLING ANCESTRY

brother, Sir Marmaduke Beckwith, a merchant in Virginia who may have had very different needs, had he deigned to write to Wotton.

In the 1730s, Wotton launched into the making of a multivolume octavo edition, this time very much in line with Beckwith's desires. But this undertaking attracted in turn many more criticisms from customers who preferred a smaller format. Case Billingsley, a London engineer and merchant from Tottenham, voiced his frustration when he learned about Wotton's project. Billingsley was a respectable entrepreneur during the Walpole ministry, first clerk in the Chatham dockyard and investor in the York Buildings Company, which provided water to London.[64] 'As a friend', he tried to convince Wotton that his compilation would sell better if he included 'all the superior degrees of honour deriv'd from the crown'.[65] His work should be of a much larger scope, with all the British baronets and peers along with all their collaterals. 'Time is money', he reminded him, and so he wondered why he was 'taking so much pain to please and oblige so small a part of our nation?'[66] His remarks were guided by a more personal interest. As stated in the 1727 preface, Wotton refused to mention the families of baronets elevated to the peerage. This seemed particularly unfair to Billingsley, as his daughter had been married to the Reverend Charles Graham, younger son of the second Baronet George Graham of Esk. His grandson might well inherit the title if the senior dynasty were to be extinct. Wotton would be wise to have a more inclusive take instead of publishing long and tedious narratives which 'the Baronets in the collateral lines will immediately cry out against and damn your book as being unjust and partial'.[67]

After the edition came out in 1741, he encountered similar criticisms from some customers. Sir Mark Stuart Pleydell, who had recently been distinguished in 1732 by a baronetage, strongly expressed his disappointment, judging his book of little use. He considered first that a classification along the county line would have made the reading much easier: Wotton should have added 'ye place of residence & county & print such as render in one county separately from another, by wch anyone will easily cast his eye on his county at once [...]. The end of publishing genealogys is that ye reader may know what familys are allied to ye party.'[68] Instead of producing a *Baronetage* organized chronologically, thus placing the new baronets in the last volume, Wotton would have been better advised to take a county-based perspective which would have made more apparent the actual county elite. Pleydell may have been inspired by the *Alphabetical Account of the Nobility and Gentrey* published by Richard Blome in 1673.[69]

---

[64] 1739, ibid., fol. 392.   [65] Ibid.   [66] Ibid., fol. 395.
[67] Ibid.   [68] 26 Mar. 1742, ibid., fol. 172.
[69] *An alphabetical account of the nobility and gentry, which are (or lately were) related unto the several counties of England and Wales: as to their names, titles, and seats by which they are (or have been) generally known and distinguished; according as they were received from the hands of divers persons experienced therein in each county by their publick offices, or otherwise; the like never before published* (London, 1673).

THE MANY WAYS OF READING AND SELLING   83

However, the crux of his criticisms dealt with its lack of portability. He wondered indeed about the poor practicality of such a large volume and argued that it should have been of a manageable size, unlike the heavy volumes. Compilation should be like the 'size-letter of the British compendium printed for Bettesworth in 1738'.[70] He was referring to Francis Nichols's *British Compendium* discussed in the first chapter. According to Pleydell, the superiority of the *Compendium* was not only its small format but also its organization as a proper dictionary 'wch people consult on occasion & may be carried up and down but wch one can hardly suppose anyone will formaly put upon a desk in his study in order to read it thro'.[71]

Like many readers, Pleydell did not set out the exact nature of his needs clearly. One may safely assume that a portable *Baronetage* would have enabled him to identify families in the counties and London. He was then residing in his estate of Coleshill in Berkshire but often visited London. He may have wished to better liaise with his aristocratic counterparts. Jon Stobart rightly pointed out that 'travel remained an important, if not defining, feature of elite life [...] and yet journeys were major undertakings that required careful planning'.[72] On that matter, pocket directories as well as travel guides were useful tools. Five years after this letter, Pleydell managed to marry his daughter to William Bouverie, the earl of Radnor.[73] There may have been a link between the timing of his writing and his plan for his eligible daughter, though we do not have much material to substantiate this idea.

Another criticism deals with the absence of any blank pages which the reader could use to record their own updates or comments. In 1739, Thomas Egerton, a younger brother to the fourth baronet and rector of Sefton and Cheadle, wrote to Wotton suggesting that 'it would please better if after the account of each family there were a blank of a page left for making such alteration with a pen as may hereafter happen in each family for want of this the book in ye course of 8 or 10 years becomes in many respects useless'.[74] Before the first edition of the *Life and Opinions of Tristram Shandy* in 1759, there were already many fictional works and almanacs left with blank pages.[75]

From the 1720s to the 1820s, the many letters sent by clients to publishers demonstrate that, far from being restricted to the aspiring middling sort, reference books were essential in aristocratic social intercourse. The reasons were the same as those set out in the first chapter: the complexity of multiple alliances and descents, the growth of honours and titles, the increasing geographical mobility in Britain, and the crucial London season. However, from the late eighteenth century

---

[70] 26 Mar. 1742, BL, Add. MS 24120, fol. 172.   [71] Ibid.

[72] Jon Stobart (ed.), *Travel and the British Country House: Cultures, Critiques and Consumption in the Long Eighteenth Century* (Manchester, 2017), 12.

[73] 25 Oct. 1768. NA, PROB 11/943/117.

[74] Nov. 1739. Thomas Egerton to Wotton, BL, Add. MS 24120, fol. 295.

[75] Anne C. Henry, 'Blank Emblems: The Vacant Page, the Interleaved Book and the Eighteenth-Century Novel', *Word and Image*, vol. 22, no. 4 (2006): 363–71.

84   SELLING ANCESTRY

onwards, when pocket directories rose in number, most polite customers started voicing their concerns. As they were progressively seen as part of one class, the landed elite and the upper-middle sorts alike demanded some specific directories be better tailored to their needs and tastes. Publishers and book merchants were mindful of this growing anxiety and strove to conciliate profit with selectivity. Many efforts were made to reassure the customers that competing demands could be reconciled. Burke's *Dictionary* represented a compromise between different impulses. Earlier on, some compilations managed to define generic borders. Joseph Edmondson, the herald who had published in 1764 a very expensive folio, advertised in 1775 his one-shilling *Companion to the Peerage*. His main selling point was the up-to-date account of the latest marriages, 'subject of so fluctuating a nature, changes will arise every day'.[76] His *Companion* would be sold in a serial manner in order to annually register all the deaths and new titles. He recommended his publication to the 'Persons not conversant with the nobility' who are 'at a loss to know from what House her Ladyship is descended. The Maiden Name being lost and merged in that of the Husband.'[77] His *Companion* followed an alphabetical arrangement thus disregarding all precedence and he left a blank for some families that readers would be able to fill up 'with a pen at pleasure'.[78]

Such products would fit into the category of the reference books for any would-be gentleman. However, Edmondson refused to make it a pocketbook. Presented as an 'appendage', he sold it as a twenty-two-page octavo in 'the size of Collins's Peerage, so that it may be bound up with it or by being interleaved, to receive additions as they arise, it may swell to a size that may give it the Honour of being a Parlour-window book'.[79] A 'parlour window book' was later defined by the bibliophile Edward Mangin as a 'book to be taken up by anyone who, for a quarter of an hour now and then, has nothing better to read or to do [...] while waiting for breakfast or dinner'.[80] Hence this cheaper product was to be used as a complement to more expensive compilations in the library. Edmondson's cunning device underpinned the complementary nature of many directories. Similarly, the publishers of the *Polite Repository* advertised their product as a precious 'home accessory' fit for cabinets and libraries.[81] The luxury almanac was sold with expensive engraving from Humphry Repton.

---

[76] *A companion to the peerage of Great-Britain and Ireland, being an alphabetical list of such of the daughters of dukes, marquises and earls, (now living) who are married to commoners* (London, 1764), ii.
[77] Ibid.   [78] Ibid.   [79] Ibid.
[80] *The Parlour Window, or Anecdotes. Original Remarks on Books* (London, 1841), i; see also Laurence Sterne: 'As my life and opinions are likely to make some noise in the world, and [...]—be no less read than the *Pilgrim's Progress* itself—and, in the end, prove the very thing Montaigne dreaded his Essays should turn out, that is, a book for a parlour window', *The Life and Opinions of Tristram Shandy, Gentleman*, vol. 1 (Oxford, 1983), 7.
[81] Nigel Temple, 'Humphry Repton, Illustrator, and William Peacock's "Polite Repository" 1790–1811', *Garden History*, vol. 16, no. 2 (1988): 161–73 at 161. On the way, publishers tried to better meet the demands of their polite customers, see also James Raven, *Judging the New Wealth: Popular Publishing and Responses to Commerce in England, 1750–1800* (Oxford, 1992), 61–82.

However, from their correspondence, it seems that many customers failed to agree on a definite formal layout and went on to use different formats in a supplemental manner. This may be explained by the fact that, along with the usual cultural distinctions between elites and middling sorts, a further layer of interpretation should be added. Namely, social elites were divided from the middle between those who were more attached to the provincial community and those who had their eyes set on national society.[82] Sir Roger Beckwith may have hoped that Wotton's *Baronetage* in 1727 would serve as a monument of all the county elites, as a celebration of their local status, while Case Billingsley, Sir Mark Stuart Pleydell, and Thomas Egerton all insisted on the need for a synoptic, national based directory. The latter distinction, though helpful in many respects, should not be pushed too far as most of these amphibious families were evolving from the local scene to the metropolis. Increased geographical mobility and the commercialization of literary production benefited not only the London scene but also many counties and towns whose histories and chronicles circulated on a wider scale.[83]

2. Editorial strategies and copyrights

Another aspect which tends to blur an overly strict categorization is related to the structure of the book industry. One of the defining features in the London bookselling business was the extent to which copyrights were shared and traded among a few individuals. This enabled the most prominent booksellers to balance risks and costs by having large and diversified sale catalogues.[84] Their investment in expensive compilations was offset by remunerative gazettes and some lucrative titles. This remarkable concentration in a few hands had several consequences.

It meant first that the same title could be configured and advertised in different formats and at different prices. The changes in Collins's *Peerage*, from 1709 to 1769, provide a good case-study. First conceived as a cheaper serial publication, Collins turned into a luxury product when more booksellers stepped in to share its copyright. The same title could be destined for diverse audiences. Secondly, the publishers were able to transfer part of the content from one format to another. Collective ownership meant that data could easily be abridged and could migrate

---

[82] Dror Wahrman, 'National Society, Communal Culture: An Argument about the Recent Historiography of Eighteenth-Century Britain', *Social History*, vol. 17, no. 1 (1992): 43–72.

[83] Rosemary Sweet on the national appeal of many urban histories: 'History of the town was important, not because it could be used for explanatory purposes but because it represented continuity and tradition. This was all the more important in view of the palpably transient nature of urban life; high levels of mobility, immigration, and mortality created a fluid and impermanent society in which a sense of the past was needed as an anchorage.' *The Writing of Urban Histories in Eighteenth-Century England*, 77.

[84] Raven, *Publishing Business in Eighteenth-Century England*, 90.

86   SELLING ANCESTRY

from expensive formats to more accessible supports such as literary journals and pocketbooks. Hence under John Nichols's direction, *The Gentleman's Magazine* became a gateway between expensive volumes and reference books. Finally, these London booksellers, through their shops and their extended sales networks in Britain and throughout the Empire, were in a position to distribute their compilations to a much wider audience than previously assumed. The growth of circulating and local libraries in particular, whose catalogues contained both cheap and costly directories, played a crucial role.

The changing fortunes of Collins's *Peerage*

Many studies have underpinned the fact that, despite the Copyright Act in 1710 that excluded any permanent copyright, London booksellers were organized into small groups which enabled the pursuit of monopolistic practices. By meeting up informally in some coffee houses such as the Queen's Head Tavern in Paternoster Row or the Globe Tavern in Fleet Street, they would trade most of their portfolio among themselves, thus ostracizing outsiders. From the few auction catalogues which have survived, notably those annotated by Aaron Ward and Thomas Longman (1704–69), we can see that family directories were owned by the most prominent booksellers, who were the proprietors of most gazettes.[85] For example, at the Anderton coffee house on 6 January 1770, Thomas Lowndes divided the copyright of *The London Packet* into twenty shares of £25 each which were bought by the same partners investing in the most recent 1768 edition of Collins's *Peerage*.[86] He published a successful merchant directory from 1772.[87] Through their various publications, they were well equipped to meet buyers' demands. As acute businessmen, they were trying hard to adapt their product to the changing moods of their customers and the variable depths of their purse.

Although the interpretation of the constant exchange of shares among booksellers has been described as complex and misleading, one may venture to suggest some general explanations in the case of the Collins compilations. The changes in its copyright and its capital, which was split into many more shares throughout the eighteenth century, demonstrate the transformation of an isolated initiative into a well-established brand.

---

[85] Original Assignments of Copyrights of Books and other Literary Agreements between various Publishers, (1703–1810) BL, Add. MS 38728, Add. MS 38729; Terry Belanger, 'Booksellers' Trade Sales, 1718–1768', *The Library*, vol. 30, no. 4 (1975): 281–303.

[86] 6 Jan. 1770, Anderton coffee houses. Those were R. Baldwin, H. Woodhall, W. Strahan, R. Davis, W. Lowndes. BL, Add. MS 38729, fol. 106.

[87] *London directory* [...] *containing an alphabetical list of the names and places of abode of the merchants and principal traders of the cities of London and Westminster environs, with the number affixed to each house* (London, 1772).

THE MANY WAYS OF READING AND SELLING   87

At first, Collins's *Peerage* started as a serial edition for the middle end of the market, which the publishers celebrated as an 'extraordinary success'.[88] Each year, Collins and Roper set out to provide an octavo volume of the old and new peers by order of precedence and so readers were pushed to acquire the whole set year after year. The annual series made each part less expensive and enabled the publishers to furnish a regular update. Their marketing method was very similar to the one applied in selling *Post Boy*. The first edition in 1709 appeared conjointly with the reform of the copyright legislation in 1710 which guaranteed the ownership of any new publication for fourteen years. In an effective commercial ploy, they multiplied the advertisements well before and long after the publication. The first volume was simultaneously marketed in the *Post Boy* (owned by Roper), *London Gazette*, *Evening Post*, and *Tatler*.[89] Collins and Roper, the initial projectors, were later joined by Egbert Sanger, John Morphew, and William Taylor, the publisher of Peter Heylyn's *Help to English History*, a useful reference book which included only the name of peers without further details on their origins.[90] After the initial copyright expired in 1723, a few more booksellers stepped in. William Innys made his first investments by buying the shares of William Taylor for £7.[91] It is hard, however, to account for these transactions. Taylor may have been disappointed by the formula or eager to invest in other subjects. Whatever his motives, the *Collins* represented for Taylor an insignificant amount compared to his popular novels, such as *Robinson Crusoe*, which brought in more than £1,000.[92] As for the buyer, William Innys was printer to the Royal Society and his stock, including some famous antiquaries and historians such as Le Neve, Clarendon, and Spelman, was estimated at £30,000.[93] In 1731, Robert Gosling bought one-third of the shares from Roper's stock for £1. 1s.[94] He was mostly engaged in publishing law dictionaries (*The Office and Authority of the Justice of Peace*) and parliamentary statutes aimed at the gentry and legal professionals for their everyday affairs. He had published in 1714 *The laws of honour: or, a compendious account of the ancient derivation of all titles* which was aimed at

[88] *The Peerage of England* (London, 1710), i; Collins, Sanger were already engaged in the serial edition of John Stevens, *A View of the Universe; or, a New Collection of Voyages and Travels* (1708–10), see R. M. Wiles, *Serial Publication in England Before 1750* (New York, 1957), 87–8.

[89] *Post Boy* (20–2 Oct. 1709); *London Gazette* (4–6 Oct. 1711); *The Tatler* (29 Oct. 1709, Issue 87).

[90] *Books printed for William Taylor at the Ship in Paternoster Row* (London, 1717).

[91] 'Queen's Head Tavern in Pater-Noster-Row, on Thursday, the 3rd of Febr. 1725, exactly at ten in the morning, (at one of the clock the company will be entertained with a good dinner) the following copies and parts of copies of the late Mr. W. Taylor, will be disposed of by auction to the highest bidder, in 88 lots'. *Longman trade sales* (1718–68), BL, C170.aa.1.

[92] Asa Briggs, A *History of Longmans and Their Books, 1724–1990* (New Castle, Del., and London, 2008), 38.

[93] 16 Jan. 1725. *A catalogue of books in quires, and copies, being part of the stock of the late Mr William Innys, to be sold At the Queen's-Arms Tavern* (London, 1725).

[94] *A catalogue of books in quires, and copies; containing the remaining part of the stock of Mr Robert Gosling, deceas'd; which will be sold by auction to the booksellers of London and Westminster* [. . .] *on Tuesday the 27th of October, 1741.* Bod. Lib. *John Johnson, Trade Sale Catalogues*, no. 89.

88   SELLING ANCESTRY

explaining the legal validity of the claims to peerages, as well as precedents in Court and Parliament.

The growing number of stakeholders led to the publication of a new Collins's *Peerage* in 1735. Along with Innys and Gosling, the driving force behind this new attempt was Thomas Wotton, who had previously invested in religious and historical publications (*Mr Rapin's History and Mr Tindal's Continuation*) and court almanacs. The three partners opted for three volumes in octavo format, with improved engravings of the arms and crests. Unlike in the previous edition, they obtained the patronage of several prominent men (the duke of Rutland, the earl of Shaftesbury, Viscount Lymington, and Robert Walpole). It sold for 24 shillings, and its copyright rose to £8. 8s. in 1736. For the second edition in 1741, the publishers were joined by a fourth investor, Samuel Birt, who invested £23.[95] They added a fourth volume which sold for £1. 4s. According to William Bowyer's ledgers, it appears that 1,000 copies were printed and its copyright amounted to £138.[96] From this date, enough London publishers started to see the selling of a luxury directory a profitable commercial prospect. The growth of the copyright reached a high point in 1756 at £432. It was then owned by twenty-four shareholders. According to William Strahan's ledgers, its printing cost (1,000 issues) rose to £51. 3s.[97]

After the beginning of the Seven Years War, the *Collins's* copyrights started to decline in value, down to £122 just before Collins's death in 1760. The latter figure may well be due to the fact that Collins had not been able to compile the last edition himself.[98] His *Peerage* was no longer the unique reference and was faced with the growth of comparable and cheaper directories which integrated Scottish and Irish peers such as Salmon's *Short Views of the Families* and Almon's pocket guides. Influential booksellers such as Longman sold £20 of his investment in 1759. It was divided into 48 shares in 1760 and even briefly into 114 shares. Between 1756 and 1768, Collins's copyrights changed hands many times.[99] Some new investors came in, such as John Rivington (£16. 14s.), William Johnston (£28), and John Almon (£12). In 1768, they consented to finance a new edition, comprising seven volumes and 200 engravings.

In the 1768 edition the publishers had, for each peer, a full page with the paternal coat of arms, crest, supporters and motto, engraved on copper-plates, along with the colours needed to paint the coat. A luxury item was more likely to be stolen. On 7 September 1768, a servant, William Vickers, was indicted for

---

[95] Ibid.

[96] Keith Maslen and John Lancaster (eds), *The Printing Accounts of William Bowyer, Father and Son. With a Checklist of Bowyer Printing. 1699–1777* (London, 1991), ref. 2918.

[97] BL, Add. MS 48803, fol. 30.

[98] In a letter to the duke of Newcastle, Collins alluded to his inability to read and the need for 'a person to transcribe for me'. 30 Apr. 1754. BL, Add. MS 32735, fol. 217.

[99] Appendix 2: The copyright of Collins's *Peerage* (1755–1768).

stealing part of a barrister's library in the Temple, notably eight printed books: 'the works of Dr. Jonathan Swift, value 20 s. seven printed books, bound in leather, of Collins's *Peerage*, value 40 s'.[100] Judging from the decline of the copyright value to £144, one can assume that this new edition was not a commercial success. The market for luxury compilations may have been overrated. Losses were limited by the fact that the publishers simultaneously invested in cheaper versions, produced by Edward Kimber between 1766 and 1768. Thomas Lowndes paid William Strahan £16. 13s. for the printing of 2,000 copies and the extra corrections.[101] Kimber's and Collins's directories were seen on the market as complementary, one for the county library, the other a pocket version for the London season.

In the latter editions, 1778 and 1785, Collins's value reached a new peak when its proprietors sold an even more expensive version (£3. 1s. 6d.) dedicated to George III with better engravings by Barak Longmate. Its copyright rose again to £370 and it was issued at 1,250 copies in eight volumes. The driving force this time was Thomas Lowndes' son, William, who acquired 1/48 of the Collins copyright from John Donaldson for £7. 7s. in 1777.[102] Another key player was John Murray, who had purchased several shares from Edward Johnston for £2. 12s. The publishers managed to bring the production cost down to £24. 14s., half the price of the 1756 edition. Murray obtained 26 copies at £1. 10s. each, and sold them for £39 with a profit of £8. 12s.[103] After a supplement edition in 1785, Lowndes failed to secure sufficient backing from his partners, 'Mrs Rivington, Baldwin, Longman, Nicolls, Byfield'.[104] In the years following the French Revolution, the Collins's copyright went down to its pre-1740 level (around £48). A last attempt to relaunch the brand occurred in 1812 under the supervision of Egerton Brydges. But the brand had lost its pre-eminence and was successfully challenged by cheaper formats sold by Debrett's.

Through the example of Collins's *Peerage*, one may note that publishers were investing simultaneously in grand publications for a few customers and more accessible reference books. The prestige acquired in selling the former benefited in turn the marketing of the latter. Sometimes, though, the same brand underwent considerable changes in the hopes of reaching the upper end of the market. A similar adaptation has been observed among publishers of urban histories. The history of Birmingham by William Hutton went through two successive editions.[105] The first one in 1781 aimed at a more middling sort of public and its author was even dismissive about the value of genealogies. The commercial

---

[100] Vickers was a servant hired by George Booth Tyndale. The Old Bailey Online, *Proceedings of the Old Bailey*. Retrieved 21 Jan. 2020 from <https://www.oldbaileyonline.org/browse.jsp?div=t17680907-23>.

[101] July 1766, BL, Add. MS 48803, fol. 75.   [102] 27 Feb. 1777, BL, Add. MS 38730, fol. 51.

[103] William Zachs, *The First John Murray and the Late Eighteenth-Century London Book Trade: With a Checklist of His Publications* (Oxford, 1998), 285.

[104] 19 Feb. 1787, BL, Add. MS 38730, fol. 119.

[105] Sweet, *The Writing of Urban Histories in Eighteenth-Century England*, 112–13.

90 SELLING ANCESTRY

success of the book and the increasing number of visitors to the city led the year after to a second and larger edition which contained all the gentry seats around Birmingham.

Expanded and abridged versions

Another consequence of the tight control over copyrights was the booksellers' ability to copy and transfer some content from one format to another. This phenomenon has already been described in the history book market. The success of the *Universal History* (1736–65) relied on its capacity to reconcile both 'high' and 'popular' histories by borrowing much from expensive publications.[106] By the same token, family directories drew from a vast array of sources and in turn were extensively plagiarized in travel guides, biographies, and gazettes. Robert Gosling, while investing in Collins's *Peerage*, was in contact with his former apprentice Cæsar Ward and his brother-in-law Richard Chandler. They had a business in York and Scarborough, a seaside resort which, like Bath, attracted many gentrified visitors.[107] They published Thomas Cox's *Magna Britannia* (1738) and *A Journey from London to Scarborough* including a 'List of the Nobility, quality and gentry at Scarborough'. In their *History and Proceedings of the House of Commons* (1741), they added the state of the Peerage which was entirely copied and pasted from Collins.[108] Similarly, several pocket traveller guides contained some extracts from Collins. In *The Kentish Traveller's Companion* (1776), Collins's *Peerage* was used to complete the description of the festivals at Eltham where in 1515 Henry VIII created Sir Edward Stanley Baron Monteagle 'for his service at Flodden-field'.[109] Collections of biographies borrowed largely from Collins's directories such as *The Biographia Britannica*, also partly owned by Lowndes.

Literary magazines, in particular the monthly *Gentleman's Magazine*, constituted a timely device for these circulations. From its foundation in 1731, it was a satisfying substitute for many readers who could not or would not buy a more expensive directory. As an enriched literary almanac, it contained a monthly account of the births and deaths in titled families. The monthly *Gentleman's Magazine* was mostly composed of news and extracts pillaged from many weekly journals as well as excerpts of books: 'the underlying economics and dominant cultural practices of eighteenth-century journalism worked against the very idea

---

[106] Karen O'Brien, 'English Enlightenment Histories, 1750–1815' in José Rabasa, Masayuki Sato, Edoardo Tortarolo, and Daniel Woolf (eds), *The Oxford History of Historical Writing*, vol. 3 (Oxford, 2012), 520.

[107] C. Y. Ferdinand, 'Ward, Caesar (bap. 1710, d. 1759), bookseller and historian', *ODNB*, 2003. Retrieved 23 Dec. 2019 from <https://doi-org.janus.bis-sorbonne.fr/10.1093/ref:odnb/64292>.

[108] *History and Proceedings of the House of Commons* (London, 1741), 1–7.

[109] *The Kentish Traveller's Companion* (Canterbury, 1776), 18.

of treating news as property'.[110] In their book reviews, the editors devoted considerable space to the publication of extracts. Their readers could enjoy reading them without any obligation to purchase. To promote the highly pricey *Peerage* by Guthrie, a journalist in the *Gentleman's Magazine*, for which Guthrie had been working as compiler, wrote a long and very favourable review. In turn one author from the *Critical Review* complained that the *Gentleman's Magazine* review was in fact a transcription 'almost verbatim, from Mr Guthrie's work'.[111] Later, as co-owner and editor from 1778 onwards, John Nichols further turned the magazine into a prime provider of genealogies. Julian Pooley's extensive study of the Nichols archives and correspondence has demonstrated that his publications could not be easily broken down into different categories.[112] Nichols had been a printer of parliamentary proceedings and also demonstrated a keen interest in gazettes, almanacs, and newsletters.[113] To these ephemeral data, he added some more substantial genealogical narratives and pedigrees, thus turning the magazine into a hybrid product between court almanacs and larger family directories.[114] The son of an Islington baker, Nichols managed to create a vast network of collaborators, from modest antiquaries to members of the landed elites. By all accounts, Nichols made sure the magazine remained congenial to the tastes of the gentry as well as to those of the middling sort.[115] Its success relied on the collaborative effort of its readers, who gained more personal gratification from having their name published in a polite magazine which circulated far beyond antiquarian circles.[116] As a consequence, the magazine was extensively used by compilers. William Betham, in his preface to his *Baronetage*, presented his various sources: *The Biographia Britannica*, printed narratives of parliamentary and judicial transactions, as well as the 'enquiries in the Gentleman's Magazine, the learned editor of which is entitled to the thanks of every traveller in the road of genealogical information'.[117]

With regard to the higher end of the market, Nichols invested in costly projects such as the re-edition of Collins's *Peerage* in 1779 and in 1784, the *Biographical*

---

[110] Will Slauter, *Who Owns the News? A History of Copyright* (Stanford, Calif., 2019), 85.

[111] *The Critical review, or, Annals of literature*, Sept. 1764, 162.

[112] I wish to express my gratitude to Julian Pooley for allowing me to work on the Nichols Database at the Surrey History Centre in Woking.

[113] 'A Copious Collection of Newspapers': John Nichols and his Collection of Newspapers, Pamphlets and News Sheets, 1760–1865' at <https://www.gale.com/c/17th-and-18th-century-nichols-newspapers-collection>.

[114] See Julian Pooley, ' "Minutely Attentive to Every Circumstance": John Nichols and the Culture of Genealogy in the Late Eighteenth Century' in Stéphane Jettot and J.-P. Zuniga (eds), *Genealogy and Social Status in the Enlightenment* (Liverpool 2021), 153–85.

[115] Gillian Williamson, *British Masculinity in the 'Gentleman's Magazine', 1731–1815* (London, 2016), 79–80.

[116] Emily Lorraine de Montluzin, *Daily Life in Georgian England as Reported in the Gentleman's Magazine* (New York, 2002); James M. Kuist, 'A Collaboration in Learning: "The Gentleman's Magazine" and Its Ingenious Contributors', *Studies in Bibliography*, vol. 44 (1991), 302–17.

[117] William Betham, *The Baronetage*, vol. 1, x.

92 SELLING ANCESTRY

Peerage by Brydges in 1808 and his new Collins's edition in 1812. Printer to the
Royal Society and the Society of Antiquaries, Nichols was personally involved
in the making of expensive county histories. He described his *History of Leicester*
as being inspired by Dugdale's *Baronage* and intended to sell it at a cost of 5
guineas.[118] These investments did not prevent him from supporting less high-
priced compilations. At the end of his life, in 1825, Nichols agreed to publish a
Synopsis Peerage by a former naval officer, Nicholas Harris Nicolas. The *Synopsis*
might be best defined as intermediary product between a pocket version and a
hefty folio. Nicolas, in his preface, saw his work as designed for the 'general
reader', unlike the heavy folios which were 'little consulted by the more numerous
classes of the literary world'.[119] His aim was to help readers answer their difficulty
in linking one family to one title, as the latter had often been borne by four to ten
different families. The understanding of family links had been made difficult by
the numerous remarriages and deaths. In a letter to Nichols, Nicolas wrote that
'the Synopsis will be a very heavy and I hope a profitable work to print'.[120] He
obtained from Nichols the promise of a distribution of 2,000 copies and a positive
review in the *Gentleman's Magazine*.

Hence, the diverse genealogical interests of the Nichols family provide a
convincing example of the porosities between the various sorts of directories.
With regard to the printing business, many overlaps enabled a wider circulation of
genealogical knowledge.

Shops, sales networks, and circulating libraries

The various sales networks that London booksellers developed throughout the
eighteenth century enfranchised different groups of readers in their ability to pick
and choose from a whole gamut of directories. Many bookshops were coming to
rival coffee houses as centres for information exchange and polite sociability, even
though in fact they were closely interrelated.[121] They were designed to encourage
the customers to stay longer and to browse through their vast stock on display,
especially as many stores were used as circulating libraries. Thomas Becket
described his shop not 'as a repository of rational amusement but as a museum
from where can be withdrawn materials capable of forming the minds of readers
to solid virtues, true politeness, noblest actions and purest benevolence'.[122] As for
the gazettes which were supplemented by poetry and news sent by their readers,

---

[118] Nov. 1808, Nichols to William Bedford. Bod. Lib., MS Eng. Lett b. 18, fol. 13.
[119] Nicholas Harris Nicolas, *Synopsis Peerage* (London, 1825), 8–9.
[120] 15 Sept. 1824, Nicolas to Nichols, BL, Add. MS 36987, fol. 87.
[121] Adrian Johns, 'Coffeehouses and print shops' in L. Daston and K. Park (eds), *The Cambridge
History of Science: Early Modern Science*, vol. 3 (Cambridge, 2006), 320–40.
[122] Raven, *The Business of Books*, 113–14.

THE MANY WAYS OF READING AND SELLING 93

the 'public' was invited to visit the bookshops and to participate in the making of directories. These invitations were not only aimed at obtaining information, they were part of a marketing tool. Whether it be the pocket compendium or the larger octavo, anyone was urged to come and provide some information. Recently, commenting on Thomas Payne's bookshop, David Fallon has stressed the crucial role of sociability in his commercial success.[123] Precious folios were lent in order to obtain the goodwill of certain antiquarians. Nichols, in particular, as he was engaged in antiquarian enquiries, was quite eager to lend expensive books from his sales catalogue.[124]

In the later eighteenth century, London booksellers were also able to supply many accessible second-hand directories at discounted prices. One of the most prominent London booksellers was James Lackington, who left some interesting memoirs. Alluding to his modest origins—his father was a shoemaker—he commented ironically, 'who would not boast of their genealogy in having a *prince* for their ancestor in being a Son of the renowned PRINCE CRISPIN?'[125] His sales catalogue included 30,000 volumes in 1784. A decade later, his library had experienced an exponential growth, reaching 200,000 books by 1796. In his 1792 catalogue, he sold sixteen editions of *Peerages*. The heavy folios were still very expensive: Edmondson's *Peerage* was sold for £17, Catton's for £4, but his clients could acquire various editions of Collins's, Salmons's and Kimber's *Peerages* for around 1s. each.[126] Apart from his bookshop in London (temple of Muse), he owned outlets in Oxford, Cambridge, Bath, Coventry, Bristol, and Newcastle.[127] Most booksellers were dispatching their publications directly to their customers. From 1747 to 1810, Thomas Lister, later made Lord Ribblesdale in 1797, was a rich owner of lead mines in the Pennines. He kept all his bills from various London booksellers, notably from John Stockdale.[128] When he was not residing in his house in London (Hanover Square), Lister lived in Gisburn Park near Leeds and ordered some of his books directly from Stockdale. On an annual basis, he spent around £10 on gazettes (*Evening Post, Universal Magazine*), parliamentary journals, and miscellaneous collections of tracts. For the year 1801, he left a bill of £48, including the *Naval Chronicle, The Navy List*, and the pocket Debrett's *Annual Peerage & Baronetage*.[129] In 1808, Stockdale sent him a £10 bill for various books, notably the more expensive *Longmate Peerage* for 18s. Like many other

---

[123] David Fallon, '"Stuffd up with books": The Bookshops and Business of Thomas Payne and Son, 1740–1831', *History of Retailing and Consumption*, vol. 5, no. 3 (2019): 228–45.

[124] Nichols Archive Project, see <http://www2.le.ac.uk/centres/elh/research/project/nichols/the-nichols-archive-project>.

[125] Crispin and Crispianus were the patron saints of shoemakers. *Memoirs of the First Forty-Five Years of the Life of James Lackington* (London, 1794), 7.

[126] *Lackington and Allen's catalogue for Feb. 1794 to March 1795: consisting of near two hundred thousand volumes, in all the various languages and classes of learning* (London, 1796), 78, 384.

[127] Raven, *The Business of Books*, 290.

[128] University of Leeds, Special Collections, Yas MD335/1/7/2.   [129] Ibid., Yas MD335/1/7/2/2.

94   SELLING ANCESTRY

booksellers with the exception of James Lackington, Stockdale extended credit to his customers.[130] From these bills, it appeared that many nobles were buying different sorts of directories. Further down the social scale, the Reverend Walter Collins from Bradley (Staffordshire) received in 1758 a £16 bill from Debrett's for the shipment of the *Parliamentary Register* and Collins's *Peerage* (£1. 4s.), among other books.[131]

Provincial booksellers, who mostly supplied stationery and schoolbooks, were not cut off from the London book trade. The direct correspondence between the London booksellers and their remote customers did not prevent the former from keeping close ties with their provincial counterparts. Some of these ties dated back to their childhood. William Innys lived in Bristol until his apprenticeship in London with Benjamin Watford started in 1702. John Almon remained strongly attached to Liverpool, where he was born. Numerous booksellers of Scottish descent (Millar, Strahan, Donaldson) kept their connections with Glasgow and Edinburgh. Many provincial retailers presented their customers with the majority of London catalogues. In their shops in Daventry, Rugby, Lutterworth, and Warwick, Clay & Sons carried most reference books, including Collins's *Peerage*, for the same price as in London.[132]

Borrowing was increasingly an option for those who did not have the means to invest in their own libraries. London and provincial booksellers also started lending their books at a nominal fee, thus making a vast range of publications accessible.[133] From 20 or so before 1760, their number grew to more than 1,000 in 1800 in London and most cities. As early as 1740, for 3 shillings per quarter, subscribers could access hundreds of volumes on history and antiquity from Thomas Taylor's circulating library, including the various editions of Collins's *Baronage*.[134] Most of the other circulating libraries provided the same references which were designated by a number to facilitate their ordering and by their purchase price. John Noble in 1746 afforded a large choice of *Peerages* and *Baronetages* in the category of 'History, antiquities, biographies'.[135] In 1757, William Bathoe at the Blue Bible (Strand) made known to the public that his library was 'being the first of its kind in London' for having more than 5,000 references, including most directories, in exchange for a yearly subscription of 10

[130] In a further letter (6 Sept. 1810) Stockdale complained of being wrongly accused of ungratefulness by Lister, arguing that 'the length of credit taken by some gentlemen leaves the tradesmen without profit and very frequently with loss'. Ibid.

[131] Ibid., Yas MD335/1/9/2/8.

[132] Jan Fergus and Ruth Portner, 'Provincial Bookselling in Eighteenth-Century England: The Case of John Clay Reconsidered', *Studies in Bibliography*, vol. 40 (1987): 147–63; John Feather, *The Provincial Book Trade in Eighteenth-Century England* (Cambridge, 1985).

[133] E. H. Jacobs, 'Eighteenth-Century British Circulating Libraries and Cultural Book History', *Book History*, vol. 6 (2003): 1–22.

[134] Norbert Schürer, 'Four Catalogues of the Lowndes Circulating Library, 1755–66', *The Papers of the Bibliographical Society of America*, vol. 101, no. 3 (2007): 329–57 at 341.

[135] James Raven, 'The Noble Brothers and Popular Publishing, 1737–1789', *The Library*, vol. 6, no. 4 (1990): 293–345.

THE MANY WAYS OF READING AND SELLING   95

shillings.[136] Later, circulating libraries grew in size and included a wider choice of directories. As a main publisher of Collins's and Kimber's compilations, it is hardly surprising to see them in the catalogues of Thomas Lowndes's circulating library.[137] In his 1774 catalogue, one could find one copy of the 1768 edition of Collins's *Peerage* but eight copies of Kimber's pocket edition.[138] Demand for smaller formats was higher but for the same price the reader, if patient, could borrow more expensive compilations. Although in his first advert, Lowndes aimed his library at 'the Nobility, Gentry, &c', it has been rightly suggested that the '&c'. 'leaves the tantalizing possibility that members of other classes might meet nobility or gentry, the main addressees of the advertisement, in the library'.[139] Peter Hudson, in his successful *New Introduction to Trade and Business* (1758; 5th edn, 1791) argued that a subscription (10s.) to Lowndes's library was a good investment for any aspiring merchant.[140] John Bell made available costly compilations such as those of Collins and Lodge as well as Salmon's *Short Views*.[141] In Newcastle, R. Fisher's circulating library included expensive directories as well as several editions of Smith's and Salmon's *Pocket peerages* (2s.).[142]

These circulating libraries thrived on a strong associational life and many commercial associations, which blurred the segregating effects of the book market. As pioneer reading venues, the owners of coffee houses invested in larger libraries which provided not only ephemeral materials but also larger volumes liable to attract even exacting antiquarians. The proportion of folios and quartos made up to 60 per cent of their catalogues.[143] Then later in the eighteenth century, an increasing number of library societies collected sufficient funds to buy a vast range of publications. As reference works, family directories figured prominently in their catalogues. Depending on the city, there were different categories of subscribers. Subscribers in cathedral cities such as Lichfield and York were mostly church parsons. In Liverpool, the literary society featured 300 members in 1778, where professional and landed elites could meet: 'voluntary associations funded by private subscription were in fact essentially inclusive in their view: with their typically non-factional membership and strongly integrative roles'.[144] In Leeds, four subscription libraries 'provided the townspeople of Leeds with a selection of

---

[136] *A New Catalogue of the Curious and Valuable Collections of Books* (London, 1757), i.

[137] BL, S.C. 707. (10.) T. Lowndes's catalogue for 1778: Douglas's *Peerage* (£1. 5s.), 18; Collins's (£2. 12s.), 67; Kimber's (3s.), 84.

[138] Ibid. T. Lowndes's catalogue for 1774, 1778, and 1779.

[139] Schürer, 'Four Catalogues', 335.

[140] *New Introduction to Trade and Business* (London, 1791), 43.

[141] *A new catalogue of Bell's circulating library* (London, 1778), 181–2.

[142] *A catalogue of R. Fisher's circulating library, in the High-Bridge* (Newcastle, 1791), 36, 40, 129.

[143] Markman Ellis, 'Coffee-House Libraries in Mid-Eighteenth-Century London', *The Library*, vol. 10 (2009): 3–40 at 27.

[144] Rebecca Bowd, 'Useful Knowledge or Polite Learning', *Library & Information History*, vol. 29, no. 3 (2013): 182–95 at 183.

96 SELLING ANCESTRY

books far beyond the financial capabilities of any one individual'.[145] The first one, founded in 1768, included many merchants as well as members of the gentry. Its 1785 catalogue contained a broad category related to history, antiquity, and biography, notably Douglas's Scottish *Peerage*, Kimber's and Johnston's.[146] In Bristol, the borrowing records of the literary society confirms the availability of less affordable volumes to a larger public.[147] Even private libraries were sometimes accessible to a wider reading community, notably among women from different social backgrounds. In rural north-east Scotland, for example, private libraries were 'a practical resource for the wider community, providing books that could not be acquired elsewhere'.[148]

To account for the extensive network of literary distribution, one can refer to various clues scattered among personal diaries. A rural shopkeeper such as Thomas Turner in Sussex had access to much that was on the bookshelf of many a London gentleman. At first, he did not mention in his diary any interest in family lineage, but later in life, when he became a property owner and a father in his own right, he 'constructed a sense of patrilineal descent'.[149] In his diary, he noted: 'Thurs. 27 Apr. At home all day. Read part of *The Peerage of England*. Oh, what an unspeakable pleasure it is to be busied on one's trade and at a leisure hour to unbend one's mind by reading'.[150] In Ireland, near Tipperary, Dorothea Herbert, daughter of the Reverend Nicholas Herbert, witnessed a confrontation between Mrs Robbins, daughter of Lord Massy and her mother. The latter used Lodge's *Peerage* to demonstrate that her family was more ancient than the Massy and were therefore entitled to the head pew in the church.[151]

With respect to colonial towns, various studies have underlined the similarities between the provincial and Atlantic bookselling networks. In terms of cost and time, they were roughly equivalent.[152] As in Britain, circulating libraries were instrumental. The Library Company of Philadelphia, the Corporation of New York, or the Annapolis Circulating Library all had several *Peerages* and

---

[145] Geoffrey Forster, Alice Hamilton, Peter Hoare, and Elaine Robinson, '*A Very Good Public Library': Early Years of the Leeds Library* (Newcastle, 2001), 4.

[146] *A compleat catalogue of the books in the circulating-library at Leeds; a copy of the laws, as they are now in force; and a list of the subscribers* (Leeds, 1785) 33, 36.

[147] Sweet, *The Writing of Urban Histories*, 117.

[148] Mark Towsey, '"I can't resist sending you the book": Private Libraries, Elite Women, and Shared Reading Practices in Georgian Britain', *Library & Information History*, vol. 29, no. 3 (2013): 210–22 at 211.

[149] Naomi Tadmor, *Family and Friends in Eighteenth-Century England: Household, Kinship, and Patronage* (Cambridge, 2001), 81.

[150] Thomas Turner and David Vaisey (eds), *The Diary of Thomas Turner* (Oxford, 1984), 145–6.

[151] Barbara Hughes (ed.), *Between Literature and History: The Diaries and Memoirs of Mary Leadbeater* (Bern, 2010), 51.

[152] Richard Beale Davis, *A Colonial Southern Bookshelf: Reading in the Eighteenth Century* (Athens, Ga, 1979); Mark Towsey and Kyle B. Roberts (eds), *Before the Public Library: Reading, Community, and Identity in the Atlantic World, 1650–1850* (Leiden, 2018).

Baronetages in their catalogues accessible to the public.[153] In Williamsburg, the Library of the General Court ordered Guthrie's *Peerage* as soon as it was published and the compilation found its way into the 'Esteemed Bookes of Lawe'.[154] James Raven has published the 'Copy Book of Letters' between various London booksellers and the Charleston Library Society from 1758 onwards. The copy book was used to preserve the memory of all the transactions, which turned out to be crucial in re-establishing commercial relations after 1783. In May 1767, the Charleston Library Society ordered Edmondson's *Peerage* as well as the *Court Calendar*.[155] A few years later, in October 1770, they complained that the copy sent from London was missing several sheets, notably the genealogical table of Harley.[156] Whether it be an expensive folio or literary gazettes, 'each was of major value in re-establishing the connection between the members and the literary and intellectual heart of the empire'.[157]

3. Genealogies and social shaming

In contextualizing the publication of several directories, such as those issued in 1709 or in 1808, we have seen they were aimed at warding off former revolutionary events. Their underlying ideological assumption was to provide a disciplined and reassuring picture of the social fabric. Genealogical practices are indeed linked to a wide range of emotions. They may be guided by an irenic and reverential impulse, though in Brydges's case, an overriding sense of nostalgia and anxiety is visible. Reading these directories and writing on them was a way to express family affection, or even anger in Old Osborne's case, crossing out his disobedient son. We should now consider also the comical and subversive potential of ancestry. It has been argued above that one of the key steps in the making of directories was collecting data from gazettes and ephemerals. To build the reputations of their clients, compilers had to sift through thousands of pages, gathering information from obituaries, biographies, and reviews. In the process, they had to discard all the gossip, innuendo, and partisan attacks. As always, the creation of memory, whether public or private, relied simultaneously on forgetfulness and censorship. Any complacent enquiry creates its own by-product of malevolent stories which could be kept for the sake of amusement or even for a moral and partisan agenda.

---

[153] *The charter, laws, and catalogue of books, of the Library Company of Philadelphia* (1770); *A catalogue of books, belonging to the incorporated Charlestown Library Society Charlestown* (1770); *A catalogue of the library, belonging to the Corporation of the City of New-York* (1766); *A catalogue of the Annapolis Circulating Library* (1786); *Catalogue in the circulating library at Halifax* (1786).

[154] Warren M. Billings and Brent Tarter (eds), *'Esteemed Bookes of Lawe' and the Legal Culture of Early Virginia* (Charlotteville, Va, 2017), 37–56.

[155] James Raven, *London Booksellers and American Customers: Transatlantic Literary Community and the Charleston Library Society 1758–1811* (Columbia, SC, 2002), 51, 233.

[156] Ibid., 263.   [157] Ibid., 112.

98   SELLING ANCESTRY

The constructive side of genealogies in the family identity is equivalent to its destructive potential.[158] Family secrets and scandals were potent tools to undermine the dignity of any title-holder. On a few occasions, notably in the 1770s and 1780s, during the growth of a reformist movement, many readers among the urban middling sorts were eager to consume voyeuristic and outrageous tales about their elites. They expressed a general anxiety about the moral failings of the 'aristocrats' and their repercussions on the social fabric. Although, it should be noted that 'aristocracy' was also a term 'used to describe a body of men rather than a system of government', and several Whig magnates in their crusade against the undue influence of the 'King's Friends' contributed to this climate of defiance.[159]

'All this is for your own amusement as such anecdotes are not for the public'

In 1801, an informer to Reverend William Betham, Gamaliel Lloyd, a former Leeds major (1778–9), a cloth merchant, member of the Yorkshire Association and of the Society for Constitutional Information, imparted to him a large amount of data on the Yorkshire baronets and a great deal of gossip. While praising Captain Charles Wood of Barnsley, the younger brother of the first baronet, who died in the East Indies in 1782 in the engagement with Suffren, the French admiral, he wrote:

> Their Uncle Tho Pigot Esq was a respectable councellor residing at Manchester. I remember very well. Having a lost his wife many years, when he was old he had a favourite chambermaid well known by the title of Molly [. . .] he was guilty of a cruel action, he obliged his nephew Capt Charles Wood to marry Molly. Fortunately, she did not live long. All this is for your own amusement as such anecdotes are not for the public.[160]

Even though Lloyd was much engaged in the reformist movement, he did not see this story as proper for the public. His intention was rather to maintain a friendly tone with his correspondent by trusting him with confidential gossip. Thomas Pigot, the owner of Bolling Hall, first married the daughter of the third baronet Ralph Ashton of Middleton. Without descent, it seemed that he had planned to transmit his property to Captain Wood on the condition of his marrying his maid. The 'amusement' which Betham may have derived from this anecdote may be understood in different ways. Pigot's behaviour may be entertaining for its

---

[158] On contemporary genealogy, see Tanya Evans, 'Secrets and Lies: The Radical Potential of Family History', *History Workshop Journal*, vol. 71, no. 1 (2011): 49–73; Deborah Cohen, *Family Secrets: The Things we Tried to Hide* (London, 2013).

[159] Langford, *Public Life and the Propertied Englishman*, 535.   [160] BL, Add. MS 21033, fol. 53.

THE MANY WAYS OF READING AND SELLING 99

inconstancies, as he tried at first to fit into the landed elite and then broke its rules by trying to impose an unconventional union. Many anecdotes are shared not only for the sake of 'amusement' but in a more moralistic spirit. The reformist movement in which Lloyd had been engaged drew its origins in the Reformation period. Sobering tales of vain or despotic kin were used among god-fearing families to better improve their behaviour. As a clergyman, Betham may have been sensitive to this side of Pigot's story.

Most of these rumours circulated incognito. A small note was sent to Wotton about several Yorkshire baronets. Though anonymous, it may have come from Roger Beckwith, the former Leeds mayor, as the writing is similar. Beckwith was also Wotton's main provider of news in the county. In the note, Sir Walter Brownlow was described as a journeyman, a blacksmith working for the London engineer Mr Richard Newsham of Cloth Fair, Sir Thomas Rudstone as a black-smith or farrier at Hayton who died when 'the hond fell to him', and Sir Matthew Peirson in East Riding as a 'waggoner' of the Stricklands in the time of Charles I.[161] It would be challenging to verify the exactness of these accusations. Walter Brownlow does not appear in the different baronetcies created in 1641. Only Rudstone and Peirson are easily identified, the first as a baronet who died childless in 1709 and the second as a knight and high sheriff of Yorkshire in 1706, before Beckwith stepped in to replace him. In both cases, these rumours, though highly improbable, alluded to the dramatic and humiliating decline of baronets turned mechanics. Richard Newsham was an engineer and the inventor of a water pump.[162] Rudstone and Peirson as a farrier and a waggoner would have been at the low end of an otherwise polite activity: horse-riding. There may have been some jest in the accusation about Peirson. Sir Matthew was famous for having bred a stallion, 'Bay Bolton', who descended from one of Sir William Strickland's studs.[163] Again, one should be cautious in attributing a clear meaning to this gossip. It may have been a personal feud which had led Beckwith to denounce some of his neighbours.

As they were extinct baronets, Wotton ignored these notes but kept them in his archives, which is worth stressing. He himself expressed much interest in the miserable ends of some families. Regarding Sir Henry Appleton, he desired to know from one correspondent whether 'ye family is reduced to poverty & to know what is become of Sr Henry who sold his estate & what issue remains'.[164] Wotton was curious to learn the fate of extinct or impoverished families, even though he erased them from his compilation. He was clearly expressing a personal interest in his enquiries.

---

[161] BL, Add. MS 24121, fol. 370.

[162] Anita McConnell, 'Newsham, Richard (d. 1743), maker of fire engines', *ODNB*. Retrieved 10 Apr. 2020, from <https://doi-org.janus.bis-sorbonne.fr/10.1093/ref:odnb/20041>.

[163] Harry Harewood, *A Dictionary of Sports: Or, Companion to the Field, the Forest, and the Riverside* (London,1835), 35.

[164] Wotton to Holman (1724), Essex RO D/Y 1/1/199/1.

100 SELLING ANCESTRY

The reader as a judge of families' highs and lows

Sometimes readers would use their compilation to record various stories gleaned among the gazettes, obituaries, and judicial memoirs (factums).[165] Wotton's *Baronage* copy in the British Library is interleaved with a copious number of annotations from 1741 to 1760 by the Reverend Robert Smyth of Woodston.[166] Dean of Rochester and member of the Spalding Society, Smyth had been working on a *History of the English Sheriffs* which never came to fruition. One can assume that he used Wotton's compilation to this purpose. He wrote many notes to complete some entries, adding the latest births and deaths after 1740. He proceeded in the same manner with his copies of Walker's *Suffering of the Clergy* and Le Neve's *Fasti Anglicani*, as well as Cave's *Parliamentary Register*.[167]

Smyth took upon himself the role of a family judge, allocating eulogy and blame. Apart from a few exceptions, baronets who were much praised tended to belong to the High Church side. On the fifth baronet, Sir John Rivers, who died in 1743, he added: 'Sir John died at Windsor, in Berks in ye 24th year of his age [...] tho his fortune did not descend to him so ample as he deserved, he supported his title with great credit.'[168] Nephew to the fourth baronet, he was the son of the Reverend Thomas Rivers, rector of Easton (Hants) and obtained a BA at Oxford.[169] He fitted well into the category of respectable baronets for his studies in Oxford and his attachment to the Church, values to which Smyth could relate. Sir Henry Harpur, sixth baronet, was the son of an affluent Derbyshire family whose father was returned as a Tory MP. Smyth copied an extract of a gazette which detailed Harpur's birthday party on his estate of Calke Abbey in July 1760:

> Many thousands of Sir Henry's tenants and neighbours were present and tents and other conveniences prepared for the reception of all without distinction: a fat ox, great plenty of venison and provisions of every sort, with thirty hogsheads of strong beer, the utmost plenty of punch and wines of various sorts were provided for their entertainment [...]. The bells of all the neighbouring towns rang incessantly and the whole was conducted with the utmost regularity and decorum. The universal joy that appear'd on every face present, was the clearest

---

[165] On the importance of factums in the creation of a non-professional French public sphere, see Sarah Hanley, 'Social Sites of Political Practices in France: Lawsuits, Civil Rights, and the Separation of Powers in Domestic and State Government, 1500–1800', *The American Historical Review*, vol. 102, no. 1 (1997): 27–52.

[166] John Nichols, *Literary Anecdotes of the Eighteenth Century* (London, 1812), vol. 3, 441. His letters are in the Spalding Gentlemen's society archives.

[167] *A selection of curious articles from the Gentleman's magazine* (London, 1811), vol. 4, 258.

[168] BL, Add. MS 24115, fol. 189.

[169] G. E. Cokayne, *Complete Baronetage*, vol. 1 (London, 1900), 170.

THE MANY WAYS OF READING AND SELLING 101

token of the high esteem and veneration which the inhabitants of Derbyshire have so long continued to pay to the very ancient and worthy family of the Harpurs.[170]

The year after, Sir Henry was elected unopposed for the county.[171] Harpur represented for Smyth the ideal of the propertied gentleman, who despite a large fortune and a promising career in London, did not neglect his tenants and neighbours. He was thus duly celebrated and elected the following year. Antiquarian baronets were viewed favourably, even if they came from a nonconformist background. Sir Richard Ellys, third baronet, sat in the Commons on the Whig side. Like Smyth, he was also a member of the Gentlemen's Society at Spalding and built up a considerable theological library which was liberally opened to most enquirers.[172] Ellys embodied the values of charity and neighbourliness. On his death in 1742, he noted that: 'Sr Richard had an hospitable custom observd at Nocton, wch was to keep a constant table there every day in ye week for all comers tho he never used to be there himself where the company was entertain'd in a generous manner as if he was present.'[173] Other families such as the Twisdens, the Ashtons, the Chardins were described with much affection.[174] Like Lloyd, Smyth was also imbued with the notions of charity and community service, Christian values which have been so often repeated in the prescriptive literature since the Renaissance.[175]

Other marginalia provided an alternative view to the complacent perspective of the *Baronetage* and its seamless dynastic narratives. About some families, Smyth had collected a great deal of gossip which would be more likely to be found in the gutter press and judicial memoirs. With much detail, he included many anecdotes about fraudsters, unpleasant characters, pointless deaths, seedy murders, and succession crises.

Smyth paid much attention to the various trials in which baronets were involved, some relating to murder cases, felonies, and robberies.[176] Concerning the fourth baronet, Sir John Aubrey, he recounted the discovery of a young corpse dug out by a dog in the family seat at Boarstall.[177] Soon, the inquiry established

---

[170] BL, Add. MS 24117, fol. 30.
[171] Mary M. Drummond, 'Sir Henry, Harpur, 6th Bt', in L. Namier and J. Brooke (eds), *The History of Parliament: The House of Commons 1754–1790* (London, 1964).
[172] Paula Walson, 'Richard Ellys', in R. Sedgwick, *The History of Parliament: The House of Commons 1674–1742* (London, 1970).
[173] BL, Add. MS 24117, fol. 133.
[174] BL, Add. MS 24117, fol. 233; on the Twisdens, BL, Add. MS 24114, fol. 244.
[175] On the pervasive influence of the early modern books of conduct since Brathwait's *English Gentleman* (1630), see Raven, *Judging New Wealth*, 95–108.
[176] Smyth may have used the *Complete Collections of State Trials and proceedings for high-treason, and other crimes and misdemeanours*. The first edition was edited by Thomas Salmon in 1719.
[177] 'A husbandman looking in a wood near Boarstall in Bucks for a sheep he had lost his dog tow up some fresh earth and ye country man coming to ye place & digging up the earth found ye child buried, this being noised about ye country', BL, Add. MS 24116, fol. 160.

that the likely perpetrator was Sir John's eldest son, who 'some years ago, got one of his fathers' maid with child and kept it conceal'd'.[178] Though indicted in the assize session, Sir John Aubrey was never punished and 'lives somewhere in obscurity & Sr John settled all he had on his second son'.[179] It could be that Aubrey's influence led the case to be unfairly dismissed. Smyth provided the missing link as to why the title was transmitted to the cadet, Thomas Aubrey.[180] About Berney, he wrote that Sir Richard, son and heir, was hanged at Norwich for killing Thomas Bodingsfeld, Esq.[181] The fifth baronet, Simon Peter Clark, was convicted of robbery 'on ye highway [...] but great interest was made and he was transported with his companion' to Jamaica.[182] He was nonetheless able to transfer his title to his son, Sir Simon Clarke, who became a wealthy slave owner.[183] The heir of Sir Richard Everard, fourth baronet, governor of the province of North Carolina, was Hugh, who 'when the title came to him he was in the marshals prison on suspicion of having acted with pirates'.[184] From other sources, he was assisting captain William Cole on the *Swift* and upon the latter's death was reported to have sold the cargo and 'spent all of the sayd mony in drinking and extravagant Living'.[185]

Smyth commented on less compromising stories which leaned rather towards the comical side of life related to cuckoldry or ridiculous deaths which undermined manly virtues. He explained how Sir Erasmus Philipps, fifth baronet, MP for Haverfordwest, was drowned in the river Avon in 1743 from a narrow bridge, after some pigs frightened his horse.[186] Also the son of Paul Methuen: his only heir George who was 'unfortunately drownd by falling in ye moat at Southcot, near Reading'.[187] Some died like James Tyrell, in the junior branch of the baronetcy, leaving behind them a despicable reputation: 'a kind master, when servants would be slaves to caprices and harsh usage without wage, a sincere friend when no favour was requir'd; a staunch patriot when he could vote without fear of losing his commission'.[188] Some were caught red-handed falsely claiming a title. Concerning Ernle, Smyth consulted the Rolls in Chancery Lane and found that the title had actually been extinct since the death of Sir John Ernle in 1734, despite Walter Ernle's claim.[189] He noted that Sir George Bridges Skipwith 'was tried at the Old Bailey for Buggery with his foot boy (but ye evidence was spirited away) and he was acquitted'.[190]

---

[178] Ibid. [179] Ibid.

[180] Aubrey's elder son is merely noted as 'unmarried' in *The Baronetage*, vol. 3, 112.

[181] BL, Add. MS 24115, fol. 123. [182] BL, Add. MS 24115, fol. 26.

[183] The Centre for the Study of the Legacies of British Slave-ownership. <https://www.ucl.ac.uk/lbs/person/view/2146646377>.

[184] BL, Add. MS 24116, fol. 175.

[185] Quoted by Marcus Rediker, *Between the Devil and the Deep Blue Sea: Merchant Seamen, Pirates and the Anglo-American Maritime World* (Cambridge, 1987), 147.

[186] BL, Add. MS 24115, fol. 208. [187] BL, Add. MS 24118, fol. 40.

[188] BL, Add. MS 24116, fol. 106. [189] BL, Add. MS 24116, fol. 270.

[190] BL, Add. MS 24118, fol. 309.

THE MANY WAYS OF READING AND SELLING   103

Many stories related to the baronets' wives or daughters. As for the men, some were dealt with respectfully while others were painted as disobedient and mean. He copied from *Country News* the obituaries dedicated to Lady William Wynn in 1749: once married, 'instead of launching into publick life, she retired to her closet to pray for the welfare of her country, while her husband endeavour'd to promote it in the Senate'.[191] On Juliana Beale, the wife of Robert Newdigate of Hillington, he transcribed a laudatory account: 'her eminent piety, extensive charity and uncommon generosity so well known, and felt by the poor in the neighbourhood parishes'.[192] As for the baronets, virtues of piety and charity were celebrated in the wives, though Smyth insisted on the importance of a more secluded life.

On the other hand, Sir Thomas Hanmer's reputation was ruined by his union with Isabella Bennet: 'She was an odd woman thin pale, sickly woman. She left Sr Tho & went abroad with ye Hon Thomas Harvey, son to ye earl of Bristol who wrote a letter after her decease to Sr Tho relating to her leaving him her fortune wch he printed wherein he endeavourd to render Sr Tho ridiculous for having not consummated ye nuptial.'[193] Similarly, the daughter of Sir Thomas Smyth, Athania, married against her parents' will a dangerous thug: 'Nathll Parkhurst of Catesby (who was hang for ye murder of Lewis Pleura in ye fleet prison) at Tyburn (May 1715)'.[194] Anne, daughter of Sir Marmaduke Gresham, married 'a Common low man and lived very meanly sometimes at last her mother took him and her to live with her in 1751. They lived privately at Acton & my Lady had a proper master to polish him. She was a tall and gentle young lady when she threw themselves away, she afterwards grew melancholic & went out of her mind.'[195]

Lastly, some comments relate rather to carnivalesque situations where a few women defying the usual conventions. Of Lady Chester, Sir William Chester's widow, it was said that she married a fourth husband, Charles Atherley of Ham Hall, and that the motto on her ring was 'If I survive I will have five'.[196] Mottoes were a suitable device to make some jokes by diverting their initial solemn meaning into plays on words and puns. Concerning the third wife of Sir Edmund Prideaux, Mary, daughter of Spencer Vincent, alderman of London, and widow or 'relict' of Sir John Roger, he commented that the baronet met her in an inn and hearing her piping some music upstairs: 'he said if it was some woman he would marry her, her coming downstairs he asked who had laid over his head, she reply I, then he said she should be his wife & married her, she married Sr Edmond Prideaux bart, and at 90 years of age, was married in Pink and

---

[191] BL, Add. MS 24119, fol. 64.   [192] BL, Add. MS 24118, fol. 278.
[193] BL, Add. MS 24115, fol. 158.
[194] BL, Add. MS 24117, fol. 408; Paul Lorrain, *The ordinary of Newgate: his account of the behaviour and declaration of Nathanael Parkhurst, Esq.; who was executed at Tyburn on Friday the 20th of May, 1715* (London, 1715).
[195] BL, Add. MS 24117, fol. 172.   [196] BL, Add. MS 24115, fol. 119.

104   SELLING ANCESTRY

silver to Coll. Arundell'.[197] Smyth was expressing both his disapproval and the pleasure of telling an unusual story with some sexual innuendos.

In Smyth's marginalia one could find a wide range of stories and gossip related to the baronets and their families. Some were rather respectful and celebratory, others pointed out their scandalous misbehaviours. Many convicted for murder, robbery, and some minor offences managed to run free, due to their connections and status. Some, as in the case of the Clarkes, even managed to make a fortune after being deported to Jamaica and preserve their dynasty. Smyth shared a growing belief among the public that many titled families did not live up to their honorific status. This critical stance relied on a middle-class culture which remained strongly influenced by Christian values.

Satirical directories

In a few cases, in the 1770s and 1780s, some publishers even went so far as to publish snippets of gossip and incidents which had for a long time remained handwritten in the margins. This fitted into the growth of radical and reformist movements from the 1760s onwards. The conflict with the American colonists, the repression against Wilkes and his partisans, as well as the parliamentary dispute over the right to publish debates contributed to a stronger radicalization among some political writers and journalists.[198] As Helen Berry argued convincingly, 'by the end of the eighteenth century, artisan and tradesmen were increasingly political in their awareness that politeness could not gloss over the social and economic equalities upon which society was based'.[199] This shift has been amply documented from a generational perspective and from the promotion of 'the natural, or unpolished, inner self'.[200] Changes in print culture facilitated the rise of a public debate about the elites and their moral shortcomings. Some publishers such as John Almon had expressed the need for greater accountability and voiced concern about certain peers created by George III.[201] Far from restoring trust, the increased public scrutiny on parliamentary debates and on corruption generated 'vicious cycles in which distrust

[197] The anecdote appeared in a different version in Henry Moore, *The Life of Mrs Mary Fletcher, consort and relict of the Rev. John Fletcher, Vicar of Madeley, Salop* (London, 1860), 85.

[198] Hannah Barker, *Newspapers, Politics, and Public Opinion in Late Eighteenth-Century England* (Oxford, 1998); W. C. Lowe, 'Peers and Printers: The Beginning of Sustained Press Coverage of the House of Lords in the 1770s', *Parliamentary History*, vol. 7 (1988): 241–56.

[199] Helen Berry, 'Polite Consumption: Shopping in Eighteenth-Century England', *Transactions of the Royal Historical Society*, vol. 12 (2002), 393.

[200] Barbara Crosbie, *Age Relations and Cultural Change in Eighteenth-Century England* (Woodbridge, 2020), 40.

[201] John Almon, *The Political Register; and impartial Review of New Books*, vol. 7 (London, 1770), 138–9; see also *The Farmer's and Monitor's letters, to the inhabitants of the British colonies* (London, 1769), 26.

THE MANY WAYS OF READING AND SELLING 105

could become a destructive feedback loop'.[202] Plays, sermons, and published judicial memoirs included many stories about sexual scandals and wrongdoings amongst peers.[203]

George III's claims to magnificence were also publicly sneered at by radicals. L. Colley recalls that when the Royal Academy commemorated his birthday 'by exhibiting an illuminated royal coat of arms at Somerset House', a Wilkite crowd tried to set fire to it, thus running the risk of destroying the whole building.[204] Biographical compilations were used with great success by radical authors in their attack on an unworthy elite as private vices and social ills were seen as interconnected in the contemporary mind. In the work of Thomas Oldfield (1755–1822) and his *History of the Original Constitution of Parliaments* (1797), the length of the lineage could become the consequence of deeply entrenched corruption. In an encyclopedic manner, Oldfield exposed the powerful family connections and their control over the boroughs and counties. About Yarmouth, he stated that 'the town is under the influence of Leicester, and has for many parliaments been represented by some of his lordship's family, with only one exception'.[205] Even among publishers of mainstream family directories, unusual comments appeared after 1770 alluding to the potential conflict between virtue and birth. Kimber in his preface to his *Baronetage* noted: 'It has been observed by some, in opposition to publications of this nature, that heroic virtue and integrity redound more to the honour of mankind than the longest train of ancestors'.[206]

In this general context, gossip about noble families came to be more politicized. A few publishers even proceeded to sell rather satirical directories by using false imprints and deceptive title pages to conceal their subversive aim. This case is well illustrated by a *peerage*, allegedly published by the vicar of Burton, Frederic Barlow, author of a successful English dictionary and a manual of grammar in 1772. His identity is, however, fraught with doubt and cannot be found in the Church of England database. Barlow's compilation was advertised as a weekly edition of twenty-four 'papers' sold for sixpence each, making two large volumes in octavo (12s.). In the first paper dedicated to his subscribers, Barlow 'engages to deliver gratis, all that shall exceed twenty-four numbers' adding that 'Number I. may be perused gratis, and returned if not approved'.[207] The aim of the

---

[202] Mark Knights, *Trust and Distrust: Corruption in Office in Britain and its Empire, 1600–1850* (Oxford, 2021), 8.

[203] On the use of pamphlets, sermons, and newspapers to promote a moral reformation of the elite see Donna T. Andrew, *Aristocratic Vice: The Attack on Duelling, Suicide, Adultery, and Gambling in Eighteenth-Century England* (New Haven, 2013); John Brewer, *A Sentimental Murder: Love and Madness in the Eighteenth Century* (New York, 2004).

[204] Linda Colley, 'The Apotheosis of George III: Loyalty, Royalty and the British Nation 1760–1820', *Past and Present*, vol. 102 (1984): 94–129 at 96.

[205] *History of the Original Constitution* (London, 1797), 482; see also Linda Colley, *Britons: Forging the Nation*, 152.

[206] Edward Kimber and Richard Johnson, *The Baronetage of England* (London, 1770), vi.

[207] *Number I of an entire new work* (London, 1772), preface.

106 SELLING ANCESTRY

compilation was to expose the corruption and vices of many peers and members of the royal family and went through two successive editions in 1772 and 1775: the author 'will put aside the ermine to show the corruption which lies hidden behind'.[208] Several extracts were inserted in various gazettes such as *The Oxford Magazine, or, Universal Museum*.[209] The work was presented to the public as a conventional compilation, borrowing the title and the illustration from that of Guthrie's *Peerage*, the publisher adding ironically that 'the arms will be blazoned by the best Heralds and engraved by the best master'.[210] It was advertised as being 'calculated for general instruction and amusement [...] on a plan entirely new. Embellished with copper-plates, satirical, political, and scientifical, from original designs.'[211] Former directories were accused of covering the stains and the corruption of the elite, and Barrow intended 'to look down on the Frowns of High Birth' and to seek only for 'those who are lovers of Truth, and the admirers of real nobility'.[212]

In the second edition, he inserted a fake list of subscribers including some joke figures such as the 'Honorable Dodington Egerton, Gentlemen of the most Honorable privy chamber'.[213] The name alluded to one of Pope's poems on Bubb Dodington, who despite his dubious activity, had been distinguished by Walpole. According to John Nichols, Dodington had written a letter to the herald Edmondson in May 1773 asking to be called 'Honourable' like any peer.[214] He introduced himself as the oldest son of the youngest son of John earl of Bridgewater. The herald replied that he was the youngest and seventh son of his father. Admitting his lie, Dodington enquired about the cost of painting his arms on 'the body and carriage of his post chaise' and asked him to modify his book of Precedence to consider his particular situation. His dogged and repetitive attempt to be called 'Honourable' against all the precedents displayed the ridiculous behaviour of some remote collaterals in the peerage. Apart from this Dodington, the so-called Barlow mentioned a long list of citizens in all the major British cities with little parliamentary representation such as Manchester, a 'Henry Bine' from New York and a 'John Low' residing at 'Petty' in France. This long list of fake names was supposed to incarnate the modest and honest citizens who supported this salutary project.

Apart from Pope, Barlow was much inspired by the many sexual scandals that were revealed to the public in the 1770s.[215] In the initial pages, the first target

---

[208] Ibid.   [209] *The Oxford Magazine, or, Universal Museum*, vol. 9 (Oxford, 1772), 150.
[210] Ibid.   [211] Ibid.
[212] 'Instead of being faithful historians, they have been little more than mere panegyrists [...]. They imagined it was necessary to ennoble all the descendants, by attributing virtues to them, which they never exercised and by burying those vices in oblivion.' *The Complete English Peerage*, vol. 1, Advertisement.
[213] Ibid., iii.   [214] John Nichols, *Illustrations of the Literary History* (London, 1774), 543–5.
[215] Matthew Kinservik, *Sex, Scandal, and Celebrity in Late Eighteenth-Century England* (Basingstoke, 2007); Nicholas Rogers, 'Pigott's Private Eye: Radicalism and Sexual Scandal in Eighteenth-Century England', *Journal of the Canadian Historical Association*, vol. 4, no. 1 (1983): 247–63.

THE MANY WAYS OF READING AND SELLING   107

was the royal family and the King's Friends. While the first two Georges were celebrated for having imposed themselves as 'the arbiter of the fate of Europe', George III's brother, the duke of Cumberland, saw his vices exposed through his relationships with the actress Miss Elliot and Lady Grosvenor. In his first paper, Barrow republished part of the letters and documents first printed in 1770 during the case for adultery brought by Lord Grosvenor. Along with a very graphic depiction of the lovers caught in the act, the editor inserted a good deal of letters to Lady Grosvenor which included several French expressions: 'je vous adore ma chère petite bejoux l'amant de mon cœur'.[216] The divorce which ensued became one of the prominent *causes célèbres* in England. Concerning other peers, Barlow went on to satirize several of Guthrie's genealogies. The Howards may have stemmed from Brus, earl of Passy in Normandy, but the author wondered whether 'the uncertainty of the ancient descents in this illustrious family is a proof of its great antiquity', therefore ridiculing the notion of immemorial origins.[217] About the Seymours, he provides a more preposterous account of the death of Francis, fourth duke of Somerset, who 'in company with some French gentlemen, whom he had met with in his travels, when they affronted some ladies of quality [. . .] was shot dead at the door of the inn, by the husband of one of them, A. D. 1678'.[218] Other Tories were mocked, such as the Bunburys and 'Lady S. B' (Sarah Lennox) and her 'conjugal infidelity [. . .] with Lord W. G' (William Gordon).[219]

Barlow had a go at some prominent Whig peers, too. Some peers were only to be commemorated for their insignificance: William Vane, the first duke of Cleveland 'never made any noise in the world'.[220] With much irony, the author deplored 'the sneers of newspaper politicians' against the duke of Grafton, an attack so unjustified as the duke had only a 'correspondence with the celebrated Miss Nancy Parsons [. . .]' and was 'seen at Newmarket when he should have been found at Whitehall'.[221] On another Whig magnate, the impoverished second duke of Chandos, it was said that 'His Grace married secondly, Mrs Anne Browne, tho' brought up in her youth in the most abandoned scenes of low life'.[222] Barlow was referring to a rumour according to which Chandos married a chambermaid he had bought from a brutal husband for half a crown in 1744.[223] As for the third duke of St Albans, it is said of him that 'finding all his efforts to confine his expenses within the bounds of his income ineffectual, he resolved to retire abroad for some time, unwilling to live voluptuously (a case too frequent among the nobility) at the expense of his tradesmen'.[224]

---

[216] *The Complete English Peerage*, 29. It was an extract from *The Genuine Copies of Letters which Passed Between His Royal Highness the Duke of Cumberland and Lady Grosvenor [. . .]. To which is annexed a clear and circumstantial account of the Trial in the Court of King's Bench, on the 5th of July 1770.*

[217] *The Complete English Peerage*, 40.   [218] Ibid., 74.   [219] Ibid.

[220] Ibid., 79.   [221] Ibid., 87.   [222] Ibid., 209.

[223] The whole story was later published in *GM*, vol. 102, part 1 (1832).

[224] *The Complete English Peerage*, 95.

108 SELLING ANCESTRY

Several Scottish peers received their share of blame. John the third duke of Athol received £70,000 to make up for the transfer of the Isle of Man to the Crown in 1764 and a pension of £2,000: 'an example as highly to be applauded, as it is rarely to be met with in these times of dissipation'.[225] Athol was a strong opponent of the London publishers who argued for the right to comment on and publish the Lords' parliamentary debates.

The general picture was that of a continuing decline in the value of nobility. Barrow wrote that if the present William Cavendish 'does not promise to add much to the glory of his ancestors', his forebear, the fourth earl who had accompanied Mr Montagu to his embassy to France in 1669, should be celebrated as a genuine hero for his patriotic behaviour:

> Indeed, and having been once grossly insulted at the opera by some French officers, he gave one of them a blow in the face. [...] He defended himself so bravely, though he received several wounds, that the affair was noised all over Europe as much to the honour of his lordship.[226]

Listing in many sordid details their shortcomings, his views triggered some angry comment from polite magazines such as the *London Review of English and Foreign Literature*: 'This reverend author [...] is as complete a grub as ever abused the liberty of the press. The impertinence and imprudence with which he hath here treated some of the first personages in the kingdom justify this remark.'[227] It was more kindly considered in *The Critical Review* as a piece of 'entertainment' and a brave initiative which 'distinguishes the historian from the parasite'.[228] The depiction of some baronets as sexual predators was echoed in some polite magazines such as *The Lady's Magazine*. In 1775 appeared a story of Sir James S—— 'who understood women as well as any man' and managed to seduce a defenceless Aurelia one night at a ball.[229] In the years following, Barlow's *Peerage* continued to be distributed and could be seen in most sales catalogues up until 1790. In Poole's catalogue in Chester, it was still available in 1792. It was displayed as a true directory and sold with Collins's supplement for 15s.[230] One should not overestimate its radical potential, as it inferred along with these undeserving nobles that there were still worthy families commanding much respect. It was more of an attack from a country perspective rather than a radical call to overturn the social order.

Another device was the comical potential of translated aristocratic mottoes. Barrow had played with their meaning. After having described all the weaknesses

---

[225] Ibid., 455.   [226] Ibid., 128–33.   [227] *London Review*, vol. 4 (London, 1776), 469.
[228] *The Critical Review, Or, Annals of Literature*, vol. 40 (London, 1775), 81.
[229] *The Lady's Magazine*, vol. 6 (London, 1775), 652.
[230] *A satirical peerage of England* (London, 1782, 1785), 17.

of the duke of Grafton, he informed the public that his motto truly conveyed the family's virtues: *Et Decus et Pretium Recti* meant, 'Both the glory and reward of rectitude'.[231] The irony was not lost on the reader. But the same device was later exploited to the full by Charles Coleman (Esq.) in *A satirical peerage of England; including a satire on mottoes* (1782), sold for 2s.[232] Again presented as a didactic work 'calculated for the present times', it offered to the public a 'literal translation and criticism on all the mottoes which now decorate the arms of the English nobility, the present sixteen Peers of Scotland'. It was a radical parody of the last *Peerage* published by Longmate the same year in which many pages were dedicated to explaining the meaning of the mottoes. The preface started with a historical summary of the symbolic devices since the Greeks and their utility in inspiring soldiers and convincing them to fight 'with ardour'. The glorious time of the Crusades was celebrated for having generated 'an infinity of beautiful expressions, coats of arms and other insignia of honour'. These remote times were opposed to the general mediocrity of the current peers. Mocking the latest mottoes created by George III for Lords Rodney, Courtenay, Brownlow, and Loughborough, 'such absurdities were unknown to our ancestors', he proposed to the public their translations in plain English.[233] The mysteries surrounding the French or Latin mottoes as well as the complex coats of arms were laid bare to the public to demonstrate their inanity (Table 2.1).

Coleman played with the pious statements of some mottoes, such as Grafton's *Et Decus et Pretium Recti*: 'Both the ornament and reward of virtue. Peers get rewarded all their lives, Can you say this—on both your wives? The Duke was first

Table 2.1 A parody of mottoes

Names	Genuine mottoes	Coleman's translation
W. Courtenay Ld Courtenay (1762)	Ubi lapsus? Quid feci!	Where am I fallen! What have I done!
Sr Fletcher Norton Ld Grantley (1782)	Avi numerantur avorum	Like among alike
George Brydge Ld Rodney (1782)	Non generant aquilae columbus	Eagles do not bring forth pigeons
George Vernon Ld Vernon (1762)	Ver non semper viret	The spring is not always green

---

[231] Ibid.

[232] See Paul Langford's views on Coleman's *Satirical peerage*: Coleman displayed 'an interest in peers as a class rather than the few who had happened to be prominent in politics and were on that account naturally exposed to public criticism and ridicule'. *Public Life and the Propertied Englishman*, 541.

[233] 'It is with great concern we find the major part of these absurd words or meanings have been assumed by peers created by his present Majesty', *A satirical peerage of England*, vi.

110 SELLING ANCESTRY

married to the present Lady Upper Ossory, but divorced, and since married the now Duchesse of Grafton, both ladies living.'[234] The attack on the dubious morality of most peers still figured prominently in the 1780s as new scandals and affairs kept hitting the headlines. Similarly, the earl of Derby's *Sans changer* attracted the following comment: 'Constant indeed,—let's hear no more, You've chang'd your wife, and took a w-re. *Miss F—n the actress is supposed to be the lady that supplies the place of the Countess'.*[235] Other mottoes were used to attack other peers for homosexual practices (earl of Exeter), or impotence (duke of Dorset). The humiliating defeat in America was laid at the door of the ruling class. Commenting on the motto, *By faith and courage*, he added ironically that it was 'better adapted to Lord North, Prime Minister during the American War' who was to blame for the loss.[236] Charles Howard's motto (*Virtue alone is invincible*) attracted the following remarks: 'Invincible *virtue*—long since chang'd her station, And now we're convinc'd she has quite left this nation. *It may be gone to America.*'[237]

Against the military exploits of the ancients, the current peers were reminded of their uselessness. About the earl of Eglinton's *Take care*, he recalled that 'the late Earl was killed in his own ground attempting to take a gun from Mr. Campbell'.[238] The author was referring to changing times and to hope for major political reforms. In this context, no motto seemed timelier than St Albans's *A pledge of better times*: 'We may hope with good reason the times are now mending, from the many petitions the counties are sending. *This alludes to the Petitions which have been sent to Parliament for a Reform.*'[239] Unlike Barrow's *Peerage*, Coleman's called explicitly for an immediate parliamentary reform and its radical agenda was this time dismissed by most literary gazettes: 'A dull attempt at ill-natured wit. Happily, for those at whom it is levelled, it is as feeble as it is malignant.'[240]

The latter publication represented the most extreme case of satire in which the whole principle of social distinction was turned on its head. Its author was trying to transform a sententious subject into a laughing matter in a carnival spirit. In the comedy *The New Peerage, or, Our Eyes May Deceive Us* (1787) by Harriet Lee, the character of Lord Melville complained that memoirs of peers were sold in London 'for the amusement of my footmen and the emolument of some hackney scribbler'.[241] A conventional genre was turned upside down for the pleasure of a radical public. Another publication aimed at enabling the public to judge the respective merit of the political elite came from Edinburgh and with the patronage of Adam Smith. In 1786, Robert Beatson criticized the 'many imperfect lists that have been published of the Peerage, the Great Officers of State' which prevent the

---

[234] Ibid., 10.   [235] Ibid., 15.   [236] Ibid., 30.
[237] Ibid., 9.   [238] Ibid., 59.   [239] Ibid., 10.
[240] *The Monthly Review*, vol. 71 (London, July–Dec. 1784), 229; *The Critical Review*, vol. 58 (London, 1784), 319.
[241] Harriet Lee, *The New Peerage* (London, 1787), 39.

reader 'to know the individual meant to be the object of condemnation or of applause'.[242] As 'the titles have so frequently fluctuated from one family to another', he devised a detailed index in order to help the public to assess, 'when a Nobleman may be the subject either of panegyric or censure'.[243]

In the late century, *Peerages* and *Baronetages* were sufficiently known to the public to be diverted from their initial aim and transmuted into satirical pieces or instruments of accountability. As they were located on the fringes, we do not know much about these radical authors who turned conventional directories into subversive tools. Again, one should not overestimate their destructive potential compared to the more effective media represented by republican pamphlets which articulated more elaborate attacks on the principles of hereditary.[244] In the first years following the French Revolution, hostile comments were still directed at many peers. The last compilation published in spring 1790 was dismissed as the 'registry of unmerited honours', though the reviewer contrasted the poor state of the peerage with its supposed former glory, regretting that 'a knight with his arms blazoned on his coat, if seen at present, would be considered as a hero of a puppet-shew'.[245] Like Barlow or Coleman, the journalist still presumed that the noble order had once been a source of pride for the whole nation and was mainly in need of reform. This moderate radicalism should be compared with Paine's view, according to which William the Conqueror was a 'French bastard landing with armed banditti and establishing himself King of England against the consent of the natives'.[246]

In the 1790s, most of the publishers took a clear royalist stance and harshly condemned the egalitarian excesses on the other side of the channel. The ideological context of the French Revolution led to the rehabilitation of a lineage culture in a Burkean manner as opposed to the new definition of honour which rose in France and was based on lists of worthy citizens. John Nichols's *Gentleman's Magazine* defended British values much along the lines of Burke's pamphlet. John Debrett as a successor to John Almon had been accused in 1789 of spreading the 'Poyson' of radical ideas for having supported the American Revolution.[247] Four years later, he became an active member of the London Association for Preserving Liberty and Property against Republicans and

---

[242] Robert Beatson, *A Political index to the Histories of Great Britain and Ireland, or, A complete register of the hereditary honours, public offices and persons in office from the earliest periods to the present time* (Edinburgh, 1786, London, 1788), preface.

[243] Ibid.

[244] Laurent Curelly and Nigel Smith (eds), *Radical Voices, Radical Ways: Articulating and Disseminating Radicalism in Seventeenth- and Eighteenth-Century Britain* (Manchester, 2016).

[245] 'On the English peerage', in *The Monthly Review, or, Literary Journal* (London, July 1790), 339.

[246] Thomas Paine, *Common Sense* (Philadelphia, 1776), 13.

[247] 1 Aug. 1789, Hester Lynch Piozzi (formerly Thrale; née Salusbury) to Penelope Sophia Pennington. Edward A. Bloom and Lillian D. Bloom (eds), *Electronic Enlightenment Scholarly Edition of Correspondence* (2014).

112   SELLING ANCESTRY

Levellers, which met at the Crown and Anchor.[248] Its chairmen were John Reeves and Charles York and among the subscribers was John Nichols. The association distributed in its 2,000 local branches several pamphlets intended to demonstrate the superiority of the British Constitution and the usefulness of the peerage. In their 'Protest against T. Paine's 'Rights of Man', they argued that:

> The Peers of Great Britain, though not actually deputed, do virtually possess a representative character, obliging them cautiously and firmly to protect those rights which they enjoyed in common, and which they can enjoy only in common with the People at large; while the existence of such a rank in the State, besides its other advantages, is conducive to the promotion of a spirit of virtuous enterprise and of honourable emulation; and its hereditary nature, is necessary both to render it independent of the Crown, and to ensure its stability and its permanence.[249]

Although Debrett was known for his cheap pocket *Peerages* and *Baronetages*, he committed himself to publishing 'an elegant and convenient edition, in royal octavo [...] the Declaration of a whole People in favour of their Established Government' furnishing all the necessary documents for its completion.[250] The many resources Debrett had accumulated for the completion of his various compilations were this time mobilized in the loyalist cause. Even in Paris, Robert Darnton conceded that 'the bottom of the literary world', populated with impoverished compilers and hacks, could not equivocally be seen as a revolutionary force.[251] He stressed their opportunistic dispositions as well as the blurred ideological fault lines. There will be much to gain by developing further Franco-British comparison on the ways Grub Street writers were dealing with their social superiors. If they behaved like entrepreneurs, Wotton, Collins, Barlow, or Guthrie should not be dismissed as marginal actors or neutral bystanders. Their directories, whether they were complacent or satirical, contributed to a culture of accountability and to a public debate on the duties and responsibilities of the titled families.

One should not establish too strict a boundary between the diverse sorts of directories. From many readers' points of view, such a distinction did not exist. We should be aware of the difficulties raised by each source, from the novels

---

[248] On its crucial role, see Boyd Hilton, *A Mad, Bad, and Dangerous People? England 1783–1846* (Oxford, 2006), 69.

[249] Circulated by the East Kent and Canterbury Association: John Bowles, *A protest against T. Paine's 'rights of Man', Printed by order of the society for preserving liberty and property* (London, 1793), 18. See on the similar lines: William Combe, *A word in season, to the traders and manufacturers of Great Britain; A plain and earnest address to Britons, especially farmers* (London, 1793).

[250] *The Critical Review, Or, Annals of Literature*, vol. 7, (London, 11 Jan. 1793), 1.

[251] Robert Darnton, 'Two Paths through the Social History of Ideas', in Haydn T. Mason (ed.), *The Darnton Debate: Books and Revolution in the Eighteenth Century* (Oxford, 1998), 254.

and the prominent characters of the retired gentlemen to the customers' correspondence and memoirs. Each requires a narrow contextualization and great prudence in analysing them. Furthermore, the integrated nature of the book industry led to the circulation of similar genealogical narratives in different formats, whether it be pocketbooks, magazines, or expensive compilations. The dominant position of a tight-knit group of influential London booksellers loomed large in the commercial success of these directories. Their shops as well as circulating libraries ensured a wide audience, from provincial communities to the colonial elites. The accessibility of these compilations should be assessed through the many channels via which they circulated. We would argue that this broadened the public's familiarity with genealogical culture, whose unintended consequence was to generate a good deal of sarcasm and parody. Praise of titled families was interspersed with some violent criticism. The arguments deployed in the latter section were not necessarily endowed with a political agenda. It was a form of 'amusement' among antiquaries involved in tedious enquiries. There is no denying, however, that many genealogists and publishers related to the moral condemnation of the aristocrats' vices. These directories in their diversity were not the sign of a resilient dynastic culture or a debased form of knowledge. They accounted for an ever-changing interest which could be used in many contexts.

Conclusion to part I

The categorization carried out in the first chapter had considerable relevance in the eighteenth century. Booksellers, customers, and many authors were keen to find some clear distinctions between various social groups, each with their own type of book. They responded to an expanding and socially differentiated readership by tailoring their titles towards distinct sections. Most of all, these compilations should reflect a well-ordered society where each group could be defined by diverse needs. Libraries, bookshops, and sales catalogues, by distinguishing different formats, were consonant with such an aspiration. However, in practice, these publications were multi-purpose and to be used in a complementary manner. Pocket handbooks, historical treatises, and rare commodities: these three main functions are not easily separated and do not cover the full variety of historical reading practices. In the 1830s, the publishers of Debrett's explained that their compilation and that of Burke 'always formed a harmonious partnership', 'the comprehensive family history given by Burke being complemented by Debrett's impartial listing'.[252] Most customers desired to read practical reference

---

[252] Debrett's, *Complete Peerage* (London, 1830), preface.

books as well as elegant and well-crafted compilations where their names could appear in an advantageous form.

Beyond the apparent wish to conform to a strict hierarchy by selling different sorts of directories, publishers were in fact quick to respond to changes in the social make-up. A narrow approach in terms of social status would not cover the diversity of reading experiences. Antiquarian and historical interests were not only shared by the landed families but were also part of the concerns of the middling sorts. They failed to agree on the ultimate functions of these compilations, whether it was to provide a synoptic view of the national elite or to defend resilient local identities. The taste for satire and gossip was widespread beyond clear-cut social categories. To better define the needs and expectations of the customers, we should now turn to a more detailed perspective based on several case studies.

PART II
THE PUBLISHERS AND THEIR CUSTOMERS

Inspired by the Baconian method of ordering knowledge, English antiquaries throughout the early modern period proceeded to send out an ever-increasing number of printed questionnaires.[1] Individuals of varying social status (clerics, landowners, professionals) were solicited, to enable the gathering of a vast array of observations on nature, population, topography, and so on. The nobility and gentry as well as the clergy were the prime targets of data collectors such as John Aubrey or Gregory King, as they were deemed to have a closer expertise of their area of residence. Adam Fox pointed out that to optimize the answer rate by speaking to respondents' interests, some questionnaires included a line about names of persons of note, the present lords, 'their genealogies, coats of arms, crest, &c'.[2]

However, despite these efforts, this wide circulation of surveys did not usually achieve the expected results. Some among many landed correspondents expressed a great reluctance or apathy. They simply could not be bothered or did not see what advantage it was to them personally. Some even may have feared that such enquiries could be tax-related or invade their privacy. Others were hostile by principle to more commercially oriented initiatives such as *The Gentleman's Magazine* or the various London directories. They were unwilling to share their manuscripts beyond their county and a narrow circle of trustworthy local antiquaries.

Publishers of family directories desired to adapt these antiquarian knowledge-gathering practices for their commercial (but speculative) projects. They made sure to mention in their preface the importance of family participation. Whatever their format or price, the exchange of letters was systematically encouraged and was welcomed in their advertisements. More often than not, families would provide the latest updates about their alliances, births, and deaths.[3] However,

---

[1] Adam Fox, 'Printed Questionnaires, Research Networks and the Discovery of the British Isles, 1650–1800', *The Historical Journal*, vol. 53, no. 3 (2010): 293–621 at 595.

[2] Ibid., 608.

[3] See, for example, in the case of Nichols's pocket compendium: 'if the Noblemen whom he had already waited on, have anything more to add, or those he has not been with, or many not have opportunity to see, will be pleas'd to send their instructions to the said author Francis Nichols, at R. Nutt's printer'. *Daily Post*, 3 Aug. 1726, issue 2140.

116 SELLING ANCESTRY

several compilations triggered more consistent correspondence, as they were seen as particularly engaging or because their publication coincided with a major political event. Three cases will be considered: the first complete *English Baronetage* by Thomas Wotton, in two editions (1727–41), the first *British Baronetage* by William Betham (1801–5), and the first volume of John Burke's *Commoners* (1832–8). These schemes generated many interactions between the publishers and their clients, whether verbal or written. In the *Craftsman*, Wotton, a self-described 'undertaker', claimed that 500 baronets had provided him with documentation either through correspondence or through visits to his shop in the City.[4] What remains in his archive are letters related to 151 customers. The second sample is smaller in size and was linked to the publication by subscription as a luxury quarto in five volumes. Part of Betham's correspondence may also have been dispersed, since only forty-three letters have been preserved for the years 1804–5.[5] A much larger sample, of 397 correspondents, relates to the rigorous preparation of the first volumes of *A Genealogical and Heraldic History of the Commoners* by John Burke in 1828–9, when the emancipation of Catholics and ambitious parliamentary reform were being much discussed.[6]

Considering the unequal survival rate of the letters sent to the London publishers, one should not extrapolate too much from these three samples. They are not necessarily representative of the many oral or epistolary exchanges between families and publishers that shaped the content of these directories. Other surviving historical records in the beginning of the nineteenth century, on peers or on the Irish and Scottish gentry would provide a different picture. However, the three selected samples are relevant, in the sense that they are scattered through a long eighteenth century and so are more likely to reflect a sense of change over the period.

In a third chapter, each sample has been treated separately, as they relate to very distinct editorial projects. Each has a unique contemporary appeal which should be closely contextualized. It is particularly challenging to provide a general picture of hundreds of customers who are not equally recognizable. Some were famous individuals who have been studied in numerous biographies, while others were obscure landowners.[7] For those who cared enough to the point of not only buying these compilations but also participating in their completion, it is worth trying to identify part of their motives. Some were guided by personal and intimate reasons, but in the third chapter, the surviving letters will help us first to make sense of

---

[4] *The Craftsman*, 10 Mar. 1727; *The London Evening Post*, 19 Dec. 1727.

[5] BL, Add. MS 21033: 'Letters &c. addressed to the Revd. William Betham, of Stonham Aspal, Suffolk, Editor of the Baronetage of England, etc. etc. etc'. 1783–1805.

[6] Letters to John Burke for the edition of *The Commoners*, CA, vol. 56 (A–F), vol. 57 (F–0), vol. 58 (0–X).

[7] Several biographical resources have been drawn on: *The History of Parliament*, ODNB, *The UCL legacy of slave ownership* (https://www.ucl.ac.uk/lbs), as well as *The Clergy of the Church of England Database 1540–1835* (<www.theclergydatabase.org.uk>).

their political claims. To do so, three general databases were therefore devised, including the customers' names, their age and place of residence, their public positions, and, sometimes, profession.[8] These data have been supplemented by varying extracts from the correspondence which conveyed the clients' own narratives.

There are inevitably methodological issues, as, for example, that their urban dwellings are rarely mentioned, except among Burke's customers. It may well be that customers would rather be associated with their county address than a London location, which was often rented. The name of their county 'estate', however small or degraded, was a key ingredient of their identity. Furthermore, many families owned lands in several counties but they chose to relate to one county in particular. They were willing to support the notion of a rooted county community even though their kinship and their political interest were scattered throughout the country. These directories project an idealized view of a landed elite which conjured the violence of political and religious disorders and the difficult assimilation of the newly ennobled. Despite considerable differences within the titled families and the landed gentry, they claim to demonstrate the existence of a coherent and united group. One should not underestimate the performative potency of such enterprise.

A fourth chapter focuses less on the particulars of each group and more on the internal logic at work within the kinship group. Whenever possible, the position of each correspondent within her/his own family will be defined. As well as being conciliatory and inclusive, directories provide a very conventional and patriarchal image of the family order. The publishers directed their enquiries towards the head of the family, as both prime heir to the title and guardian of the ancestral memory. However, against these prescriptive representations, the letters reveal a much more diverse and complex vision of family life. Cadets, uncles, and cousins played a key part in the data gathering. By the same token, women, as wives, daughters, sisters, or aunts, also played a significant role, even though their contribution was often derided and given little formal recognition. Moreover, the letters exposed many conflicts and disagreements among the family members when they failed to agree on the construction of their memory.

---

[8] See Appendices 3–5.

3

Hundreds of Customers

Looking for Some Common Patterns

The nature of their contribution was to a great extent determined by the ways in which these projects were thought through and advertised. By supporting these genealogical projects, many families were able to influence their content and to propose a specific view of the past. Beyond the impulse to have one's name vindicated, it seems that for each publication a core of customers expressed specific needs and the social profiles within the landed elite were indeed often markedly different from each other.

1. Wotton and the threat of 'displeasing accounts'

In 1725 Thomas Wotton posted several advertisements in the London gazettes to inform the general public of his intention to publish a complete *Baronetage*.[1] As a well-established bookseller in London, Thomas Wotton succeeded to his father in his shop at the 'flower de Lys' and then at the Three Daggers and the Queen's Head against St Dunstan's church in Fleet Street. His father's catalogue was considerable and diversified, including parts of copies of Cowley's works, Hobbes's *Leviathan*, Rushworth's *Historical Collections*, Selden, and Chamberlain's *State of Great Britain*.[2] Wotton was able to spread word of his project in most London gazettes. He sent personalized letters to all the baronets, with a draft of their genealogies and a letter asking for 'a perfect account of them but also that nothing might be inserted that should be displeasing to them'.[3] The last part of the sentence could be interpreted as a sort of veiled threat in order to obtain a response. Right up to the publication of the first edition in 1727, he publicized in the press a list of some who had not yet sent in their accounts, requesting the help of 'their friends or relations', as he hoped to convince the recalcitrants that 'no Baronet needs be averse to sending in his account for there's no secret history to be in'.[4] He dedicated his volumes to Sir Holland Egerton of Heaton (4th baronet) 'for the use of his Collection and

---

[1] *Daily Post*, 20 Aug. 1725, 3; *The Mist's Weekly Journal*, 30 Oct. 1725, 3.
[2] *A catalogue of copies and parts of copies lately belonging to Mr Matthew Wotton* (1729).
[3] Wotton correspondence 1724–41, BL, Add. MS 24120, fol. 1.   [4] *Daily Post*, 10 Apr. 1727, 2.

Selling Ancestry: Family Directories and the Commodification of Genealogy in Eighteenth-Century Britain. Stéphane Jettot,
Oxford University Press. © Stéphane Jettot 2023. DOI: 10.1093/oso/9780192865960.003.0004

120 SELLING ANCESTRY

Draughts of arms'.[5] He proceeded in the same manner for his second edition in 1741, insisting on the need to transmit many more 'memoirs and monumental inscriptions'.[6] Judging from Wotton's repeated pleas, many baronets were reluctant to communicate their genealogies. They ignored the publishers' requests or dismissed them as trivial or irrelevant. In 1740, Henry, the second son of Thomas Bond, third Bart, of Peckham, wrote to Wotton that he would 'insist upon yours not mentioning our Branch in your baronetage'.[7] Henry may have been unwilling to divulge the secrets and whereabouts of a well-known Catholic and Jacobite family or he may have been in conflict with his elder brother, who had just inherited the title in 1734. Some were more enthusiastic and went on to participate, either (in Wotton's words) in order to avoid any 'displeasing account', or for other motives. Henry's cousin, William Gage, who came from another Catholic family, was happy to help Wotton in his endeavour.[8] In many cases, we can only make hypotheses on the behaviour of the compilers' customers.

The enduring legacy of the Restoration

Out of the 144 families of baronets who answered Wotton's letter, 98 had been created in the aftermath of the Restoration. There had been an unprecedented number of new creations (402 titles) in 1660, mainly for the benefit of Cavaliers and repentant republicans. The extinction rate was considerable, and by 1740, 217 titles survived. As a result of this high level of mortality, by 1740 the title had been already transmitted some distance into the collaterals in most of these families.

It appears that about half of the surviving baronets from the Restoration wrote to Wotton whereas the proportion is much lower for the more ancient or the more recent titles. Out of the thirty-six titles created by the first Hanoverians up to 1740, only twelve agreed to answer Wotton's queries. This may sound counter-intuitive, as one might have expected that a new baronet would have been more likely to make his new status known to the public. How can we account for the over-representation of Restoration baronets? It is worth noting that Wotton's initiative stemmed from an unfinished project undertaken by Arthur Collins as early as 1711. The commercial success of his serial *Peerage* led him to launch a subscription for a similar compilation for the baronets.[9] Nine years in the making, the first volume, dedicated to the baronets created by James I, was published in 1720. In its preface, Collins pointed out that a 'Baronettage' should mention the two British revolutions of 1640 and 1689: the celebration of the martyrs who 'suffer'd for their

---

[5] Wotton's *Baronets*, 4. [6] BL, Add. MS 24121, fol. 20. [7] BL, Add. MS 24120, fol. 125.
[8] A double marriage took place in 1675 between the Bonds and the Gages in the presence of the duke of York. BL, Add. MS 24120, fol. 372.
[9] *A Proposal for printing, a genealogical history of all the families of the Baronets of England* (1711).

loyalty to King Charles the First', and the 'patriots who endeavour'd the redressing the grievances of the Nation and the exorbitant Power of the Crown' in 1689.[10]

This initial plan may explain why so many Restoration baronets were involved in Wotton's scheme. Out of ninety-eight Restoration baronets who answered Wotton's enquiry, sixteen had or still held a seat in Parliament. Their biographies in *The History of Parliament* show that they mostly belonged to the Tory side and overwhelmingly represented seats in the east and the north.[11] They were inactive backbenchers and five of them (Glynne, Keyt, Howe, Rous, Trevelyan) had been suspected of Jacobite activities. Sir William Keyt in 1715 'was turned out of the commission of the peace for proclaiming the Pretender'.[12] Elizabeth Hanham, the mother of the third baronet was imprisoned in the Tower of London in 1689 for her open hostility to the new regime.[13] Both Long and Morgan have been described as hostile to the Walpole and Pelham administrations but their speeches have not been recorded.[14] In his answer to Wotton, Sir Roger Bradshaigh (third baronet) took great pride in his 1695 election for Wigan and for having 'sat in Parliament as a Member for that place ever since, which is now above 32 years, this is more than can be said of any gentleman of his age in England'.[15] He first supported the Tories until 1715 and then sided with the Whigs. Those listed on the Whig side were quiet backbenchers.[16] Sir James Ashe is said to have kept away from London, a town he 'hated so much'.[17] Sir Charles Crisp only represented Woodstock (on the interest of the duchess of Marlborough) for a year.[18] Sir Harvey Elwes, deprived of any connection in London, used to spend much of his time secluded in Stoke-by-Nayland (Suffolk), and though a wealthy land-owner, he was reputed to be 'perhaps the most perfect picture of human penury that ever existed'.[19]

---

[10] A. Collins, *The English Baronettage* (1720), preface, 6.

[11] Sir George Barlow (Cardigan Boroughs, 1713–15, Haverfordwest, 1715), Sir Roger Bradshaigh (Wigan, 1695–1747), Sir John Glynne (Flintshire, 1741–7), Sir Robert Hildyard (Hedon, 1701–2), Sir James Howe (Hindon, 1701–9), Sir William Keyt (Warwick, 1722–35), Sir Robert Long (Wotton Basset, 1734–41); Sir John Morgan (Hereford, 1734–41), Sir John Rous (Eye, 1685), Sir John Trevelyan (Minehead, 1708–22).

[12] Shirley Matthews, 'Sir William Keyt', in R. Sedgwick (ed.), *The House of Commons 1715-1754* (London, 1970).

[13] CSP Dom. 1689–90, 245.

[14] John Brooke, 'Sir John Morgan' and R. S. Lea, 'Sir Robert Long', ibid.

[15] BL, Add. MS 24120, fol. 140.

[16] Sir James Ashe (Downton, 1701–5), Sir Robert Cotton (Cheshire, 1727–34), Sir Charles Crisp (New Woodstock, 1721–2), Sir Archer Croft (Leominster, 1722–7, Bere Alston, 1728–34), Sir Harvey Elwes (Sudbury, 1713–22), Sir James Lowther (Carlisle, 1694–1702, Cumberland, 1708–22, Appleby 1723–7, Cumberland, 1727–55); Sir William Wentworth (Malton, 1731–41).

[17] D. W. Hayton, 'Sir James Ashe', in D. Hayton, E. Cruickshanks, and S. Handley (eds), *The History of Parliament: The House of Commons 1690-1715* (London, 2002).

[18] Ibid.

[19] Edward Topham, *Life of the Late John Elwes* (London, 1790), 3; see also the coloured etching of 'two celebrated misers', *Sir Hervey Elwes and his nephew John Elwes* (London, 1825). Welcome Trust, ref. 32,323.

122   SELLING ANCESTRY

Croft, Lowther, and Wentworth may be the only exceptions to this portrait of inactive county MPs. Sir Archer Croft was a zealous Court supporter and made several speeches, notably during the debate against a bill for excluding pensioners in 1731. He held a seat on the Board of Trade and thus obtained a yearly pension of £1,000.[20] Sir James Lowther was an independent Whig who endorsed the cause of Frederick, prince of Wales. He made a speech in favour of the South Sea Company, which he briefly supervised (1733–6).

Apart from the MPs, it is worth mentioning the presence among the correspondents of five high sheriffs: Sir Ralph Asheton (Lancashire, 1739), Sir Roger Beckwith (Yorkshire, 1706), Sir Robert Cann (Gloucestershire, 1726), Sir Charles Lloyd (Montgomeryshire, 1706), and Sir Thomas Palmer (Northamptonshire, 1740). These families who received their titles from the Restoration held influential public positions which were a certain measure of rank.

With respect to their wealth, their landed income was considerable. In the late seventeenth century, baronets' revenue was estimated at an average of £1,200 a year by Edward Chamberlain in his *Angliae Notitiae*.[21] Ashe's properties were worth £4,000 per annum and he defended them in Parliament against a project to make the Avon navigable between Christchurch, Dorset, and Salisbury.[22] Sir William Wentworth prospered during the reign of George I and managed to double his estate to 17,200 acres.[23]

Many correspondents had a mercantile background but most had moved away into their estates, such as Charles Crisp, who acquired Dornford castle in the late seventeenth century. Those engaged in industrial activities such as Bradshaigh, Ramsden (fulling mills), or Lowther (colliery, copper) omitted to mention them and distanced themselves from the source of their wealth.[24] Similarly, nothing was reflected of their urban investments. The Tempests held many properties in Durham, the Croft and Gage families owned houses in Bury St Edmunds, John Cullum owned houses in Hardwick (17 hearths) and three houses in various smaller towns in Suffolk (58 hearths). Several members of colonial gentry appear, such as John Colleton, who had high pretentions in regard to their ancestry but hardly any documents to substantiate their claims: 'I am ye worst genealogist in ye world but in answer to yours ye best account I will give you I believe the family came in with the Conqueror.'[25] As slave owners from Barbados, members of the colonial elite in Carolina, and recently returned to England (Exeter), the Colletons

[20] A. N. Newman, 'Sir Archer Croft', in R. Sedgwick (ed.), *The House of Commons 1715–1754* (London, 1970).

[21] Edward Chamberlain, *Angliae Notitiae* (London, 1694), 442.

[22] D. W. Hayton, 'Sir James Ashe', *The History of Parliament*.

[23] Peter Roebuck, *Yorkshire Baronets 1640–1760* (Oxford, 1980), 307.

[24] Bradshaigh owned the Haigh Colliery, one of the largest in Lancashire. Richard D. Harrison, 'Sir Roger Bradshaigh', *ODNB*, 2004. Retrieved 21 Feb. 2020 from <https://doi-org.janus.bis-sorbonne.fr/10.1093/ref:odnb/63021>.

[25] BL, Add. MS 24120, fol. 213.

felt the need to establish some Norman extraction. To combat the animus and prejudices against colonials, they had to compensate for the relative obscurity of such families.[26] Creole absentees had to reconfigure their identity to fit with the cultural framework of their mother country. Another prominent representative of the planters' interests, Sir John Yeamans (Antigua) was closely linked to William Beckford, a 'transatlantic figure' between Britain and Jamaica.[27]

Just a few insisted on mentioning the source of their wealth. In 1727, Sir Edward Blackett, a Newcastle merchant and a rich coal and lead miner, did not comment on the origin of his income, adding to the draft text simply that the first baronet had received his title in 1673.[28] In 1739, Sir Richard, his successor in the title, complained to Wotton about the lack of substance in their article: 'You have not done justice to ye family of the Blackett, [...] they made such a contemptible figure in ye first edition.'[29] He demanded that for the second edition, it should be mentioned that the first baronet 'by the product of his mines and collieries, acquired a very great fortune' and 'was member of Parliament for Newcastle'.[30] His wealth did not prevent him from being 'a gentleman of extraordinary bounty to those in want'.[31] Would it be far-fetched to suppose that in the 1740s, the title-holder was more disposed to divulge these details? A similar observation can be made for another correspondent, Sir Robert Barnardiston. In 1726, he referred only to the fact that they were 'one of the most ancient and illustrious families of the equestrian dignity in the kingdom, having flourished in the direct line for about 29 generations',[32] whereas the second edition included many particulars about the family's role in the City and their East India interests, though the provider of the latter information is unknown.

In the sample, baronets created after 1685 were more closely linked to the Hanoverian court and more likely to occupy state positions (Army, Customs, Treasury). Sir William Irby was chamberlain to the princess of Wales. Sir Adolphus Oughton was elevated in 1718 'to represent his Royal Highness the Duke of York, as his proxy, at his instalment as Knight of the Garter'.[33] Sir Samuel Armytage was employed as a supervisor in the excise service in Wales in the 1720s. Among the correspondents whose title was created after 1685, eight held a seat in Parliament.[34] Some were very active, such as the merchant and industrialist Sir Abraham Elton, MP for Bristol in 1727 and the instigator of various petitions in

---

[26] On the Colleton Family, *The South Carolina Historical and Genealogical Magazine*, vol. 4, no. 1 (1900): 325–41.

[27] Perry Gauci, *William Beckford*, 54–6.   [28] *Baronets*, vol. 2, 489.

[29] BL, Add. MS 24120, fol. 64.   [30] *Baronetage*, vol. 4, 551.   [31] Ibid., 552.

[32] BL, Add. MS 24120, fol. 40.   [33] *Baronetage*, vol. 3, 192.

[34] Sir John Evelyn (Helston, 1708–10), Sir Abraham Elton (Taunton, 1724–7; Bristol, 1727–42), Sir John Dutton (Gloucestershire, 1727–41), Sir Cordell Firebrace (Suffolk, 1735–59), Sir William Irby (Launceston, 1735–47), Sir John Lade (Southwark, 1713–27), Sir Adolphus Oughton (Coventry, 1715–36), Sir John Rogers (1713–22), Sir Thomas Cookes Winford (Worcestershire, 1707–10).

124 SELLING ANCESTRY

favour of the mercantile interest and against the Excise Bill.[35] Sir John Evelyn, due to 'his accommodating attitude towards successive administrations', managed to hold on to his commissionership of customs from 1721 to 1763.[36] He obtained a pocket borough with the support of Lord Godolphin and switched to the Tory side in 1712. Sir John Lade was a Southwark brewer who claimed to have 'raised a very considerable fortune [...] by 'his prudent management' but also argued that his family was established seated in Kent since 1445, according to an old bible in his possession.[37] Apart from Lade who openly boasted his recent rise to fortune, it may well be that younger baronets were unwilling to contribute to Wotton's project. They were markedly different from the Restoration county magnates, who were keen to vindicate their deeds.

Unequal memories of two British revolutions

For the Restoration baronets in particular, the Civil War provided an opportunity to explore the heroic circumstances of their rise in status. Whether they were of a Whig or a Tory sensibility, they insisted on the nature of the first baronets' endeavours, even though many did not descend directly from the first baronet. They could rely on a vast store of accumulated knowledge about the Civil War, which was available in their own papers as well as in recognized historians such as Clarendon or Burnet. On the other hand, far fewer mentioned the 'Glorious Revolution'. In a climate of uncertainty and change, many families preferred to remain safely ambiguous.[38]

Sir Archer Croft sent a long letter about the heroic bishop Herbert Croft, who preached against the parliamentarians in Hereford Cathedral and nearly got shot by 'a guard of musqueteers'.[39] Sir Robert Cotton complained that his first account was 'grossly mistaken' and unsatisfactory, Wotton having only noted in 1727 that one Philip Cotton, a captain, was 'killd in the service of K. Car. I'.[40] He should have

---

[35] Shirley Matthews, 'Sir Abraham Elton', in *The History of Parliament: The House of Commons 1715–1754*.

[36] Perry Gauci, *The History of Parliament: The House of Commons 1690–1715*.

[37] BL, Add. MS 24121, fol. 23; *Baronetage*, vol. 4, 229.

[38] On the conflicting memories of the two revolutions, Mark Stoyle, 'Remembering the English Civil Wars', in Peter Gray and Oliver Kendrick (eds), *The Memory of Catastrophe* (Manchester, 2014), 19–30; Gabriel Glickman, 'Political Conflict and the Memory of the Revolution in England 1689–c. 1750', in Stephen Taylor and Tim Harris (eds), *The Final Crisis of the Stuart Monarchy: The Revolutions of 1688–91 in their British, Atlantic and European Contexts* (Woodbridge, 2013), 243–71; Edward Vallance, *Remembering Early Modern Revolutions: England, North America, France and Haiti* (London, 2019); Edward Legon, *Revolution Remembered: Seditious Memories after the British Civil Wars* (Manchester, 2019).

[39] 'Some officers then present began to mutter amongst themselves and a guard of musqueteers in the church, were preparing their pieces, and ask'd whether they should fire at him; but the colonel Burch, the governor, prevented them.' BL, Add. MS 24120, fol. 229; *Baronetage*, vol. 1, 539.

[40] *Baronets*, vol. 2, 531.

HUNDREDS OF CUSTOMERS 125

added that the first baronet had been elected for Chester, Cotton being himself an MP for the city. After the Restoration a strong link existed between loyalty to the Stuarts and gentility in county towns, especially in Cheshire and Yorkshire.[41]

Tory MPs demonstrated a similar eagerness to set out in detail their ancestors' position. Sir Thomas Palmer answered Wotton's enquiry by stating that Sir Geoffrey Palmer, the first baronet, had been involved in the prosecution of the earl of Strafford.[42] He then proceeded to quote Lord Clarendon, who wrote that Palmer later came to prove himself, 'a man of great reputation [...] and in the debate about the remonstrance, his speech not being agreeable to the prevailing party in the house, he was committed to the Tower'.[43] Sir Roger Bradshaigh proudly informed Wotton that his grandfather, the first baronet, was also the 'first Protestant of this family' and a fierce opponent of the rebels who had beheaded his protector Lord Derby at Bolton in 1651.[44] The desire of Sir Roger to convert to Protestantism was in itself a mark of merit and loyalty. Briefly a prisoner in the Castle of Chester, he remained loyal to the Cavaliers and was then elected for Lancashire in 1660. His successor produced a long extract from Dr Richard Wroe, *Memorials and Characters of Eminent Persons*, in which the first baronet had 'retrieved from the errors of Popery', which was clearly a way to disperse all allegations about any pro-Jacobite inclination.[45] Bradshaigh's letters to Wotton aimed at demonstrating that since the first baronet the family had been consistently loyal to the monarchy and the Church. To stress this point, he added that one brother, James, was a captain in the army, and another one, Thomas, the rector of Stratford St Mary in Suffolk. Several repentant republican families managed to ingratiate themselves in 1660. Sir William Beaumont's father had taken the parliamentary side during the Civil War, served on the committee for the New Model Army, and represented Leicestershire under the Protectorate. He was made a 'baronet' by Cromwell in 1658 and the baronetcy was regranted by Charles II at the Restoration.[46]

From an archival point of view, the Civil War was providential for those who did not have much evidence to support their title. Sir James Musgrave tried to explain the shadowy circumstances during which the title was created: 'you complained yt ye steps from the conquest to the Civil war was too wide, ye reason for this is yt all the records of that family perished in ye flames in Scalibye Castel [...] burned by ye usurpers partisans'.[47] He was referring to the destruction of

---

[41] See, for example, the case of the urban elite in Chester who were integrated into the ranks of the gentry at the Restoration: F.-J. Ruggiu, 'The Urban Gentry in England, 1660–1780: A French Approach', *Historical Research*, vol. 74, no. 185 (2001): 249–70 at 258.

[42] BL, Add. MS 24120, fol. 140, 1739; see also *Baronetage*, vol. 3, 19.

[43] BL, Add. MS 24120, fol. 140, 1739.

[44] 'Ye time of the civill warrs when that noble lord was beheaded at Bolton in Lancashire he was taken prisoner by ye rebells & confined in ye castle of Chester but nothing could alter his unshaken loyalty to his prince from whom he received many marks of his favour'. BL, Add. MS 24120, fol. 139.

[45] Ibid.   [46] BL, Add. MS 24120, fol. 42.   [47] BL, Add. MS 24121, fol. 335.

126 SELLING ANCESTRY

Scaleby Castle in 1645 and in 1648. Margaret Vaughan, the daughter of Sir Evan Lloyd, second baronet, bemoaned that her grandfather, the first baronet, had not been included in the first edition, though she was unable to inform Wotton of the date of creation: 'I believe it was some years before ye sivel war begun.'[48] Some, such as the Yeamans and the Stapeltons, wished to record that their loyalty to the Stuarts had led them to complete ruin, which in turn had forced them to settle in the West Indies.[49] Their arrival in the Caribbean is described as a choice dictated by political allegiance rather than by opportunism. Even those whose titles were created after the Restoration could not resist the attraction of the Civil War as the founding event of their prosperity. James Edwards, a baronet since 1691, argued that he was 'of opinion yt the name of a family adds no real lustre to any man's person', though he went on to depict in great detail his ancestors' deeds in the 1640s.[50]

In contrast, accounts related to the 'Glorious Revolution' were much more elusive. In the first edition, only a few baronets were explicit in their rejection of James II. Many baronets left their reminiscences of the political crisis of the 1670s and 1680s voluntarily vague. The third baronet Thomas Mainwaring suggested the need to allude to the last revolution but ultimately left it to Wotton's judgement: 'I leave it to you whether to insert somewhat of my father's assisting at the revolution but think you should.'[51] Wotton inserted the exploits of the grandfather, the first baronet, before the 'Happy Restoration', along with those of his father, Sir John Mainwaring, in favour of the 'Happy Revolution'.[52] The details of his contribution to the latter were not clearly spelt out, however. Sir George Warrender of Lochend, who was created baronet in 1715, wrote Wotton an enthusiastic letter on the 'happy revolution' without elaborating on his family's involvement.[53] Only a few families went on to explain in detail the sources of their opposition to the later Stuarts. We will consider two examples: the Crisps and the Duttons.

Sir Charles Crisp wrote that 'the case of our family was so far unlike other gentlemen, what Sr Nicholas Crisp, my Great Grand Father spent for K. Cha ye 1st altho as much as any private gentleman in England spent, was all lost'.[54] According to his great-grandson, Sir Nicholas Crisp spent most of his fortune, acquired in his pioneering slave and gold trade in Guinea and in the East India Company, in supporting the cause of Charles I. In 1660 he was sent to Breda as a commissioner by the City and was warmly embraced by Charles II and later distinguished with a baronetcy.[55] In his will, the first baronet required that his

[48] BL, Add. MS 24121, fol. 45.
[49] Sir William Stapleton, BL, Add. MS 24121, fols 260–2; John Yeamans, first baronet, BL, Add. MS 24121, fol. 366.
[50] 8 Nov. 1725, BL, Add. MS 24120, fol. 293.   [51] BL, Add. MS 24121, fol. 65.
[52] *Baronetage*, vol. 2, 160.   [53] BL, Add. MS 24121, fol. 325.
[54] Dec. 1739, BL, Add. MS 24120, fol. 225.
[55] Robert Ashton, 'Crisp, Sir Nicholas, first baronet', *ODNB*, 2004. Retrieved 20 Feb. 2020 from <https://doi-org.janus.bis-sorbonne.fr/10.1093/ref:odnb/6705>.

heart be placed in a marble urn with a bust of the martyr-king.[56] Crisp drew a parallel between the financial burden willingly borne by his ancestor and the many thousands of pounds he spent himself as an MP 'for the Good of the ye publick'.[57] Despite their fidelity to the royal cause, Crisp accounted for the family's economic ruin as a consequence of the setting up of the Royal African Company by the duke of York. They distanced themselves from the later Stuarts and claimed to have been harassed by the Chancellor Finch and James II. Regarding the Duttons, Wotton recognized the contribution of Mary Arnold, the wife of John Dutton Colt, a nephew to the first baronet, referring to her as 'the lady to whom I am greatly obliged for the many curious particulars, which she sent me, from her father's mss'.[58] Her son had inherited the title because Sir Harry Dutton Colt had died childless. With the title came his papers, including a very detailed narrative of Sir Henry Dutton Colt's tribulations under the later Stuarts. While in his first edition, Wotton merely mentioned that the first baronet 'was advanced to that dignity, by K. William, for the great services he did at the Revolution', the second version abounded with many details on the persecutions endured by the family under the later Stuarts.[59] In his manuscript, the first baronet explained how his father George Colt and his elder brother John Dutton, though a 'little boy', fought at the battle of Worcester, but, despite Charles II's promises to give a reward, he 'never did anything for them after his restoration'.[60] This injustice was all the more unforgivable in that George Colt was drowned while crossing the Channel on a secret mission in 1658. Found on the shore, his corpse carried a warrant for him to be made an earl. For speaking ill of James of York during the Popish Crisis, his brother was convicted upon the statute *scandalum magnatum* in 1684 and sentenced to three years in a Southwark prison.[61] The first baronet then related a dramatic encounter between James II and his brother in 1687. When Colt kissed the king's hand on being freed from jail, James II 'observed that he was turned gray' and seemed much older than him, upon which Colt asked the favour of never being 'put into any publick employment again to which the king smiled'.[62] Not only in this case, but in many others, the second edition in 1740 abounded with many details of the former king's cruelty. Mary Dutton Colt justified her initiative in supplying this material by stating that 'nothing will be more instructive and useful to posterity than a true history of the family in England for lesson for the future age'.[63] It may well be that she was attempting to kill two birds with one stone. On the one hand, she displaced attention from the baronet to his elder brother, her own husband's grandfather, the ancestor of her own son, the heir to

---

[56] BL, Add. MS 24120, fol. 227.   [57] 15 Dec. 1739, BL, Add. MS 24120, fol. 224.
[58] *Baronetage*, vol. 5, 51.   [59] *Baronets*, vol. 2, 50.   [60] *Baronetage*, vol. 5, 48.
[61] John Dutton Colt was accused of having said in the last Parliament that: 'The Duke of York is a papist, and before any such papist dog shall be successor to the crown of England, I will be hanged at my own door'. Ibid., 49.
[62] Ibid., 50.   [63] BL, Add. 24120, fol. 216.

128 SELLING ANCESTRY

the title. On the other hand, she inserted her own family into the mix, by adding that her father, John Arnold of Llanvihangel Court (MP), had also been the victim of a *scandalum magnatum* in 1682, which had cost him £10,000 in damages as well as time in prison.[64]

It may well be that before 1745, many in the landed elite were still reluctant to explicitly condemn the Jacobite cause and therefore chose a constructive ambiguity when relating the 'Glorious Revolution'. In many ways, it has been demonstrated that the political stability of the Walpoleian era should not be overstated.[65]

Family solidarities and county networks

It is worth noting that in the instance just discussed, the Duttons and the Arnolds were closely related to each other. Their letters allow a partial reconstruction of the connections between customers as many were linked by marriage, geographic proximity, or bonds of friendship. In numerous cases, the decision to answer the publisher's circular letters was not taken in isolation. These correspondents were organized in clusters and they collectively mobilized their networks and their archives to give a common image of themselves. Sir Thomas Winford was married to the daughter of Sir Henry Parker. Blount, Mainwaring, Blackett, and Charlton were linked by alliances, as were the Bradshaighs, to the Lowthers, the Canns to the Yeamans, and the Keyts to the Pakingtons. They contributed to Wotton's enquiry in a concerted manner. The third baronet Sir Jacob Astley agreed to provide Wotton with many details about his ancestors and informed him that he would use Sir Thomas L'Estrange's expertise.[66] Sir Jacob was married to Lucy L'Estrange, Sir Thomas's sister, and the two families had been Cavaliers. Their commitment was described in Wotton's articles along with a long extract from Clarendon: 'The famous Sir Roger L'Estrange' had been declared a spy by the Parliament in London, jailed in Newgate for four years, and was then tried again in 1653.[67] Similarly, Sir Isaac Astley was, during the Great Rebellion, governor of Oxford and Reading. He distinguished himself in several battles and was made Lord Astley of Reading.[68] Alongside alliances, a sense of community was instrumental to the success of Wotton's enquiries. Sir Harvey Elwes, who was portrayed by the playwright Edward Topham as a comic figure, had two close friends in Suffolk, the baronets Sir Cordell Firebrace and Sir Robert Barnardiston, who used

[64] *Baronetage*, vol. 5, 51.

[65] On the role and resilience of Jacobitism in the social life of the gentry, see Paul K. Monod, *Jacobitism and the English People 1688–1788* (Cambridge, 1989).

[66] BL, Add. MS 24120, fol. 23, Sir Thomas L'Estrange carried out extensive research into his ancestry which can be reconstituted in the Norfolk Record Office: Papers relating to the pedigree and history of the L'Estrange and related families, containing transcripts of deeds, wills, settlements (File LEST/DM 1–2).

[67] *Baronetage*, vol. 2, 145–9.   [68] *Baronetage*, vol. 3.1, 66.

to gather in their local club to debate which of the three was the richest.[69] All three baronets exchanged letters with Wotton.[70] Yorkshire offers a relevant case study as the county was overrepresented among Wotton's correspondents, supplying 20 per cent of them (Map 3.1).

It may well be that the extinction of many titles before 1730 generated a genealogical impulse among the survivors. Those baronets who escaped oblivion consolidated and extended their properties. As a large county, Yorkshire had a more autonomous marriage market.[71] In 1725, Roger Beckwith, a former high sheriff of the county in 1706, provided plenty of details about his neighbours: 'I am always an encourager of useful knowledge [...]. I have several memoirs relating the Yorkshire families and I am willing to assist you if occasion be.'[72] The Beckwiths were not long-established members of the Yorkshire gentry: Roger's brother was a merchant in Virginia and other members were scattered outside the county. They did not figure in the collection of pedigrees and arms created in 1580.[73] Nonetheless, Roger Beckwith was keen to portray himself to Wotton as a key purveyor of knowledge on Yorkshire. His recent ascent to gentry status may account for his antiquarian interest, though he had no living male heir himself. Perhaps he hoped to project himself into posterity or to express his local patriotism. Whatever his motives, Beckwith had previously engaged with similar projects. He volunteered to help Ralph Thoresby in writing *The Topography of Leeds* (1715) by providing him with many details, and he then hosted the antiquary and herald John Warburton.[74] In the late eighteenth century, other Beckwiths from Leeds were enlisted in similar endeavours, notably Josiah and Thomas Beckwith, who were both connected to the London Society of Antiquaries and who accumulated a considerable collection of manuscripts on the Yorkshire gentry.[75] At about the same time, Roger Beckwith's efforts were supported by various baronets around Leeds: the Ramsdens (Byram), the Pilkingtons (Chevet Hall), the Jacksons (Hickleton), and the Hildyards (Patrington). The same phenomenon took place during the production of the second edition in 1741, though in a wider area beyond Leeds. In 1739, many more families lent their backing to the crowdsourcing: Anderson (Kilnwick), Armitage (Kirklees), Boyton (Bramston), Cayley (Brompton), Marwood (Little Busby), Pennyman (Ormsby), Graham

---

[69] Edward Topham, *Extraordinary lives of Sir Harvey and John Elwes, two celebrated misers* (London, 1805), 5.

[70] Barnadiston to Wotton, BL, Add. MS 24120 fol. 40. Firebrace to Wotton, ibid., fol. 323.

[71] The Beaumonts made 25 purchases between 1639 and 1764 which enabled them to increase their property around the seat in Lepton. Roebuck, *Yorkshire Baronets*, 292–3.

[72] BL, Add. MS 24120, fol. 46.

[73] Yorkshire gentry pedigrees and arms, Leeds University, YAS/MD335/13/1.

[74] Ralph Thoresby, *Ducatus Leodiensis, or Topography of the Ancient and Populous Town and Parish of Leedes* [...]. (London, 1715), 132; see also his name in Francis Drake's *History of York, Eboracum* (York, 1736), 355. On map making and Yorkshire, Harold Whitaker (ed.), *A Descriptive List of the Printed Maps of Yorkshire and Its Ridings, 1577–1900* (Leeds, 1971).

[75] Josiah Beckwith Collection (1767–85), Bod. Lib., MS Eng. c. 4782.

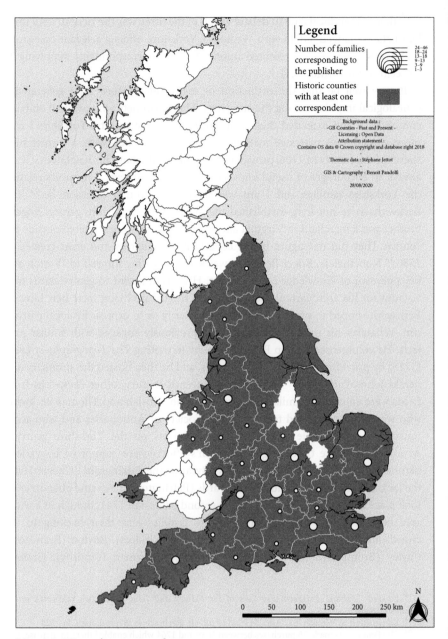

Map 3.1 Wotton's correspondents

(Norton Conyers), Tancred (Boroughbridge), Tempest (Bracewell), Wentworth (Bretton), Vavasour (Hazelwood), and Ashton (Middleton). Along with the decisive contribution from Beckwith and the above-mentioned baronets, it is very likely that Wotton's initiative was mentioned in Leeds and York during civic balls or assizes or quarter sessions. The annual feast at the Merchant Taylors' Hall in York provided a timely opportunity to discuss their participation.

Hence, between his first and second editions, Wotton collected a considerable number of documents from the baronets. His success rate was uneven, attracting above all the interest of the Restoration baronets and of those in the northern counties.

It may well be that Wotton's customers mistrusted the College of Arms, as the institution was suspected of being biased towards the Whigs, with the nomination of Sir John Vanbrugh as Garter King of Arms in 1715. A member of the Kit-Kat Club, he was commissioned to build Castle Howard and Blenheim Palace. Vanbrugh and many other club members were celebrated by a series of portraits with their coats of arms painted by Sir Godfrey Kneller and sold in a single volume by Jacob Tonson in 1735.[76] By contrast, Wotton's scheme may have been viewed as a more inclusive endeavour. Most of his contributors were wealthy land-owners with prominent county positions. The exploits of founding baronets during the Civil War constituted a key element in their successors' personal and collective identity. Providing information was a way to compensate for the baronets' inability to preserve the appearance of a direct line after a challenging period when mortality rates had been higher and fertility lower than in the second half of the seventeenth century. Unlike the recent baronets, who did not participate with equal enthusiasm in Wotton's enquiries, these older families enhanced their distinction by their civic engagement and were unwilling to identify the economic basis of their elevation. They portrayed themselves as men of landed property and as residing on their estates, immune to the deep-seated changes of their times.

2. The Bethams and the making of the first British *Baronetage*

In the late eighteenth century, William Betham's position was markedly different from that of Thomas Wotton. Betham, a modest provincial clergyman, was a stranger to the prosperous world of London booksellers and had to rely on the support of noble patrons. In 1809, a gazette recorded that the Revd William Betham had received an extra sum of £115 for the upkeep of his fourteen children from the governors of the Sons of the Clergy.[77] Ordained in 1773, he was first employed as chaplain to Brownlow Bertie (1729–1809), later the fifth duke of Ancaster in 1779, and then as headmaster in a Suffolk school, at Stonham Aspall,

---

[76] *The Kit-Cat Club done from the original paintings of Sir Godfrey Kneller*, engraved by Mr Faber and sold by J. Tonson (London, 1735).

[77] *Universal Magazine* (July 1809), 12, 76.

132 SELLING ANCESTRY

from 1784.[78] Endowed with a small income, he struggled to make ends meet and may have hoped by his publications to gain more rewarding positions.[79]

First, he conceived *The Genealogical Tables of the Sovereigns of the World* (1795), a folio volume with the trees of all the royal families, beginning with the 'Antediluvian Patriarchs', the British Royal Races, and the European nobility. In the *Monthly Review*, it was judged superior to Anderson's *Royal Genealogies* as it included all the 'Nobility of these Kingdoms descended from Princes'.[80] The work was dedicated to George III and fitted into the loyalist fervour which followed the French Revolution. It was aimed at celebrating dynastic principles from biblical times to the French Revolution. Its purpose was to establish that most of the British nobles had royal ancestry: Betham's protector, the fifth and last duke of Ancaster, happened to derive from William of Nassau, the Montagus, and Edward I. In the index, Ancaster's name is listed between the dukes of Amalfi and the kings of Andalusia. The *Tables* gathered the support of 283 subscribers: the members of the royal family, 59 peers, 21 bishops, the Speaker of the House of Commons, and 15 baronets.

In 1795, he announced in the press his intention to launch another subscription to finance an improved edition of the *Baronetage*. He deplored the poor quality of the pocket *Baronetages* which had followed Wotton's editions, as they ignored 'much of the historical matter, relating to families, which ought to have been preserved'.[81] He argued that the 262 families of baronets who had newly gained the title since 1741 deserved to be fully commemorated by a prestigious publication in five volumes, in quarto.

Betham set himself the task of accounting for all the families involved in 'the enlargement of empire, the extension of commerce, the advance of wealth and the polite arts, the frequent recurrence of wide operations of war' and celebration of the 'glory of the British names' against 'the extravagant demolition of all honours in France'.[82] Each subscriber would receive an engraving of his coat of arms, upon a separate sheet. The initial cost was to be 4 guineas for a 'common paper' and 6 guineas for a fine paper set. Unlike the baronets created under the first Georges who contributed so little to Wotton's enterprise, a new generation of baronets was at the centre of this new project: 302 individuals are listed as subscribers (191 baronets, 19 peers and bishops).[83] Among the subscribers, 95 baronets were created after 1760 and 50 after 1789. From his surviving correspondence, only 43 names have been recovered and most of them could also be found in the

---

[78] From the Clergy of the Church of England Database. The Berties were among the MPs who dominated many seats in the Commons: in term of years of service, 'the Berties, dukes of Ancaster, rise to the top of the list with 1001 years', Ellis Archer Wasson, 'The House of Commons, 1660–1945: Parliamentary Families and the Political Elite', *The English Historical Review*, vol. 106, no. 420 (1991): 635–51 at 641.

[79] GM, Dec. 1853, 632–5.   [80] *Monthly Review*, vol. 21, Oct. 1796, 236.

[81] Betham's *Baronetage*, x.   [82] Ibid., xiii–xiv.

[83] List of subscribers, Betham's *Baronetage*, vol. 4, appendix (Oxford, Queen's College collection).

subscribers' list. This sample is rather representative of the corpus of subscribers as a quarter of the correspondents had been recently elevated by Pitt. They wrote to Betham in the years 1804–5 either to insert some addenda to the first volumes or in order to be published in the last two volumes. Almost half of them held a seat in Parliament.[84] In many ways, they were far from the model of the country gentleman depicted above. Concerned by the threat of radicalism, these Court baronets supported a new brand of British patriotism, predicated both on a more tolerant approach towards dissenters and Catholics and on a wider family involvement in imperial expansion.

A family affair

Inspired by the success of his *Genealogical Tables*, Betham introduced in his *Baronetage* a new presentation of the several stages of descent through a series of tables, containing the names, alliances, and collateral branches with darker lines for the principal descent. The latter was also marked by Roman letters as opposed to the collateral lines and their Arabic 'letters'. He described his graphic method as the only way to insert both the senior and the collateral lines and to distinguish them easily. This new configuration was better suited to the increased fertility of the late eighteenth-century landed elite (Illus. 3.1).[85]

The compilation took ten years to complete, from 1795 to 1805, and was first printed at Ipswich and then at London for two prominent London booksellers: William Miller and Edmund Lloyd.[86] While Betham remained in Suffolk, part of his correspondence with the baronets was handled by two of his children who resided in Chancery Lane with their uncle. The elder daughter, Matilda, established strong bonds with several influential Catholic families while his elder son, William Jr, was quickly involved with the most influential antiquaries in the Society of Antiquaries. Matilda became a respected miniaturist and a literary figure, publishing in 1804 *A Biographical Dictionary of the Celebrated Women of Every Age and Country*. In her autobiography, she lamented that her 'father's hopes of preferment were one by one disappointed. By death and translation of

---

[84] Sir John Aubrey (Aldeburgh, 1796–1812), Sir Martin Browne Ffolkes (King's Lynn, 1790–1821), Sir John Callander (Berwick-Upon-Tweed, 1795–1802), Sir George Colebrooke (Arundel, 1754–74), Sir Henry Fletcher (Cumberland, 1768–1806), Sir Harbord Harbord (Norwich, 1756–86), Sir John Hippisley (Sudbury, 1790–6. 1802–18), Sir Robert Harry Inglis (1802–6), Sir William Lygon (Worcestershire, 1775–1806), Sir Henry Mildmay (Westbury, 1796–1802), Sir John Henniker (New Romney, 1785–90, Steyning, 1794–1802), Sir Robert Peel (Tamworth, 1790–1820), Sir John Rous (Suffolk 1750–1827), Sir Richard Sullivan (New Romney, 1787–96, Seaford, 1802–6), Sir John Trevelyan (Somerset, 1780–96).

[85] T. H., Hollingsworth, 'Mortality in the British Peerage Families since 1600', *Population*, vol. 32, no. 1 (1977): 323–52 at 332.

[86] William Todd, *A Directory of Printers and Others in Allied Trades. London & Vicinity. 1800–1840* (London, 1972), 16.

134 SELLING ANCESTRY

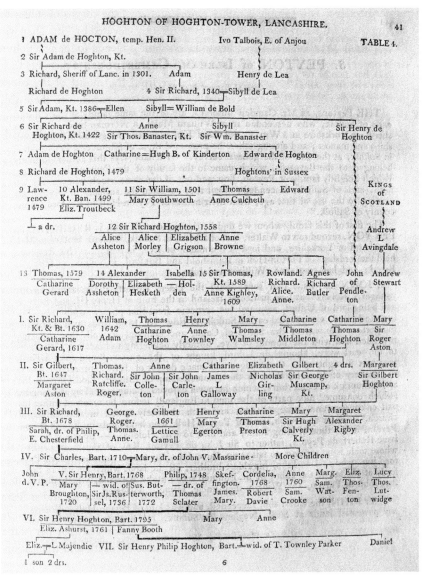

Illus. 3.1 Reorganizing a family tree: the example of the Hoghtons (Lancashire) (Betham, vol. 1, 41)

© All Souls College Library, 4:SR.39.c.3/1

bishops; and once by having delayed his request a little time after he knew of the lapsed living, because he would not call about it on a Sunday.'[87] However, the

---

[87] Her autobiography (*Crow Quill Flights*) is in the Ipswich Record Office. See E. Bailey, 'Matilda Betham: A New Biography', *Wordsworth Circle*, vol. 38 (2007): 144.

HUNDREDS OF CUSTOMERS   135

Bethams benefited from the patronage of a powerful Catholic family, the Jerningham's. They held several estates in Suffolk and Norfolk and were hoping to obtain the attainted barony of Stafford.[88] Sir William Jerningham and his wife, Lady Frances, the daughter of Viscount Dillon, had previously bought four copies of Betham's *Genealogical Tables*. Betham established the connection between Sir William Jerningham and Mary, daughter of William Stafford.[89] He also dedicated the fourth volume of his *Baronetage* to them, in 1804, and Matilda painted Lady Frances Jerningham's bust.[90] Matilda, through her literary and artistic activities, befriended the Jerninghams and behaved as a conduit between them and her father in Suffolk. She obtained from Frances Jerningham a much longer and more precise narrative than had been published in the former *Baronetages*.[91] Jerningham's active contribution coincided with the reconciliation of former Jacobite families to the Hanoverians. As a remarkable ancestor, she chose Henry Jerningham, commander of the forces under the duke of Norfolk during the rebellion of Sir Thomas Wyatt. He had built the current manor of the family at Cossey, 'one of the largest in the county of Norfolk'.[92] Though loyal to Queen Elizabeth, the Jerninghams, for their 'attachement to ye ancient religion and to which his posterity has inviolably adhered', were unjustly sidelined.[93] Back in favour during the Stuarts, Henry Jerningham was made a baronet in 1621 but the narrator failed to describe their role during the two revolutions. She avoided any disparaging comments on these events, other than dwelling on the martyrdom of one of their remote relations, William Howard, attainted and beheaded in 1680: 'a victim of perjury and [...] the credulity of the times'.[94] Delving instead into the eighteenth century, Lady Frances did not shy away from describing Jerningham's presence on the continent, their marriages with French families (such as the Jonquet de l'Epine), and their links to the Jesuit order. The fifth baronet 'passed the greater part of his youth on the Continent' and one of his sons was 'a general officer in the service of the late King of France'.[95] While openly recognizing their Jacobite involvement, she added that her son by the present baronet was now an 'officer in the English army, and lately in the Austrian service; where, during the hard and perilous campaigns, from 1792 to the Treaty of Campo Formio, he signalized himself by distinguished bravery and judgement'.[96] As the example of

---

[88] Papers relative to the two baronies of Stafford, claimed by Sir William Jerningham, 1807. On the family correspondence, 1779–1824, Staffordshire Record Office, D641/3/P/4/14/20.

[89] *The Genealogical Tables of the Sovereigns of the World* (London, 1795), table 615.

[90] BL, Add. MS 21033, fol. 44. On the considerable correspondence of Frances, wife of Sir William Jerningham (dated 1796–1823), Stafford RO, D641/3.

[91] Betham, *Baronetage*, vol. 1, 223–33. To compare with the short article in Wotton, *Baronetage*, vol. 1, 450–3.

[92] BL, Add. MS 21033, fol. 44.   [93] Betham, *Baronetage*, vol. 1, 229.   [94] Ibid., 232.

[95] Ibid., 231; M. J. Mason, 'Nuns of the Jerningham Letters: Elizabeth Jerningham 1727–1807 & Frances Henrietta Jerningham 1745–1824 Augustinian Canonesses of Bruges', *Recusant History*, vol. 22 no. 3 (May 1995): 350–69.

[96] Betham, *Baronetage*, vol. 1, 231.

136 SELLING ANCESTRY

the Jerninghams illustrates, the *Baronetage* aimed to celebrate the strength of the loyalist spirit among Catholic and Protestant elites alike. Sir Henry Mildmay shared similar convictions. He set up a committee with some leading churchmen at Winchester to review the status of Roman Catholics.[97] Faced with the threat of radicalism, Catholics and Protestants had to support a conservative coalition and enlist all religious minorities against the French republicans.[98]

Another asset in Betham's family was his elder son, William, who became connected to some prominent literary figures and antiquaries, notably John Nichols, who subscribed to the *Genealogical Tables* and was printer both to the Society of Antiquaries and the Royal Society.[99] It was probably through Nichols that William Betham Junior was introduced to Richard Gough, the Director of the Society of Antiquaries from 1771 to 1797.[100] In the late eighteenth century, many members of titled families joined the Society of Antiquaries and several of them could be found on the list of Betham's correspondents: John Coxe Hippisley, Martin Brown Folkes, and John Smith. Betham Jr was employed by Gough to work on a revised edition of William Camden's *Britannia*, which appeared in 1806. He was on the receiving end of most of the baronets' letters and was heavily involved in the archival research in London and Ireland. In London, he worked closely with the heralds, in particular the Garter King of Arms Isaac Heard.[101] In 1805, to complete the last volume on the Irish baronets, he went to Dublin to meet several families, notably the Revd Sir Henry Aston Bruce and the Sullivans. The latter title was created in 1804 and they were one of the largest landowners in Londonderry.[102] Like Matilda, Betham Jr was in contact with various Catholic baronets, especially Sir John Coxe Hippisley, whose activity in favour of Catholic emancipation has been explored by several historians.[103] Hippisley was rightly hoping that the radical threat posed by the French Revolution, particularly in Ireland, would force Parliament and the Church to reconsider the Penal Laws and re-establish normal diplomatic relations with Rome. In their compilation, the Bethams gave him a great deal of space—thirty pages—to vindicate his position. Betham wrote that 'Sir John possesses many local advantages, which greatly facilitated his intercourse with the court of Rome [...], he was nearly allied, by

---

[97] BL, Add. MS 21033, fol. 62; Betham, *Baronetage*, vol. 4, 383.

[98] On some other Catholic correspondents: John Aubrey (BL, Add. MS 21033, fol. 4), Sir John Trevelyan (BL, Add. MS 21033, fol. 87). See also J. J. Sack, *From Jacobite to Conservative: Reaction and Orthodoxy in Britain c.1760–1832* (Cambridge, 1993).

[99] Julian Pooley and Robin Myers, 'Nichols family', *ODNB*, 2004. Retrieved 26 Mar. 2020 from <https://doi-org.janus.bis-sorbonne.fr/10.1093/ref:odnb/63494>.

[100] Rosemary Sweet, 'Antiquaries and Antiquities in Eighteenth-Century England', *Eighteenth-Century Studies*, vol. 34, no. 2 (2001): 181–206 at 182.

[101] See his contribution on the article related to the Baronet William Pepys, 14 June 1803, BL, Add. MS 21033, fol. 11.

[102] Sir Henry Hervey Aston Bruce to Betham, BL, Add. MS 21033, fol. 6.

[103] Susan M. Sommers, 'Sir John Coxe Hippisley: That "Busy Man" in the Cause of Catholic Emancipation', *Parliamentary History*, vol. 27, no. 1 (2008): 82–95.

marriage, to a Patrician family of Rome [...]'.[104] He was able to end 'the estrangement which had subsisted between the Government of the British Empire and that of Rome for more than two centuries and the existence of certain penal laws (though the occasions which gave birth to them had long ago ceased to exist)'.[105] Extensive diplomatic documents in English, Latin, French, and Italian were included to demonstrate his negotiating skills. Hippisley may have obtained in return from the Pope the condemnation of the 'ill-advised Catholics, who had suffered themselves to be led away by Democratic principles'.[106] In England, as in Ireland, the Catholic elites were presented as a useful tool against democratic contagion. Finally, Betham inserted a letter from the duke of Portland in April 1796 stating that the many merits and services of Hippisley had earned him the title of baronet in that year.[107] Betham's *Baronetage* was closely linked to the political debate around the Catholic emancipation issue, which emerged into the public sphere during and after union with Ireland.[108] Through his involvement in the editing process, Betham Jr gathered archival experience, as well as connections with prominent antiquaries. In a later text, Betham reflected on these formative years, during which he established an extensive collection of records and indexes to the London and Irish archives: 'so that all persons of one name appear under one head, and all matters and names may be found with as much ease as a word in a lexicon'.[109] This experience later enabled him to attain rewarding positions. He obtained the charge of custodian of the Bermingham Tower in Dublin, where many state records were preserved. Knighted in 1812, he was appointed Genealogist Attendant in the Order of St Patrick and in 1820 Ulster King of Arms.

An army of Pittite baronets

The Bethams' correspondence mostly featured supporters of Pitt's religious policy.[110] Pitt's agenda was consistent with the reintegration of loyalist Catholics and repentant Jacobites in Britain before and after the Irish Act of Union. In the 1790s, dynasticism was no longer separated from loyalism as it had been during the last Jacobite invasion. It was in a sense reconfigured to play a crucial role in the emerging national and imperial identities.[111] This renewed form of dynasticism was later used against Napoleon and his attempts to create a nobility bringing

---

[104] Betham's *Baronetage*, vol. 4, 327.   [105] Ibid., 338–9.   [106] Ibid.   [107] Ibid., 341–2.

[108] On the growth of literature around the sufferings and loyalty of the Catholics, see, for example, Charles Butler, *Historical Memoirs of the English, Irish and Scottish Catholics, since the Reformation* (London, 1819) and John Milner, *Supplementary memoirs of the English Catholics* (London, 1820).

[109] P. B. Phair, 'Sir William Betham's Manuscripts', *Analecta Hibernica*, no. 27 (1972): 1–99 at 21 and 30.

[110] Jeremy Black, *Pitt the Elder* (Cambridge, 1992), 19 and 39, 243–7.

[111] My thanks to Joanna Innes for bringing this dichotomy between loyalism and dynasticism to my attention. Ilya Afanasyev and Milinda Banerjee argued that the reinvention of the term 'dynasty' in the

138 SELLING ANCESTRY

together *ancien régime* and republican elites.[112] However, Stuart Semmel mentioned also the destabilizing effects of a new French dynasty: 'even as Napoleon's apparent embrace of hereditary dynasty repelled some republicans, it opened up rhetorical pathways along which other radicals could assault loyalist pieties'.[113] If the various strands of British loyalism were indeed reinforced, much collective anxiety and doubts subsided about the outcome of the Napoleonic war, about a dysfunctional royal family, and about the risk of domestic disturbances. Betham's *Baronetage* aimed at demonstrating the martial superiority of the British elites, old and new. And by doing so Betham presented the memory of republican families in more positive light. Regarding the Harringtons, when Collins and Wotton simply mentioned that James had been degraded of his dignity and estates, he celebrated the quality of his *Oceana*: 'a work of genius and invention'.[114]

Another difference from Wotton was the large place given to the many Scottish and Irish families whose members had been promoted under Pitt, to the point where the volume might better have been labelled the first British *Baronetage*. In fact, the subtitle to volume 5 was 'Baronets of the United Kingdom'.[115] The publisher appealed to many families of Scottish and Irish descent who were part of the new British power elite that emerged under Pitt and Henry Dundas.[116] The Anglo-Irish Union precipitated the making of the British landed elite into a powerful interest which survived Pitt's death, thus changing the 'status structure' of the country. Betham's initiative was very much in line with the strengthening of the honours system around the king and the creation of various British Orders (the Thistle for Scotland, St Patrick for Ireland).[117] This proximity to the Court was reflected in the geographical location of the correspondents. Unlike Wotton's baronets, their estates were no longer concentrated in the northern counties, but also scattered around the metropolis (Kent, Surrey, Somerset, Berkshire, Bedfordshire) (Map 3.2).

Out of the forty-three correspondents, only eight held a seventeenth-century title (Aubrey, Davie, Jerningham, Liddell, Murray, Rous, Trevelyan, Whichcote) and eighteen had been elevated to the baronetage after 1780. Like most new

---

late eighteenth century became 'an essential part of ideological, material, and power landscapes of the globalized world in the nineteenth to twenty-first centuries', in 'The Modern Invention of "Dynasty": An Introduction', *Global Intellectual History*, vol. 7, no. 3 (2022): 407–20 at 410.

[112] See, for example, in *The Times*, a journalist mocked Napoleon's own dynasty: 'Joseph Buonaparte married her imperial highness MM Clart, daughter of a ship broker at Marseilles' and as for 'Citizen Lucien Buonaparte, his first wife was a pot girl in the tavern of one Maximin near Toulon, she died in Neuilly for bad treatment. His second wife is Madame Jauberton, the divorced wife of an exchange broker of Paris' (23 Nov. 1804). On a similar theme, see also James Gillray, *New Dynasty—or The Little Corsican Gardiner Planting a Royal-Pippin-Tree* (1807).

[113] *Napoleon and the British* (New Haven, 2004), 109.

[114] Betham, *Baronetage*, vol. 1, 108.   [115] Ibid., vol. 5, 427.

[116] David Cannadine. 'The Making of the British Upper Classes', in D. Cannadine, *Aspects of Aristocracy: Grandeur and Decline in Modern Britain* (New Haven, 1994), 23–6.

[117] Alvin Jackson, 'Ireland, the Union and the Empire, 1800–1900', in Kevin Kenny (ed.), *Ireland and the British Empire* (Oxford, 2005), 128–30.

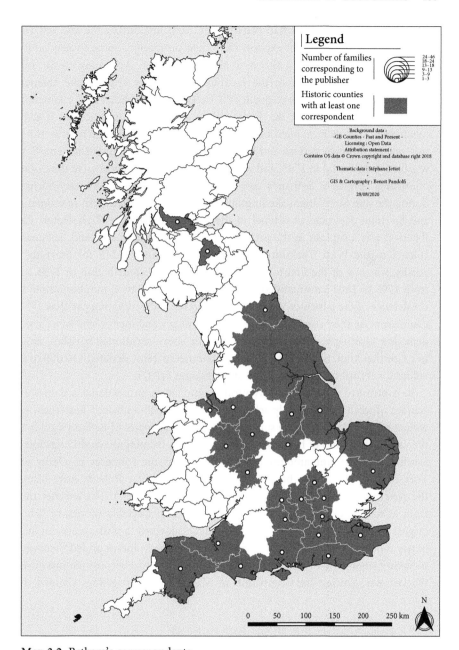

Map 3.2 Betham's correspondents

baronets, they were generally from a professional background rather than from landed families: mostly army officers, governors, lawyers (Ffolkes, Hanmer Sullivan, Lygon), merchants and financiers (Colebrooke, Henniker) and industrialists and coal owners (Peel, Liddell). As volunteers in the militia or officers in the

140 SELLING ANCESTRY

army, many new baronets had been on the front line during the last war with France. It was an important experience to their promotion. Some contended that France had always been a threat to the social order. According to Sir John Callander, Louis XIV before the Jacobins had already applied 'the shameful invention of seizing people of quality'.[118] Referring to the Edict of Fontainebleau in 1685, he claimed that the French state had a long tradition of levelling hierarchies. Callander applied countless times to Pitt for preferment after thirty-two years of military service and having long shown loyalty in Parliament.[119] He was finally successful in 1798, and was made baronet of Westertown in the County of Stirling. Several of Betham's customers served in various Voluntary Societies during the war: Sir William Skeffington, as colonel of the Leicestershire yeomanry, and Sir John Meyrick, as colonel of the Fulham volunteers.[120] Sir Henry Carr Ibbetson was a captain in the prince of Wales's dragoon guards and lieutenant-colonel of the West Yorkshire militia.[121] John Henniker, MP for Steyning in Sussex, was one of the first to celebrate the voluntary contribution in 1794, and from 1798 to 1802 'commanded a body of infantry, ninety in number, raised for the defence of the parish of Worlingworth and the eight adjoining parishes'.[122] To commemorate their deeds, he presented his officers and men with a silver medal depicting Worlingworth in Suffolk and all the above-mentioned parishes, united in a Gordian knot. Sir Robert Peel, made baronet in 1800, donated £10,000 to the voluntary contribution against a French invasion (1797).

In contrast to the pattern in Wotton's compilation, professional activities and sources of wealth were openly acknowledged. John Milnes from Chesterfield was willing to pay £7. 10s. for the subscription to several copies of Betham's guide for the various branches of his family from Dunstone, Brimington, and Longsdon.[123] Sending a significant amount of information on the Milneses in Derby and Yorkshire, he claimed to be from the same 'stock' as Sir Robert Shore Milnes, the governor of Martinique (1795) and of Lower Canada.[124] The baronet came from a 'romantick village' in Derby and from a 'respectable yeomanry' whose origins could not be traced as their descendants, devoted to trade, 'were not likely to pay much attention to genealogical studies'.[125] The Milneses prided themselves in having among their ranks since 1801 a baronet who had become famous during the last war. During the occupation of Martinique, John Milnes claimed that

---

[118] Callander to Betham, 1800, BL, Add. MS 21033, fol. 108.

[119] J. M. Collinge, 'Sir John Callander' in R. Thorne (ed.), *The History of Parliament: The House of Commons 1790–1820* (London, 1986).

[120] R. J. Morris, 'Voluntary Societies and the British Urban Elite, 1780–1850', *The Historical Journal*, vol. 26, no. 1 (1983): 95–118 at 95.

[121] BL, Add. MS 21033, fol. 50.   [122] Betham, *Baronetage*, vol. 3, 320.

[123] Ibid., vol. 5, 445; several members of the Milneses consented to subscribe to the last volume: James Milnes (MP), John Milnes of Wakefield, John Milnes of Beckingham, Richard Milnes of Barlow Grange, Robert Pemberton Milnes, and Richard Milnes of Crow Nest.

[124] Ibid., vol. 5., 431.   [125] Ibid.

'the inhabitants of that country [...] presented to him an address of thanks, accompanied with a present of three thousand pounds'.[126] This pride was increased by the family's wealth 'resulting from industry and perseverance in commerce'.[127] Edward Hanmer, barrister-at-law, was the younger brother of the second baronet. As a 'favour', he required to see the article on his family before printing and wished a copy to be directed at the Enrolment office at Chancery Lane for his clerk to 'get a sight of it'.[128] Regarding the Lombes of Great Melton, it was the son-in-law of Sir Edward Lombe, the attorney Meadows Taylor, who had been commissioned to answer Betham's query: 'I have introduced some additions to your narrative marked ABCD.'[129] Among the key points, Taylor insisted on the fact that the Lombes should be described as the first to introduce the making of silk in Derby and to receive a parliamentary grant of £14,000. This industrial feat was seen as more valuable than any gentrified lifestyle, all the more so as John Lombe died in heroic circumstances, poisoned by some Italians as a punishment for his technological robbery. In this case, noble ideals were nicely reconfigured to suit the industrial age. Others were unapologetic about their modest origins. Sir Henry Etherington simply started with his father, a merchant from Hull, twice mayor of the town in 1769.[130] His pedigree was indeed very short, without any elaborate claims (Illus. 3.2).[131]

However, Betham's *Baronetage* managed to preserve a polite gloss and some country values. Betham wanted to defend the reputation of his work since some of his customers had been publicly lampooned for their aspirations. Hippisley, whose father was a haberdasher, was dubbed 'Sir John Coxe Hippisley MP FRS SAS XYZ etc'.[132] Many baronets who bought their way into the upper gentry still did not want to display their commoner origins. Whatever the origin of their wealth, many still conformed to a gentrified lifestyle. Sir Henry Carr Ibbetson came from powerful cloth merchants in Leeds who exported their goods throughout the continent. The third surviving son of James Ibbetson had amassed a substantial art collection, including works by Rubens, on the Ibbetsons' Denton Estate, as they moved away from their urban origins.[133] The last baronet did not

---

[126] Ibid., vol. 5, 450, 461.   [127] Ibid., vol. 5, 450, 461.

[128] BL, Add. MS 21033, 30 Mar. 1803, fol. 36. John Hanmer, *A memorial of the parish and family of Hanmer in Flintshire out of the thirteenth into the nineteenth century* (1876). Betham, *Baronetage*, vol. 3, 432.

[129] BL, Add. MS 21033, fols 100–8; Betham, *Baronetage*, vol. 4, 142; on the collection of papers gathered by Meadows Taylor, see also NRO, MC 257/59, 684X3—Genealogical notes and rough pedigrees of the Lombe, Meadows, and Taylor families.

[130] BL, Add. MS 21033, fol. 25.   [131] Betham, *Baronetage*, vol. 4, 11.

[132] See James Gillray on an inflated baronet: 'Scientific researches!—new discoveries in pneumaticks!—or—an experimental lecture on the powers of air' (23 May 1802, NPG D13036); Roland Thorne, 'Sir John Coxe Hippisley', *ODNB*, 2004, retrieved 27 Mar. 2020, from <https://doi-org.janus.bis-sorbonne.fr/10.1093/ref:odnb/13361>.

[133] R. G. Wilson, *Gentlemen Merchants: The Merchant Community in Leeds, 1700–1830* (Manchester, 1971), 214.

142 SELLING ANCESTRY

ETHERINGTON, OF KINGSTON-UPON-HULL, YORKSHIRE.   11

319. ETHERINGTON, of KINGSTON-UPON-HULL, Yorkshire.

Created Baronet, Nov. 11, 1775.

THIS family is descended from the Etheringtons, of Great Driffield, in Yorkshire. One of the ancestors of Sir George Etherington was knighted after the battle of Bosworth, and is interred at the above place: the present is of a younger branch.

Henry Etherington, the father of the present Baronet, was a merchant, and married Jane Porter, by whom he had two daughters, Jane, who died unmarried, and Margaret, wife of John Mons, of Wolsingham, in Durham, Esq.; and two sons, George, who died an infant, and,

I. HENRY ETHERINGTON, Esq. who was created a Baronet, and married Maria-Constantia, daughter of Sir Thomas Cave, Bart. M. P. They have no issue.

ARMS—Per pale, argent and sable, three lions rampant counterchanged, two and one.

CREST—A tower decayed on the sinister side, argent, on the battlement a leopard's face, proper.

SEAT—At North Ferriby, near Hull, Yorkshire.

TABLE.

HENRY ETHERINGTON=JANE PORTER

Jane	Margaret	George,	I. Sir Henry Etherington
	John Mons	d y	Maria-Constantia Cave

320. HAMILTON, of MARLBOROUGH-HOUSE, Portsmouth, Hants.

Created Baronet, July 6, 1776.

JOHN HAMILTON, captain of his Majesty's ship the Hector, was created a Baronet, July 6, 1776.

Illus. 3.2 From pedigree to horizontal kinship: Sir Henry Etherington (Betham, vol. 4, 11)

© All Souls College Library, 4:SR.39.c.3/4

expatiate much on his forebears, stating only that 'the family is of considerable antiquity' and that the first baronet was the son of an 'eminent merchant'.[134]

---

[134] Betham, *Baronetage*, vol. 2, 244.

HUNDREDS OF CUSTOMERS   143

While professional and mercantile activities were more openly celebrated, industrialists were more discreet about their activities. Peel's pedigree mentioned an estate, named 'Peel Cross', which had 'for many generations been in the possession' of the family, but nothing was disclosed about the cotton spinning mills at Bolton.[135] The return correspondence included wealthy landowners from Ireland (Bruce, Crofton), Scotland (Callander, Inglis), and the West Indies (Cunliffe, Champneys, Heron, Trevelyan), giving the compilation a more landed profile.[136] Sir Foster Cunliffe enthusiastically paid his subscription as he presented himself as a passionate genealogist.[137] In his article, he dwelt at length on his Saxon origins and on family deeds during the Civil War, omitting the fact that their slave trade initiated from Liverpool.[138] Similarly, Sir Thomas Champneys introduced himself as the head of a very ancient West of England family dating back to the Norman Conquest, although since 1776 he had actually lived in Jamaica.[139] Sir Robert Heron asked for '25 copies on the best paper' and volunteered to help Betham in his data collection by promising to send a volume to his 'Northern Friends, as they may know from their own families of marriages of some of the men mentioned in the table which I have not been able to discover'.[140] Heron was notably connected to the north through Sir John Trevelyan, as they held properties and slaves in common in Grenada.[141] They commented mostly on their charitable practices and Trevelyan in particular gave a long depiction of his Catholic engagement.[142] It is worth adding that some baronets were instead on the abolitionist side, notably Sir Harbord Harbord.[143]

These landed magnates imparted a more traditional character to the *Baronetage*. As the peerage grew in number, many baronets were hoping to obtain a peerage in the near future and several had their wishes fulfilled.[144] Whether they acquired a large fortune, were instrumental in the political machine, or displayed military courage, their claims to ennoblement in the times of Pitt were likely to succeed. Like the Jerninghams, the Lygons schemed for the revival of the barony of Beauchamp of Powick, a title which they finally regained in 1806. As he considered the baronets and peers to be deeply connected, William Lygon

---

[135] Ibid., vol. 5, 491.

[136] 'After 1800 it was the creations from Scotland and Ireland that sustained the traditional character of the peerage as the bastion of great landed proprietors.' Michael McCahill and Ellis Archer Wasson, 'The New Peerage: Recruitment to the House of Lords, 1704–1847', *The Historical Journal*, vol. 46, no. 1 (2003): 1–38 at 10.

[137] BL, Add. MS 21033, fol. 17.   [138] Betham, *Baronetage*, vol. 2, 612.

[139] BL, Add. MS 21033, fol. 19. Betham, *Baronetage*, vol. 3, 347.

[140] July 1803, BL, Add. MS 21033, fols 38–9.

[141] On the important link between slavery and Northern local industries, see in particular John Charlton, *Hidden Chains: The Slavery Business and North East England, 1600–1865* (Newcastle upon Tyne, 2008), 125–39.

[142] Heron, Betham's *Baronetage*, vol. 4, 33; Trevelyan, ibid., vol. 2, 307.

[143] R. G. Thorne, 'Sir Harbord Harbord', *The House of Commons, 1790–1820*.

[144] A. Malcomson, 'The Irish Peerage and the Act of Union 1800–1971', *Transactions of the Royal Historical Society*, 6th ser., vol. 10 (2000): 289–327.

144 SELLING ANCESTRY

encouraged Betham to add to his baronetage a 'revisal of Collins's Peerage brought down to the present times'.[145] He claimed to 'have a great deal of information which I consider as valuable to communicate to you, if you cannot get it from other hands', notably concerning the Hanmers (his mother was Sarah Hanmer), the Inglises, and the Burroughs.[146] Lygon had dropped his initial name Pyndar and adopted that of his grandmother, Margaret Lygon, a descendant of the Beauchamps. Lygon asked Betham to change his account in the third volume, which he found highly improper. In a footnote about William Jennens, first cousin to Lygon's mother, Betham indicated that Lygon had 'obtained administration of his immensely large personal estate' (£800,000).[147] It was not considered a timely comment as the case was not closed and many claimants had rushed to the Chancery Court to establish their rights to parts of Jennens's fortune.[148] It was a lawsuit which had already generated too much publicity. Though not a baronet, Lygon's participation in Betham's project was closely linked to his hopes of becoming a peer. Similarly, when Sir John Henniker wrote in 1803, he was about to inherit the Irish title of Baron Henniker of Stratford-upon-Slaney (Wicklow), which his father had received in 1800.[149] Sir Harbord Harbord in his letter wondered 'whether it would be arguable in your plan to insert it, the baronetage being now extinct', as he was made Lord Suffield in 1786.[150] Like Lygon, he was in favour of such an insertion as it would strengthen the links between titled families.

The East India interest

Another defining pattern in the group of correspondents is their strong links with the East India Company (EIC), which Pitt had consistently supported. Sir John Rous, for example, voted against Fox's East India bill, which he condemned as 'violating public faith, and invading private property'.[151] Several studies have underlined the growth of the colonial administration and its reliance on family patronage and networks.[152] This was particularly the case as far as the EIC was concerned: family connections and correspondence were essential in the daily

---

[145] BL, Add. MS 21033, fol. 54.   [146] BL, Add. MS 21033, fol. 57.

[147] Betham's *Baronetage*, vol. 3, 430.

[148] On a case which inspired Dickens in *Bleak House*, see Patrick Polden, 'Stranger than Fiction? The Jennens Inheritance in Fact and Fiction Part Two: The Business of Fortune Hunting', *Common Law World Review*, vol. 32, no. 4 (2003): 338–67.

[149] Betham's *Baronetage*, vol. 3, 313. *Some Account of the Families of Major and Henniker* (London, 1803).

[150] BL, Add. MS 21033, fol. 73.

[151] Winifred Stokes, 'Sir John Rous', in *The History of Parliament: The House of Commons 1754–1790*.

[152] Sir George Colebrooke, Sir John Hippisley, Sir Henry Fletcher, Sir Hugh Inglis, Sir John Smith-Burges, Sir Richard Sullivan, Sir George Wombwell, Sir Francis Wood.

working of the Empire.[153] The second volume of Betham's *Baronetage* was dedicated to Lord Cornwallis, governor-general of India and lord lieutenant of Ireland (1798–1801). As the Cornwallis family had long been settled in Suffolk, Betham was keen to stress a common bond. Cornwallis embodied the efforts of the successive governments to quash the independentist rebellion in Ireland while planning to concede some religious and political rights to loyalist Catholics. Furthermore, it has been argued that Cornwallis did much to open the EIC to Scottish merchants. Dominant in the Houses of Agency between the Indian settlement and London, they amassed considerable wealth, which was then invested in Scotland and England in landed acquisitions. Lord Bute and later Henry Dundas, as head of the new India Board, made it a systematic policy to involve the Scots more closely in the expansion of the British Empire in India. The massive benefits generated helped to turn many reluctant Scots into staunch loyalists.

The fifth volume was dedicated to a prominent Scottish merchant, Sir Hugh Inglis, who received a baronetcy in 1801, after having served as director of the EIC. His elder son Robert Harry wished to supplement the article drafted by Betham 'with the little additions which may be made to the account of our family [...] and a few epitaphs on Baronets or their families which I have collected'.[154] Again, as for Lygon and many others, their own family history was always conceived in a collaborative manner, with the inclusion of many other baronets. He provided in fact a long genealogy (10 pages) which would later be used as the framework for his father's biography (*Sketch of the Life of Sir Hugh Inglis*, 1821). Robert Harry was to Anglicize his origins and insist on the marriage of his father into the Bedfordshire gentry. Several pages were dedicated to demonstrating that, although the family had been living in Scotland for several centuries, their name allegedly came from the first English settlers, according to 'the old language of Scotland' and to many other authorities.[155] He added that initially the family had been opposed to the Act of Union, notably Robert Inglis, who represented Edinburgh during the reign of Anne and was a director of the Bank of Scotland.[156] Like the Jerninghams, previous sources of discontent were made irrelevant by the French Revolution and the defence of a truly British Empire. His father's aunt Rachel married a major in the EIC and a cousin Robert, serving in the Bombay Army, died after the capture of Seringapatam, in 1800. Another relation, James, was enlisted in the EIC's marine service and was killed in Ceylon.[157] As for Hugh Inglis, he went to the East Indies in 1762 and was elected a director of the Company in 1784, and chairman in 1800.

---

[153] Margot Finn has stressed the importance of family networks by establishing interconnected biographies, in 'Anglo-Indian Lives in the Later Eighteenth and Early Nineteenth Centuries', *Journal for Eighteenth-Century Studies*, vol. 33, no. 1 (2010): 49.

[154] BL, Add. MS 21033, fol. 48.   [155] Betham's *Baronetage*, vol. 5, 438–42.

[156] Ibid., 446.   [157] Ibid., 448.

146 SELLING ANCESTRY

Among the English families, Betham dedicated a long narrative to the Colebrooke's in India.[158] The son of the present baronet was described as a very prominent judge of appeal in Bengal and a Persian translator to Governor Hastings. Extracts from Hastings's correspondence were added along with extended footnotes on his Digest of 'Hindoo Law'. He had been a judge at Mirzapoor and 'made himself master of the Sanskrit language' and had authored several treaties on agriculture and commerce in Bengal.[159] Another correspondent, Sir Henry Fletcher, briefly mentioned his Norman descent 'as there was a family of their name and arms in the southern part of Normandy', but went into great detail about his role as a director in the service of the EIC from 1763 to 1784.[160] Similarities between the Irish and Indian colonization have been described by many historians and the case of the Fletchers illustrates this point. One of their relations was Major Philip Fletcher, who had been surveyor-general of the province of Ulster until his death in 1758. His son Philip died in Bengal, while Edward was administering the district of Santipur in Bengal, and James was a physician for the Company.

Experience in the EIC seems to connect several of Betham's correspondents into a tightly knit group. John Coxe Hippisley had served with John Sullivan, a lawyer from Cork who was resident in Tanjore from 1781 to 1785 and was then Under-Secretary of State for War and Colonies (1801–4).[161] John's brother, Sir Richard Sullivan, also corresponded with Betham and had just been made a baronet in 1804 after serving as minister at the court of the Nawab of Arcot (1781–3). They both benefited from the help of their kinsman, Laurence Sullivan, the director and a chairman of the Company, and obtained parliamentary seats with the help of Pitt. The Sullivans of Thames Ditton (Surrey) were said to be descended from Olioll, king of Munster, 'whom the Irish chronicles deduce from Heber Fionn, one of the sons of Milesius'.[162] In 1804, William Betham Jr had already determined upon rehabilitating the Irish medieval period, which later became his main subject of expertise.[163] He quoted Dr Johnson and his positive view of Ireland as 'the school of the West, the quiet habitation of sanctity and learning'.[164] Just as these Irish connections were later beneficial in his career in Dublin as Ulster King of Arms, so the acquaintances made in the EIC during the publication of the *Baronetage* were useful to other members of the Bethams.

---

[158] BL, Add. MS 21033, fol. 23, May 1805. Betham's *Baronetage*, vol. 3, 281. The Colebrooke were also slave owners in Antigua. H. V. Bowen revised by Anita McConnell, 'Colebrooke, Sir George', *ODNB*, 2004. Retrieved 27 Mar. 2020 from <https://doi-org.janus.bis-sorbonne.fr/10.1093/ref:odnb/37301>.

[159] Betham's *Baronetage*, vol. 3, 287.   [160] Ibid., vol. 4, 101–5.

[161] Ibid., vol. 5, 556–68.   [162] Ibid.

[163] In his publication of the book of Armagh, he states: 'in it will be found evidence to convince the more sceptical, that Ireland in the seventh century was a cultivated and civilised country, and had been so for centuries'. *Irish Antiquarian Researches*, vol. 1 (1827, Dublin), 245.

[164] *Irish Antiquarian Researches*, vol. 1 (1827, Dublin), 245.

HUNDREDS OF CUSTOMERS   147

Indeed, in the Revd William Betham's obituary, it is noted of his many children that George, Edward, and Robert all served as officers in the EIC, that John was a captain in the Indian Navy, and that a daughter, Mary-Ann, married a captain who served as Persian interpreter at Hyderabad.[165]

Again, we can see that many correspondents were linked by alliances and/or business connections. The long-lasting presence of the Bethams in Suffolk and Norfolk led them to benefit from many useful contacts among the local baronets (Henniker, Rous, Hippisley, Browne, Harbord, Jerningham, Lombe). As with Roger Beckwith for Wotton, some individuals were particularly active as brokers between various families—for the Bethams, it was Gamaliel Lloyd who fulfilled this function. He provided a wealth of information on several baronets around Leeds, where he had been an apprentice in the cloth trade in 1760 and mayor in 1778. Among the many names to which he connected himself were Sir William Horton, Sir Henry Ibbetson, Sir George Savile, Sir Francis Lindley Wood of Barnsley, recorder at Leeds, as well as Sir Thomas Beevor:

> I find I am very distantly related to one family which I did not know before, I mean the Beevors. In the 3rd vol page 312 (Hortons of Chaderton) Eliz eldest daught of Wm Horton marr. William Batt of Oakwell Hall in the parish of Burstall [. . .]. Whether Eliz Batt who marr. Wm Beevor was a daught or a grand daught of W. B & Eliz Horton I cannot tell but I think probably the former in the case Sr Tho Beevor and myself are fourth cousin.[166]

Lloyd's mother was Susanna Horton, sister to the first baronet Sir William Horton, high sheriff of Lancaster. He also knew the Bolds in Lancashire. Anna-Maria Bold passed the property on to her nephew, the MP Peter Patten of Bank Hall, another Pitt supporter, 'who distinguished himself last winter in the House of Commons'.[167] And lastly it was through the mediation of Lloyd that Sir William Skeffington came to write to Betham, offering to send him 'some particulars which might be an advantage to his valuable baronetage'.[168] Lloyd may have met Betham the elder when he moved in 1789 to Bury St Edmunds, Suffolk, or his son when he later bought a residence in Hampstead.[169]

Although the Bethams managed to obtain prestigious patronage and the support of some wealthy baronets, their expensive work in five quarto volumes did not sell. They transferred the copyright to William Miller, who brought out an

---

[165] GM, vol. 12 (Dec. 1839). See also J. Nichols, Literary Anecdotes of the Eighteenth Century, vol. 9 (London, 1815), 51.

[166] BL, Add. MS 21033, fol. 52.   [167] BL, Add. MS 21033, fol. 53.

[168] Skeffington to Betham, 19 Dec. 1803, BL, Add. MS 21033, fol. 79.

[169] Daniel Webster Hollis, 'Lloyd, Gamaliel', ODNB, 2004. Retrieved 27 Mar. 2020 from <https://doi.org/10.1093/ref:odnb/39688>.

148 SELLING ANCESTRY

abridged and pocket edition in two volumes in 1804.[170] Deprived of all the family trees and long historical narratives, Miller's new baronetage was better suited to challenging war times. However, Betham's undertaking reflected the decisive integration of rich Irish and Scottish landowners into the first UK baronetage, a trend very much in line with the reorganization of the peerage.

3. Burke's *Commoners*: 'A picture of England to future times as the Doomsday Book is to us of England'

By this flattering comparison between the *Commoners* and the Domesday Book, Arthur James Jones, a Welsh lawyer from Chancery Lane, expressed strong enthusiasm for Burke's project, arguing that it could serve as a snapshot of the current landed gentry.[171] Among the urban elite, a similar excitement could be found: John Harvey, the mayor of Norwich and chairman of Merchants & Manufacturers, believed that this *Commoners* would be 'of interest to the large portion of the reading public'.[172] Many members of the Church of England, notably those who were represented on the Bench, showed their support. The vicar of Llandyfaelog, William Evans, congratulated Burke for his invention of a new product: as 'novelty breeds notoriety', his compilation will 'recommend itself to the curiosity and approval of that class in society'.[173] Among the untitled gentry, Charles Goring, the son of Sir Charles Matthew Goring's second marriage, rejoiced that, unlike former *Baronetages* which had favoured the senior line at the expense of collaterals, his name would at last appear: 'I am the first person of my family belonging to the class of society to which your letter refers.'[174]

Other correspondents were more critical. A wealthy magistrate from Thornhill, Shakespeare Reed, the son of John Reed, a modest London artisan in Sun Tavern Fields and later a famous dramatist, wrote back arguing that the *Commoners* would simply maintain the undue taste for ancient lineages. The compilation would be only 'a most valuable acquisition to those who can boast of any other hereditary ancestry than that of Adam, which not being my case say for several generations. I cannot in any instance find the dignity of our family to have arrived at a higher honour than that of Halter maker.'[175] Another correspondent derided Burke's project, stating that Mr Crawshay 'has something else to do than enter

---

[170] Miller deplored that Betham 'did not meet with the success his industry merited' but pointed out that his new edition 'has the benefit of the very numerous original communications with which Mr Betham has been favoured'. *New Baronetage*, preface, vii.

[171] 'I believe it will be as interesting a picture of England to future times as Doomsday book is to us of England in the days of the Conqueror'. Apr. 1829, CA, Burke's *Commoners* (hereafter BC), vol. 57, case 291.

[172] CA, BC, vol. 57, case 230.   [173] CA, BC, vol. 56, case 167.

[174] CA, BC, vol. 57, case 204.

[175] Shakespeare Reed, Thornhill, 16 July 1828, CA, BC, vol. 58, case 457.

into what he considers idle, particular and totally uninteresting to any one'.[176] William Crawshay (1764–1834) was the wealthy owner of the Cyfarthfa Ironworks in Wales and son of Richard Crawshay, one of the first British millionaires. From a humble background, Richard was a pioneer in iron refining and among the main iron traders. Instead of claiming remote ancestors, William chose rather to commission a series of portraits of the main iron founders, thus expressing rather a sense of 'corporate fraternity'.[177] Others criticized Burke for opening the gate to all the upstarts and unworthy nouveaux riches. Thomas Newcome, rector of Shenley, presented himself as the scion of a prestigious family whose 'clerical line' derived from the Elizabethan Reformation in 1590.[178] Since, however, he was not a rich landowner, he regretted that Burke's initiative would be mainly popular among those imbued with 'national vanity and for the new rich'.[179]

These conflicting views were expressed by reviewers in the gazettes. *The Gentleman's Magazine*, praising an original and useful initiative, welcomed the inclusion of families of talent as well as wealth, such as Henry Dymock (the king's champion), William Allan (antiquarian), and John Latham (physician and naturalist).[180] We have already mentioned in the Introduction the indignant review by Sir Egerton Brydges in the ultra-Tory *Fraser's Magazine*.[181] Ancient and charitable families were replaced by reckless parvenus such as Lord Brougham and 'his salary fixed at £14,000 a year': this state of affairs would only encourage 'the radical mob of incendiaries' and machine breakers and lead to the despair of the worthy poor.[182]

Whatever their positive or negative views, most contemporaries would have agreed that the innovation of the *Commoners* was a commercial success. The first volume went through four new editions from 1832 to 1835 and was followed by three supplemental volumes from 1835 to 1838. The compilation was then republished in 1846–8 and again after 1860. For all four volumes of the *Commoners*, it has been calculated that 4,776 pedigrees were collected (2,879 English, 1,166 Irish, 515 Scottish, 216 Welsh).[183] To account for such a success, we will point to the efficient marketing campaign by its publisher Henry Colburn, as well as the favourable context created by the debates on parliamentary reform. With much astuteness, Burke chose not to clearly define what he meant by 'commoners' and his initiative generated a considerable amount of publicity and interest. He then went on to select the families in various categories, from those

---

[176] George Forest on behalf of William Crawshay to Burke, Cyfarthfa Castle, 17 Nov. 1728. CA, vol. 56, case 116.

[177] Chris Evans, 'Richard Crawshay', *ODNB*, 2004. Retrieved 21 Feb. 2020 from <https://doi-org.janus.bis-sorbonne.fr/10.1093/ref:odnb/45891>; J. P. Addis, *The Crawshay Dynasty: A Study in Industrial Organisation and Development, 1765–1867* (Cardiff, 1957).

[178] CA, BC, vol. 57, case 389.   [179] Ibid.   [180] *GM*, Dec. 1832, vol. 102, 541–2.

[181] *Fraser's Magazine for Town and Country*, vol. 8 (June 1833).   [182] Ibid., 645.

[183] *Notes and Queries*, vol. 6, issue 152 (Jan.–June 1882), 191.

150 SELLING ANCESTRY

who emerge in the first volume to those who appeared in later volumes, as well as those whose pedigree remained unpublished.

A timely commercial and political operation

The originator of the project was John Burke, a Roman Catholic, the elder son of Peter Burke, a JP for Tipperary and King's County.[184] He moved to London in 1811 to work as a journalist and indexer for the *Examiner*. He then joined the Colburn press and worked on different serial publications such as *The Royal Kalendar* and *The Naval and Military Gazette*. In the middle of the economic crisis, Colburn agreed to finance Burke's first and very successful *General and Heraldic Dictionary of the Peerage and Baronetage* (1826). Burke saw his *Commoners* as a continuation of his previous work. In June 1828 Colburn announced in most newspapers the forthcoming appearance, 'published during the present season', of *The Genealogical and Heraldic History of the Commoners*. He informed the public that 'circular letters (so successfully adopted in the case of the Peerage and Baronetage) have been transmitted to the eminent persons who come, it is presumed, within the limitation of the work, and their replies to the accompanying printed interrogatories are most earnestly solicited, with as much despatch as possible'.[185] The 'interrogatories' in question were easy to fill out and could be sent back free of postage, a significant outlay considering its rising cost after 1790.

The latter detail drew attention to the role of the publisher Henry Colburn, who had the financial resources and extended sales networks to make *The Commoners* an achievement. Colburn was a very enterprising bookseller who owned many copyrights of novels and gazettes (*New Monthly Magazine and Literary Journal, Literary Gazette, The Athenaeum, The John Bull*).[186] He reinforced his position during the 1826 financial crisis and was one of the few to emerge with a stronger position in the publishing business.[187] He invested in many 'silver fork novels' about the style of prominent aristocrats by such writers as Thomas Lister, Benjamin Disraeli, or Theodore Hook. Colburn's novels belonged to 'a vital subgenre in the development of new middle-class readership for the novel and the recognizable culture of literary celebrity that developed during the Regency'.[188]

---

[184] Thomas Woodcock, 'John Burke', *ODNB*, 2004. Retrieved 3 Mar. 2020 from <https://doi-org.janus.bis-sorbonne.fr/10.1093/ref:odnb/4021>.

[185] *The Times*, 23 June 1828; see also a similar advert in *The Edinburgh Review* and *The Quarterly Review*.

[186] John Sutherland, *Victorian Novelists and Publishers* (London, 1976), 327.

[187] Thomas Woodcock, *ODNB*, 2004. Retrieved 5 Mar. 2020 from <https://doi-org.janus.bis-sorbonne.fr/10.1093/ref:odnb/4021>.

[188] Clara Tuite, 'Celebrity and Scandalous Fiction', in Peter Garside and Karen O'Brien (eds), *English and British Fiction, 1750–1820: The Oxford History of the Novel in English*, vol. 2 (Oxford, 2015), 400.

HUNDREDS OF CUSTOMERS   151

Colburn also invested in translation of foreign novels: 'These carefully up-market items [...] helped keep Colburn and his library in the public eye, and occasionally reaped the rewards of daring.'[189] He possessed a considerable circulating library in New Bond Street and benefited from a vast sales network in Britain, notably with Richard Bentley in England, Bell and Bradfute in Edinburgh, and Cumming in Dublin.[190]

As early as 1820, Colburn aimed at challenging the domination of Debrett's compilation. He used his *Literary Gazette*—which he owned jointly with Longmans—to launch a well-organized campaign of denigration overseen by its editor, William Jerdan. Since 1802, John Debrett had published a series of alphabetical pocket compilations on a nearly annual basis. From 1820, the *Literary Gazette* opened its pages to many readers who railed against the dubious quality of Debrett's works. The core of the argument was that they insulted the dignity of many titled families which were 'miserably recorded' and that 'it contains at least as many errors as there are articles'.[191] Faced with a public trial by the editor, Debrett was invited to defend himself. Against the accusation of 'scandalous errors', he complained of the 'scandalous meanness' of the attack.[192] His intervention seems only to have been an invitation for further complaints, staged in the following issues. One reader wondered why Debrett, if he could not attain perfection, was not at least trying to aim at it.[193] A further list of 'scandalous' or comical mistakes was exposed: the marriage of the marquess of Winchester with Martha Ingoldsby in 1812 though she had died in 1796, the fact that 'the late Marchioness of Winchester had a grand-child before she had a husband' or that the earl of Mexborough was married to his countess on 25 September 1782, while their daughter Eliza 'came into the world on the 20th of June preceding. Upon my word, Mr Debrett, this is taking a shocking liberty with Lady Mexborough's character!'[194] In short, as summarized in the *Gazette*, many readers were 'out of pocket for Mr Debrett's bundle of inaccuracies'.[195] It was about time that a new reference book appeared on the market. It was then, in a concerted manner, that Burke and Colburn came up with a new product, beginning in 1825. Colburn made a significant profit from selling Burke's compilations, and Strickland's *Lives of the Queens of England* were together estimated in 1832 at £2,000 and were sold after his death for £6,900.[196]

---

[189] Peter Garside, 'The English Novel in the Romantic Era', in Peter Garside, James Raven, and Rainer Schöwerling (eds), *The English Novel 1770–1829: A Bibliographical Survey of Prose Fiction Published in the British Isles*, vol. 2 (Oxford, 2000), 88.

[190] Winifred Hughes. 'Silver Fork Writers and Readers: Social Contexts of a Best Seller', *Novel*, vol. 25 (1992), 328–34; Edward Copeland, *The Silver Fork Novel: Fashionable Fiction in the Age of Reform* (Cambridge, 2012).

[191] *The London Literary Gazette*, 24 June 1820, no. 179, 409.

[192] Ibid., 5 Aug. 1820, no. 185, 504.   [193] Ibid., 26 Aug. 1820, no. 188, 552–4.

[194] Ibid. 552.   [195] Ibid. 553.

[196] Frank A. Mumby, *Publishing and Booksellings* (London, 1956), 229.

152 SELLING ANCESTRY

Another decisive factor was the implicit political agenda followed by Burke and Colburn. In the *Age of Equipoise*, William L. Burn argued that printed genealogies such as those published by Burke and Debrett should be understood as 'a defensive reaction on the part of established families against the threat of the new industrialists, leading to a desire to divorce the concept of gentility from that of economic status'.[197] However, it seems that Colburn and Burke's position, far from being only reactionary, praised the ongoing restructuring among the elites. In their celebration of the 'non-titled aristocratic class', they intended to promote a moderate version of political reform against the ultra-conservatives and the Chartists. To do so they had to tread carefully. In April 1829, Colburn and Burke successfully petitioned Sir Robert Peel to obtain permission to dedicate the second edition of their *Peerage and Baronetage* to the king. Burke considered that 'in all future advertisement, it gives us a great advantage over our foes'.[198] Alluding to his latest reforms, Burke wrote a laudatory article on Peel, presenting him as a middle-ground politician between radicals and reactionaries:

> Since he has filled his present office [...] there has been no invasion or suspension of the Constitution, there have been no alarms of treasonable plots [...] no needless display of military force [...]. The choice of Juries has been placed on a fair and honest footing; he has put a stop to the distribution of judicial patronage in Scotland for political purpose [...]. He has done more than any man living to improve the tone of the government towards the people and the people towards the government.[199]

Burke obtained the honour of being presented to the king at his levée on 30 April 1829.[200] The conservative nature of the Reform Bill has been stressed in many recent studies and depicted as a middle way between the democratic agenda of the radicals and the reactionary positions of the Tories.[201] Middle-class reformers such as Thomas Attwood in Birmingham, the first MP in the election of 1832, were more hostile to the London monied interests than to the local county gentry. Attwood contended that 'all landowners are with me although few of them have the courage to own it'.[202] Among the metropolitan Whigs, the editors of *The Times* dedicated several articles to the need to reform the pocket boroughs by

---

[197] William L. Burn, *The Age of Equipoise: A Study of the Mid-Victorian Generation* (New York, 1964), 254.

[198] Burke to Colburn, CA, BC, vol. 55, 25 Apr. 1829, fol. 145.

[199] Burke on Peel, CA, BC, vol. 55, 25 Apr. 1829, fol. 147. See the edited version of the article, in *A General and Heraldic Dictionary* (1832), vol. 2, 289.

[200] *The Times*, 30 Apr. 1829.

[201] John Phillips, *The Great Reform Bill and the Boroughs: English Electoral Behaviour* (Oxford, 1993).

[202] Quoted by Asa Briggs, 'The Background of the Parliamentary Reform Movement in Three English Cities, 1830–1832', *The Historical Journal*, vol. 10 (1952), 301.

HUNDREDS OF CUSTOMERS   153

using former directories as proof of the resilient Old Corruption: 'Look for this to the Peerage, the Baronetage [...] and you will see what a source of honours, offices and emoluments [...] the possession of close boroughs has been to their owners, relatives and protégés.'[203] Leaving aside the moral argument in favour of fairness, the journalist referred to the political damage caused by an unreformed Parliament. Hence during the War of American Independence, when peace could have been negotiated in 1780 under the pressure of many urban and county MPs, the move was prevented by 106 rotten boroughs.

In contrast, the forthcoming *Commoners* was praised in *The Times* as the sign of changing times. It was announced as early as September 1831 as a work which would 'connect in many instances the new with the old nobility'.[204] In his *Dictionary of Dormant and Extinct Peerage*, Burke already tried to demonstrate the absence of strict boundaries between the gentry and the nobility: the English gentleman is 'a grade in society [that] has arisen amongst us, not to be found in any other country of Europe, a grade inferior to the noble in nought beside the artificial importance attached to rank [...]. The English gentleman stands hardly one step, if at all, below the English nobleman.'[205] After the passing of the Reform Bill, *The Times* informed its readers in November 1832 of the imminent publication of the directory, commenting that 'this highly influential and extensive class to whom it refers have at present no work of reference'.[206] While hardly necessary, the dedications and the portraits included in the first edition left little ambiguity as to the publisher's intentions. They were closely linked to the evolution of the parliamentary debates before and after the Reform Bill.

Thomas William Coke and Lord Brougham were among the main promoters of the Reform Act. The former finally accepted a peerage (as earl of Leicester in 1831) when 'every measure for which I was most eager will be completed upon the Reform being carried'.[207] Lord Brougham had been among the founders of the *Edinburgh Review* and was a close friend of the editor of *The Times*, Thomas Barnes. Brougham was considered an outsider to the rest of the political class. His decisive involvement in parliamentary reform did not mean that he was oblivious to his own origins. Burke introduced him as 'the representative of two very ancient families in the North of England'.[208] An article in the *Edinburgh Review* mentioned the legal claims of Brougham to the Vaux of Harrowden. In 1832, Burke had already dedicated a long narrative to them, their ennobling patent

[203] *The Times*, 18 Apr. 1831.   [204] *The Times*, 12 Sept. 1831.

[205] *Dictionary of Dormant and Extinct Peerage*, vi.

[206] See also a comparative initiative by John Briton on the Reform Act and the metropolis: Steven Daniels, 'Mapping the Metropolis in an Age of Reform: John Britton's London Topography, 1820–1840', *Journal of Historical Geography*, vol. 56 (2017): 61–82.

[207] Quoted by J. Beckett, 'Coke, Thomas William, first earl of Leicester of Holkham' *ODNB*, 2004. Retrieved 3 Mar. 2020 from. Michael Lobban, 'Henry Brougham and Law Reform', *EHR*, vol. 115 (2000): 1184–215.

[208] *Commoners* (1833), vol. 1, preface.

154 SELLING ANCESTRY

in April 1573, and the many princes of that name in Normandy and Provence including several emperors of Greece.[209] In the first volume, Burke placed Charles Manners-Sutton in first place. The incumbent Speaker of the House of Commons, Manners-Sutton was presented as a nonpartisan Speaker who had received 'the unanimous thanks of all parties'.[210] Though a Tory, Manners-Sutton had served under Wellington and remained Speaker throughout the lengthy debate over the Reform Bill.

The second volume was dedicated to John Maude, deputy lieutenant of the West Riding combined with a portrait of Hon. Edward John Littleton. While the former held a local position, the latter was highly influential in Parliament (Staffordshire, 1812–32). A Whig sympathizer, he supported Catholic Emancipation and parliamentary reform and was then made chief secretary to Ireland.[211] John took the name of Littleton to inherit the vast estates of his great-uncle, Sir Edward Littleton, and hoped that Burke would connect him to the *Baronetages* sold by Betham and Wotton, a desire which the publisher fulfilled.[212] The dedication took place in 1835 when he was created Baron Hatherton of Hatherton, a striking example of a commoner elevated to the peerage.

The third volume honoured James Abercromby, Whig MP for Edinburgh in the first reformed Parliament and the first Scottish Speaker of the Commons elected after Manners-Sutton, who defended a liberal agenda.[213] The reasons behind the dedication to the Carys of Follaton are more difficult to establish. It may well be that the family helped Burke materially or financially in his research. The Carys may have been linked to two fundamental reforms, the emancipation of the Catholics and the abolition of slavery. Burke mentioned in his 1835 edition that the Carys were connected with the noble Catholic families of Stafford: the Petres, the Cliffords, and the Dillons. They had 'extensive possessions in the West Indies inherited from his maternal great-grandfather, Hon Gilbert Fleming', governor-general of the Leeward Islands.[214] The dedication coincided with the compensation scheme which followed the abolition of slavery in 1833. In 1835, the Carys obtained several thousands of pounds for the emancipation of their slaves in St Kitts.[215] This decision could be seen in the context of the anti-slavery campaign, as the end of a bitter struggle and enduring peace enabled by the compensation scheme. Hence the *Commoners* was narrowly linked to a process

---

[209] *A General and Heraldic Dictionary of the Peerage and Baronetage of the British Empire* (1832), 156–8.

[210] *Commoners*, preface, 2; Norman Gash, 'Sutton, Charles Manners', *ODNB*, 2004. Retrieved 3 Mar. 2020 from <https://doi-org.janus.bis-sorbonne.fr/10.1093/ref:odnb/17965>.

[211] G. Barker and H. Matthew, 'Littleton Edward John', *ODNB*, 2004. Retrieved 6 Mar. 2020 from <https://doi-org.janus.bis-sorbonne.fr/10.1093/ref:odnb/17965>.

[212] CA, BC, vol. 57, 3 Aug. 1828, case 319.

[213] T. Henderson and H. Matthew, 'Abercromby, James', *ODNB*, 2004. Retrieved 6 Mar. 2020 from <https://doi-org.janus.bis-sorbonne.fr/10.1093/ref:odnb/41>.

[214] *Commoners* (1835), vol. 2, 38.

[215] *Legacies of British Slave-ownership* project. <https://www.ucl.ac.uk/lbs/person/view/43950>.

of improvements and reforms aimed at counteracting radical and democratic movements. Described as open and inclusive, the new British 'aristocratic class' was vindicated in Burke's compilation as a remedy against revolutionary threats. Burke struggled, however, to select his hundreds of *Commoners*, as there was no title on which he could rely.

The 'Commoner' and its fruitful ambiguity

Walter Reeding from Derby wondered about what the editor understood by 'Commoner': 'an extensive meaning according to Dr Johnson, that it is not easy to know to what extent Mr Burke means to carry it in his dictionary'.[216] Indeed in Johnson's *Dictionary*, a commoner was defined as '1. One of the common people, a man of low rank. *Addison*. 2. A man not noble. *Prior*. 3. A member of the house of commons. 4. One who has a joint right in common ground. *Bacon*. 5. A student of the second rank at the university of Oxford. 6. A prostitute. *Shakespeare*.'[217] Considering the various meanings of the term, one could well understand Reeding's perplexity. It was all the more troubling as Burke kept changing the scope of his project from 1828 up to the publication of the fourth volume in 1838. As he did not follow any alphabetical order, Burke was able to integrate different categories of gentlemen in his later volumes.

At first, his 1828 circular letter was aimed at the landowners who could qualify to be elected as knight of the shire: those who had property of at least £600 of annual revenue.[218] A partial edition in 1832 counted only eighty-one families who more or less corresponded to those who sat in Parliament as knights of the shire, and was later turned into a larger volume which was republished between 1833 and 1835. In 1833, Burke chose the following title: *A Genealogical and Heraldic History of the Commoners* [. . .] *enjoying territorial possessions or high official rank but uninvested with heritable honours*. He had dropped the selective criterion of knight of the shire for those of 'territorial possession' and 'high officials'. The 1833 volume included the 'lineage of nearly four hundred families, enjoying in the aggregate probably a revenue of two million sterling and deriving many of them, their territorial possessions from William of Normandy'.[219] It reflected well on the first effect of the Reform Act, which led at first to an increase in country gentlemen in the Commons.[220] They were supposed to be independent landowners whose

---

[216] Reeding to Burke, 18 May 1828, CA, BC, vol. 28, case 454.

[217] Samuel Johnson, *A Dictionary of the English Language*, 3rd edn (London, 1768).

[218] *History of the commoners of Great Britain and Ireland qualified by landed property to become member of Parliament* (London, 1832).

[219] *Commoners* (1833), preface.

[220] Arthur Burns and Joanna Innes (eds), *Rethinking the Age of Reform: Britain 1780–1850* (Cambridge, 2003), 46.

156 SELLING ANCESTRY

standing would increase through the suppression of pocket boroughs and the weight of larger constituencies. They were families sitting on the fence, on the porous border between commoners and titled gentry. Among his most distinguished correspondents were the following county MPs: Edmund Pollexfen Bastard (Devon), John Bennet (Wiltshire), Thomas Duncombe (Hereford), Edward J. Littleton (Staffordshire), John Luttrell (Somerset), John Marshall (Yorkshire), Francis Munby (Derby), Robert Palmer (Berkshire), Evelyn Shirley (Monaghan), and George Wilbraham (Cheshire). Edmund P. Bastard sent him several letters on his ancestors' settlement since the Conquest and on their role as sheriffs of the county for many generations. He recalled how his grandfather William in 1779, when a French fleet appeared in front of Plymouth, conducted all the French prisoners in the port to Exeter, 'assisted only by the gentry and peasantry of the neighbourhood [...] [and] was created Baronet by his late Majesty. The title was gazetted in 1779 but had never been assumed.'[221] By mentioning this anecdote, Bastard seemed willing to claim the title for himself and was convinced that it was only a matter of time before the Bastards would join the titled families. John Bennett (or Benett) was celebrated as a just and prominent figure in a trying context. His political authority had been violently challenged during the Swing Riots in 1830 by a crowd who attacked his seat, Pythouse, near Hindon. Bennett confronted the rioters with the help of the local yeomanry and was even injured.[222] Several of his threshing machines were destroyed and the riot led to the death of 252 people in the county. Weathering the storm and after the passing of the Reform Act, he was re-elected for Wiltshire. By celebrating his ancient origins, with a lineage supposedly deriving from a sheriff of Wiltshire in Henry III's reign, Bennett embodied a resilient county elite reinforced by the current reforms.[223] Similarly Major Hugh Blaydes introduced himself as an effective high sheriff in Nottingham who had managed to suppress a Luddite rebellion in 1812.[224] John Marshall was described first as deputy lieutenant, knight of the shire, and a large landowner in Yorkshire, Cumberland: 'an affluence which Mr Marshall has attained, has been chiefly acquired by his successful introduction of mechanical improvement into a branch of the linen manufactory, the spinning of flax, in which he has formed extensive establishments, at Leeds and at Shrewsbury'.[225]

Burke included many wealthy landowners without parliamentary involvement, such as Fowler Hickes, who described his manor as one of the 'highest ridges in

---

[221] CA, BC, vol. 56, case 25.

[222] Letter from Mr Minty, Salisbury Post Office, [Wiltshire], to Francis Freeling, General Post Office, London. 'The city continues to be quiet but an assault took place at Pyt House, near Hindon, the home of John Bennett MP for Wiltshire. A crowd was meet by the Hindon Yeomanry and a "regular battle" took place with shots fired and sabres used. Two of the crowd was killed, many wounded and 37 now in gaol. Mr Bennett and Captain Wyndham were both injured.' Nov. 1830, NA HO 52/11/27 fols 56–8. On the Swing Riots, see Eric Hobsbawm and George Rudé, *Captain Swing* (Harmondsworth, 1973).

[223] *Commoners* (1833), 248.   [224] CA, vol. 56, case 40.   [225] *Commoners* (1833), 295.

the county, near the great road leading from York to Newcastle'.[226] William Allan saw himself as a representative of the 'wealthiest family and most respectable family in the County'.[227] He had just inherited from his uncle George Allan the property of Blackwell Grange in Durham. George, moreover, had been a prominent member of the Society of Antiquaries. Wealth and knowledge disposed Allan to be an eminent part of the Commoners. Robert Foote admitted that his property was below £600 yet thought that his family history deserved to be mentioned. His mother was the sister of the first baronet, Horace Mann, fifty years a diplomat at the court of Tuscany, and she was also linked to the Revd James Cornwallis, bishop of Lichfield and later fourth earl.[228]

There were several prominent landowners in the West Indies: the Ricketts and the Sullivans in Jamaica or the Senhouses in Barbados. George Ricketts, Thomas's father, had been His Majesty's attorney in Jamaica and a member of the Honourable Council in the island. On returning to England, he settled at Ashford Hall near Ludlow and Combe in Herefordshire.[229] The elder branch of the Senhouses invested in Cumberland in 'the flourishing town of Maryport', from which coal and iron were exported.[230] The Senhouses and alternatively the 'Sewynhouses' or the 'Sevenhouses' had been established in the county since at least Richard I although their grants were 'without date'.[231] The present proprietor, Humphrey Senhouse is presented by Burke as 'having inherited the antiquarian skill and hospitality of his ancestor, John Senhouse, the friend of Camden'.[232] Their involvement in the West Indies is hardly mentioned. Thomas Fowler, Joseph Hosken, and John Newton Lane also figured among the list of the families compensated for the abolition of slavery. John Hosken took the name Harper under the will of his father-in-law William Harper. William Harper (1749–1815) was a major slave-trader in Liverpool with fifty-two voyages between 1784 and 1799 and left £7,000 at his death. As for Lane, not a word is mentioned about his colonial property, although he resided in the West Indies; he was depicted instead as a landed gentleman from Kings Bromley in Staffordshire and whose first ancestor—Adam de Lone—was again 'without date'.[233] Unsurprisingly, the volume did not contain one reference to 'slaves' or 'slavery'. The West Indies are mentioned in relation with the heroic naval battles which took place against the European enemies.

Also present in the first volume were a great many collaterals to noble families: Edmund Lechmere-Charlton (Lord Lechmere), Arthur Aylmer (Lord Aylmer), George Danvers (Lord Lanesborough), Thomas-Henry Lister (Lord Ribblesdale),

---

[226] CA, vol. 57, case 258.   [227] 19 Oct. 1828, CA, vol. 56, case 7.
[228] 15 Sept. 1828, CA, BC, vol. 56, case 182.   [229] *Commoners* (1833), 22.
[230] CA, vol. 58, case 484. See their papers in the Cumbria Archives Center; *Commoners* (1833), 238.
[231] *Commoners* (1833), 218.   [232] Ibid.
[233] *Commoners* (1833), 174. Alan Howard, *The Lane Inheritance: Kings Bromley and Barbados* (Kings Bromley, 2011). <https://www.ucl.ac.uk/lbs/person/view/2927>.

158 SELLING ANCESTRY

William Wyndham (Lord Egremont), Simon Yorke (Lord Hardwicke). One could add a few celebrities such as David Ricardo, whose father was introduced as 'a gentleman of Jewish origin', a member of the Stock Exchange and 'writer upon Finance', and 'whose most important production was his treatise upon *Political Economy and Taxation*, a work said to rank with the celebrated *Wealth of Nations* by Adam Smith'.[234] Ricardo was a prominent spokesperson in favour of the abolition of the Corn Laws, another aspect of the reformist agenda which was quietly presented in the volume as a positive policy. In his scathing review of *The Commoners*, Sir Egerton Brydges—along with attacking the Jews—also referred to the shortcomings of Adam Smith as he reflected on 'the moral and political effect' of his theories.[235] Smith's ideas were accused of being the driving force behind Pitt's promotion of manufactures and free trade at the expense of the nobility. The end of the Corn Laws would prove to be the last episode in the destruction of the landed gentry.

After the commercial success of the first volume—three re-editions in 1833, 1834, 1835—came the second, third, and fourth volumes, from 1835 to 1838: 1,154 families in total. Much to Burke's surprise: 'the circulation of the book has surpassed and is surpassing the utmost that could have been anticipated [...]. The work has experienced much favour while contributions valuable and interesting have poured into me from all quarters of the kingdom.'[236] Families in the latter volumes were less likely to hold high positions in the county (MP, high sheriff) than those of the first volume but were still large landowners and mostly JPs, deputy-lieutenants, and clergymen. Many articles included a celebration of the county magistrates and their social standing. George Whieldon, a Staffordshire JP, wrote that he had 'the gratification of receiving from his friends and neighbours, in 1826, an elegant silver candelabrum, value one hundred guineas, "as a small tribute" expressive of their sense of his able and upright discharge of the responsible duties of the magistracy'.[237] The third volume was presented as a work of 'national importance [...]not a mere biographical history of wealthy or high-born commoners, it will provide an interesting account of many English worthies who have been eminent in the art either of war or peace and whose names are intertwined with the most glorious and valuable records of their country'.[238] The latter definition was highly flexible and allowed an even larger definition of gentry. It includes a hotchpotch of social profiles which defies any classification. Wealth, offices, and the connection to a prominent political figure could be vindicated. Among the many profiles was Charles Collinson, whose father spent 35 years in the EIC and whose uncle Peter had been a member of various antiquarian societies (London, Berlin, Stockholm). Collinson added that his

---

[234] *Commoners* (1833), 373.

[235] Ancient Country Gentlemen of England', *Fraser's Magazine*, vol. 7 (June 1833), 633, 643.

[236] Burke to Phillipps, 23 July 1834, MS Phillipps-Robinson, Bod. Lib., MS c 450, fol. 206.

[237] *Commoners* (1836), vol. 3, 116.   [238] *New Monthly* (1838), vol. 4, 507.

uncle corresponded with scientists such as Franklin, who sent him his first *Essays on Electricity*.[239] Edward Esdaile came from a Huguenot family who escaped Louis XIV's persecution and settled in London. His father William is described as 'an eminent banker in the City of London'.[240] Also a London banker, he invested in Jamaica (Carrick Folye estate, Trelawney) and appeared on the list of claimants in 1833.[241] As in the first volume, the West Indies planters could be traced back through their property: men such as the Walronds, Werges, Willises, and Pennants. For instance, the first Pennant to arrive in Jamaica in 1655 was a military officer. As usual, it was the zeal of the Pennants for the royal cause which compelled the family to emigrate. The house was plundered and they were forced to live on a bag of oatmeal. Most of the narrative is dedicated to Thomas Pennant, the 'celebrated naturist and traveller', member of the Royal Society of Uppsala and of London, in contrast to their presence in the West Indies, which is merely touched upon.[242] In their 1736 probate, the Pennants owned 610 slaves, of whom 324 were recorded as male and 286 as female. Eighty-seven were listed as boys, girls, or children.[243] Along with being MP for Saltash and then Sudbury, from 1825 to 1832, Bethell Walrond had inherited some estates in Antigua from his mother's family, the Codringtons.[244]

At last, a well-established literary reputation was accepted by Burke as a legitimate claim. From 'Kenwyn, near Truro', the Revd Richard Polwhele wondered why Burke had not sent him a form: 'Mr Polwhele has seen in the hands of several of his neighbours Mr Bourkes' prospectus of the Commons of England and cannot express his surprise (as the representant of the most ancient and not many generations ago the most opulent family in Cornwall) that no such paper has reached him.'[245] In the provincial literary world, information travelled fast and Polwhele could not help voicing his frustration at being unknown to Burke. Though he could not qualify as knight of the shire, he argued that he had corresponded with Sir Walter Scott and acted for thirty years as a Justice of the Peace. 'An anti-Jacobin Church and King reactionary', he made a name for himself by expressing strong views against the radicals and the Methodists.[246] In his letter, he provided a long account of his deeds, which convinced Burke of his important local status. Polwhele felt unjustly treated by Burke as he had been particularly active in promoting a better historical knowledge of Cornwall and

---

[239] CA, vol. 56, case 110; *Commoners* (1835), vol. 2, 539.   [240] *Commoners* (1836), vol. 3, 606.

[241] *Legacies of British Slave-ownership* project. <https://www.ucl.ac.uk/lbs/person/view/14668>.

[242] *Commoners* (1836), vol. 3, 33–5.

[243] On the considerable wealth of the Pennants, see Christley Petley (ed.), *Rethinking the Fall of the Planter Class* (London, 2017).

[244] *Commoners* (1835), vol. 2, 557–60.   [245] 21 Nov. 1828, CA, vol. 58, case 435.

[246] For a balanced opinion on his career and his poetical works, see Dafydd Moore: 'Polwhele, for all his apparently old-fashioned views and values, creates an imagined national community and deploys what is more usual to think of as a modern, secular imaginative construct in order to offer an essentially religious defence of traditional social order', *Richard Polwhele and Romantic Culture: The Politics of Reaction and the Poetics of Place* (London, 2021), 16.

160 SELLING ANCESTRY

Devon through many poetic and antiquarian publications (*The Influence of Local Attachment with Respect to Home*, 1796; *A History of Devonshire*, 1797; *A History of Cornwall*, 1803). He felt that his impecuniousness should be counterbalanced by his illustrious ancestry and his literary achievements. To further oblige Burke, Polwhele was willing to send him a copy of his latest work, *Traditions and Recollections*, published by John Nichols & Son in 1826, a work which contained a selection of letters sent by various celebrities such as Sir Walter Scott, Sir Isaac Heard, or Erasmus Darwin. It was depicted by John Nichols as 'honest vindication of a literary character, which has either been unaccountably neglected, or unfeelingly calumniated'.[247] He wanted to convince Burke that he still had some connections with the London literary world. An old clergyman retired in his remote Cornish land, Polwhele was keen to maintain his reputation on a national stage. In its inclusion of rising individuals and declining worthies, *The Commoners* displayed a considerable range of trajectories.

Those in, those left out

In the course of the publication, many other correspondents warned Burke against the risk of an overly inclusive approach which would debase the value of his *Commoners*. Edward Littleton, whose name appeared in the first volume, criticized Burke for relying excessively on the Sheriff's Court Rolls and the rolls of the Justices of the Peace.[248] These lists contained many families not resident in the county and many poor clergymen living in manufacturing districts, modest attorneys, and many 'manufacturers, scarcely of respectable connexion'.[249] Burke's scheme would attract mainly 'residents of low birth & connexion for the sake of giving their names a better repute than belongs to them'.[250] Public offices such as sheriff or JP were not a source of significant income if they were not paired with a large landed fortune. With regard to Staffordshire, Littleton went on to suggest 'a list of such persons now residing in this county as may be considered representative of gentleman families, qualified to become county member'.[251] From Devon, the clergyman and magistrate Holland Coham, who was in the first volume, provided Burke with a list of fifty names from the 'true' gentry in Devon, and he volunteered to 'look over your list of the families in this obscure county [...] in which I live'.[252] He feared that, given the number of 'people who

---

[247] Richard Polwhele, *Traditions and Recollections: Domestic, Clerical and Literary* (London, 1826), advertisement by John Nichols.

[248] See his notes on the lists printed in the *London Gazette*, CA, vol. 58.

[249] CA, vol. 57, case 319.   [250] Ibid.   [251] Ibid.

[252] William Arundell (Lifton Park), Joseph Basset (Watermouth House, Ilfracombe), Lewis Buck (Daddow, Bideford), George Acland Barbor (Fremington, Barnstaple), James Wentworth Buller (Downes, Crediton), Edmund P. Bastard (Kitley house), etc. Coham to Burke, 13 July 1828, CA, BC, vol. 56, case 96.

have made their money and are pushing their noses into society God Knows how, you must make up your mind to send forth some twenty volumes to the world instead of two'.[253] He also provided the pedigree of his mother from the Bickfords of Dunsland and added that his younger brother was a deputy-lieutenant in the county. Later, in October, he insisted on meeting Burke at the Russell Hotel or at Colburn's bookshop in order to show him all his 'papers relative to the families in Devon'.[254] It seems hardly a coincidence that among his list, several families had already written to Burke to recommend their neighbours as well, such as William Harris Arundell, Henry-George Cary, Paul Treby, Richard Tuckfield, Bethell Walrond, and John Aysford Wise. The latter, recorder for Totnes and a deputy-lieutenant, commented that 'it would be almost impossible to have a perfect list'.[255] Like Coham, John A. Wise was in a position to guide Burke since his family had 'a direct descent from father to son during the space of 728 years', an outstanding claim which he supported by sending a printed pedigree.[256] From Hereford, John J. Garbett Walsham agreed to help Burke in identifying the main families. According to Walsham's account, his ancestors descended from the Flavii and landed with the Conqueror, finally establishing themselves 600 years earlier at the manor of Knill.[257] On receiving Burke's list two months later, Walsham added a zero to the new names and a cross to only twelve 'ancient' families.[258] The fact that Walsham received a baronetcy in 1831 further reinforced the value of his assistance. As had happened in 1740 with Wotton, some prominent members in the counties had acted as self-proclaimed guides in 1800 for Betham. Now, from a quantitative point of view, Burke's correspondents were more widely scattered all over Britain, though as usual the northern counties were over-represented, notably Yorkshire, Lancashire, as well as the area of East Anglia (Map 3.3).

Even though, according to many correspondents, *The Commoners* should have been pruned more extensively, Burke had in fact filtered out many families. Out of his 397 correspondents, 236 failed to figure in the volume, although many were reintegrated in the second edition in 1846 by Bernard Burke. There had been, then, a selection process, though it is sometimes difficult to fathom its criteria.

In order to account for those left out, four rough categories have been established. A first group includes those who claimed prestigious forebears but who willingly disclosed their impecunious state. For instance, William Turbutt lamented that his family was 'formerly of great distinction in the county of York [...] the estate possessed by them there was wasted by an ancestor addicted

---

[253] Coham to Burke, 9 Sept. 1828, ibid.; see also *Commoners* (1833), 459.
[254] CA, BC, vol. 56, case 96, 14 Oct. 1828.
[255] Wise to Burke, 13 Dec. 1828, CA, BC, vol. 58, case 609.
[256] See the printed pedigree: *Commoners* (1833), 21.
[257] Walsham to Burke, 22 July 1828, CA, BC, vol. 58, case 578.   [258] Ibid., 12 Sept. 1828.

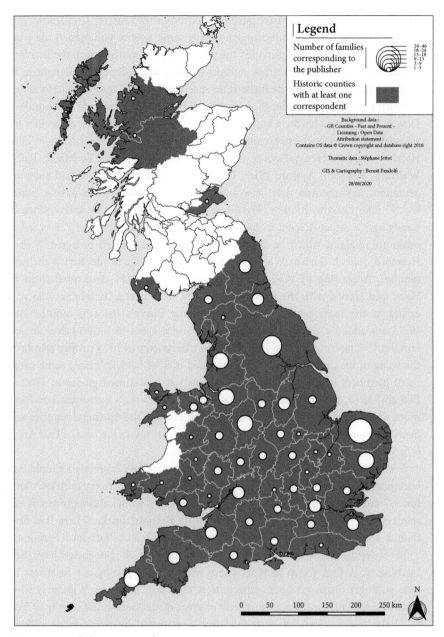

Map 3.3 Burke's correspondents

to gaming'.[259] Similarly Captain Edward William Leyborne-Popham alluded to his family's pedigree in the College of Arms, though he claimed to have

---

[259] Turbutt to Burke, 5 Aug. 1828, ibid., case 560. Turbutt was no longer living in the family estate of Ogston Hall. See their family papers in the Derbyshire County Council D37.

HUNDREDS OF CUSTOMERS   163

lost everything through 'the extravagance' of his grandfather.[260] The latter was William L. Leyborne, governor-general of Grenada, who married Anne Popham, the heiress of Littlecote. Although his origins derived from Sir John Popham, Lord Chief Justice in the time of Elizabeth, he was reluctant to have his ancestry published, considering it was now of little consequence.[261] William Spurdens, who presented himself as a humble vicar, wrote: 'You will hardly find me to belong to the class of personages to whom your work is intended to refer. As I believe I am professionally unqualified for a seat in Parliament. My property in land also, is not much.'[262] Richard B. Podmore was from an Irish family, established in Chester: 'my father Richard, from very humble parents, was a clergyman' while he himself was the youngest of the three sons with very few resources, being merely a small 'lay-freeholder'.[263] William Roberts, from Bromley in Kent, wrote that he came from a very ancient family, mentioned by Lambarde in 1574 and in Hasted's county history but suspected that he would not be included as 'my landed property is very inconsiderable'.[264] However, despite his financial predicaments, Roberts expressed some hope of being included by Burke for the various anecdotes he provided.

A second group omitted to refer to their modest incomes but tried to make up for them by describing fantastic pedigrees. George Geary Bennis from Limerick informed Burke that his ancestors came from Thermopolis and then, after passing through Grenada and Guyenne, had followed William in his Conquest. Hoping to be incorporated, he added an extract from d'Hozier's *Armorial Général* which linked him to the Bennis family, and another from the *Dormant Peerage* by Christopher Banks linking him to the 'Beneses'.[265] He sent him a page from *Le Dictionnaire Biographique Universel* with a narrative on Anne-François Benit (1796–1825), a noble author and writer on the European army (*Idée d'un jeune officier sur l'état militaire*, 1820).[266] Bennis saw himself as a genuine scion of an ancient European nobility from immemorial times. In fact, however, he worked as a grocer, librarian, and also occasionally as a literary editor. When he wrote to Burke, he was living in Paris, where he published different works such as *Traveller's Pocket Diary* and a *Treatise on Life Assurance*.[267] Another customer, Henry Mountford, flatly stated that 'with respect to an account of my Family I must refer you to the History of England as I am Heir at Law (or in other words) next of kin on the male line to Simon de Montford'.[268] Edward Latimer, a solicitor,

---

[260] Popham to Burke, 23 Nov. 1828, CA, BC, vol. 58, case 429.

[261] Part of the family papers on the years 1582–1650 were later published by the Historical Manuscript Commission Report on the manuscripts of F. W. Leyborne-Popham, esq., Littlecote, co. Wilts (Norwich, 1889).

[262] Spurdens to Burke, 23 July 1828, CA, BC, vol. 58, case 508.

[263] Podmore to Burke, vol. 58, case 436.   [264] Roberts to Burke, 10 July 1828, vol. 58, case 466.

[265] Bennis to Burke, vol. 56, case 31.   [266] Ibid.

[267] W. Axon, N. Banerji, 'Bennis, George Geary', *ODNB*, 2004. Retrieved 25 Mar. 2020 from <https://doi-org.janus.bis-sorbonne.fr/10.1093/ref:odnb/2132>.

[268] Mountford to Burke, CA, BC, vol. 57, case 379.

164 SELLING ANCESTRY

wanted to establish his link to Bishop Latimer, as his 'uncle the Rev. Rob. Walker, an eminent man and head of the church always told me that we were descendants of the Bishop Latimer'.[269] Henry Pilkington, a barrister from Doncaster, complained of having been left out of the consultation, whereas his family 'is one of the oldest in the kingdom and which has flourished in the brightest periods of British chivalry'.[270] It seems that Burke ignored his request but 'Henry Pilkington, Esq., Park Lane' already appears in a wide range of directories such as *An Authentic alphabetical list of the nobility, clergy and gentry* (1817), *The General Short-Horned Herd-book* (1822), *Paterson's Roads* (1822), and Pigot and Co.'s *National commercial directory* (1829). As for Charles Clifton, a small Welsh owner, he claimed to be a lineal descendant of Brychan, prince of Brycheiniog, a fifth-century Welsh saint who brought up many children who later became saints in Cornwall, Ireland, and Brittany.[271]

A third group was composed of individuals who did not try to devise an outstanding ancestry or to hide their industrial interests. Raisbeck Lucock Bragg asserted that he had 'no long genealogy to boast of' and 'suppose[d] it useless to say, his great grand-father has prosper'd in trade and established his family' by becoming high sheriff of Cumberland 'in the year of the last Scotch rebellion'.[272] Richard Swallow was a comb maker in Sheffield and proudly mentioned the first in his line, Richard Swallow, a yeoman who died in 1703 at the age of 101.[273] Richard Llewellin, a student at Lincoln's Inn, informed Burke that he had inherited property in Bristol, where his father had built a brewery, and his mother was the daughter of Levi Ames, a prominent alderman.[274] William Jessop notified Burke that he came from a modest Irish family. His grandfather was a government officer in the dockyards of Plymouth though his current wealth enabled him to be part of the *Commoners*: 'although I have property in land sufficient for qualification referred to, yet my property consists principally in extending the coal mines situated at Butterley'.[275] He went on to explain how his father had established on the estate a foundry and a forge, describing him as an 'eminent civil engineer' who had been involved in the construction of the Bristol docks, the City Canal, and the Caledonian canal. William Jessop Jr, also an engineer who built Vauxhall Bridge, strangely did not appear in the *Commoners*. John Brindley of Union Hall in Staffordshire reminded Burke that his grandfather John was the projector of navigable canals. As well as ungentrified industrialists, some prominent scientists were left out. John Lind introduced himself as a physician of the Royal Hospital of

[269] Latimer to Burke, ibid., vol. 57, case 303.
[270] Pilkington to Burke, 20 Aug. 1828, ibid., vol. 58, case 424.
[271] Clifton to Burke, ibid., vol. 56, case 92. On Brychan, see John T. Koch, *The Celts: History, Life, and Culture* (Oxford, 2012), vol. 1, 135.
[272] Bragg to Burke, CA, BC, vol. 56, case 52.
[273] Swallow to Burke, Oct. 1828, ibid., vol. 58, case 534.
[274] Llienwellin to Burke, 21 Nov. 1828, ibid., vol. 57, case 323.
[275] Jessop to Burke, ibid., vol. 57, case 285.

HUNDREDS OF CUSTOMERS   165

Haslar, one of the first hospitals designed for marines and sailors. His father's fame came from his discovery of the means of freshening seawater and of combating 'scurvy and diseases of hot climate'.[276] Even if the majority of barristers and clergymen in this group probably called themselves gentlemen, if they did not have sufficient land they were excluded from the compilation. As a fellow of the London Society of Antiquaries and of the Linnean Society, Thomas Walford hoped that 'the publication will embrace the great majority of families in the Kingdom as I should not wish to appear with a few to affect notoriety'.[277] Walford insisted on the need to incorporate a large category of landed gentlemen as it would interest a larger public and prevent the *Commoners* from being seen as snobbish and exclusive. Despite his reputation as a prominent antiquary, it is telling that Walford did not figure in the compilation. Walford had told Burke that his landed property was very limited: 'The Estates formerly in the family have been divided into so many different branches that I have but little left.'[278]

A fourth category could be seen as oddities, for they presented all the signs of well-established political elites. David Pugh, a tea trader who wished to be recognized as descended from the Cadwalladers of Llanerchydol, was an MP and deputy-lieutenant in Montgomeryshire.[279] George Scholey, a distiller and a former Lord Mayor of London in 1812–13, was also left out of the *Commoners*, a decision which is very hard to account for.[280] Similarly, Horace Twiss, a prominent Tory MP, is strangely absent. It could perhaps be explained by his opposition to the Reform scheme and his view that 'the disfranchisement of boroughs, he argued, was "a violation" of the constitutional settlement of 1688'.[281] However, this explanation is not convincing given that some Whig MPs are not included either. James Mangles, son of a ship chandler and oilman of Wapping, was elected in 1831 and was a fervent supporter of the Grey ministry's reform bill.[282] Other MPs, too, were not mentioned, such as Lewis Weston Dillwyn, Joseph Hume, or John Cheesment Severn, but then again it would be adventurous to account extensively for the absence or the integration of all of Burke's correspondents.

The first edition of Burke's *Commoners* was in many ways a work of compromise, designed to satisfy the moderate core of the political class around the themes of rank and property. He celebrated the gentry as a bulwark against the threat of social disorder, insisting on the authority of the local and county magistrates. Though a Catholic himself, Burke avoided mentioning the Emancipation Act, an omission that may have alienated some High Church customers like Evelyn John Shirley, who was violently opposed to the act. He omitted referring to the debate on slavery, publishing instead the accounts of both

---

[276] Lind to Burke, ibid., case 320.   [277] Walford to Burke, Aug. 1828, ibid., vol. 58, case 579.
[278] Ibid., 12 Sept. 1928.   [279] Pugh to Burke, ibid., case 445.
[280] Scholey was the subject of several caricatures notably by Charles Williams, *Benefits of a Plentiful Harvest* (1813).
[281] Twiss to Burke, CA, BC, vol. 58, case 562.   [282] Mangles to Burke, ibid., vol. 57, case 354.

166 SELLING ANCESTRY

slave owners and abolitionists such as Gamaliel Lloyd or Harbord Harbord. By the same token, as the industrialists and the monied interests generated great antipathy from the public, Burke either eluded such men's activities or else filtered them out by using anecdotes. His appeal to Norman ancestry, followed up by many customers in a frenzy of gothic inventiveness, was instrumental in creating a common narrative. He demonstrated that aristocracy was a distinct class and yet closely interwoven with the whole framework of British society.

Burke's considerable surviving correspondence poses different interpretative challenges from that of either Wotton or Betham. No clear definition existed of who could be inserted in the directories. Many correspondents were dismissed as being insufficiently endowed or reputed. Eventually, after 1838, the term 'Commoners' came to be seen as an awkward label and it was later replaced by the expression of 'Landed Gentry' in the later editions, whose commercial success testified to the delicate balance that Burke had managed to achieve within a polarized landed elite. For the second edition, which he prepared from 1832 onwards, he also changed his way of classifying families, hitherto by order of prominence: he promised that from now on 'those who communicate earliest with the Editor obtain priority of insertion'.[283] This led to a much more heterogeneous *Landed Gentry* and a growing presence of mercantile and industrialist interests.

The success and the extent of family involvement depended on the ability of the compilers and publishers not only to draw attention to their work's preparation but also to gain the customers' trust throughout the editing process. They had to rely on intermediaries in the counties who would spread the news and vouch for the relevance of a new directory. Hence each publication generated its own particular reaction and a different kind of participation from the public. The letters sent to the publishers reflected the political claims and self-justifications of different parts of the social elite—notably Wotton's sometimes Jacobite Restoration baronets, Betham's Pittite supporters, or Burke's slave-trading country gentlemen and industrialists.

The three case-studies each put forward different conceptions of memory and honour. For the majority of baronets involved in Wotton's undertaking, their centres of interest mostly focused on the first British revolution. While newly created baronets might be unwilling to come forward, well-established county gentry, especially in the north, were keen to link the acquisition of their titles to their families' financial sacrifices and to military deeds of the 1640s. This memory dominated their narrative even to the point of obstructing other aspects, such as wealth, professions, and political activities, as well as the divisive 'Glorious Revolution'. They were remote from the core government in London and saw their seventeenth-century titles as a source of pride and independence.

---

[283] Prospectus, 'A genealogical and heraldic history of the Landed Gentry', *The Literary Gazette: A Weekly Journal of Literature, Science, and the Fine Arts*, 21 July 1832.

Unlike Wotton, the Revd William Betham did not rely on extensive commercial networks and his *Baronetage* (1801–5) was financed through subscriptions. Most correspondents had been elevated by the younger Pitt and were eager to stress their current contributions in the struggle against France and expansion of the Empire. They belonged to the new British elite which was also strengthened by the integration of the old Irish colony by the Act of Union with Ireland. Most of their narratives were closely linked to recent decades and dealt with the seventeenth-century confessional and political divisions with more equanimity. Republican as well as Catholic and Jacobite families were incorporated in a patriotic and inclusive memory.

John Burke's *History of the Commoners* (1832–6) differed in many ways from Wotton's and Betham's *Baronetages*. His plan was to create a directory of the untitled gentry as a sequel to his former compilations dedicated to peers and baronets. He saw all three guides as forming an entity, that of a new aristocratic class distinguished by its landed wealth and political positions from the emerging urban middle and working classes. The Reform Act reinforced this distinction. Narratives about the Norman Conquest and the Middle Ages also contributed to a cultural divide. While the perception of the past was considered essential by the publishers' correspondents, they did not share the same historical interest.

Despite their own specificity, each directory aimed at bridging a gap between the old and new elites and was conciliatory in nature. In the three case-studies, local and regional identification were also deeply engrained and were instrumental in the data-gathering. Even though it has been demonstrated that in terms of economic and bonds, the 'county community' was a myth, as the property market and matrimonial alliances far exceeded the territorial and social limits of the counties, sub-national networks and affinities remained resilient throughout the modern period. County histories were a bottomless source of inspiration for the gentry even though they gravitated to the metropolis.

4

Family Ties and Publishers' Enquiries

Far from reflecting an intense collaboration among relatives, most of the innumerable pedigrees found in the directories were in fact supplied by a few individuals. Martine Segalen noted a common pattern, in that for each generation there was one distinctive member in charge of the family's past.[1] The Lloyds of Welcombe provide a striking example of the limited consultation that took place despite appearances to the contrary. We saw above that Gamaliel Lloyd had been one of Betham's key contributors for his *New Baronetage* in 1800. Later, it was his son, William Horton Lloyd, 'Esq., FLS of Bedford Place' who replied enthusiastically to John Burke's inquiry in 1828.[2] He imposed himself as the unique storyteller of the Lloyds of Welcombe by producing a transformed narrative which could read from both a vertical and a horizontal perspective.

First, he distanced himself from his paternal account by endorsing his remote mercantile origins. His father had insisted on his alliances, notably his brother-in-law's baronetcy and his connections with several northern baronets. His son chose instead to draw attention to the Lloyds in Leeds and Manchester. He was more interested in his seventeenth-century ancestors, Benjamin of the London company of Painter Stainers and his younger brother Gamaliel (d. 1661). Judging it impolite, Burke, however, failed to mention Benjamin Lloyd's professional activities. The latter established himself in Manchester as a 'merchant manufacturer', and it was only after two generations that George, born in 1708, took a degree at Cambridge, became a fellow of the Royal Society, and later invested in a country estate outside Manchester.[3] His eminent grandfather may have eclipsed his modest forebears but for Burke's *Commoners*, William Horton chose instead to reaffirm his urban and mercantile origins.[4] While many facts and anecdotes were devotedly transmitted from one generation to the next, it was often the case that narratives went through a continuous process of reconfiguration (Tree 4.1).

---

[1] 'In every genealogy, there is a relative who can be seen as a pivot, a kind of junction point in the structure, either because he is important from the point of view of such matters or because of his knowledge of the ramifications of the family tree.' Martine Segalen, *Historical Anthropology of the Family* (Cambridge, 1986), 90.

[2] 29 Sept. 1828, CA, BC, vol. 57, case 324.

[3] 31 Jan. 1829, CA, BC, vol. 57, case 324. See his handsome portrait by Isaac Seeman (1734) with a silk velvet coat and floral waistcoat. Manchester Art Gallery, accession number 1982.157.

[4] However, he informed Burke that, if needs be, he was also able to provide abundant material about the baronetcy of his great uncle and to 'furnish several alterations and corrections for the next edition of your baronetage', 31 Jan. 1829, CA, BC, vol. 57, case 324.

Selling Ancestry: Family Directories and the Commodification of Genealogy in Eighteenth-Century Britain. Stéphane Jettot, Oxford University Press. © Stéphane Jettot 2023. DOI: 10.1093/oso/9780192865960.003.0005

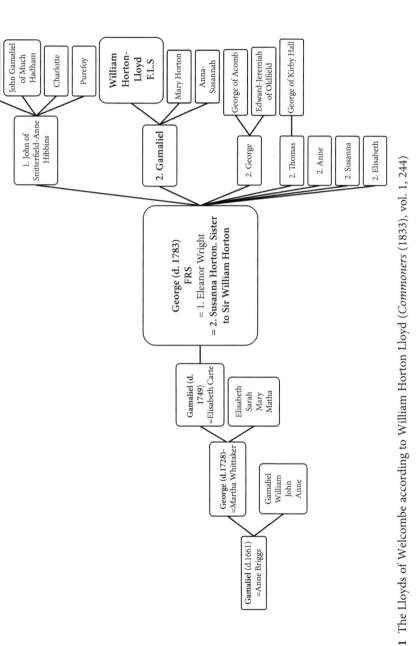

Tree 4.1 The Lloyds of Welcombe according to William Horton Lloyd (*Commoners* (1833), vol. 1, 244)

170 SELLING ANCESTRY

Furthermore, William Horton, though from the junior branch, provided an account for all his collaterals. Cautiously at first, he claimed to have many 'particulars of the families of four cousins, Mr Lloyd of Welcombe, Mr Lloyd of Much Hadham, Mr Lloyd of Acomb & Mr Lloyd of Oldfield Hall' but did not 'like to send them to Mr Burke, without their permission & revisal'.[5] He waited first for the assent of the elder line, the Lloyds of Welcombe and Hadham, from the first union of his grandfather George with Eleonor Wright. His elder cousins had inherited the properties in Warwickshire and Lancashire and both had served as deputy lieutenant and high sheriff. In the published article, the Lloyds of Welcombe and their coat of arms featured in the first position along with the name of the current representative, John-Gamaliel, then high sheriff for Warwickshire. Eventually, however, either because the elder branch failed to add any detailed information or because their contribution was ignored by William Horton, the space dedicated to them was somewhat dwarfed by that filled by their younger cousin.

William Horton only mentioned in passing John Gamaliel's father, who had been a fellow of the Royal Society and the first acquirer of the estate of Welcombe. He could have written in much detail about the property: how it was transformed by John and his eldest son George into a magnificent place, and how it was celebrated in various poems.[6] In *The Gentleman's Magazine*, it was reported that many remarkable discoveries had been made there: old skeletons and weapons, including flints comparable to those engraved by Dugdale.[7] By the same token, Horton also failed to write about John Gamaliel's mother and his two sisters, Charlotte and Purefoy. Charlotte, by marrying the Revd Thomas Ward, gave an heir to the Welcombe estate.[8] Her husband in 1828 was already a well-established architectural historian who had accumulated a considerable collection of documents on Warwickshire houses.[9] Such details are usually highly valued and singularly enrich a narrative like nothing else, yet they were discarded by William Horton. Instead, he transmitted many more particulars about his own uncles, aunts, and siblings. Regarding his uncles, George and Thomas, he stated that the former would not reply to his letters and that the latter deemed 'his landed property was not sufficient to bring him within the class you propose to give an account of'.[10] George was a lawyer from Manchester, Thomas was a Leeds merchant and councilman in the corporation. As they chose not to contribute,

[5] Horton to Burke, 29 Sept. 1828, ibid.
[6] John Jordan, *Welcombe Hills, near Stratford Upon Avon. A Poem, Historical and Descriptive* (London, 1827).
[7] *GM*, vol. 64 (1794), 505.
[8] See a highly detailed account in John Burke, *Genealogical and Heraldic Dictionary of the Landed Gentry* (1847), vol. 1, 751.
[9] Geoffrey Tyack, 'Thomas Ward and the Warwickshire Country House', *Architectural History*, vol. 27 (1984): 534–42.
[10] Ibid.

FAMILY TIES AND PUBLISHERS' ENQUIRIES 171

their nephew had considerable leeway in writing his story. Between the county magnates of the elder branch and the middle sorts from the second union, William Horton produced a bespoke narrative of the Lloyds. A member of various London societies (*The Royal Literary Society, The British Association for the Advancement of Science, The Linnaean Society,* and *The Society for the Encouragement of Arts, Manufactures, and Commerce*), he had the resources and social connections to develop his own hybrid account of the gentrified and professional branches of his family in which he took centre stage position. He also made an unsolicited suggestion for a new interpretation of the coat of arms and crest, according to 'the old drawing' in his possession.[11]

The example of the Lloyds introduces the main theme of this chapter, namely the distinctive role of certain relatives in the crafting of narratives at the expense of others. In the 1830s, compared to previous editions, genealogical directories were no longer focused exclusively on the elder male line, as their making relied on the participation of many collaterals who blurred the conventional order in the kinship network.[12] This is not to say that the heads of families disappeared altogether. They remained the central figures and were still the first person to be contacted throughout the period. However, for pragmatic as well as commercial reasons, with or without the heir's consent, many other members got involved. Lloyd's article reflected Burke's inclusive policy, namely, to generate 'so vast a portion of family history as perhaps the annals of no other country could produce'.[13] William Horton's description held a central position even though he was from the second branch. Such an editorial strategy was prone to attract criticism. These all-encompassing compilations were accused of obscuring differences between elder lines and collaterals. Alexander Maitland, the elder son of the first baronet of Westerham in Kent made this point forcefully:

It could be clearer if the editor were numbering the first generation from the head of families with roman numbers, the second with Arabic, those of the third putting a broad black line [...]. By distinguishing each generation in this manner, it will prevent (as it is often the case) our confounding aunts & uncles with their nephews & nieces, the children of their senior brother and sisters & will have the advantage also of showing you at once by how many generations the individual is removed from the head of the family.[14]

---

[11] 29 Sept. 1828, CA, BC, vol. 57, case 324.

[12] On the rise of a 'kinship-hot society, one where enormous energy was invested in maintaining and developing extensive, reliable, and well-articulated structures of exchange among connected families over many generations', see David Warren Sabean, Simon Teuscher, and Jon Mathieu (eds), *Kinship in Europe: Approaches to Long-Term Development (1300–1900)* (Oxford, 2007), 3; For a critical review of the notion: François-Joseph Ruggiu, 'Histoire de la parenté ou anthropologie historique de la parenté? Autour de *Kinship in Europe*', *Annales de démographie historique*, vol. 119, no. 1 (2010): 223–56.

[13] Burke quoted by a reviewer in *The Times*, 28 Feb. 1837.

[14] Maitland to Burke, Dec. 1826, CA, WC 62, fol. 53.

172 SELLING ANCESTRY

Maitland felt family representatives were unfairly treated. The *Annual Peerage* published from 1826 onwards came closer to Maitland's wishes: first the peer, then his children, his siblings and their posterity, then uncles and aunts and other collaterals.[15] But the latter was only a reference book and did not supply any narratives or anecdotes. With regard to Burke, while the head of the family was still displayed on the front page, the core of the narrative was provided by whoever agreed to contribute to the article. Publishers depended on the goodwill of a variety of family members even though their participation was unequally acknowledged. How and why did some protagonists come to the fore at the expense of others? Answering this question may explain why family trees did not fit well in these directories, as they were more likely to expose these informal arrangements. Comparisons between the published version and the correspondence enable us to better identify the key contributors. It is essential to reflect on the language used by the correspondents and the ways in which they adapted to received norms in a given situation. Moreover, these letters shed light on the many protagonists who were made invisible in the publishing process, whether they were cadets, uncles, women, or collaterals. Another aspect worthy of attention relates to the conflicts which arose during the enquiries. Family members would often collaborate in a constructive and affectionate manner as they were linked by mutual obligation and a sense of shared identity. However, their letters betrayed strong resentment and sometimes led the publishers to get involved in lengthy litigation.

1. The 'fountain-head' and the publishers

It is best to start with the household's head, who was invariably portrayed as the guardian of the past. In his directories, Burke advertised first that 'information has been sought at the fountain-head' of each family.[16] It was a potent metaphor which conveyed the idea of a continuous stream of memories from the remotest ancestor to living contemporaries. As principal heirs, the heads of family were theoretically in charge of the ways in which close and distant forebears were to be remembered. They were entitled to classify and filter memories, to choose which records were worth keeping. They placed themselves in a continuous male line which sustained their privilege to inherit and transmit the name, lands, and other properties.[17] Recounting parentage and ancestry helped elder sons to formulate their family identities in terms of social status and personal worth. In the early modern period, the links between patriarchy and archival practices have often

---

[15] *The Annual peerage of the British empire* (London, 1826).

[16] Burke, *Genealogical and Heraldic dictionary of the English Peerage*, vi.

[17] Eric Ketelaar, 'The Genealogical Gaze: Family Identities and Family Archives in the Fourteenth to Seventeenth Centuries', *Libraries & the Cultural Record*, vol. 44, no. 1 (2009): 9–28.

been underlined. While young cadets and daughters moved away from the household and broke free from its legacy, the eldest son was supposed to be the custodian of collective memory and to enable its intergenerational transmission. It was both a privilege and a constraint. In the College of Arms, most of the heralds' pedigrees and grants of arms were personally signed by the family head.[18] Some, like Sir Daniel Fleming of Rydal Hall, who inherited the paternal estate at the age of 20, went even further and distinguished himself by his antiquarian skills. Being an heir and an archival expert were connected, as both related to a moral responsibility.[19] In the case of the Verneys, it was the baronets as household heads who were in charge of assembling and maintaining a large private collection of manuscripts.[20]

Family historians now consider the earlier paradigm of the declining patriarchy and the rise of the 'affective family' with great caution.[21] Despite repetitive attacks, notably from Adam Smith, heads of family were still able to enjoy many of the legal, patriarchal, and normative privileges of their forebears. Henry French has noted the resilient strength of a 'timeless, deep-level habitus of patriarchal male virtue, honour and power'.[22] By the same token, patriarchal norms in practice did not hinder many forms of accommodation and uncertainty. Both primogeniture and entail (which prevented estates from being alienated) limited what the family representative could do. Martin J. Daunton has stressed the need not to overestimate the concentration of landed property in the hands of the elder brother and the strength of his position, although the debate is far from over.[23] What is generally agreed is that, in a constant flux of change and unpredictable life cycles, family power relations were continually reconfigured. Cadets or nephews were likely to inherit the name, thus requiring memories and archives to be widely shared and commented upon among close relatives.

Keepers in chief of material and oral memories

In 1725, Wotton sent a personal letter to all living baronets, including a draft of their pedigree and a printed message, encouraging them to provide some

[18] Adrian Ailes, 'Can we trust the Genealogical Record of the Heralds' Visitations? A case study (the 1665–66 Visitation of Berkshire)', in Jettot and Lezowski (eds), *The Genealogical Enterprise*, 143–57.

[19] Alan Macfarlane, *The Justice and The Mare's Ale* (Oxford, 1982), 200.

[20] Susan E. Whyman, *Sociability and Power in Late-Stuart England: The Cultural Worlds of the Verneys 1660–1720* (Oxford, 1999).

[21] Helen Berry and Elizabeth Forster, *The Family in Early Modern England* (Cambridge, 2007), 1–4.

[22] Henry French, *Man's Estate: Landed Gentry Masculinities, c.1660–c.1900* (Oxford, 2012), 35.

[23] Martin J. Daunton, *Progress and Poverty: An Economic and Social History of Britain* (Oxford, 1995), 79; Linda Pollock, 'Rethinking Patriarchy and the Family in Seventeenth-Century England', *Journal of Family History*, vol. 23, no. 1 (1998): 3–27. Edward Bujak, while insisting on its flexibility, argues that the strength of the strict settlement should not be underestimated, *England's Rural Realms: Landholding and the Agricultural Revolution* (London, 2007), 24.

174   SELLING ANCESTRY

Table 4.1 Wotton's untitled correspondents

Cadets	Wives	Cousin	Daughter	Nephew
Erle, Edward	Blois, Jane, Boynton,	Alleyn, Marie,	Dutton,	Hildyard,
Hildyard, Christopher	Frances Charlton,	Beaumont, William	Mary	John
Middleton, Thomas	Mary D'Oyly, Susanna	Blackett, Richard		
Musgrave, James	Guldeford, Clare	Broughton,		
Osborn, Thomas		Christopher		
Twisden, Thomas		D'Oyly, Samuel		
		Freke, William		
		Hildyard, Francis		
		Tempest, Stephen		

information about the past of their families. He later insisted on the masculine value of his enterprise, dedicated to the heirs 'which are animated to a pursuit of noble and worthy actions, by seeing the examples of others and especially of their forefathers'.[24] In 1741, he celebrated the commitment of exemplary baronets, such as Sir William Egerton, for the quality of 'his collections and his draughts of arms, (from which most of the coats, in the front of the work, are engraved)'.[25] In fact, of his 151 correspondents were baronets, apart from six younger sons, five wives, eight cousins and a few others (uncle, nephew, servant).

With a few exceptions, the latter's names were not mentioned in the published version, either in the main text or in the footnotes. In demographic terms, his correspondents were middle-aged men aged 30–60, and most already had inherited their title.

In Betham's sample, the proportion of non-baronets was even smaller. Most of his correspondents had been created baronets and were eager to answer the publisher directly. He received the letters from two baronet's wives (Anne Davie, Frances Jerningham), one brother-in-law (Gamaliel Lloyd) and two cousins (Meadow Lombe, William Lygon). As for Burke, even if he tried in his advertisements to reach as many relatives as possible, his correspondents were mostly the representatives of the family. Out of almost 400 correspondents, one can find only twelve women.[26] Their dates of birth are never mentioned. Compared to Wotton's younger sample, Burke's correspondence includes a significant proportion of older correspondents, aged 40–60. As there was no title at stake, the desire to participate in Burke's project corresponded to a form of leisure for retired politicians.

If the head was too old, the responsibility was transferred to his elder son. Ann, the wife of Sir Andrew Hammond the first baronet, informed Burke that

---

[24] *The English Baronets*, i.   [25] *The English Baronetage*, vol. 1, ii.

[26] Dorothy Allanson, Sarah Barnard, Etheldred Bennett, Alexandra Campbell, Augusta Cracford, Mary Coham, Anne Dod, Blandina Harrington, Ann Norcliffe, Marie Ann Saltern, Eliza Sullivan, and Emma Tatton.

'Sir Andrew's great age prevents his taking the trouble of looking into his pedigree' and instructed him to contact his son, Rear Admiral Hammond, at Norton Lodge, 'telling him it is by his Father's desire you do so'.[27] Cadets and collaterals felt it their duty to redirect Burke's enquiry to the elder line. Robert Jenkins from Charton Hill wrote that 'the family estates are in the possession of my brother-in-law, Richard Jenkins of Bicton Hall, I have transferred your letter to him'.[28] George Deering, half-brother of the seventh baronet Sir Edward Cholmeley Deering, and uncle of the eighth baronet, though he had been 'his guardian for 17 years', asked him to send the enquiry to 'his nephew, Sir Edward Deering [who] is the head of our house and the 8th Baronet'.[29] Though they had shared the same household for many years, the uncle still believed it was his nephew's responsibility to answer. Richard Lowndes, a lieutenant in the Navy, found it 'very unreasonable to apply to every individual of a family. Your application should be made to the head of a family and not to the younger or collateral branch.'[30] The authority of the senior line was reinforced by the fact that they usually held the most important political positions. As a member of the younger branch, Richard added that the head of the elder branch, William Selby Lowndes, 'has represented his native county in parliament as four other ancestors have done'.[31] The analogy often used between the household and polity was still effective in the nineteenth century. As a well-established MP, William S. Lowndes was expected to rule over the family narrative.[32]

The authority of the heads of household was, furthermore, enhanced by the assumption that they would be in possession of the most significant archives and artefacts.[33] In fact, very few were able to send a ready-made pedigree, with a few exceptions such as John Evelyn, the son of the diarist and gardener John Evelyn (1620–1706) and also a fellow of the Royal Society. He was known to have built a 45-foot-long library at his family seat in Surrey and he dispatched Wotton a very detailed account.[34] Thomas Pope Blount of Tittenhanger gave a forty-page narrative including all the proofs one can imagine, but he drew most of his references from a 1695 printed biography of his ancestor Charles Blount.[35] Pope Blount recalled

---

[27] Hammond to Burke, 24 Nov. 1826, CA, BC, vol. 57, case 232.

[28] Robert Jenkins to Burke, 12 Aug. 1828, CA, BC, vol. 57, case 286.

[29] George Deering to Burke, 15 July 1828, CA, BC, vol. 56, case 135.

[30] Richard Lowndes to Burke, 12 Aug. 1828, CA, BC, vol. 57, case 332.   [31] Ibid.

[32] On the much-discussed notion of 'separate spheres', see the stimulating bibliographical summary by Karen Harvey, *The Little Republic: Masculinity and Domestic Authority in Eighteenth-Century Britain* (Oxford, 2012), 1–24.

[33] On the materials of memory, see Andrew Jones, *Memory and Material Culture* (Cambridge, 2007); Heather Wolfe and Peter Stallybrass, 'The Material Culture of Record-Keeping in Early Modern England', *Proceedings of the British Academy*, vol. 212 (2018): 179–208; D. Brenton Simons and Peter Benes (eds), *The Art of Family: Genealogical Artifacts in New England* (Boston, 2002).

[34] Inglis to Betham, 1804, BL, Add. MS 24120, fols 311–14.

[35] BL, Add. MS 24120, fols 78–123; *The Miscellaneous Works of Charles Blount* [...]: *To which is Prefix'd the Life of the Author* (London, 1695).

176 SELLING ANCESTRY

that Charles was a friend of the antiquaries William Dugdale and Anthony Wood and had been nicknamed the 'Socrates of ye age' for all his publications.[36] Sir Robert Harry Inglis informed Betham that he would 'call on' him 'with the little additions which may be made to the account of our family [...] and a few epitaphs on Baronets or their families which I have collected'.[37] At 18 years old, still a student in Oxford, he was already engaged in antiquarian activities, deciphering many funeral inscriptions around the family estate. Later called to the bar, he pursued the same line of interest, being elected in 1816 Recorder of Devizes and fellow of the Society of Antiquaries, being appointed Trustee of the British Museum in 1834. From the pedigree sent to Betham, Inglis published himself a more extended family account (*Sketch of the life of Sir Hugh Inglis*, 1821).[38]

To make up for their shortcomings, most heads of household tapped into accessible printed references in their libraries. As a period of increased cultural consumption, the eighteenth-century book market provided a wide gamut of historical materials. Most baronets drew the majority of their knowledge from William Camden, William Dugdale, or Peter Heylyn's *Help to English History*, which went through many editions. The young Henry Tyrwhitt (1824–94), son to Sir Thomas, second baronet prided himself on his ownership, along with 'original sources', of the whole set of *Baronetages* since the first volume in 1720:

> I have made a very considerable collection relating to the extinct baronets from original sources (I do not allude to any Baronetage in print, though I possess every one printed from 1720 to the present time).[39]

Many heads of family were in possession of manuscripts which were mentioned as 'treasures' or 'relics' and regarded as essential pieces of evidence. Among the most coveted documents were original grants of arms. Thomas Henry Lister was eager to show Burke a copy of his own pedigree certified by William Dugdale.[40] Often the ownership of ancient documents was complemented by several deictic references which testified to their familiarity with and their understanding of what they possessed. Langham Rokeby described a manuscript on his desk before him and went on to explain his scholarly activities: 'I have a book which I copied a few years ago from an ancient transcript in my possession and which I have had an opportunity of correcting from a parchment roll'.[41] Others had less precious documents though they were enriched by autographs: Sir Robert Adam from London alluded to a copy of 'a printed sermon dedicated to my father' by

---

[36] BL, Add. MS 24120, fol. 78.   [37] BL, Add. MS 21033, fol. 48.

[38] *GM*, June 1855, vol. 43, 640–1.

[39] Henry Tyrwhitt to Burke, 22 Apr. 1836, BL, Add. MS 16569, fol. 214. His father was represented by Robert Muller in mezzotint, standing up in front of his library. NPG D36731.

[40] CA, BC, vol. 57, case 321.

[41] Langham Rokeby to Burke, 31 Jan. 1836, BL, Add. MS 16569, fol. 184.

FAMILY TIES AND PUBLISHERS' ENQUIRIES 177

Dr Nathaniel Hardy from St Martin Parish, a figure of enduring loyalty to the king during the Civil War and a commissioner sent to The Hague to prepare Charles II's restoration.[42] His father, the fourth baronet, had just died, and for Sir Robert, Wotton's *Baronetage* was a way to project himself into a new status. Some dedicated several pages to certain significant objects in their possession: a bible, a grant of arms, heraldic glass, rings, goblets, textiles, or furniture; portraits which, far from expressing intimacy and affection, fitted into a strong and defiant dynastic agenda.[43] Those artefacts had the capacity to store and give credence to countless memories. One Robert Barnardiston owned a sculpture of his ancestor, which 'seems to be very ancient'.[44] Commenting on his rich collections deposited in Hengrave Hall, Sir William Gage referred to 'a very curious specimen of embroidery, being the fine lawn shirt that belonged to Arthur, Prince of Wales, son of King Henry VII and which was given to the late Mr. Gage Rokewode by the Countess de Front [...] and a small mazer or grace cup, with silver band'.[45] The Countess de Front was related to the Lord of the Bedchamber of Henry VII. By contracting a marriage with Mary Charlotte Bond, daughter of Sir Thomas Bond, William Gage obtained many artefacts in possession of the Bonds: ancient devotional books and a picture of Henrietta, duchess of Orléans, and several van Dyck portraits. His son, John Gage had married the heiress of the Rokewodes, another influent Roman Catholic family in Suffolk. Hence the Gages, through their local alliances, became the repository of many Catholic treasures.[46] While relics had lost some of their confessional connotation, they were still used by Catholic families to express a distinctive sense of the past. It is quite telling that none of these artefacts is mentioned by Wotton in his editions. His aim, as we have seen earlier, was to display a homogeneous picture of the baronets which led him to erase the distinctiveness of their confessional culture. It is only in the nineteenth century that the exceptional richness of their patrimony was revealed to the public by John Gage and later by various antiquarian publications.

To establish his credentials William Greaves, 'from a prolific race' since the Norman Conquest, presented a wide range of several artefacts in his possession.[47] First, a parchment on the Greaves family of Darby recorded in the 1634 visitation

---

[42] BL, Add. MS 24120, fol. 4. On Nathaniel Hardy, see Anthony Wood, *Athenae Oxonienses: An Exact History of All the Writers*, vol. 3 (London, 1817), 896–8.

[43] Kate Retford, 'Sensibility and Genealogy in the Eighteenth Century Family Portrait: The Collection at Kedleston Hall', *The Historical Journal*, vol. 46, no. 3 (2003): 533–60 at 540; on consumption, material culture, and status, see Mark Girouard, *Life in the English Country House* (New Haven, 1978); Jon Stobart and Mark Rothery, *Consumption and the Country House* (Oxford, 2016).

[44] BL, Add. MS 24120, fol. 398.   [45] Ibid., fol. 372; Wotton, *Baronetage* (1741), vol. 3.2, 367.

[46] For a whole list of their belongings, see John Gage, *The History and Antiquities of Hengrave, in Suffolk* (London, 1822); *Proceedings of the Bury & West Suffolk Archæological Institute*, vol. 1 (Bury St Edmund's, 1853), 335–9. A large collection of Hengrave manuscripts were purchased by the Cambridge University Library in 2006. CUL, GBR/0012/MS Hengrave.

[47] William Greaves to Burke, 13 Aug. 1828, CA, BC, vol. 57, case 206.

178 SELLING ANCESTRY

by Henry Chitting, Chester herald. Second, a 'beautiful silver medal about the size of half a crown but thicker, which was presented by Prince Edward to Colonel Goring'.[48] The medal commemorated the friendship between the Greaves and the Gorings, who distinguished themselves during the Civil War and against the Jacobite uprising in 1745. He also owned an 'original portrait' of Sir Isaac Newton which proved that they were related by marriage to him. Finally, he described a chimney piece in Mayfield with the inscription 'A. L. 1608 J. L.', standing for Alan and Jane Ley. Through this detail, he demonstrated his connection to the Leys 'of considerable antiquitye'.[49] Henry George Cary, a magistrate who had recently inherited from his uncle Torre Abbey in Devon, had various documents from the time of the Normans to an original pedigree, made by a herald to the order of Queen Anne Boleyn and a silver box with miniatures of James of York and Henrietta-Maria, admittedly used at the Restoration as 'royal bond for monies lent and estates alienated'.[50] Richard Broun informed Burke that he was in possession of the magical and 'famous Colstoun-pear', previously owned by Hugh de Gifford of Yester who died 1267.[51] One of Gifford's remote ancestor was 'famed for his necromantic power' and 'was supposed to have invested [the pear] with an enchantement which rendered it invaluable, viz that any family possessing it shall be attended by unfailing prosperity. This palladium is preserved in Colstoun, with the care due to no singular an heir-loom & without regard to superstition must be considered as a very singular curiosity, having existed for more than five centuries (Vide Chambers' Picture of Scotland).'[52] While Broun sought to vindicate his ancient origins, Chambers used the story in a different context. For the visitors, the 'Colstoun pear' was presented as a relic of an extinct family, a local curiosity with no connection to the Brouns. Chamber described 'the seat of the ancient family of Brown, which has at length terminated in the present countess of Dalhousie. This place is chiefly worthy of attention here, on account of a strange heir-loom with which the welfare of the family was always supposed to be connected.'[53] Unsurprisingly, it was a Lady at an unspecified time who caused the demise of the Browns, 'taking a longing for the forbidden fruit, while pregnant, [and inflicting] upon it a deadly bite'.[54]

Allusion to emblematic places, monuments, and architectural details occurred extensively in the enquiries. Like manuscripts and prints, paintings and funerary monuments convey a powerful sense of continuity, perhaps hiding the end of a male line or the transfer of titles. Some correspondents explained in detail how they went to neighbouring churches to find the funeral escutcheons and

---

[48] Ibid. and *Commoners* (1833), vol. 1, 388.   [49] *Commoners* (1833), vol. 1, 388.
[50] *Commoners* (1835), vol. 2, 35.   [51] Broun to Burke, 4 Dec. 1828, CA, BC, vol. 55, n.p.
[52] Ibid.   [53] Robert Chambers, *The Picture of Scotland*, vol. 2 (Edinburgh, 1827), 135.
[54] Ibid.; the story is now mentioned on the family website: 'The Brouns have protected this Pear for centuries and the full story of The Pear is only told at the house.' <https://www.colstoun.co.uk/the-house>.

inscriptions.[55] Castles were used as proof, even when they had been acquired recently. Edmund Lechmere Charlton mentioned the 'fine specimen of Queen Elizabeth's style of architecture' at his seat in Whitton Court as proof of his ancient origins.[56] Lewis Clutterbuck described 'the original gothic beautiful front' and the 'windows embellished with fine specimens of stained glass' along with their coats of arms.[57] Kiffin John Lenthall depicted the mansion of Hampton Court (Herefordshire) as well as his ancestors' deeds at Agincourt: 'they took more prisoners there, with whose ransom they completed the new building at Hampton Court. In this house was preserved a picture, which was engraved by Vertue & is said to be an undoubted original of Henry the fourth.'[58] His painting was indeed so famous that a copy had been made in 1732 by George Vertue, a highly regarded engraver.[59] The description of the castle, the portrait, and an eighteenth-century engraving: all were combined to reinforce the idea of a prestigious lineage. The accumulation of these objects turned the estates into miniature museums which gradually became accessible to the public. However, one should be careful not to systematically impose a correlation between the ownership of genealogical artefacts and the willingness to provide a rich family narrative. John Hugh Smyth Pigott first wrote to Burke in 1828 and gave only the names of his wife and children. Such a meagre account was only published in the second edition of 1846.[60] He was in possession of a considerable number of objects, which could have enriched his pedigree. In the sale catalogue of his goods, we learn that he owned a pair of 'state Chairs, chimeroe legs, boldly carved and richly guilt'.[61] The author of the catalogue commented on the fact that 'these relics formerly belonged to Strongbow, Earl of Clare. His arms and coronet from the back, the seats are covered in velvet.'[62] Smyth Pigott commissioned a painting by Thomas Barker of a view near his estate at Brockley Hall with 'the Severn stretching horizontally across the Picture, and the Monmouth and Glamorganshire Hills in the distance.'[63] He was also the keeper of the portrait of the 1st Baronet Sir Edward Fust, whose 'arms and pedigrees are painted on the picture', and in his library, he collected the volumes of Dudgale's, *Baronage,* Guillim's *Heraldry,* Betham's *Baronetage,* and Burke's *Peerage.*[64] Yet none of these artefacts and books are inserted in his account, an absence which could be interpreted in so many ways.

When documents and objects were missing, the heir might come up with anecdotes from his memory and the family 'tradition'. One could argue that their social status made up for their lack of reliable sources. Heads of family got

---

[55] Sir Francis Head gave Wotton a detailed account of his wanderings in the local churches of Rochester: BL, Add. MS 24120, fol. 415.

[56] Edmund Lechmere Charlton to Burke, 16 Aug. 1828, CA, BC, vol. 56, case 76.

[57] CA, BC, vol. 56, case 91.   [58] CA, BC, vol. 56, case 318.   [59] NPG D23723.

[60] Bernard Burke, *A Genealogical and Heraldic Dictionary of the Landed Gentry* (London, 1846), vol. 2, 1197.

[61] *Catalogue of the Costly and Highly Interesting Effects of John Hugh Smyth Pigott* (Bath, 1849), 8.

[62] Ibid., 8.   [63] Ibid., 19.   [64] Ibid., 11, 30–1, 51.

180   SELLING ANCESTRY

away with telling fabulous stories. Oral sources were still common currency but to be more credible, they were meant to be applied to a context where written sources were unavailable—for instance, during their childhood, or in remote places such as the colonies where records were scarce. Charles Streynsham Collinson, 'a silk contractor', simply wrote: 'I must consequently be governed in great measure by the oral testimony of my relations in the days of my youth.'[65] The validity of the testimony was guaranteed by its source, namely, his grandfather Peter Collinson, a respected botanist and fellow of the Royal Society. In a colonial context, unpredictable witnesses could be mentioned. Henry Archbold, the last male heir of wealthy planters in Jamaica, claimed to be both the great-grandson of Sir Henry Morgan (c.1635–1688), the privateer and governor of Jamaica and the remote cousin of Sir John Morgan of Kinnersley. He was hoping to demonstrate his connection to Henry Archbold, who in 1671 had married Joanna Morgan, daughter of the deputy governor of Jamaica (1664). Although he admitted having 'no voucher to prove any connection between Sir John and Sir Henry', and also acknowledged that Morgan was 'a mighty common name in Wales', his trump cards were 'a miniature picture of Charles the Second done in enamel which the king presented to Sir Henry Morgan' and his mother's recollections about her childhood in Jamaica:

> It is usual for people in Jamaica to name their favourite negroes after their own family and my mother now living remembers a slave belonging to my grandmother who was Sr Henry's only daughter, being call'd Lewis which was the Christian name of Sr John's father.[66]

While the first proof was a conventional argument, the second piece of evidence deserves further comment as it relates to the practice of slave-naming in Jamaica. The point made by Archbold was all the more dubious, as many slave owners gave the same first name to thousands of slaves who were listed in their inventories. Planters thought themselves fundamentally different from the 'negroes' and did not make much effort to try and individualize them even though they were distinguished from their livestock. Slave-naming did not reflect slaves' family relationships but mostly the planters' mindset. It has been demonstrated that slaves were not in a position to name themselves: 'the names given to blacks indicate that white Jamaicans thought of Africans (whom they invariably denoted as "negroes" rather than slaves) to be people entirely different from themselves'.[67] However as the name 'Lewis' was not recorded among the twenty most popular

---

[65]   CA, BC, vol. 56, 1828, case 110.

[66]   Henry Archbold to Mark Noble, 24 June 1789, Bod. Lib., Eng. Misc. d. 155, fol. 29.

[67]   Trevor Burnard, 'Slave Naming Patterns: Onomastics and the Taxonomy of Race in Eighteenth-Century Jamaica', *The Journal of Interdisciplinary History*, vol. 31, no. 3 (2001): 325–46 at 326. In Thistlewood diaries, several slaves were named Johnnie, a common name in the family.

names given to slaves, Archbold might have felt it was a remarkable occurrence and the proof of a special relationship between the two branches of the Morgans. In the London metropolis, slave naming patterns were as obscure as medieval etymologies and Archbold may have hoped to get away with this flimsy piece of evidence.[68]

His was not the only family alleging to be linked to the privateer. Jones of Llanarth claimed to descend from a 'sister and heir of Henry Morgan, Esq. of Penllwyn (a branch of the Morgans of Tredegar)'.[69] These competing allegations may be explained by the continuous uncertainties about Morgan's origins. The first controversy was triggered by the publication of Alexandre Olivier Exquemelin's *Buccaneers of America* in London in 1684. Exquemelin introduced Morgan as an indentured servant, a derogatory contention that Morgan managed to have erased following a successful lawsuit. In the later English editions, he was labelled 'a Gentleman's son of good quality in the County of Monmouth'.[70] In the eighteenth century, when his reputation was further consolidated, some authors preferred to see him as a modest but worthy upstart, while others continued to stress his genteel background. For Charles Leslie, Morgan was 'a man born of mean and obscure parents', whereas Edward Long, discussing his alleged massacres, argued that:

> It is but justice to Sir Henry Morgan, the most celebrated of all the English leaders, to affirm, it does not appear that he ever encouraged or approved of any such inhumanities. [...] This gentleman has been unhappily confounded with the piratical herd.[71]

Morgan was seen as an imperial British hero for his brave raids on Panama in 1671 and his conversion from buccaneer to a respectable official. He entered the pantheon of navy heroes such as Francis Drake and Admiral Vernon. For a West Indies family, a connection to Morgan was to be cherished. The creation of the baronetcy of Morgan of Tredegar in 1792, given to Charles Gould, further increased the value of the name. Sir Henry Morgan's parentage was later described in *The Gentleman's Magazine* as 'one of the great clans of the Morgans of Monmouthshire of which the House of Tredegar was the head'.[72]

---

[68] In his genealogical collection of Jamaican families, Charles Edward Long traced Henry Archbold back to one Elizabeth, with no surname and the son of Major William Archbold. BL, Add. MS 27968, fol. 42.

[69] Burke, *Commoners*, vol. 4 (1838), 728.

[70] Mark G. Hanna, *Pirate Nests and the Rise of the British Empire, 1570–1740* (Chapel Hill, NC, 2015), 139.

[71] Charles Leslie, *A new history of Jamaica, from the earliest accounts, to the taking of Porto Bello by Vice-Admiral Vernon* (London, 1740), 107. Edward Long, *The History of Jamaica*, vol. 1 (London, 1774), 300.

[72] *GM*, 1832, vol. 151, 128.

182 SELLING ANCESTRY

Finally, claims of immemorial origins could be based in the inscrutable medieval past. In *The Antiquities of Arundel* (1766), Charles Caraccioli made the point that 'the uncertainty of the origin of the illustrious family of Howard is proof of its antiquity'.[73] Sir John Trevelyan recalled an oral tradition in his parentage and 'amongst the inhabitants of Cornwall [...] that one of the Trevelyans at the time of the inundation swam from thence to land on horseback and saved himself from the Deluge whence the family in memory thereof have born in their coat armour a land horse issuing out of the wave'.[74] The Egerton family, according to its head, the ninth baronet Philip Grey, was famous 'for having continued its uninterrupted male descent from a period to which few families can trace themselves', namely from the Norman baron of Malpas.[75] One Colonel Henry de Montmorency explained that he had among his ancestors 'the greatest man of the name, the constable Anne de Montmorency, who neither knew how to read or write' as 'in former uneducated ages when scarcely any one except the priest of the parish knew how to write'.[76] It was therefore perfectly normal to be devoid of written sources and so plenty of anecdotes could be safely used. Charles Chad 'does not pretend that the origin of his family derived from any other sources than that of tradition supported by facts which give the greatest weight to the supposition'.[77] One Colonel William Beckwith was even less specific about his Norman origins. According to 'an old manuscript', he came from Lady Beckwith Bruce of Castle Levington, an estate which belonged 'to my family beyond record [...] but I should think an inspection of ancient records in Publick libraries might settle that point'.[78] We have seen above that his ancestor by maternal descent, the baronet Sir Roger Beckwith, had been heavily involved in the making of Wotton's baronetage. Sir Roger's narrative was very much rooted in the seventeenth-century political crisis and the Restoration, when the family obtained the baronetcy, whereas William's imagination went much further back into an immemorial past, as he put it, 'beyond record'.

Audacious name swappers

The central position of family representatives was reinforced by the increasing trend to change names and/or absorb the spouse's pedigree, thus connecting an ever-larger number of names together. In the late eighteenth century,

---

[73] *The Antiquities of Arundel. The Peculiar Privilege of its Castle and Lordship: With an Abstract of The Lives of The Earls of Arundel* (London, 1766), 154.

[74] BL, Add. MS 24121, fol. 292.

[75] Philip Grey Egerton to Courthope, 1828, CA, WC 63, fol. 120.

[76] Henry de Montmorency to Courthope, 3 Oct. 1823, CA, WC 69, fol. 47.

[77] Charles Chad to Courthope, 13 June 1828, CA, WC 62, fol. 221.

[78] Beckwith to Burke, 11 Jan. 1836, BL, Add. MS 16569, fol. 23.

FAMILY TIES AND PUBLISHERS' ENQUIRIES   183

in order to limit the extinction of titled names, heirs—by petitioning the Crown or conforming to the instructions in a will—came to supply narratives about family to which they were distantly related. Sometimes married women gave up their rights not only on most of their property but also on their past. 'There is in my possession a very accurate pedigree in that family,' wrote Sir Harbord about his spouse, Mary, the daughter of Sir Ralph Assheton of Middleton.[79] Harbord set himself the task of describing Mary's parentage with great zeal. His own name had been in fact Morden until he became heir to his maternal grandfather's name, arms, and property. Similarly, Sir Richard Brooke de Capell was the son of Richard Supple of Cork and of the daughter of Arthur Brooke of Great Oakley.[80] He had been trained a barrister in Lincoln's Inn and then held a position of colonel in the Northamptonshire militia. From his mother, he inherited the Brooke estates and surname and from the king he obtained a licence to use the surname of 'de Capell'. Hence the new baronet attached himself to two different eminent families, Capell and Brooke. As a member of the Royal Society from 1797, Sir Richard had the archival resources and the connections to establish a detailed story of both lines with ample footnotes, funerary inscriptions, and endless Latin quotations.[81] The Brooke family 'appears, by a very ancient pedigree now before me to owne its origin to the House of Lathan' in the reign of King Stephen.[82] By doing so he managed to connect together different Brooke baronetcies in Chester, Yorkshire, and Ireland. Concerning the Capells, he put the Harleian manuscripts in the British Museum to extensive use, as well as some charters allegedly from the Birmingham Tower in Dublin. Quoting Sir Henry Piers in the *Collectanea de Rebus Hibernicis*, Sir Richard reminded the public that 'a corruption of sound' was common in Ireland and that it was usual 'to describe the same person by two names, spelt almost entirely different'.[83] Hence the English Capell became in Lower Irish, the Supple of Cork, a family of considerable importance by their reputation and possessions. The inventive baronet used the re-edition of Camden's *Britannia* by Richard Gough to explain the connection between the Sussells, Sapells, and Supples. The latter in particular came from oral sources—the 'common neighbouring Irish, who had several traditional stories relative to their first settlement'—and topography, notably a hill 'where the Irish suppose the numerous dead were buried after the Chappels or Suppels achieved a victory' and an island: 'Capell Island the name its distinguished by in all ancient maps'.[84] Landscape, antiquarian knowledge, and etymological extrapolations were used by the young baronet with the help of Betham in order to create an inclusive account which embraced the whole of English and Irish history. In the late eighteenth century, the book market and local and national archives offered sufficient

---

[79] Sir Harbord to Betham, 20 Oct. 1798, BL, Add. MS 21033, fol. 75.
[80] Sir Richard Brooke to Betham, 19 Apr. 1805, BL, Add. MS 21033, fol. 7.
[81] Betham, *Baronetage*, vol. 5, 514–34.   [82] Ibid., 514.   [83] Ibid., 526.   [84] Ibid., 528.

184 SELLING ANCESTRY

resources and guidebooks to enable zealous amateurs such as Sir Richard Brooke to conceive extensive pedigrees.

Playing on different spellings proved to be the easiest way to claim someone else's origins. John Coxe Hippisley, the son of William Hipsley, a haberdasher, changed the spelling of his name to be connected to the Hippisleys in Camely, Somersetshire, and to Richard 'born in the 14th Edward III'.[85] He pointed out that, in a compilation of early modern documents (*Cabala, sive, Scrinia Sacra, Mysteries of State*), John Hippisley, MP for Dover in the time of James I, was spelt John Hipsley and during the Civil War, 'the name is also sometimes written Hipsley as in the letters published in the *Scrinia Sacra*'.[86] He is then indicated that in the time of Edward VI, 'in the parish register of Yatton, the name is variously written: Hippisley, Hipsley, Hipsly and Hippesley', thus demonstrating that from the Middle Ages to the seventeenth century, his family name had been spelt in different ways. [87] John Coxe could then use the same argument to claim a large number of prominent ancestors.

Among Burke's commoners, many of them branched themselves out into titled names.[88] John Conway, the son of the Revd John Potter, obtained 'by his Majesty permission to drop the name of Potter' and to use the surname of his mother. Retracing his ancestry further back, he established a link with the extinct baronetcy of Conway of Bodrythan and also claimed the arms of the marquess of Hertford.[89] William Francis Booker, whose father was 'esq of the 53 regiment' obtained in 1825 a royal licence to use the surname of Gregor.[90] Erasing any reference to Booker, he constructed his account around the richer potentials of the Cornish Gregors, landed gentry with a few high sheriffs, MPs, and various worthies such as the Revd William Gregor, a painter and chemist 'celebrated throughout Europe'.[91] Booker composed an advantageous and balanced past which combined the values of rural antiquity, political dedication, and personal merit. In Ireland, William Gore, MP for Leitrim, assumed the additional surname of Ormsby. By marrying Mary-Jane Ormsby, 'who represented the ancient noble

---

[85] Ibid., vol. 4, 327.

[86] He was referring to a famous compilation of letters: *Cabala, Sive, Scrinia Sacra Mysteries of State & Government: in Letters of Illustrious Persons, and Great Agents, in the Reigns of Henry the Eighth* (London, 1691). Betham, *Baronetage*, vol. 4, 328–9.

[87] Ibid., 331.

[88] John Potter-Conway, James Hayhurst-France, William Francis Booker-Gregor, Joseph Hosken-Harper, Gordon William Francis-Gregor, William Grieves-Goring, William Hodgson-Hinde-Compton, Edward John Walhouse-Littleton, John Fownes-Luttrell, Peter Rickards-Mynors, George Pollen-Boileau, William Stanhope-Roddam, Abraham Spooner-Lillington, George Hutchinson-Sutton, Edward Swainston-Strangwayes, Emma Egerton-Tatton, John Plumb-Tempest, Richard Hippisley-Tuckfield, Charles Kemeys-Tynte, John Tippet-Vivian, Charles Watkins-Shakerley.

[89] John Conway to Burke, Apr. 1828, CA, BC, vol. 56, case 104.

[90] William-Francis Booker to Burke, CA, BC, vol. 57, case 211.

[91] 'The Gregor family first known as landed proprietors in the middle of the 17th century, ended Feb. 1825 in a female who bequeathed her property to Loveday Sarah wife of the above G. W. Booker'. Ibid.

family of Godolphin', he was able to extend his narrative well beyond his Irish origins. The Ormsbys had been previously allied to the Owens of Porkington, and thus William gathered together the three names by presenting himself as William Ormsby Gore of Porkington. Two years after writing to Burke, he published a description of the Porkington manuscripts to further enrich his account.[92] Henry Fownes took his wife's patronym, Luttrell, and their son, John Fownes-Luttrell, MP for Minehead, sent a very detailed pedigree of his maternal lineage.[93] Very much involved in the lengthy reconstitution of the Luttrells, John directed Burke to contact James Savage, from the library of the Somerset and Taunton Institution, who was about to print a history of the western division of the county of Somerset.[94]

It is worth pointing out that a change of name, whether by testament or by royal commission, opened up new vistas and multiplied the paths to prestigious memories but led to the reduction of the paternal line. Edward Swainston could have chosen to mention his father's publications as a York physician but only cited his name in passing: 'Allen Swainston, M.D. of the City of York'.[95] In contrast he provided the very detailed pedigree of his mother's lineage—Frances Strangwayes, a family linked to Lord d'Arcy—adding in a footnote that 'a moiety of that baron has become vested in the descendant of this alliance, the present Edward Swainston-Strangwayes'.[96] A few counter-examples can be found. Abraham Lillingston-Spooner, the son of an industrialist, could have been tempted to focus on the genteel origins of his wife, Elizabeth-Mary, the daughter of Luke Lillingston of Ferriby Grange. However, although he did not mention his father's activities as a prominent banker and industrialist, he drew a balanced and equal account between his paternal line and that of his wife.[97] Along with the paternal line, siblings were sidelined in many narratives. In their attempts to forcibly insert themselves into the most prominent branch, family representatives were led to forget their siblings. In 1822, George William Hutchinson took the name and arms of the Suttons according to the terms of his great-uncle's will. He drew a family tree aimed at illustrating this link as well as showing the prestigious lineage of his mother from Bathurst baronetcy. His father, a prosperous banker in Stockton-on-Tees, appeared squeezed in the corner in addition to his siblings, briefly noted along the lower branch.[98]

While heads of family were at the forefront, their letters demonstrate nevertheless that they were often acting as a broker, a legal façade between the publishers and other relatives.

---

[92] *Manuscripts at Porkington: The Seat of William Ormsby Gore Esq. Near Oswestry* (Salop, 1830).
[93] CA, BC, vol. 57, 8 Nov. 1828, case 338. Burke, *Commoners*, vol. 1, 142.
[94] CA, BC, vol. 57, 8 Nov. 1828, case 338.   [95] Burke, *Commoners*, vol. 1, 665.
[96] Ibid.   [97] Ibid., 185.   [98] CA, BC, vol. 58 (1828), case 531.

186 SELLING ANCESTRY

With a considerable help from close kin

Many reasons required the need to involve a wider number of relatives. First, the publishers complained that many household heads failed to answer. Wotton criticized their inconsistencies and was aggrieved 'to see, how very indifferent some [baronets] are still about their ancestors and with what difficulty others were persuaded to take any the least pains in furnishing the accounts of them'.[99] In his final advertisements before the completion of his editions, he had to ask for collaterals to come forward and provide missing links.[100] The role of kinship in the making of Wotton's compilations has been explored in a collective publication entitled *Genealogical Knowledge in the Making*.[101] In the late century, to increase the channels of communication (as well as enlarge the number of potential buyers), publishers invited most of the kin to participate. To prepare the new edition of his *Directory* in 1829, Burke addressed himself in the *Times* to all collaterals of baronets and peers, 'all those who come within the most remote remaindership of family honours'.[102]

It should be noted that the involvement of a wider family circle was often welcomed and encouraged by family heads. Some admitted to having nothing in their possession that related to their ancestors. Sir Ralph Assheton confessed: 'I found no manner of authority in any memoirs of mine. I should be glad if you could recollect from whom you had the material or the account of my family that I might apply to them for further information.'[103] Assheton expected Wotton to reconnect him to collaterals whom he had lost sight of. The ease with which most heads of family contacted their siblings, uncles, or nephews testified to the continuous ties they managed to maintain through physical encounters or correspondence. Family relations have been best described as a 'dynamic process, which involved a constantly changing interaction of personalities rather than a view of the family as a monolithic entity'.[104] Collaboration between fathers and sons, uncles and nephews can be documented. But siblings in particular were the most active protagonists as 'siblinghood was the only lifelong aspect of kinship'.[105] Amy Harris has argued that research on nuclear families or the development of self and individuality led to underestimating the importance of sibling relations.

---

[99] Wotton, *English Baronets*, 1727, x; also in the second edition: 'some were such strangers to the Glory of their ancestors and the future honour of their families, as not to be prevailed on, by repeated solicitations to spare a moment in furnishing one single material', *English Baronetage*, vii.

[100] 'If any of their friends or relations will favour the undertaker with any of the aforesaid account', *The Craftsman*, 10 Mar. 1726.

[101] Stéphane Jettot, 'Family Input in the Making of London Genealogical Directories in the 18th Century', in V. Bauer, F. Markus, and J. Eickmeyer (dir.), *Genealogical Knowledge in the Making: Tools, Practices, and Evidence in Early Modern Europe* (Oldenburg, 2019), 169–98.

[102] *The Times*, 23 Jan. 1829.   [103] Sir Ralph Assheton to Wotton, BL, Add. MS 24120, fol. 21.

[104] Tamara K. Haraven, 'What Difference Does it Make?', *Social Science History*, vol. 20, no. 3 (1996): 317–44 at 326.

[105] Amy Harris, *Sibling and Social Relations in Georgian England* (Manchester, 2012), 15.

An 'imaginary household' often persisted between siblings well into their adult life. A strong sense of reciprocal duties was maintained between the heir and his younger siblings.[106]

Through letters and regular encounters, family members worked together in various sorts of endeavours related to education, economics, and cultural activities. The conjugal and parental family did not weaken the enduring strength of sibling interactions. A discrepancy is often visible between the actual owner of the archives and the storyteller. Sometimes family records were too remote to be easily perused. Among the Firebraces, Samuel was allowed by his elder brother, 'the Captain Firebrace of the 58th Regiment at present quartered at Ceylon', to answer Burke's enquiry, although he complained about his poor documentation: 'I do not speak from documentary but from oral evidence received from my late father, having quitted home at too early an age to read such papers the family possessed and which are now in possession of my eldest brother'.[107] Sometimes, the sudden death of the father compromised the transmission process. Sir Edmund Anderson wrote: 'my father died & left me young so that I can say nothing of my own knowledge', and so he could give no better information than what his uncle had told him.[108] Alternatively, some heads of household confessed to having little curiosity for their ancestors. John Foster advised Burke to see his nephew, John Frederick Foster, at Manchester as he 'had paid more attention to the history of our family than I have'.[109]

In many cases, the family repository was insufficient, fragmentary, and even non-existent. Other sources of knowledge were then required. Thomas Bond, a vicar in Dorset, informed Burke that as his nephew who succeeded to the estates of his elder brother, 'took no interest in the matter & to which I have given some attention, he had desired me to answer your query'.[110] Bond, who was of Wadham College in Oxford, had developed a taste for antiquities. He looked after his elder brother's properties while the latter was MP for Corfe Castle (1801–7) and one of the lords of the Treasury. As younger siblings were more likely to become clergymen or lawyers, they were better placed to collect reliable data in public records. Like Thomas Bond, rectors and curates referred for their enquiries to parish registers but also to their networks of colleagues and local antiquaries.[111] In 1804, the article on the baronets of Lombe was entirely conceived by Meadows

---

[106] 'Connected to the individual household run by masters and mistresses were links to sibling households (whether married or not) that established a virtual, or imagined, household shared by families of origin even after the dispersal of the physical household into new marital or nuclear units'. Ibid., 117.

[107] Samuel Firebrace to Burke, 14 Dec. 1832, BL, Add. MS 16569, fol. 83.

[108] Edmund Anderson to Wotton, 23 Sept. 1739, BL, Add. MS 24120, fol. 11.

[109] John Foster, 19 July 1828, CA, BC, vol. 56, case 184.

[110] Thomas Bond to Burke, 1828, CA, BC, vol. 56, case 48.

[111] On this subject, see Jettot, 'Family Input', 175–8.

188 SELLING ANCESTRY

Taylor, the baronet's father-in-law, a prominent attorney in London.[112] William Helyar, sheriff for Somerset and plantation owners in Jamaica, wrote that he had only a few artefacts, notably a locket with Charles I's picture in enamel and the distant memory that his ancestor William had raised a troop of horse for King Charles and was fined £1,500.[113] He added that his brothers, George and Charles Helyar, barristers-at-law in London, would be able to 'give an exact genealogical account of my family'.[114] Because of their professional expertise and their privileged access to the London records, lawyers were the voice of authority and their contribution was always underlined.

Finally, responses to such enquiries were also guided by self-interest, as many younger brothers, nephews, uncles, and cousins were potential heirs. Premature death of the firstborn son and his lack of offspring constantly reorganized birth-order dynamics and kinship interactions. As we have seen above, the notion of a continuous male line documented by a succession of eldest sons was in reality a fiction. Especially in the first half of the eighteenth century, few families actually followed direct male line descent for more than three or four generations. The parents, the eldest son, and his siblings were acutely aware of the effect of the high mortality rates on their prospects. The more fragile the dynasty, the more likely siblings were to be treated kindly in the father's will.[115] When siblings or nephews came in turn to inherit the title or the land, they were well aware of their temporary and fragile position.

Table 4.2 shows the declining proportion of the eldest son in Wotton's *Baronetage* after the first succession. For the more recent baronetcies, created after 1700, eldest sons were still the majority in 1727, but for those established during the Restoration period, the title was only rarely preserved in the senior line. Between 1661 and 1739, the baronetcies of Clavering and Glynne were transmitted six times to younger brethren, nephews, and uncles. The seventh baronet Ernle owed his title to Walter Ernle in 1660. Dying without heir, the first baronet left his

Table 4.2 Transmission of baronetcies among Wotton's correspondents

	Eldest son	Younger sons-nephews, collaterals	
2nd baronet	20	6	26
3rd baronet	23	17	40
4th–6th baronets	3	30	33
	46	53	99

[112] Betham to Taylor, 1804, BL, Add. MS 21033, fol. 107.
[113] William Helyar to Burke, 22 Jan. 1829, CA, BC, vol. 57, case 257. [114] Ibid.
[115] Lloyd Bonfield (ed.), *Marriage, Property, and Succession: Comparative Studies in Continental and Anglo-American Legal History* (Berlin, 1992), 308.

title first to his cousin, then to the latter's cadet who died childless, and then to another cousin, the son of the first baronet's brother. It later fell into the hands of his younger brother and then was assumed by a descendant of the first baronet's youngest brother, Sir Michael Ernle.[116] Wotton had been informed that the original lineage was in fact extinguished in 1734, but chose not to omit the current claimant to the title.

There are a few remarkable exceptions, such as the Bickleys or the Packingtons, with a succession of eldest sons who bore the same name and forename.[117] Sir Francis Bickley, the fourth baronet, was aware that this continuous line was in itself remarkable and did not bother to invent any fanciful narrative about his ancestors, alluding to the fact that the first baronet had been a London draper before the Civil War and had married the daughter of Richard Parsons, a City Merchant. The second baronet wedded the daughter of an alderman from Norwich and the third that of a Dutch engineer, Vermingden. However, this continuous line did not mean that the memory was better safeguarded. The last Sir Francis Bickley apologized for his vague recollection, as 'having no pedigree preserved amongst us'.[118] It was his half-brother, the Revd Humphrey Bickley, from the daughter of another baronet, who provided most of the data on the Bickleys, notably from the funeral monuments in the church of Attleborough (Norfolk). Like names, lands and family knowledge circulated among many branches.

2. Women in the publishing process

In July 1728, Etheldred, the younger sister of John Bennett, MP for Wiltshire, scolded Burke for having addressed his letters to the 'junior member of the junior branch' instead of to her brother, 'the head of the family [... who] represents his native county in Parliament'.[119] Two months later, she insisted that her brother was the 'chief of my family and who is not likely to be superseded by any other branch'.[120] In a persistent manner, she was keen to assert the control of the elder branch and, simultaneously, she presented herself as the Bennetts' genealogist: Burke may 'be surprised to hear that your correspondent is a lady' but he had to

---

[116] BL, Add. MS 24120, fol. 305; Wotton, *Baronetage*, vol. 3, 221.

[117] Sir Francis Bickley: 1st bt (1582-1670); 2nd (1623-81); 3rd (1644-87); 4th (1667-1746) in Wotton, *Baronetage*, vol. 2, 225; Sir John Packington (1st bt: 1600-24); 2nd (1621-80); 3rd (1649-88); 4th (1671-1727); 5th (1701-48) in Wotton, *Baronetage*, vol. 1, 188.

[118] BL, Add. MS 24120, Sept. 1725, fols 60-1.

[119] 'It is somewhat singular that in prosecuting inquiries of such a nature you should have fix'd on the junior member of the junior branch of the family to apply to, when the Head of the family has for the last nine years represented, and still represents his native county in Parliament'. Etheldred to Burke, 10 July 1828, CA, BC, vol. 56, case 32.

[120] Ibid., 6 Sept. 1828.

190 SELLING ANCESTRY

accept that 'the pedigree can only be procured from myself'.[121] With the assistance of her youngest brother, she sent him all the relevant information: a very detailed account of the Bennetts of Pythouse since the sixteenth century along with extracts from a 1623 Visitation. She dispatched an engraving along with a description of the seat 'commanding an extensive prospect of hill, wood and vale [...] and an abrupt hill covered with shrubs and trees'.[122] All these elements, she added, had already been collected for Sir Richard Hoare's *History of Modern Wiltshire*.[123] The female line must have been essential in Etheldred's own genealogical interest, as she was named after her grandmother Etheldred Wake, the daughter of the archbishop of Canterbury and after her great-grandmother Etheldred Howell. One of her aunts, who is not mentioned in Burke's account, was also named Etheldred and left in her will all her belongings, as well as a gold medal of the Queen Caroline, to her sister Catherine.[124] Finally, one of her nieces is called Etheldred-Catherine and had just married in 1827 Lord Charles Spencer-Churchill, second son of the duke of Marlborough. The Wake's lineage enabled her father, Thomas, to obtain 'a fellowship at Oxford, as founder's kin, through his mother Etheldred Wake to Archbishop Chichely'.[125] In 1833, she edited the genealogy of the Wakes which she found among the archbishop's papers, 'in his own writing' and in the preface she stated that no apology was needed 'from his Granddaughter for giving it to the Public'.[126] Furthermore, far from being a discreet and submissive figure in the shadow of her brother, Etheldred had already established her reputation within and outside the family circles as a natural historian and fossil collector.[127] Her contribution to Hoare's county compilation involved the fields of natural and family histories. Her interest in geology and genealogy clearly converged. In both cases, several layers of time could be reconstituted from scattered material clues. For many contemporaries, the limits between family history and natural sciences were still not easily distinguished.

Whether they provided a full-length narrative or a few particulars, female participations were seldom acknowledged in the printed edition. Unmarried as well as financially independent, Etheldred wished to be seen by Burke as the family genealogist. Yet, despite all that she communicated, she had only her first name

[121] Ibid.

[122] Sir Richard Hoare, *The History of Modern Wiltshire: The Hundred of Dunworth* (London, 1829), vol. 5, 131–3.

[123] Sir Richard Colt Hoare, a famous antiquarian, had launched into the publication of a multivolume county history in 1822.

[124] Will of Etheldred Bennet or Benett, 'Spinster of Bath', 2 Nov. 1778, NA, Prob 11/1047/3.

[125] Burke, *Commoners*, vol. 1, 249.

[126] *William Wake, Enquiry into the Antiquity, Honour, and Estate of the Name and Family of Wake, with Autog. Letter of Sir R. Colt Hoare* (London, 1833).

[127] On her correspondence with G. B. Greenough, the first president of the Geological Society, in 1813, see M. R. S. Creese and T. M. Creese, 'British Women who Contributed to Research in Geological Sciences', *British Journal for the History of Science*, vol. 27 (1994), 26–7. She also published a *Catalogue of the Organic Remains of the County of Wiltshire* (Warminster, 1831).

FAMILY TIES AND PUBLISHERS' ENQUIRIES 191

and that of her sisters registered. In most compilations, it was assumed that men were in charge of the official history of their relatives and that women could at best add a few snippets of information. This is why the letters sent to the publishers are worth considering. They confirmed the existence of a widespread bias shared by many customers and some publishers towards women who, by congenital weakness or mere disinterest, were seen as a potential threat to the preservation of the past. While the letters abound in misogynistic comments, they testify to the fact that Etheldred Bennett belonged to the long list of sisters, wives, daughters, and mothers at the centre stage of the publication process, either as the main correspondents or as providers of data to their husbands or sons. The extent of their involvement is not limited to their letters, as many male correspondents recognized their importance. John Edmund Dowdeswell, MP and recorder for Tewkesbury, was able to prove his connection to the baronetcy of Sir Dudley Digges thanks to 'a very good portrait of him by Cornelius Jansen, which was brought to the place by my grandmother'.[128] James Walwyn claimed to descend from the Wakes of Clevedon through 'a pedigree in my mother's handwriting'.[129] With respect to their direct involvement, it is worth noting that it was usually justified by various arguments. They were allowed to step in if they were themselves of prestigious origins themselves or to make up for their husbands' incapacities (due to distance, disease, or old age).[130]

Women as a liability and a threat

'I cannot let young ladies meddle with my documents. Young ladies are too flighty.'[131] With great irony, George Eliot in *Middlemarch* depicted the patronizing behaviour of a useless old uncle towards his astute niece Dorothea Brooke.[132] He even rejected the possibility that she could be a valuable secretary while he was unable to order his archive from A to Z. Dorothea's future husband, the Revd Casaubon, was no more spirited than her uncle in his vain and misguided work on etymologies. In both cases, two male characters supported widespread sets of beliefs which disqualified women from mastering history and even from being allowed access to archives and muniment rooms.[133] That said, this highly

---

[128] John Edmund Dowdeswell to Burke, 22 Dec. 1835, BL, Add. MS 16569, fol. 77.

[129] Ibid., fol. 233.

[130] On the essential role played by Lady Barlow, the wife of a baronet in Calcutta, see Margot C. Finn, 'The Barlow Bastards: Romance Comes Home from the Empire', in Margot C. Finn, Michael Lobban, and Jenny Bourne Taylor (eds), *Legitimacy and Illegitimacy in Nineteenth-Century Law, Literature and History* (Basingstoke, 2010), 30–1.

[131] George Eliot, *Middlemarch* (Oxford, 3rd edn, 2019), 14.   [132] Ibid.

[133] Leonore Davidoff and Catherine Hall have used another novel by George Eliot, *The Mill on the Floss*, to describe the emergence of 'the distinct and separate spheres of male and female which provided the basis for a shared culture among the middle class by mid-century', *Family Fortunes. Men and Women of the English Middle Class, 1780–1850* (Routledge, rev. edn, 1987, 2013), 74.

192   SELLING ANCESTRY

gendered language was mild compared to the ruthless punishment inflicted by the legendary Bluebeard on any woman who dared step into his study. Drawing on an analogy with the story of Bluebeard, Christiane Klapisch-Zuber underlines the disappearance of women from Italian family memories.[134] Women's exclusion from the past can be traced back to the early modern period in their weakening power over land as well as in the redefinition of history as a patriarchal-oriented exercise. The stereotypical old wives' tales are to be found in a large range of archives, whether public or private.[135] The promotion of military and political events led to the abasement of family history, increasingly seen as anecdotal and irrelevant to a wider public. In the late eighteenth century, it has been contended, women's progressive confinement to the private sphere may have accelerated the disqualification of their knowledge, since it was regarded as based merely on hearsay and even suspicious.[136] We have seen in the introduction how Burke's attack on Lord Bedford was gender based. Bedford was accused of complaisantly believing women's stories, thus raising questions about his ability to govern. Deprived of sufficient education or supplied with excessive imagination, women in the household were complicit in the making of fanciful pedigrees. They were indeed suspected of been more prone to snobbery. One of Burke's informers from Cork considered that most of the fictions came initially from some influential female members:

> I do not know whether it has ever occurred to you to notice how often families of the highest respectability are led into erroneous ideas relative to their own ancestry from relying implicitly on accounts derived from maidens, aunts, grandmothers.[137]

He criticized both the fanciful nature of their narrative but also their enduring impact on later generations. To drive his point home, he alluded to the female lies peddled among the Rices of Mount Eagle. Fooled by old women's tales, the new baronet Wedale Rice believed himself to be descended from Marchweithan, the founder of the fifteen tribes that settled in Wales. It was only through 'a cool inspection' of the written archives that truth would finally be restored.[138] The expression was a direct reference to the masculine capacity to temper heated passion and patiently scrutinize difficult texts.

---

[134] *La maison et le nom: stratégies et rituels dans l'Italie de la Renaissance* (Paris, 1990), 29.

[135] See my article, 'Family Input', 188–90.

[136] Adam Fox, *Oral and Literate Culture in England*, 174; Natalie Zemon Davis, 'Women as Historical Writers, 1400–1820', in Patricia H. Labalme (ed.), *Beyond Their Sex: Learned Women of the European Past* (New York, 1980), 153–82.

[137] Francis Elvans of Rathcormack to Burke, 14 July 1828, CA, BC, vol. 55, fol. 197.

[138] Ibid., fol. 198.

FAMILY TIES AND PUBLISHERS' ENQUIRIES   193

Along with their taste for fiction, another common bias towards women related to their excessive vanity. In *The Tatler,* Joseph Addison described a 'Welsh harp' as 'a certain Lady, who is one of those Female Historians that upon all Occasions enter into Pedigrees and Descents, and finds herself related, by some Off-shoot or other, to almost every great Family in England'.[139] Another example was that, according to John Burke, many women had refused to give their real age. Unmarried ladies, in particular, were even ready to pay in exchange for post-dating their date of birth. Dismissing these rumours as unfounded or limited to a few 'silly women', an influential reviewer in *The Gentleman's Magazine* regretted that these arguments were used to account for incomplete family directories. He laid the blame at Burke's door, complaining that in his *Commoners,* 'the dates of the births of sons are given but those of daughters suppressed, which combined with his practice of placing all the females after the males, is a loss of accuracy and of information'.[140] Despite these criticisms, it was still very rare after 1830 to read the birth date of peers' and baronets' daughters and even to see their children's names mentioned.

Worse than perpetuating baseless superstitions or concealing their dates of birth, some women were accused of iconoclasm and heedlessness. Following the French Revolution, the destructive power of women was exposed in the context of the various commissions on the state of public records which took place after 1800. The reorganization of the national repositories aimed at protecting private and public manuscripts from neglect and the threat of political radicalism. Several antiquaries and compilers were involved in the committees such as Nicholas Harris Nicolas, William Betham, Thomas Phillipps, and Stacey Grimaldi.[141] Public records were to protect the aristocratic past from the incidents of daily life. The commissioners gave various examples of careless women as well as unruly children who were responsible for the destruction of public archives. In the town of Lewes, the clergy had for long '[kept] the old registers in a cupboard, where the children, or any one else, could have got at them'.[142] In some cases, their registers were turned into 'kettle-holders for the curate's wife or widow' in Christchurch, or in another instance, where the 'keeper's daughters being lacemakers, it has been

---

[139] Joseph Addison, *The Lucubrations of Isaac Bickerstaff, Esq.* (London, 1712), vol. 3, 214.

[140] *GM,* Oct. 1833, 348.

[141] Nicholas Harris Nicolas, *Observations on the State of Historical Literature, and on the Society of Antiquaries* (London, 1830). Later, in July 1838, Thomas Phillipps wrote to John Russell, the Secretary of State, about 'the importance of preserving records to all ancient noble families (of which that of Russell is not the least)' which 'is to my view so great that I am astonished they have not so long since united together in a desire & determination to save the only memorials of their ancestors from total destruction. Some day a mad fit will seize the Populace of London (like that of Bristol) when all the depots of records will be set fire to and not one authentic document may remain to prove the existence of their forefathers.' A. N. L. Munby, *The Formation of the Phillipps Library up to the Year 1840* (Cambridge, 1954), 106.

[142] After the Act for Registration of Births, Deaths, and Marriages in 1827, several magazines published an abridged version of the inquest since 1828. *The Lancet,* vol. 2 (1839), 309.

194 SELLING ANCESTRY

used in that manufacture, in another, it has been transformed into the tester of a bed'.[143] These destructions were prejudicial for the landed elite but also for the whole nation. In the 1828 edition of *The Cyclopaedia*, it was pointed out that family records provide 'information highly important to those who are studying critically the biography of the distinguished persons of the English nation'.[144] However, in some cases, the eradication was described as intentional and morally justified. George Croker Fox, the self-styled 'chief of the Cornish families of Fox' wrote in great detail about the first common ancestor, Francis Fox, who during the Civil War had joined the Society of Friends in Cornwall:

> I cannot trace the descent before the said Francis Fox, nor can I say that I have taken pains to investigate it. And if you can throw any light on the subject, it will oblige me, having no documents to illustrate it, which as I have heard it said, were destroyed by an old woman of my predecessors, that her descendants might not be inflated with vanity.[145]

George Fox did not censure the old woman's behaviour as he himself did not seem to take many pains to look further into his origins. Despite his reservations, he pressed Burke to consult some reference books in order to enhance his descent. He wanted to insert that in Collins's *Peerage*, Francis Fox was linked to Sir Stephen Fox, an ancestor of the earls of Ilchester. Concerning the name Croker, George required Burke to look into John Prince's *Worthies of Devon* in which it was written, 'by the old proverbial distich: "Croker, Crewys, and Copplestone, When the Conqueror came, were at home".'[146] In his letter George Croker Fox paid homage to an old woman and her condemnation of vanity, though he seemed to believe that such prevention was no longer relevant in his time.

Another weakness attributed to women was the fact that they were expected to follow their husband, thus leaving their elder brother in charge of the papers and giving up their birth family. One Charles Claude Clifton, high sheriff of Brecknockshire, regretted that his mother had followed his father to India when she was too young: 'being only 14 when married she was not and did not become inquisitive'.[147] Neither was she able to keep any document on her husband and so 'singular as it may seem I have not the smallest clue to trace my Father's Pedigree'.[148] Born at St Thomas Mount in Madras, Clifton assumed that his mother would have been in charge of both her and his father's past. Far from being extraordinary, this was a widespread belief among other customers.

There are indeed many instances in which a female member of the kinship played a decisive role in the preservation of the past. Various studies underline the

---

[143] Ibid., 310.   [144] Article 'Pedigree', *The Penny Cyclopædia*, vol. 17 (London, 1828), 366.
[145] CA, BC, vol. 56, 7 Aug. 1828, case 183.   [146] Burke, *Commoners*, vol. 4, 314–15.
[147] CA, BC, vol. 56, 13 Dec. 1828, case 92.   [148] Ibid.

fact that women had access to most of the printed guides consumed by men and used their letter writing as a resource to record their own memories.[149] However, while the participation of the heads of household was assumed and even required, female contributions needed to be justified and closely contextualized.

'Celebrated' and 'distinguished' females

Beyond the binary opposition between patriarchal values and affective relationship, many aristocratic women led their lives in a complex and unpredictable manner. Scholarship on this subject abounds with stimulating perspectives.[150] Diaries, wills, and correspondence provide many examples of household literacies and ideas of ancestry. As in many female diaries, Elizabeth Isham (1609–54) included in her *Book of Remembrance* both an account 'of traditional genealogy (which descends through the generations) as well as less formalized types of inheritance, which may in fact be passed laterally through peers, friends, or servants'.[151] Reverence for patrilineal forebears and male inheritance has been distinguished from the extreme form of 'patriarchism', the one defined by Laurence Stone as the 'despotic authority of husband and father'.[152] The correspondence of Lady Isabella Wentworth, the duchess of Marlborough, and the duchess of Portland testified to their commitment to continuation of the male line and their pride in giving birth to boys.[153] Their increased participation in the household led them to be more involved in the transmission of the past of their own birth family. Far from generating egalitarian behaviour, the emerging discourses on patriotism and empire-building reinforced the role of elite women as the mothers of future military heroes and worthy statesmen. Country houses, which have so often been described as male sanctuaries of retired politicians, were cared for and transformed by their own wives. However, it seems that their ability

[149] George L. Justice and Nathan Tinker (eds), *Women's Writing and the Circulation of Ideas: Manuscript Publication in England, 1550–1800* (Cambridge, 2002); Amanda Vickery, *The Gentleman's Daughter: Women's Lives in Georgian England* (New Haven, 2003).

[150] The best introduction to this subject is provided by Daniel R. Woolf. 'A Feminine Past? Gender, Genre, and Historical Knowledge in England, 1500–1800', *American Historical Review*, vol. 102 (1997): 645–79.

[151] Jennifer Kolpacoff Deane, Julie A. Eckerle, Michelle M. Dowd, and Megan Matchinske, 'Women's Kinship Networks: A Meditation on Creative Genealogies and Historical Labor', in Merry E. Wiesner-Hanks (ed.), *Mapping Gendered Routes and Spaces in the Early Modern World* (London, 2015), 237.

[152] On the useful distinction between patriarchy and patriarchism, see Ingrid Tague, 'Aristocratic Women and Ideas of family', in Berry and Forster (eds), *The Family in Early Modern England*, 186; Susan D. Amussen, 'The Contradictions of Patriarchy in Early Modern England', *Gender & History*, vol. 30, no. 2 (2018): 343–53.

[153] 'Daughters required explanation and apology, both because husbands wanted sons and because women identified with the dynastic priorities of their families, through which they were able to establish a significant role as the bearers of heirs': Tague, 'Aristocratic Women and Ideas of Family', 197.

196 SELLING ANCESTRY

to make decisions in their own homes usually occurred after the husband's death.[154] As a widow in Welbeck, Lady Oxford amassed a considerable number of portraits and memorabilia associated with her own lineage and that of her deceased husband. Her interest in lineage did not exclude attention to her close kin. On the same premises, different family cultures coexisted. Lady Irwin, another widow with a sizeable wealth inherited from her father, succeeded in refashioning Temple Newsam, her 'country house', in a homely manner. Her coats of arms appeared on china and silver along with more intimate portraits and bedrooms available for close kin. Lady Irwin's dynastic concern was not simply a homage to the past but was guided by political interest, namely the defence of the parliamentary borough of Horsham against the duke of Norfolk.[155]

It has been established that the unmarried Mary Leigh was actively involved in strengthening her own lineage by 'marking all her silverware as well as her coach with the arms, supporters, and coronet'.[156] Like Etheldred Bennett, her single status did not prevent her from expressing a strong interest in ancestry.

We saw above that many husbands embedded their pedigrees in that of their wives of high rank, though it was rarely done without their consent and effective participation. For aristocratic women, the knowledge of their parentage was not just a resource that could be mobilized by their husbands. As well as their own personal wealth, they used it to assert their authority in various circumstances: sociability, marriage negotiations, and legal disputes. Furthermore, they were able to rely on their birth or their marriage, on their paternal or maternal side. It has been justly underlined that women had in a sense 'more options than men in identifying their families, and that their early prominence in the field of family history may reflect not only their more domestic preoccupation but also their less flawed possession of family identity'.[157]

Whether it be Wotton, Betham, or Burke, all agreed that some women of highest rank were endowed with greater genealogical literacy than their husbands. Wotton published the letter of Sir John Packington in which it was asserted that the educational treatise, *The Whole Duty of Man* had been written by Lady

---

[154] On the early modern gentle widow in Richard Brathwaite's frontispiece and her role as a 'familial genealogical guardian', see the stimulating introduction by Marie H. Loughlin, *Early Modern Women Writers Engendering Descent: Mary Sidney Herbert, Mary Sidney Wroth, and their Genealogical Cultures* (London, 2022), 1–11.

[155] 'Her sense of the lineage family is one oriented toward the future, toward stewardship and preservation, rather than in glorifying the past,' Judith S. Lewis, 'When a House Is Not a Home: Elite English Women and the Eighteenth-Century Country House', *Journal of British Studies*, vol. 48, no. 2 (2009): 336–63 at 355. On an internalized 'new-style patriarchy'.

[156] Jon Stobart and Mark Rothery, *Consumption and the Country House* (Oxford, 2016), 146.

[157] Katharine Hodgkin, 'Women, Memory and Family History in Seventeenth-Century England', in Erika Kuijpers et al. (eds), *Memory before Modernity: Practices of Memory in Early Modern Europe* (Leiden, 2013), 302.

Packington, the wife of the second baronet.[158] Dorothy Packington, as the daughter of Sir Thomas Coventry, the Lord Keeper, came from a higher family than her husband. Due to her eminent origins, she was in a situation to use her own parentage as a didactic tool in child rearing or more generally in moral guidance. The growing place attributed to women in the domestic sphere impacted on advice literature. In *The relative duties of parents and children, husbands and wives*, William Fleetwood recognized that some wives 'have a faithfulness and strength of memory' superior to that of their husbands.[159] Similarly, when William Betham was working on his *Baronetage*, he let his daughter Matilda publish *A Biographical Dictionary of the Celebrated Women* in which she referred to several 'female worthies' who displayed great reverence for their ancestors and their memories. Among the various portraits, Elizabeth Burnet, the daughter of Sir Richard Blake and successively married to Robert Berkeley and Gilbert Burnet, was described as the main guardian of the family papers in both her marriages and the maker of fair wills which preserved peace in the kinship.[160] Blanche Parry was introduced as a lover of Welsh antiquities, an attendant of Queen Elizabeth and the author of a remarkable pedigree.[161] Long before Betham, George Ballard in his compilation on literate women had already commented on the genealogical skill of Blanche Parry. Her pedigree proved not only 'her taste and genius' but 'the gentility of her descent'.[162] Hence, a faithful memory and the ability to transmit to the younger generations the deeds of the past, notably the notion of self-sacrifice and fidelity, were seen as female qualities. Their sensibility and their taste for evocative details enhanced the ancestors' deeds more than a disembodied lineal account. Even Burke, though reluctantly and mostly in footnotes, paid homage to some female aristocrats. In his two volumes of *The Portrait Gallery of Distinguished Females* (1833), he included a few 'female perfections' who contributed to the posterity of their husbands.[163] With few exceptions, it was through their portraits and beauty rather than thanks to their intellectual faculties, that their superiority was recognized. In his time, Mrs Andriane O'Sullivan, the author of *A genealogical and chronological game*

[158] Sir John Packington to Wotton, BL, Add. MS 14121, 1726, fol. 142; 'She has the reputation of being thought the author of the Whole duty of a man [...] though her modesty would not suffer her to claim the honour of it, but as the manuscript under her own hand now remains with the family, there is hardly room to doubt it'. Wotton, *Baronetage*, vol. 1, 188.

[159] William Fleetwood, *The relative duties of parents and children, husbands and wives* (London, 1737, 3rd edn), 134.

[160] *A Biographical Dictionary of the Celebrated Women of Every Age and Country* (London, 1804), 182–4.

[161] Ibid., 671. See also the articles on Anne Pembroke (677), Katherine Philips (688), Laetitia Pilkington (693), Elizabeth Row (750), and Martha Roper (737).

[162] George Ballard, *Memoirs of several ladies of Great Britain, who have been celebrated for their writings or skill in the learned languages, arts and sciences* (London, 1752), 177.

[163] On Lady Jane Savage, wife to John Paulet, marquess of Winchester: John Burke, *The Portrait Gallery of Distinguished Females including beauties of the courts of George IV. and William IV* (London, 1833), vol. 1, 162.

198 SELLING ANCESTRY

(1818) provides a more convincing example of female involvement in ancestry. While Newbery's game could be used as a modified goose game, Andriane O'Sullivan used her small textbook as a way for children to memorize the main kings, queens, and politicians as well as their parentage. She may have been inspired by previous games such as the one published in 1791 by Elizabeth Newbery, *Royal genealogical pastime of the sovereigns of England* (1791) which was presented as a 'scientific game' intended to 'amuse' and 'to make the Players acquainted with the Genealogy of their Own king'.[164] Andriane O'Sullivan's book was dedicated to Lady Anne Holroyd, the daughter of Lord North and the countess of Sheffield, presented as a patron and model in terms of family values. The young reader inspired by her should 'attend to the precepts of your enlightened parents; follow their example; emulate their virtues; and in your turn, as others have done for ages past, you will add fresh lustre to your elevated rank'.[165] Similarly, the Innes sisters dedicated their *Peerage* to Victoria Maria Luísa, duchess of Kent, who embodied 'the exemplary virtues of a female character'.[166] In the obituary of Anne, the eldest of the sisters, she was recognized for her 'prompt and correct judgement, enlarged intellect' and 'eager patriotism'.[167] Still, it was promptly added that her successful *Annual Peerage* would not have come to fruition without the kindness and instruction of the herald Edmund Lodge and her father Charles Innes.

With regard to the publishers' correspondents, most mentioned their mothers or their wives whenever they had a higher parentage. Henry Barnard replied to Burke following his mother's directions. Sarah Barnard-Gee is described as an heiress from 'a very old family' in York and for further details, she would take 'a great pleasure in giving you a very possible information in her power'.[168] Henry portrayed himself as the last male figure in the family, after his father's and brothers' deaths, yet he let his mother complete the article. She sent a letter in which she depicted both funerary monuments, respectively in white and black marble, dedicated to her younger son and her husband.[169] She gave a highly detailed rendition of the Gees of Rothley and their alliances to the Yorkshire baronetcies of Hotham, Parker, Carew, and Penyman. As the heiress of her father's property and a widow, she was the driving force behind the Barnard-Gee article. Similarly, the Revd Holland Coham answered Burke's enquiry at the request of his mother Mary Holland, who was 'anxious' to know more about his scheme.[170] As the clergyman was then staying in London, she asked him to meet Burke with a button of her armorial crest and a 'complete pedigree of the

[164] E. Newbery, *Royal genealogical pastime of the sovereigns of England*, Bod. Lib., Bodleian Library Games folder (33).

[165] Ibid., preface.   [166] *The Annual peerage of The British Empire* (London, 1827).

[167] *GM*, Sept 1856, vol. 201, 253.   [168] CA, BC, vol. 56, 21 July 1828, case 28.

[169] CA, BC, vol. 56, 28 Dec. 1828, case 28.

[170] 'I received last week from my mother (who resides in Devon) containing an advertisement of a work you are about to publish [...] and of which she is anxious to obtain some further information'. CA, BC, vol. 56, 13 July 1828, case 96.

FAMILY TIES AND PUBLISHERS' ENQUIRIES 199

Hollands' copied out of an original done in metal which Segar Somerset saw in the possession of Mr Garter'.[171] From these various elements, it appears that her ancestors had belonged to 'one of the most ancient and illustrious' families in England since Edward II.[172]

Unexpected and exceptional situations

In several exceptional situations, wives were required to step into their husbands' shoes. Major political events were such as they brought about a reconfiguration of gender roles. The English civil wars which led to the exile or imprisonment of royalists promoted many women to unconventional responsibilities. The extensive genealogical narratives composed by Anne Clifford, Anne Fanshawe, and Anne Hutchinson have been amply scrutinized. Unlike Clifford's, the writing of Fanshawe and Hutchinson was closely linked to political upheavals.[173] Claire Gheeraert-Graffeuille rightly insisted on Hutchinson's 'act of genealogical inscription' at the beginning of her *Memoirs* as she 'establishes a genealogy of virtue, honour, and piety, and grounds it in Nottinghamshire, in order to legitimize the long narrative that follows.'[174]

By the same token, their contribution to the preservation of the aristocratic identity among Jacobite refugees was crucial. Sean J. Connolly in *The Making of Protestant Ireland* argued that being a refugee did not involve being entirely cut off from the Irish or even the British community.[175] John Bossy and several recent historians have pointed to the central role played by women in the cultural and material life of the exiled community. Restrictions and repression brought about by the penal laws were mainly directed at men and thus reinforced women's responsibilities, notably their role in the preservation of archives and in various writing practices (didactic treatises, correspondence, devotional texts).[176] In Paris, late in the reign of Louis XIV, James Terry was established as the Irish herald for the exiled families.[177] Terry held a strategic position for the many Irish officers

---

[171] Ibid., 14 Oct. 1828.   [172] Ibid.

[173] See the recent edition by Jessica Malay of some of Anne Clifford's archives and the memoirs of her mother Margaret Russell, *Anne Clifford's Great Books of Record* (Manchester, 2015); Derek Hirst, 'Remembering a Hero: Lucy Hutchinson's Memoirs of Her Husband', EHR, vol. 119 (2004), 682–91.

[174] Claire Gheeraert-Graffeuille, *Lucy Hutchinson and the English Revolution: Gender, Genre and History-Writing* (Oxford, 2022), 45.

[175] Sean J. Connolly, *Religion, Law, and Power: The Making of Protestant Ireland 1660–1760* (Oxford, 1992).

[176] Liesbeth Corens, *Confessional Mobility and English Catholics in Counter-Reformation Europe* (Oxford, 2019), 94; Gabriel Glickman, *The English Catholic Community 1688–1745: Politics, Culture and Ideology* (Cambridge, 2009).

[177] BN MS Anglais 111–13: correspondence of Jacques Tyrry (Terry). Stéphane Jettot, 'Les vaincus des guerres civiles: exil et réinvention de soi dans la gentry jacobite irlandaise (XVIIe–XVIIIe siècle)', in E. Dupraz and C. Gheeraert-Graffeuille (éds), *La guerre civile: représentations, idéalisations, identifications* (Rouen, 2014), 240–60.

200 SELLING ANCESTRY

who needed to be recognized as noble in France. To certify their pedigree, he used several compilations, notably a fifteenth-century codex called the Book of Lecan: an ornamented vellum tome of 315 folios displaying hundreds of pedigrees. Some close female relatives were central in his attempt to assert authority over a community which did not easily accept his position. Terry claimed that his mother, Mary Ronan, was the 'daughter to William Ronan of Cratalagh (Clare) and of Ellen Stricht. [...] the said William Ronan [...] descended from Ronan king of Ireland of milestones races'.[178] His daughter Margaret married into the MacGillicuddy family of county Cork, whose members were enrolled on both sides of the conflict, in the French army and the imperial army.[179] In 1713, she was living in Surrey and conducted several transactions with the College of Arms on behalf of her father.[180] Terry received many letters from the wives of Jacobite army officers and merchants.[181] They were heavily involved in defending the status of their husbands and some complained that they had to pay a fee to be recognized as noble whereas their gentility was undisputed. Marguerite Thoumy complained to Terry's wife about her husband's rough behaviour, reminding her that in Ireland she had been on familiar terms with the nobility while the Ronans came from 'poor parents':

> My husband and I never did you but pleasure and goodness. My mother yt keep in her own 3 chambermaid in silk to serve her, & her children receivd ye Duke of Ormond, ye Earl of Mongomry and ye best gentry of her country in her own house, had breeding, plate, gold, and richness to do it and she had her sister ye spouse of capt grant, Vice-Admiral, justice of peace and high sheriff, joint with ye honest parents I come from ought to oblige you to show me some civility at least. I never spook of you but great and good, I never told of your poor parents, how they strove to live [...] by selling a poor cup of beer.[182]

The herald wrote to Lieut. William Griffin about the latter's wife, Françoise Margaret Griffin, who had dealt with him in the most 'barbarous manner', 'stayning his reputation' at the court of Saint-Germain.[183] The tense relationship the herald had with many officers' wives testified to the latter's persistent involvement. Furthermore, it is worth mentioning that while Revd Mervyn Archdall was

---

[178] BN MS Anglais 111, fol. 131.

[179] W. M. Brady (ed.), *The McGillicuddy papers* (London, 1867).

[180] BN MS FR 32964, fol. 320.

[181] Eleanor and Helena MacCarthy of Clanrickard, Margaret Hamilton, 'Françoise' Margaret Griffin, Catherine O'Hara, Lady Percival of Kinsale, Mannsell, Margaret Roch, Catherine Barnenvalle, Marguerite Thoumy.

[182] Marguerite Thoumy to Mary Terry, 1723, BN MSS Ang 113, fols 103–4.

[183] 'Sir I doe not understand the barbarous manner I am used by your wife, she gives herself the liberty to stayn my reputation [...]. She is pleased to say that I made a blacksmith's son an armes.' James Terry to William Griffin, 6 Dec. 1704, BN MSS Ang 113, fol. 57.

celebrated as an 'Irish worthy' for the quality of his *Peerage* published in 1789, Richard Ryan, his sycophant, recounted that it was in fact his wife, Abigael Young, a clergyman's daughter, who managed to decipher and reassemble all the manuscript notes left by John Lodge, the author of the first edition.[184] We also saw above the considerable contribution of Frances Jerningham, the daughter of Viscount Dillon, who relied on her close kin and their continental networks, notably in various monasteries, to provide an extensive pedigree in Betham's *Baronetage*.

At last, the more usual circumstances in which women were expected to step in, were related to sudden deaths, diseases, and travels. Anne Dod was keen to explain that it was the brutal disappearance of her father the year before that had led her to answer Burke's letter.[185] Anne and the elder daughter were still unmarried and she felt it was her turn to take on this responsibility. Her brother John Anthony had died a bachelor in India and she introduced her elder sister 'Miss Charlotte' as presently the head of the 'Dods of Edge' (Chester). Along with many references drawn from J. H. Henshall's *History of the County Palatine of Chester* (1823) and G. Ormerod's *History of Cheshire* (1818), Anne furnished a very personal description of the property, its various styles, its moat and its parks overseeing a sublime and picturesque view over Wales:

At the back is a parklike enclosure, ascending gently to a terrace, on the summit of a rocky eminence well planted with trees, through the interstices of which the eye commands the high Broxton and Bickerton hills behind and in front the Clwydian range, with loftier mountains above them, seen over the broad vale of Chester. On the right the estuaries appear in the distance, and on the left is a boundless continuation of the magnificent vale below, broken in some places by the Montgomeryshire hills, and completely losing itself in the vista.[186]

In her case, Dod's article borrowed much from the romantic sublime and from travel guides. Like most antiquaries, she was conscious of the public appetite for such a picturesque description: 'the landscape, rural and urban, became a theatre of religious history and national memory, a manifestation of the consuming interest in the classical, British, and Gothic past that gripped the upper classes of Britain and Ireland in the long eighteenth century'.[187] Other correspondents

---

[184] 'Mr Lodge had left numerous additions to his work in MS. but written in a cypher declared to be totally inexplicable by all the short-hand writers in Dublin, these MSS. were about to be given up in despair, when Mrs Archdall, (his surviving relict) a woman of considerable ability and ingenuity, applied the arduous task, and after a short time happily discovered the key, and thereby greatly enriched the edition.' Richard Ryan, *Biographia Hibernica: A Biographical Dictionary of the Worthies of Ireland* (London, Dublin, 1819), vol. 1, 18.

[185] 'The person & head of this family to whom your letter is addressed died May 18th 1827 leaving 4 daughters', Anne Dod to John Burke, 17 July 1828, CA, BC, vol. 56, case 145.

[186] Burke, *Commoners* (1836), vol. 3, 551.

[187] Alexandra Walsham, *The Reformation of the Landscape: Religion, Identity, and Memory in Early Modern Britain and Ireland* (Oxford, 2011), 324.

202 SELLING ANCESTRY

noted the frail state of the household head. Eliza Sullivan, the daughter of Sir Richard Joseph Sullivan, was entrusted with providing an account as her father was highly 'indisposed'.[188] Dorothy Allanson, the daughter of the Revd George Allanson, mentioned the inability of her father 'to act for himself'.[189] One Francis Burton, from the cadet branch of the Burton of Galway, had received the formula from his wife's uncle. He answered that he was 'deprived of sight' and that his wife was devoutly engaged in decoding all his papers, stressing:

> The difficulty of deciphering the name in some old papers, wills and title deeds which having been kept in the family between one and two centuries in a large oak chest have been gnawed by mice which have eaten their way through the bottom. My wife spent five weeks in piecing them together and had made out several clearly but others seem almost hopeless. She will persevere and they shall be forwarded as speedily as possible.[190]

Sophia-Alethea Burton, the youngest daughter of a military surgeon, proceeded very swiftly to deliver a complete pedigree enriched with literary details such as their connection with Robert, the author of the *Anatomy of Melancholy*, along with various comments by Anthony Wood and Lord Byron on his work. Making up for her husband's disability, she composed a remarkable narrative.[191]

Lastly, we may consider the case of a wandering baronet. While away on his grand tour Sir George Lucy entrusted Philippa Hayes, his housekeeper at Charlecote (Warwickshire), with digging into the family papers. In her letter to Wotton, Philippa, a highly literate woman, wrote back with an exhaustive pedigree. She acknowledged the help of George's former tutor at Oxford, a certain Godwyn, depicted as a 'bookworm, fellow of Balliol College'.[192] Charles Godwyn (1701–70) was indeed a respected antiquary and fellow of Balliol mostly renowned for his collection of coins and medals. A widow with grown-up children, Hayes was particularly active and was involved in a wide network of correspondents.[193] William Masson, while his father was away from home, also benefited from the help of dedicated women. It was first by his 'mother's desire' that he agreed to help Burke in his task; he was seconded by his great-aunt, Mrs Elizabeth Blomefield, the daughter of the author of *History of Norfolk*, who despite being 91 years old, 'possessed her recollections from the earliest period':

---

[188] BL, Add. MS 21033, 1804, fol. 80.   [189] CA, BC, vol. 56, 1828, case 8.

[190] CA, BC, vol. 56, 22 Nov. 1828, case 65.

[191] Burke, *Commoners* (1836), vol. 3, 271. Her genealogical interest may have been strengthened by a legal case regarding some land in East Riding (Surrender and admission relating to land in Igglemire, May 1833. ERYA: DDX31/171).

[192] BL, Add. MS 24121, fol. 59.

[193] On Mrs Hayes, see the recent work by Jon Stobart, 'Housekeeper, Correspondent and Confidante: The Under-told Story of Mrs Hayes of Charlecote Park, 1744–73', *Family & Community History*, vol. 21, no. 2 (2018): 96–111.

Her observations are of some value, particularly as her mother died many years ago 93 years of age and possessed her faculty to the last and her grandmother, 87, also a person perfectly living in her recollection and as her family was intimate with my grandfather, her record of generations long gone by I think may be relied on.[194]

Masson relied on an exceptionally long chain of transmission from his female kin. From the many cases explored above, it is worth pointing out that in many ways, men were far from holding a monopoly on the family past. Whether it be from personal recollection or from long hours of work in the archives, transcribing, 'piecing together' various documents and in the case of Etheldred Bennett even editing, women played a central role in these directories. The numerous traces of their hidden participation make these letters particularly valuable. Their contribution did not differ significantly from male recollection and contributed to resilient patriarchal values. There was no reason to believe that an aristocratic woman would not take pride in a long line of male ancestors. The idea that women were excluded from the family past does not hold ground, and in many occasions they fulfilled the role of storytellers on their own. The many examples considered previously demonstrate the existence of an interesting space between 'masculine' intellectual knowledge networks, and 'feminine' interest in family history, and inheritance.

3. Family feuds and legal claims

While wives' higher social origins allowed them to participate openly in the publishing process, they could also generate much resentment in the household. Several studies have been dedicated to the miseries occurring in a marriage between a genteel wife and a commoner. The diaries of Elizabeth Shackleton contain a sobering tale of the mismatched union between John Shackleton, a local woollen merchant, and Elizabeth, from a well-established gentry. John failed 'to bolster his identity as an elite adult man' and greatly suffered from his financial dependence.[195] Without any descendants, John was said to be consuming vast quantities of alcohol and to be acting with increasing violence towards her. To make up for this social imbalance, she even ventured to visit the College of Arms to discover what arms belonged to her husband's name. Here is an extreme case of a wife trying desperately to restore her husband's sense of honour.

---

[194] William Masson to Burke, 21 July 1828, CA, BC, vol. 57, case 355. His mother was Elizabeth Colombine, daughter of Paul Colombine DD, rector of Plumstead (Norfolk).
[195] French, *Man's Estate: Landed Gentry*, 200.

204 SELLING ANCESTRY

However, with respect to the making of directories, conflicts and acrimonious relations occurred mostly among siblings and competing collaterals. They arose when relatives failed to agree on a consensual narrative. A whole spectrum of rationales might account for these conflicts, from the usual jealousies and competition between siblings to the anxieties raised by inheritance issues. Accusations of illegitimacy could serve to disqualify the other competing party. Most often letters referred to discontents or tensions which never reached the law courts. Some alluded to cases in which ancestry and lineage were expected to play a role in the litigation process. Caught between competing parties, the publishers tried, although often unsuccessfully, to avoid becoming involved in the conflict.

Tyrannical elder brothers

Tensions arose when members of the kinship felt that the balance between duties and privilege was no longer respected. Some heads of family were suspected of abusing their dominant position and committing various excesses: a theme which abounds in many novels and can also be found in customers' correspondence. There are several instances in which an elder brother expressed a proprietorial and defiant attitude towards his siblings, jettisoning a sense of common purpose and mutual obligation.

Some were accused of unjustly erasing some relatives from the narrative. Sir William Wentworth of Bretton dictated a very short account to Wotton: 'I would have no more of what related to our family inserted in our Baronetage, except what is above.'[196] Forbidding him to look for further sources of information, he introduced himself as 'the 15th in a lineal descent from their branching from Earl Strafford's family', omitting to mention that he was in fact the second surviving son.[197] Keen to be positioned into a continuous male lineage, he erased the memory of his elder brother, a misdeed that his sisters condemned. To prevent their involvement, he successfully discouraged Wotton from getting in touch with them. Similarly, Sir James Ashe, the second baronet, asked Wotton 'not to seek out for any farther information whether true or false' from his sisters.[198] The origin of this sign of distrust may have come from an ancient feud with his own mother, Mary Wilson. After her husband's death, she was in control of considerable property left by her father. Opposing her son's union to the daughter of Sir Edmund Bowyer, she complained of 'his perverseness to me, and crossness in not marrying where I desired'.[199] It seemed that Ashe's sisters rallied around their

---

[196] Wentworth to Wotton, 1 Dec. 1725, BL, Add. MS 24121, fol. 329.
[197] *The English Baronets* (1727), vol. 2, 407.   [198] Ashe to Wotton, BL, Add. MS 24120, fol. 19.
[199] Quoted by David Hayton, *The House of Commons*, vol. 3, 68.

mother and he decided to sever all ties with them. Wotton complied with his wishes, stating merely that the father 'had issue several daughters and one son'.[200]

In some other cases, the genealogical investigation offered an opportunity to revive old disputes and rivalries. Answering Wotton's letter, Annabella Blount born Guise, the wife of Sir Edward Blount of Soddington, informed Wotton that her husband 'commanded me to answer that part of yr letter which concerns my own family'.[201] She was frank in demonstrating that she was not acting on her own. Furthermore, her participation was justified by her elder brother's lack of response:

> I have already written twice to my Br, importuning him to give an account of his race, which if carefully done would be rewarding but since you say he neglected it, you shall have what my memory furnishes. I not having any archive of the family.[202]

By 'race', she did not mean the hereditary qualities assigned to noble birth but the patrilineal narrative for which her brother was to be accountable. Since he had failed to answer both her letters and Wotton's, she perceived that her deferential behaviour was not reciprocated. As he did not fulfil his responsibility as head of the family, she felt justified in stepping in. The elder son of the second baronet, John Guise (1678–1732), was the owner of a rich collection of papers left by their grandfather, Christopher Guise, who had composed a long account of his life and ancestors (equivalent to a 'Libro di ricordanze' or 'Livre de raison').[203] Sir John Guise's refusal to participate in Wotton's enquiry was all the more surprising since he was actually passionate about ancestry. As a sign of devotion to his forebears, he continued writing in his grandfather's record books, possibly for the sake of instructing his own son. While he praised his grandfather and father's behaviour, he made a few harsh comments on some female members, starting with his grandfather's second wife, 'a woman who, living with Sir Christopher in his latter days, had so far imposed upon his weakness as almost to cause the ruin of his family'.[204] Similarly his mother and sisters were accused of threatening the continuation of the male lineage. He described his mother as being 'of an indolent temper and ill versed in the business of the world'.[205] About his two sisters, he resented the fact that his estate was charged with £6,000 to them and that he was obliged to maintain them 'though they were in better circumstances

---

[200] Wotton, *English Baronets* (1727), vol. 2, 152.

[201] Annabella Guise to Wotton, 4 Feb. 1726, BL, Add. MS 24120, fol. 401. On the Blounts, see Jettot, 'Family Input', 187–9.

[202] Annabella Guise to Wotton, 4 Feb. 1726, BL, Add. MS 24120, fol. 401.

[203] *The Memoirs of the Guises* has been published by the Camden Society (new series, 28, 1917). My thanks to Henry French for bringing this source to my attention.

[204] Ibid., 132.   [205] Ibid., 137.

206 SELLING ANCESTRY

then myself'.[206] In providing too little for himself, he felt that his parents had weakened his position. Far from being grateful and obedient, both his sisters married against his wishes. Along with the bitterness accumulated throughout their childhood, the sisters' new marital status did not improve the dynamics. It seems that Anne Guise had refused to consider his reservations about marrying an impoverished and older man. The fact that Anne got a local painter to place a heraldic over the mantle displaying the impaled arms of Blount and Guise, with the motto: *Lux Tua Via Mea* ('Your light is my path') may have upset him. He accused his mother of having spoilt his sister and fortified her 'bookish humour', which had led to her being fooled by Blount. This was a common bias according to which, instead of being enriched by her erudition, a *femme savante* became vain and more likely to be manipulated by her husband. He finished his account by warning his reader against any wife who 'will not, with her person, give up all her affaires' and against any man who will not be able to 'preserve the dignity and authority of a husband'.[207] He supplemented his grandfather's memoirs with a new agenda, namely the defence of endangered patriarchal values. He quoted the Gospel to demonstrate that husbands were to be respected in their natural authority yet expressed much anxiety about his ability to perform this function.[208]

Moreover, Guise's hostility to his sister may have come from the fact that she allied herself to the Catholic arch-enemy to the point of converting herself to the much-abhorred faith. Their grandfather Christopher Guise was a fervent Protestant and a Protectorate MP. Guise mentioned in his memoirs the fears of his grandfather at the time of the threatened Spanish invasion in 1588 and of his father's support for the 'silent ministers and non-conformists' against the Arminians.[209] As he refused to allow her access to his archives, Guise worried that his papers would fall into the wrong pair of hands. Issues of politics, gender, and religion were at stake. Her husband was certainly no friend to John Guise. One of his correspondents and friends, Alexander Pope, on a visit to the Guise seat at Rendcomb Hall, had exchanged with Blount a joke about John Guise's dynastic pride. Pope described a haunted place inhabited by agitated ghosts. He felt possessed by the family portraits, their 'faces all upon me', and the grandfather Sir Christopher 'being in his shirt seems as ready to combat me'.[210] After the Reformation, the seams between the worlds of the dead and the living occasionally burst open. Along with the memories of confessional strife, the invasion of ghosts

---

[206] Ibid., 140; see also the trust deed of Edward *Blount* of Blagdon (Devon) esq. and Annabell, daughter of Sir John Guise, bt of Rendcomb, 1704. GA, D326/F17.

[207] *Memoirs of the Guises*, 152.

[208] On anxiety and masculinity, see Alexandra Shepard, 'From Anxious Patriarchs to Refined Gentlemen? Manhood in Britain, circa 1500–1700', *The Journal of British Studies*, vol. 44, no. 2 (2005): 281–95.

[209] *Memoirs of the Guises*, 110 and 113.

[210] 'I am well pleased to date this from a place so well known to Mrs Blount, where I write as if I were dictated to by her ancestors, whose faces are all upon me'. 3 Oct. 1721 (quoted ibid., 98.)

has been interpreted as a symbol of dysfunction and guilt among patriarchal families.[211]

The conflict between John Guise and his sister was linked not only to access to the archives but also to the right to shape the past. The accounts of both Christopher and John Guise ignored medieval stories, dismissed the value of the College of Arms, and were centred around the strife and violence of the recent political crisis, while Anne's narrative went far back to the time of the Norman Conquest, a remote past which dwarfed the confessional and political oppositions of later times.[212] Remote origins helped to bridge the confessional gap which arose at the Reformation. Anne displayed a remarkable knowledge of alternative sources. She relied on a wide variety of resources, ranging from county histories to personal recollections. She strove to make up for her brother's reluctance by providing various clues from Sir Robert Atkyns's *History of Gloucester*, and even considered travelling to London to supply Wotton with further details.[213] Although her contribution is not mentioned in the footnotes, Wotton faithfully printed most of her letters. In contrast to John Guise's insecure and solitary behaviour, his sister seems to have been well supported by her husband as well as certain good friends such as Alexander Pope. Her confident manner, which is reflected in her letters, may later have been strengthened by her effective matrimonial strategy. Of her four daughters, Maria married Edward the ninth duke of Norfolk, Elizabeth the third Baron Clifford, and Henrietta, the ninth duke's younger brother Philip Howard.[214] Although they were weak in terms of political influence, these Catholic magnates had succeeded in preserving their social standing.

Another conflict among siblings took place during the re-edition of Debrett's *Peerage* by William Courthope. Amid his correspondents was Sholto Henry Maclellan, Lord Kirkcudbright, nicknamed 'Lordly Elevation' for his alleged haughtiness and aspirational spirit. He was the target of caricaturists such as John Cawse and James Gillray, and was portrayed as a foppish coward and a ridiculous dwarfish hunchback who stood on a baron's coronet to appear taller.[215]

These attacks may arise from his personal behaviour as well as from the modest origins of the family. His forename 'Sholto' was said to derive from

---

[211] 'Ghosts wove their way between members of a lineage, redefining the place of individuals and, crucially, gender relations within the family.' Caroline Callard, *Spectralities in the Renaissance: Sixteenth and Seventeenth Centuries* (Oxford, 2022), 131.

[212] 'If you will take the pain to look into Doomsday book & the other records in the Heralds office, you will find (as I had it from my father) in Doomsday Book that Sr Wm Guise a younger Bt of an illustrious family in France followed the fortune of William the Conqueror.' Annabella Blount to Wotton, 4 Feb. 1726, BL, Add. MS 24120, fol. 400.

[213] Ibid., fol. 402.   [214] Wotton, *Baronetage*, vol. 3.1, 315–16.

[215] *Town fops including L. Skeffington, J. Penn and Lord Kirkcudbright, feigning fashionable wounds after the return of the troops from Holland.* Coloured etching after J. Cawse (London, 1799); James Gillray, Sholto Henry Maclellan, 9th Baron Kirkcudbright ('Lordly Elevation') published by Hannah Humphrey (1802), NPG D12776.

208 SELLING ANCESTRY

'Sholto Douglas', the mythical figure of the Clan Douglas. The family received a glorious account in most peerages, with their roots dating back to Sir William Wallace and Edward I, including many anecdotes about their military deeds at Flodden and fighting a gang of Moors who invaded Ireland in the reign of James II.[216] Sholto Henry had inherited the title from his grandfather, William McLellan, a glover in Edinburgh, and from his father John, an army officer who successfully petitioned the House of Lords in 1767 against other claimants to the barony.[217] Considering his modest origins, the ninth Lord was mocked for his genealogical pretensions and for impersonating a decadent aristocrat. In 1823, he notified Courthope of an 'affair of much delicacy', namely that the wife and daughter of his brother were 'as I am informed what is professionally termed nullius filiae, or no mans' daughters, they being in fact illegitimate children and so being were not entitled to be introduced into the pedigree'.[218] Like Blount and Ashe previously, the holder of the title was without issue and felt he was permitted to exert strict control over the narrative. He asked Burke to erase their names from the pedigree. Despite the increase in the illegitimacy ratio over the eighteenth century, the social stigma attached to out-of-wedlock unions was very potent. The lord felt that the supposedly illegitimate daughter fathered by his brother was a stain on his pedigree. Informed by Courthope of his older sibling's claims, the younger brother, Camden Gray, wrote back to him with a copy of his marriage certificate as well as his daughter's birth certificate and christening documents, adding in a rather pleading tone:

> I can in no way submit to the degradation of persons so dear to me. I am called upon as a man, a father and a husband to protect them. [...] I therefore caution and entreat you sir on no account to attend to any future misrepresentation or misstatement relative to my family.[219]

While his older brother was using the language of honour and lineage, Camden Gray chose to underline that of the close bonds between husband, wife, and daughter. Trying to mediate between the estranged brothers, Courthope wrote back to Sholto Henry about the various certificates which established the legitimacy of his brother's family. Far from appeasing him, he only caused further offence. The documents were dismissed as 'a fabrication and a gross imposition on

---

[216] Debrett, *Scottish Peerage* (1803), vol. 2, 441.

[217] *Proceedings relating to the Peerage of Scotland*, from 16 Jan. 1707 to 29 Apr. 1788, William Robertson (Edinburgh, 1790), 329. On William McLellan, see his portrait as a Scottish glover by John Burke, *The Patrician* (1846), vol. 1, 133.

[218] CA, WC 69, 6 June 1823, fol. 10. On the figure of the younger brother, see Ronda Arab, 'Sir George Sondes *His plaine Narrative to the World*: The Envious Younger Son and the Inequality of Inheritance in Seventeenth-Century England', *Journal of Medieval and Early Modern Studies*, vol. 49, no. 2 (2019): 403–26.

[219] Camden Gray to Courthope, 15 Sept. 1824, CA, WC 69, fol. 50.

FAMILY TIES AND PUBLISHERS' ENQUIRIES   209

your weak credibility'.[220] Sholto Henry further denigrated his 'degraded brother' and warned Courthope against 'wilfully sully[ing] the page of my Honors':

> You are bound at your peril, to obey my injunction and set him down as a bachelor [...]. If you wantonly insult my name and therefore the whole Peerage of Scotland [...] then I shall sue you for £20,000 damages.[221]

It was a rather eccentric threat to scare the publisher. More interestingly, he then explained what was at stake financially, namely that their mother had left 'a considerable part of her property' to any of her sons' legitimate children.[222] As he was himself childless, if his brother's child was recognized, he would be excluded from the reversionary interest established in the will. But he added that the provision had never been intended for his niece, a 'love child' who was known to his mother and should have been barred 'from her will as any other bastard from the inheritance'.[223] Hence Courthope was forced to choose between two competing causes. Initially he complied with the older brother's wish in the following edition, erasing the younger brother's family while, at Sholto Henry's death in 1827, he pragmatically reintroduced it.[224]

Treacherous stepfamilies

As premature deaths and remarriages were so widespread, stepfamilies, half-brothers, and half-sisters were a part of a ubiquitous form of family life. The stepfamily has often been described as an inclusive place where stepchildren used to gather around to defend their mutual interest.[225] Several studies have under-lined the peaceful relations that were the rule among recomposed families. Co-residence usually led to strong bonds which were advocated by the parents. In his letter, Peter Rickards-Mynors mentioned the death of his father Peter and his mother's remarriage to Jasper Farmer, who held the property of Treago as a jointure. He seemed to be living on good terms with his stepfather, and the latter encouraged him to be in charge of both his father's and his mother's pedigree.[226] Jasper Farmer was not keen to appear in the narrative and Peter Mynors, as for him, went on to present his mother as 'Meliora Baskerwill of Erdesley', descending from a proud line of ancestors whose name could be seen in the roll at Battle Abbey and who were 'for many reigns champions to the kings of England and were sheriffs of the county of Hereford twenty-one times'.[227]

---

[220] Sholto Henry to Courthope, 18 Dec. 1824, CA, WC 69, fol. 32.   [221] Ibid., fol. 33.
[222] Ibid.   [223] Ibid.   [224] Debrett, *Peerage* (1824), vol. 2, 834; ibid. (1827) vol. 2, 601.
[225] Lyndan Warner (ed.), *Stepfamilies in Europe 1400–1800* (London, 2018).
[226] Peter Richards-Mynors to Burke, 1828, CA, BC, vol. 57, case 388.   [227] Ibid.

210 SELLING ANCESTRY

It has been argued, however, that the change from vertical bonds to stronger horizontal ties gave more power to stepmothers at the expense of the children from the first union. A fear which prevailed was that the interest of the latter would be sidelined. The commonplace of the wicked stepmother raised its ugly head in many sobering tales. In a letter to Wotton, the herald Charles Townley referred to a story from the time of James I recorded by John Aubrey, about Sir Walter Long, who 'disinherited his eldest son John at ye justification of his second wife Catherine Thynne'.[228] Again, as in the Guises' case, injustice led to the occurrence of supernatural events. Catherine Thynne, the second wife, did everything she could to make her stepson odious to his father. She even asked a clerk to modify the will to the advantage of her own son. Aubrey wrote that during the night the clerk worked on the will he saw a 'fine white hand interposed between the writing and the candle'.[229] Refusing to proceed after a third apparition, the clerk was replaced by another writer who managed to alter the will. The plot did not come to fruition as Sir Walter died shortly afterwards and 'his body did not go quiet to the grave, it being arrested at the church porch by the trustees of the first Lady'.[230] Finally, ousting the wicked stepmother, the stepchildren agreed to share the inheritance equally. In the case of Anne Guise, by attacking her friend Alexander Pope, the spectre of her grandfather seemed to have taken on his grandson's cause and to be impersonating a dying patrilineal culture. With regard to Sir Walter Long, we may safely assume that it was probably the first wife who came back from the dead to uphold her son's rights. Even in the eighteenth century, ghosts were often mobilized in the defence of abused women.[231] Among the publishers' correspondents, no such extraordinary event took place, although the anger expressed against a stepmother could be quite strong. Thomas Whitaker apologized for his shortcomings:

> I cannot give you so full an account as I could wish my mother having died in my infancy and my father having married a second wife who was a widow with children by her former husband and consequently, she did all in her forces to deprive me of the affection of my father that she might get as much of his property as possible for her own children.[232]

As we have seen previously, access to archives was closely linked to inheritance. As he was the only surviving son of the first union, Whitaker felt that his rights were being undermined by the larger and dominating stepfamily. Fortunately, his

---

[228] Townley to Wooton, BL, Add. MS 24118, fol. 26.

[229] John Aubrey, *Miscellanies, Upon the Following Subjects* (London, 1721), 76.   [230] Ibid.

[231] Ghosts were increasingly involved as arbiters in succession crises and marital violence. See Sasha Handley, *Visions of an Unseen World: Ghost Beliefs and Ghost Stories in Eighteenth-Century England* (London, 2007).

[232] Whitaker to Burke, 8 Aug. 1828, CA, BC, vol. 58, case 587.

stepmother had recently died, and he managed to find some particulars among the notes left by his uncle, who has been the rector of Ashton since 1730.

Another interesting case related to the succession of the barony Saye and Sele in 1824. The present and twelfth lord, William Thomas, was without issue and his uncle, the Revd Thomas-James Twisleton, archdeacon of Colombo and the presumptive heir to the title, had just died. His death triggered a bitter confrontation between the children from his two marriages. In the 1822 edition of Debrett's *Peerage*, the children of the first line disappeared whereas those of the second union were named and introduced as the next in line, in particular the elder son Frederick-Benjamin, a fellow of New College (Oxford) (Tree 4.2).

Julia Eliza Twisleton, the daughter from the first union, complained about being left out of the edition and about 'a disposition in the world to misrepresent the situation in the life of the first Mrs Twisleton', namely that she was an actress with two illegitimate children.[233] This was a strange occurrence since in the 1816 edition, she had been mentioned along with her brother Charles and with the children of the second union.[234] Julia and her half-siblings had been brought up together in Ceylon. They may have later fallen out prior to the 1822 edition, and she suspected the second branch of being responsible for the faulty article, as well as for the insulting obituary in *The Gentleman's Magazine*. Presented as a cautionary tale, the unknown writer of the magazine recounted how Thomas James Twisleton, once a serious student, 'took a most imprudent step' of playing in a tragedy with a 'very beautiful young lady of the name of Wattel':

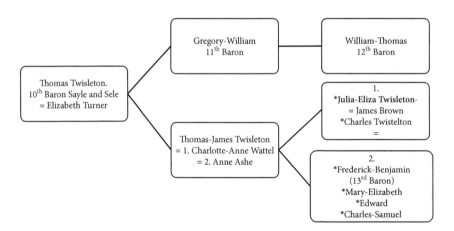

Tree 4.2 The illegitimate Julia Eliza Twisleton

---

[233] Julia Eliza Twisleton to Courthope, June 1825, CA, WC 69, fols 96–7, Debrett, *Peerage*, vol. 1 (1822), 462.

[234] Debrett, *Peerage*, vol. 1 (1816), 433.

212 SELLING ANCESTRY

Like most other early unions, this turned out to be an unfortunate one. The lady was extravagant and otherwise misconducted herself, and the marriage, after the birth of a daughter and a son, was in consequence dissolved by Act of Parliament.[235]

The text above inferred that the divorce was caused by the dissolute behaviour of the actress, the usual 'sexual suspect'.[236] The lady in question was Charlotte-Anne Wattel and the couple were at the time famous actors from a genteel background, who proceeded to act after their union in 1788 in various tragedies, notably at the Covent Garden Theatre.[237] His family managed to persuade him to stop acting while Charlotte continued a professional career on the London stage. As a mother and a married gentlewoman, Wattel was transgressing the usual social boundaries. She was criticized for having undermined her husband's authority by obtaining an engagement at the Covent Garden Theatre without his consent.[238] Exposing herself to the public gaze in a marketable manner, she was contravening her domestic duties. Such an 'unnatural' and defiant attitude could only lead to adultery and bad motherhood. When their marriage fell apart, Thomas James petitioned the Lords for divorce, on the grounds that his wife's illegitimate son, Charles, could be imposed upon him to succeed to his estate and fortune:

> The Act contains the usual provisionary clauses, viz, 1. To dissolve the marriage of Mr and Mrs Twisleton. 2. To empower Mr Twisleton to marry again. 3. To declare the issue which Mrs Twisleton may hereafter have, to be illegitimate. 4. To bar Mrs Twisleton from all claims of dower and thirds. 5. To exclude Mrs Twisleton from all claims on Mr Twisleton's property.[239]

Throughout the long trial, he attempted to demonstrate that they had already been living apart since 1796. The case was also considered in 1797 in the Court of Chancery and generated much publicity: it led to various testimonies and gossip from servants, friends, and some local clergy. After the divorce in 1798, the

---

[235] *GM*, Jan.–June 1825, vol. 137, 275.

[236] Actresses were seen as victims and a threat to the social order: Kristina Straub, *Sexual Suspects: Eighteenth-Century Players and Sexual Ideology* (Princeton, 1992), 106; Jane Moody (ed.), *The Cambridge Companion to British Theatre, 1730–1830* (Cambridge, 2007), 202.

[237] Jane Austen, was remotely related to the Twisletons. She mentioned in her pocketbook the various plays in which the couple was involved: 'May 1788. Thomas James Twisleton acts in public, taking the role of Mentevole in Jephson's tragedy Julia, this title role is taken by Charlotte Wattell'; published by Deirdre Le Faye (ed.), *A Chronology of Jane Austen and Her Family* (Cambridge, 2006), 115. According to Sybil Marion Rosenfeld, the couple may have inspired Austen in the writing of *Mansfield Park*. See *Temples of Thespis: Some Private Theatres and Theatricals in England and Wales, 1700–1820* (London, 1978), 128.

[238] 'She despised his authority and went to Mr. Harris, the proprietor of Covent Garden Theatre to apply for an engagement without his knowledge.' William Woodfall, *An Impartial Report of the Debates that Occured in the Two Houses of Parliament* (London, 1798), vol. 2, 350.

[239] As reported in the *Oracle*, Tuesday, 24 Apr. 1798, issue 1915.

obituary stated that as an act of atonement, Mr Twisleton took holy orders, resided in a vicarage at Northampton, and then married Anne, the respectable daughter of Captain Ashe, from the East India Company. He was later sent as archdeacon to Colombo. As for Charlotte, she continued with her career as an actress in England and in Boston. In 1801, Jane Austen remembered having met the 'Adultress' at a ball in Bath: 'she was highly rouged, & looked rather quietly & contentedly silly than anything else'.[240]

While Charles was officially recognized as adulterous, Thomas James considered Julia as his legitimate daughter. In 1825, it seems that her stepbrother was painting both children of the first union with the same brush. In order to defend herself, she put forward several lines of argument around the social and moral status of her mother. First, she reminded Courthope that Wattel, far from being an impoverished actress, was linked to the baronets of Stonehouse and had brought her husband £4,000: 'The truth is she was descended from a family nearly as respectful as that of the Twisletons, I mean the Stonehouse whose baronetcy is one of the most ancient and she brought him no inconsiderable fortune.'[241] Secondly, she laid the blame on her father, claiming that her mother 'never acted on the stage until she went on it at his desire and it became the means of leading her to the misconduct which occasioned her divorce'.[242] Furthermore, Julia's son had been received at Winchester College as a 'founders' kin', according to the strictest rules allowing a descendant of the Twisletons privileged access to the school.[243] Thirdly, she relied on the help of her mother's first cousin, Edward Vansittart Neale, vicar of Taplow in Buckinghamshire, who reminded Courthope that 'at the time of her birth and for many years after there was not the slightest imputation on her mother's conduct [...]. I know that Mr Twisleton always acknowledged her as undoubtedly his child.'[244] He produced several documents to substantiate her claims: a birth certificate, letters from former servants and from her maternal grandmother, and even a testimony from his own relative, the late George Vansittart, MP for Berkshire, 'who entered fully into the whole business at the time of the divorce (and) was fully satisfied that there was no reason to doubt the legitimacy of Mrs Brown'.[245] He went on to pay 4 shillings to search the Rolls of Parliament, stating that she was not included in the bastardy clause. He reminded Courthope that the incumbent Baron Saye and Sele, William Thomas, was her son's godfather and that 'his mother Lady Saye and Sele always received her as a legitimate member of her family, had her as an intimate at her house and

---

[240] Deirdre Le Faye (ed.), *Jane Austen's Letters* (Oxford, 1995), 85.

[241] Julia Eliza Twisleton to Courthope, 1825, CA, WC 69, fol. 98; in the Bill of Complaint of Charlotte Wattel-Twisleton, it is stated that her father consented to 'advance to the said Thomas James Twisleton the sum of one thousand pounds' as he was 'in great distress for money'. 16 Jan. 1796, NA, CC, C12/220/9.

[242] Ibid.   [243] Ibid., fol. 99.   [244] Neale to Courthope, 7 Mar. 1825, CA, WC 70, fol. 46.

[245] Ibid., 12 May 1825, fol. 51.

214 SELLING ANCESTRY

I am told actually died in her arms'.[246] Descriptions of a close and intimate family, even in its most dramatic moments such as the death of the grandmother, fitted into the attempt to demonstrate that Julia was a legitimate child. The clergyman obtained 'His Lordship's assurance that he had not interfered in any way to prevent the insertion of her name' and insisted that 'the omission of her name in your work is to her in many respects an injury which she feels deeply'.[247] His support was not purely altruistic, as he simultaneously required the publisher to add his own family account. Neale's intervention in the name of his younger cousin was decisive. Unlike the vulnerable and isolated widow, he was a respected figure in Buckinghamshire and had maintained close links with the maternal as well as the paternal sides. As a seemingly impartial broker, his testimony could not be easily discarded. In the following edition of Debrett's *Peerage*, a compromise was reached. Julia Eliza and her deceased husband were reinserted, though her brother and her son were omitted. As for the second line, the elder son Frederick, he finally received the lordship of Saye and Sele after a final trial in the House of Lords against Charles Twisleton in 1848.[248]

A series of letters sent to Burke also exposed the bitter relations between three competing lines. In 1836, George Vandeput Drury, from a first union, complained about the unfair treatment his family had suffered from previous compilers. He referred notably to the way his line had been evicted in Betham's *Baronetage* by the second branch of the Vandeputs: 'It was attempted notwithstanding to impose upon the Revd. William Betham and other genealogical authorities that his natural child by Miss Gery before marriage was born in wedlock.'[249] By contrast with the case of the Twisletons, it was the second branch and the widow who were accused of concealing the existence of an illegitimate son (Illus. 4.1).

Sir George Vandeput, the second baronet, had married twice, first to Mary Schutz, whose name and descent were not even mentioned by Betham, and second, Philadelphia Gery, who allegedly gave birth to the third baronet, Sir George Vandeput. According to Burke's correspondent, it was an outrageous lie:

> It was permitted to be introduced into the Court Peerage and list of Nova Scotia Baronets [. . .] in giving the family title to the late Admiral George Vandeput, or more correctly George Fonnereau, he being the illegitimate offspring of an Italian woman of that name.[250]

---

[246] Ibid.   [247] Ibid.

[248] Debrett, *Peerage*, vol. 1, (1828), 305, vol. 2, 99. 'The Lords Committee for Privileges answered by the affirmative to the petition of Frederick Benjamin Twisleton on his claim to the Title, Honour and dignity of Lord or Baron of Saye and of Sele.' *The Sessional Papers, printed by Order of the House of Lords*, vol. 22 (London, 1847–8), 137–205.

[249] Drury to Burke, 1836, BL, Add. MS 16569, fol. 221.

[250] Ibid.; on the case in 1750, 'Fonnereau v Vandeput', NA, CC, C 11/328/39.

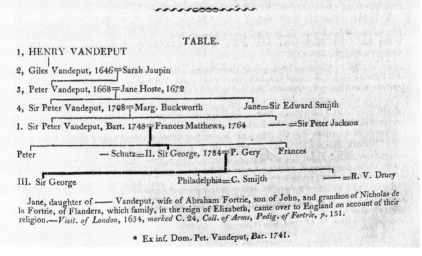

Illus 4.1 The complaint of Vandeput Drury (Betham, vol. 3, 205)
All souls 4:SR.39.c.3/3

He assumed this fake account had been 'intentionally submitted to Mr Betham by the parties concerned in giving a fictitious description to that gentleman' when he was himself away in the service of the East India Company.[251] He argued that the culprit was Philadelphia, who accepted George as her own son and defended his

---

[251] Drury to Burke, BL, Add. MS 16569, fol. 221.

216 SELLING ANCESTRY

claim to the baronetcy.[252] As the principal legatee, she survived the second baronet for twenty years and left most of his wealth to her child and to George's sons.[253] In this case, the half-siblings who had been living together were not excluded by the widow. This may have incensed the children of the first union and notably George Vandeput Drury who, thirty years later, denounced Philadelphia's intrigues and Betham's spineless behaviour, asserting that the latter was complicit in degrading a once well-respected family. Betham alluded to his 'remarkable contest with Lord Trentham' in the Westminster election of 1749–50. To Trentham, who had hinted at his foreign origins, Vandeput presented himself as 'a gentleman who never deviated from the principles of his ancestors [...] an ancient and wealthy family of the Netherlands, who about two Hundred Years ago, were obliged to leave their Country for their Steady support of the Protestant religion'.[254] Though he failed in the contest, he nonetheless acquired the reputation of an independent and patriotic figure, which made him popular among the London middling sort. George Vandeput pointed out that for such a remarkable dynasty, it was a disgrace that the title should have ended up in the hands of the son of an Italian nobody.

In the new version published by Burke in 1841, the first line was expanded in terms of size and prominence. His grandmother was now introduced as the daughter of Baron Augustus Schutz and his mother as the wife of Richard Vere Drury from 'an ancient and highly connected family settled in Normandy' (along with an extra pedigree). George Vandeput Drury of the EIC informed the public that he was 'the heir-at-law and residuary legatee of the Schutz family'. His letter was motivated not only by the desire to rectify past narratives but by the new balance established among the Vandeputs' competing lines. Indeed, George Vandeput Drury informed Burke that he was now 'the living descendant of that House' and the heir of a large Wiltshire estate (Standlynch Park near Salisbury), the 'seat of Lord Nelson'.[255] Before being acquired by Act of Parliament in 1813 as a gift to Admiral Nelson's brother, the seat had belonged to the first baronet, Sir Peter Vandeput.

As for the second branch, severely pruned off, it was dealt with rather dismissively in the footnote according to which 'Sir George Vandeput, the last baronet, left by different mothers, two illegitimate children, a daughter Philadelphia [...] and a son George Vandeput Admiral in the R. N. who appears to have assumed the title of baronet'.

---

[252] See his laudatory obituary in the *Naval Chronicle* (May 1800), 332; J. K. Laughton and Nicholas Tracy, 'Vandeput, George (d. 1800), naval officer', *ODNB*, 2010. Retrieved 10 Apr. 2020, from <https://doi-org.janus.bis-sorbonne.fr/10.1093/ref:odnb/28066>.

[253] *The Ancestor: A Quarterly Review of County and Family History* (1903), vol. 4, 43.

[254] *T—t—m [Trentham] and V—d-t [Vandeput]. A collection of the advertisements* (London, 1749), 10–11.

[255] George Vanderput Drury to Burke, 1836, BL, Add. MS 16569, fol. 221.

Soon to be the owner of the family seat, which was now linked to the memory of Nelson, he hoped to eclipse the memory of George Vandeput, alias 'George Fonnereau'. This was the sweet revenge of a modest country gentleman over the heroic admiral.

Endless litigation and inheritance disputes

Along with facing long-lasting family feuds, the publishers found themselves in the middle of ongoing legal battles. Sir William Blackstone in his *Commentaries* had stressed the fundamental weakness of pedigrees in judicial proceedings. He stated that most documents from the College of Arms were not relevant in inheritance cases, notably in the Court of Chancery. As they were based on the declaration of the head of the household, many excluded all younger sons and daughters as well as their spouses and own children. He even went further, by claiming that ancient medieval pedigrees were more reliable than the ones made by early modern heralds.[256] Nonetheless, pedigrees were still used in various legal proceedings. In *An Essay on Collateral Consanguinity* (1750), Blackstone also condemned those who were trying to gain access to some public schools and Oxford colleges by tracing a relation to the founders. Pointing out the injustice and absurdity of such a principle, Blackstone argued that it should be dismissed: 'If therefore the Founders' statute is to be interpreted as his Will would have been in our Present Courts of Equity, it must be entirely disregarded, and his fellowship distributed, as if, *quoad hoc,* he had made no statute, for that is the method in Chancery of disposing of such general Legacies.'[257] Despite this comment, many families hoped, by establishing a connection with a founder, to bypass the selection process. As indicated by the aforementioned Twisleton case, in the *c.*1820s pedigrees could still be used to gain privileged access to Winchester College and All Souls College.[258] Throughout a long eighteenth century, family directories would also prove valuable in various legal cases related to inheritance. Unlike heralds' pedigrees, which recorded the patrilineal transmission of title, they contained an up-to-date account of kinship and affinity which enlarged the range of potential successors.

---

[256] 'For the failure of inquisitions *post mortem*, by the abolition of military tenures, combined with the negligence of the heralds in omitting their usual progresses, has rendered the proof of a modern descent, for the recovery of an estate or succession to a title of honour, more difficult than that of an ancient.' W. Blackstone, *Commentaries on the Laws of England* (Oxford, 7th edn, 1775), vol. 3, 106.

[257] *An Essay on Collateral Consanguinity, its Limits, Extent, and Duration; More particularly as it is regarded by the Statutes of All Souls College* (London, 1750), 65. On his role in repelling founders' kin from All Souls College, Wilfrid Prest, *William Blackstone: Law and Letters in the Eighteenth Century* (Oxford, 2008), 75–96.

[258] See, for example, John Edmund Dowdeswell asking Burke for 'a pedigree shewing the claim of the issue of the late George Dowdeswell of Gloster, M.D., to fellowships of All Saints College, Oxford, as Founder's kin, A.D. 1776'. 22 Dec. 1835, BL, Add. MS 16569, fol. 74.

218   SELLING ANCESTRY

Mary Alleyn wrote to Wotton in order to correct some mistakes in her lineage. It was not, she argued 'to satisfy everybody's vanity', but for her niece, 'for whose sake only I give myself any trouble in this affair having no issue of my own now living'.[259] The daughter of Esther Alleyn-Stephenson, the niece was involved in a case where she sought to be recognized as heiress of an estate since the male line had become extinct. Similarly, Christopher Broughton of Longdon (Staffordshire), 'from the younger branch', sent Wotton his original pedigree and required him to send it back to him swiftly so he could use it in a lawsuit over some disputed lands: 'if you print it pray let it be done as this [...]. I beg you to let me have it again for I must make use of both at my tryall.'[260] The Parkers of Honington were also bitterly divided over the succession of the title. In 1739, an anonymous letter from a family 'friend' was dispatched to Wotton presumably at 'the order of Sir Henry-John Parker'.[261] It accused his uncle Harry Parker of trying to smuggle his illegitimate son in as the rightful owner to the title. In 1739, the third baronet had only two daughters but the 'friend' reminded Wotton that Harry was without issue as 'he has not cohabited with his wife these 30 years upon ye account of her adultery'.[262] Wotton cautiously stated that Sir Henry-John Parker was the present baronet with only two daughters and corrected his previous edition by inserting that Harry, 'who married a daughter of Dr. Harrison, master of St Cross, at Winchester, by whom he has no issue'.[263]

Arthur Collins was also involved in similar issues and published a guidebook into the matter.[264] He helped Elizabeth Perry, the sole heir to the Sidneys, earls of Leicester, and presented a petition to Lord Newcastle, as 'she desired as I knew the state of the Barony to draw a Petition to his Maty setting forth her right'.[265] From the late eighteenth century onwards, legal proceedings relating to the succession to a title, a peerage or a baronetcy, became commonplace. Collins's compilations were used in many peerage claims. In 1796, 'as a matter of great consequence', John Archer, from Birmingham, asked Mark Noble, a respected antiquary, for a copy of the Collins editions of 1750 and 1770 to assist him in tracing his pedigree:

---

[259] 'Mrs Alleyn the sole surviving daughter and heir of Samuel Stephenson, filed this bill, to have the estate reconveyed to her'. Mary Alleyn to Wotton, 20 Jan. 1740, BL, Add. MS 24120, fol. 8. On the case *Alleyn v. Alleyn* in the Chancery, see William Mosely (ed.), *Reports of Cases argued and determined in the High Court of Chancery* (London, 1803), 262.

[260] Christopher Broughton to Wotton, 3 Dec. 1740, BL, Add. MS 24120, fol. 160; NA, CC, C 11/481/1: *Broughton v. Bayley*. Christopher Broughton and his mother Frances were engaged in a lawsuit with the tenants of Christopher's father Christopher Broughton of London (Staffordshire). The first bill of complaint was issued in 1724.

[261] A letter to Wotton, BL, Add. MS 24121, fol. 155.   [262] Ibid.

[263] 'Parker of London', *The English Baronetage*, vol. 3.2, 692.

[264] Arthur Collins, *Proceedings, precedents and Arguments on Claims and Controversies* (London, 1734).

[265] Collins to Newcastle, 4 Apr. 1758, BL, Add. MS 32879, fol. 54.

After being informed by many gentlemen in this town that you have made it your study for many years to search into antiquity concerning the pedigree of noble-men's families. I having traced my pedigree down very clearly so as to joining mine into the late Lord Archers. The reason of my doing this is there being a large estate which was given by the crown to this family in the reign of Henry 2nd [...]. The purpose of my letter is to request the favour to know whether you have in your possession any old peerages (particular Collins, years 1750 & 1770) which give a very particular account of the Archer family.[266]

As John Archer clearly stated, a considerable property was at stake in many peerage claims. Genealogists and compilers, such as Thomas Christopher Banks and Nicholas Harris Nicolas, specialized in such claims. The latter printed various pamphlets on several dubious cases.[267] In 1825, Harris Nicolas's *Synopsis of the Peerage* was published and dedicated to Lord Redesdale, who was involved in the 'Lords' committees appointed to search for documents touching the dignity of a Peer'.[268]

Among several others, two cases related to the succession of the Paynes of St Kitt and the Codringtons of Barbados will be considered. It is striking to notice that the publishers involved in these cases did not each take the same view. In September 1828, Peter Payne of Knuston Hall (Northamptonshire) wrote to William Courthope about his case against his younger sister and his nephew Charles: 'I have been compelled lately to defend my legitimacy against a declar-ation, which a younger sister was advised to make in the Court of Chancery stating that she was the only legitimate child'.[269] Peter had just been recognized by the Court in June 1828 as the rightful heir of Sir Gillies Payne. He complained about the inclusion of his father's name in the list of extinct baronets and wished 'to make a formal application to you to expunge in your next edition now coming out and insert the name of Peter Payne as the late son of Sir Gillies Payne Bt'.[270] In an exchange of angry letters throughout September, Payne failed to convince the editor. As his sister and nephew contested the Court's decision, Courthope's answer was rather cautious and dilatory:

It is my duty to the public to request more detailed accounts of the nature & points of the Chancery suit [...] before I would have felt justified in altering a statement which was certainly not made unadvisedly nor without considerable enquiry.[271]

---

[266] Archer to Noble, 24 Oct. 1796, Bod. Lib., Misc d. 156/1, fol. 99.

[267] *An Analysis of the Genealogical History of the Family of Howard* (London, 1812).

[268] *Synopsis of the Peerage of England, exhibiting under alphabetical order arrangement, the date of creation, descent &c.* (London, 1825).

[269] Peter Payne to Courthope, 4 Sept. 1828, CA, WC 62, fol. 99.

[270] Ibid., fol. 100.   [271] Ibid.

220   SELLING ANCESTRY

Courthope also reminded him that the entries in the local church made 'all Sr Gillies Payne's children illegitimate' and wondered why his own nephew had continued 'to claim & use it [the title] & has done for twenty years at least unquestioned by you'.[272] As a herald of Arms, Courthope felt he had enough authority to step in and act as a judge. He considered that the case was quite improbable and likely to be dismissed on appeal. Since the death of his elder brother in 1803, Peter Payne had never contested the fact that he had been born out of wedlock in 1760. Payne reacted angrily to the publisher's disparaging tone and threatened litigation, pondering on what authority he went against the court's decision. Courthope replied that his authority came from the moral duty he owed to the 'public' which 'prevents my complying with any individual request I may receive as an editor, but I should very ill perform that duty if in any case I permitted threats of legal responsibility to influence my conduct'.[273] In the end, Courthope refused to give in and the Court's decision was cancelled in 1829 by the Lord Chancellor. Nonetheless, Peter Payne continued to style himself baronet after his election as MP for Bedfordshire in 1831 as a Whig candidate. While Courthope placed him in the *Extinct Baronetage*, he was presented as a living baronet in Burke's *Peerage and Baronetage* and in the first edition of the *Commoners*.[274] As a public figure, Payne's claims were tacitly accepted by Burke, despite an opposing view from the Chancellor. Through the commercial success of his directories, Burke was able to reinforce many allegations whether genuine or false. Even a judicial decision was unable to turn the tide.

As for the Payne family, litigation over lineage of the Bethells fell within the scope of the contested integration of West Indian families into the British aristocracy. In 1829, Henry Walrond expressed the desire to meet Burke in person in order to discuss the case of an impostor:

> The present person calling himself Sir Bethell is disallowed at the 'Doctors' Commons' (which he is) as well as at the herald college which last he pretends to despise whilst the legal authority of the former cannot be disputed.[275]

He was alluding to Sir Christopher Bethell Codrington, who was presented in the 1826 edition as fourth baronet of Codrington, on the grounds that his cousin, the third baronet, had died in France in 1816 without lawful issue.[276] Bethell Codrington had inherited from the second baronet's property in the West

---

[272] Ibid.   [273] 12 Sept. 1828, ibid., fol. 108.

[274] 'Sir Peter Payne succeeds to the title in 1828 in consequence of a decree of the Court of Chancery, confirming a report finding him the eldest son born in wedlock of his late father', Burke, *A General and Heraldic Dictionary* (1832), 287. In the article his elder brother's and his nephew's names were erased. See Burke, *Commoners* (1833), xxxiv.

[275] Henry Walrond to Burke, Jan. 1829, CA, BC, vol. 58, case 574.

[276] Burke, *A General and Heraldic Dictionary* (1826), 66.

FAMILY TIES AND PUBLISHERS' ENQUIRIES 221

Indies in exchange for providing his cousin an annuity of £2,000. Bethell Codrington was a powerful political figure and belonged to the absentee planters who were forcefully defending their interests during the anti-slavery campaign.[277] He used his knowledge of West Indian families to discredit several abolitionists, pointing out in particular that the first baronet, Thomas Fowell Buxton, a prominent abolitionist, was descended from a slave trader. In 1833, he was awarded nearly £30,000 for almost 2,000 enslaved people in Barbuda.[278] As Henry Walrond pointed out, Bethell Codrington was indeed embroiled in litigation with his cousin's son, William Raimond Codrington, who, in 1827, had obtained from Doctors' Commons and the College of Arms recognition as the legitimate heir.[279] As Garter King of Arms, it was Sir George Nayler who acknowledged Raimond Codrington as the true heir. He may have relied on the letters sent by the third baronet from France and from various papers left in Rennes.[280] Raimond Codrington and his French lawyer convinced Nayler that his father had been married by a priest, a union which, though deemed illegal by the French revolutionaries, was valid on the other side of the Channel. Hence, Burke was urged by Henry Walrond to mention this lawsuit and to erase Bethell Codrington in his next edition.

However, in 1828 Burke had received a printed pamphlet stating the death of the third baronet in 1816 as a Catholic as well as his doubtful union in France with his nurse Eleanor Kirk (*Narrative of Mr Powell's Enquiries relative to the supposed Marriage of the Late Sir William Codrington*). As a solicitor, John Allen Powell had been hired by Bethell Codrington to demonstrate his right to the title.[281] Powell described his visit to the local archives in Rennes and to various witnesses who vouched for the fact that the third baronet's son had been born out of wedlock. It was assumed in France that 'Sir William had repeatedly since his wife's death told, [...] his son would never have the title'.[282] Several manuscript letters from Bethell Codrington, are pasted to a copy of Powell's *Narrative*.

---

[277] Nicholas Draper, 'Codrington, Christopher Bethell (1764–1843), slave owner and politician'. *ODNB*, 2016. Retrieved 10 Apr. 2020 from <https://doi-org.janus.bis-sorbonne.fr/10.1093/ref:odnb/107410>.

[278] Natalie Zacek, 'West Indian Echoes: Dodington House, the Codrington Family and the Caribbean Heritage', in Madge Dresser and Andrew Hann (eds), *Slavery and the British Country House* (London, 2013), 106–13; Michael Taylor, 'The British West India Interest and Its Allies, 1823–1833', *EHR*, vol. 133, no. 565 (2018): 1478–511.

[279] See, in the collections of the Wedgwood Museum, the Copper Plate produced as an armorial ware at the request of Sir William Raimond Codrington in 1825. (<http://www.wedgwoodmuseum.org.uk/collections/collections-online/object/copper-plate-codrington-esq->)

[280] In his account of the *Englishmen in French Revolution*, John Goldworth Alger alluded to the existence of these documents, which he received from the third baronet's grandson. *Englishmen in French Revolution* (London, 1889), 148; Burke, 1828, CA, BC, vol. 55, fol. 55.

[281] Born in Jamaica in 1781, Allen Powell was on good terms with many planters and was awarded £4,002 in 1833 by the Slave Compensation Commission. <https://www.ucl.ac.uk/lbs/person/view/45181>.

[282] *Narrative of Mr Powell's Enquiries relative to the supposed Marriage of the Late Sir William Codrington* (London, 1828), 14.

222   SELLING ANCESTRY

In one of them, Bethell Codrington commented on his distribution of the *Narrative* to various friends and raged against Nayler's unfounded position:

> Raimond Codrington cannot proceed without proving his father's marriage. If married, by the laws of France it must be register'd and being register'd, every man can claim a copy of the registers. Sir G. Nayler has admitted him without any such certificate (for in fact none exists), and Sir G. N. has so admitted him altho fully aware of the Content of the Narrative.[283]

He reminded his correspondent that the third baronet's exile to France had been requested by his father after leaving various debts, which amounted to £5,000 per annum. In 1782, he was even jailed by his creditor and then later cut off from his inheritance. According to Bethell Codrington, the fact that his nephew had allegedly married his Catholic nurse did little to strengthen his case. Bethell Codrington may have been all the more willing to cling to his baronetcy as his income from Barbuda was declining and the demise of slavery had become inevitable. One could further suggest that his title may have been instrumental in his daily financial transactions. What was at stake was not simply his social status but his credit as a borrower. Christopher Bethell Codrington relied on his lenders for various loans, notably on his consignee, the London merchant Marmaduke Trattle.[284]

Moreover, in denouncing Bethel Codrington, Henry Walrond may have had a personal axe to grind. If he warned Burke against the so-called baronet and his dismissal of the court's decision, it was because he suspected that his own cousin, Bethell Walrond, was seeking to claim precedence over his own branch. He complained about the clients who did not have pedigrees 'vouched by proper testimonials, not mere assertion' and reminded Burke that he was the only one from 'the senior branch of my family', established since the time of Henry II.[285] Henry Walrond feared that his young cousin might be inspired by the audacity of Sir Christopher Bethell Codrington as the two knew each other. On his mother's side, Bethell Walrond was Christopher's nephew and his father, Joseph Lyons Walrond, had been the manager of the Codrington plantations in Antigua (Tree 4.3).[286]

Joseph Walrond attended the Merchant Taylor's School in London and won in 1770 a fellowship to St John's College (Oxford), before moving to Antigua and

---

[283] Bethell Codrington to Mrs Bliss, Dodington, 17 Jan. 1829. *Narrative of Mr Powell's Enquiries*, BL Store 1414. c.29.

[284] On the consigneeship between London merchants and slave owners, Catherine Hall, Nicholas Draper, Keith McClelland, Katie Donington, and Rachel Lang (eds), *Legacies of British Slave-Ownership: Colonial Slavery and the Formation of Victorian Britain* (Cambridge, 2014), 113.

[285] Henry Walrond to Burke, Jan. 1829, CA, BC, vol. 58, case 574.

[286] <https://www.ucl.ac.uk/lbs/person/view/44946> <https://www.sjc.ox.ac.uk/discover/about-college/st-johns-and-colonial-past/blog/joseph-lyons-walrond-alumnus-and-slave-owner-antigua>.

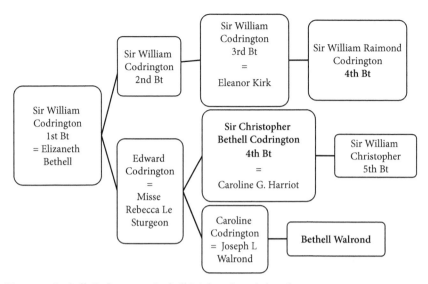

Tree 4.3 Bethell Codrington, Bethell Walrond, and their kin

marrying Caroline Codrington. He complained in 1792 that 'mistaken humanity of the Abolition has done much mischief in all the Islands, by putting wrong notions into the negroes heads and making their lives less content and happy than they were'.[287] At his death in 1815, he left his son the considerable sum of £14,000. In 1828, Bethell Walrond wrote to Burke in order to appear among the *Commoners*. He did not refer to his father's connections with the Merchant Taylor's School or with Oxford, and instead chose rather to focus on the civil wars. Like many slave owners, he explained that his family shift to the West Indies had not been driven by the hope of making money but by political motives. Their departure, he reminded Burke, was the consequence of their enduring loyalty to the Stuarts in the 1640s.[288] For Bethell Walrond, it was essential to defend his ancestors against the widespread allegations directed at slave owners, namely that they were originally indentured servant and fortune seekers. He mentioned the ownership of an 'estate in the West Indies since 150 years', a property in Devon of more than 3,000 acres, and his union with the only daughter of the earl of Rosslyn.[289] He was elected MP for Saltash and then for Sudbury between 1825 and 1832. Finally, he was hoping to be declared as a coheir to the ancient barony of Welles, in direct line from Elizabeth Devenish since 1570.

Henry Walrond was determined to prevent his younger cousin from reaching this goal. He might not have sufficient landed wealth to appear himself in the

---

[287] Joseph Walrond to Christopher Bethell Codrington, 16 Jan. 1792. GA, D 1610, C.15, fol. 9.
[288] The family crest had allegedly been 'granted by Charles I to Colonel Humphrey Walrond, for his services during the civil wars'. Burke, *Commoners* (1835), vol. 2, 557.
[289] Henry Walrond to Burke, case 574.

224 SELLING ANCESTRY

Commoners, but as the head of the elder line he sought to discredit his ambitious cousin. Burke adopted a pragmatic position. Regarding Christopher Bethell Codrington, he followed Henry's guidance and published Sir George Nayler's decision in favour of Sir William Raimond Codrington.[290] The editor of Debrett's followed suit but other compilers, such as Edmund Lodge, supported the assertion of Christopher Bethell Codrington and of his son.[291] As for Bethell Walrond, Burke remained sitting on the fence, merely informing the public that his claim to the barony of Welles had been referred to the attorney-general, 'and so the matter at present rests'.[292] The feud between the two branches continued right until Bethell Walrond's death in 1876 and it could be documented in the Court of Chancery as well as in the High Court of Justice.[293]

By sticking to various epistolary conventions, the letters sent from clients were likely to deliver a more formal picture of family relations than spontaneous face-to-face interactions. However, they also demonstrated that participation in the publisher's enquiries was limited to a few members of the family. Judging from the publishers' correspondence, there does not seem to have been extended consultation among close kin and collaterals. The heads of family were the prime recipients of the formulas and exercised tight control over their families' archives and the making of the narrative. Very few had a precise knowledge of their own past beyond three generations, though they owned quantities of domestic artefacts which enabled them to go further back in time and provide some picturesque anecdotes. Increasingly, in the latter part of the century, they absorbed their wives' pasts and transformed these into plurisecular accounts. Lineage was both a legal and a fictional entity arranged with different voices from a variety of memories, whether textual or oral in origin.

Though in possession of remarkable documents and striking anecdotes, the heads of household often did not have the resources to compose a narrative. Then their close kin, whether it be young sons, nephews, or uncles, would come to the fore. Heads of households increasingly relied heavily on them to fill in some gaps or even to provide the whole narrative. A few families managed to pool their resources in a very effective manner, to produce some extensive narratives. Similarly, women, despite the usual misogynistic bias, held a central place. They contributed, like the other relatives, to a resilient patriarchal culture. The letters contain many snippets of family life, ranging from affection to conflict. As such they provided an alternative view, beyond the dull and formal skeleton offered by

---

[290] 'Sir William's son has, however, established his right in *Doctors' Commons*, and has been acknowledged by the Heralds' College'. Burke, *Commoners* (1833), 270.

[291] See, for example, E. Lodge, *The Peerage of the British Empire* (London, 1843), 56.

[292] Burke, *Commoners* (1835), vol. 2, 557.

[293] *Walrond v. Walrond*, CC: C15/580/W157 (1858); C 15/718/W57 (1859); C16/174/W129 (1863); C16/239/W27 (1864); C16/834/W101 (1872); Court of Probate and Supreme Court of Judicature, J 165/36 (1863–70); J 121/2854 (1876)/3043 (1877).

the published pedigree. From one generation to another, from the head of family to his kin, customers had many options available to construct their identity in the past. Far from considering them as mundane and anecdotal, many contemporaries felt that family narratives, whether short or plurisecular, did matter. As family was an organic structure, the notoriety of one branch could either benefit or be detrimental to the other lines.

Conclusion to part II

The analysis of hundreds of letters has provided a good vantage point on the individuals and families involved in the making of these compilations. The historicization of these documents may be appreciated from different angles. First, they have been studied from a larger social and political point of view. Whether it be in 1727, in 1800, or in 1828, they related to a heterogeneous landed elite. These publications were closely linked to major historical events such as the Hanoverian Succession, the French Revolution, the Irish Union Act, and the 1832 Reform Act. Wotton's customers belonged in the majority to the county elite descended from the Restoration period, while Betham's *Baronetage* attracted rising British families who had been elevated during the revolutionary wars, in the EIC, or in the army. Burke's *Commoners* ignited considerable interest from the local landed elite who often came from mercantile and industrial origins. Second, from a micro perspective, these letters enable us to give due credit to the everyday life, emotions, and competing expectations raised by the enquiries.

Comparisons between the published versions and family correspondence highlight the extended participatory nature of these enquiries. From the various examples mentioned, it appears that the most active protagonists belonged to the narrow kinship group. The patriarchal values of a continuous male line were still given much currency and to be frank required many highly fictional accounts. The making of such compilations was closely influenced by structural patterns such as vertical and horizontal kinship, primogeniture, and rules of inheritance. This resilient culture was upheld not only by the household heads but also by many of their close kin. Whether old or new, many families were involved in the creation of a common identity attached to their name. Within this general framework, competing demands were made over the extension and content of the narrative. Some kin and even whole branches were arbitrarily pruned off while other individuals were given more prominence. Far from being set in stone, the family order was negotiated and reframed one edition after another. As a broker between contending versions, the publishers were placed in a strong but often awkward position. Compilation was in and of itself a balancing act in which the reputation as well as the social status of the publishers were key ingredients in the success or failure of these directories.

PART III

COMPILERS AND THE MAKING OF CREDIBLE NARRATIVES

> There are so many impostors nowadays, perambulating the country with catch-penny prospectuses of one thing or another, that any person may be excused for regarding any of them with a suspicious eye. [...] More than one person who taking advantage of the prevailing whim for long pedigree had been round the country, soliciting and obtaining subscription for whatever trash he had in mind.[1]

Edmund Lechmere Charlton, a Shropshire landed gentleman, was rather blunt about his distaste for fake genealogists and their continuous harassment of the public. He considered that these literary projectors were fooling credulous families into spending a considerable amount of money and time in supporting their commercial ploys. In the three years preceding Charlton's letter in 1828, there had been indeed at least seven compilations on titled families.[2] To Charlton's mind, families were on the losing end, on several scores. Most of the expense fell on them, such as the cost of the subscription and of exchange of letters back and forth. Moreover, their honour was poorly treated in these hasty and 'trashy' compilations.

It is worth noting that, despite his reservations, Charlton now consented to subscribe to Burke's *Commoners*. After all, was Burke not the well-respected 'author of the Dictionary'?[3] Although a former Oxford MA and a trained barrister, Edmund Lechmere Charlton could not resist the attraction of providing a fabulous pedigree. He launched himself into an account of his ancestors, from the last prince of Powys, Madog ap Maredudd, to the many lords, bishops, and baronets related to the Charltons, along with another very ancient pedigree of the Lechmeres. He added 'there is a great deal about the Charlton family in the

---

[1] Edmund Charlton to John Burke, 16 Aug. 1828, CA, BC, vol. 56, case 77.

[2] John Debrett, *Peerage and Baronetage* (1825); Charles White, *Compendium* (1825); H. Nicolas, *Synopsis of the Peerage* (1825); John Burke, *Heraldic Dictionary* (1826); Ann Innes, *Annual Peerage* (1826); Saunders & Otley, *Manual of Rank* (1827); William Berry, *Encyclopaedia Heraldica* (1826–7).

[3] Edmund Charlton to John Burke, 16 Aug. 1828, CA, BC, vol. 56, case 77.

228 SELLING ANCESTRY

British Museum but I have never had the curiosity to look at it'.[4] As with so many customers, an initial condemnation of genealogy was followed by an eagerness in answering the publishers in great detail.

Why did Edmund Lechmere finally decide to trust Burke after having dismissed so many previous schemes? From Lechmere's point of view, Burke had more credibility than his other competitors. However, it would be difficult to support the argument that his reputation stemmed from more rigorous editing. Burke was often derided for releasing extraordinary genealogies. His *Heraldic Dictionary* had met with much criticism and sarcasm. One competitor, Harris Nicolas, a member of the Society of Antiquaries, alluded to some of his reckless inventions:

> We are informed, for example, that the present earl of Aldborough traces his pedigree to the time of Alfred! [. . .] And the Tollemache would come from the Saxon word Tolling the Bell and that 'Sir Robert Williams' deduces his pedigree, with singular perspicuity, from Brutus! Son of Silvius Posthumus!! Son of Ascanius!! Son of Aeneas!!![5]

Burke's anecdote about the Tollemache was recycled in later compilations and gazettes.[6] It was later picked up by Edward Augustus Freeman, the eminent historian of the Norman Conquest, in his attack on the 'pedigree-makers', but he laid the blame on Burke's son, Sir Bernard, Ulster King of Arms and Keeper of the State Papers in Ireland. It was used as an example of his etymological inventions:

> In what language 'tollmack' means 'toll the bell' is not explained. Nor is it easy to see the connexion of cause and effect between tolling of the bell and flourishing with the greatest honour since the first arrival of the Saxons in England.[7]

Freeman did not wish to dismiss the social value of pedigrees. Whether short or long, they were a precious inheritance and should be treated respectfully.[8] While he was eager to forgive families for their credulity, he laid the blame on the compilers for their 'guilty', 'perverse', and 'monstrous fictions'.[9] In the Victorian period, his definition of lying and deception had a strong moral undertone and

---

[4] Ibid.   [5] N. H. Nicolas, *The Retrospective Review*, vol. 2 (1828), 171.

[6] The story about the bell tolling is then repeated and expanded in countless publications: *The New Monthly*, vol. 37 (1833), 497; *The British Gazetteer* (1852), 477; *The Art Journal*, vol. 6 (1853), 67; *The Brights of Suffolk* (1858), 79; Francis Open Morris, *A Series of Picturesque Views of Seats*, vol. 4 (1880), 57.

[7] Edward Augustus Freeman, 'Pedigrees and Pedigree-Makers', *Contemporary Review*, vol. 30 (1877), 27.

[8] 'A true pedigree, be it long or short, is a fact; and like any other fact, it is to be respected [. . .] The inheritance of a really great name [. . .] should be matter, not of pride but of responsibility', ibid., 40.

[9] Ibid., 13, 15, 23, 26.

COMPILERS AND THE MAKING OF CREDIBLE NARRATIVES   229

was associated with the notions of personal responsibility and strength of will. In his own way, Freeman was historicizing the notions of truths and lies by distinguishing different periods according to their own epistemological rationales. In contrast to his progressive time, Freeman alluded to the former 'states of the human mind', when fake genealogies grew in collective and holistic communities out of the belief in hagiographies and natural metaphors. The latter in particular were embedded in the early social mindset which led ancestors 'into thinking that a story really grows of itself, as a tree grows'.[10] The ancients did not peddle lies due to a lack of moral values but because they were still living in an enchanted place. There was an anti-Catholic subtext in his complaint about the fictitious accounts of saints and the vanity of families who chose to 'blot out the weaver who was burned for his religion, but who kept the knight who was hanged for treason'.[11] Freeman worried that a misplaced interest in factious medieval barons had led too many families to ignore the decisive moment of the Reformation.

The comments by Lechmere and Freeman illustrate the complex relation between truth and fiction in a specific context. The former established a distinction between Burke and his 'trashy' competitors, while the latter retrospectively painted all the pedigree-makers with the same brush, holding that they did not apply the same understanding of truth and credibility.[12] We need therefore to suspend our 'positivist' mindset to determine, throughout the eighteenth century, the rationales on which truths and lies were established. The ambiguous attitude oscillating between dismissing and celebrating genealogies, apparent in letters of Lechmere as well as of many other customers, has been noted in other periods.

Roberto Bizzocchi, in his stimulating work on early modern Europe, explored the contradictory statements made by humanists and antiquaries on the 'incredible' genealogies'. Instead of rejecting or condemning errors and lies, positivist historians would be more inspired to engage with the complex notion of credibility.[13] While Annius of Viterbo was unanimously denounced for his fanciful invention, he was also read, imitated, and even surpassed by more creative authors. Bizzocchi studied on what grounds Annius, who retraced the Borgias' parentage back to Isis and Osiris, was criticized in the context of the schism between Catholics and Protestants and the discovery of America. In Germany, anti-Italian scholars such as Albert Krantz attacked the childish creations of Annius while establishing a link between Noah and the German nobles.[14] Along with classical sources, the Bible was used as

---

[10] Ibid., 15.   [11] Ibid., 35.

[12] On the historical mindset in the Victorian period, see Philippa Levine, *The Amateur and the Professional: Antiquarians, Historians and Archaeologists in Victorian England, 1838–1886* (Cambridge, 1986).

[13] 'Adopter une attitude moqueuse et [...] ne voir en eux que des moments de défaillance dans le cadre d'une évolution conduisant des ténèbres de l'erreur à notre vérité rationnelle, n'est donc sans doute pas la meilleure manière pour en saisir le sens.' Roberto Bizzocchi, *Généalogies fabuleuses: inventer et faire croire dans l'Europe moderne* (Paris, 2010) [first published Bologna, 1995], 73.

[14] Ibid., 49.

230 SELLING ANCESTRY

the central reference to construct Protestant and Catholic pedigrees as well as the emerging 'European' race.[15] Hence, it was from both confessional and anthropological points of view that the credibility of historical discourse was to be assessed. Everywhere in Europe, whether it be Spain, England, or France, Annius's narrative was simultaneously dismissed and reconfigured to provide far-reaching origins to these emerging nations. Many dubious histories were borrowed and circulated as long as they conformed to certain social and scholarly expectations. In Renaissance Europe, Bizzochi referred to an 'epistemology of presuppositions' according to which knowledge was not directly drawn from documents.[16] Rather, the latter were used to validate the preconceptions that were intended to build an unbroken line between a cherished antiquity and the present time. Antiquarian searches were aimed at providing the missing link. In the commercial eighteenth century, Annius was condemned for having a more materialistic motive. According to Pope in *The Dunciad,* the monk was mostly engaged in enriching himself by trying to talk noble families into trading precious artefacts in their possession for objects from his fake collections.[17]

How then was the credibility of family directories to be established in the eighteenth century? To better historicize the notion of truth and lies, following Bizzocchi's method, we will consider, in a first chapter, the nature of the criticisms directed at the London compilers. Based neither on the moral agenda framed by E. A. Freeman nor on the humanist aspiration of the Renaissance, the rejection of these works was closely linked to a more general distrust of urban society and its uncontrolled growth.[18] Compilers as well mercenary authors were dismissed for being exploited by London booksellers or being under the thumb of courtiers and ministers. This did not mean that these negative opinions were necessarily upheld by landed gentlemen, while even in London they were widely shared views among some middling-sort authors. Most compilers of humble birth were in situations of financial dependence which made it harder for them to be recognized as trustworthy and honest. The urban scene, whether it be the monstrous metropolis or booming industrial towns, provided a hiding place for swarms of impostors and fraudsters.

And yet, as we have seen in Edmund Lechmere's letter, among the bevy of dubious schemers who invaded his rural tranquillity, some compilers were given due credit. In the final chapter, we will consider the reasons why some of them managed to be acknowledged as worthy antiquaries despite all the negativity

---

[15] Giuliano Gliozzi, *Adam et le nouveau monde: la naissance de l'anthropologie comme idéologie coloniale: des généalogies bibliques aux théories raciales* (Lecques, 2000).

[16] R. Bizzochi, *Généalogies fabuleuses,* 208.

[17] Richard Nash, 'Translation, Editing, and Poetic Invention in Pope's "Dunciad"', *Studies in Philology,* vol. 89, no. 4 (1992): 470–84 at 472; Paul Baines, '"Our Annius": Antiquaries and Fraud in the Eighteenth Century', *British Journal for Eighteenth-Century Studies,* vol. 20, no. 1 (1997): 33–51.

[18] On this point, see Dror Wahrman, 'National Society, Communal Culture: An Argument about the Recent Historiography of Eighteenth-Century Britain', *Social History,* vol. 17, no. 1 (1992): 43–72.

associated with their work. Moving away from the great paradigms about the scientific revolution or the Enlightenment, it is through their collecting practices and their collaboration with respected scholars that their activities were perceived in a more positive light. The gentlemanly qualities which were often retrospectively attributed to them played a role in the making of their reputation. These values which proved so instrumental in the balancing act between belief and scepticism in seventeenth-century England were still relevant in our period. They were recomposed to fit into the changing world of antiquarian studies.[19] London imposed itself as a scientific centre of accumulation and exchange where reputations could be made or destroyed. As in other periods, family truths and lies were historicized and relocated in a specific social culture of knowledge.

[19] Steven Shapin, *A Social History of Truth, Civility and Science in Seventeenth-Century England* (Chicago, London, 1994), ch. 3; Rosemary Sweet, *The Discovery of the Past in Eighteenth Century Britain* (Hambledon and London, 2004); Susan M. Pearce (ed.), *Visions of Antiquity: The Society of Antiquaries of London 1707–2007* (London, 2007); Jan Broadway. *'No historie so meete': Gentry Culture and the Development of Local History in Elizabethan and Early Stuart England* (Manchester, 2006).

associated with their wider. Moving away from the great paradigms about the scientific revolution or the Enlightenment, it is through their collecting practices and their collaboration with respected scholars that their activities were perceived in a more positive light. The gentlemanly qualities which were often retrospectively attributed to them played a role in the making of their reputation. These values which proved so instrumental in the balancing act between belief and scepticism in seventeenth century England were still relevant in our period. They were compelled to fit into the changing world of antiquarian studies. London in itself as a scientific centre of accumulation and exchange where reputations could be made or destroyed. As its own epistemic model with truth on Elite were fabricated and collected in a specific social culture of knowledge.

5

The Protagonists of a 'Shoddy Industry'

In 1983, in his re-edition of Cokayne's *Baronetage*, Hugh J. Massingberd contrasted the emergence in 1850 of a 'ruthlessly reforming school of genealogists' with the 'shoddy industry' of previous compilers:

> The eighteenth century had seen the appearance of works on the peerage and baronetage by Collins which were full of fairy tales. Most pride of popular Peerages in the nineteenth century were to copy these legends. It was the golden age of bad genealogy: a whole shoddy industry propped up the pretensions of the parvenus to social status by supplying bogus evidence of gentility.[1]

A *Telegraph* journalist and an amateur scholar, Massingberd had worked as an editor of Burke's *Guide to the Royal Family* and *Guide to Country Houses* (1978–81). He implied that the Burke compilations for which he was responsible had undergone considerable changes since the time of their foundation. The expression 'shoddy industry' appears well suited as it relates to the remote past of the industrial recycling and wool remanufacturing in Yorkshire.[2] It is a powerful analogy between narratives and clothing, both being re-spun into useful material. Used in a derogatory manner, it relates to a distinctly inferior order of work in industrial towns. Those pedigree-manufacturers were condemned for their plagiarism and mystifications in a growing society where social identities were being redefined. At the time of Massingberd's statement, as in Freeman's era, the assumption was that hierarchies had by then been firmly reinstated. However, the term 'industry' also pertains, in a more general sense, to a tedious and repetitive activity such as that of the London 'hacks' or 'scribblers'. Used by Swift and Pope as literary tropes, these terms referred to the deceitful and mercenary practices of some London booksellers and their foot soldiers, who would write and publish anything for a few pennies.[3]

In the eighteenth century, the gist of the argument employed against many compilers was indeed their financial dependence on either the meagre allowances

[1] Hugh J. Massingberd (ed.), *G. E. Cokayne, The Complete Baronetage* (Gloucester, 1983), 1.
[2] James Hepworth, 'Rags and Shoddy', *Journal of the Textile Institute Proceedings*, vol. 45 (1954), 62–4.
[3] Brean S. Hammond, *Professional Imaginative Writing in England, 1670–1740: 'Hackney for bread'* (Oxford, 1997); George Justice, *The Manufacturers of Literature: Writing and the Literary Marketplace in Eighteenth-Century England* (Newark, NJ, 2002).

Selling Ancestry: Family Directories and the Commodification of Genealogy in Eighteenth-Century Britain. Stéphane Jettot, Oxford University Press. © Stéphane Jettot 2023. DOI: 10.1093/oso/9780192865960.003.0006

234 SELLING ANCESTRY

of booksellers or servile ministerial patronage. Unable to impose themselves as 'authors', their task was repetitive and devoid of creativity. If the expression of hacks has sometimes been applied to literary celebrities such as Defoe or Pope, who called himself 'a hackney scribbler', the compilers in question belonged to the small fry, the very marginal sub-category of journalists, indexers, proof-readers, and printers whose names are little known. Their urge to produce many sorts of prints rapidly and in considerable quantities allegedly led them to compose dubious pedigrees. A second category related to mercenary authors, such as Arthur Collins, William Guthrie, and Alexander Jacob who designed several compilations under the patronage of prominent ministers and courtiers. In the hopes of better prospects, they were led to forge complacent accounts. Finally, to complete the sorry picture of this 'shoddy industry', one should include a third category of authors, namely those whose fictions were self-serving and directed at hiding their own humble origins or deficient social status.

1. 'At the risk of some booksellers' and 'unfortunate authors'

In the early Victorian period, a reviewer in a conservative journal expressed his dismay at the consequence of the genealogical directories being 'published at the risk of some booksellers' and 'unfortunate authors'.[4] He regretted that the landed elite have ceased its involvement in family. This was a trend confirmed by several historians in the eighteenth century. In the Early Modern period, antiquaries were of gentlemanly status. Edward Lhuyd was helped by his widespread Welsh connections, both his expertise and his gentle status managed to attract a considerable amount of interest in the composition of his *Parochial Queries* (1696).[5] A few decades later, county history writers were increasingly recruited from a middling sort background. In 1755, several gentlemen rallied around Sir Thomas Cave to entrust a schoolmaster, Peter Whalley, with writing the history of Northamptonshire.[6] But the reviewer wondered: if the lower middle sorts were to turn into genealogists, would they not inflict some irreparable damage to elite's prestige? He quoted the derogatory comment of Edward Gibbon about Ezra Cleaveland and his *History of the Noble and Illustrious Family of Courtenay* (1735): 'the rector of Honiton had more gratitude than industry and more industry than criticism'.[7] These repeated criticisms had already been voiced in

---

[4] *London Quarterly Review*, vol. 72 (1843), 165.
[5] Huw Pryce pointed out that 'his family background did help him to realize his plans, as his kinship connections facilitated collaboration with antiquarian-minded Welsh gentry, clergy, and school masters and opened doors to patrons in Wales willing to support his scholarly endeavours'. Huw Pryce, *Writing Welsh History: From the Early Middle Ages to the Twenty-First Century* (Oxford, 2022), 177.
[6] Sweet, *Antiquaries: The Discovery of the Past*, 42.
[7] *London Quarterly Review*, vol. 72 (1843), 171.

the early modern age by prominent heralds such as Dugdale, who deplored 'the liberty taken by divers mechanicks since the commencement of the late unparallel'd rebellion' in providing coats of arms and even pedigrees.[8] In particular, he castigated Richard Blome, a London bookseller, for his re-edition of Camden's Britannia and an *Essay to Heraldry* [...] *being a treaty of the nobility and gentry* (1684): Blome was '*a most impudent* person [...], he gets a livelihood by bold practices'.[9] Like the anonymous reviewer in 1843, Dugdale saw the involvement of unqualified commoners as a threat to the political order. Before considering the 'unfortunate authors', we will deal with the attacks directed at the booksellers.

Booksellers and their poor reputation

In his letter to Lord Chesterfield, Samuel Johnson celebrated a new literary age, which moved away from aristocratic patronage to hinge on the beneficial association between booksellers and their authors.[10] He alluded to some considerate booksellers who made up for the small incomes of their authors by treating them well. The brothers Edward and Charles Dilly were renowned for their hospitality towards most authors. David Hume was on very good terms with the printer William Strahan. Their long-lasting correspondence illustrates how Strahan helped Hume to navigate in the bookselling business and defend his interests against the greedy Andrew Millar.[11] Tobias Smollett established a dominant position for himself by selling 20,000 copies of his *Complete History* and retaining the copyright of his novel *The Expedition of Humphry Clinker*, which he later sold for £210.[12] For their creativity and independence, they could be considered professional authors, easily distinguishable from hackney scribblers. However, they were exceptional cases. Most authors were still poorly paid, if compared to the profits generated by the London book trade. Booksellers were likened by the poet Thomas Campbell to 'ravens' feasting on their victims.[13] Many compilers and printers felt ill-used by publishers and complaints can be traced back in the archives. The same Strahan who was so helpful to Hume also printed Collins's *Peerage*, Nichols's *Compendium*, and Owen's *Irish Peerage* for Thomas Lowndes and other booksellers. In various sources, he was accused of bullying and notably of having 'for twenty years past employed constantly more journeymen that any

[8] William Dugdale, *The Antient Usage of bearing such ensigns of Honour* (London, 1682), 3.
[9] 'A most impudent person, and the late industrious Garter (Sir W. D.) hath told me that he gets a livelihood by bold practices.' Anthony Wood, *Athenae Oxonienses*, vol. 1 (London, 1691), 389.
[10] 'Now learning is itself a trade. A man goes to a bookseller and gets what he can. We have done with patronage', quoted in E. Clery, C. Franklin, and P. Garside (eds), *Authorship, Commerce and the Public: Scenes of Writing 1750–1850* (Basingstoke, 2002), 9.
[11] Raven, *Publishing Business in Eighteenth-Century England*, 235.
[12] J. W. Saunders, *The Profession of English Letters* (London, 1964, 2000), 154.   [13] Ibid., 163.

236　SELLING ANCESTRY

other printers in London'.[14] A memorial published in his favour in 1770 retorted that his accusers were mostly pressmen, 'indolent and drunken fellows'.[15]

Furthermore, they were, despite their wealth, still looked down upon by their social superiors. In his *Autobiography*, Dr Alexander Carlyle, a founding member of the Royal Society of Edinburgh, commented on Andrew Millar on his trip to Harrogate in 1763 and how 'all the baronets and great squires' were civil enough to obtain his newspaper:

> yet when he appeared in the morning in an old well-worn suit of clothes, they could not help calling him Peter Pamphlet; for the generous patron of Scotch authors, with his city wife and her niece, were sufficiently ridiculous when they came into good company.[16]

Some booksellers were accused of being illiterate and only interested in making a profit. John Stockdale, who first worked with John Almon and then published his own family compilations, was described in a very hostile manner by William Hamilton in his *Intrepid* (1784). The demeaning portrait was illustrated by a caricature by Thomas Rowlandson:

> That booksellers are no longer men of letters [...] excepting Mr J. Nichols, and barely one of decent reading except the younger Lowndes. Stockdale is the son of a blacksmith in Cumberland. [...] He got to be admitted porter to Mr Almon's pamphlet shop. This was at a period of about ten years back, and at that time, this now-celebrated bookseller could not write, and could hardly read.[17]

While booksellers' lack of gentility was underlined, their compilers were in an even direr situation. They did not belong to the category of authors who broke free from any form of dependence. It should be recalled that booksellers held a dominant position over these poorly paid men, many of whom lived literally in the garrets situated above shops. As the owners of most copyrights, the booksellers often used their own name in the title, such as Almon's, Kearsley's, Debrett's, or Stockdale's *Peerages*. Robert Chambers, the Scottish journalist and scholar, complained about the fate of the 'Industrious Obscure who busy themselves in the compilation of Tourist's Guides, Peerages, School-Books, and Almanacks. Such publications are usually anonymous, and the purchaser thinks no more of the unknown author than he thinks of the man who made his hat or tanned the leather of his shoes.'[18] About Debrett, who presented himself as an author,

---

[14] Strahan's papers, BL, Add. MS 48904, fol. 16.　　[15] Ibid.

[16] *Autobiography of the Rev. Dr Alexander Carlyle, Minister of Inveresk: Containing Memorials of the Men and Events of His Time* (London, 1861), 434.

[17] William Hamilton, *The Intrepid* (1784), 53.

[18] Robert Chambers, *The Picture of Scotland*, vol. 1 (Edinburgh, 1827), preface.

Chambers added that 'no distinct idea is attached to the words [...] anymore than to the maker's name on the blade of a table-knife'.[19] Indeed, for the few compilers whose names were mentioned, hardly any documentation remains to enable us to reconstitute their existence. It could only be pieced together from a few lines in the literary gazettes, memoirs, and ledgers. Those who were famous authors, such as William Godwin, did not dwell much on their occasional hack work.

Kimber the obscure

Of Francis Nichols, who published many *British Compendia* from 1717 to 1750, little is known, apart from the fact that his work was severely criticized by John Lodge in his preface: Nichols was 'a person employed by the English booksellers to furnish an Irish compendium' which turned out to be so 'lame and erroneous that I dared not rely on any circumstance or date'.[20] While Nichols had been 'employed twenty years in compiling' it, he admittedly 'never consulted the records of the kingdom'.[21] Although Lodge was himself the son of a husbandman, he managed to secure a respected status by obtaining a Cambridge BA and a position as deputy clerk and keeper of the rolls (Dublin Castle).

Slightly more is known about Edward Kimber, a prolific writer of memoirs and novels, and a key indexer for gazettes such as *The Gentleman's Magazine* (1754), the *Universal Magazine* (1750), and the *Westminster Journal* (1751).[22] Much of his work was published anonymously. His name is linked to many *Peerages* and *Baronetages* in the 1760s printed for the most influential booksellers such as John Almon and Thomas Lowndes. He was acknowledged by John Nichols as 'a very useful corrector of the Press and Editor for the booksellers'.[23] Between 1766 and 1767, Lowndes's ledger book included a few receipts related to his work. Kimber received '10 guineas for compiling the Peerage in full of all accompts' and a further 14 guineas 'for copying of the Peerage of Scotland' and '5 guineas, being with 10 received before, in full for the copy of the Peerage of Ireland'.[24] Their remuneration was comparable to the one gained by hack writers employed literary magazines, such as Joseph Trapp who received in 1791 12 guineas from George Robinson—the owner of *The Town and Country Magazine* and *Lady's Magazine*—for his translation of a French novel.[25] In contrast to the sums mentioned above for the more established 'professional authors' such as Hume

---

[19] Ibid.   [20] John Lodge, *Peerage of Ireland* (1754), vi.   [21] Ibid.
[22] Jeffrey Herrle, 'Kimber, Edward (1719–1769)', *ODNB*, 2004. Retrieved 1 June 2020, from https://doi-org.janus.bis-sorbonne.fr/10.1093/ref:odnb/15547>.
[23] John Nichols, *Literary Anecdotes of the Eighteenth Century*, vol. 3 (London, 1812–15), 604.
[24] Lowndes Papers, BL, Add. MS 38728, fol. 59.
[25] Gillian Hughes, 'Fiction in the Magazines', in Peter Garside and Karen O'Brien (eds), *English and British Fiction, 1750–1820: The Oxford History of the Novel in English*, vol. 2 (Oxford, 2015), 464.

238 SELLING ANCESTRY

or Smollett, these were indeed poor allowances. Before his death in 1769, Kimber teamed up with Richard Johnson, described as 'a very useful corrector of the Press and Editor for the booksellers'.[26] In their preface, they cautiously expressed their unwillingness 'upon mere presumption to deprive any family of its honours'.[27] Commenting on one of their articles, in *The Herald and Genealogist*, Nichols underlined their carelessness. As in other compilations by John Almon, there was 'an air of studied incompleteness, framed in order that it might wear the appearance of being the result of imperfect information'.[28] Errors and lies were dissimulated under the pretence that pedigrees were still under investigation. Both Kimber and Johnson were labelled as 'bookseller's hacks, not genealogists by profession or predilection'.[29] In his preface, Richard Johnson paid tribute to Kimber, his former colleague, claiming that Kimber had died 'a victim, in the meridian of his life, to the indefatigable toils in the Republic of letters'.[30] The latter expression conveyed the sense of a common good to which Kimber allegedly dedicated his life. It assumed that all writers, whatever their social position, were engaged in a relationship of trust and reciprocity in order to develop the sharing of knowledge.[31] Though of a very humble social standing, Kimber, who had travelled to the American colonies in his prime, may have wished to be seen as a member of an Atlantic Republic of Letters. However, this attempt by Johnson to create an enduring reputation failed, as Kimber's name was dropped from later re-editions and replaced by that of the copyright owners, John Almon and then John Debrett. Well-established literary gazettes such as *The Gentleman's Magazine* and prominent antiquaries did not acknowledge him as one of their own.

However, one could argue that some of the compilers' articles went beyond mere carelessness and may have had a political agenda. Their complacent view, guided by a commercial interest, opened the gate to dubious claims which had far-reaching consequences. In the third volume of his *Baronetage*, the bookseller Thomas Lowndes added that while 'the family of Perrott is omitted', he wished 'to do strict justice to all mankind' by inserting the 'curious' pedigree of an army officer, Sir Richard Perrott from Surrey. Johnson and Lowndes published the warrant recognizing him as rightful baronet signed by his Majesty and authenticated in the College of Arms in January 1767.[32] Perrott's pedigree, which was transmitted to Kimber, introduced him as the descendant of remote Welsh ancestors and from 'a most numerous race of Kings, monarchs of Britain,' according to the 'British Annals which will bear record of the truth'.[33] Perrott's

---

[26] C. H. Timperley, *A Dictionary of Printers and Printing, with the Progress of Literature* (London, 1839), 784.

[27] Kimber and Johnson, *Baronetage* (1771), preface, i.

[28] John Gough Nichols, *The Herald and Genealogist*, vol. 8 (1874), 316.   [29] Ibid., 317.

[30] *Baronetage*, i.

[31] Dena Goodman, *The Republic of Letters: A Cultural History of the French Enlightenment* (Ithaca, NY, and London, 1994), 12–15.

[32] Kimber & Johnston, *Baronetage*, vol. 3 (1771), 458.   [33] Ibid., 460.

THE PROTAGONISTS OF A 'SHODDY INDUSTRY' 239

extraordinary claims was used by Nichols as a proof of Kimber's amateurism. In a Welsh manuscript received by Kimber, Perrott was linked to 'Brutus, who first inherited this land, which after him was called Britain. This about the year of the world 2855 and 1116 years before the birth of Christ.'[34] These were unusual claims, even by scribblers' standards, which smacks of parody and may have had a political undertone. To publish the royal warrant validating someone's extraordinary assertions was in itself potentially subversive. It exposed the dysfunctions of a Court which had already been derided in a public campaign the year before. In 1770, during the Wilkite crisis, Perrott presented the prince of Wales and the king with an address of loyalty in the name of the Welsh people, 'whose lives and fortunes His Royal Highness may at any time call forth'.[35] Perrott astutely linked his alleged Welsh origin to his loyalism and was well rewarded as he received a medal and the grant of a manor.[36] His rapid rise to fortune despite his unknown origin was exploited by the radical opposition. In the *North Briton*, Perrott's petition was denounced as an outrage as he 'affects to talk in the name of all the Welsh [...] whereas he has not the least authority' and by offering the king 'the assistance of such a pitiful corporation, to subject the yoke of slavery of nine or ten millions of people'.[37] A song mocked the Court's gullibility in acknowledging dodgy adventurers such as Perrott, 'the valiant knight':

> We're told how once a valiant Knight, Amongst the Ancient Britons, To Court went with a Paper Kite, and met with free admittance, Nay there Sir Richard so' tis said, The King not only saw, Sir, But with young George the honour had, To Play a game at Taw, Sir.[38]

The *Monthly Review* in their account of the pamphlet, *The Life, Adventures, and Amours of Sir R—P—t*, pointed out that 'every news-paper has been of late, filled with anecdotes, true or false, of Sir R—d P—t. This anonymous pamphlet account seems to be of equal authenticity.'[39] Even more conservative periodicals such as *The Gentleman's Magazine* joined the fray and supported in this context a 'middling-sort public opinion from men who saw themselves as independent of the corruption of places and pensions'.[40] In the latter periodical, Perrott was exposed as 'Dick Perrott, the second son of Perrott, a decayed distiller of Mardol in Shrewsbury, who managed during the Seven Years War to pass himself

[34] Ibid., 460.   [35] *The London Evening Post*, 30 Dec. 1769.
[36] Roger T. Stearn, 'Perrott, Sir Richard, second baronet (1716–1796)', *ODNB*, 2004. Retrieved 1 June 2020, from https://doi-org.janus.bis-sorbonne.fr/10.1093/ref:odnb/21989>.
[37] *The North Briton*, 27 Jan., vol. 147 (1770), 298; *The Life, Adventures, and Amours of Sir R—P who so recently had the Honour to present the Flint address at the English court* (London, 1770).
[38] *The political songster or a touch of the times*, 6th edn (London, 1790), 84.
[39] *The Monthly Review*, vol. 42 (1770), 251.
[40] Gilliam Williamson, *British Masculinity in the 'Gentleman's Magazine', 1731 to 1815* (Basingstoke, 2016), 135.

240   SELLING ANCESTRY

for a knight of the order of the Eagle of Prussia and to seduce various girls'.[41] Allegedly, he left a trail of abused women left destitute and with child. Whenever anyone read Perrott's account in the *Baronetage*, he would not be fooled by the fake pedigree but would rather relate it to the avalanche of parodies directed at him and the Court. Instead of showing a lack of critical judgement, the editors of this compilation were doubling down on the radical campaign against Court corruption.

Godwin and his anonymous Peerage

The potentially subversive impact of literary hacks may be illustrated by the case of William Godwin, the author of *Enquiry concerning Political Justice*, an attack on political institutions. The Robinson family in Paternoster Row was well known for publishing eminent radical authors during the French Revolution.[42] As well as Godwin's *Political Justice*, George Robinson and his brothers, John and James, supported Thomas Paine and Anne Radcliffe. Robinson the elder, in particular, nicknamed the 'King of the Booksellers', was reputed to be a generous employer, enabling Godwin to make ends meet by financing his 'writing different things of obscure note'.[43] Among the 'different things' was the *New Annual Register* from 1784 to 1791 and, in 1786, *The English Peerage*, which he wrote for the sum of £10. 10s.[44] It was a rather generous allowance compared to the sums received by Kimber. In the 1780s, however, family compilations were even more successful and generated more profit. In 1788, William Lowndes paid Philip Luckombe 30 guineas for the new *Pocket Peerage* and 4 guineas for the plates.[45] Luckcombe was the son of a tailor from Exeter and composed various dictionaries, travel books, and a successful *Concise History of the Origin and Progress of Printing* (1770). His *Concise History* was a close adaptation of John Smith's *The Printer's Grammar* (1755) and most of his later writings consisted of unacknowledged appropriations.[46] Despite the rise of their income, other

[41] *GM*, vol. 40 (Feb. 1770), 59.

[42] G. E. Bentley, 'Robinson family (per. 1764–1830), booksellers', *ODNB*, 2008. Retrieved 10 May 2020, from https://doi-org.janus.bis-sorbonne.fr/10.1093/ref:odnb/74586>.

[43] '[B]y the liberality of my bookseller, Mr. George Robinson, of Paternoster Row [...] for nearly ten years [...] while writing [for him] different things of obscure note', *Godwin's Diary*, quoted by G. Bentley, ibid. William West called the elder Robinson 'the most enterprising, intelligent, and communicative bookseller with authors of his day', *Fifty Years' Recollections of an Old Bookseller* (London, 1837), 92.–

[44] G. E. Bentley, 'Copyright Documents in the George Robinson Archive: William Godwin and Others 1713–1820', *Studies in Bibliography*, vol. 35 (1982), 89.

[45] 'Rec of William Lowndes the sum of thirty guineas for the copy of the new Pocket Peerage [...]. Memorandum of mr Lowndes having paid to mr Luckomb the sum of four guineas for the copy of the plates of the Peers, Peeresses and Baronets of England'. 5 Jan. 1788, BL, Add. MS 38728, fol. 65.

[46] Jocelyne Hargrave, 'The First Appropriation of Editorial Style: Philip Luckombe's *A Concise History of the Origin and Progress of Printing*', in J. Hargrave, *The Evolution of Editorial Style in Early Modern England* (Basingstoke, 2019), 153–83.

THE PROTAGONISTS OF A 'SHODDY INDUSTRY' 241

compilers still complained of being poorly used. Barak Longmate, the editor of
Collins's *Peerage* in the 1780s for Lowndes and Rivington, wrote to the antiquary
Mark Noble to confirm his unfavourable bias towards most publishers. Although,
he made an exception for the Robinsons: 'I am sorry your experience of London
publishers confirms the unfavourable idea I have of them in general, yet the
Robinsons are reckoned of very respectable character.'[47]

After three years of work, Godwin noted in his diary, 'Finish the Peerage,'
on 28 June 1789 when the French Revolution had already erupted.[48] As
a radical author who warmly welcomed this event, it is easy to understand
why he never acknowledged his *Peerage*. When the guide was published in
1790, its preface contained a statement which could not be further from
Godwin's views: 'We are delighted to observe virtue becoming as it were
hereditary in certain families, and to recollect how much England is indebted
to the Montagus, the Percies, and the earls of Dorset.'[49] In his *Political Justice*,
Godwin had dismissed the idea that as between a 'new born son of a peer and a
mechanic', a 'more generous blood' would circulate in the former's heart.[50]
With much irony, he represented to his public the 'burden' which each lord
carried with him every time he acquired a new title and had to come up with a
new narrative:

> History labours under the Gothic and unintelligible burden; no mortal patience
> can connect the different stories of him, who is today Lord Kimbolton, and
> tomorrow earl of Manchester; today earl of Mulgrave, and tomorrow marquis of
> Normanby and duke of Buckinghamshire.[51]

The *Peerage*, which held a marginal place in Godwin's career, could be seen as an
anecdotal experience, an insignificant piece of hack writing. As in the case
of Kimber, his compilation may have little relevance to the rest of his work beyond
underscoring his early financial insecurity. Not all publications by radical booksellers were aimed at making political points. However, we could equally well
argue that this compilation, which was three years in the making, may have
contributed to Godwin's critical views on the nobility and hereditary privileges.
As we have seen above through several cases, from the 1770s onwards, family
directories were instrumentalized in unpredictable ways.

---

[47] Longmate to Noble, 22 Oct. 1787, Bod Lib., MS Eng. Misc d. 153, fol. 187.
[48] William Godwin's Diary, Bod. Lib. MS Dep. e.197, fol. 8r. Retrieved 18 May 2020, from <http://
godwindiary.bodleian.ox.ac.uk/diary/1789.html>.
[49] *The New Peerage*, ii.
[50] Mark Philp (ed.), *William Godwin, An Enquiry Concerning Political Justice* (Oxford, 2013),
246–7.
[51] Ibid., 254.

242   SELLING ANCESTRY

2. Servile authors and senior ministers

In a letter to George Montagu, Horace Walpole admired the dedication of Sir Philip Sidney in his vindication of his uncle Leicester:

> I am got deep into the Sidney papers [...] and there is a little pamphlet of Sir Philip Sidney's in defence of his uncle of Leicester [...]. In his little tract, he is very vehement in clearing up the honour of his lineage. I don't think he could have been warmer about his family, if he had been of the blood of the Cues. I have diverted myself with reflecting how it would have entertained the town a few years ago if my cousin Richard Hammond had wrote a treatie to clear up my father's pedigree, when the Craftsman used to treat him so roundly with being nobody's son [...]. Yours ever, The Grandson of Nobody.[52]

Walpole was referring to *A Discourse in Defence of the Earl of Leicester* (1584), in which Sir Philip defended his worthy ancestors against the aspersion that they were newcomers. He may have been nostalgic for a golden age of chivalry. Sidney as a scholar and gentleman even went so far as to offer a fight against his uncle's enemies at court.[53] As a platform intended to rally the Country Whigs and Tories against Walpole's ministry, the newspaper was accused by Horace Walpole of attaining the honour of his family. In particular, the authors in the *Craftsman* made a good number of comparisons with historical figures such as Cardinal Wolsey.[54] Both were men of low birth who only achieved high positions through alleged corruption and various misdeeds. These attacks were repeated in several editions, notably in 1732, with a reference to 'Ranulf', a minister 'of a very mean birth who raised himself to the head of the Treasury' after the Norman conquest under the much-vilified reign of William Rufus.[55]

Horace Walpole was convinced that his father's honour would have been better vindicated by his cousin, Richard Hammond, First Clerk of the Pells in the Exchequer. As a respectable figure in the kinship, he would have been in a preferable position to defend his kin than outsiders. In the early modern period, genealogical writing was a common form of service which linked secretaries, lawyers, or clergymen to a noble family[56] since they praised both the dynastic longevity of their patrons and the exceptional quality of their archives. In the eighteenth century, aristocratic patronage has been somewhat overlooked, as it

---

[52] Walpole to George Montagu, 22 May 1746, John Wright (ed.), *The Letters of Horace Walpole*, vol. 1 (Philadelphia, 1842), 480.

[53] On this affair, Katherine Duncan-Jones, *Sir Philip Sidney, Courtier Poet* (New Haven, 1991), 269.

[54] *The Craftsman*, vol. 1, no. 8 (1728), 67.   [55] Ibid., vol. 9, no. 308 (1732), 130.

[56] On Etienne Baluze and Jean Boutier (dir.), *Étienne Baluze, 1630–1718: érudition et pouvoirs dans l'Europe classique* (Limoges, 2008); Valérie Piétri, 'Une offrande à la vanité des *puissants*: l'écriture généalogique comme service littéraire (France méridionale, XVIIe–XVIIIe siècle)', in Jettot and Lezowski (eds), *The Genealogical Enterprise*, 171–89.

THE PROTAGONISTS OF A 'SHODDY INDUSTRY' 243

does not fit into the progressive narrative of a society moving away from old forms of sociability to celebrate independent literary geniuses and their ever-larger pool of passionate readers. However, recent historians no longer take the view that aristocratic literary patronage was a dying cultural practice. Far from being eclipsed by booksellers, peers and ministers were still much engaged in protecting authors, although their involvement took new forms such as 'foundation grants, tax policies, fellowships, academic appointments'.[57] We have seen above in the case of William Betham that early nineteenth-century compilations were still financed through a small pool of wealthy subscribers. The patronage economy was well adapted to the book market industry and to a growing commercial society. It is hardly surprising that several authors should have tried to escape furnishing hack works and sought to obtain more respected appointments through ministerial patronage. Many Scottish authors 'enjoyed professional positions with regular, secure and often substantial incomes, as well as pensions and sinecures from the government'.[58] However, when it came to writing pedigrees, some grandees, like Horace Walpole, warned about the consequence of placing one's honour in mercenary hands.[59]

Collins and the Whig magnates

Though his training as a stationer is undocumented, Arthur Collins had worked as apprentice to the bookseller Roper, probably as indexer to his gazette *The Post Boy*. He does not seem to have gained much from the commercial success of the *Peerage* in 1709 as the copyright was owned by Roper and other booksellers. As he struggled financially, Collins advertised the rental of a small house which he possessed in Guildford.[60] In his attempt to look for aristocratic patrons, he may have been inspired by Simon Segar, great-grandson to the early Stuart Garter King of Arms, Sir William Segar. Segar benefited from the patronage of Edward Harley for his publication of his *Honores Anglicani or Titles of Honour* (1712), an inventory of the English nobility. Already a well-known collector, Harley was hailed by Segar for his library and collections, 'that great magazine of History and

---

[57] Dustin Griffin, *Literary Patronage in England, 1650–1800* (Cambridge, 1996), 4. Paul Korshin, 'Types of Eighteenth-Century Literary Patronage', *Eighteenth-Century Studies*, vol. 7, no. 4 (1974): 453–73.

[58] Sher, *The Enlightenment and the Book*, 204.

[59] On the relation between genealogists and French nobles, see also Nicolas Schapira, 'Les secrétaires particuliers sous l'Ancien Régime: les usages d'une dépendance', *Les cahiers du Centre de Recherches Historiques*, vol. 40 (2007), 111–25.

[60] 'A Convenient House at Guildford in Surry ready f'rnish'd, having 4 Rooms on a Floor, with a pleasant Garden wall'd round, is to be Lett, (with, or without the Goods) for the Summer Season, or a longer Term, if desired: Enquire of Mr. Arthur Collins at the Black-Boy in Fleetstreet', *Pax, Pax, Pax, Or a Pacifick Post Boy* (1713), Thursday 7 May 1713.

244　SELLING ANCESTRY

Antiquities'.[61] Segar hoped his patronage would 'infallibly screen him from all Picque and Censure'.[62] Segar added in his introduction that the legitimacy of his work stemmed from his qualities 'by nature and birth right' as he was a former Oxford student and belonged to 'the fourth generation in this way of learning'.[63] He was entitled to criticize the *Peerage* published by Collins and Roper, an erroneous 'abridgment' which bore little comparison to Dugdale's *Baronage*. Segar died two years after his publication and no longer represented a threat. However, Segar's success in obtaining the protection of a patron, as well as the opportunities offered by the change of regime, may have induced Collins to move away from the bookselling trade and seek a more secure position in the administration. In May 1716, he petitioned for the place of Collector of the Customs at Dartmouth with the support of Josiah Diston, a director of the Bank of England.[64] Most of the Civil List places were in the Office of the Treasury, the Pipe Office, the Customs and the Excise. Collins relied on the backing of Lord Stanhope, for whom he started collecting manuscripts 'of every branch of his family which he presented to his Lordship'.[65] Retrospectively, he considered that he deserved a position comparable to the ones occupied by Elias Ashmole, who was both herald and 'comptroller' of the Excise, and by William Dugdale 'who was knighted by King Charles 2d and made Garter King of Arms for writing his Baronage of England'.[66] He claimed to be more useful to the government than Dugdale, who had been 'deficient in his account of those advanced to the Honr's in his own Time'.[67] Much nostalgia was expressed in his comments about a declining royal patronage which used to protect eminent genealogists. Due to the intricacies of high politics, Collins failed to obtain the much-coveted appointment in the Customs, blaming Lord Carteret and Lord King for having pressed Stanhope to give up his support on behalf of a creature of their own.[68] As compensation, Charles Stanhope, who was acting as secretary to the Treasury, put him temporarily on the Commission of the Lottery. When Sunderland succeeded Stanhope at the Treasury, Collins hoped once more to trade some genealogical enquiries for the office of Landwaiter of London (£80 per annum). Again, he was thwarted in his plan, this time by the bishop of Winchester who secured the position for his

---

[61] The dedication. On the Segar dynasty, see June Schlueter, 'Segar, Francis, the younger (b. before 1564, d. 1615)', *ODNB*, 2016. Retrieved 10 May 2020, from https://doi-org.janus.bis-sorbonne.fr/10.1093/ref:odnb/109694>.

[62] Simon Segar, *Honores Anglicani, Or, Titles of Honour. The Temporal Nobility of the English Nation* (London, 1712), dedication.

[63] Ibid., iii.

[64] 'They [the Bank Directors] recommend to my Lords Mr. Arthur Collins to be Collector of the Customs at Poole, which is now vacant. My Lords say they will put him into some employment in the Customs', Minute Book: August 1715, William A Shaw and F. H. Slingsby (eds), *Calendar of Treasury Books*, vol. 29 (London, 1957), 288.

[65] See his annotated copy of his memoir: *The Case of Arthur Collins, Esq, Author of the Book entitled the Peerage* (London, 1753). BL, Add. MS 32885, fol. 90.

[66] Ibid.　　[67] Ibid.　　[68] Ibid.

THE PROTAGONISTS OF A 'SHODDY INDUSTRY' 245

brother-in-law. These repeated failures led him to have a nervous breakdown and he spent a few months in Chelsea Hospital.[69]

From 1720 onwards, however, Collins started appearing on the royal bounty list with a yearly pension of £200.[70] It was not an insignificant sum though less than the one received by the Historiographer Royal (£300), or the Inspector of Plays (£400).[71] It has been estimated that the expenditure of Walpole's ministry on various publications and journalists such as Matthew Concanen and William Arnall amounted to £20,000 per annum.[72] Influential 'newspaper propagandists' were indeed crucial in Walpole's public strategy, but by the same token, his politics of honour and status should also be considered at face value. Collins may have benefited from the failure of the Peerage Bill in 1719. As the creation of many peers became a sensitive issue, Walpole 'may have been quick to acknowledge that a new order of knighthood offered an attractive alternative though not acceptable to all peerage-seekers'.[73] This new strategy was seconded by the second duke of Montagu, who played a significant role in rallying heralds and genealogists to the Whig cause.[74] Montagu and Walpole managed to get John Anstis, the leading herald at the College of Arms and former Tory MP, involved in the setting up of a new order of knighthood including peers and gentry alike. It is hardly a coincidence that Collins dedicated his *Baronettage of England* to Anstis in 1720, when the latter had been reconciled to the Whig ministry and had received a royal warrant to start work on a history of the Garter Knights.

Walpole's distribution of pensions was seen at first as the triumph of personal interest over ideology. According to Lewis Namier, the promises of pensions and places would have relegated convictions and ideas to background noise or, to use his metaphor, to 'a libretto'.[75] But his creation of the Order of Bath in 1725 should not be perceived 'simply as "a fund of favours", mainly to curry the support of

---

[69] Collins to Townshend, 28 May 1721: 'he having been promised employment in the Customs, which was given to others. This so affected his senses that he was unfit for business'. NA SP 35/26, fol. 182.

[70] Collins received a yearly pension of £200 in 1722 and 1729 and £100 in the following years: 1720, 1731, 1732, 1733, 1734, 1736, 1738, 1737, 1739, 1740, 1743, 1742, 1744, 1745. Joseph Redington (ed.), *Calendar of Treasury Books and Papers*, vols 6–7 (London, 1889).

[71] Korshin, 'Types of Eighteenth-Century Literary Patronage', 458; Simon Targett, 'Government and Ideology during the Age of Whig Supremacy: The Political Argument of Sir Robert Walpole's Newspaper Propagandists', *The Historical Journal*, vol. 37, no. 2 (1994): 289–317.

[72] Korshin, 'Types of Eighteenth-Century Literary Patronage', 462.

[73] Andrew Hanham, 'The Politics of Chivalry: Sir Robert Walpole, the Duke of Montagu and the Order of the Bath', *Parliamentary History*, vol. 35, no. 3 (2016): 262–97 at 264.

[74] 'Nowhere did Montagu's antiquarian sallies feature so obsessively than in his preoccupation with the history of his own family. His father had entered the higher aristocracy with an earldom in 1689, but had been anxious to project himself and his descendants as one of the nation's premier aristocratic dynasties'. Ibid., 263.

[75] 'What matters most is the underlying emotions, the music, to which ideas are a mere libretto, often of a very inferior quality.' L. B. Namier, *Personalities and Powers* (London, 1955), 4.

246   SELLING ANCESTRY

wealthy independent Whig MPs'.[76] Whig magnates had a genuine desire to defend the prestige of their lineages along with that of the Hanoverian dynasty. A new chivalric order played the role of a political nexus between the Court and the state elite as Walpole and Montagu negotiated the backing of powerful courtiers such as Newcastle, Halifax, and Leicester in the appointment of knights.

In December 1728, for his *Baronagium Angliae, or an Historical account of our English nobility*, Collins obtained a royal licence giving him 'sole right and title of the copy of the said book'.[77] A four-volume folio, Collins's *Baronagium* was strikingly different from the cheap serial peerages that he had previously published. For the first time, Collins's name appeared on the cover as an 'author' and 'Esquire'. The compilation contained detailed pedigrees of a select list of eleven Whig magnates: Cavendish, Churchill, Pelham, Sackville, Compton, Lumley, Cholmondeley, Hervey, Carteret, Stawel, and Walpole. It was hardly a coincidence that all these Lords were to be part of the new Order of the Bath. According to Collins, Walpole's high birth and his deeds were vindicated against the 'Kennel-Dirt', the false aspersions in the *Craftsman* (no. 16) about his 'plain habit and manner of address', exposing him 'to be hunted and worried by the Populace'.[78] In the *Craftsman*'s issue alluded to by Collins, that was a semi-fictional story about a political turmoil in which appeared 'a man dress'd in a plain habit, with a purse of gold in his hand. He threw himself forward into the Room, in a bluff, ruffianly manner. [...] In an instant, I saw half the august assembly in chains'.[79] Like the Hanoverians, the Walpoles, of 'brave and worthy stock', were rooted in the cherished Saxon times, when royal prerogative and parliamentary freedom were equally respected.[80] Introducing Walpole as 'my great Patron', Collins used a natural metaphor according to which 'not unlike the most generous sorts of fruit-trees, that put forth their buds, and blossom out for fruit, some time before there is any appearance of the proper ornaments for themselves'.[81] Collins was alluding to the fact that Walpole only allowed his own son Robert to be elevated to the peerage in 1723.

This attempt to revive a medieval order, a 'theatre of honour', was quickly abandoned as it did not meet the expectations of its founders and turned out to be counter-productive. It only exacerbated the mockery and the puns directed at 'King Robin'.[82] Many country Whig and Tory magnates such as Stanhope, Bedford, or Bolingbroke were probably not impressed by the extraordinary

---

[76] Hanham, 'The Politics of Chivalry', 262; On patronage and court politics see Hannah Smith, *Georgian Monarchy: Politics and Culture 1714–1760* (Cambridge, 2006).

[77] Dec. 1728, NA SP 36/9/2/8.

[78] *Baronagium Angliae, or an Historical account of our English nobility*, published by Robert Gosling (London, 1727), vi–vii.

[79] *The Craftsman*, 27 Jan. 1727, no. 16, 95.

[80] According to Camden 'the Walpole in Norfolk, was in England before the conquest', *Baronagium*, 651; Simon Keynes, 'The Cult of King Alfred the Great', *Anglo-Saxon England*, vol. 28 (1999): 269–74.

[81] *Baronagium*, iii.   [82] Hanham, 'The Politics of Chivalry', 270.

THE PROTAGONISTS OF A 'SHODDY INDUSTRY'   247

pedigrees attributed to Walpole's friends by an unknown London scribbler. Collins's initiative came at a time when Walpole had already divested his funds away from the Order of Bath. Although he remained on the bounty list, Collins failed to obtain a stable and rewarding official position. He wrote to Walpole again in 1730, hoping for the position of Keeper of the Records in the Tower. He described himself as a well-connected scholar: 'I have corresponded with most of the antiquaries in the kingdom [...] and by having that office I shall be able to discover and publish those particulars which will be to the honour of the nation'.[83] In 1734, he tried again to solicit him, claiming that his compilations 'have the design'd effect to silence such as raise groundless clamours against you'.[84]

> I observ'd with peculiar pleasure; that since my publication of the account of your family (among others of the nobility) just before his present Majestys accession to the throne, those who envied your services and the royal Favour, have forbore endeavouring to asperse you in your birth and hereditary fortunes.[85]

These repeated pleas do not seem to have been any more successful. In a rather desperate move, Collins tried in vain to involve Newcastle and then Horace Walpole. He reminded the former that he had spent his fortune 'to retrieve the memory of those who have deserv'd well of their country' and he deserved 'some favour from the government'.[86] He asked for an ensign commission for his son John, who helped him in copying manuscripts. Two years later, on Christmas Day, despite his pension, he described himself as 'left in starving condition with a large family growing up' and pleaded Newcastle to speak to Walpole in his favour, insisting on his specific expertise, he 'being the only author not preferred that ever wrote on the subject'.[87] He asked the latter to intervene in order to obtain the available position of keeper of the records in the Pipe office.[88] His letter to William Pitt was no more successful.[89] Collins had to resort to occasional work for various peers such as the Sidneys, Cavendishes, and the Holles, which led to a series of limited editions of family papers.[90] Few peers were eager to support literary tasks

---

[83] 20 Aug. 1730. TNA SP 36/20/1/62.

[84] Collins to Walpole, 11 Aug. 1734, Cambridge Lib., Cholmondeley Papers, vol. 1, 2307, fol. 1.

[85] Ibid., fol. 4.   [86] To Newcastle, 31 Mar. 1734, BL Add. MS 32689, fol. 178.

[87] Ibid., fol. 208.

[88] 'I don't doubt of meeting with some particulars both of your ancestors and Sr Robert', 21 Sept. 1739, BL, Add. MS 32692, fol. 314.

[89] 'Having occasion to copy some particular relating to Families in the Prerogative Office, as likewise in the Heralds Office, I have met with some Wills, one of Thomas Pitt in the beginning of Henry 8th's Reign and two pedigrees of your family [...] and a remarkable Certificate of the Funeral of Sr William Pitt [...] From the Honr and Respect I bear to you, I will forthwith copy whatever I meet with your Family, if you please to accept thereof.' Collins to Pitt, 18 June 1746, NA SP 30/70/5/299.

[90] *Letters and Memorials of State* [...] *by Sir Henry Sydney, the famous Philip Sydney* (London, 1746); *Historical Collections of the Noble Families of Cavendish, Holles, Vere, and Harley and Ogle* (London, 1752).

248 SELLING ANCESTRY

and were reluctant to pay.[91] In many cases, he complained of being poorly remunerated for his services and even of being publicly humiliated. He referred to his copying work for Philip York, second earl of Hardwicke, which failed to be rewarded. As he was 'ashamed to mention this to Mr York', he asked one of his protégés, Thomas Birch, secretary to the Royal Society, 'to hint to him that they really cost me upwards of ten guineas'.[92] In another letter to Newcastle, he wrote that his brother openly ignored him 'at his levee' and 'hardly admitted me to speak to him'.[93] Nor did his many dedications to various peers in his *Peerages* bring in much cash. Multiplying his imploring letters to Newcastle, in which he contrasted the generous behaviour of Walpole with the latter's ingratitude, he finally managed to obtain the promise of a pension of £400 for his last *Peerage* in 1756. He dedicated his first volume to George II and the second to Anthony, earl of Shaftesbury, whose 'great ancestor' stood in 'defence of the Protestant Religion, the Liberty and Property of the Subjects'.[94] In the third volume, Collins was 'induced to beg' another minister's 'Patronage': Robert d'Arcy, whose forebears 'served the conqueror in his victorious expedition.'[95] The promise of a pension failed to materialize, however. In one of his last letters, he begged him to meet at the Treasury, explaining that the warrant he received could not be validated in his absence. In a dramatic and pleading tone, he wrote, 'I humbly hope you wont let me dye for want of Bread, who am, Your most afflicted and most Devoted servant'.[96]

Collins seems to have been placed in an awkward spot, both being poorly treated by booksellers for his succeeding editions of the Peerage and unable to obtain a secure position in government.

William Guthrie, Alexander Jacob, and their competing patrons

Collins died in 1760, the year of George III's accession to the throne. The new reign revived the possibility of more generous aristocratic patronage. The much-advertised compilations by Guthrie and Edmondson in 1762 and 1763 have already been considered. The significance of their undertaking has been dismissed by historians. For Lewis Namier, Guthrie belonged 'to the canaille, to

---

[91] 'Even if, in 1750, there were as many as 100 peers and wealthy commoners (an extremely liberal estimate) willing and able to make personal patronage grants to authors, this degree of beneficence would not have gone very far toward supporting England's writing community', Korshin, 'Types of Eighteenth-Century Literary Patronage', 461.
[92] Collins to Birch, Mar. 1746, BL, Add. MS 4303, fol. 9.
[93] 'You said to me why don't you go to my brother and when I have done myself that Honr at his levee, he has reacted very coldly and hardly admitted me to speak to him'. 7 Aug. 1751, BL, Add. MS 32725, fol. 21.
[94] Collins, *Peerage* (1756), vol. 2.   [95] Ibid., vol. 3.
[96] 1 Nov. 1758, BL, Add. MS 32725, fol. 180.

THE PROTAGONISTS OF A 'SHODDY INDUSTRY'   249

hired journalists and pamphleteers'.[97] He was one of a group of mercenary authors who were no match for the skilled press team around Almon and Wilkes. Similarly, after mentioning his first-hand work as reporter for *The Gentleman's Magazine* and the writing of a scatological pamphlet, Guthrie's latest biographer has referred to him as an unprincipled author, receiving pensions from Henry Pelham and then from Bute.[98] His *Peerage* is dealt with in a single terse sentence:

> His *Complete List of the English Peerage* (1763) was useful in intent though not always accurate in its execution, containing numerous errors even in relation to George II's very recent reign.[99]

As in the case of Godwin, this compilation is described as a faulty one-off of little importance compared to his later enlightened contributions, such as his *General History of the World* (1764–7) and his highly successful *Geographical, Historical, and Commercial Grammar* (1770). It should be noted, first, that his compilation was actually named *A complete history of the English Peerage* and second, while not bearing scrutiny from a factual point of view, that it should not be dismissed as entirely irrelevant to his later work. We saw in the first chapter that his compilation was aimed at celebrating a new political order under George III and was directed at the Whig ministers of the previous reign. It could be seen as very similar to Collins's *Baronage*, as both compilations were restricted in scope to twelve peers and openly favoured noble courtiers. Furthermore, Guthrie's publications should not be considered as separate from each other. The considerable amount of knowledge he accumulated in his previous work was used in his *Peerage* and, reciprocally, his compilation had some influence on his later compositions. Already in his *General History of England* (1744–51), published under the patronage of Chesterfield, Guthrie had vindicated the importance of the Country opposition against the Court Whigs and drew much of his inspiration from Bolingbroke's ideas on the Patriot King.[100] These condemnations were reformulated in his *Peerage*. In both publications, Rapin de Toyras's views were criticized and the royal prerogative's role in social harmony and the defence of commercial interests was similarly praised.[101] By the same token, his censure of Walpole was rehearsed for his later *Geographical, Historical, and Commercial*

---

[97] *The Structure of Politics at the Accession of George III* (London, 1957), 229.

[98] The significance of Bute's patronage has been studied by Richard B. Sher in the case of the dramatist John Holme, who became his private secretary. *The Enlightenment and the Book*, 205. His protection of the Scottish universities and William Robertson has been explored by Edward Andrews, *Patrons of Enlightenment* (Toronto, 2006), 133.

[99] David Allan, 'Guthrie, William (1708?–1770)', *ODNB*, 2004. Retrieved 10 May 2020, from https://doi-org.janus.bis-sorbonne.fr/10.1093/ref:odnb/11792>.

[100] Laird Okie, *Augustan Historical Writing: Histories of England in the Enlightenment* (Lanham, Md, 1991), 171.

[101] William Guthrie, *General History of England*, vol. 1 (London, 1744), iii, and *Complete History of the English Peerage*, vol. 1, 172.

250 SELLING ANCESTRY

Grammar.[102] Guthrie's leitmotivs circulated throughout his publications, in his *Peerage* as well as in his historical essays.

Moreover, it is worth stressing that his compilation was not ignored by his contemporaries. The attacks directed against Walpole's patronage compromised Collins's reputation and in the same vein, the ferocious campaign against Bute had a detrimental effect on Guthrie. His mistakes were indeed all the more unforgivable as they were linked to a disgraced ministerial figure. Much in the vein of Pope's *Dunciad*, 'Author', a satirical poem composed by Charles Churchill in 1763, dealt with the corruption of science and literature under the patronage of incumbent ministers. Churchill was a close ally of John Wilkes and contributed to the publication of the *North Briton*.[103] On Guthrie, he had this to say:

> With rude unnatural jargon to support,
> Half Scotch, half English, a declining court;
> To make most glaring contraries unite,
> And prove beyond dispute that black is white;
> To make firm Honour tamely league with Shame,
> Make Vice and Virtue differ but in name; [...]
> Is there not Guthrie? Who, like him, can call
> All Opposites to proof, and conquer all?
> He calls forth living waters from the rock;
> He calls forth children from the barren stock;
> He, far beyond the springs of Nature led,
> Makes Women bring forth after they are dead;
> He, on a curious, new, and happy plan,
> In wedlock's sacred bands joins Man to Man;
> And, to complete the whole, most strange, but true,
> By some rare magic, makes them fruitful too,
> Whilst from their loins, in the due course of years,
> Flows the rich blood of Guthrie's English Peers.[104]

This dismissal of his work came partly from his Scottish origins and his 'rude unnatural jargon'. The ability of some Scots to speak proper English was even open to question. By a 'curious, new, and happy plan' and 'rare magic', Guthrie attributed descendants to barren families and transformed unknown

---

[102] The prince of Wales 'complained that through Walpole's influence he was deprived not only of the power but the provision to which his birth entitled him'. William Guthrie, *Geographical, Historical, and Commercial Grammar* (London, 1794), 340. See also his passage on honours and titles, ibid., 286–7.

[103] James Sambrook, 'Churchill, Charles (1732–1764)', *ODNB*, 2004. Retrieved 10 May 2020, from https://doi-org.janus.bis-sorbonne.fr/10.1093/ref:odnb/5397>.

[104] Charles Churchill, *Poems*, vol. 2 (London, 1766), 30.

THE PROTAGONISTS OF A 'SHODDY INDUSTRY' 251

individuals into glorious ancestors. The spirit of such criticism related to a powerful anti-Scottish bias and to the alleged persistence of a mystical world up north which allowed fairy tales to subsist. Like their Irish counterparts, Scottish genealogists were suspected of recycling old myths and bardic poetry. It was sometimes contended that 'the prevailing ignorance among Scots of their origins had resulted in the filling of this void with Irish tales'.[105] Despite the strength of a British assimilationist policy, many English authors still failed to recognize the existence of a specifically Scottish enlightenment and for all his successful publications, Guthrie was still held in low esteem. The gist of the argument was repeated later by Samuel Johnson in his 1773 *Tour of the Western Islands of Scotland*. It was only recently, he observed, that among the local elite, hereditary poets and bards had ceased to be taken at face value. He celebrated the dawn of an age founded on 'written learning [...] a fixed luminary, which after the cloud that had hidden it has passed away, is again in its proper station'.[106] Protestant England was presented as a beacon of modernity when compared to the Scottish northerners and the Catholic southerners.

Another element worth stressing is that Guthrie's initiative generated a counter-attack from Alexander Jacob, an Anglican clergyman and chaplain to the second duke of Chandos. Jacob was husband to Elizabeth, second daughter of the first duke, James Brydges, and was later buried in 1785 in the Chandos family vault.[107] Although the strength of the Chandos patronage network in Church and Parliament had collapsed after the death of the first duke in 1744, the second duke felt it necessary to defend the memory of his father and other Whig magnates. On the frontispiece of his *Complete Peerage*, Jacob is depicted presenting his compilation to the king and, in contrast to Edmondson's *Peerage*, no herald is represented. The king is displayed directly distributing noble honours without interference from courtiers and heralds.

Dedicated to Henry, duke of Chandos, knight of the order of the Bath, Jacob's *Peerage* was intended to vindicate the memory of the Walpole era against the aspersions cast by Guthrie. His history was unapologetically Whig, mentioning the 'violent opposition of the Tories, with the Earl of Nottingham' against the bill for the succession of the Crown in the Protestant line in 1701 and how the Tories, until 1710, had 'frowned upon every measure that tended to strengthen the Hanover Succession'.[108] Against this constant Jacobite threat stood a few heroes such as James Brydges, first duke of Chandos, 'from Arnolph of Brugge',

---

[105] Colin Kidd, *Subverting Scotland's Past: Scottish Whig Historians and the Creation of an Anglo-British Identity 1689–1830* (Cambridge, 2003), 235.

[106] Arthur Murphy, *Works of Samuel Johnson*, 3rd edn, vol. 2 (New York, 1845), 651.

[107] Clergy of the Church of England database, Alexander Chandos. Preacher throughout diocese of Bath and Wells. Person ID: 43950. Retrieved 10 May 2020 from <https://theclergydatabase.org.uk/jsp/search/index.jsp>.

[108] Jacob, *A Complete English Peerage*, vol. 1, 39.

252 SELLING ANCESTRY

Robert Walpole would be descended from Reginald of Norfolk, and Thomas Pelham from Ralph Pelham, all in the Domesday book.[109] James Brydges, 'a genius equal to the most arduous employs of state, and [of] an integrity that made him capable of the highest truths', was raised to the peerage by his various deeds.[110] As 'one of the best accomptants in the nation', he discovered the most amazing 'scene of corruption' in the Tory ministry and succeeded in restoring the value of the pound by a great recoinage. Walpole was described as an effective manager in the Commons against the 'artful insinuations' of Henry Sacheverell against 'the rights and liberties of the people of England, the happy revolution'.[111] Lord Pelham, during his 34 years in government, 'was enabled, by prudent degrees, to effect a reduction of the interest upon the national debt'.[112]

Jacob was dismissed by several reviewers for copying former works: 'the present author has been too sparing in his references, even to those from whom he has mostly freely borrowed'.[113] While Guthrie had been mocked for his Scottish invention, Jacob was repudiated for his plagiarism.

The perfect George Allan and his aborted Peerage

Between these dubious schemers supported by powerful ministers and courtiers, one honest antiquary might have managed to write a good peerage if he had not been sidelined by the partisan politics of the 1760s. This was in a nutshell the point made in an article published by John Nichols in his *Literary Anecdotes* (1814). Nichols alluded to George Allan Esq, 'this very meritorious antiquary' and his various documents transmitted by his son.[114] Allan was described as a man with a pedigree registered in the College of Arms and with a large fortune which he inherited from Ann Allan of Blackwell Grange. Through various intermarriages, the Allans were depicted as connected to the Killinghalls and the Pembertons and were owners of vast estates in Darlington. Unlike the servile and impoverished authors, Allan is portrayed as a generous and hospitable figure. His son revealed that he tried to publish a *Peerage* in 1763 despite similar projects by Guthrie or Edmondson.[115] He hoped to obtain the patronage of Lord Lincoln and the contribution of at least 200 subscribers to cover publication costs, estimated at £3,000. Eventually, his work would have been

---

[109] Ibid., vol. 1, 390, vol. 2, 124.   [110] Ibid., vol. 1, 398–9.
[111] Ibid., vol. 2, 128.   [112] Ibid., vol. 1, 352.
[113] *The Monthly Review*, vol. 43 (1771), 443; see later *The Life of George Allan: To Which Is Added, a Catalogue of Books and Tracts Printed at His Private Press at Blackwell Grange* (1829).
[114] John Nichols, *Literary anecdotes*, vol. 8 (1814), 351.
[115] A work 'printed on large imperial paper with a neat and beautiful type and embellished with proper ornaments', ibid., 355.

THE PROTAGONISTS OF A 'SHODDY INDUSTRY'   253

able to preserve the dignity of each nobleman as Allan offered all the families the possibility of supervising the editing of their articles: 'should any mistakes be discovered, they may be carefully corrected before publication'.[116] His scheme was compromised by the 'two similar works having been published about the same time' whose authors were unknown in polite society.[117] Allan was a collateral victim of the ministerial rivalries that plagued the 1760s, whereas he would have been in a better position to use the 'valuable lights now opened, by the beneficence of Parliament, in the British Museum'.[118] The latter repository was accessible in 1759 only with the agreement of its trustees, Peter Collinson and William Watson, both fellows of the Royal Society. Competing with other national collections in Paris and Edinburgh, the British Museum had been enriched with vast collections formed by Sir Hans Sloane and the Harleys.[119] Allan's genteel expertise was contrasted with the dubious activities of Edmondson: Edmondson's 'tables are disposed in so obscure and intricate a manner' while 'Mr. Allan's are beautiful, plain and explicit, *even to the meanest capacity*'.[120] Allan was even offered a position in the College of Arms in 1764 by Ralph Bigland who complained about Edmondson, who had demonstrated 'many disagreeable proofs of his behaviour'.[121] Once an apprentice to a barber, he had been imposed upon the other members of the College by Lord Suffolk and was accused of continuing his lowly activity of coach-painting.[122]

Later a fellow of the Society of Antiquaries, and the owner of a private press, Allan collected a considerable number of wills, visitation books, and many other curiosities (birds, arrows, shells), preserved in what his son called his 'museum' which was open to genuine antiquaries such as Thomas Tennant or Mark Noble.[123] In his collections, he acquired more than 500 pedigrees of the Yorkshire nobility and gentry. He identified himself with Dugdale and, like him, was eager to defend his honour, writing memoirs that were later revised by his son and published in 1829.[124] He even had his portrait done after Wenceslaus Hollar's engraving of Sir William Dudgale (Illus. 5.1 and 5.2).

---

[116]   Ibid., 356.

[117]   An anonymous reviewer who described himself as 'a great lover of the noble science of heraldry' wrote that 'both the authors are unknown to me and if any preference ought to be given to merit, perspicuity and ingenuity, I think Mr Allan's tables have the claim thereto'. Ibid., 357.

[118]   Ibid., 356.

[119]   Edward Miller, *That Noble Cabinet: A History of the British Museum* (London, 1973); K. G. W. Anderson (ed.), *Enlightening the British: Knowledge, Discovery and the Museum in the Eighteenth Century* (London, 2003).

[120]   Nichols, *Literary Anecdotes*, vol. 8, 356.

[121]   Ralph Bigland to George Allan, 15 Jan. 1765, ibid., 359.

[122]   Adrian Ailes, 'He was disliked by his brother officers for his low origins and for encroaching on their prerogatives', 'Edmondson, Joseph (bap. 1732, d. 1786)', *ODNB*, 2008. Retrieved 27 May 2020 from https://doi-org.janus.bis-sorbonne.fr/10.1093/ref:odnb/8491>.

[123]   Nichols, *Literary Anecdotes*, vol. 8, 356.

[124]   Robert Henry Allan (ed.), *The life of the late George Allan* (Sunderland, 1829).

Illus. 5.1 George Allan. Engraving by T. A. Dean after a painting by T. L. Busby. ©Durham County Record Office D/XD 124/1

Allan was in many senses the perfect antiquarian hero who would have been an ideal *Peerage*-maker, had it not been for the hostile environment created by the book industry and competing aristocratic patronages.

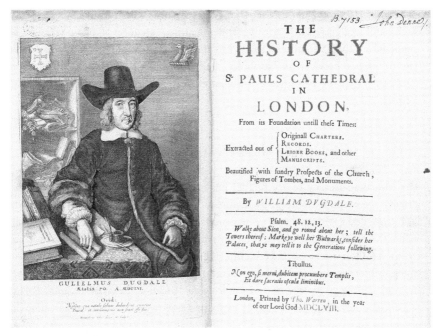

Illus. 5.2 Sir William Dugdale (1656). Etching by Wenceslaus Hollar. Used as frontispiece to Dugdale, *The History of St Paul's Cathedral in London* (1658).
© The Metropolitan Museum of Art, 2017.320.1

3. Impersonators and forged identities

Another compiler, William Playfair, and his *British Family Antiquity* (1809) might simply be pigeonholed in the category of unworthy projectors if it were not for the fact that he was also accused of fraud. After his death, he was described as a man of a 'mechanical genius' and 'too volatile a disposition, even in literary pursuits, to confine himself to the dull labour of tracing out a family pedigree'.[125] Due to a 'very extravagant price', his compilations did not sell well and their 'proprietors, who were no booksellers, became bankrupt in the undertaking'.[126] In an obituary, Playfair was represented as both a scribbler and a mercenary author. He 'had neglected his own interests to promote those of the British government', a reference to the fact that he worked under the patronage of Pitt and several other ministers (Liverpool and Perceval).[127] A ruined Playfair was then accused of

---

[125] *The Literary chronicle and weekly review*, no. 200 (1823), 172.   [126] Ibid.
[127] Ian Spence, 'Playfair, William (1759–1823)', *ODNB*, 2004, retrieved 10 Apr. 2020, from https://doi-org.janus.bis-sorbonne.fr/10.1093/ref:odnb/22370; on Playfair's attempted extortions,

256 SELLING ANCESTRY

extortion at the end of his life, trying to sell some fake family papers to Lord Archibald Douglas. This case illustrates a third category of compilers, no less unappealing than the others, related to the world of impersonators and forgers. The difference between the scribblers and mercenary authors and these impersonators is that the inventions of the latter dealt with their own identity or their sources.

Literacy, social identity, and fraudsters

The idea that literacy might further engagement in various illegal activities was already a common theme in the eighteenth century, for instance in the growing literature dedicated to 'writing prisoners' and their worrisome reading skills: 'while the expansion of written literacy was imagined as a way to spread sociability, the counterfeiter occupies the flip side of this coin (or bill)'.[128] Like fake bank notes, impersonation relied on trust and prowess. In his provocative self-help manual, *The Way to be Rich and Respectable, Addressed to Men of Small Fortune* (1775), the Reverend John Trusler explained how a country gentleman may 'live as well as, and make an appearance in life equal to, a man of £1000 a year and not expend £400'.[129] In his criticism of the consumption of luxuries, he argued that in the 'infectious' metropolis, social boundaries and identities became easier to cross and blur. Books could be used to boost false claims and, by the same token, corrupt heralds were part of this dissolution process. In his memoirs, he recalled his visit to the heralds' office in 1758 and his encounter with a young herald. The latter suggested that 'for the small sum of forty pounds', he could make him 'a coat of arms and ally you to some of the first families in this kingdom'.[130] Trusler mentioned the old story about a prisoner in Ludgate, who managed to escape by tying a robe to the statue of King Lud. After a long stay on the continent where he succeeded in enriching himself, he came back to London where he was recognized by the heralds as 'lineally descended from King Lud'.[131] The story may have originated in John Stow's *Survey of London* in which Ludgate is described as having been restored under King Henry III and adorned with a statue of the British king. It was later turned into a prison and was given the name of Newgate

---

see Howard Wainer, *Graphic Discovery: A Trout in the Milk and Other Visual Adventures* (Princeton, 2005): 9–27; J. F. Dunyach, 'Le *British Family Antiquity* de William Playfair (1809–1811), une entreprise généalogique', in Jettot and Lezowski (eds), *The Genealogical Enterprise*, 319–39.

[128] Jodi Schorb, 'Crime, Ink: The Rise of the Writing Prisoner', in Jodi Schorb, *Reading Prisoners: Literature, Literacy, and the Transformation of American Punishment, 1700–1845* (New Brunswick, NJ, 2014), 70.

[129] *The Way to be Rich and Respectable* (London, 1775), 16.

[130] *Memoirs of the Life of the Rev. Dr Trusler* (London, 1806), 7.

[131] Ibid., 9. The story already appeared in various books, notably in John Kelly, *A New Plain and Useful Introduction to the Italian* (London, 1739), 427.

THE PROTAGONISTS OF A 'SHODDY INDUSTRY' 257

during the reign of Queen Elizabeth.[132] In 1727, a story circulated about an Irish dancing-master in Ipswich, who was convicted as a cheat and imposter for assuming the title and functions of a king of arms, and took large fees in so doing.[133] Such stories were plentiful enough, but more exceptionally in a few cases, compilers used their work to elevate their own status. Initially devised to detect impersonators, their guides were at the same time unparalleled resources for refashioning identities. Some writers employed false titles and others went so far as to mutilate documents or forge entirely new ones. They fit in a period when the notion of fraud was itself redefined and discussed in many social arenas, becoming a major preoccupation in common law.[134] They corresponded to an age when 'so far as literary forgery is concerned, as they were publicly exposed, these authors contributed to the poor reputation of printed genealogies'.[135]

Several compilers, notably William Berry and Sir Egerton Brydges, were accused of making false claims and their convictions were closely linked to attempts by the heralds of the College of Arms to reassert their rights over allegedly dubious pedigree-makers. A petition in the State Paper enunciated various rules in order to avoid 'confusion parity and contempt in the degrees and dignities of persons'.[136] Hoping to revive the writs of 1417 restricting the right to bear arms, its author suggested the need for the heralds to 'have power to reverse, or deface' any unlawful arms 'wherever placed and to give notice thereof in the Gazette as a mark of infamy'.[137] The Parliament was required to regulate the printing of Coats of Arms and to prevent any artificer to paint or carve them without authority of the College. If these strict recommendations were not acted upon, we have seen in the first chapter that after 1760, the College had received official backing from the king. It was later closely involved with most of the enquiries conducted by the House of Lords on peerage claims. As early as 1767, Blackstone in his *Commentaries* had stressed the need to remedy the situation 'for the future, with respect to claims of peerage, by a late standing order of the House of Lords, directing the heralds to take exact accounts and preserve regular entries of all peers and peeresses of England'.[138] With respect to the baronets, George III had ordered in 1782 that 'no Baronet in future, shall have his name and title inserted in any deed or other instrument, until he shall have proved his right to such title in the Heralds' Office'.[139] This more visible public role for the College of

---

[132] William J. Thoms (ed.), John Stowe, *A Survey of London: Written in the Year 1598* (London, 1876), 15.

[133] Richard Wagner, *English Genealogy* (London, 2nd edn, 1972), 133.

[134] Paul Baines, *The House of Forgery in 18th-Century Britain* (Brookfield, 1999), 4.

[135] On a literary and general approach to mystification and forgeries, see in particular Peter Knight and Jonathan Long (eds), *Fakes and Forgeries* (Amersham, 2004).

[136] Petition 'touching coats of Arms and registering pedigrees', NA 35/66, part 2, fol. 92.

[137] Ibid., fols 93–4.

[138] Wilfrid R. Prest and David Lemmings (eds), *Commentaries on the Laws of England*, vol. 3 (Oxford, 2016), 71.

[139] *The European Magazine, and London Review*, vol. 5 (Jan. 1784), 32.

258 SELLING ANCESTRY

Arms is illustrated by the second edition of *The Peerage of Ireland* in 1789 by Mervyn Archdall. Member of the Royal Irish Academy, this respected antiquary re-edited the preface written by John Lodge in 1754 for the first edition. In retrospect, Lodge was celebrated as a pioneer in the 'science of heraldry' for his precocious stand against unworthy compilers such as Aaron Crowley, a herald-painter, and the journalist Francis Nichols. Lodge had denounced their 'sorry performance' and their lack of support from the Irish nobility.[140] Like Lodge, Archdall described his directory as patronized by the heralds, notably the Ulster King of Arms, and by a long list of Irish peers. In the late 1790s and as in England, the Irish peerage was to be placed under the protection of well-established antiquaries. The regained authority of the College and its growing influence in the commercialization of ancestry led to several cases in which the manipulations and fabrications of compilers were publicly exposed.

William Berry, the fake clerk

In August 1830, William Berry 'of Kennington' was accused in *The Gentleman's Magazine* of fraudulent deception and notably of lying about his position.[141] Berry was a compiler of several works, including an *Introduction to Heraldry* (1810), an *Encyclopaedia Heraldica* published in monthly issues from 1824 to 1828, and a series of *County Histories*, starting in 1829 with Kent. As the latter edition was allegedly based on the heralds' Visitations, the unknown reviewer attacked him for wrongly asserting that he had been for fifteen years the 'registering clerk in the Heralds' College', adding that this title never existed and that his name did not appear in the register of the Corporation.[142]

Berry decided to sue the magazine for libel and a trial took place in November 1830 in the court of the King's Bench. Henry Brougham represented the plaintiff while the attorney-general conducted the defence. In November 1830, *The Times* and *The Gentleman's Magazine* published a report of the trial summarizing the gist of the accusation. Beyond the question of his dubious office, it was his position as a genuine antiquary and a representative of the College which was contested.[143] In the 1829 edition of *GM*, the reviewer not only questioned Berry's position but also made broader historical statements. He complained that, following the end of Visitations in 1689, heralds had been succeeded by persons who were 'not members of their Corporation' and were deprived of any 'liberal education'.[144] A genealogist, if not of 'gentle blood' himself should at least be 'the allowed equal

---

[140] 'Mr. Lodge's preface', M. Archdall, *The Peerage of Ireland*, vol. 1 (London, 1789).
[141] G. Boase and M. Lloyd, 'Berry, William (1774–1851)', *ODNB*, 2004. Retrieved 28 May 2020 from https://doi-org.janus.bis-sorbonne.fr/10.1093/ref:odnb/2267>.
[142] *GM*, 1st ser., vol. 99 (1829), 99–101.   [143] *GM*, 1st ser., vol. 100, part 2 (1830), 409–11.
[144] *GM*, 1st ser., vol. 99 (1829), 99.

THE PROTAGONISTS OF A 'SHODDY INDUSTRY'   259

and associate of those who are so, with a very quick perception of the truth'.[145] The latter statement clearly established the correlation between 'a quick perception of truth' and gentility, whether acquired by birth or by a liberal education. As Berry was deprived of both, the reviewer was inclined to call into question his ability to collaborate with the best families of Kent. It was assumed that he used his spurious position in the College to gain their trust.

In a speech for his defence, Henry Brougham stressed that 'Mr Berry complained not of an attack upon his book, but upon his character for truth and honesty'.[146] The plaintiff was unjustly libelled by 'zealous heralds' who out of jealousy had rejected his expertise and his 'interference into their mysteries'.[147] In the preface to his *Encyclopaedia Heraldica*, Berry presented himself as a conduit between the 'increasing class of persons who are now desirous of an acquaintance with Heraldry' and the 'professional men, or professed antiquaries' who had kept the science of heraldry 'solely into their hands'.[148] As a 'historical writer', he believed he had sufficient authority to dismiss the 'fabulous' stories and draw a 'line between ancient and modern history'.[149] Berry was implicitly challenging other antiquaries and their rather consensual and authorized view of the College of Arms, such as the history published by Mark Noble in 1804. Noble's tone was overwhelmingly celebratory, passing over the crisis of the College and insisting on its national relevance:

> I cannot but most earnestly plead for an institution absolutely essential to a civilised, a polished nation, and for the Monarch whom they serve, a Sovereign whose dominions are immensely large.[150]

Similarly, the article on 'Pedigree' in a new edition of the *Penny Cyclopaedia* pointed to the usefulness of family records, particularly in the College of Arms or the British Museum, as they provide 'information highly important to those who are studying critically the biography of the distinguished persons of the English nation'.[151]

In contrast to these favourable comments, Berry embarked on a more critical account of the institutions and brought in the 'Public' as a legitimate judge on their activities. He mentioned the increasing mistrust which had characterized the relation between the heralds and society. He argued that it was not until the 'great political revolutions', in the sixteenth and seventeenth centuries, that the heralds realized that 'their only hope to retain some influence with their refractory

---

[145] Ibid., 100.   [146] *GM*, 1st ser., vol. 100, part 2 (1830), 411.   [147] Ibid., 410.
[148] *Encyclopedia Heraldica, or complete Dictionary of Heraldry* (London, 1828), ii.   [149] Ibid.
[150] *History of the College of Arms: and the Lives of all the Kings, Heralds, and Pursuivants* (London, 1804), 406.
[151] *The Penny Cyclopædia of the Society for the diffusion of useful knowledge*, vol. 17 (London, 1828), 366.

260 SELLING ANCESTRY

subjects was in offering a friendly embrace to all who were willing to approach'.[152] He recounted the 'growth of the spirit of freedom' in the Elizabethan period against the 'monopoly of honour', the end of the Court of Chivalry in 1640, 'which had no hopes to maintain itself but by terror' or 'the fall of arbitrary power' in 1689, and the end of all 'that was arbitrary in the constitution of the College of Arms'.[153] He stated that the Whigs considered the 'arbitrary interference of the heralds' with great hostility, and were accused of being instrumental in the end of the Visitations.[154] Therefore it was the 'power of opinion' and the 'altered state of society' which had lessened its influence and prevented further abuse. As the College had been restored to its rightful place, the science of heraldry was no longer a 'mystery in the hands of its professional followers'.[155] His work was then intended to 'gratify the wants of the Public' by opening the gates of useful collections to historians, biographers, and even novices. He therefore saw his initiative as a transgressive move to divulge the secret science of heraldry in order to make it accessible to a wider audience.

In alphabetical order, Berry provided the essential keys to navigate one's way in a once exclusive source of knowledge, demystifying its jargon and symbols. Understandably, this account probably did not go down too well with many heralds and their friends, notably the Nichols family of publishers. During his trial, Berry produced a witness, a Major Hook, who had been following him during his enquiries among the main families of Kent. He confirmed Berry's ability to conduct genuine genealogical investigations. His testimony was corroborated by Clement Taylor Smyth, a solicitor from Maidstone. A dozen families in Kent had subscribed to his undertaking and their signatures were presented during the trial.

Then the defence convened several heralds who demonstrated that Berry had falsely assumed a position in the College and that he had only occasionally served as footman to some heralds. George F. Beltz, Lancaster Herald, produced all the books of grants of arms to prove that Berry was nowhere to be found. The attorney-general added that 'The Gentleman's Magazine was one of the most ancient publications in the country and it had been distinguished for its literature, its moderation and its learning.'[156] The defence managed to convince the jury that Berry was indeed guilty of deluding the public in his statement and had been 'sailing under false colours'.[157] As a result of the proceeding, Berry was convicted of falsehood on several counts, firstly that he invented a position in the College which never existed and then that he was not sufficiently socially connected to conduct an enquiry among the landed elite. Berry's condemnation was displayed

---

[152] *Encyclopedia Heraldica*, iv.   [153] Ibid.

[154] 'As the spirit of constitutional liberty became more universally established by the revolution of 1688, the arbitrary interference of the heralds lost its authority.' *A Weekly Journal of Literature, Science, and the Fine Arts*, 29 July 1820, 333.

[155] *Encyclopedia Heraldica*, v.   [156] *GM*, vol. 100, part 2 (1830), 413.   [157] Ibid.

as a victory for the College and its reputation. More recently commenting on the 'breakdown in heraldic authority', Anthony Wagner, both a herald and a historian, took issue with Berry's views. Wagner chose to blame the Whig grandees for the decline of the College of Arms as 'they had little interest in the strict regulation of a privilege—that of bearing arms—which they and the poorest gentry shared'.[158]

Brydges: a self-serving and devious gentleman

Whereas the fraud of William Berry was quite easily exposed by the College of Arms and *The Gentleman's Magazine*, G. F. Beltz later had to deal with a much more challenging impersonator. In 1834, in his *Review of the Chandos Peerage Case*, the herald uncovered at great length the many mystifications of Sir Egerton Brydges, who had been trying since 1789 to be recognized as entitled by descent to the barony of Chandos.[159] Unlike Berry, Brydges was of a liberal education, a Cambridge student, a landowner, a fellow of the Society of Antiquaries from 1795 and the author of many publications. He had served as MP for Maidstone, 1812–18, and was made baronet in 1814.[160] As a consequence, Brydges's fictions were far more difficult to expose publicly. In 1803, after a long trial, the House of Lords rejected the claims of the Brydges of Harbledown to the title of Chandos. Far from being of a collateral branch of a sixteenth-century barony, the Brydges family was proved to descend from yeomen and grocers in Canterbury. What moved Beltz into writing his essay was that while many 'spectators' of this case had died by 1834, the main protagonist, Sir Egerton Brydges, continued to proclaim himself peer by the 'Law of the Land' in his last publication in 1831.[161] Beltz was worried that his false title would eventually be recognized.

According to Beltz, the extraordinary nature of the case was that Brydges used all possible means to vindicate himself, to the point of publishing several *Peerages*, notably the re-edition of Collins's *Peerage* in 1812: 'He even stooped to the drudgery of editing a peerage of nine volumes, in order that a few of its pages might transmit a record of his family wrongs to posterity.'[162] Indeed, relying on his authority as a recognized antiquary, Brydges had convinced prominent booksellers such as Thomas Payne, John Nichols, and the Rivingtons of the need for a new edition of Collins's work. He peppered all the volumes with various remarks

---

[158] Wagner, *English Genealogy*, 117.
[159] G. F. Beltz, *Review of the Chandos Peerage Case: Adjudicated* (London, 1803).
[160] K. A. Manley, 'Brydges, Sir (Samuel) Egerton, first baronet, styled thirteenth Baron Chandos', *ODNB*. Retrieved 29 May 2020, from https://doi-org.janus.bis-sorbonne.fr/10.1093/ref:odnb/3809>.
[161] Brydges, *Lex Terrae, a Discussion of the Law of England regarding Claims of inheritable Rights of Peerage* (London, 1831), viii.
[162] Brydges, *Collins' Peerage*, vol. 1, vi.

262 SELLING ANCESTRY

about the barony of Chandos, alluding to his link to the third son of John Bridges, created lord of Chandos in 1554.[163] Previously, in his *Biographical Peerage of the Empire* (1808) and later in his *Biographical Peerage of Ireland* (1817), he had managed to insert additional comments on his family.[164] *The Monthly Mirror* heralded his *Biographical Peerage* and its genteel author, who, unlike the servile quacks of past publications, was an 'independent and enlightened mind, [and] a widely informed and accomplished writer'.[165] In a rather obsessive and repetitive manner, Brydges saturated his compilations with his own personal claims. In his *Autobiography*, he justified his initiative by the shortfalls of former compilers who were 'intellectual labourers, working at the direction of others, or upon other men's capital'.[166] Collins was wanting 'of education on a liberal scale' and his 'narrow sphere of life which restrained him from any familiar acquaintance with elevated society, made him contemplate rank and titles with too indiscriminate respect and flattery'.[167] In contrast, Brydges fashioned himself as a worthy antiquary not unlike George Allan:

> A love of reading, more especially works of fancy, history, and biography, and the dreams of authorship, have been the ruling passions of the Editor's life. In these pursuits no mercenary considerations ever mixed themselves for a moment: for these he has neglected interest, and ever more profitable ambition.[168]

But predictably, he reserved his strongest criticisms for Alexander Jacob, the chaplain of Lord Chandos, declaring that the latter's *Peerage*, 'a catchpenny book', made 'a loose statement without a single detail or authority'.[169] It might have passed unnoticed by Brydges if it had not been for the fact that Jacob's *Peerage* was used against his claims. At the end of his trial in 1803, a member of the Committee of Privileges 'has got that great folio in his hands, and is busily showing it to all the lords who are waiting about the benches'.[170] As a result, Brydges felt obliged to publish a series of new *Peerages* in order to erase the memory of these faulty peerages. In this task, he was confronted with two main enemies: the noble patrons of mercenary writers such as Jacob or Collins and the complicity of the College of Arms. Alexandre Jacob had worked under the protection of the second duke of Chandos, a family which obtained a dukedom during the 'robinocracy'. Similarly, the 'new Lord' in the Committee for Privileges

---

[163] Ibid., vol. 1, 151, 282, 323, 388, vol. 2, 57, 109, 421, 601, 616, vol. 3, 7–8, 82, 189, vol. 4, 473, 479, vol. 5, 338, 536, vol. 6, 704–6, 729, 719, 723, vol. 8, 20, vol. 9, 486.

[164] Revd E. T. Brydges 'was directly descended from the royal blood of Tudor and Plantagenet, through the great houses of Egerton, Stanley, Clifford and Brandon', *Biographical Peerage*, vol. 2, 94.

[165] *The Monthly Mirror*, Nov. 1808, 284.

[166] *The Autobiography, Times, Opinions, and Contemporaries of Sir Egerton Brydges, Bart. K.T. (Per legem terrae) Baron Chandos of Sudeley*, vol. 1 (London, 1831), 109.

[167] *Collins' Peerage*, iv. [168] *Collins' Peerage*, vol. 4, 733.

[169] Brydges, *Autobiography*, 339–40. [170] Ibid.

THE PROTAGONISTS OF A 'SHODDY INDUSTRY' 263

who had used Jacob's *Peerage* to dismiss his claim was 'gorged with the spoils of public money'.[171] This was a veiled reference to Baron Ellenborough, the Attorney-General who drafted the report for the Committee. Ellenborough belonged to the group of new peers created by Pitt in 1802.[172] As this 'modern' aristocracy, as Brydges called it, could not stand the pre-eminence of the old, they engineered mercenary *Peerages* to destroy the memory of the latter.

He declared that these brand new nobles had various accomplices in the College of Arms. He recalled how some heralds such as Francis Townshend were enrolled to prepare evidence against his claim in 1790. He suspected that his 'enemy' Townshend had dismissed the manuscript pedigrees of the Ashmole Library at Oxford, which 'named several sisters of James, the eighth Lord Chandos, omitted in all the peerages printed before that time'.[173] When asked during his trial why his ancestors had not been registered in the 1663 Visitation, Brydges replied that the veracity of his arms did not rely on the heralds' view. They were well known to his neighbours and he recalled how they were occasionally displayed in the main street of Canterbury:

> Here is a large funeral achievement publicly *blazoned forth to the world*, about 1663 or 1665 with the Chandos arms and crest, distinguished by the mullet, the mark of the third branch, *telling to the world* of what family and what branch the bearer claimed to be; and this *put in the most frequented street of the large city of Canterbury.*[174]

Like William Berry, Brydges resorted to the Restoration period to demonstrate the growing chasm between the public and the heralds, who, he argued, were increasingly discredited in the eyes of the gentry in their narrow and self-interested enquiries:

> A large portion of those who now form no inconsiderable part of the comparatively ancient gentry of the kingdom appears not in the Registers of this Society, while the lowest upstarts, East-Indians, brokers, contractors and often tradesmen, who has not even a pretention to birth […] crowd to the office.[175]

The abasement of honourable families in the hands of the heralds was described as particularly dramatic in Kent, where 'there is no district where property has oftener changed hands'.[176]

---

[171] Ibid.
[172] Michael Lobban, 'Law, Edward, first Baron Ellenborough (1750–1818)', *ODNB*, 2004. Retrieved 9 June 2020 from https://doi-org.janus.bis-sorbonne.fr/10.1093/ref:odnb/16142>.
[173] Brydges, *Autobiography*, 138.   [174] *Brydges's Lex Terrae*, 198.
[175] Sir Egerton Brydges, *Censura Literaria*, vol. 3 (London, 1809), 87.
[176] Brydges, *Autobiography*, vol. 1, 47.

264   SELLING ANCESTRY

To further discredit Brydges's claim, Beltz alluded to several striking irregularities in many local archives. Along with forging dubious and self-serving *Peerages*, Brydges might have tampered with crucial evidence. During the trial, Townshend had been sent to search for diverse papers in the registrar's office at Canterbury and in parishes. He observed that some documents were missing and that a good deal of registers showed signs of several 'mutilations' for various periods (1591–4, 1608–9) that had been made recently 'by cutting out a leaf at each place'.[177] For the years 1640–2, duplicates in the Archdeaconry Court and the parish differed in their contents. During the trial these irregularities were accounted for by the chaos created by the start of the Civil War. In his memoir, Beltz made these veiled allusions in passing. He may have been weary of formulating more explicit accusations against a respected antiquary and public figure. Local scholars such as John Boys of Margate and William F. Boteler, recorder of Canterbury, sent Beltz further proof of Bridges's forgeries. The two men were also well known to Brydges, who dismissed them in his *Autobiography* as two examples of the 'petittesses of antiquarianism'.[178] Boteler was described as a retired surgeon whose vanity came from the grants of arms given to his ancestor, and Boys was another surgeon who composed 'a dry and full history' of the town.[179]

Boys established that on the register in the parish of Ore near Canterbury, several entries related to the Brydges family had been added with fresh ink, which 'marks the transcript as a modern performance'.[180] No previous case, he stated, had generated 'so much system of Criminality [...] in the fabrication of documents' and this should be disclosed to the public.[181] Beltz failed to follow his advice. At the death of Brydges in 1837, his obituary in *The Gentleman's Magazine* was rather forgiving, alluding to Brydges's 'merits' and 'defects', and considering that he had rendered 'good service to the studies of poetical and genealogical antiquaries'.[182] In unmasking a fraudster after several decades, Beltz was magnanimous in his victory and refrained from ruining his reputation entirely. Despite having appealed to the public against well-established institutions such as the Lords and the College, Brydges belonged to the same conservative environment.[183] Forgeries are often seen as a subversive tool. In the case of Brydges, however, they were enrolled to defend strong anti-modernist views. A journalist in the more radical *Edinburgh Review* portrayed him as a mad 'advocate of the ancient system' which 'cheats, soothes, flatters, to the verge of

---

[177] Beltz, *Review of the Chandos*, 113.

[178] Brydges, *Autobiography*, vol. 1, 49–50.   [179] Ibid.

[180] Boys to Beltz, 18 Jan. 1835, in R. H. Goodsall, 'Lee Priory and the Brydges Circle', *Archaeologia Cantiana*, vol. 77 (1962), 12.

[181] Boys to Beltz, 15 Feb. 1825, ibid., 15.   [182] *GM*, Nov. 1837, 537.

[183] See his pamphlet against the Reform Act. *An Exposition on the Parliamentary Reform Bill* (London, 1831).

the abyss' and hoped that the Reform Bill would lead to 'the rising generation of literary men with a more wholesome and masculine frame of mind'.[184]

The considerable number of family letters surviving from the publication process facilitates an enquiry into the expectations and the social profiles of the customers. In contrast, compilers of directories left hardly any documents and it is mostly through printed sources in the gazettes or in a few memoirs that we can obtain some insight into their lives and posterities. Unlike the canonical authors of the Enlightenment, they remain largely obscure literary figures. The frequently derogatory comments that most received about their work were closely linked to their subordinate position, either as booksellers' scribblers or as patronized writers. As they were constrained to publish quickly and/or to please their superior, the title of 'author' was often denied to them, as it related to a sense of creativity and independence. For those few who were recognized as such, for instance William Guthrie and William Godwin, their *Peerages* have been seen as one-off publications, with little relationship to their later pieces. We would argue otherwise, suggesting that this experience, long in the making, informed their views on politics and nobility. Most compilers, either to make ends meet or to gain a coveted position, were likely to commit some mistakes and repeat fanciful stories. A few of them were publicly accused of lies and forgeries although, as we have observed in the cases of William Berry and Sir Egerton Brydges, double standards did apply. Brydges was only exposed three decades after his trial while Berry was convicted very swiftly. Despite their authors' poor reputations, the directories themselves were on the whole commercially successful. We will now see that some compilers even succeeded in ultimately making a name for themselves.

---

[184] *The Edinburgh Review*, vol. 59 (1834), 439.

6

The Keys to a Rewarding Posterity

In 1805, in a letter to Sir Joseph Banks, Thomas Christopher Banks sought to obtain his patronage in order to publish a *Peerage* of extinct titles. As a member of the Society of Antiquaries, of the Spalding Gentlemen's Society, president of the Royal Society since 1778 and a member of the Privy Council, Sir Joseph's support would have been a great asset.[1] T. C. Banks sent him a prospectus, emphasizing the commercial relevance of the project as it would help any 'existing branch of such families at a loss to trace its lineage'.[2] He argued, moreover, that as Sir Joseph Banks was renowned for his 'deep research into natural and ancient history', he had every reason to support him in his desire 'to promote historical, biographical and genealogical knowledge'.[3] In order to further convince Sir Joseph Banks, he developed a more personal line of argument: that the ancient origins of the Bankses would be fully vindicated. Nature as well as history concurred in establishing their origins: names 'were mostly assumed from places & Lands. It seems to me the Rivers and the Banks owe their rise to the same common ancestors.'[4] From the Old Danish 'Banke', their name confirmed that their shared origins were to be found before the Norman Conquest.

Despite all his efforts to spin his proposal in the most favourable manner, Thomas Banks's arguments fell on deaf ears. First, Sir Joseph Banks answered that such a letter should have been addressed to the president of the Society of Antiquaries, not to the 'President of the Royal Society whose business is to encourage natural knowledge'.[5] Second, he retorted that 'general antiquities has been always with me a favourite pursuit of relaxation, though I have never delighted in the genealogical Parts'.[6] Through his refusal, Sir Joseph Banks was reminding him of the clear hierarchy between natural knowledge, antiquities, and, at the lower end, genealogy. The latter was not even recognized as a form of ancillary knowledge. For his failure, Thomas Banks could be added to the gallery of scribblers and impoverished writers considered in the previous chapter. Later in life, he suffered further setbacks. Lacking financial support, he failed again to publish in 1811 another compilation, intended as an improved

---

[1] John Gascoigne, 'Banks, Sir Joseph, baronet (1743–1820), naturalist and patron of science', *ODNB*, 2003. Retrieved 11 May 2020 from <https://doi-org.janus.bis-sorbonne.fr/10.1093/ref:odnb/1300>.
[2] 8 Aug. 1804. Letters to Sir Joseph Banks, BL, Add. 33981, fol. 160.   [3] Ibid.   [4] Ibid.
[5] Royal Botanic Gardens Library, Kew. 2992, 10 Aug. 1804. Banks's answer is quoted by John Gascoigne in *Joseph Banks and the English Enlightenment* (Cambridge, 1994), 121.
[6] Ibid., 123.

Selling Ancestry: Family Directories and the Commodification of Genealogy in Eighteenth-Century Britain. Stéphane Jettot, Oxford University Press. © Stéphane Jettot 2023. DOI: 10.1093/oso/9780192865960.003.0007

THE KEYS TO A REWARDING POSTERITY   267

version of Dugdale's *Baronage* (1675), in a grand folio edition of four volumes.[7] He subsequently specialized in disputed inheritances in his London 'Dormant Peerage Office' and was accused of forgery in cases related to the earldoms of Stirling and of Salisbury.[8]

Sir Joseph Banks may have been slightly disingenuous in claiming that his taste for the antiquarian was only recreational. Although he established his reputation through his naval exploration with James Cook, Banks dedicated a considerable amount of time and money to gathering collections of papers and artefacts in Lincolnshire. His antiquarianism was in fact closely linked to his agricultural investments and his parliamentary career. Banks's interests were deeply rooted in his county, where 'he was following a tradition of gentlemanly inquiry into the history and antiquities of localities'.[9] Distancing himself from some premises shared by global historians, Julian Hoppit underlines the significance of Banks's provincial tropism, from his knowledge of local history to his various schemes related to drainage, enclosures, and turnpikes. Furthermore, as an antiquary, Sir Joseph Banks was not necessarily representative in his harsh dismissal of geneal-ogy as a valid source of knowledge. In 1805, when he rebuked Thomas Banks, William Betham had just finished the fifth and last volume of his *Baronetage*, with the support of the most influential patrons at Court. We have seen earlier how he managed to count among his subscribers three members of the Society of Antiquaries. Betham's success demonstrated that many antiquaries took ancestry to heart. The main contributors to Betham's accomplishment were not only the assistance of respected antiquaries, but also the participation of his son and daughter in London and their ability to handle customers' demands. Even though their *Baronetage* was too expensive and did not sell well, it was recognized at least as a reputable publication. It even opened the door to a position as herald in Dublin for Betham's son.

Hence, the posterity of these compilers should be considered in a larger social context where a few historical actors, namely antiquaries, family members, and customers, played a prominent role. The first were crucial as their authority and renown made them qualified to vouch for the compilers' seriousness and expert-ise. Antiquaries were part of the long-term process of attestation and verification which distinguished reliable scholars from booksellers' hacks. Compilers' des-cendants contributed greatly to the reputation of their forebears by reframing the

---

[7] In the prospectus, he hoped to reproduce the original text with the additional accounts since 1675 and 'all the connection and degree of consanguinity between the respective branches': Notes and additional matter for a new edition of Sir William Dugdale's 'Baronage of England', BL, Add. MS 27585, fol. 2.

[8] T. F. Henderson and Michael Erben, 'Banks, Thomas Christopher (1765–1854), genealogist', *ODNB*, (2004). Retrieved 15 June 2020 from <https://doi-org.janus.bis-sorbonne.fr/10.1093/ref:odnb/1303>.

[9] Julian Hoppit, 'Sir Joseph Banks's Provincial Turn', *The Historical Journal*, vol. 61, no. 2 (2018): 403–29 at 412.

268   SELLING ANCESTRY

nature of their publishing activities in a politer manner, often succeeding in improving their own status, even if sometimes at the expense of erasing all memory of their ancestors. Lastly, the power relationship established between compilers and customers must be considered. As compilers were financially dependent, they were expected to be subservient to the demands of their clients. To combat accusations of complaisance, records of conflicts and tensions were kept and instrumentalized in order to place the compiler in a better light.

1. Antiquaries and their prescriptive authority

Sir Joseph Banks's attempt to establish a clear-cut distinction between antiquaries and genealogists belonged to a long-standing tradition. In the late seventeenth century, county historians were already making similar statements. Edward Gibson, in his revision of Camden's *Britannia* (1695), complained that 'the eternal vanity of English gentlemen was a threat to serious antiquarian studies, forever trying to make the past illustrate their own lineage'.[10] But these repeated complaints in fact displayed the difficulty of severing all ties between two intertwined relations to the past. Both were embedded in the social and cultural practices of their contemporaries. They were framed by the same genteel interest for land-ownership and education: 'an informed appreciation of antiquities demanded learning, and the issues of property and genealogy with which antiquarian top-ography was particularly concerned, rendered it the natural preserve of the gentleman'.[11] Right up until the late nineteenth century, natural science, heraldry, topography, and genealogy were not easily distinguished.[12] Science was still open to a variety of approaches, whether it be 'speculative', 'useful', 'mundane', or even 'severe'.[13] More generally, John Pickstone has stressed the need to look for similarities of practice rather than for clear-cut categories of knowledge.[14] Science is not simply experimental and several historians have considered the comparable epistemological value of collecting in various fields of science and

[10] Graham Parry, *The Trophies of Time: English Antiquarianism of the Seventeenth Century* (Oxford, 1995), 333.

[11] Rosemary Sweet, 'Antiquaries and Antiquities in Eighteenth-Century England', *Eighteenth-Century Studies*, vol. 34, no. 2 (1991): 181–206 at 189.

[12] Philippa Levine, *The Amateur and the Professional: Antiquarians, Historians, and Archaeologists in Victorian England, 1838–1886* (Cambridge, 1986), 72.

[13] 'A la fin de l'Ancien régime, une ligne de partage s'accentue entre les "sciences spéculatives" (abstraites), et les "sciences utiles", qui intéressent directement l'État et la société; une autre entre les représentants des "sciences mondaines" et les savants tenants d'une "science sévères", ayant alors les mathématiques pour modèle.' Patrice Bret, 'Figures du savant, XVe–XVIIIe, in Liliane Hilaire-Pérez, Fabien Simon, and Marie Thébaud-Sorger (eds), *L'Europe des sciences et des techniques: un dialogue des savoirs, XVe–XVIIIe siècle* (Rennes, 2016), 97.

[14] 'I use my "ways of knowing" to bridge between esoteric, technical worlds and the worlds of "everyday", both past and present.' John V. Pickstone, *Ways of Knowing: A New History of Science, Technology and Medicine* (Manchester, 2000), 5.

antiquity.[15] We have seen previously how Etheredge Bennett, from her letters to John Burke in 1828, collected and ordered family manuscripts as well as fossils. Both geology and genealogy could be understood as uncovering accumulated layers of the past by looking for scattered materials. The family tree as a 'cognitive metaphor' was used to organize knowledge and observations on history, plants, and animals. More than ever, in the Enlightenment, it proved to be an efficient epistemological tool to explain, for example, the internal hierarchies within the natural order or within the various races of men discovered in the Pacific.[16]

Secondly, we should be wary of extrapolating too much from the view of a single scholar, however eminent he might be. Along with the porous boundaries between several fields of knowledge, the unity of the antiquarian 'community' has been called into question. Rosemary Sweet has alluded to the misconceptions which may arise by thinking in terms of 'networks'.[17] This metaphor, which was not yet used in the eighteenth century, conveys ideals of collaboration and transparency. In fact, in London, informal networks were created both against and inside established institutions such as the Society of Antiquaries or the Royal Society. Rejection was as common as collaboration. Antiquaries were divided by personal interests, affinities, and religious or political biases. Similarly, in Edinburgh, another 'cultural capital', the influence of the antiquarian societies was compromised by a lack of institutional support, absenteeism, and divisions.[18] In this state of affairs, there was no such a thing as an immutable pantheon of prominent antiquaries. In the beginning of the nineteenth century, William Dugdale's reputation benefited from the rehabilitation by the College of Arms and attracted a growing number of positive comments.[19] Yet the quality of his

---

[15] Richard Landon, 'Collecting and the Antiquarian Book Trade', in R. Gameson (ed.), The Cambridge History of the Book in Britain, vol. 5 (Cambridge, 2014), 711–22; Bruno J. Strasser, 'Collecting Nature: Practices, Styles, and Narratives', Osiris, vol. 27, no. 1 (2012): 303–40.

[16] Carlo Ginzburg, 'Family Resemblances and Family Trees: Two Cognitive Metaphors', Critical Inquiry, vol. 30, no. 3 (2004): 537–56; see 'La généalogie des rois des Moluques (1780)', in Claude-Olivier Doron, L'Homme altéré: race et dégénérescence (Seyssel, 2016), 48. Mary Bouquet, 'Family Trees and Their Affinities: The Visual Imperative of the Genealogical Diagram', Journal of the Royal Anthropological Institute of London, vol. 2, no. 1 (1996): 43–66.

[17] 'We do, however, need to think harder about what work the network metaphor is doing when we apply it and exercise a greater degree of reflexivity in its use […]. Is there a danger of assuming a degree of connectivity that was simply not felt at the time?', Rosemary Sweet, the 'Institutions as Networks' workshop (London, 2017) <http://institutionsofliterature.net/2017/07/22/roey-sweet-on-institutions-and-networks/>.

[18] 'Contrairement à une vision répandue, ces institutions restent fragiles malgré leur reconnaissance royale. Trois types de problèmes sont récurrents: les difficultés financières, l'absentéisme et l'engage-ment trop mesuré des membres; la faible légitimité des sciences antiquaires.' Stéphane Van Damme, 'La grandeur d'Édimbourg: savoirs et mobilisation identitaire au XVIIIe siècle', Revue d'histoire moderne & contemporaine, vol. 55, no. 2 (2008), 178.

[19] See, for example, James Dallaway, Heraldic Miscellanies, consisting of the Lives of Sir William Dugdale and Gregory King (London, 1796), 20–3; Thomas Moule, Bibiliotheca Heraldica Magnae Britanniae (London, 1822), 200–2.

270　SELLING ANCESTRY

work remained much debated. An eminent peerage lawyer, Stacey Grimaldi, considered his *Baronage* too faulty to be used in court proceedings.[20] In the numerous peerage claims that were made at this time, many compilations were seen as unreliable. The antiquaries engaged in legal cases had a very different perception of what a useful pedigree was. They argued that historical anecdotes should be discarded in favour of detailed accounts of the maternal and paternal lines, although they failed to agree on the most authoritative compilation.

At the beginning of the nineteenth century, the epistemological status of genealogy was still being discussed. And while it was dismissed by Sir Joseph Banks as not even a worthy source of recreation, other antiquaries felt inclined to vindicate its relevance. To interpret narratives praising the work of certain genealogical compilers, such rehabilitation merits precise contextualization. Through the examples of Wotton, Collins, and Burke, we will consider several influential antiquaries who contributed significantly to their improved reputation.

'A great reputation both as an Author and Bookseller'

It was in those terms that John Nichols in his *Literary Anecdotes* described Thomas Wotton's legacy as 'author' of the first complete *Baronetage*.[21] *Literary Anecdotes* is regarded as an incomparable repository of biographical detail about London publishers and minor authors: 'in an age of biography and anecdote, John Nichols collected, preserved and printed more biographical information about the book trade, antiquaries and writers than all of his contemporaries combined'.[22] Nichols had previously published several essays on William Hogarth and several London printers, and his work could be compared to that undertaken in *The Miscellanies* of Isaac d'Israeli (1796). In both cases, publishers with a strong antiquarian mindset hoped to open the minds of their general readers by including an unprecedented range of subjects.[23] For many little-known authors who did not leave much in the way of archives, Nichols's writings were often the sole source and would later be exploited extensively in the *DNB* and *ODNB*. Nichols

---

[20] 'It has determined that Dugdale's Baronage is not evidence, to prove a descent', Stacey Grimaldi, *Origines Genealogicae; or The Sources Whence English Genealogies may be Traced from the Conquest to the Present Time* (London, 1828), 304.

[21] John Nichols, *Literary Anecdotes of the Eighteenth Century*, vol. 3 (London, 1813), 440–1.

[22] Julian Pooley, '"A Copious Collection of Newspapers": John Nichols and his Collection of Newspapers, Pamphlets and News Sheets, 1760–1865'. An essay for the 2017 digital publication of the Nichols Newspaper Collection at the Bodleian Library. Julian Pooley, '"A Laborious and Truly Useful Gentleman": Mapping the Networks of John Nichols (1745–1826), Printer, Antiquary and Biographer', *Journal for Eighteenth Century Studies*, vol. 38, no. 4 (2015): 497–509 at 497; Edward L. Hart (ed.), *Minor Lives: A Collection of Biographies by John Nichols* (Cambridge, Mass., 1971).

[23] *Biographical Anecdotes of William Hogarth* (London, 1781); *Biographical Memoirs of William Ged* (London, 1781); *Biographical and Literary Anecdotes of William Bowyer* (London, 1782); Isaac d'Israeli, *Miscellanies, or Literary Recreations* (London, 1796).

composed his biographies from memory as well as the many articles previously published in the *GM* which he had been editing and printing since 1778. The authority of his compilation came from the prominent reputation he had built for himself as a publisher and literary scholar. When many local gentlemen questioned the ability of commercial compilers to deal with antiquarian matters, Nicols used to stand up in their defence. In the *GM*, he argued in 1792 that 'from the general complexion of our Magazine, it would be heresy to doubt our readiness to assist the researches of a topographical correspondent'.[24]

Nichols's note on Wotton relied on scattered sources in his own possession. While working on the publication of the memoirs of John Dunton, one of the founders of the 'Athenian Society', he found a quotation about Wotton's father: Matthew Wotton, a 'rising man' but 'just to his word that, if he was immortal, it would be altogether as good dependence as his bond'.[25] Dunton epitomized the involvement of London booksellers in the rise of political parties. Both Dunton and Wotton were placed by Nichols in the pantheon of esteemed and trustworthy London citizens. They belonged to the small group of professionals who took pride in their business while displaying polite virtues. Nichols was a member of the Society of the Antiquaries and was engaged in civic life. Both he and Wotton were elected Masters of the Stationers' Company. Dunton's *Athenian Mercury* could be seen as a source of inspiration for the *GM*. Dunton, Wotton, and Nichols embodied the possibility of reconciling the profession of bookseller with antiquarian taste.[26]

Their shops were located close to London's main archival repositories (the Tower of London, the College of Arms, the Cotton and Harleian Collections in the British Museum). While they remained acutely attuned to the tastes of landed elites, they did not turn their back on their civic origins. The City, as the main publishing location in the kingdom and seat of a prime social scene where new and old elites came to meet in its many coffee houses, was a central laboratory in the promotion of antiquarian knowledge. In his published history of the Society of Antiquaries (1818), Mark Noble insisted on the role of polite booksellers among antiquaries: 'It is not unusual for booksellers to be learned men [. . .] in infant literary society a person of this trade in London who was intelligent might be very useful by directing the members to suitable works proper to investigate.'[27] However, Dunton like Wotton embodied the uncertainties of the booksellers'

---

[24] In this extract, Nichols was defending the relevance of a questionnaire inserted in the *GM* by Richard Polwhele in order to compile his *History of Devon*. On this 'clash of ideas about antiquarian method', and 'the tension between the worlds of gentlemanly amateurism based on an (albeit extended) coterie and professional print', see Dafydd Moore, *Richard Polwhele and Romantic Culture: The Politics of Reaction and the Poetics of Place* (London, 2021), 40–2.

[25] Nichols, *Literary Anecdotes*, 440.

[26] With respect to antiquarian methods, urban record keeping provided a stimulating environment: 'no less important than the ancestral preoccupations of gentry', Woolf, *The Social Circulation of the Past*, 281.

[27] SAL MS 269, fol. 3.

272 SELLING ANCESTRY

lives and reputations. Financially ruined and briefly jailed in the Fleet, Dunton at the end of his life was mocked as a 'beggar' and 'abusive scribbler'.[28] Wotton did not die destitute, although his achievements were hardly recognized. A terse note in the *GM* records on 1 April 1766 the death of 'Tho. Wotton, formerly an eminent bookseller at Point Pleasant, Surrey'.[29] Hence Nichols sought to make up for the dismissive tone of a previous publisher of the *GM* by insisting on Wotton's legacy as the 'Author' of several baronetages. Nichols quoted Richard Johnson in his 1771 re-edition of the *Baronetage*, who introduced Wotton as:

> That indefatigable Labourer in the golden mines of Antiquity, whose Avenues were rendered almost inaccessible by the destructive Hand of Time, and the cruel Ravages of barbarous Nations, has cleared the paths which lead to the perfection of this intricate science.[30]

In this quotation, Johnson brought together 'genealogy' with 'antiquity' and 'science'. As for the 'cruel ravages of barbarous Nations', it was a common expression often employed by William Dugdale to account for the many invasions since the times of the Saxons.[31] He was implicitly comparing Wotton to Dugdale. Nichols would likely have been aware of the preface to the new edition of the *Baronetage* in 1801 by William Betham, with whom he worked closely. Like Johnson, Betham was highly impressed by his predecessor: Wotton's *Baronetage* was 'unquestionably the best' as 'it contains a great deal of information; the indexes are copious and correct; and, upon the whole, it is not only a laborious, but useful performance'.[32] As a further source of documentation, Nichols had acquired various manuscript collections from the Revd Robert Smyth, including his annotated copy of Wotton's *Baronetage*.[33] That Wotton's compilations had been carefully preserved and commented upon by a respected antiquary from the Spalding Gentlemen's Society was, in itself, a sign of the high esteem in which the *Baronetage* was held. Nichols had access to the correspondence between Wotton and Smyth, as well as three folio volumes on the same subject. He celebrated the fact that Wotton acknowledged his debt to various antiquaries, notably Peter Le Neve; a part of the latter's collection of manuscripts was bought by Wotton in 1731, who praised its usefulness.[34] The ability to recognize the importance of others' work was rare among antiquaries, and according to Nichols, Wotton's homage was 'more than ordinary obligation, as having been of the greatest use to him'.[35]

---

[28] John Nichols, *The Life and Errors of John Dunton, Citizen of London*, vol. 1 (London, 1818), vi.
[29] *GM*, vol. 36 (1766), 199.   [30] Kimber and Johnson, *The Baronetage*, iii.
[31] R. Harbin (ed.), Sir William Dudgale, *Monasticon Anglicanum: or, The History of the ancient Abbies, Monasteries, Hospitals, Cathedral and Collegiate* (London, 1718), 14.
[32] Betham, *Baronetage*, viii.   [33] Nichols, *Literary Anecdotes*, vol. 5, 48.
[34] *List of catalogues of English Book sales, 1676–1900 now in the British Museum* (London, 1915), 50.
[35] Nichols, *Literary Anecdotes*, vol. 5, 48; Wotton, *Baronetage of England*, iii.

THE KEYS TO A REWARDING POSTERITY   273

Son of a London upholsterer, who as such was involved in heraldic funerals, Le Neve was recruited as herald in 1690 and later was made fellow of the Royal Society and became president of the revived Antiquarian Society. At his death, he left a three-volume manuscript on 'Pedigrees of baronets'.[36] Wotton acquired these collections not as a status symbol, but to use them in his compilations.

As well as acknowledging his debt to Le Neve's work, Wotton expressed his gratitude to several 'skilful antiquaries' scattered throughout the country who made up for the reluctance of 'some families to give the least assistance', notably Arthur Collins, William Holman of Halstead (Essex), Arthur Brooke (Northampton), Philip Gurdon (Norfolk and Suffolk), John Thorpe (Kent), and Francis Peck (Lincolnshire).[37] He acknowledged their participation not only in the preface but in the many footnotes which now appeared for the first time in a family compilation and reinforced the general impression of a collaborative endeavour.[38] Footnotes better displayed the collective nature of any scientific enquiry. Concerning Collins, Wotton obtained all his working papers used in the first *Baronetage* published in 1720. As for William Holman, he was a non-conformist cleric based in Halstead from 1700 until his death in 1730.[39] Holman's long-term social standing in Essex and the vast network of correspondents he built up throughout those years enabled him to gain the trust of many families. Arthur Brooke, an attorney-at-law in Kettering, was connected to the baronets Isham and Brydges. The Revd Philip Gurdon, vicar of Bures, was allied through his mother to Bt William Cooke. John Thorpe was an Oxford student in medicine and from 1705 a fellow of the Royal Society. He assisted Hans Sloane in the publication of the *Philosophical Transactions* and then established himself in Rochester for thirty-five years. A member of the Society of Antiquaries, Thorpe maintained close connections with London and the City, where Wotton was living. As for Francis Peck, he was elected to the Society of Antiquaries in 1732 and had already published his much-respected *Desiderata Curiosa* [...] *relating chiefly to matters of English History* (1732–5) and the *New Memoirs of the life and Poetical Works of John Milton* (1740). His notes on Leicestershire were later used by Nichols in his own history of the county.[40]

Wotton relied on these men's collaboration to obtain data on the many baronets who had ignored his request. Holman, who was on friendly terms with

---

[36] Thomas Woodcock, 'Le Neve, Peter (1661–1729), herald and antiquary', *ODNB*, 2009. Retrieved 18 June 2020, from <https://doi-org.janus.bis-sorbonne.fr/10.1093/ref:odnb/16440>.

[37] Wotton, *English Baronets*, iv; Wotton, *Baronetage*, iii.

[38] On the inspiring example provided by Bayle's *Dictionary*, see Anthony Grafton, *The Footnote: A Curious History* (London, 1997), 194–5.

[39] 'The Revd Mr Holman of Hastead in Essex who is writing the antiquities of that County has also favourd me with what he had collected of the famillies of those baronets who were his neighbours.' Wotton, *The English Baronets*, iii.

[40] On Peck and his reputation, see David B. Haycock, 'Peck, Francis (1692–1743), antiquary and apothecary', *ODNB*, 2004. Retrieved 23 June 2020, from <https://doi-org.janus.bis-sorbonne.fr/10.1093/ref:odnb/21738>.

274 SELLING ANCESTRY

various Whig baronets and the main heralds of the College of Arms, had direct access to repositories that were closed to Wotton. His research into the history of Essex benefited from 'a male gentry sympathetic and even mildly interested' and the zealous assistance of many 'wives, aunts and sisters for reliable genealogical information'.[41] Through Arthur Brooke, Wotton obtained the pedigrees of the families of Bridges, Bunbury, Dryden, Haveling, Cotton, Seabright, and Parson.[42] Concerning Sir William Parsons's pedigree, Brooke wrote: 'Mr Wotton may easily fill up the blanks wch I have left for ye purpose.'[43] This response provides some insight into Wotton's working methods. First, he composed a draft account which he sent to the families and then he relied on his antiquarian friends to fill in the gaps. In Kent, John Thorpe had collected a large number of pedigrees and local records which were published after his death. In the preface of his *Registrum Roffense*, he is described as tracing out sepulchral inscriptions and coats of arms on monuments, and searching 'in the midst of woods, over-run with bushes and brambles'.[44] His support was valuable as Wotton complained of the refusal of most Kentish baronets to assist him, where only eight families out of a total of thirty-two of the living baronets in the county replied.[45] Wotton asked for help in gaining access 'to any other baronets accts not here mentioned or [in putting] me into a method how to get them' and gave him some further specimens to distribute among them.[46] Wotton believed that the lack of cooperation from some families derived partly from their declining social position. He alluded to the case of the Heymans: 'ye ffamilly is reducd & very poor & that reason may in a great measure satisfy ye world, why an acct of yt ffamilly could not be got'.[47] Francis Peck sent him a 'full drawn' account of Sir Cyril Wyche, '5 folio pages, pretty close wrote', starting from the Saxon Wiccia.[48]

In return for their assistance, he was able to give or lend them various books from his own catalogue.[49] To Holman, he dispatched a copy of Thomas Fuller's *Worthies of England* and David Lloyd's *Memoires of the Lives Actions, Sufferings and Deaths of Those Excellent Personages* (1668) and *The Works of Sir Francis Bacon* in four volumes (1706).[50] Arthur Brooke borrowed a copy of *The Case of Dr Ayliffe at Oxford* (1716), *The Topography of Norfolk*, and Bayle's *Dictionary*.[51]

---

[41] Woolf, *The Social Circulation*, 116.

[42] Brooke to Wotton, 11 May 1741. BL, Add. MS 24120, fol. 144; 7 May 1740, BL, Add. MS 24121, fol. 29.

[43] Brooke to Wotton, BL, Add. MS 24120, fol. 168.

[44] John Thorpe (ed.), *Registrum Roffense or a collection of antient records, charters and instruments of divers Kinds* (London, 1769), iii.

[45] Wotton to Thorpe: 'The baronets in Kent are very numerous & to most, if not all, I have sent specimen but have heard from few', 16 Nov. 1725. Sal MS 150, fol. 268.

[46] 9 July 1726, ibid., fol. 270.   [47] 15 Oct. 1726; SAL MS 150, fol. 273.

[48] Peck to Wotton, 1740, BL, Add. MS 21421, fols 353–4.

[49] On the 'nexus of this gift economy' which was central to antiquarian practices, see Sweet, *Antiquaries*, 65.

[50] Wotton to Holman (1724), Essex RO, D/Y 1/1/199/1.   [51] BL, Add. MS 24121, fol. 168.

THE KEYS TO A REWARDING POSTERITY   275

Wishing to stay abreast of the intellectual debates in London, he asked Wotton for some gossip about the re-edition of Holinshed's *Chronicles* and 'the Castration account wch makes so much noise'.[52] He was referring to the re-edition by two rival booksellers with the pages that had been censored in the 1587 edition for reasons of state now being reinserted.[53] In the first re-edition, in 1722, by Christopher Bateman under the patronage of Thomas Jett, more than 200 errors were found and both the booksellers and patrons were accused of 'vilely' deceiving the public.[54] County pedigrees here were traded for London gossip from the bookselling world. Wotton obliged Brooke by including him, as well as his wife and children, in his *Baronetage*. Brooke was married to a daughter of Zaccheus Isham, a family related to the Northamptonshire baronet Sir Edmund Isham.[55] Similarly, Francis Peck was inviting Wotton to start a long-term association grounded on a mutual exchange of books and manuscripts. He wrote that he had the pedigrees 'of most families in England by divers hands for which reason I desire an exchange of books with you that I may interleave your baronetage & improve it'.[56]

Like Nichols in the 1780s and 1790s, Wotton managed to obtain the contributions of well-established antiquaries in various counties in exchange for opening his rich collection of books. As an 'Author and Bookseller', Wotton was singled out in the *Literary Anecdotes* for his ability to obtain the cooperation of the most eminent scholars. In his case, the two occupations are hard to separate. His 'authorship' did not depend on his creativity but rather on his skill in gathering the knowledge of others. We have seen that his bookselling business was essential in gaining the trust and support of most county antiquaries. By his collaborative mindset and his modest standing, he embodied one of the most cherished principles in the antiquarian ethos, as retrospectively expressed by John Nichols. As such, Wotton deserved to be distinguished from the unscrupulous compilers.

The unknown hero in 'the dust of the closet'

By the same token but for different reasons, Arthur Collins, who died in 1760, was deemed worthy to be inserted in Nichols's collection of eminent literary figures. In 1812, Nichols reproduced a letter written to the *GM* in 1799 by the biographer

[52] Brooke to Wotton, 7 May 1740, BL, Add. MS 24121, fol. 29.
[53] Dr Drake, *Holinshed's Chronicles of England: A complete set of the Castration* (London, 1728). K. Maslen, 'Three Eighteenth-Century Reprints of the Castrated Sheets in Holinshed's Chronicles', *The Library*, 5th ser., vol. 13 (1958): 120–4.
[54] On this affair, see Nichols, *Literary Anecdotes*, vol. 1 (1812), 251.
[55] Arthur Brooke was presented by Wotton as a gentleman and his father-in-law depicted as 'that learned and eminent Divine [...] Prebendary of Canterbury and St Paul's and several times Proctor in Convocation for the City of London'. *Baronetage*, vol. 1 (1741), 276.
[56] Peck to Wotton, 1740, BL, Add. MS 21421, fols 353–4.

276 SELLING ANCESTRY

Stephen Jones, who deplored that Collins 'who immortalized others [. . .] has been wholly disregarded by posterity':

> Justice demands that we rescue the memory from oblivion [. . .] of a man whose works have done so much honour to his own industry and so much service to his country.[57]

Unlike Wotton, Collins's badge of honour was not to have coordinated the expertise of various scholars. Instead, he was praised for having spent his fortune and many years of his life 'in the dust of the closet, with poring over mss, scarcely legible, and rescuing half-devoured sentences from the combined attacks of Time and the moth'.[58] He was presented as a genuine archivist, the 'historiographer of the "Baronage" and "Baronetage" of England'.[59] He embodied another virtue in the antiquarian ethos, the devotion to manuscripts as a heightened source of authenticity. Palaeography emerged very slowly as a distinct discipline in the eighteenth century. Archives were no longer seen in their early modern sense as a 'juridical treasury', but rather as 'an object of historical analysis and critique'.[60] An analytical use of archives was becoming the characteristic sign of genuine enquiry. Hume, for example when preparing his acclaimed *History of England*, was believed to have been in touch with 'all the families which have papers relative to public affairs transacted in the end of the last and beginning of this century'.[61]

Nichols's interest in Collins may have originated first from his financial participation in the re-edition of the *Peerage* in 1779 and 1784. Previous editors of the *GM* did not pay much attention to Collins's *Peerage* when he was alive. His pro-Whig agenda and his open attack on the *Craftsman* made him unsuitable for a rather pro-Tory magazine. His obituary in 1760 was brief: 'Arth. Collins, Esq., author of the *Peerage*'.[62] The re-edition of his *Peerage* in the 1770s and 1780s led first to the discovery of his intense archival work. In the preface to the 1779 edition, Barak Longmate reminded the public of 'the labour of a long life' which Collins had dedicated to genealogical enquiries.[63] Though initially an engraver, Longmate was a regular contributor to the *GM* and assisted Nichols in various works. He described himself as walking in his footsteps by looking into 'a great number of the most curious manuscripts in the British Museum' and in the 'register books of several parishes'.[64] In his letters to Mark Noble, he detailed his

---

[57] *GM*, Apr. 1799, 282. Nichols, *Literary Anecdotes*, vol. 2, 16.

[58] Nichols, *Literary Anecdotes*, vol. 2, 16.   [59] Ibid.

[60] Randolph C. Head, 'Documents, Archives, and Proof around 1700', *The Historical Journal*, vol. 56, no. 4 (2013): 909–30 at 909. Francis X. Blouin and William G. Rosenberg, *Processing the Past: Contesting Authority in History and the Archives* (Oxford, 2011); Markus Friedrich, *The Birth of the Archives: A History of Knowledge* (Ann Arbor, 2013); Élisabeth Décultot (ed.), *Lire, copier, écrire: les bibliothèques manuscrites et leurs usages au XVIIIe siècle* (Paris, 2003).

[61] John B. Burton, *Life and Correspondence of David Hume*, vol. 2 (London, 1846), 246.

[62] *GM*, 1760, vol. 30, 154.   [63] Longmate, *Collin's Peerage* (1779), vi.   [64] Ibid.

visits to various family archives, such as the Howards at Audley End, ten miles from Cambridge.[65] He left his own considerable assortment of manuscripts and notes to the Society of Antiquaries and other repositories.[66] The richness of Collins's collections had already become cause for interest after his library was sold by auction in February 1761.[67]

The catalogue of Collins's library, distributed gratis by Samuel Baker, provides a detailed picture of the many tools and resources in his possession:

> The proprietors think it proper to inform the Public, that these scarce and valuable papers may not be looked as Papers made use of by Mr Collins in his Peerage and Baronetage of England but that many of them are Originals and Collections from Manuscript hitherto unpublished.

His library included first all the main reference books required in any serious antiquarian investigation: Sir Thomas Littleton's *Tenure* (1617), *The Harleian Miscellany* (1744), Dugdale's *Origines Juridiciales* (1671), Weever's *Funeral Monuments* (1631), Prynne's *Abridgement of Cotton's Records* (1657). His own books were enriched with manuscript notes which made them even more valuable. Rusworth's *Historical Collection* contained a 'manuscript of some speeches, left out in the Editions'.[68] His copy of Dugdale's *Baronage* included 'additions as large as the printed work and numberless corrections'.[69]

A second category in his library was the many copies of manuscript pedigrees which he obtained from well-known antiquaries. In 1708 Collins made contact with Richard Rawlinson, the outstanding collector of manuscripts and coins. He would meet him at Robert Gosling's bookshop, to acquire monumental inscriptions about the Cope Family in Oxford.[70] Rawlinson, in his perambulations in and around Oxford, had already copied many pedigrees from the neighbouring gentry. Gosling specialized in printing legal works, which led him to publish several manuscripts from Sir Robert Cotton's library on common and ecclesiastical law. He paid Charles Bush £41 for a transcript of the Statute Rolls in the Tower of

---

[65] Longmate to Noble, Oct. 1785: 'I was obliged to set off to Lord Howard set at Audley end about 10 miles from Cambridge'. Bod. Lib., MSS Eng Misc d. 151, fol. 202.

[66] Barak Longmate left a large collection of monumental inscriptions on various churches. SAL MS 430–82; Alphabet of arms collected by Barak Longmate, BL, Add. MS 30373; *A catalogue of a valuable collection of books, and heraldic manuscripts. The property of the late Barak Longmate*, 10 Mar. 1794. Clive Cheesman, 'Longmate, Barak (1737/8–1793), genealogical editor and heraldic engraver', ODNB, 2003. Retrieved 24 June 2020 from <https://doi-org.janus.bis-sorbonne.fr/10.1093/ref:odnb/16993>.

[67] *A catalogue of the printed books, and curious manuscripts, of Arthur Collins, Esq; deceased. Author of the peerage of England. Many of the printed books are with manuscript additions and notes of learned men; and many of the manuscripts unpublished, and relate to the antiquities and history of Great Britain. Many others in heraldry, and the pedigrees of all our nobility, baronets, and other gentlemen, and most of them very ancient* (London, 1761).

[68] *Catalogue of the Printed Books*, 4.   [69] Ibid., 7.

[70] Collins to Rawlinson, 11 Oct. 1708, Bod. Lib., Rawl. MS letters 114, fol. 89.

278 SELLING ANCESTRY

London.[71] As both a bookseller and a banker, Gosling embodied the many connections between finance, antiquaries, and the law. Far from being a self-contained profession, bookselling was open to a large gamut of knowledge, whether practical or speculative. Gosling was even admitted to the Society of Antiquaries in 1718. Finally, thanks to Humfrey Wanley, the first keeper of the Harleian Library, Collins was able to peruse the collection formed by Thomas Coles, which abounded with old visitations.[72] Wanley was eager to help Collins as he confessed that the genealogy of his ancestors had 'some weight' with him:

> The reflexion upon their examples makes a deeper impression on me than that of others and 'tis from them that I had rather learn, & practice what to do & what to lett alone.[73]

Interestingly, the publishers of Wanley's diary added in the index that Collins was a 'bookseller, of late years Gentleman'.[74] They considered that his archival work elevated him from a professional to a gentle status.

A third category in Collins's catalogue relates to notes taken by him in the London repositories, namely the collections of wills at Lambeth Palace, the Prerogative Office, and the Tower of London. The catalogue displayed the technical expertise he allegedly acquired by reading medieval Latin, charters, and wills. His collections were used not only to compile pedigrees but also to 'illustrate the history of our nation'.[75] He bought some documents bearing on crucial national events: the Norman Conquest (No. 39), Thomas Cromwell on the 'first Progress of the Reformation' (No. 34), the 'Irish Establishment' by Sir Henry Sidney (No. 44), the Civil War, with George Monck's notes (No. 37), Lord Clarendon's Journal (No. 80) and the Glorious Revolution with Dugdale's diary for 1688 (No. 50). He was given access to exclusive family papers, notably at Penshurst Place, at the seats of Lords Dursley, Berkeley, and other peers. His archival work on the Sidney family was considered as a decisive contribution to Irish history in the sense that it led to influential printed compilations. Hume made regular reference to Collins's *Letters and Memorial of State* (1756), an unprecedented collection of printed documents which upheld the reputation of Sir Henry Sidney as governor of Ireland and Lord President of Wales. Describing Collins both as an antiquary and an authority, Nicholas Canny argued that he 'provided an alternative elite

---

[71] Frank Melton, 'Robert and Sir Francis Gosling: Eighteenth-Century Bankers and Stationers', in Robin Myers and Michael Harris (eds), *Economics of the British Book Trade 1605–1939* (London, 1985), 63.

[72] C. E. Wright and Ruth Wright, *The Diary of Humfrey Wanley: 1715–1726*, vol. 1 (London, 1966), 141–7, 156, 158, 175, 211, 265, 334. Under his custody, and in terms of quality and diversity, the Harleian collection soon became comparable to the Cottonian library. See Daniel Woolf, *Reading History in Early Modern England* (Cambridge, 2000), 57.

[73] Wanley to Collins, BL, Lansdowne MS 841/30, fol. 36.

[74] Wright and Wright, *The Diary of Humfrey Wanley*, vol. 1, 203.

[75] *Catalogue of the Printed Books of Arthur Collins*, ii.

interpretation of Ireland's history during the sixteenth and seventeenth centuries to what has been advanced by Carte and the Clanricard memorialists'.[76]

Hence, the catalogue distributed gratis offered for the first time an overview of Collins's considerable endeavour. Before 1760, he had only left some scattered and restricted accounts limited to a few patrons and a narrow audience. In the preface to his *Collection of the Noble Families of Cavendishe, Holles, Vere, Harley and Ogle*, he described himself as writing 'from early in the morning till twelve at night to compleat a history of the Peers' (preface, 1752). We have little information on how he obtained such a remarkable collection. In a memoir published in 1753, he recalled that he went 'twice to Oxford, copied out of the public libraries there and hired persons to transcribe for him, wherein he has expended seven hundred pounds [...] in taking extracts of records in the Tower, Cotton Library and purchasing of manuscripts'.[77] In his *Letters and Memorial of State*, financed by a narrow pool of subscribers, he described the manuscript repository at Penshurst and in His Majesty's Paper Office and the documents which could not be found to have been printed in Rymer's *Feodora*.[78]

In 1746, his work was mainly seen as a pro-Whig undertaking and its archival value was dismissed given Collins's dependence on patronage. In 1799, his writing took on another meaning. Collins was praised for his dedication to aristocratic families. This celebratory biography by Stephen Jones was enlarged from a first version drawn from his *New Biographical Dictionary* (1794), which ran to eight editions.[79] It may well be that the loyalist culture which arose from the war made the domestic partisan struggle of the first part of the eighteenth century irrelevant. In these troubled times when social hierarchies were threatened, Jones retrospectively turned Collins into a Burkean disciple: 'while there remains a spark of veneration for ancestry', Collins should be remembered as historian of the aristocracy, 'that splendid and necessary part of the British constitution'.[80] In his article for the *GM*, Jones added that this aristocracy 'has been so happily termed the "Corinthian column" of the British Constitution'.[81] Burke defined true nobility as 'a graceful *ornament* to the civil order. It is the *Corinthian capital* of polished society'.[82] For Jones, it was a way to advertise his biographical dictionary by

---

[76] *Imagining Ireland's Pasts: Early Modern Ireland through the Centuries* (Oxford, 2021), 149.

[77] *The Case of Arthur Collins, Esq, Author of the Book entitled the Peerage.* 1753 BL, Add. MS 32885, fol. 90.

[78] *Letters and Memorial of State [...] Transcribed from the Originals at Penshurst Place* (London, 1746), 4.

[79] H. J. Spencer, 'Jones, Stephen (1763–1827), journal editor and compiler of reference works', *ODNB*, 2004. Retrieved 23 June 2020 from <https://doi-org.janus.bis-sorbonne.fr/10.1093/ref:odnb/15083>.

[80] *New biographical dictionary: Containing a Brief Account of the Lives and Writings* (London, 1799), 141.

[81] *GM*, 1799, Apr., 282.

[82] *Reflections on the Revolution in France* (London, 1790), in F. P. Lock, *Edmund Burke*, vol. 2 (Oxford, 2006), 302.

280 SELLING ANCESTRY

providing an article on a personality likely to interest the reader. From one publication to another, one can see how Collins's posterity came to be redefined and on the whole improved in a different political context. When, posthumously, Collins started to be hailed for his archival mastery in 1799, the preservation of family and public repositories had become a burning political issue. The French Revolution led to the creation of a state-sponsored archival system in France, which ignited many debates on the other side of the Channel.[83]

Fictions and historical novels in Burke's compilations

Burke's compilations from 1826 to 1838 took place in a context which was markedly different from the one in which John Nichols had lived. Their credibility came mostly from their proximity to two successful branches of literature, namely the social satires of the Regency Era and Scott's historical novels. Burke assisted Henry Colburn in publicizing and marketing 'silver fork novels'.[84] The idea was to advertise 'fashionable novels' as written by supposedly genteel authors. Titles such as *Pelham or the Adventure of a Gentleman* (1828) by Edward Bulwer, *The Hamiltons* (1834) by Catherine Gore, or *Henrietta Temple, a Love Story* (1837) by Benjamin Disraeli, celebrated the epiphany of a renewed landed class, integrating Catholics and the rising elites into an ancient mould. A general vindication of aristocratic principles coexisted with the denunciation of a few vile and haughty nobles. This was not only escapist literature. Its commercial success was closely linked to the hopes and promises generated by the forthcoming Reform Act. As such, fiction intimately described the ongoing social changes and enabled them to take place.

The self-fulfilling nature of a few of these novels can be best illustrated by the case of Thomas Henry Lister, the author of *Ganby* (1826) and *Herbert Lacy* (1828).[85] His two works relate the adventures of aspiring young men wishing to marry above their rank. Along with social prejudice, Lister deals with the difficult hopes and obstacles of Catholics. His novels are reflected in his own life: a marriage to the daughter of a lord (George Villiers), a property (Amitage Park). Lister was personally committed to Catholic emancipation and in 1834 was hired as a commissioner to inquire into the state of religion in Ireland.[86] By including

---

[83] Dominique Poulot, *Musée, nation, patrimoine, 1789–1815* (Paris, 1997); Stefan Berger, 'The Role of National Archives in Constructing National Master Narratives in Europe', *Archival Science*, vol. 13, no. 1 (2013): 1–22.

[84] Winifred Hughes, 'Silver Fork Writers and Readers: Social Contexts of a Best Seller', *Novel*, vol. 25, no. 3 (1992): 328–47; Edward Copeland, *The Silver Fork Novel: Fashionable Fiction in the Age of Reform* (Cambridge, 2012).

[85] 9 Aug. 1828, CA, BC, vol. 57, case 321.

[86] Donald Hawes, 'Lister, Thomas Henry (1800–1842), writer and civil servant', *ODNB*, 2012. Retrieved 29 June 2020 from <https://doi-org.janus.bis-sorbonne.fr/10.1093/ref:odnb/16768>.

him in *Commoners*, Burke was turning fiction into reality. In a letter to Burke, Lister displayed great skill in sketching the dramatic situation in which his ancestor Thomas Lister had found himself. Lister described how the latter was ordered to attend the trial of Charles I. However, breaking ranks with the regicides, Thomas Lister declined to sign the death warrant, even after four meetings.[87] Despite the different nature of their publications, Burke and Lister were part of the same literary world, where fiction and fact both reflected the reality of the recomposition of the British elite. In the silver fork novels as well as among the landed families, directories such as Burke's were used to chart one's way through the London season, expose fraudsters, or mock certain extravagant pedigrees. Far from dismissing this crossover of genealogy and literature, the well-established antiquary Sir Thomas Phillipps congratulated Burke on his *Commoners*, which, he claimed, provided firmer roots for the elite promoted by the Reform Act: 'the ancestor should not share a little in the glory of their descendant'.[88] Prestigious ancestry not only brought about eminent descendants. Men of talent had the right to enrich their past retrospectively. An illegitimate son of a calico manufacturer in Manchester, Phillipps became a vast book collector and was part of a new elite integrated in the political system. His father had bought a seat in Worcestershire and was the high sheriff in 1802.[89] Phillipps spent much of his wealth buying a considerable number of manuscripts (over 60,000).[90] He was on friendly terms with influential antiquaries such as Sir Richard Colt Hoare and William Betham, and was elected fellow of the Royal Society in 1820. From 1830 onwards, Phillipps was involved in Burke's enquiries. Before the publication of the *Commoners*, he encouraged Burke to broaden his spectrum further by including the 'genealogies of the esquires', which may be called a 'knightage', and in a more distant future by composing an 'esquirage', which would also prove useful for the public.[91] Burke replied by inviting him to peruse the first volume of the *Commoners* prior to its publication: 'Mr Burke will have great pleasure in shewing him the mss of the commoners.'[92]

However, Phillipps was more reserved about Burke's handling of the Saxon era. When a re-edition of *Commoners* was on its way, Phillipps advised Burke to be more selective in the family accounts: 'the four former volumes require much

---

[87] 9 Aug. 1828, CA, BC, vol. 57, case 321.

[88] 'When men by their talents rise to eminence & reflect a lustre on their families it is unfair that the ancestor should not share a little in the glory of their descendant'. Phillipps to Burke, 22 July 1839, Bod. Lib., C. 438, fol. 34.

[89] A. Bell, 'Phillipps, Sir Thomas', *ODNB*, 2004. Retrieved 25 Mar. 2020, from https://doi-org.janus.bis-sorbonne.fr/10.1093/ref:odnb/22143.

[90] A. N. L. Munby, *The Formation of the Phillipps Library up to the Year 1840* (Cambridge, 1954). Toby Burrows, '"There never was such a collector since the world began": A New Look at Sir Thomas Phillipps', Toby Burrows and Cynthia Johnston (eds), *Collecting the Past: British Collectors and their Collections from the 18th to the 20th Centuries* (London, 2019), 45–63.

[91] Phillipps to Burke, 2 June 1832, Bod. Lib., MS Phillipps-Robinson, c. 438, fol. 170.

[92] Burke to Phillipps, 6 June 1632, Bod. Lib., MS Phillipps-Robinson, c. 438, fol. 174.

282 SELLING ANCESTRY

condensation, much judicious pruning and much correction. I recommend you reject all of Saxon descent unless people will shew you documents to prove them.'[93] Phillipps's advice on the medieval period should not be seen simply as a positivist condemnation. Although he criticized Burke's handling of the Saxons, he did not object to his using unverifiable sources such as Scott's novels for other periods. Along with his enormous collection of manuscripts, Phillipps possessed one of the most complete libraries of gothic novels. The new generation of antiquaries and historians in the pre-Victorian period were deeply influenced by ubiquitous historical novels.[94] As president of the Royal Society of Edinburgh, Scott was interested in mundane material culture, revealed by the discovery of random rings, coins, and other odd artefacts.[95] Richard Hoare, the highly respected antiquary from Wiltshire, considered that Scott's novel should be merely not seen as a source of knowledge but of 'edification and even moral improvement'.[96]

Some compilers before Burke had used historical novels as authentic sources, especially once they started to embrace the British elite as a whole. Commenting on Sir Robert H. Inglis's pedigree, William Betham explained that his name was of Latin origin: 'Inglis: Ingles (Lat. Inglisius) was brother of Ina, King of West Saxon' and their rise to power came from their 'system of marauding' from both sides of the Border:

> It is nevertheless well known, according to the observation of a later very ingenious author that either in their names, their mottoes, or the symbolical representations of their Heraldic bearings, the predatory occupations and nightly excursions of the borderers were designated. (See Walter Scott's *'Minstrelsy, &c'*. vol. 1, iii.)[97]

Similarly, Betham's son, Sir William, Ulster King of Arms, is mentioned in a footnote in Lady Morgan's novel *O'Donnel: A national Tale* (1814) as a key authority and a provider of various documents.[98] But what had been scattered

[93] Phillipps to Burke, 22 July 1839, Bod. Lib.,uuhuu MS Phillipps-Robinson, c. 438, fol. 34.

[94] On the 'novelization' of history and the 'historization' of the novel, see Foteini Lika, 'Fact and Fancy in Nineteenth-Century Historiography and Fiction: The Case of Macaulay and Roidis', in Rens Bod, Jaa Maat, and Thijs Weststeijn (eds), *The Making of the Humanities*, vol. 2 (Amsterdam, 2012), 149–67.

[95] 'The convergence between antiquarianism and literature—as in the revival of interest in ballads, minstrelsy, and bardic literature—reinforced this tendency, helping to make antiquarian scholarship more amenable to female readers and writers.' Andrew Lincoln, *Walter Scott and Modernity* (Edinburgh, 2012), 55.

[96] David Allan, 'Circulation', in Peter Garside and Karen O'Brien, *English and British Fiction, 1750–1820: The Oxford History of the Novel in English*, vol. 2 (Oxford, 2015), 53.

[97] Betham, *Baronetage*, vol. 5, 438. Betham was referring to the 1801 edition in Edinburgh.

[98] 'The letter of King James to Irish chief on granting him the patent is extremely curious: it is on the Irish rolls. Through the kindness of Sir William Betham, Ulster King at Arms, I have been permitted to get a copy.' Lady Morgan, *O'Donnel: A National Tale*, vol. 1 (1815), 183.

THE KEYS TO A REWARDING POSTERITY   283

allusions to historical novels in the 1800s became a flood under John Burke's pen. As an Irish Catholic, Burke was eager to insert in the otherwise dominant Protestant narrative of previous directories alternative stories about struggling Irish and Scottish Catholic families. He intended to compose an inclusive account, in which the distinct family agendas would be reintegrated into a shared national and British tale. Burke's notices are strongly influenced by the narrative structure of 'gothic plots' and 'national tales', which valued 'doubled or traumatized identities' and a constant 'movement between private and public life'.[99] In this regard, Burke's enterprise borrowed much from Walter Scott's literary ambitions.

As in many county and urban histories, Scott staged in his fiction the conflicts between modernity and tradition, between the rural and urban landscapes. Voices from the past which had been formerly suppressed were given unexpected leeway. In *The Antiquary*, Jonathan Oldbuck, a descendant of a Westphalian printer during the Reformation, was finally reconciled with his neighbours, baronets of Wardour, who were marginalized for their Jacobite involvement after 1688.[100] The baronet was given a voice in order to remind the public of the unfair treatment of Jacobites at the hands of Protestant officials. In a frank dialogue born of friendship, Sir Arthur related their unfair treatment:

When I was sent to the Tower with my late father in the year 1745, it was upon a charge becoming our birth,—upon an accusation of High treason, Mr Oldbuck; [...] At least, said Oldbuck, you have now the company of a dutiful daughter and a sincere friend, if you will permit me to say so, and that may be some consolation.[101]

Thanks to his antiquarian interest, Oldbuck was able to pay tribute to the ancient Scottish lineages, thus paving the way to reconciliation and enabling the British elites to face the prospect of a French invasion. In 1825, John Burke published a *New History of England by Hume and Smollett* in the same spirit.[102] The edition was enriched with many engravings for a wider public in which both Protestant deeds and the heroic Jacobite resistance were commemorated.[103] As well as fictitious accounts, pictures were indeed instrumental in the efficiency of this inclusive historical imagination. Whigs as well Jacobite martyrs were embedded

[99] Claire Connolly, 'The National Tale', in Peter Garside and Karen O'Brien, *English and British Fiction, 1750–1820: The Oxford History of the Novel in English*, vol. 2 (Oxford, 2015), 233.

[100] Sir Walter Scott, *The Antiquary* (London, 1827), 9 and 33.   [101] Ibid., 344.

[102] John Burke Esq. (ed.), *The History of England; from the invasion of Julius Caesar to the Revolution in 1688: by D. Hume. With a continuation, from that period to the death of George the Second, by Tobias Smollett. and Chronological Records to the coronation of his present Majesty, George the Fourth* (London, 1825), 6 vols.

[103] On the consequence of Culloden, 'the men were either shot upon the mountains, like wild beasts, or put to death in cold blood, without form of trial: the women, after having seen their husbands and fathers murdered, were subjected to brutal violation, and then turned out naked with their children, to starve on the barren heaths.' J. Burke (ed.), *A new History*, vol. 11 (1825), 231.

284 SELLING ANCESTRY

in the same narrative. The ruthless execution of Lord Russel by the Tories was followed a few pages later by a graphic description of the Glencoe massacre in 1692.

In his 1826 *General and Heraldic Dictionary*, Burke provides a tragic pedigree of the Scotts:

> He [Walter Scott] is descended from Sir William Scott of Harden, through his third son, Walter Scott, of Raeburn, which Walter, or, as more frequently and familiarly designated, 'Auld Watt', was forcibly deprived of the education of his children, had part of his estate wrested from him, and was himself thrown into the prison of Edinburgh, while his wife was incarcerated in that of Jedburgh, for daring to embrace the mild and benevolent tenets of Quakerism.[104]

In this passage, Burke gathered in one quotation extracts from different works by Scott, notably from the *Minstrelsy* (1801) and a Waverley novel, *The Heart of Mid-Lothian* (1818).[105] Burke may have had access to an unpublished version of Scott's memoirs. Like many, Scott denied paying attention to pedigree, as 'the passport which my poetical character afforded me into higher company than my birth warranted'.[106] However, in April 1808, Scott consigned in his memoirs a long narrative around his ancestors and 'Auld Watt':

> Every Scottish man has a pedigree. It is a national prerogative as unalienable as his pride and his poverty. [...] According to the prejudices of my county, it was esteemed gentle [...]. My father's grandfather was Walter Scott, well known in Teviotdale, by the surname of *Beardie*. He was the second son of Walter Scott, first laird of Raeburn, who was third son of Sir William Scott, and the grandson of Walter Scott, commonly called in tradition *Auld Watt*, of Harden.[107]

As in the *Antiquary*, Catholic families in Burke's compilations were given the chance to appear alongside the successful Protestant gentry. There were the Massingberds who obtained many confiscated Irish lands and a title during the Protectorate, next to the O'Byrnes from Leinster, who were deprived of their domain in the same period and established themselves in Bordeaux.[108] After the Emancipation Act of 1829, Burke's *Commoners* was a cultural statement about the diversity of British history. Furthermore, Burke used Scott's novels for other purposes: to provide an authoritative view on matters of etymology, to enrich picturesque

---

[104] *A General and Heraldic Dictionary*, 286.

[105] In the *Minstrelsy*, Auld Watt is the husband of 'Flower of Yarrow'. *Minstrelsy of the Scottish Border* (Edinburgh, 1802, vol. 1, 226); on the Quaker side of the story see, the edition by Claire Lamont, *Heart of Midlothian* (Oxford, 1982).

[106] John Gibson Lockhart, *Memoirs of the Life of Sir Walter Scott*, vol. 1 (Edinburgh, 1837), 2–3.

[107] Ibid.   [108] *Commoners*, vol. 1 (1834), 433; vol. 2, 107.

descriptions, and to add some biographical elements to a dry pedigree. In the first case, Burke explained that the Kempes or Kampions of Rosteage belonged to an ancient family of warriors:

> The word 'Kempe' signifies a combatant or man at arms: it is used frequently in that sense in the early period of our language, and will be found revived in its original meaning by Sir Walter Scott.[109]

He used Scott's poem *Lady of the Lake* (1810) to depict the Grahams of Dumbarton and Stirling, as well their heroic deeds from the battles of Falkirk in 1298 to that of the first Jacobite uprising in Killiecrankie in 1688.[110] He quoted several ballads from *Rokeby* (1813) to enrich his lyrical description of a family seat in Wiltshire: 'Littlecott House stands in a low and lonely situation [...]. Close on one side of the house is a grove of lofty trees, along the verge of which runs one of the principal avenues, etc.'[111] In the many biographies that featured in his pedigrees, Burke cited Scott to express the characters' emotions. He described Sir William Forbes as a banker in Edinburgh, adding that 'Sir Walter Scott says, in his notes to *Marmion* that he was unequalled, perhaps, in the degree of individual affection entertained for him by his friends as well as in the general esteem and respect of Scotland at large.'[112] Burke was inspired by the success of the edition of the Waverley Novels to suggest to Colburn and his partner Richard Bentley a series of the cheapest reprints, to be coined 'The Standard Novels', adorned with various embellishments and engravings. He signed an agreement with his publisher in April 1830 by which he 'was to receive £100 as a premium and £50 yearly for the life of the series in return for the idea and for his assistance'.[113]

The frequent use of Scott's novels as a source of inspiration and authority by pedigree-makers can be better understood only if, *a contrario*, one bears in mind that historical novels had been composed with the help of family directories. As with the silver fork novels, they were part and parcel of the same matrix. In the late eighteenth century, novelists drew a lot of their inspiration from the material available in family compilations, as well as literary gazettes such as the *GM*. The influence of the *Peerage* and its endless list of names on Jane Austen's narrative in *Persuasion* has previously been explored.[114] In 1824, Scott wrote to his school friend, the printer James Ballantyne: 'I wish you could get & forward to me the

---

[109] Ibid., vol. 2, 530.

[110] 'The ancient and powerful family of Graham says Sir Walter Scott, in the Lady of the Lake'. *A General and Heraldic Dictionary of the Peerage and Baronetage* (London, 1832), 537.

[111] *Commoners* (1835), vol. 2, 200.   [112] *A General and Heraldic Dictionary* (1832), vol. 1, 485.

[113] Royal A. Gettmann, *A Victorian Publisher: A Study of the Bentley Papers* (Cambridge, 1960), 44.

[114] Obsession with family name had been a well-established trope since the early modern period up to the Victorian period, D. J. Greene, 'Jane Austen and the Peerage', *Modern Language Association*, vol. 68 (1953): 1017–31; Sophie Gilmartin, *Ancestry and Narrative in Nineteenth-Century British Literature: Blood Relations from Edgeworth to Hardy* (Cambridge, 1998).

286 SELLING ANCESTRY

newest set of Debretts Baronetage.'[115] In 1830, he noted in his diary a dinner with 'honest John Wood, my old friend' and commented on his 'very powerful memory, and much curious information'.[116] Wood had published an enlarged edition of Sir Robert Douglas's *Peerage of Scotland* in 1813. Scott's fictions are no longer considered as simply driven by nostalgic and conservative impulses. Their appeal went far beyond the world of antiquaries. Between documentation and fiction, they explored the dark corners that remained in most factual and progressive narratives. His novels gave a voice to disquiet, forgotten voices, and unsolved dilemmas. The triumph of modernity was taunted by 'the unsettling and powerful survival of the past'.[117] Scott's novels should not be seen as a straightforward epic celebration of the British Empire. Dialects, pedigrees, memoirs, and state papers led to the creation of a 'linguistic texture' which prevented any simplistic reading.[118]

Against a retrospective definition of science as rational and narrowly experimental, it was now widely accepted that there was an epistemological value to fiction and legends. Even Darwin was passionately interested in Walter Scott's novels and, far from being of anecdotal interest, they were reported to be influential in the shaping of his scientific hypothesis: 'Darwin's extensive investment in the novel, particularly in historical fiction, inculcated a comparative understanding of the past that emphasized the complexity and indeterminacy of previous events.'[119] He was a keen reader of county histories, such as Gilbert White's *Natural History and Antiquities of Selborne* (1789).[120]

Whether it be the silver fork novels or Scott's historical sagas, fiction was not rejected by its readers as worthless invaluable knowledge. It is with this intellectual background in mind that the credibility of Burke's compilations should be appraised. Burke demonstrated a remarkable capacity for enmeshing his pedigrees within a broader literary world. His proximity to literature did not at first bring his publication into disrepute. We have seen that some antiquaries were more

---

[115] Sir Herbert Grierson (ed.), *The Letters of Sir Walter Scott* (London, 1832–7), vol. 8 (1823–5), 203. About Burke, ibid., vol. 10, 237.

[116] On Wood, National Library of Scotland, Acc.12047. John Gibson Lockhart, *Memoirs of the Life of Sir Walter Scott* (Edinburgh, 1839), vol. 9, 351–2.

[117] Devin Griffiths, *The Age of Analogy: Science and Literature between the Darwins* (Baltimore, 2016), 86.

[118] 'Even as they invoke the imperial logic of stadial history, however Scott's novels mount a resistance to it in the local experience of reading [...]. Contemporary readers were variously dazzled, delighted, bewildered, and annoyed by the unprecendeted heterogeneity of the novels' linguistic texture.' Ian Duncan, 'Walter Scott and the Historical Novel', in Peter Garside and Karen O'Brien (eds), *English and British Fiction, 1750–1820: The Oxford History of the Novel in English*, vol. 2 (Oxford, 2015), 319.

[119] Ibid., 235.

[120] Susan B. Lipscomb, 'Introducing Gilbert White: An Exemplary Natural Historian and His Editors', *Victorian Literature and Culture*, vol. 35, no. 2 (2007): 551–67. More generally on the combination between science and fiction, see Frédérique Aït-Touati, *Contes de la lune, essai sur la fiction et les sciences modernes* (Paris, 2011).

THE KEYS TO A REWARDING POSTERITY   287

supportive of his works while others, such as Nichols's grandson John Gough
Nichols, were fairly dismissive. Elected a Fellow of the Society of Antiquaries in
1818, and a founding member of the Surtees Society in 1834, John Gough Nichols
in his *Collectanea topographica et genealogica* commented on Collins in a favourable
manner and chose instead to ignore Burke.[121] Later, in *The Topographer and
Genealogist*, Nichols insisted that Collins had been a 'very industrious compiler'
though limiting his 'labours to existing families', but he denounced the negligence of 'our modern genealogists, Messrs. Burke'.[122] Unlike his grandfather and
his inclusive *Literary Anecdotes*, John Gough Nichols was part of the increasing
professionalization of historical research in Victorian Britain.

To the antiquaries, one should now add another category of important actors,
namely the compilers' descendants, as they were involved in their uncertain
posterity.

2. Family devotion and reputation

The importance of family origins in the genealogists' reputations should not be
underestimated. This point has been well illustrated in France by the case of André
Duchesne (1584–1640). One of most prominent French historians and genealogists, Duchesne identified himself as a *Tourangeau* ('native of Touraine').[123]
Though he obtained the title of royal geographer under the protection of
Richelieu for his many editions of medieval texts and urban histories, he saw
himself as a provincial antiquary. As in early modern England, most antiquarian
enquiries were conducted outside the metropolis on the basis of the personal links
strengthened in the provincial community. It was only in the late seventeenth
century that provincialism became either a 'stain' or a 'claim against the intoler-
able domination of Paris'.[124] His son wrote an 'encomium' which established the
family origins in the thirteenth-century nobility of Touraine. Whereas Duchesne
came in fact from humble Parisian printers, his son felt the need to reconstruct a
prestigious pedigree, which survived through various biographies over the following centuries. Such a retrospective invention may have been guided by filial
affection as well as by self-interest, as the son, by reprinting many of Duchesne's
works, 'managed to live off this inheritance, just like other people live off a
business stock or the invention of a patent'.[125] The Duchesne family provides a

[121] On Collins, *Collectanea Topographica*, vol. 1 (London, 1834); vol. 2 (1835), 58; vol. 3 (1836), 295–7.
[122] *Topographer and Genealogist* (London, 1846), vol. 1, 2, 497.
[123] Olivier Poncet, 'The Genealogist at Work', in Eickmeyer, Friedrich, and Bauer (eds), *Genealogical Knowledge in the Making*, 203.
[124] Ibid.   [125] Ibid., 216.

288 SELLING ANCESTRY

striking example of genealogists from a modest urban background who did not claim any gentility but were subsequently ennobled in later generations.

Son of a Gentleman Usher?

Omitted in the first edition of the *Biographie universelle ancienne et moderne* by Louis-Gabriel Michaud (1843), Arthur Collins appeared in the 1854 edition, just above the biography of his grandson David, judge advocate in the settlement of Botany, writer and governor of 'Van Diemen' in New South Wales.[126] Both articles were written by 'D-Z-S' (Dezos de la Roquette). A royalist and diplomat, Dezos de la Roquette composed an armorial of French cities, published in 1816, and he translated several English historical works.[127] It was probably from the article by Jones in the *GM* that he obtained his information. Jones himself indicated that all his data came from Collins's grandson David.[128] One may question why David Collins felt the need to send a biography of his grandfather. After having served as a secretary to the governor of New South Wales, he came back to London in 1797. He failed both to keep his salary as Judge-Advocate and to recover his rank in the army.[129] Struggling to make a living, he launched into a detailed account of his residence in the newly established colony (*An Account of the English Colony in New South Wales*, 1798).[130] His work included many developments on natural sciences, descriptions of landscapes, and comments on the Maori languages. He started corresponding with Joseph Banks and obtained his patronage to be sent back to Hobart as lieutenant-governor. Several extracts from his *Account of the English Colonies* were published in the *GM*, notably one passage on the alleged discovery of a gold mine by a convict.[131] It was certainly the case that his account of his grandfather was linked to his attempt to be acknowledged in antiquarian circles. He placed himself in a lineage of polite authors. According to David, Arthur Collins was born in 1682, 'the son of William Collins, esq. (Gentleman Usher to Queen Catherine in 1669) by his wife Elizabeth, daughter of Thomas Blyth, daughter of John Horwood esq. of Okely, in the county of Southampton'.[132]

---

[126] L. G. Michaud (ed.), *Biographie universelle ancienne ou moderne* (Paris, 1854), vol. 8, 604.

[127] See his antiquarian collection at the Bibliothèque Ste Geneviève, MS 3586–3641. William Wilkinson, *Tableau historique, geographique et politique de la Moldavie et de la Valachie, traduit de l'anglais par M. Dezos de la Roquette* (Paris, 1824).

[128] 'It is chiefly from data which I procured from this gentleman, that the foregoing sketch of his grandfather has been written', *GM*, Apr. 1799, 282.

[129] 'When absent, he had been passed over when it came to his turn to be put on full pay; nor was he permitted to return to England to reclaim his rank in the corps.' *Memoirs of the late Colonel David Collins, GM*, vol. 80 (1810), 480.

[130] Brian Fletcher, 'Collins, David (1756–1810), colonial official and army officer', *ODNB*. Retrieved 25 June 2020 from <https://doi-org.janus.bis-sorbonne.fr/10.1093/ref:odnb/5937>.

[131] John Currey (ed.), *David Collins. Letters to Sir Joseph Banks: London & the Derwent 1798–1808* (Malvern, 2004); *GM*, vol. 68 (1798), 325–6.

[132] *GM*, vol. 69 (1799), 282.

THE KEYS TO A REWARDING POSTERITY   289

On the maternal side, Jones's account was rather confusing. He juxtaposed the families of Blyth and Horwood. He meant that the Blyths descended from the dynasty of Horwood in Hampshire. As with many hack jobs, spelling mistakes were numerous: 'Okely' stands for the parish of Oakley. As time went on, William Collins became in the French version 'gentleman to Queen Caroline in 1649'.[133] Lost in translation, Queen Catherine became 'Caroline'. Despite various tweakings, his account provided a template for the following centuries. However, in the 1887 edition of the *DNB*, Collins's birthdate was postponed to 1690 and the Southampton connection to the Horwoods was dropped.[134] In the biography published in 2016 by the genealogist Cecil R. Humphery-Smith, Arthur Collins was born either in 1681 or in 1682, and is declared to be:

> Son of William Collins, a gentleman usher to Charles II's consort, Queen Catherine of Braganza, and his wife, Elizabeth Blyth, daughter of Thomas Blyth. It seems likely that the family was Roman Catholic and that record of birth and marriage would have been found among the records of the Portuguese embassy chapel, which have not survived.[135]

It is quite telling that Collins's biography was entrusted not to a professional historian but to a genealogist, the founder of the *Institute of Heraldic and Genealogical Studies* in Kent and the editor of *Family History*.[136] From one biographer to another, there are conflicting accounts in terms of birth date, parentage, and even religious affiliation. In a database of English Court Officers, William Collins is presented as an 'extraordinary quarter waiter' only for 26 March 1669.[137] His temporary post was 'to open the door and if necessary to open the way into the presence chamber' and was to be distinguished from the gentleman usher of the privy chamber who had many more duties at Court.[138] Why then should William Collins be remembered for a position held for one day? Arthur Collins left several papers and letters which contradict his grandson's assertion. His origins seemed to be located, instead, in the City and in the world of brewers and excisemen. In a letter to Newcastle, he gave many details about his own grandfather John:

---

[133] 'Un laborieux antiquaire', 'son père gentilhomme de la reine Caroline en 1649, avait possédé et dissipé une grande fortune'. *Biographie universelle*, 604.

[134] Francis Espinasse, 'Collins Arthur', *DNB* (1882), vol. 11, 364.

[135] Cecil R. Humphery-Smith, 'Collins, Arthur (1681/2–1760), genealogist', *ODNB*, 2016. Retrieved 9 June 2020 from <https://doi-org.janus.bis-sorbonne.fr/10.1093/ref:odnb/5934>.

[136] See Cecil Humphery-Smith, Esq, OBE, FSA on the Debrett's website.

[137] J. C. Sainty, Lydia Wassmann, and R. O. Bucholz (eds), Household of Queen (from 1685 Queen Dowager) Catherine 1660–1705. Retrieved 9 June 2020 from <http://courtofficers.ctsdh.luc.edu>.

[138] R. O. Bucholz, *The Augustan Court: Queen Anne and the Decline of Court Culture* (Stanford, Calif., 1993), 121.

290   SELLING ANCESTRY

> My great-grandfather spent an estate in Warwickshire which had been in his family for 300 years, leaving my grandfather with a poor pittance, which he managed so well and by honest industry, became one of the greatest brewers in London, so that on the Restoration of King Charles the 2nd he had so plentiful a fortune that he left of business and was one of the first farmers and Commissioner of the Excise.[139]

The setting up of the Excise benefited the Corporation of London Brewers, which during the Commonwealth, obtained the farming of duties on ale and beer.[140] However, there is no trace of John Collins among the Commissioners of the Excise or in the records of the Brewers' corporation in London.[141] More work needs to be done to identify both the grandfather and his father. John Collins, Arthur's elder son, who obtained a position in the army during the War of the Austrian Succession, wrote a notebook in which he introduced himself as the son of 'Arthur Collins of Kenilworth, Warwickshire'.[142] According to Arthur Collins, his mother Elizabeth Blyth 'in her right enjoys upward 2000£ a year' and he inherited from her leases of four properties in St Brides.[143] Her sister, Sarah, was married to Henry Coghill in 1699 and their own daughter Sarah was married to Robert Hucks, another prominent London brewer in St Giles in the Fields and MP for Abingdon in 1722. Breweries may have been the common link between the Collinses and the Huckses, but so far there is no substantial evidence.

It is hard to believe Arthur's claim that he was 'the son of misfortune, my father having run through more than 30,000'.[144] An astronomical sum indeed! What is more certain is that Arthur Collins's City identity is further established by his marriage at St Dunstan's in the West in 1707 to Elizabeth, the daughter of John Tooker. The latter petitioned the Treasury for a position to obtain a pension for his son-in-law.[145] John Tooker the younger was the General Accountant in the excise (malt and hops).[146] His father, John Tooker the elder had been acting as deputy and receiver for the county of Somerset and city of Bristol of all land taxes granted by Act of Parliament ever since the return of King Charles II.[147]

---

[139] Collins to Newcastle, 27 Mar. 1746, BL, Add. MS 32693, fol. 302.

[140] Edward Hughes, *Studies in Administration and Finance 1558–1825* (Manchester, 1934) 123.

[141] I am very grateful to Perry Gauci for his help on this point in trying to identify John and William Collins.

[142] Notebook of John Collins, son of Arthur Collins of Kenilworth, Warwickshire, Plymouth Archives, The Box, 1305/6.

[143] Collins to Newcastle, 27 Mar. 1746, BL, Add. MS 32693, fol. 302; Collins to Newcastle, 14 May 1753, 'My mother inheriting from her brother four houses in new street in the parish of St Brides of 56 per annum, held by lease of 61 years from the Goldsmith company which on her death in 1720, she bequeaths to me, and the lease did not expire till 1733'. BL, Add. MS 32731, fol. 453.

[144] Collins to Newcastle, 5 Feb. 1752, BL, Add. MS 32726, fol. 108.

[145] Letters, memorials and memoranda, relating to grants of pensions. BL, Add. MS 4188, fols 233–4.

[146] John Chamberlayne, *Magnæ Britanniæ Notitia* (London, 1725), 525.

[147] William A. Shaw, *Calendar of Treasury Books*, vol. 8 (1685–1689) (London, 1923), 264.

THE KEYS TO A REWARDING POSTERITY 291

The Collinses and the Tookers may have been acquainted with each other as there was a Richard Collins, supervisor of the excise in Bristol during the Commonwealth and Restoration.[148] Again, to date there is no evidence to substantiate this hypothesis. Arthur Collins, who made a living from publishing the pedigrees of hundreds of peerages, left contradictory accounts of his own origins which allowed his grandson to provide a much more genteel version of their family past.

Burke and the 'great De Burgho house of Clanricarde'

Like Arthur Collins, John Burke did not leave a ready-made pedigree of his own family. He may have considered it as unnecessary or improper in his compiling activity. It was therefore his son, Sir Bernard Burke, who undertook this task. Again, the genealogical statement made by his son took place at a peculiar moment in time. In 1853, Sir Bernard Burke had just been made Ulster King of Arms, for which he produced a confirmation of arms for his family, the descendants of Peter Burke of Elm Hall (Co. Tip.).[149] This pedigree was later vindicated and commented upon in various gazettes published in Ireland, England, and even in the United States.

In *The Irish Literary Gazette*, Sir Bernard Burke was praised as a principal restorer of the Irish past. After the 'bygone times of almost continual feud, disturbances and distraction', he was able to satisfy 'the public anxiety to repair the past and amend the future'.[150] He introduced himself as 'the scion of a highly respectable Irish family (his grandfather was an active magistrate for two counties), which claims descent (What Burke family does not?) from the great De Burgho house of Clanricarde'.[151] Burke may have been inspired by the *Memoirs and Letters of Clanricarde* published by the earls of Clanricarde in 1722 and in 1757: 'these editions provided a pretext for offering general appraisal of the positive role played by their family in Ireland's history since medieval times but most especially since the mid-sixteenth century'.[152] As the Butlers of Ormond, the Clanricard Burkes were depicted as ancient and loyal Irish nobles. While faithfully publishing Burke's account, the journalist inserted an ironic remark in the facts indicating that all Burkes descended from the powerful Clanricarde. A Gaelic name which referred to Richard Mor de Burgh in the thirteenth century, Burke was spelt in many ways—'De Burgh', 'Bourg', 'Burc, 'Bourke', 'Burgho'—which

---

[148] Joseph Trutt mentioned an engraving of Richard Collins in his *Biographical Dictionary containing an historical account of all the engravers* (London, 1785), vol. 1, 151. Richard Collins was the author of *The Countrey Gaugers Vade Mecum* (London, 1677).

[149] Copy of confirmation of arms to the descendants of Peter Burke of Elm Hall, Co. Tipperary. 30 Mar. 1854. National Library of Ireland, Genealogical Office, MS 108, fols 75–6.

[150] *The Irish Literary Gazette*, 14 Nov. 1857, 248.   [151] Ibid.

[152] Canny, *Imagining Ireland's Pasts*, 126.

292 SELLING ANCESTRY

enabled limitless variations. According to Sir Bernard Burke, 'the Norman name of *De Burgh* became, in process of time, corrupted into *Burke*'.[153] In his account published in the Irish gazette, Burke did not dwell much on his recent family. His close ancestors were described as moderate and free 'from all party bias' although rather from 'the old, higher Whig school'.[154] He briefly alluded to his father's successful settlement in London in this 'sister country'. A year later, in 1858, Sir Bernard Burke published in the London *Patrician* a 'biographical notice of John Burke. ESQ':

> The author of 'The Peerage', paternally sprang, was seated in high repute for several successive generations at the Castle of Meelick in the West of Ireland, an inheritance conferred on its immediate founder, John Burke, by his father Richard, second earl of Clanricarde. Maternally, Mr. Burke had an equally honourable ancestry, deriving, [...] of the late Sir Robert Barnevall, Bart. from the distinguished Anglo-Norman house of Barnevvall of Crickstown Castle.[155]

In the *Memoirs and Letters of Clanricarde* (1757), Richard, the second earl of Clanricarde, was 'called by the Irish Sassanagh the Englishman' and described as a loyal subject to the Tudors.[156] Along with this new pedigree, which now included his English maternal ancestors, Sir Bernard Burke dedicated much space to his father's career in London. Skipping the seventeenth and eighteenth centuries, he argued that his father had received a good 'classical education' and, after a brief experience as a merchant, was attracted to 'the excitement of politics and literature'.[157] He is not described as a compiler or indexer, which in fact he was for *The Times*, but as an author, whose 'genius' was first expressed in various political articles and poetry.[158] About his politics, his son mentioned his articles in the prestigious *Examiner,* which attracted prominent writers such as Byron, Keats, and John Stuart Mill. John Burke's articles were so widely read that his 'squibs' allegedly angered the Tory Prime Minister, George Canning. The allusion is not very clear but we can speculate that Burke may have commented upon the fact that, as Canning married his daughter to the first marquess of Clanricarde, they belonged to the same family. On the prime qualities attributed by Sir Bernard Burke to his father were his 'friendly dispositions' and his 'unbounded' sense of hospitality which led to creating a 'social roof' around him.[159] His generosity was directed at the worthy poor, the beggars 'especially women and children': 'he would not give them money, but would walk with them after him to a baker's shop'. As a further example of his 'kindness and benevolence', Sir Bernard mentioned his father's long-lasting friendship with the bookseller Sir Richard

---

[153] John Bernard Burke, *A Genealogical and Heraldic Dictionary* (1845), 210.
[154] *The Irish Literary Gazette* (1857), 249.   [155] *The Patrician*, vol. 5 (1858) 501.
[156] Canny, *Imagining Ireland's Pasts*, 131.   [157] Ibid., 502.   [158] Ibid.   [159] Ibid.

Phillips.[160] Phillips was a radical figure, publishing the *Leicester Herald* during the French Revolution and selling Paine's *Rights of Man*. The owner of the *Monthly Magazine*, he specialized in cheap publications, reference books, and school books.[161] For his activities as well as his connections, John Burke appeared as a new type of intellectual figure, moderate but progressive, literate but sociable, a compiler and a creative author.

In 1859, *The New England Historical and Genealogical Register* published a shorter account of John Burke which borrowed from the *Irish Literary Gazette* as well as from the *Patrician*, adding that Burke's father was introduced as 'the late Sir John Burke'.[162] It seems that, on the other side of the Atlantic, Sir Bernard was able to make his father a knight without too much fuss. He added further comments on his father's compilations that were omitted in the Irish and English versions. His aim was probably to advertise to an American public the quality of their family dictionary: 'that most popular and useful book now universally known' which sold 'fifteen hundred copies every year'.[163]

Even if Sir Bernard Burke was inclined to vindicate his glorious ancestry in Britain as well as on the other side of the Atlantic, we can see that the account of his father's life took different directions. In Dublin, he insisted on the Irish side of his family, while in London his father was termed esquire and presented as a major author in politics and literature. On the other side of the Atlantic, John Burke was elevated to the dignity of knight and the commercial success of the family's products was heavily stressed. Sir Bernard Burke's position was in many ways comparable to that of Sir William Betham. Both held the position of Ulster King of Arms thanks to their involvement in their fathers' genealogical enquiries. Both were eager to vindicate their fathers' memories and in doing so, before their fathers' deaths, it became increasingly difficult to disentangle their respective role in the making of the compilation.

Thomas Wotton of Little Cannons

In contrast to Collins and Burke, the memory of the publisher Thomas Wotton was retrospectively absorbed in the pedigree of a more genteel family, the Abneys of Mesham Hall. His name appeared in Burke's *Commoners* as 'Thomas Wotton of Little Cannons, Herts, Esq'.[164] The denomination 'Little Cannons' came from

---

[160] Ibid., 503.

[161] Pamela Clemit and Jenny McAuley, 'Phillips, Sir Richard (1767–1840), author and publisher', *ODNB*, 2004. Retrieved 20 June 2020 from <https://doi-org.janus.bis-sorbonne.fr/10.1093/ref:odnb/22167>.

[162] 'Memoir of the late sir John Burke', by his son, Sir John Bernard Burke, Ulster King of Arms at Dublin, *The New England Historical and Genealogical Register*, vol. 12, no. 3 (1858), 194–5.

[163] Ibid., 195.   [164] Burke, *Commoners*, vol. 1 (1833), 572.

294 SELLING ANCESTRY

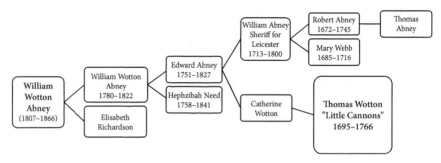

Tree 6.1 The Wotton–Abney family in Burke's *Commoners*

the fact that after the publication of his first *Baronetage*, Wotton invested in 1730 in a small property in the parish of Shenley, Hertfordshire, and in the deeds he was referred to as 'esquire'.[165] Wotton chose a place located less than thirty miles from the City, where he continued to work till his death. It was the high sheriff, William Wotton Abney of Mesham Hall (Derby), who provided a family account in 1828 (Tree 6.1).[166]

Although the name 'Wotton' was transmitted to his father by his grandparents and then to himself, William was only interested in the Abney side of the family. Introducing himself as 'the representative of the family', he mentioned a 'tradition held from father & son', namely that they allegedly came from Aubigny, according to Mme de Maintenon's *Mémoires*.[167] William predictably chose to link the Aubignys to the Norman Conquest, after which he jumped several centuries to focus on Sir Thomas Abney, knighted by William III and one of the directors of the Bank of England. The prestigious pedigree of the Abneys erased all other alliances, notably that of his grandmother, Hephzibah Need, who was only quoted in passing although she was still alive in 1828. The daughter of Samuel Need, she might have given him the opportunity to mention the spectacular invention of her father in Nottingham. Samuel, a successful hosier and burgess from Nottingham, partnered with Jedediah Strutt in the creation of the 'Derby rib machine' which produced ribbed stockings of quality.[168] Their device afforded cheaper stockings and became immensely popular. These 'heroes of invention' were increasingly celebrated by the urban middle sorts and were no longer feared as a force that might destabilize the social fabric.[169] Ignoring this sort of celebrity, however, William Wotton Abney chose rather to focus on his grandfather, Edward

---

[165] 'Of Thomas Wotton, Esq. to Pieces of land waste of manor, part of which now converted into a fishpond, on road from Shenley Hill to Well End, etc. Manor of Shenley Hall'. 16 Oct. 1730, Herts Arch, DE/HCC/27.
[166] CA, BC, vol. 56, case 1.   [167] Ibid.
[168] J. J. Mason, 'Strutt, Jedediah (1726–1797), inventor and cotton manufacturer', *ODNB*, 2006. Retrieved 12 June 2020, from <https://doi-org.janus.bis-sorbonne.fr/10.1093/ref:odnb/26683>.
[169] Christine Macleod, *Heroes of Invention: Technology, Liberalism and British Identity 1750–1914* (Cambridge, 2007).

Abney, 'a gentleman of genuine old English hospitality'.[170] William Wotton chose to ignore anything related to industry, bookselling activities, and female lines. He merely alluded to his great-grandmother, Catherine Wotton, and chose instead to highlight her husband, William Abney, who as a Leicester high sheriff figured in Nichols's county history. He was 'one of the last of that old-fashioned race of English proprietors [...] a man of very vigorous mind, a Whig of the revolution'.[171] By perusing a good deal of polite gazettes, he would have been able to provide many details on Wotton's publications, but he chose not to do so.

In William Wotton Abney's account, the strength of the patriarchal mindset as well as the exclusive taste for a landed culture led to making Thomas Wotton's identity as a prominent London bookseller invisible. In marrying his only daughter to a country squire, Thomas unwittingly compromised his posterity, at least in genealogical compilations. It is worth noting that during his life, Wotton had been reluctant to create an impressive pedigree for himself. When he was assembling his second *Baronetage* in 1740, he drew a sketch of his family tree.

His father, Matthew, appeared on the second branch, as the younger son of a grocer, Thomas Wotton of Bewdley (Worcestershire). He did not mention the name of his grandmother, 'sister of Robert Hill of Bewdley, mercr'. At the centre of the tree stood his uncle Thomas Wotton, 'banker' in Fleet Street, who had been apprenticed to Thomas Fowle, a goldsmith banker at the sign of the Black Lion.[172] Thomas is represented as married to the 'daughter of Hiccocks' along with their three children (William, Elizabeth, Susanna). Whether or not Wotton ran out of space, he placed his close family outside of the tree, linking it with a long line on the recto page. His mother, Jane (1667–1741), is mentioned, as well as his sisters Mary and Elizabeth. All were buried at St Dunstan's. In his roughly sketched family tree, Wotton thought it useful to add a reference to a personal trauma. He wrote that his mother was sister to John Perry, who was murdered in 1741.[173] In gruesome detail, the press reported the murder of Perry, a Principal of Clement's Inn and Deputy Paymaster of the Pensions, who in June was clubbed to death and had 'his Throat cut from Ear to Ear' by his servant James Hall.[174] Executed on 14 September and hung on a gibbet at Shepherd's Bush, Hall gave an account of his behaviour. He mentioned the importance of Thomas Wotton in the discovery of the crime.

Hall had gone to meet him the day after he got rid of the body and Wotton asked him about his uncle's health. Growing suspicious, Wotton brought Hall before a magistrate and later found some missing bank notes. Wotton must have been traumatized by his uncle's murder, which coincided with the publication of

---

[170] *Commoners*, vol. 1, 574.   [171] Ibid., 593.

[172] John Orbell and Alison Turton, *British Banking: A Guide to Historical Records* (London, 2001, 2017), 215.

[173] BL, Add. MS 24121, fol. 351.

[174] *The ordinary of Newgate, his account of the behaviour, confession, and dying words, of James Hall* (London, 1741); see also *GM*, vol. 10 (1741), 159.

his *Baronetage*. In a note in the press, he informed the public that he 'having been so taken up for these three months last past in bringing to Justice that notorious villain James Hall [...] is obliged to postpone the publication of the English Baronetage'.[175] In his own tree, Wotton was more interested in retracing his immediate family history, the prosperity of his uncle as a banker, and his subsequent murder. He left these scattered notes after the death of his mother (1742) and of most of his kin. Neither his wife nor his children were mentioned. While spending a considerable amount of time in publishing baronets' pedigrees, Wotton was not interested in claiming landed origins for himself. His family tree was firmly rooted in the City corporations (Mercers, Goldsmiths, Stationers). The conflicting accounts of Wotton's family convey the difficulty for John Burke of transforming a London bookseller into a proper gentleman. This may be explained by the strained relations between the middle class and the landed elite in the years before the Great Reform Act. In contrast to the memory of Collins and Burke, that of Wotton was absorbed and made invisible by a senior branch.

3. Conflicts with the customers and their rewarding potential

The compilers' posterity relied on the assessment of well-established antiquaries and on their social background, and one could add another crucial ingredient, namely the nature of the relationship they managed to create with their customers. The latter's participation in the main stages of preparing for publication was both a threat and an opportunity. To have a large number of participants was in itself a sign of success, a badge of honour, as it demonstrated the ability to involve the public in formerly well-guarded knowledge. We have seen above, in the example of William Berry, how in his preface he portrayed himself as the representative of the public interest against the monopolistic practices of the College of Arms.

However, any commercial undertaking raised suspicions of complaisance and incompetence by allowing fake and genuine pedigrees to coexist. The compilers' socially inferior position did not help and they had to defend themselves against accusations of being 'mercenaries'. To safeguard their reputation, compilers were forced to perform a fine balancing act between accommodating clients' desires while yet maintaining public esteem by refusing the most unacceptable accounts. Conflicts with a few customers were inevitable and sometimes even necessary. The few scattered documents available, both printed and manuscript, have allowed us to reconstitute this power relationship with the customers that so greatly contributed to shaping the publisher's reputation. When conflicts arose, the memory of the compiler was sometimes preserved in order to place them in a more favourable light.

---

[175] *London Daily Post*, 5 Dec. 1741, issue 2222.

A working relationship based on trust

Through their enquiries and in their prefaces, most compilers considered all appropriate means to gain their clients' trust. We have seen before how letters were essential to establish a working relationship. More often than not, customers demanded to meet the compiler in person. In the 1760s, many publishers moved away from the City to settle in the politer venues of Westminster. Almon's, later Debrett's, bookshop was located opposite Burlington House in Piccadilly. In 1781 John Stockdale and James Ridgway also migrated to Piccadilly, while Colburn set up in Mayfair. The latter shop was even fashioned as a private residence: 'the Said Premises shall not externally bear the appearance of other than a private residence' and the shop should look like 'the property of a gentleman rather than of a shopkeeper'.[176]

One common criticism which Wotton was very keen to express dealt with the ignorance or lack of interest of many customers in their ancestors. In a letter to William Holman he gently mocked the 'romantic' creativity of most families: 'to see all the accounts Baronets have sent me, you'd be amazed some being so romantick in order to prove themselves of an ancient stock [...]. I found the Baronets in general very backward in sending their account and in answering trifling questions.'[177] Of the Keates of the Hoo (Hertfordshire), whose title was bestowed by Charles II in 1660 on Jonathan Keate, Wotton scoffed at their pretensions, declaring that 'ye family is of no antiquity, ye principal rise of it was from William Keate a sugar baker of London'.[178] Wotton's most damaging verdict on these families, whether they were new or old, was their refusal or their inability to help him. On Sir Harvey Elwes, second baronet, who inherited the title but lived in extreme poverty, Wotton considered that 'he deserved to be omitted for his carelessness'.[179] He provided many other examples of ignorant families among the colonial elite such as Sir Richard Everard, governor of North Carolina, and worse, among men of letters such as Sir Thomas Sebright, 'though reckoned a bookish man'.[180] Sebright, fourth baronet, was a respected book collector, praised by Thomas Hearne, and served as MP for Hertfordshire from 1715 to 1734. He is represented drinking wine with his friends under a coat of arms hanging on the wall with the following motto: 'You all say another day what jolly brave boys were we.'[181]

---

[176] Clause in the Sun Fire Insurance contract (1823), quoted by John Sutherland and Veronica Melnyk, *Rogue Publisher: The 'Prince of Puffers'. The Life and Works of the Publisher Henry Colburn* (Brighton, 2018), 86.

[177] Thomas Wotton to William Holman, 1724, ERO, D/Y 1/1/199/1/8.

[178] Thomas Wotton to William Holman, 1724, ERO, D/Y 1/1/199/1/30.

[179] Thomas Wotton to William Holman, 1724, ERO, D/Y 1/1/199/1/30/19.

[180] Thomas Wotton to William Holman, 1724, ERO, D/Y 1/1/199/1/10.

[181] <http://www.histparl.ac.uk/volume/1715-1754/member/sebright-sir-thomas-saunders-1692-1736>. See the portrait by Benjamin Ferrers with the coat of arms against the wall: 'A Group Portrait of Sir Thomas Sebright, Sir John Bland and Two Friends' (1723). Private Collection.

298 SELLING ANCESTRY

Continuing the theme of alcoholism, Wotton struggled to obtain anything from Sir John Swinnerton Dyer, fourth baronet, and wondered why he and his friends 'don't kill themselves at drinking'.[182] Implicitly, Wotton assumed that with the dignity of a title came the duty to provide historical knowledge for the sake of the public. As a broker between families and the general public, many publishers took the moral high ground and fiercely condemned those who refused to lend their support.

Nonetheless, Wotton, Betham, and Burke's correspondence abounds with details about their constructive meetings with various family members in coffee houses and hotels. Sometimes they were even invited to the family's urban lodgings or their landed estates. Customers trusted the publisher to release the best account of the family and even to fill in the gaps in their memory. A certain Adolphus Oughton asked Wotton to come to his London house in Hanover Square in order to show him his coat of arms engraved on his furniture, adding that he was 'not herald enough to know how to blazon' and that Wotton 'may take them singly or with their quartering off some escutcheons'.[183] He admitted to being 'so little skilled in genealogical affairs' and trusted Wotton to 'methodize in the manner most suitable to your design'.[184] Among various confusing statements on ancestors, Oughton recalled that in the fifteenth century 'John the Grandson of Robert very much impaired the estate which however Thomas the grandson of John and my great-great-grandfather in some measure repaired.'[185] Wotton tried to make sense of the last passage by reformulating it in simpler and shorter sentences.[186] In the same vein, Joseph Grove urged Burke to visit him at his lodging, 6 Montagu Street, to show him a gold cup given by George II to his wife Louisa.[187] He was invited for a few days by Henry Lawson to Brough Hall near York to inspect his manuscripts. He met Thomas Bourke Ricketts at Colburn Library to discuss several competing versions of the Ricketts' pedigree.[188] As the Colburn circulation library held hundreds of books related to antiquarian studies, Ricketts and Burke would have had all the resources on hand to find an acceptable version. One George Pochlin wrote that he felt 'particularly anxious of having my pedigree extended from the representation of it in Nicholl's history'.[189] He complained that Nichols's *History of Leicester* was too short on his family and asked for a 'personal interview' in the summer: 'as I am sheriff of this County and have to serve for the summer afaires on the 8th day of August, after that period I shall be

---

[182] Thomas Wotton to William Holman, 1724, ERO, D/Y 1/1/199/1/17.
[183] Sir Adolphus Oughton, in *Wotton correspondence 1724–1741*, BL, Add. MS 24121, fol. 135.
[184] Ibid.   [185] Ibid.
[186] 'John Oughton, from which the present baronet is descended [...] settled about the year 1400. [...] Robert, grandson of John Oughton purchased the Parks of New-Fillongley [...] till the father of the present baronet, John, the Grandson of Robert, impaired the Estate. Which Thomas (Grandson of John) greatly repaired.' Wotton, *The English Baronet*, vol. 3, 191.
[187] Grove to Burke, CA, BC, vol. 57, case 228.
[188] Lawson to Burke, case 300. Ricketts to Burke, CA, BC, vol. 58, case 461.
[189] George Pochlin to Burke, 8 July 1828, CA BC, vol. 58, case 437.

glad to personally wait upon you'.[190] Country houses fulfilled different functions: sites for hospitality, polite museums, and temples of memory.[191] Wotton, Burke, or Nichols were not simply considered as visitors but rather as respectable guests. Even if they belonged to various social worlds, compilers benefited from their daily interactions with many landed families. An invitation to the home of a family could be regarded as a gift rewarding the time spent by a compiler in covering their ancestry. Social boundaries were not suppressed but only briefly suspended during the enquiry.

However, these informal meetings could deteriorate into a more argumentative or intimidating relationship. Some customers used their purchasing power as a source of leverage. John Twemlow asked to be added to the article on the Fletcher baronets. John Fletcher Fenton Boughey, the second baronet, had just died in 1823 and his sister was married to one of their relatives. John Twemlow gently nudged Burke into accepting his narrative: 'if you do comply with my wishes, I shall want two or three copies'.[192] However, certain kinds of pressure turned into open conflicts. The publishers and their descendants preserved various letters which documented the way they had been poorly treated.

Bullying and ungrateful customers

William Betham kept several letters from angry clients. Some sent intimidating letters insisting on the need not to 'mutilate' their account, threatening to not pay the subscription or to discourage friends from investing in the scheme. One John Smith, from Sydling House (Dorset) wrote an incensed letter, 'feeling much hurt as well as disappointed in finding that you have not perform'd your promise'.[193] As there was much confusion in Smith's story, Betham had treated the entry carefully and suppressed several first names, replacing them by dashes: '—Smith, grandson of the last-mentioned Sir George, was consul general at Cadiz' and '——' married to 'Sir George Monk, Knt'.[194] John Smith, incensed by such precautionary measures, appealed to his honour: 'I so fully relied on your word as well as from a specimen you sent me of ye corrections requir'd that I sent up for the 4th vol.' Smith accused Betham of perjury and 'a particular disrespect if not contempt' of his honour as Betham had not taken Smith's instructions into consideration. Oscillating between threatening or a warmer tone, Smith commanded him to

[190] Ibid.
[191] On the growing practice of country house visiting, see Jon Stobart (ed.), *Travel and the British Country House: Cultures, Critiques and Consumption in the Long Eighteenth Century* (Manchester, 2017) and Peter Mandler, *The Fall and Rise of the Stately House* (New Haven, 1997).
[192] Twemlow to Burke, 10 Dec. 1825, CA, BC, vol. 55, case 23.
[193] Smith to Betham, 30 Aug. 1804, BL, Add. MS 21033, fol. 83.
[194] Betham, *New Baronetage*, vol. 3, 450.

300 SELLING ANCESTRY

publish a supplementary sheet reminding him that he was 'one for your first subscribers and one may say one of the warmest'.[195] He finished with a blunt statement: 'if ye above is comply'd with, it may be for your advantage, as it may lay in my power to promote ye sale of yr work'.[196] As a fellow of both the Society of Antiquaries and the Royal Society, Smith was in an influential position and it was much to Betham's credit that he refused to give in.

This exchange was not published but may have circulated among various hands in order to vindicate Betham's integrity. Conversely Arthur Collins's struggle with some families did not remain in the relative confidentiality of his diary. The diary is now missing from the Collinses' archives and we have only the extracts published by Nichols in 1814. He chose to select a few humiliating situations which turned out to be, in the long term, more embarrassing for his customers than for Collins's reputation. His meeting with the Portlands was described in much detail:

> Jan. 30, 1752. I breakfasted with their Graces the Duke and Duchess of Portland, with their two eldest daughters, Lady Elizabeth Cavendish Bentinck and Lady Henrietta Cavendish Bentinck, both very beautiful in their persons [...]. The discourse between us gave me an opportunity to say how I was descended and the misfortunes that attended my family and myself, on which they seemed to pity me, but said nothing more.[197]

The extract was intended to display the indifference of the wealthiest magnates to the plight of a hard-working publisher who had just carried out an exhaustive search of their papers. He then described the meanness of the duchess of Portland, who 'thinking of the expense', decided to have only two portraits of her ancestors printed, namely the countess of Shrewsbury and Lord Vere, at the expense of others.[198] Another extract dealt with the collective responsibility of the peers in leaving one of the brightest genealogists in a state of poverty. Collins depicted himself at the King's Levee. None of the peers thought of presenting him to the king: 'I stood so as to be seen by the Lords, as also the King, but, having never had the honour of being introduced to his Majesty, was unknown to him.'[199] Later, only Lord Gage ventured to defend him and chastised the other peers: he 'said to other Lords present at the same time: "Here is Collins, who has served us, and we do nothing for him", to which all the answers made was, "that the Ministry ought to show me more favour".'[200] None of them did much to help him. These were empty promises which failed to materialize. Nichols added that Collins was a 'most able and indefatigable writer', who finally obtained a more respectable

---

[195] Smith to Betham, 30 Aug. 1804, BL, Add. MS 21033, fol. 83.
[196] Ibid. [197] Nichols, *Literary Anecdotes*, vol. 8 (1815), 392–3.
[198] Ibid. [199] Ibid., 394. [200] Ibid.

THE KEYS TO A REWARDING POSTERITY   301

pension of £400, just at the end of his life.[201] Collins's reputation was further increased in these extracts by the ungratefulness of his patrons and clients. Collins appeared in Nichols's publication as a martyr to the genealogical cause and a living proof of the little interest that Whig magnates then had in their history. By his work and sacrifice, he displayed heroic virtues in contrast to vain Ladies and indifferent courtiers. Such tales helped to forge the misconception that Whig peers were not interested in their own genealogies. This view is not supported by documentary evidence but was formed in the early nineteenth century and has subsequently been repeated, notably by Anthony Wagner.[202]

Other publishers left a different legacy, a more positive image of themselves in a more dominating position. This was the case in particular of Thomas Wotton, who as a well-established bookseller was able to successfully confront certain difficult customers.

'Of great service to the Publick'

In his letter sent to all baronets, Wotton reminded them that his account of them 'will be of great service to the Publick'.[203] He depicted his scheme not as a commercial operation but as a selfless cooperative scheme, akin to a republic of letters. He had to strike a delicate balance between the flattery, the deference due to his customers, and the need to defend his credentials as a reliable publisher. Families were free to compose their articles as they pleased: 'the accounts which are here inserted, will be seen to vary pretty much, (gentlemen taking their own method in putting them together)'.[204] However Wotton did not neglect to mention the issues raised by the many errors found among his correspondents and in most sources. Honesty as well as his wide network of correspondents were instrumental in the making of his reputation.[205] He should not only be considered as a passive intermediary between his customers and the various antiquaries involved in his *Baronetage*. Implicitly, he endorsed a significant editorial role

---

[201] Ibid.

[202] On the considerable investment of Lady Oxford in genealogical practices, see Judith S. Lewis, 'When a House Is Not a Home: Elite English Women and the Eighteenth-Century Country House', *Journal of British Studies*, vol. 48, no. 2 (2009): 341–243. Commenting on the 'breakdown in heraldic authority', Anthony Wagner blamed the Whig grandees for the decline of the College of Arms: 'they had little interest in the strict regulation of a privilege—that of bearing arms—which they and the poorest gentry shared', *English Genealogy*, 117.

[203] Wotton correspondence, BL, Add. MS 24120, fol. 1.   [204] Wotton, *Baronetage*, iii.

[205] For a useful comparison with other London tradesmen and collectors, see Tim Somer: 'Tradesmen in Virtuoso Culture had a strong sense of their identity and hierarchical position. They were able to self-consciously justify their activities in terms of their use, value and "honesty." Turning to these activities highlights their important creative roles in the culture of curiosity.' 'Tradesmen in Virtuoso Culture: "Honest" John Bagford and His Collecting Network, 1683–1716', *Huntington Library Quarerly*, vol. 81, no. 3 (2018): 359–86 at 364.

302 SELLING ANCESTRY

which can be assessed by comparing family accounts and printed genealogies. He reserved the right to correct these errors and in particular, with the help of the clergy, when monumental inscriptions were concerned. He openly expressed doubt about certain families' claims, even naming a few of them, such as the J'Ansons, Bunces, and Courtenays, as 'their ancestors procured a sign manual for this title, but never took out their patents for it'.[206] In order to vindicate the seriousness of his publication, he even justified his intention to exclude them.

With regard to the Bunce and Courtenay families, Wotton did not take many risks. Sir James Bunce, allegedly the 6th baronet, died in 1741, and the 4th baronet Courtenay had died in 1700. The case of J'Anson was potentially more problematic as the claimants were still alive and desirous of appearing in the *Baronetage*. In a letter to Wotton, Sir Thomas J'Anson had vowed to give a substantial and 'liberal' amount of money to finance the publication: 'I look on mine (family) to have a place therein.'[207] As he had been forgotten in the first edition, he complained about this unfair treatment: 'should you pass my family by in silence on this occasion, it will be particularly injurious [...]. Yr complying with my request shall be recompensed in a present adequate to your own desire.'[208] Mixing threats with promises of gratification, Thomas J'Anson hoped to convince Wotton of his rightful claims. To establish the veracity of his assertions, Sir Thomas relied on several arguments. First, in the conventional manner, he explained that the destruction of the patent took place during the 'troubles' of the civil war 'which cost him a great part of his fortune and estate'.[209] Second, his brother was in possession of crucial evidence, namely a letter from Charles II in Paris written to 'Sir Bryan Janson' in 1651 in which the title was recognized. An attorney in the City, his brother 'who uses ye temple exchange coffee houses every evening [...] can more particularly inform you about ye patent given to my father for places in king James times'.[210] As often, it was when their claims were difficult to establish that customers insisted on meeting the publisher. Third, he came up with a story about the origin of his name, from the French noble of Janson who 'gives rise to the jansénistes at present (much) talk'd of there (France) [...]. After some continued residence in England they new modelld their name by putting a stop between ye J and ye A.'[211] Thomas J'Anson may have hoped that the Jansenists were little known in England, not to mention their founder Cornelius Jansen, Catholic bishop of Ypres. He may himself have believed in his own story. However, he underestimated the fact that during the Restoration the debates between the Jesuits and their opponents were followed on the other side of the Channel by many Anglican clerics as it fitted into the attempts to pave the way for a *via media* between two perceived extremes: the most uncompromising Calvinists and the abhorred Jesuits. Antiquaries and scientists such as Robert

---

[206] Wotton, *Baronetage*, vi. [207] J'Anson to Burke, May 1739, BL, Add. MS 24121, fol. 10.
[208] Ibid. [209] Ibid., fol. 12. [210] Ibid. [211] Ibid.

Boyle and John Evelyn expressed much interest in the controversy.[212] As Wotton's target audience included many clergymen, J'Anson's extraordinary claims would not have gone down too well. One could easily allege to descend from the Normans but a dubious reference to the eighteenth-century *jansénistes* was more problematic. The public was more lenient about many fictions relating to remote ancestors but contemporary phenomena—such as the Jansenist crisis, which was much discussed in Britain—were seen with a more critical eye. There were in fact many other families who did not have a copy of their patent but J'Anson's narrative was dismissed for other motives. An impoverished family in Kent, Wotton took little risk in ignoring their appeal and gained much profit in advertising the fair exclusion of certain dubious claims.[213]

On other occasions, Wotton tried to convince baronets to amend specific details when he had some more reliable sources. Concerning the Martins of Long Melford, when we compare the two pedigrees in Wotton's possession, we can reconstitute a complete redrafting of the family's version. William Holman established from some funeral inscriptions in Essex that the first ancestor, Laurence Martin, was the 'first that occurs to our enquiry. He deceased about 1460, lyed burried in Melford Church under a large tomb.'[214] Wotton's customer, Sir Roger Martin, claimed to go back further, to the time of the 'Heptarchie, with the kingly race, by the marriage of Joan de la Piddle' in Dorset.[215] Wotton was eager to balance Sir Roger Martin's groundless account with all the data provided by Holman. To convince Sir Roger of the need to change his narrative, Wotton attempted to engage with him at a more personal level. Hence, he invited him to 'drink a bottle together' in the City and so, finally Martin, this 'hearty and merry old gentleman', accepted the modifications.[216] Most of the time, Wotton was trying hard to please his customers and, in doing so, he let the inconsistencies between accounts remain visible. Wotton managed to strike the difficult balance between integrating as many family elements as possible while maintaining the general credibility of the publication.

Conclusion to part III

Family participation was not in itself sufficient. An extra layer of certification was required and provided from dozens of antiquaries spread all over in Britain. By

---

[212] Mark R. F. Williams, 'Translating the Jansenist Controversy in Britain and Ireland', *English Historical Review*, vol. 134, no. 566 (2019), 59–91.

[213] J'Anson did not appear in Hasted, *History and Topography of the County of Kent* (Canterbury, 1797).

[214] See the manuscript accounts provided by Holman and the baronets, BL, Add. MS 24121, fol. 72.

[215] *The English Baronetage*, vol. 3.2, 520.

[216] 'Sir Roger Martin called lately on me and we drank a bottle together, he is a hearty and merry old gentleman. He approved of his account', Wotton to Holman, Essex RO, D/Y 1/1/199/22.

304 SELLING ANCESTRY

considering the antiquarian community through its diversity and divisions, it becomes easier to understand why some compilers were taken seriously in their lifetime or posthumously, while others were denigrated and discarded. No agreement existed on the boundaries between antiquarian and genealogical forms of knowledge. The criteria used to assess their works closely depended on the specific context. The dismissal of Arthur Collins by Sir Egerton Brydges was later shared by J. H. Round with the same arguments: 'his want of means', his lack of the 'manly independence which made Dugdale refuse to flatter family pride'.[217] Round's comments were later shared by Anthony Wagner, who compared him unfavourably to Dugdale, a distinguished antiquary and, like him, a senior member of the College of Arms.[218] In the late eighteenth century, after the French Revolution, prominent publishers such as John Nichols made a case for Collins and Wotton. The multiplication of biographical dictionaries led to the reappraisal of specific skills. Though they did not fit into the category of gentle-men amateurs, some compilers were recognized as possessing a distinctive talent: Wotton for being a broker between the scattered county antiquaries and the bookselling world, and Collins for his ambitious and systematic archival mining.

The changing fortunes of some of these hard worker drudges, such as Wotton or Collins, from dismissal to rehabilitation, brings out the need to closely histori-cize the notions of trust and credibility. John Burke's reputation came from his familiarity with Scott's historical novels and the silver fork authors. Fictions were not only consumed for entertainment's sake. To a large readership, they provided some much sought-after insight into the social elites during the debates on the Reform Act. Burke's compilations were part of a larger narrative, combining fact and fiction, on the whereabouts of the upper echelons of society during the London season and on the tragic or glorious lives of their ancestors. The making of a good reputation may have been facilitated by the authors during their lifetime or even by their descendants. Collins left many manuscripts and prints which vindicated his work and were later used in his favour in *The Gentleman's Magazine* and the *Literary Anecdotes*. The nature of the power dynamic that they established with their customers was crucial. Since from the start they were suspected of complaisance and mercenary behaviour, the memories of their struggles with their customers could also be put to good use.

Other compilers were less lucky and fell into oblivion. In particular, those who did not belong to certain respectable institutions of knowledge, such as the College of Arms, the Society of Antiquaries, or the Stationers' Company, generated little interest. They were often derided for their lack of originality or financial depend-ence. Some London booksellers were dismissed for being moved solely by financial gain. These kinds of genealogical publications were viewed by many antiquaries as

---

[217] J. H. Round, *Family Origins and Other Studies* (London, 1930), 7–8.
[218] Wagner, *English Genealogy*, 329.

suspect and likely to attract the wrong kind of person: fraudsters, con men, dubious lawyers. Prejudices against scribblers and mercenary authors were transmitted from some contemporaries to later generations of historians. For respected authors such as William Godwin or William Guthrie, their compiling activities did not draw much attention either. Their *Peerages* were seen as an insignificant digression, compiled simply to make ends meet or obtain some ministerial patronage. It is worth mentioning the idiosyncratic posterity of Sir Egerton Brydges. Though a baronet and a member of several antiquarian institutions, his reputation as a fraudster and a con artist was discussed in his lifetime. Brydges, moreover, did not help his partisans by expressing in his *Autobiography* sentiments that were in direct opposition to the antiquarian ethos. He openly despised his neighbours who 'were addicted neither to literary nor intellectual pursuits, nor had they any idea of name or pedigree beyond the aboriginal plough-tail squires of the soil'.[219] He described himself as a 'lonely, melancholy, moralizing man', who 'always advocated seclusion and meditation'.[220] Such a mindset did not sit well with the implicit rules on which the study of antiquity was grounded: friendship, collaboration, and selflessness. The making of a reputation was faced with many hurdles and since a good deal of factors were at play, the outcome was rather unpredictable. The destruction of collections or their dispersal in a lot of repositories throws a veil over the work and merits of compilers.

In 2021, their reputation is still a matter for debate. In the notice displayed in the Debrett's website to advertise the first online edition of their *Peerage and Baronetage*, Collins is described as an outsider, lacking the connections 'to gain access to family records held by various title holders' and so he developed 'a tendency to flatter them' whereas John Almon was 'a well-respected and liked man'.[221] John Debrett, Almon's 'protegé', worked 'with a keen eye, removing any descents left over from Collins's work that he considered uncertain' and 'this ethos that has been the mainstay of subsequent Debrett editors and remains our number one rule to this day.'[222]

---

[219] Brydges, *Autobiography*, vol. 1, 214.   [220] Ibid., vol. 2, 247.

[221] 'The Genealogy of Books', Retrieved 10 Jan. 2021, from https://debretts.com/our-story/the-genealogy-of-books>. This interpretation is put forward by 'Dr Susan Morris, Director of Research at Debrett Ancestry Ltd.'

[222] Ibid.

Conclusion

The main objective of this research has been to re-establish the significance of family directories across the eighteenth century. Such publications merit reinstatement into a general narrative from which they were retrospectively ousted. Employed by contemporaries as reference tools to navigate through a dynamic and changing society, they should not be interpreted as signs of a surviving 'Ancien Régime'. The impulse to recover a sense of place or to claim roots was part and parcel of the commercial and imperial growth. Nor should they be considered an 'abased' product from a dying lineage society, since the notion of abasement would imply the pre-existence of an 'authentic' genealogical culture. The latter has constantly been reconfigured to meet new demands, up to the modern day. The use of family directories was not limited to iconic old squires poring over them in private libraries, since they were also carried in many pockets throughout Britain and its colonies, or annotated to mark the latest birth in the family or to record gossip.

In a first part, these directories are placed back in the context of the larger printing culture. Although it fitted into a more general process of commercialization in British society, the book market was still highly segregated and segmented into different categories. Some of the *Pocket Peerages* and *Baronetages* belonged to the growing sector of reference books which included almanacs, travel guides, and urban directories. Dedicated to a wider audience of readers, they provided an updated snapshot of the landed elite in an urban context. Some more work should be done on how these guides were precisely used by middling-sort buyers. Another type of compilation, published mostly in octavo and multi-volume sets, catered to less practical needs and fed politer tastes. Inspired by the most successful historians of the times, their authors composed long prefaces vindicating the publications' didactic and social values. Whether aimed at the general public or the scions of the landed elite, they were marketed as British histories told from a family and dynastic point of view. Monumental folios, gilded and enriched with detailed engravings, belonged to yet another category of object, clearly destined for the upper end of the market. Under the patronage of prominent lords and ministers, they were published to celebrate decisive events such as the Scottish Act of Union, the accession of George III to the throne, or military triumphs over the French during the revolutionary wars.

Such a functional breakdown into three groups should not be exaggerated, for research related to reading practices reveals a more complex picture. Pocket

---

Selling Ancestry: Family Directories and the Commodification of Genealogy in Eighteenth-Century Britain. Stéphane Jettot, Oxford University Press. © Stéphane Jettot 2023. DOI: 10.1093/oso/9780192865960.003.0008

CONCLUSION 307

directories were used by middling-sort readers in order to emulate the ways of their social superiors and in the hopes of obtaining their protection or recognition. They were acquired by members of the landed elite in their ever-increasing journeying to the metropolis and across Britain. An unresolved underlying tension continued to exist between the need for practical guides and the desire to see one's name included in a more exclusive and gratifying publication. Irrespective of format or price, most such directories belonged to the larger portfolio of copyrights held by London booksellers. Through their commercial networks, secondhand catalogues, and circulating libraries, the latter were in a position to ensure a wide distribution of their products in Britain as well as the Atlantic anglosphere, thus ensuring a larger circulation than previously anticipated. Surviving marginalia also demonstrates that readers assigned uses to their compilations for which they had not initially been destined by their publishers. They added further information about their own families, or gossip and rumours about others. It was by emulating these writing practices that, after the 1770s, several fake directories printed both praise and derogatory comments on titled families. Publishers made use of them to contribute to a patriotic campaign against aristocratic vice.

The second part of this enquiry concerns the methods used by the London publishers to gather data on families. Publishers' enquiries triggered an exchange of thousands of letters and documents between them and various family members. In such correspondence, I have endeavoured to better identify the customers' identities and demands, initially by employing a prosopographical approach to obtain an overview of the groups of correspondents involved in the publishing process. Across the long eighteenth century, three main publications have been selected: Thomas Wotton's *Baronetage* (1727–40), William Betham's *New Baronetage* (1800–5), and John Burke's *Commoners* (1827–30). This enquiry led me to look for distinctive features in those who corresponded with each selected publication: their place of residence, age, political and religious affiliations, and historical interest. During the first Hanovers, Wotton's clients mostly belonged to the northern counties landed elites who had risen to prominence during the Restoration. They were keen to elaborate on their deeds during the first British revolution in favour of the Stuarts, while at the same time distancing themselves from the Jacobite cause. Their contribution and insistence on the seventeenth-century political crisis fitted into a partisan feud between Whigs and Tories. The latter felt they were ostracized and lampooned by the former and so used Wotton's *Baronetage* to defend their past and reputation. In contrast, Betham's correspondents were recent baronets. From the first generation to hold a title, they owed their elevation to their support of Pitt the Younger's policies. Many were of Irish and Scottish descent, close to the EIC and had an interest in the Catholic cause. While keen to insist on their loyalty during the French revolutionary wars, they expressed a strong predilection for the Tudor era, when certain landed families had been sidelined by the Reformation and Irish wars. Unsurprisingly, John Burke's

308 SELLING ANCESTRY

correspondents expressed yet another set of wishes. Devised in the context of the Catholic Emancipation Act and the Great Reform Act, the first volume of the *Commoners* would regroup all the non-titled families who composed the backbone of the landed elite. Corresponding from all over the counties, hundreds of families wrote to Burke and his publisher, the successful Colburn. They were more likely to provide details about the source of their incomes since mercantile interests were no longer seen as derogatory. However, industrial activities were still deemed ill-bred. Notably older than the two other groups of respondents, Burke's clients were more likely to see genealogy as a form of leisure and expressed much enthusiasm in the medieval era. Burke's pedigrees abounded with fantastic gothic tales which later precipitated their dismissal by positivist historians.

This correspondence contains a wealth of information on customer households. It had been previously assumed that their heads were 'naturally' in charge of the family narrative. Much effort was made by the publisher in promoting the scientific value of customers' contributions. Patriarchy was celebrated both as a social virtue and as a criterion for the reliability of the articles. The diversity and the authenticity of the family archives were put to the fore and described in much detail. Heads of households were presented as co-authors of a vast historical enterprise, along with more established authorities such as famous antiquaries and historians. However, some gradual change took place across the eighteenth century. After 1800, collateral lines were increasingly recognized along with the main branch, and extended ties in kinship were more valued than previously. Generally speaking, cadets and female and lower-class correspondents were edited out of the final text although progressively their contributions were more openly acknowledged. From the letters, it seems that these vast enquiries among the kin usually took place in a spirit of goodwill and mutual interest. However, publishers encountered certain family feuds which they frequently had to arbitrate. Rivalries and resentment among siblings, different ancestral lines, or stepchildren were openly exposed.

A third part is devoted to the epistemological status of these directories and poor reputations of their authors. I saw the role played by families in the editing process and then considered the social identity of the compilers. Ideally, to secure their reputation as trustworthy publishers, they would have antiquarian expertise and some gentility. As undertakers, they were accused of lacking both. Despite their commercial success, they were often looked down upon as mere scribes and mercenary authors. Many commentators in the literary gazettes and antiquarian circles dismissed these publications as unreliable and outdated. Undisputedly, the Enlightenment period was characterized by a shift away from the typical single-male-line pedigree and the obsession with ancestry and birth. There are countless examples of letters, tracts, novels, and paintings aimed at ridiculing these compilations. However, the uncertain boundaries between truth and lies, history and genealogy were grounded in specific contexts and were open to

CONCLUSION   309

different interpretations. At the centre of the arguments formulated against family directories was the publishers' dubious social status. Through the examples of John Stockdale, William Guthrie, and Edward Kimber, the criticisms directed at them were less centred around their abilities as historians than their financial dependence. Established institutions such as the Society of Antiquaries or the College of Arms were instrumental in several smear campaigns against compilers who were suspected of false expertise and impersonations. However, offensives were more difficult to mount when, as in the case of Sir Egerton Brydges, the accused was from a genteel background.

Despite this hostile context, it is worth noting that a few compilers managed to make a name for themselves. Late in the eighteenth century, earlier compilers such as Arthur Collins or Thomas Wotton came to be rehabilitated by several influential individuals such as John Nichols: the former for his ability to build unprecedented archives and the latter for his capability to connect with the best antiquarian experts in Britain. His individual family histories were established partly through a collective endeavour by antiquaries, genealogists, and more distant family members. John Burke built up a favourable reputation by anchoring his pedigrees in the popular world of historical novels, quoting extensively from Walter Scott and his various works. Additional factors may be put forward to account for their reputation. Compilers' descendants intervened to retrospectively reconfigure their own ancestry in a more advantageous manner. The record of conflicts with bullying customers was staged to the benefit of the compilers, who portrayed themselves as defenders of the public trust against unfair manipulation.

These compilations were intended to demonstrate the existence of a stable and well-ordered social fabric but they often triggered parodies and gossip about families which were designed to be celebrated. Birth alone was never seen as sufficient basis for distinction. They praised old and well-established dynasties while simultaneously being invested by an even greater number of aspirational elites. They were aimed at materializing a comforting family order under the wise guidance of fathers and elder sons. But their completion led to bitter quarrels among kin and competing demands. Genealogical sources such as legal records enable historians to measure the gap between prescriptive discourse and actual behaviour. They demonstrate that wealth in itself is never sufficient to legitimize social superiority.

The emergence of family directories is only the beginning of the enduring success of the Debrett's and Burke's brands. In his most recent publication, Thomas Piketty pointed out the significance of these registers to the survival of noble values among the European elites.[1] In his memoir published in 1932,

---

[1] 'His lists of names and lineages soon became the ultimate reference for the study of British Aristocracy of this era. His authoritative listing filled a need because there was no official compilation of members of the gentry, even though it was the largest subgroup of the nobility. The first *Burke's*

310 SELLING ANCESTRY

a reformed criminal going under the pseudonym of Stuart Wood explained how he was using various reference works to impersonate various identities to pursue his illegal activities:

> Works of reference in public libraries furnished me with whatever data I required about particular families and professions—Burke's, 'Who's Who', Crockford, the Army List, the Navy List, the University Registers and Year Books—until in due course I was able to engage in the game of thrust and parry with all kinds of people and keep my end up.[2]

Along with a reflection on the abuses of the prison system, his memoirs provide a portrait of a self-educated criminal who managed to navigate into different worlds, notably in the military and naval service. He described the practical utility of these directories in gaining a specific cultural capital likely to be trusted by his social superiors. While regretting his crime, the memorialist underlined his remarkable skill in inventing various profiles to fit his targeted public. Some family names managed to withstand the considerable turmoil of two world wars and profound changes in the property market. Although it has little general value, in the digital age it is striking to observe the survival of several names and their narratives. The Abneys, whose family was extensively commented on by Burke, now specialize in management consulting according to the Abney Global website.[3] It would be worth studying how and to what extent current owners of county estates, either privately or in conjunction with the National Trust, tap into the narrative printed in Burke's or Debrett's.

In today's digital age, these directories no longer assume the role of arbiter of who counts and who does not; they are something of the past. These brands attempt to survive in the internet age by diversifying their activities. In 2019 Debrett's stopped publishing the printed version of *The Peerage and Baronetage*, which will henceforth be accessible in digital form only. It advertises itself

---

Peerage, published in 1826, met with such resounding success that it was revised and reprinted throughout the century. [...] One finds similar catalogs, royal almanacs, and *bottins mondains* in many other countries, starting with the *Livro de Linhagen* compiled in the thirteenth and fourteenth centuries and continuing through the annual compilation of the nineteenth and twentieth centuries. Here, nobles and their allies could take stock, sing their own praises, and express their demands'. *Capital and Ideology* (Cambridge, Mass., 2020), 174.

[2] *Shades of the prison house: A personal memoir* (London, 1932), 104–5. <http://www.open.ac.uk/Arts/reading/UK/record_details.php?id=12654>, accessed 26 June 2017.

[3] The genealogical account of the Abneys since Magna Carta and the Norman d'Aubigny family, is justified as followed: 'One-thousand years of leadership history. We firmly believe that Abney Global is more than just a business partner to our clients. Our reputation casts a lofty shadow over your reputation. That is why we urge you to investigate who we are, and what type of background we come from.' <https://abneyglobal.com/abney-family/>

as a 'professional coaching company, publisher and authority on etiquette and behaviour' and counts among its clients Ford, Airbnb, and Sotheby's.[4]

Compared to the slow growth of family compilation, the commercialization of ancestry is now 'on steroïds'. Millions of individuals are tapping into online resources or provide genetic materials in order to establish their own ancestry. This remarkable genealogical impulse owes little to the defence of or search for noble ancestry. It is described as a peaceful recreational activity or as an attempt to root one's identity, either collective or personal, in a larger time span. However, the geneticization of genealogies completely transformed the problematics around ancestry. DNA is now used on an industrial scale in legal cases or more broadly in one's thirst for one's origins (ADN MyHeritage, Ancestry DNA). The growing popularity of DNA testing via websites is a new step after the pedigree craze of the early modern period and the age of family directories, which may have dangerous consequences as it contributes to and benefits from the confusion generated between ancestry and genetics.

---

[4] <https://www.debretts.com/>.

APPENDICES

APPENDICES

List of *Peerages* and *Baronetages* (1700–1835)

	Imprint date	Title	Author	Publishers	Volume	Format	Price	Dedication
1	1709	*Peerage of England, or an Historical Account of the Present Nobility*	NS	A. Roper; A. Collins	1	8vo	6s./10s.	
2	1710	*Peerage of England or a Genealogical Account of all the Flourishing Families of this Kingdom*	NS	A. Roper; A. Collins	1	8vo	6s.	
3	1711	Id. (re-ed.)	NS	A. Collins; E. Sanger	1	8vo	6s.	
4	1712	*Honores Anglicani*	Simon Segar	J. Baker	1	8vo		Edward Harley
5	1714	*Peerage of England* (re-ed.)	NS	A. Roper; A. Collins	2	8vo	10s. 6d.	
6	1715	Id. (re-ed.)	NS	A. Collins; J. Morphew	1	8vo	10s. 6d.	
7	1716	Id. (re-ed.)	NS	A. Collins	1	8vo	10s. 6d.	
8	1716	*Peerage of Scotland*	George Crawfurd	Printed for the author	1	folio		
9	1717	*Peerage of England* (re-ed.)	NS	W. Taylor	2	8vo		
10	1718	*British Compendium: or a particular Account of all the present Nobility*	Francis Nichols	J. Smith; C. King; J. Graves; T. Griffiths	1	16mo 16mo	5s.	

Continued

	Imprint date	Title	Author	Publishers	Volume	Format	Price	Dedication
11	1719	Id. (re-ed.)	Francis Nichols	A. Bettesworth	1	16mo	5s.	
12	1720	*Baronettage of England*	Arthur Collins	W. Taylor; R. Gosling; J. Osborn	2	8vo	10s.	John Anstis
13	1721	*British Compendium* (re-ed.)	Francis Nichols	A. Bettesworth; C Hitch; R. Nutt.	1	12mo	5s.	
14	1722	*Irish Compendium*	Francis Nichols	A. Bettesworth; C Hitch; R. Nutt.	1	16mo	6s.	Gerald de Courcy, 19th Baron Kinsale
15	1725	*British Compendium* (re-ed.)	Francis Nichols	A. Bettesworth; C Hitch; R. Nutt.	2	16mo	7s.	
16	1725	*Peerage of Ireland*	Aaron Crossley	T. Hume (Dublin)	1	folio		Lord Carteret, Lord Lieutenant
17	1727	*English Baronets*	Thomas Wotton	T. Wotton	3	12mo	10s.	Sir Holland Egerton
18	1727	*English Baronage*	Arthur Collins	R. Gosling	1	4to	16s.	Sir Robert Walpole
19	1729	*British Compendium* (re-ed.)	Francis Nichols	A. Bettesworth; G. Strahan; J. Clarke; D. Browne; J. Stagg; J. Jackson	1	16mo	7s.	
20	1735	*Peerage of England* (1st)	Arthur. Collins	R. Gosling; T. Wotton; W. Innys; R. Manby	3	8vo	£1. 4s	Duke of Rutland, Lord Talbot, earl of Halifax, Robert Walpole.
21	1735	*The Irish Compendium* (re-ed.)	Francis Nichols	J. & P. Knapton; C. Hitch; T. Astley; A. Millar	1	12mo	7s.	
22	1741	*Peerage of England* (re-ed.)	Arthur Collins	W. Innys; R. Manby; T. Wotton; F. Gosling	4	8vo	£1. 4s.	Duke of Rutland, earl of Shaftesbury, Viscount Lymington, Robert Walpole

No.	Year	Title	Author	Publisher	Vols	Format	Price	Dedicatee
23	1741	*Baronetage of England*	Thomas Wotton	T. Wotton	5	8vo	£1. 15s.	
24	1750	*A supplement to the four volumes of the Peerage*	Arthur Collins	S. Birt; W. Cox; W. Innys, P. Knapton; H. Shute, D. Withers; T. Wotton	2	8vo		Lord Viscount Cobham, earl of Northumberland
25	1751	*A short View of the Families of the Present English Nobility*	Nathaniel Salmon	W. Owen; G. Woodfall	1	12mo	3s.	
26	1752	*Scots Compendium* (re-ed.)	Francis Nichols	J. and P. Knapton; C. Hitch; L. Hawes; T. Astley;R. Baldwin; A. Millar	1	8vo		
27	1753	*British Compendium* (re-ed.)	Francis Nichols	J. and P. Knapton; C. Hitch; L. Hawes; T. Astley; R. Baldwin; A. Millar	3	16mo	7s.	
28	1754	*Peerage of Ireland*	John Lodge	W. Johnston	4	8vo	£1. 4s	Marcus Beresford, earl of Tyrone, Baron Newport, Lord Southwell, Sir Robert King
29	1756	*Peerage of England* (re-ed.)	Arthur Collins	H. S. Cox; P. Davey; C. Hitch; W. Innys; L. Hawes; W. Johnston; B. Law; R. Manby; J. Richardson; J. and J. Rivington; T. Wotton; E. Withers	5	8vo	£1. 4s	George II (1)earl of Shaftesbury (2) earl of Holderness (3) earl of Northumberland (4) Lord Abergavenny (5)
30	1758	*Short View of the Families of the Present English Nobility*	Nathaniel Salmon	W. Owen	1	12mo	1s. 6d.	
31	1761	*English Compendium* (re-ed.)	Francis Nichols	C. Hitch and L. Hawes; A. Millar, H. Woodfall; W. Strahan [and 11 others in London)	3	8vo	7s.	

Continued

	Imprint date	Title	Author	Publishers	Volume	Format	Price	Dedication
32	1762	*A Complete History of the English Peerage*	William Guthrie	J. Newbery; S. Crowder and Co; J. Coote; J. Gretton;T. Davies; W. Johnston; G. Kearsley, J. Osborne	2	4to	£2. 2s.	George III
33	1762	*Peerage of Scotland*	Sir Robert Douglas	R. Fleming (Edinburgh); A. Miller, R. Baldwin; D. Wilson, T. Durham	1	folio	£1. 16s.	James Douglas, earl of Morton
34	1763	*Short View of the families* (re-ed.)	Nathaniel Salmon	W. Owen	1	12mo	1s. 6d.	
35	1764	*Baronagium Genealogicum*	Joseph Edmonson	Sold by Him at his house.	5 vols	folio	£25. 5s.	George III, duke of York, duke of Gloucester, duke of Cumberland, prince of Wales
36	1765	*List of the English, Scots and Irish Nobility*	Charles Whitworth	C. Marsh; J. Millan; R. Davies, J. Robson	1	12mo	3s.	
37	1766	*Complete English Peerage*	Alexander Jacob	J. Wilson; J. Fell;J. Robson	2	folio	£5	Duke of Chandos
38	1766	*Peerage of England.* (re-ed.)	Edward Kimber	J. Almon; R. Baldwin; W. Bathoe; J. Fuller; Johnson and Co; B. Law; T. Longman; T. Lowndes; W. Nicoll; Z. Stuart; J. Wilkie, H.& G Woodfall	1	12mo	3s.	

39	1768	Mr Collins's Peerage (re-ed.)		H. Woodfall; J. Beecroft; W. Strahan; J. Rivington; W. Sandby; J. Fuller; R. Baldwin; L. Hawes; W. Clarke and R. Collins; R. Horsefield; W. Johnston; T. Caslon; S. Crowder; T. Longman; C. Rivington, W. Griffin; M. and J. Shuckburgh; W. Nicoll; S. Bladon; M. Folingsby; T. Payne; J. Ronson; T. Davies; R. Davis; J. Almon; H. Gardner	7	8vo	£2. 6s.	George III
40	1768	New Accurate Peerage of Ireland		J. Almon	2	8vo	12s.	
41	1768	Peerage of England	Edward Kimber	H. Woodfall, J. Fuller, G. Woodfall, R. Baldwin, W. Johnston, B. Law, T. Longman, T. Lowndes; J Wilkie, J. Johnson and J. Payne, Z. Stuart, W. Nicoll, E. Johnson, and M. Bathoe	1	12mo	3s.	
42	1768	Peerage of Scotland	Edward Kimber	H. Woodfall; J. Fuller; G. Woodfall; R. Baldwin; W. Johnston; and 9 others in London)	1	12mo	6s.	

Continued

	Imprint date	Title	Author	Publishers	Volume	Format	Price	Dedication
43	1768	*Peerage of Ireland*	Edward Kimber	H. Woodfall; J. Fuller; G. Woodfall; R. Baldwin; W. Johnston, B. Law; T. Longman; T. Lowndes; J. Wilkins; J. Johnson; W. Bathoe; Z. Stuart; W. Nicoll; E. Johnson	2	8vo	6s.	Lord Clive
44	1768	*Peerage of Scotland*	Robert Douglas	J. Donaldson	1	folio		James Douglas, earl of Morton
45	1769	*Pocket Herald; or, A complete View of the present Peerage of England, Scotland and Ireland*	Edward Kimber	J. Almon; R. Balwin; S. Crowder; S. Bladon; F. Newbery; G. Law; T. Carslon; G. Kearsley; J. and T. Curtis; Richardson & Urquhart	2	18vo	7s.	
46	1769	*Extinct Peerage*	Solomon Bolton	J. Rivington; J. Robson; T. Longman	1	8vo	5s.	
47	1769	*Extinct Peerage*	Edward Kimber	J. Almon	1	12mo	3s.	
48	1769	*British Compendium* (re-ed.)		A. Millar; H. Woodfall; W. Strahan; J. Rivington; R. Baldwin; E. Stevens; L. Hawes and Co. G. Keith; S. Crowder; B. Law; R. Horsfield; J. Wilkie; J. Johnson and Co[vant]; T. Pote	3	16mo		

49	1769	*The Pocket Herald; or, A Complete View of the Present Peerage of England, Scotland and Ireland*		J. Almon; R, Baldwin; R. Beecroft; J. Bew; T. Cadell; T. Caslon; T. Crowder; S Davis; W. Dilly, J. Donaldson; J. Evans; M. Folingsby; M. Fielding and W. Fox; W. Gardner; H. Lasher; T. Longman; T. Lowndes, J. Murray; J. Nichols; W. Owen; W. Payne; T. Rivington; C. Robson; G. Robinson; W. Strahan; J. White	3	12mo/8vo	10s./12s.
50	1769	*New Peerage*		W. Owen; R. Davis	3	12mo	5s.
51	1769	*New Baronetage*		J. Almon	3	12mo	10s. 6 d.
52	1769	*A Complete English Peerage*	Alexander Jacob	J. Wilson & J. Fell, J. Robson	1	folio	£5. 5s.
53	1771	*The Baronetage of England*	Richard Johnson	G. Woodfall. J. Fuller; E. Johnson; Clarke &Collins; W. Johnston; S. Crowder; J. Wilkie; T. Longman; B. Law; T. Lowndes; T. Caslon; Robinson & Roberts; W. Nicoll; R. Baldwin; Z. Stuart; W. Davis	3	8vo	
54	1772	*The Complete English Peerage*	Frederic Barlow	T. Evans; S. Bladon	2	8vo	12s.

Continued

	Imprint date	Title	Author	Publishers	Volume	Format	Price	Dedication
55	1776	*Companion to the Peerage*	JosephEdmonson	H. Reynell, J. Ridley, J. Walter	1	8vo	1s.	
56	1778	*Pocket Peerage of Great Britain*	Barak Longmate	W. Smith	1	8vo	2s.	
57	1778	*The New Peerage* (re-ed.)	Edward Kimber	W. Owen; L. Davis; W. Davis	3	8vo		
58	1778	*Collins's Peerage* (re-ed.)	Barak Longmate	W. Strahan; J. F. and C. Rivington; J. Hinton; T. Payne; W. Owen; S. Crowder; T. Caslon; T. Longman; C. Rivington; C. Dilly; J. Robson; T. Lowndes; G. Robinson; T. Cadell; H. L. Gardner; W. Davis; J. Nichols; T. Evans; J. Bew; R. Baldwin; J. Almon; J. Murray; W. Fox; J. White; Fielding and Walker; T. Beecroft; J. Donaldson; M. Folingsby	8	8vo	£3. 1s. 6d.	George III
59	1779	*Peerage of the Nobility*	Hugh Clark; Thomas Wormull	G. Kearsley; C. Talbot	8	8vo	2s. 6d.	
60	1779	*Collins's Peerage* (re-ed.)	Barak Longmate	W. Strahan; J. F. and C. Rivington; J. Hinton; T. Payne; W. Owen; S. Crowder; T. Caslon;	8	8vo	£2. 12s.	George III

				T. Longman; C. Rivington; C. Dilly; J. Robson; T. Lowndes; G. Robinson; T. Cadell; H. L. Gardner; W. Davis; J. Nichols; T. Evans; J. Bew; R. Baldwin; J. Almon; J. Murray; W. Fox; J. White; Fielding and Walker; T. Beecroft; J. Donaldson; M. Folingsby.			
61	1782	*A New Pocket Peerage. Origin, Progress and Present State*		J. Fielding	2	12mo	2s.
62	1784	*A Supplement to the Fifth Edition of Collins's Peerage of England*	Barak Longmate	W. Strahan, J. F. and C. Rivington, T. Payne and Son, W. Owen, S. Crowder;T. Longman, C. Rivington, C. Dilly, J. Robson, T. and W. Lowndes, G. Robinson, T. Cadell, H. L. Gardner, J. Nichols, J. Bew, R. Baldwin, J. Murray; J. Debrett, W. Fox, J. White, J. Walker, T. Beecroft, and M. Folingsby		8vo	7s. 6d.

Continued

	Imprint date	Title	Author	Publishers	Volume	Format	Price	Dedication
63	1784	*The New Peerage* (re-ed.)	Edward Kimber	W. Owen; L. Davis; J. Debrett (successor to Mr Almon)	3	8vo		
64	1784	*Baronagium Genealogicum*	Joseph Edmonson	Printed for the author, and sold by him, at his house in Warwick Street Golden Square		folio	£18. 18s.	George III
65	1785	*A Satirical Peerage of England*	Charles Coleman	G. Lister		4to	2s.	
66	1786	*The New Peerage*	William Godwin	G. G. J. Robinson	3		11s.	
67	1788	*The Pocket Peerage of England, Scotland, & Ireland*	Philip Luckombe	J. F. & C. Rivington; T. Longman, S. Crowder; G. G. J. & J. Robinson; R. Baldwin [and 15 others in London]	2	12mo	7s.	
68	1788	*Heraldry in Miniature*		J. F. & C. Rivington; T. Longman; S. Crowder; G. G. J. & J. Robinson; R. Baldwin; W. Richardson; J. Bew; J. Bladon; W. Lowndes	2	12mo		
69	1789	*Lodge's Peerage of Ireland*	Archdall, Mervyn	J. Moore (Dublin); J. Robinson	7	8vo	£2. 16s	Baron Cobham
70	1789	*The Present Peerage of Great Britain*		J. Stockdale	1	12mo	7s. 6d.	

71	1790	*Pocket Peerage* (re-ed.)	BarakLongmate	J. F. & C. Rivington; T. Longman, S. Crowder; G. G. J. & J. Robinson; R. Baldwin; W. Richardson; J. Bew; J. Bladon; W. Lowndes; J. Debrett	2	12mo	9s.	
72	1790	*Complete Peerage of England, Scotland and Ireland.*		G. Kersley	1	16mo		
73	1790	*The English Peerage*	William Godwin, Charles Catton	G. G. J. Robinson	3	4to	£3. 3s.	
74	1790	*The Peerage of England, Scotland and Ireland*		W. Owen; L. Davis; J. Debrett	3	8vo		
75	1790–1800	*Complete Peerage of England, Scotland and Ireland.*		G & C. Kearsley	1	16mo		
76	1790	*Fielding's New Peerage*		J. Murray; J. Stockdale		12mo		
77	1791	*Peerage directory*		P. W. Clarke; J. Debrett		12mo	1s.	
78	1793	*Pocket Peerage* (re-ed.)	BarakLongmate		2	12mo	9s.	
79	1793	*The Peerage of Great Britain and Ireland*	Robert Pollard	C. Dilly; J. Edwards; R. White & P. Byrne (Dublin); Laurie & Symington (Edinburgh)	1	4to	£1 11s./ vol.	George III
80	1798	*The Baronage of Scotland*	George Douglas	Bell & Bradfute; W. Creech; J. Dickson; E. Balfour; P. Hill; W. Laing; A. Guthrie, J. Watson; Manners & Miller; A. Constable; Cadell & Davies.	2	folio		

Continued

	Imprint date	Title	Author	Publishers	Volume	Format	Price	Dedication
81	1801–5	*New Baronetage*	William Betham	W. Miller; E. Lloyd	5	4to	£7. 6s.	James Cecil, marquess of Salisbury (vol. 1) Earl Cornwallis (vol. 2) Lord Huntingtower (vol. 3) Sir William Jerningham (vol. 4) Sir Hugh Inglis (vol. 5)
82		*Correct Peerage of England, Scotland and Ireland*	J. Debrett	J. Debrett	2	12mo	15s.	
83	1804	*Complete Peerage of England, Scotland and Ireland.*		G. Kearsley	1	24mo	9s.	
84	1804	*New Baronetage*		W. Miller; E. Lloyd	2	12mo		
85	1806	*New Pocket Peerage*		J. Stockdale	1	12mo	11s	
86	1806	*Peerage of England, Scotland and Ireland* (re-ed.)	J. Debrett	T. Egerton; F., C. and J. Rivington; J. Stockdale; W. Miller; Clarke and Sons; Crosby and Co; Cuthell and Martin; R. Lea; J. Harding	2	16mo		
87	1806	*Dormant and Extinct Baronage*	Thomas C. Banks	F. C. and J. Rivington; T. Egerton, J. Stockdale; W. Miller; Clarke and Sons; Crosby and Co; Cuthell and Martin; R. Lea; J. Harding	3	4to	£5. 5s./£9 (royal)	George III

88	1807	*Baronetage of the United Kingdom*		J. Stockdale; J. Ridgway	3	12mo	7s. 6d.	
89	1808	*A Biographical Peerage of the Empire*	John E. Brydges	Johnson and the 'chief London Booksellers'	2	12mo	16s.	
90	1808	*Baronetage of England*	J. Debrett	C and J. Rivington	2	12mo	£1. 13s.	
91	1808	*Longmate Pocket Peerage* (4th edn since 1788)	J. Debrett	J. Asperne, R. Baldwin, Byfield and Hawkesworth, Crosby and Co, B. Law, J. Longman, J. Stockdale, Suttaby, J. Walker	2	12mo	18s.	
92	1809	*British Family Antiquity*	William Playfair	J. Gold; T. Reynolds; H. Grace	9	4to	£90	Prince of Wales
93	1812	*Collins's Peerage*	John E. Brydges	T. Payne; J. Walker, T. Bensley; F., C., and J. Rivington; Otridge and Son; J. Nichols and Son; Wilkie and Robinson;	9	8vo	£9. 9s.	
94	1813	*Peerage of Scotland*	John. P. Wood, Robert Douglas	G. Ramsay	2	folio		Marchioness of Stafford
95	1813	*Pocket Peerage*	Barak Longmate, the Younger.	W. Lowndes	1	12mo		
96	1812	*A Genealogical and biographical history of the Dormant and Extinct Peerage*	T. C. Banks	H. K. Causton	1	8vo		Prince Regent
97	1815	*Baronetage of England* (re-ed.)	J. Debrett	F. C. Rivington	2	12mo	3s.	
98	1817		John E. Brydges		4	12mo	£1. 13s.	

Continued

	Imprint date	Title	Author	Publishers	Volume	Format	Price	Dedication
		Biographical peerage of the Empire		T. Payne; J. Walker, T. Bensley; F., C., and J. Rivington; Otridge and Son; J. Nichols and Son; Wilkie and Robinson				
99	1817	*Present Peerage and Baronetage*		J. Stockdale	2	12mo	15s.	
100	1821	*The Peerage Chart*	William Kingdom,	G. and W. B. Whittaker; J. Warren	1	12mo	4s./10s.	
101	1822	*The Baronetage Chart*	William Kingdom	G. and W. B. Whittaker; J. Warren	1	12mo	4s./10s.	
102	1822	*Peerage of the United Kingdom* (re-ed.)	J. Debrett	F. C. Rivington; T. Egerton; J. Harding; B. Lloyd	1	12mo		George IV
103	1822	*Peerage, Baronetage, Knightage* (re-ed.)	J. Debrett	C and J. Rivington	2	12mo	£1. 8s.	
104	1825	*Compendium of the British Peerage*		P. for C. Wight	1	8vo		
105	1825	*A Synopsis of the Peerage of England*	Nicholas Harris Nicolas	J. Nichols	2	12mo	15s.	Lord Redesdale
106	1826	*Heraldic Dictionary of the Peerage and Baronetage of the British Empire*	JohnBurke	Knight and Lacey; Westlet and Tyreel (Dublin)	1	8vo	18s./vol.	George IV

107	1827	*Annual Peerage*	Anne, Eliza, Maria Innes	John Murray, Saunders and Otley.	4	12mo		Duchess of Kent
108	1827	*Dictionary of the Extinct and Dormant Peerages*	JohnBurke	Henry Colburn	1	8vo	28s.	Duke of Devonshire
109	1828	*Manual of Rank or Key to the Peerage*		Saunders and Otley	1	12mo		
110	1828	*A General and Heraldic Dictionary of the Peerage and Baronetage of the British Empire*	John Burke	Henry Colburn	1	8vo	31s.	
111	1829	*Debrett's Peerage of the United Kingdom*		F. C. Rivington	2	12mo	£1. 8s.	
112	1830	*Peerage of the British Empire*	John Sharpe	J. Andrew; J. Hatchard, Simpkin and Marshall, N. Hailes	2	12mo		William IV
113	1830	*County Genealogies (Kent, Sussex)*	William Berry	Sherwood, Gilbert and Piper	1	folio	£5. 5s.	
114	1831	*Debrett's Peerage of England, Scotland, and Ireland* (re-ed.)		F. C Rivington	2	12mo		
115	1831	*Genealogical and Heraldic Dictionary of the English Peerage, extinct, dormant and in abeyance*	John Burke	H. Colburn	1	8vo		Duke of York
116	1832–8	*A Genealogical and Heraldic History of the commoners of Great Britain and Ireland*	John Burke	H. Colburn	1	8vo	£1. 11s.	Baron Brougham (vol. 1)

Continued

	Imprint date	Title	Author	Publishers	Volume	Format	Price	Dedication
117	1832	*Genealogical Peerage of England, Scotland and Ireland*		W. Berry	1	folio	7s.	
118	1832	*A Manual of the Baronetage of the British Empire*	R. B.	J. Fraser	1	12mo		
119	1832	*The Genealogy of the Existing British Peerage*	Edmund Lodge	Saunders and Otley	1	12mo		
120	1833	*Sharpe's genealogical Peerage of the British Empire*	John Sharpe	J. Andrew, J. Hatchard, Simpkin and Marshall, N. Hailes	2	12mo		
121	1833	*A General and Herald Dictionary of the Peerage and Baronetage of the British Empire* (re-ed. in 1834, 1835), vol. 2, 1835, vol. 3, 1836, vol. 4, 1838.	John Burke	H. Colburn	4	8vo		
122	1833	*The Peerage of the British Empire*	Edmund Lodge	Saunders and Otley	1	8vo		Duchess of Kent
123	1834	*Debrett's Complete Peerage* (re-ed.)	William Courthope	J., G., & F. Rivington		8vo		
124	1835	*Debrett's Baronetage of England* (re-ed.)	William Courthope	J., G., & F. Rivington	2	12mo	£1. 8s.	
125	1835	*Synopsis of the extinct Baronetage* (re-ed.)	William Courthope	J., G., & F. Rivington	1	12mo		

APPENDIX 2

The copyright of Collins's
Peerage (1755–1768)

Date	Seller	Buyer	Share	Cost	Total value
Sept. 1755	Robinson	John Knapton	12th	£25. 10s.	£306
Id.	Innys	Id.	12th		
Feb. 1756	Wilkins	Birt	24th	£15	£360
Id.	Davey	Id.	24th	£16	£384
Id.	Crowder	Id.	24th	£18	£432
Feb. 1757	Johnston	Innys	24th	£10	£240
Feb. 1759	Payne	Longman	24th	£5. 2s.	£122. 8s.
Feb. 1759	Crowder	Longman	24th	£5. 2s.	£122. 8s.
Feb. 1759	Rivington	Longman	24th	£5. 2s.	£122. 8s.
Feb. 1759	Whitby	Longman	24th	£5. 2s.	£122. 8s.
Apr. 1760	Brown	Rivington	48th	£5. 15s.	£276
Nov. 1760	Braunets	Woodgate	114th	£1	£114
Id.	Braunets	Woodgate	114th	Id.	Id.
Id.	Derham	Woodgate	48th	£5. 15s.	£276
Jan. 1761	Baldwin	—	12th	£13	£156
Id.	Johnston	—	12th	£16	£192
Feb. 1761	Rivington	—	24th	£5. 5s	£126
Id.	Brown	—	24th	£5	£120
Sept. 1761	Johnston	—	24th	£5	£120
Jan. 1763	Johnson	—	27th	£2. 2s.	£56. 7s.
Id.	Horsfield	—	43th	£4. 14s.	£208. 1s.
Id.	Sandby	Manby	25th	£6. 6s.	£157. 5s.
Id.	Longman	Manby	25th	£6. 6s.	Id.
Jan. 1764	Nichols	—	24th	£6. 16s.	£163. 2s.
Sept. 1764	Rivington	—	24th	£6. 10s.	£156
June 1765	Horsfield	—	72th	£1. 11s.	£111
Nov. 1765	Griffin	—	48th	£3. 10s.	£168

Continued

332 APPENDICES

Date	Seller	Buyer	Share	Cost	Total value
Oct. 1765	Thersley	—	24th	£8. 15s.	£210
Feb. 1766	Gardner	—	48th	£4	£192
Sept. 1766	Almon	Richardson	24th	£12. 15s.	£306
Nov. 1766	Davies		24th	£12. 15s.	Id.
Jan. 1767	Horsfield		24th	£11. 11s.	£277
July 1768	Davies	Anne Shuckburgh	48th	£3	£144

Original Assignments of Copyrights of Books and other Literary Agreements between various Publishers (1703–1810). BL, Add. MS 38728; Add. MS 38729; Add. MS 48803; Bod. Lib., *John Johnson, Trade Sale Catalogues*, no. 89.

APPENDIX 3

Thomas Wotton's correspondents (1727–1740)

Abbreviations

DL   Deputy-Lieutenant
ES   elder son
HS   High Sheriff
JP   Justice of the Peace
LG   Lieutenant-General
MP   Member of Parliament
Revd Reverend

	Name	Surname	Date	Title	Date of creation	Position in the kinship in regard to the previous title-holder	Birth–Death	Age	Residence	County	Profession-Public office
1	Adams	Robert	1735	5th Bt	1660	Cadet (4th)	1668–1754	73	Wandsworth	Surrey	Solicitor
2	Alleyn	Marie	1741		1629	Cousin (7th)	—		Rugeley	Staffs	
3	Anderson	Edmund	1739	5th Bt	1660	ES (4th)	1687–1765	53	Kilnwick	Yorks	
4	Armytage	Samuel	1738	1st Bt	1738	Cadet	1695–1747	44	Kirklees	Yorks	Exciseman
5	Ashe	James	1727	2nd Bt	1660	ES (1st)	1674–1733	54	Twickenham	Wiltshire	MP
6	Assheton	Ralph	1739	3rd	1660	Nephew (2nd)	1692–1765	47	Middleton	Lancs	HS
7	Astley	Jacob	1739	3rd	1662	ES (2nd)	1692–1760	47	Melton Constable	Norfolk	
8	Barlow	George	1726	2nd	1677	ES (1st)	1680–1726	44	Slebech	Pembroke	MP
9	Barnardiston	Robert	1726	4th	1663	Cadet (3rd)	1676–1728	50	Ketton	Suffolk	
10	Beaumont-Busby	William	1741		1661	Cousin (4th)	—		Stoughton	Leics	Solicitor
11	Beckwith	Roger	1725	2nd	1681	Cadet (1st)	1682–1743	43	Aldbrough	Yorks	HS
12	Betenson	Edward	1726	3rd	1663	Cousin (2nd)	1688–1762	51	Wimbledon	Surrey	
13	Bickley	Francis	1725	4th	1661	ES (3rd)	1669–1746	56	Attleborough	Norfolk	Captain
14	Bickley	Humphrey	1725	5th	1661	Half-brother (4th)	d. 1754		Attleborough	Norfolk	Revd
15	Blackett	Edward	1727	3rd	1673	ES (2nd)	1683–1756	44	Newby	Yorks	Captain
16	Blackett	Richard	1739		—	Cousin (3rd)	—		Newby	Yorks	

17	Blois	Jane	—		1686	Mother (2nd)			Cockfield	Suffolk	
18	Blount	Appolonia	1727		1642	Wife (4th)	1704–49	23	Sodington	Worcester	
19	Blount	Harry Pope	1740	3rd		Cadet (2nd[nd])	1702–57	41	Tittenhanger	Herefords	
20	Blount	Thomas Pope	1727	2nd	1679	ES (1st)	1670–1731	57	Tittenhanger	Herefords	
21	Bond	Henry Jermyn	1741		1658	Cousin (3rd)	1693–1748	48	Bury St Edmunds	Suffolk	
22	Bowyer	William	1741	3rd	1660	Nephew (2nd)	1710–68	31	Denham	Bucks	
23	Boynton	Frances	1737		1618	Wife (4th)			Barmston	Yorks	
24	Bradshaigh	Roger	1727	3rd	1679	ES (2nd)	1675–1747	52	Haigh	Lancs	MP
25	Bridgeman	John	1726	3rd	1660	ES (2nd)	—		Blodwell	Shrops	
26	Brooke	Richard	1739	4th	1662	ES (3rd)	1719–81	28	Norton Priory	Cheshire	
27	Broughton	Bryan	1739	4th	1660	Cadet (3rd)	1717–44	22	Doddington	Cheshire	
28	Broughton	Christopher	1740			Cousin (3rd)	—		Longdon	Staffs	
29	Brown	Charles		3rd	1659	ES (2nd)	1667–1751		Kiddington	Oxon	
30	Brown	John	1726	5th	1660	Cadet (4th)	d. 1775	46	Caversham	Oxon	
31	Buswell	Eusebius	1726	1st	1714		1681–1730	46	Clipston	Northants	
32	Cairnes	Alexander	1726	1st	1708		1665–1732	61	Dublin	Ireland	Banker
33	Cann	William	1739	5th	1662	Cadet (4th)	1689–1753	58	Bristol	Gloucester	Town clerk
34	Carew	Thomas	1727	4th	1661	Cadet (3rd)	1692–1746	35	Haccombe	Devon	
35	Cayley	George	1739	4th	1661	Cadet (3rd)	1707–91	32	Brompton	Yorks	
36	Charlton	Mary	1740		1686	Wife (3rd)	—		Ludford	Shrops	
37	Chetwode	Philip	1725	2nd	1700	Cadet (1st)	1700–64	25	Oakley	Staffs	
38	Clavering	James	1739	6th	1661	Cadet (5th)	1680–1748	59	Axwell	Durham	

Continued

	Name	Surname	Date	Title	Date of creation	Position in the kinship in regard to the previous title-holder	Birth–Death	Age	Residence	County	Profession-Public office
39	Cobb	Edward	1739	2nd	1662	Cadet (1st)	1676–1744	63	Adderbury	Oxon	
40	Colleton	John	1725	3rd	1661	ES (2nd)	1669–1754	56	Ash Park	Herts	Colonel
41	Coryton	John	1725	4th	1661	Cadet (3rd)	1690–1739	35	Newton Ferrers	Cornwall	
42	Cotton	Robert	1739	3rd	1677	ES (2nd)	1695–1748	44	Combermere	Cheshire	MP
43	Crisp	Charles	1739	5th	1665	Uncle (4th)	1680–1740	59	Dornford	Oxon	HS-MP
44	Croft	Archer	1726	2nd	1671	ES (1st)	1684–1753	42	Croft	Herefords	MP
45	Cullum	John	1739	5th	1660	ES (4th)	1699–1774	40	Hardwick	Suffolk	
46	Dawes	Darcy	1726	4th	1663	ES (3rd)	1690–1732	36	Putney	Surrey	
47	De Bouverie	Jacob	1741	3rd	1714	Cadet (2nd)	1694–1761	47	Salisbury	Wiltshire	
48	Dolben	John	1725	2nd	1704	ES (1st)	1684–1756	41	Durham	Durham	Revd
49	D'Oyly	Samuel	1729		1663	Cousin (3rd)	1681–1748	48	Hadleigh	Suffolk	
50	D'Oyly	Susanna			1666	Wife (3rd)	1670–1749		Chiselhampton	Oxon	
51	Dudley	William	1727	3rd	1660	Cadet (2nd)	1696–1764	31	Clapton	Northants	
52	Dutton	John	1740	2nd	1678	ES (1st)	1684–1743	56	Sherborne	Gloucester	
53	Dutton Colt	Mary	1725		1692	Mother (2nd)	d. 1761				
54	Dyer	Swinnerton	1726	3rd	1678	ES (2nd)	1688–1736	38	Great Dunmow	Essex	
55	Eden	Robert	1740	3rd	1672	ES (2nd)	1715–55	25	West Auckland	Durham	
56	Edwards	James	1725	2nd	1691	ES (1st)	1689–1744	36	Walton-upon-Thames	Surrey	
57	Egerton	Thomas	1739		1617	Uncle (5th)	1718–63	21	Brasenose College	Oxon	

58	Elton	Abraham	1725	1st	1717		1654–1728	71	Bristol	Gloucester	MP
59	Elwes	Harvey	1726	2nd	1660	Grandson (1st)	1683–1763	43	Stoke	Suffolk	MP
60	Ernle	Edward	1739	7th	1660	Cadet (3rd)	1711–87	28	All Souls College	Oxon	Revd
61	Evelyn	John	1725	1st	1713		1682–1763	43	Wotton	Surrey	MP
62	Filmer	Edward	1728	3rd	1674	Cadet (2nd)	1683–1755	45	East Sutton	Kent	
63	Firebrace	Cordell	1739	3rd	1698	ES (2nd)	1712–59	27	London	Middx	MP
64	Fleming	George	1741	2nd	1705	Cadet (1st)	1667–1747	80	Rydal	Westminster	
65	Freke	William	1727		1713	Cousin (2nd)	—		West Bilney	Norfolk	
66	Fust	Francis	1739	5th	1662	Half-brother (4th)	1705–69	34	Hill Court	Gloucester	
67	Gage	William	1725	2nd	1662	ES (1st)	1651–1727	74	Hengrave	Suffolk	
68	Garrard	Nicholas	1726	3rd	1662	ES (2nd)	1655–1728	71	Langford	Norfolk	
69	Glynne	John	1741	6th	1661	Cadet (5th)	1713–77	28	Hawarden	Flints	MP
70	Goodricke	Henry	1728	4th	1641	ES (3rd)	1677–1738	51	Ribston	Yorks	
71	Gough	Henry	1740	1st	1728		1709–74	31	Edgebaston	Warwick	MP
72	Graham	Reginald	1730	4th	1662	Cadet (3rd)	1704–55	26	Norton Conyers	Yorks	
73	Guldeford	Clare (Monson)	1727		1686	Wife (1st)	—		Hemsted	Kent	
74	Hanham	William	1739	3rd	1667	ES (2nd)	1690–1762		Wimborne	Dorset	
75	Head	Francis	1739	4th	1676	Cadet (3rd)	1693–1768	42	Hermitage	Kent	
76	Heron	Harry	1739	4th	1660	Cadet (3rd)	1696–1749	43	Chipchase	Northumb	
77	Hildyard	Christopher	1727			Cadet (2nd)	—		Howley	Yorks	Revd
78	Hildyard	Francis				Cousin (2nd)	—				
79	Hildyard	John	1739			Nephew (2nd)	—			Wiltshire	
80	Hildyard	Robert	1726	2nd	1660	Grandson (1st)	1670–1729	56	Patrington	Yorks	MP
81	Howe	James	1725	2nd	1660	ES (1st)	1669–1736	56	Cold Barwick	Wiltshire	MP

Continued

	Name	Surname	Date	Title	Date of creation	Position in the kinship in regard to the previous title-holder	Birth–Death	Age	Residence	County	Profession-Public office
82	Humble	Sarah (Lant)	1726		1660	Wife (4th)	—		London		
83	Irby	William	1740	2nd	1704	ES (1st)	1707–75	33	Boston	Lincs	MP
84	Jackson	Bradwardine	1725	3rd	1660	Half-brother (2nd)	1670–1730	55	Hickleton	Yorks	
85	James	Cane	1727		1682	ES (2nd)	1692–1741	35	Creshall	Essex	
86	J'Anson	Thomas	1739	4th	1652	ES (3rd)	1702–1764	37	New Bounds	Kent	
87	Jenkinson	Jonathan	1725	3rd	1685	Cadet (2nd)	—		Walton	Derby	
88	Jocelyn	Strange	1725	2nd	1665	ES (1st)	1651–1734	74	Hyde	Essex	
89	Keyt	William	1739	3rd	1660	ES (2nd)	1688–1741	51	Norton	Gloucester	MP
90	Lade	John	1738	1st	1731		1662–1740	86	Warbleton	Sussex	Brewer-MP
91	Langham	John	1739	4st	1660	ES (3rd)	1670–1747	69	Cottesbrooke	Northants	
92	Lloyd	Charles	1727	3rd	1661	ES (2nd)	d. 1743		Garth	Montgomery	HS
93	Long	Robert	1739	6th	1661	ES (5th)	1705–67	34	Draycot	Wiltshire	MP
94	Longueville	Thomas	1741	4th	1638	Cadet (3rd)	d. 1759		Esclusham	Denbighs	
95	Lowther	James	1740	4th	1642	Cadet (2nd)	1673–1755	67	Whitehaven	Cumberland	MP
96	Lucy	Berkeley			1618	Servant			Charlecote	Warwick	
97	Mainwaring	Thomas	1726	3rd	1660	ES (2nd)	1681–1726	45	Over Peover	Cheshire	
98	Martin	Roger	1725	2nd	1667	ES (1st)	1667–1742	58	Long Melford	Suffolk	
99	Marwood	Samuel	1739	3rd	1660	Nephew (2nd)	1672–1739	67	Little Busby	Yorks	
100	Maynard	Henry	1725	3rd	1681	ES (2nd)	d. 1738		Walthamstow	Essex	
101	Meredith	Amos	1741		1639	ES (2nd)	1687–1744	64	Powderham	Devon	

102	Middleton	Thomas	1739		1662	Cadet (2nd)	—	39	Belsey	Northumb	
103	Morgan	John	1727	4th	1661	Cadet (3rd)	1710–1767	17	Kinnersley	Herefords	MP
104	Mosley	Oswald	1725	1st	1720		1674–1751	51	Ancoats	Lancs	Sheriff
105	Mostyn	George	1725	3rd	1670	ES (2nd)	1675–1739	50	Talacre	Flints	MP
106	Musgrave	James	1740		1638	Cadet (3rd)	1681–1747	59	Little Gransden	Cambridge	Revd
107	Oglander	William	1725	3rd	1665	ES (2nd)	1680-1734	45	Southampton	Hants	
108	Osborn	Thomas	1739		1662	Cadet (3rd)	—		Chiksands	Bedford	Revd
109	Oughton	Adolphus	1725	1st	1718		1685–1736		Tachbrook	Warwick	MP
110	Pakington	John	1726	4th	1620	ES (3rd)	1671–1727	55	Hampton Lovett	Worcester	MP
111	Palmer	Thomas	1739	4th	1660	ES (3rd)	1702–65	37	Carlton	Northants	HS
112	Parker	Walter	1739	3rd	1674	ES (2nd)	1694–1750	43	Ratton	Sussex	
113	Pennyman	James	1739	3rd	1664	ES (2nd)	1661–1745	78	Ormsby	Yorks	
114	Pilkington	Lionel	1726	5th	1635	ES (4th)	1707–78	19	Chevet Hall	Yorks	HS–MP
115	Pleydell	Mark Stuart	1739	1st	1732		1693–1768	49	Coleshill	Berkshire	
116	Poole	Francis	1727	2nd	1677	ES (1st)	1682–1763	45	Poole	Cheshire	
117	Prideaux	Edmund	1726	5th	1622	Cadet (4th)	1675–1729	51	Netherton	Devon	
118	Ramsden	William	1726	2nd	1689	ES (1st)	1672–1736	54	Byram	Yorks	
119	Robinson	James	1727	3rd	1660	Cadet (2nd)	1669–1731	58	Cranford	Northants	
120	Robinson	William	1725	1st	1690		1655–1736	70	Newby	Yorks	MP
121	Rogers	John	1725	2nd	1699	ES (1st)	1676–1744	49	Wisdome	Devon	MP
122	Rous	John	1726	2rd	1660	ES (1st)	1656–1730	70	Henham	Suffolk	MP
123	St John	Francis	1741	1st	1715		1680–1756	61	Longthorpe	Northants	
124	Sanderson	William	1727	1st	1720		d. 1727		Coombe	Kent	Capt
125	Shaw	William	1739	3rd	1665	Cadet (2nd)	1679–1752	60	Cheshunt	Here	
126	Sherard	Brownlow	1740	4th	1674	Cadet (3rd)	1702–48	38	Lopthorp	Lincs	

Continued

	Name	Surname	Date	Title	Date of creation	Position in the kinship in regard to the previous title-holder	Birth–Death	Age	Residence	County	Profession-Public office
127	Shuckburgh	Stukeley	1739	4th	1660	ES (3rd)	1711–59	28	Shuckburgh	Warwick	
128	Simeon	Edward	1739	2nd	1677	ES (1st)	1682–1768	68	Chilworth	Oxon	
129	Skipwith	Francis	1740	3rd	1670	Grandson (2nd)	1705–78	35	Newbold	Warwick	
130	Smith	Edward	1739	3rd	1661	ES (1st)	1686–1741	53	Hill	Essex	
131	Smithson	Hugh	1740	4th	1663	Grandson (3rd)	1714–86	26	Stanwick	Yorks	
132	Smythe	John	1736	3rd	1661	Cadet (2nd)	1690–1737	46	Eshe	Durham	
133	Standish	Thomas	1727	2nd	1677	ES (1st)	1703–56	24	Duxbury	Lancs	
134	Stanley	Rowland	1739	4th	1661	ES (3rd)	1707–71	32	Hooton	Chester	
135	Stapleton	William	1725	4th	1679	ES (3rd)	1698–1740	27	Bray	Oxon	
136	Stonhouse	George	1734	5th	1628	ES (4th)	d. 1737		Radley	Berkshire	
137	Swinburne	John	1725	3rd	1660	ES (2nd)	1698–1745	27	Capheaton	Northumb	
138	Tancred	Thomas	1740	3rd	1662	Cadet (2nd)	1665–1744	79	Boroughbridge	Yorks	
139	Tempest	Stephen	1741		1664	Cousin (6th)	—		Bracewell	Yorks	
140	Trevelyan	John	1735	2nd	1662	ES (1st)	1670–1755	65	Nettlecombe	Somerset	HS MP
141	Twisden	Thomas	1725		1666	Cadet (4th)	—		Bradbourn	Kent	
142	Twisden	Roger	1740	5th	1666	Cadet (4th)	1705–72	35	Bradbourn	Kent	
143	Warrender	John	1735	2nd	1715	ES (1st)	1686–1772	49	Lochend	Haddington	
144	Wentworth	William	1739	4th	1664	Cadet (3rd)	1686–1763	53	Bretton	Yorks	Capt-MP
145	Wheler	William	1726	5th	1660	Cadet (3rd)	1704–63	22	Leamington	Warwick	

146	Whichcote	Francis	1739	3rd	1660	ES (2nd)	1692–1775	47	London	Middx	
147	Williams	David	1739	3rd	1674	Nephew (2nd)	1659–1740	80	Eltham	Kent	
148	Wilson	Edward	1740	5th	1661	ES (4th)	1725–60	15	Waddon	Sussex	
149	Winford	Thomas Cookes	1725	2nd	1702	Nephew (1st)	1673–1744	52	Winford	Worcester	Lawyer– MP
150	Wright	Nathan	1725	2nd	1661	ES (1st)	1661–1727	74	Cranham	Essex	
151	Yeamans	John	1740	5th	1664	Cadet (4th)	1720–80	20	Oxford	Oxon	

William Betham's correspondents (1803–1805)

ID	Name	Surname	Letters' date	Date of creation	Date	Baronet	Birth-Death	Age	Place	County	Public offices
1	Aubrey	John	1805	6th	1660	ES	1739–1826	66	Boarstall	Bucks	MP, Lord of the Treasury
2	Beltz	George Frederick					1774–1841				Herald
3	Brooke de Capell	Richard	1805	1st	1803		1758–1829	47	Dover	Kent	
4	Browne Ffolkes	Martin	1805	1st	1774		1749–1821	56	Hillington	Norfolk	MP
5	Bruce	Henry Harvey Aston	1805	1st	1804		1788–1822	17	Down Hill	Londonderry	Reverend
6	Callander	John	1805		1798		1739–1812	66	Westerton	Stirling	MP
7	Champneys	Thomas	1805	1st	1767		1745–1821	60	Orchardley	Somerset	
8	Colebrooke	George	1805	2nd	1759	ES	1729–1809	76	Bath	Somerset	MP
9	Corbet	Corbet d'Avenant	1805	1st	1786		1752–1823	53	Adderley	Shropshire	
10	Cunliffe	Foster	1805	3rd	1759	ES	1755–1834	50	Saighton	Cheshire	HS
11	Davie	Lady	1805		1641	Widow			Crediton	Devon	
12	Douglas	John	1805				1721–1807	74			Bp Salisbury
13	Etherington	Henry	1805	1st	1775				North Ferriby	Yorks	
14	Fletcher	Henry	1805	1st	1782		1727–1807	78	Ashley Park	Surrey	MP

No.	Surname	Forename							Place	County	Role
15	Hanmer	Edward	1805	2nd	1774	ES	1747–1828	58	Bettisfield	Flints	
16	Harbord	Harbord	1805	2nd	1746	ES	1734–1810	71	Gunton	Norfolk	MP
17	Henniker	John	1803	2nd	1765		1751–1821	52	Worlington	Suffolk	MP DL
18	Heron	Richard	1803	1st	1778		1726–1805	77	Newark-on-Trent	Notts	Sec for Ireland-MP
19	Hippisley	John Coxe	n.d.	1st	1796		1747–1825		Warfield Grove	Berkshire	MP, Writer EIC
20	Ibbetson	Henry Carr	1805	3rd	1748		1779–1825	26	Denton	Yorks	Sheriff
21	Inglis	Robert Harry	1805	2nd	1801	ES	1786–1855	29	Milton Bryan	Beds	
22	Liddell	Thomas Henry	1805	6th	1642		1775–1855	30	Ravensworth	Durham	HS
23	Llyod	Gamaliel	1804				1744–1817	59	Hampstead	Middx	Mayor of Leeds
24	Lombe	Meadow Taylor	1803		1783	Cousin			Norwich	Norfolk	
25	Lygon	William	1805				1747–1816	58	Madresfield	Worcester	MP
26	Meyrick	John	1805				–1806		Peterborough	Middx	
27	Mildmay	Henry	1805	3rd	1772		1764–1808	41	Dogmersfield	Hants	MP
28	Milnes	John	1805		1801		–1833		Beckingham	Lincs	
29	Murray	John M.	1805	8th	1664		1768–1827	37	Stanhope	Peeblesshire	
30	Peel	Robert	1802	1st	1801		1750–1830	52	Drayton	Staffs	MP DL
31	Pepys	William	1803	1st	1801		1740–1825	63	Ridley Hall	Cheshire	
32	Rous	John		6th	1660		1750–1827		Henham	Suffolk	MP DL
33	Skeffington	William	1803	1st	1786		1742–1815	61	Skeffington	Leics	Lt.-Col.
34	Smith	Edward	—	2nd	1783	ES	1768–1845		Newland	Yorks	
35	Smith	John	1804	1st	1774		1744–1807	68	Sydling	Dorset	HS

Continued

ID	Name	Surname	Letters' date	Date of creation	Date	Baronet	Birth-Death	Age	Place	County	Public offices
36	Smith-Bruges	Margaret	—	1st	1804	Sister-in-law	1744–1828	68	Tring Park	Herts	
37	Sullivan	Elizabeth	1805	1st	1804	Daughter	1790–	15	Brighton	Sussex	
38	Trevelyan	John	1803	4th	1662	ES	1735–1828	68	Nettlecombe	Somerset	MP
39	Turton	Thomas	1804	1st	1796		1764–1844	40	Starborough	Surrey	MP HS
40	Whichcote	Thomas	—	5th	1660		1763–1828		Aswarby Park	Lincs	Sheriff
41	White	Thomas Woollaston	1805	1st	1802		1767–1817	38	Wallingwells	Notts	DL
42	Willoughby	Christopher	1804	1st	1794		1748–1808	56	Baldon	Oxon	
43	Wombwell	Anne	—	2nd	1778	Wife			Wombwell	Yorks	

John Burke's correspondents (1828)

ID	Name	Surname	Date of birth	Age	Place	County	City address	Public charges, military titles	Volume
1	Abney	William Wotton	1807	21	Measham Hall	Derbys		HS	1833, 572
2	Adams	Edward Hainlin	1777	51	Bailbrook House	Somerset			
3	Addenbrooke	John Homfray	1759	69	Landaff	Glamorgan		HS	1833, 236
4	Alderley	Samuel			Alderley Hall	Cheshire			
5	Allan	William	1796	32	Blackwell Grange	Durham			1833, 39
6	Allanson	Dorothy	1801	27	Broughton	Flints			
7	Allington	Marmaduke			Binbrook	Lincs			
8	Allix	Charles	1783	45	Willoughby Hall	Lincs		Revd-DL	1833, 482
9	Amherst	William	1793	35	Parndon House	Essex			
10	Anderson	James			Euxton	Lancs			
11	Anguish	George	1768	60	Somerleyton Hall	Suffolk	George St, London	Revd	1835, 419
12	Arburthnot	George	1772	56	Elderslie Lodge	Surrey	Wimpole St, London		
13	Arundell	William Harris	1758	70	Lifton	Devon		Knight, DL, HS	1834, 512
14	Aylmer	Arthur	1769	59	Walworth	Durham		JP, LG	1833, 177
15	Bacon	Nicholas	1788	40	Blundeston	Suffolk			

Continued

ID	Name	Surname	Date of birth	Age	Place	County	City address	Public charges, military titles	Volume
16	Ballard	Samuel Wrangham	1765	63	Coates Hall	Yorks	Bath		
17	Barnard	Henry Gee	1789	39	Cave Castle	Yorks	Harrogate		1835, 253
18	Barnard	Sarah				Yorks	Beverley		
19	Bastard	Edmund Bolleston	1784	44	Kitley	Devon	New St, Yealmpton	MP	1833, 18
20	Bateman	John	1782	46	Knypersley	Staffs	Brunswick Hotel, Jermyn St. London		1833, 18
21	Bates	Ralph	1799	29	Milbourne Hall	Northumb			1833, 626
22	Benett	Etheldred	1775	53	Norton House Pythehouse	Wiltshire	Albermale St. London		1833, 248
23	Bennett	John Leigh	1768	60	Thorpe Place	Surrey			1833
24	Bennis	George Geary	1793	35			Limerick		
25	Bent	Richard	1779	49	Basford House	Staffs			
26	Bethell	Richard	1772	56	Rise	Yorks			1833, 451
27	Blair	James	1788	40	Penninghame	Wigtown		MP	
28	Blaydes	Hugh	1777	55	Ranby	Notts			1833, 667
29	Blenkinsopp	John Coulson	1770	58	Blenkinsopp	Northumb			
30	Bond	Thomas	1756	72	Eggleston	Dorset		Revd	1833, 240
31	Borough	Thomas					York Terrace, London		
32	Boulton	Antony			Tiverton	Devon		Revd	

33	Bourne	Ralph	1772	56	Hilderstone	Staffs		JP-DL	1835, 31
34	Bouverie	Edward William	1807	21	Delapre Abbey	Northants			1835, 7
35	Bowes	Thomas	1758	70	Bradley	Durham	Brook St, London		1833, 182
36	Bowles	Charles	1766	62	Barton	Bucks	Shaftesbury	Revd	
37	Bowles	Thomas	1790	38	Milton	Berkshire			
38	Boyd	Edward			Merton	Cumberland	Wigton	DL	
39	Bracebridge	Charles Holte	1799	29	Atherstone	Warwick			1833, 273
40	Bragg	Raisbek Lucock	1795	33	Lorton	Cumberland			
41	Brindley	Joseph	1788	40	Union	Staffs			
42	Bristow	Samuel Ellis	1800	28	Beesthorpe	Notts			
43	Brooke	Charles	1765	63	Ufford	Suffolk		Revd	1833, 336
44	Brown	Janus	1786	42	Harehill	Yorks			
45	Browne	Thomas Henry	1789	39		Denbigs	St Asaph	Lt.-Col., Knight	
46	Buliver	William	1799	29	Haydon	Norfolk			
47	Bulkeley	James Felding	1798	30	Oak Cottage	Essex			
48	Burrough	Henry Negus	1784	44	Burlingham	Norfolk			
49	Burton	Francis	1788		Unsworth Lodge	Lancs			1836, 273
50	Butlin	John	1796	32	Turville	Bucks			
51	Caldecott	Abraham	1763	65	Caldecott Hall	Warwick	Rugby		1834, 627
52	Calverley	Thomas			Ewell	Surrey	Berkeley Square (London)		1833, 673
53	Campbell	Alexandra	1766	62		Isle of Wight	Gatcombe	Colonel	
54	Carew	George Hen	1794	34	Crowcombe	Somerset			

Continued

ID	Name	Surname	Date of birth	Age	Place	County	City address	Public charges, military titles	Volume
55	Carpenter	Charles	1756	72	Moditonham	Cornwall			
56	Cary	Henry-George	1800	28	Torr Abbey	Devon		Magistrate	1835, 33
57	Chambers	Samuel	1763	65	Bredgar	Kent		Sheriff	1835
58	Charletton	James Wakeman	1764	64	Hanley Court	Worcester			
59	Charlton	Edmund Lechmere	1789	39	Whitton Court	Shropshire			1834, 27
60	Charlton	Roberton	1789	39	Lee Hall	Northumb			
61	Chichester	Arthur	1798	30	Dunbrody	Wexford		Lt.-Col.	1838
62	Child	Wiliam	1793	35	Begelly House	Pembroke			1836, 692
63	Clarke	George	1768	60			Hyde Hall New York		1835, 189
64	Clarke	William	1766	62	Ardingdon	Berkshire		HS, Lt.-Col.	1837, 112
65	Clifton	Charles Claude	1778	50	Ty Mawr	Brecon			
66	Cludde	Edward			Orleton	Salop		DL	1833, 483
67	Clutterbuck	Lewis			New Oak	Gloucester		Horse Guard	
68	Cochram	Archibald			Hendon House	Durham		Captain	
69	Coham	Mary			Dunsland	Devon			1833, 459
70	Collinson	Charles Streynsham	1753	75	The Chantry	Suffolk		HS	1835, 538
71	Conway	John			Soughton	Northants			
72	Cook	Philip Davies	1793	35	Gwysaney	Flints		DL, Sheriff	1835, 276
73	Corbet	Athelstan	1789	39	Denbigh	Denbighs		Sheriff	

74	Courtenay	Thomas Peregrine	1782	46	Abingdon	Middx	Harley Street London	MP		1835, 306
75	Cracroft	Augusta	1783	45	Hackthorn Hall	Lincoln				
76	Dalton	John	1766	62	Hemingford	Hunts				
77	Danvers	George John	1794	34	Swithland	Leics		HS		1833, 148
78	Davies	John	1770	58	Mannington	Shrops				
79	Davison	Alexander	1750	78	Swarland Park	Northumb		DL		
80	Delafield	Joseph	1749	79	Camden Hill	Middx				1833, 542
81	Denison	Joseph	1784	44	Rushholm	Lancs				1833, 383
82	Denton	Thomas	1781	47	Ashford Lodge	Middx				
83	Denty	Arthur			Oswald House	Surrey				
84	Dering	Edward			Surrenden	Kent				
85	Dillwyn	Lewis Weston	1778	50	Penllergare	Breaconshire		MP, naturalist		
86	Dod	Anne			Edge Hall	Cheshire				1836, 548
87	Dodsley	John	1787	41	Kegby	Notts				
88	Donovan	James	1748	80	Godstone	Surrey				1834, 76
89	Dovaston	John Freeman Milward	1782	46	The Nursery	Shrops				
90	Downall	John			Ramsgate	Kent		Revd		
91	Drake	Thomas Tyrwhitt	1782	46	Donat Castle	Glamorgan				1835, 619
92	Duberly	James	1758	70	Gaines	Hunts				
93	Duke	Edward			Dovenby	Cumberland		Revd		
94	Duncombe	Philip Duncombe Pauncefort	1784	48	Brickhill	Bucks		DL		1835, 74
95	Duncombe	Thomas	1795	33	Copgrove	Yorks		MP		1833, 151

Continued

ID	Name	Surname	Date of birth	Age	Place	County	City address	Public charges, military titles	Volume
96	Edmeades	William	1766	62	Nurstead	Kent		EIC capt.	
97	Edridge	Thomas	1749	79	Monkton	Wilts			
98	Edwards	John	1770	58	Greenfield	Montgomery			
99	Ensor	John	1769	59	Rollerby	Norfolk			
100	Errington	Frederic	1763	65	High Warden	Northumb			
101	Esdaile	Edward Jeffries	1785	47	Cothelstone	Somerset		HS, JP	1836, 604
102	Evans	William	1758	70	Llandyfaelog	Camarthen		Revd	
103	Falcon	John	1767	61	Garoon House	Herts			
104	Farmar	Jasper	1777	51	Treago	Herefords			
105	Farrington	William	1783	49	Shawe Hall	Lancs			
106	Feilden	John	1769	59	Mollington	Cheshire		HS-DL	1833, 446
107	Fisher	John Landerson	1776	52	Wood Hall	Cumbria			
108	Fitzgerald	John	1775	53	Little Island	Waterford		MP	1838, 179
109	Fitzherbert	Michael John			Somersall	Derbys			
110	Fitzroy	William	1773	55	Kempstone	Norfolk		LG	
111	Foljambe	Thomas	1770	58	Hartsfield	Gloucester			
112	Folliot	William Harwood	1761	68	Stepley	Cheshire			
113	Fonnereau	Charles William	1764	63	Christchurch Park	Suffolk		Revd	1835, 110
114	Fontaine	Andrew	1770	58	Marford	Norfolk			
115	Foot	Roberton	1783	49		Kent	Charlton	HS	

No.	Surname	First name	Year	Age	Place	County	Town	Note	Ref
116	Fortescue	John	1767	61			Highfield London		1838, 549
117	Foster	Arthur-Fitz-John	1765	64	Brickhill	Bedford			1833, 376
118	Fowler	Thomas	1765	63	Gunton	Suffolk			1838, 314
119	Fox	George Croker	1785	47	Grove Hill	Cornwall			
120	France	James France	1793	35	Bostock	Cheshire			
121	Fraser	Alexander			Inchcoulter	Ross-shire			
122	Fydell	Samuel Richard	1771	57		Lincoln	Boston		1835, 260
123	Garnons	Richard	1773	55	Colomendy	Denbigh		DL	1834, 374
124	Gent	George William	1809	21	Moyn	Devon			
125	Gilbert	Robertson	1776	52	Postwick Hall	Norfolk			
126	Gollops	George	1791	37	Strode	Dorset			1833, 600
127	Goodford	John	1784	44	Chilton	Somerset			
128	Goodhart	Emmanuel	1772	56	Langley	Sussex			1833, 369
129	Gore	William Ormsby	1779	49	Porkington	Shrops		MP, Sheriff	1833, 85
130	Goring	Charles	1743	85	Wiston	Sussex			
131	Gosselin	Gerard	1769	59	Ospringe	Kent		DL	1833, 302
132	Gosselin	Thomas Le Marchant	1765	64	Bengeo	Herts		Vice-Admiral	1833, 301
133	Gough	John	1780	48	Rockland	Staffs			1835, 392
134	Gower	John Leveson	1802	26	Bill Hill	Berks			1833, 320
135	Grantham	Charles	1791	37	Ketton	Rutland		Captain	
136	Gray	John	1792	36	Hartsheath	Flints			
137	Greaves	William	1771	55	Mayfield	Staffs			1833, 386

Continued

ID	Name	Surname	Date of birth	Age	Place	County	City address	Public charges, military titles	Volume
138	Green	Henry	1794	34	Rolleston	Leics			1834, 521
139	Green	Thomas	1794	34	Slyne	Lancs			
140	Greenly	William	1741	87	Tittey	Herefords		DL	1833, 293
141	Greenwell	William Thomas	1777	51	Lanchester	Durham			1834, 114
142	Gregor	Gordon William Francis	1789	39	Trewarthenick	Cornwall			1835, 617
143	Gresley	Richard	1766	63		Staffs	Stowe		
144	Grove	Joseph	1778	50	Walbury	Essex			
145	Grylls	Richard Gerveys	1758	70	St Laurent	Cornwall		Revd	
146	Gurdon	Theophilus Thornhagh	1764	65	Letton	Norfolk		DL	1834, 396
147	Gurney	Hudson	1775	53	Keswick	Norfolk		MP	1833, 484
148	Gwynn	Henry	1779	49	Glanbran	Camarthen			
149	Haffenden	James	1788	40	Homewood	Kent			1835, 301
150	Halford	Richard	1806	22	Paddock	Kent			1836, 559
151	Halkett	Charles Craigie	1802	26	Hall Hill	Fife		Lieutenant	1833, 339
152	Hall	Benjamin	1802	26	Abercane	Monmouths		MP	1833, 202
153	Hall	Thomas Bayley	1745	84	Hermitage	Cheshire			
154	Hamerton	James	1779	49	Chisnall	Lancs			
155	Hamford	Charles Edward	1781	47	Widas	Worcester			
156	Hammond	Francis Thomas				Suffolk	Bury St Edmunds		

157	Hampton	John Hampton	1775	53	Henllys	Anglesey			
158	Hanbury	William	1780	48	Kelmarsh	Northants			
159	Harding	Thomas Wry	1783	45	Pilton	Devon			
160	Harper	John Hosken	1782	46		Cheshire	Davenham		1835, 32
161	Harries	John Hill	1783	45	Priskilly	Pembroke		DL	1834, 256
162	Harrington	Blandina	1776	52	Worden	Devon			1833, 461
163	Harvey	John	1756	72	Thorpe	Norfolk		Sheriff	1837, 399
164	Hasell	Edward William	1796	32	Dulemain	Cumberland			
165	Havers	Thomas	1787	41	Thelton	Norf			1833, 381
166	Hay	Edward			Belton	Suffolk			
167	Helyar	William	1778	50	Coker	Somerset		Sheriff	1836, 281
168	Hesketh	Lloyd Hesketh Bamford	1788	40	Bamford	Lancs		HS	1838, 523
169	Hext	John	1766	63	Trenarren	Cornwall		DL	1835, 428
170	Heygate	William	1782	46	Southend	Essex		MP	
171	Heysham	Robert Thornton	1769	60	Stagenhoe	Herts			
172	Hickes	Fowler	1765	64	Silton Hall	Yorks		DL	1833, 510
173	Hodgson	William	1773	55		Cumberland	Carlisle	MP	1838, 309
174	Hodson	James Alexander	1785	43		Lancs	Wigan	MP	
175	Holbeck	William	1774	54	Farnborough	Warwick			1834, 659
176	Holmes	John	1774	54	Redenhall	Norfolk		Town Clerk	
177	Homfray	Samuel	1762	66	Penydaren	Glamorgan		Magistrate	
178	Horton	Joshua-Thomas	1790	38	Howroyde	Yorks	Halifax	Revd	1833, 283

Continued

ID	Name	Surname	Date of birth	Age	Place	County	City address	Public charges, military titles	Volume
179	Hosken	Joseph	1773	55	Ellenglaze	Cornwall		Captain, JP, DL	1834, 94
180	Hotchkis	John			Alnwick	Shrops			
181	Howard	Fulk Greville	1773	55	Castle Rising	Norfolk		Colonel	1833, 503
182	Howard	Henry	1757	71	Corby	Cumberland		HS	1834, 196
183	Howes	James	1798	30	Morning	Norfolk			
184	Huddard	Joseph	1766	62	Brynkir	Caernavon		HS	
185	Hume	Joseph	1777	51	Burnley Hall	Norfolk		MP	
186	Humfrey	John	1772	56	Wroxham	Norfolk			
187	Hungerford	Henry	1803	25	Dingley Park	Northants			
188	Hutton	William	1781	47	Cappleside	Cumberland		Revd	
189	Irton	Samuel	1796	32	Irton	Cumberland		MP, DL	1836, 675
190	Isherwood	John	1776	52	Marple	Cheshire		HS	1837, 101
191	Jelf	James	1763	65		Gloucester	Gloucester	Mayor	
192	Jenkins								
193	Jenyns	George Leonard	1763	65	Bottisham	Cambs			1836, 582
194	Jervis	Swynfen	1797	31	Darlaston	Staffs			
195	Jessop	William	1784	44	Butterley	Derbys			
196	John	George	1769	59		Cornwall	Penzance		
197	Johnes	Arthur James	1809	19	Garthmyl	Powys	London	Court Judge	
198	Johnstone	A. G.	1789	39	Friston Hall	Suffolk			

199	Jolliffe	John Twyford	1779	49	Ammerdown	Somerset				1833, 517
200	Jones	Edward	1772	56	Hay Hill	Gloucester				
201	Kingscote	Robert	1754	73	Kingseat	Gloucester			Colonel	1833, 280
202	Lambert	Aylmer Bourke	1761	67	Boyton House	Wiltshire	botanist			1833, 66
203	Lane	John Newton	1800	28	Bromley Hall	Staffs				1833, 174
204	Latimer	Edward	1775	53		Oxon	Headington			
205	Laughton	William Gore	1760	68	Newton Park	Somerset				
206	Lawrence	Charles	1757	71	Hanlwith	Radnor				
207	Lawson	Andrew	1800	28	Boroughbridge	Yorks			DL	1835, 247
208	Lawson	William	1775	53	Longhirst Hall	Northumb			DL	1836, 105
209	Layborn	Jonathan	1780	48	Thewing	Yorks				
210	Leather	John	1789	37	Herringfleet	Suffolk				
211	Leigh	Joseph	1768	60	Belmont	Cheshire				
212	Leigh	Robert	1773	55	Bardon	Somerset			DL	
213	Lenthall	John William	1789	39	Maynan Hall	Caernavons			HS	1833, 178
214	Levett	Richard	1772	56	Milford Hall	Staffs				
215	Lewis	Charles	1777	51	St Pierre	Monmouths				1833, 221
216	Lewis	Thomas Frankland	1780	48	Harpon	Radnor			MP	1833, 335
217	Leycester	Ralph	1764	64	Toft	Cheshire			MP	1834, 73
218	Liddel	Henry Thomas	1797	31	Eslington	Northumb				
219	Lind	John	1750	78	Westmont ride	Cambria				
220	Lister	Thomas Henry	1800	28	Armitage Park	Staffs	Kent House London			1833, 219

Continued

ID	Name	Surname	Date of birth	Age	Place	County	City address	Public charges, military titles	Volume
221	Littleton	Edward John	1791	35		Staffs	Lichfield		1833, 389
222	Llewellyn	Richard			Holm Wood	Gloucester			
223	Llyod	William Horton	1784	44		Middx	BedfordLondon		
224	Locke	Wadham	1779	49	Rowdeford	Wiltshire			
225	Loftus	William Francis	1784	44	Kilbride	Wicklow		Colonel	1833, 209
226	Lowndes	Richard	1790	38	Roe Hill	Surrey		Revd	
227	Love	Edward	1782	46	Somerleyton	Suffolk		Revd	
228	Lucas	Charles	1766	62	Castleshane	Monaghan		Lt.-Col.	
229	Lucy	George	1789	39	Charlecote	Warwick		Sheriff	1836, 97
230	Lushington	Stephen	1776	52	Norton Court	Kent		Revd	1835, 185
231	Luttrell	John Fownes	1787	41	Dunster Castle	Somerset		MP	1833, 144
232	Machen	James	1743	87	Coleford	Gloucester			
233	Mangles	James	1762	66	Woodbridge	Surrey		DL, MP	
234	Manners	Otho	1794	34	Goadby Marwood	Leics			
235	Marshall	John	1765	63	Headingley	Yorks	Berkeley SqLondon	DL, MP	1833, 295
236	Marten	George Robert	1801	27	St Albans	Herts			
237	Martin	Henry	1763	65	Colston Basset	Notts		MP	
238	Massingberd	Thomas	1763	65	Candlesby	Lincs			
239	Master	William	1785	43	Knol Park	Gloucester			
240	Matthew	George	1807	21	Hawkhurst	Kent			

241	Maunsell	Robert	1782	45	Bank Place	Limerick		Supreme Council Madras	1833, 304
242	Maxwell	William Constable	1804	24	Everingham	Yorks			
243	Mayne	John Thomas	1792	36	Teffont Evias	Wiltshire			1838, 504
244	Morgan	Edward	1759	69	Golden Grove	Flints			1835, 163
245	Mountfort	Henry	1789	39	Beauhurst Hall	Staffs			
246	Mules	Charles			Barn Park	Devon			
247	Mundy	Francis	1771	57	Merkeaton	Derby		MP	1833, 25
248	Mynors-Rickards	Peter	1787	41	Treago	Herefords		DL	1833, 37
249	Needham	Matthew	1768	60	Lenton	Notts			
250	Nethercoal	John	1782	46	Moulton Grange	Northants			
251	Newcome	Thomas	1777	51	Shenley	Herts		Revd	
252	Nicholl	Richard	1802	26	Greenwich Grove	Herefords			
253	Norcliffe	Ann	1784	44	Langton	Yorks			1835, 631
254	Ovey	Thomas	1788	40	Rotherfield	Hants			
255	Packe	Charles James	1758	70	Prestwold Hall	Leics			1833, 157
256	Pain	Solomon	1761	67	Hunter's Hills	Somerset			
257	Palmer	Henry	1780	48	Whitecote	Shrops		Revd	
258	Palmer	Robert	1793	35	Holme Park	Berkshire		MP	1833, 65
259	Parker	Robert Townley	1793	37	Cuerden	Lancs		HS	1833, 116
260	Patten	John Wilson	1802	26	Bank Hall	Lancs		DL	1836, 79
261	Paynter	John	1790	38	Boskenna	Cornwall			1833, 38

Continued

ID	Name	Surname	Date of birth	Age	Place	County	City address	Public charges, military titles	Volume
262	Pennant	David	1763	69	Downing	Flints		HS	1836, 30
263	Penrice	John	1787	41		Norfolk	Yarmouth	Captain	1833, 362
264	Penyston	Francis	1794	34	Cornwell	Berkshire			
265	Peter	William	1785	37	Harlyn	Cornwall			1833, 29
266	Peyton	Henry			Turman	Oxon			
267	Philips	Francis	1771	57	Bank Hall	Lancs		DL	1835, 593
268	Pigott	John Smyth	1792	36	Brockley Hall	Somerset		HS	
269	Pilkington	Henry	1787	41	Park Lane	Yorks	Doncaster	Barrister, Tithe commissioner	
270	Pitman	James	1781	47	Oulton	Norfolk			
271	Place	Lionel	1768	60	Weddington	Warwick			
272	Plowman	John	1763	65	Normanston	Suffolk			
273	Pochin	George			Barkby	Leics		HS	1833, 234
274	Podmore	Richard B.	1780	48	Pailton House	Warwick			
275	Pollen-Boileau	George	1798	30	Bookham	Surrey		Rector	1833, 575
276	Polwhele	Richard	1760	68	Polwhele	Cornwall		Vicar-JP	1833, 424
277	Popham	Edward William	1807	21	Littlecote	Wiltshire			
278	Portman	Edward Berkeley	1799	29	Bryanston	Dorset		MP	1833, 62
279	Powell	Alexander	1782	46	Hurdcott	Wiltshire		MP	1833, 375
280	Powell	Richard Jones	1795	33	Hinton Court	Herefords			
281	Pratt	Edward Roger	1756	72	Ryston Hall	Norfolk			1834, 231

282	Prescott	William Willoughby	1776	52	Shire Hall	Middx			
283	Preston	George			Stanfied	Norfolk		Magistrate-Vicar	
284	Price	Hugh	1786	42	Castle Madox	Brecon		Sheriff	1836, 176
285	Pryce	Richard	1772	55	Guntley	Montgomery			
286	Pugh	David	1789	39	Llanerchydol	Montgomery		HS, DL	
287	Radcliffe	Walter			Warleigh	Devon		Magistrate-Vicar	1835, 28
288	Rawlings	William	1788	40	Padstow	Cornwall		JP, DL	1835, 68
289	Reed	Shakespeare			Thornhill	Durham		Magistrate	
290	Reeding	Walter				Derbys			
291	Reeve	James	1784	44		Suffolk	Lowestoft		
292	Ricardo	David	1803	25	Gatcombe	Gloucester			1833, 373
293	Ricketts	Edward			Combe	Herefords			
294	Ricketts	Thomas Bourke	1780	48	Combe	Herefords			1833, 92
295	Rickford	William	1768	60		Bucks	Aylesbury		
296	Roberts	William Roberts	1766	62	Bromley	Kent			
297	Robertson	Charles	1790	38	Kindeace	Ross-shire			1835, 77
298	Roddam	William	1793	35	Roddam Hall	Northumb			1833, 675
299	Rogers	John	1778	50	Penrose	Cornwall		Revd	1833, 299
300	Roundell	Richard Henry	1776	52	Gledstone	Yorks		Magistrate	1833, 342
301	Rous	Thomas Bates	1783	45	Courtyrala	Glamorgan			1833, 118
302	Saltern	Mary Ann			Michaelstow	Cornwall			
303	Salway	John			Elton Hall	Herefords			

Continued

ID	Name	Surname	Date of birth	Age	Place	County	City address	Public charges, military titles	Volume
304	Salway	Richard			Elton Hall	Herefords			
305	Salway	Theophilus Richard	1757	71	Elton Hall	Herefords			
306	Salwin	William Thomas	1767	51	Croasdaile	Durham			
307	Sandys	Myles	1762	66	Graythwaite	Lancs		DL	1833, 308
308	Scholey	George	1757	71		London	Old Swan Lane	Lord Mayor	
309	Scott	William Lister Fenton	1781	47	Wood Hall	Yorks			
310	Selby	Thomas	1756	72	Earle	Northumb			1835, 706
311	Senhouse	Humphrey	1763	65	Ellenborough	Cumberland		HS	1833, 216
312	Severn	John (Cheesment)	1782	46	Penybont Hall	Radnor		MP	
313	Shaw	Robert Newton	1788	40	Kesgrave	Suffolk		MP	
314	Sherwin	John	1803	25	Bramcote Hills	Notts			
315	Shirley	Evelyn John	1788	40	Eatington Park	Warwick		MP	1833, 49
316	Sikes	Joseph	1781	47		Notts	Newark		
317	Skelly	Gordon William Francis	1766	62	Pilmore	Durham		Colonel	
318	Smith	James	1771	57	Hilton	Shrops			
319	Sneyd	William	1767	61	Ashcombe	Staffs		DL	1833, 555
320	Sparrow	William Wynne	1792	36	Beaumaris	Caernarfon			
321	Spitty	Thomas	1788	40	Bowers Hall	Essex			
322		Abraham	1797	31	Elmdon	Warwick			

Spooner
Lillington

323	Spurdens	William	1777	51	The Oaks	Norfolk		Revd	
324	Spurgeon	John Grove	1745	83		Norfolk	Lowestoft	Rector-Magistrate	
325	Stanhope	John Spencer	1787	41	Cannon Hall	Yorks			1833, 467
326	Staunton	William	1765	63	Longbridge	Warwick		DL	1835, 587
327	Stead	Benjamin	1774	54	Beauchief	Derbys			
328	Stephens	Ellys Anderson	1770	58	Bowers Hall	Essex			
329	Stewart	John	1784	44	Belladrum	Inverness			
330	Storie	George Henry	1766	62	Springfield	Surrey		Revd	1833, 275
331	Stracy	John	1768	60	Beach	Cheshire		Colonel	
332	Stretton	Sempronius	1784	44	Lenton Priory	Notts		Lt.-Col.	
333	Strickland	Charles	1790	38		Lancs	Kendal		
334	Stuart	William	1798	30	Tempsford	Bedford		MP, DL	1833, 427
335	Sullivan	John	1749	79	Richings	Bucks		Sec. of State	1833, 410
336	Summer	Richard	1795	33	Puttenham Priory	Surrey			
337	Sutton	George William	1802	26	Elton	Durham			1835, 61
338	Swainston-Strangwayes	Edward	1782	46	Alne	Yorks		DL	1833, 665
339	Swallow	Richard	1797	31	Sheffield	Yorks			
340	Symonds	Charles	1784	44	Rudham	Norfolk			
341	Symonds	James	1779	49	Great Ormsby	Norfolk		Revd	
342	Symons	William	1786	42	Hatt House	Cornwall			
343	Talbot	Thomas	1778	50	Tivetshall	Norfolk		Revd	

Continued

ID	Name	Surname	Date of birth	Age	Place	County	City address	Public charges, military titles	Volume
344	Tatton	Emma	1809	21	Northenden	Cheshire			
345	Tempest-Plumbe	John			Tong Hall	Yorks		DL	1833, 289
346	Teward	John	1764	64	Southgate	Middx			
347	Thompson	Charles	1782	46	Witchingham	Norfolk			
348	Thornhill	Bache	1747	81	Stanton	Derbys		JP, HS	
349	Towneley	William	1770	58	Cartmel	Lancs			
350	Trafford	Edward	1783	45	Swythamley	Staffs			
351	Treby	Paul	1758	70	Plympton	Devon			
352	Trevanion-Bettesworth	John TrevanionPurnel	1780	48	Caerhayes	Cornwall		Colonel	1833, 253
353	Trevelyan	Raleigh	1781	47	Netherwitton	Northumb			1835, 329
354	Trotter	John	1768	60	Hetton	Durham			
355	Trye	Henry Norwood	1798	30	Leckhampton	Gloucester		Magistrate	
356	Tuckfield	Richard Hippisley	1774	54	Fulford Park	Devon			
357	Tunnard	Charles Keightley	1788	40	Frampton House	Lincoln		Major-Magistrate	
358	Turbutt	William	1768	60	Arnold Grove	Notts			
359	Turnon	Edmund	1754	74	Panton House	Lincoln			
360	Twemlow	John	1764	64	Hatherton	Cheshire			1837, 334
361	Twiss	Horace	1787	41			London	MP	
362	Tynte	Charles Kemeys	1779	49	Halsewell	Somerset		Colonel, DL, MP	1838, 182
363	Vivian	John	1784	44	Pencalenick	Cornwall			1833, 407

No.	Surname	First name	Year	Age	Seat	County	Address	Titles	Reference
364	Walker	George Townshend	1764	64	Bushey Hall	Herts	Harley street London	LG	1833, 313
365	Wall	Charles Baring	1795	33	Tytherley	Hants	Stockbridge	MP	
366	Wall	Samuel	1775	53	Worthy Park	Hants		Lt.-Col, DL, HS, banker	1833, 121
367	Waller	Harry Edmund	1804	24	Farmington Lodge	Kent		JP, DL	
368	Walmesley	Charles	1781	47	Westwood	Lancs			1833, 278
369	Walrond	Bethell	1802	26	Montrath	Devon		MP	
370	Walsham	John James Garbell	1805	25	Knill Court	Herefords			
371	Warde	George	1760	68	Woodland Castle	Glamorgan			
372	Wastek	Henry	1765	63	Thornley	Durham			
373	Watson	John Farside	1803	25	Bilton Park	Yorks			
374	Watts	Edward	1752	76	Hanslope	Bucks			
375	Werge	Edward			Heygrave	Notts			
376	Whieldon	George	1787	41	Cotton Hall	Staffs			
377	Whitaker	Thomas	1769	59	Caldewell	Worcester			
378	Wilbraham	George	1779	49	Delamere Hall	Cheshire		MP	1833, 315
379	Wilkinson	George Hutton	1791	37	Harperley	Durham			
380	Wilkinson	Walter	1777	51	Wallsworth	Gloucester			
381	Williams	James Rice	1787	41	Lee	Kent		DL	
382	Williams	Orlando Harrys	1783	45	Ivy Tower	Camarthen		HS	
383	Williams	Owen	1764	64	Temple House	Berkshire			
384	Williams	Robert	1767	61	Moor Parks	Herts			
385	Willis	Richard	1760	68	Halsnead	Lancs			
386	Wilson	John							

Continued

ID	Name	Surname	Date of birth	Age	Place	County	City address	Public charges, military titles	Volume
387	Wilson	Richard Fountayne	1783	45	Melton Park	Yorks		Sheriff, MP	
388	Winstanley	Clement	1775	53	Branston	Leics			
389	Wise	John Aysford	1786	42	Ford House	Devon			
390	Wodehouse	Edmund	1784	44	Lennox lodge	Norfolk		MP	
391	Wolfenstan	Stanley Pipe	1785	43	Stafford Hall	Staffs			
392	Wood	Henry Richard	1786	42	Hollin Hall	Ripon			
393	Wyndham	William	1769	59	Wyndham	Wiltshire		JP, DL	
394	Wynn	Charles Watkins Williams	1775	53	Llangedwyn	Denbigh		MP, President of the Board of Control	1833, 566
395	Yeates	Anthony	1743	45	Kirkland	Westm			
396	York	Simon	1771	57	Erthig	Denbigh		HS, MP	

Bibliography

Manuscripts

Bibliothèque Nationale
BN MS Anglais 111–13: correspondance de Jacques Tyrry (Terry): héraut d'armes anglais à Paris.
BN MS FR 32964: Preuves de noblesse recueillies par James Tyrry.

Bodleian Library
MS Eng. misc. d. 151–7: Letters to Mark Noble.
MS Phillipps C. 425: Sir Thomas Phillipps to John Burke.

British Library
Add. MS 19819: Pedigrees of families of Great Britain, 1784–6.
Add. MS 21033: Letters &c. addressed to the Revd William Betham, of Stonham Aspal, Suffolk, Editor of the *Baronetage of England*, 1783–1805.
Add. MS 24114–19: Notes on Wotton's *Baronetage*.
Add. MS 24120: Letters &c. addressed to Thomas Wotton (A–M).
Add. MS 24121: Letters &c. addressed to Thomas Wotton (M–Z).
Add. MS 27585: Notes and additional matter for a new edition of Sir William Dugdale's 'Baronage of England' continued to 1811, by Thomas Christopher Banks.
Add. MS 32689–93: Collins's letters to duke of Newcastle.
Add. MS 32715–26: Arthur Collins, Author of the *Peerage in England*: Letters to the duke of Newcastle.
Add. MS 36987: Letters addressed to Richard Gough, the antiquary, and to John Nichols.
Add. MS 38728: Original Assignments of Copyrights of Books and other Literary Agreements between various Publishers (1703–1810).
Add. MS 48800–901: Strahan papers.
Add. MS 48904: Strahan letters.

College of Arms
WC 55: Letters &c. addressed to John Burke (*Dictionary of the Peerage and Baronetage*, 1826).
WC 56–8: Letters to John Burke for the edition of *The Commoners* (1828), 3 vols.
WC 62–4: Courthorpe MS on Debrett's *Baronetage*.
WC 69–70: Courthorpe MS on Debrett's *Baronetage*.

Essex RO
D/Y 1/1: Wotton to Holman (1724).

366 BIBLIOGRAPHY

Irish Cultural Centre in Paris

John Lodge, *The Peerage of Ireland* (London, 1789), Annotated ed. CCI, B 674.

National Archives

C 5/175/17: Short title: *Mynors v Mynors.*
C 5/582/120: *Wotton v Eccleshall.*
C 11/328/39: Short title: *Fonnereau v Vandeput.*
C 11/481/1: Short title: *Broughton v Bayley.*
C12/220/9. Bill of Complaint of Charlotte Wattell.
PROB 11/123/206 Will of John Debrett.
PROB 11/1047/3 Will of Ethelred Bennet.
PROB 11/1236/89 Will of Barak Longmate.
PROB 11/1563/280 Will of John Stockdale.
PROB 11/1919/255 Will of William Betham.

National Art Library, Victoria & Albert Museum

Forster Collection: Correspondence and papers related to the *Peerage* (1826–40).

National Library of Scotland

APS.5.204.03: Subscribers to the British Family Antiquity: from 6 April to 18 May 1808, in the order they were received. London: Glendinning 1808.
Acc. 12047: Two volumes of Sir Robert Douglas of Glenbervie's Peerage of Scotland, 2nd edition, Edinburgh, 1813, edited by John Philip Wood, heavily annotated by the Edinburgh genealogist and family historian Alexander Sinclair (1794–1877).
Adv MS 19. 1. 21: Sir Robert Douglas. Genealogical material collected by Sir Robert Douglas, some of which was used in his Baronage of Scotland.
Adv MS 20. 1. 6–11: Sir Robert Douglas. Genealogical material collected by Sir Robert Douglas, some of which was used in his Peerage of Scotland.
Adv MS 35. 6. 14: Peerage of Scotland. An Eighteenth-century MS Used by John Phillip Wood in his edition of Sir Robert Douglas's *Peerage of Scotland.* 1813.

Society of Antiquaries of London

SAL MS 150: John Thorpe/Thomas Wotton.
SAL MS 173: A large collection of Kentish pedigrees transcribed by John Thorpe, senior.
SAL MS 508: Thorpe Papers.
SAL MS 691: Yorkshire pedigree by Thomas Beckwith of York (FSA, 1776).
SAL MS 982/1–3: Around bastardy by Thomas Christopher Banks in the Peerage.

Surrey RO

Surrey History Centre, G85/1: William Bray (1736–1832), Surrey lawyer and antiquary, kept a detailed diary of his personal and professional life.

University of Leeds, Special Collection

Yas MD335/1/7: Lister family papers.
MD335/1/9 Correspondence and papers of Rev Walter Collins of Bartin, in the parish of Bradley, Staffords.
MD335/3 Pilkington of Chevet, Family and Estate Records.

BIBLIOGRAPHY 367

Printed primary sources

Joseph Addison, *The Lucubrations of Isaac Bickerstaff, Esq.* (London, 1712).

James M. Adair, *Unanswerable arguments against the abolition of the slave Trade* (London, 1790).

Jane Austen, *Persuasion* (London, 1983).

G. F. Beltz, *Review of the Chandos Peerage Case: adjudicated* (London, 1803).

The Miscellaneous Works of Charles Blount [. . .]: To which is Prefix'd the Life of the Author (London, 1695).

Biographical and Literary Anecdotes of William Bowyer (London, 1782).

The Printing Accounts of William Bowyer Father and Son. With a Checklist of Bowyer Printing. 1699–1777, ed. Keith Maslen and John Lancaster (London, 1991).

The Autobiography, Times, Opinions, and Contemporaries of Sir Egerton Brydges, Bart. K. T. (Per legem terrae) Baron Chandos of Sudeley, vol. 1 (London, 1831).

John Burke, *The Portrait Gallery of Distinguished Females including beauties of the courts of George IV. and William IV* (London, 1833).

James Dallaway, *Inquiries into the origin and progress of the science of Heraldry in England* (London, 1793).

James Dallaway, *Heraldic Miscellanies, consisting of the Lives of Sir William Dugdale and Gregory King* (London, 1796).

Isaac d'Israeli, *Miscellanies, or Literary Recreations* (London, 1796).

Francis Drake, *History of York, Eboracum* (York, 1736).

William Fleetwood, *The relative duties of parents and children, husbands and wives* (London, 1737, 3rd edn).

Biographical Memoirs of William Ged (London, 1781).

Stacey Grimaldi, *Origines Genealogicae; or The Sources Whence English Genealogies may be Traced from the Conquest to the Present Time* (London, 1828).

Mary Ann Hanway, *Ellinor: Or, The World as it is* (London, 1798).

John Jordan, *Welcombe Hills, Near Stratford-upon-Avon: A Poem, Historical and Descriptive* (London, 1827).

John Gibson Lockhart, *Memoirs of the Life of Sir Walter Scott* (Edinburgh, 1837).

William Mosely (ed.), *Reports of Cases argued and determined in the High Court of Chancery* (London, 1803).

Thomas Moule, *Bibiliotheca Heraldica Magnae Britanniae* (London, 1822).

J. N. Nichols, *Literary Anecdotes of the Eighteenth Century,* 34 vols (London, 1812–15).

Thomas Osborne, *Catalogus bibliothecae Harleianae* (London, 1743).

Thomas Salmon, *An Impartial Examination of Bishop Burnet's History of His Own Times* (London, 1724).

Alan Saville (ed.), *Secret Comment: The Diaries of Gertrude Savile, 1721–1757* (Nottingham, 1997).

Richard Steele, *The Plebeian. By a Member of the House of Commons* (London, 1719).

Laurence Sterne, *The Life and Opinions of Tristram Shandy, Gentleman* (Oxford, 1983).

William Makepeace Thackeray, *Vanity Fair* (London, 1993).

Ralph Thoresby, *Ducatus Leodiensis, or Topography of the Ancient and Populous Town and Parish of Leedes* (London, 1715).

John Thorpe (ed.), *Registrum Roffense or a collection of antient records, charters and instruments of divers Kinds* (London, 1769).

Nicholas Tindal, *The History of England. Written in French by Mr. Rapin de Thoyras. Continued from the revolution to the accession of King George II,* 4 vols (London, 1744).

Memoirs of the Life of the Rev. Dr. Trusler (London, 1806).

David Vaisey (ed.), *The Diary of Thomas Turner* (Oxford, 1984).

The Way to be Rich and Respectable (London, 1775).

368 BIBLIOGRAPHY

Printed secondary sources

Books

Frédérique Aït-Touati, *Contes de la lune, essai sur la fiction et les sciences modernes* (Paris: Gallimard, 2011).

K. G. W. Anderson (ed.), *Enlightening the British: Knowledge, Discovery and the Museum in the Eighteenth Century* (London: British Museum Press, 2003).

Donna T. Andrew, *Aristocratic Vice: The Attack on Duelling, Suicide, Adultery, and Gambling in Eighteenth-Century England* (New Haven: Yale UP, 2013).

Edward Andrews, *Patrons of Enlightenment* (Toronto: University of Toronto Press, 2006).

James Ayre, *Art, Artisans and Apprentices: Apprentice Painters & Sculptors in the Early Modern Tradition* (Oxford: Oxbow Books, 2014).

Joanne Bailey, *Parenting in England 1760-1830: Emotion, Identity, and Generation* (Oxford: Oxford UP, 2012).

Paul Baines, *The House of Forgery in 18th-Century Britain* (Farnham: Ashgate, 1999).

Janine Barchas, *Matters of Fact in Jane Austen: History, Location, and Celebrity* (Baltimore: Johns Hopkins UP, 2012).

Hannah Barker, *Newspapers, Politics, and Public Opinion in Late Eighteenth-Century England* (Oxford: Clarendon Press, 1998).

John V. Beckett, *The Aristocracy in England, 1660-1914* (Oxford: Basil Blackwell, 1986).

Maxine Berg, *Luxury and Pleasure in Eighteenth-Century Britain* (Oxford: Oxford UP, 2007).

Ann Bermingham and John Brewer (eds), *The Consumption of Culture, 1600-1800: Image, Object, Text* (London: Routledge, 1995).

Gianenrico Bernasconi, *Objets portatifs au Siècle des Lumières* (Paris: Éditions du comité des travaux historiques et scientifiques, 2015).

Hilary J. Bernstein, *Historical Communities: Cities, Erudition, and National Identity in Early Modern France* (Leiden and Boston: Brill, 2021).

Helen Berry and Elizabeth Forster (eds), *The Family in Early Modern England* (Cambridge: Cambridge UP, 2007).

Helen Berry and Jeremy Gregory, *Creating and Consuming Culture in North-East England, 1660-1830* (London: Routledge, 2019).

Warren M. Billings and Brent Tarter (eds), *'Esteemed Bookes of Lawe' and the Legal Culture of Early Virginia* (Charlottesville, Va: University of Virginia Press, 2017).

Roberto Bizzochi, *Généalogies fabuleuses: inventer et faire croire dans l'Europe moderne* (Paris: Éditions Rue d'Ulm, 2010).

Francis X. Blouin and William G. Rosenberg, *Processing the Past: Contesting Authority in History and the Archives* (Oxford: Oxford UP, 2011).

Lloyd Bonfield (ed.), *Marriage, Property, and Succession: Comparative Studies in Continental and Anglo-American Legal History* (Berlin: Duncker & Humblot, 1992).

Peter Borsay, *The Urban Renaissance: Culture and Society in the Provincial Town 1660-1770* (Oxford: Clarendon Press, 1989).

Richard Bourke, *Empire and Revolution: The Political Life of Edmund Burke* (Princeton: Princeton UP, 2015).

Jean Boutier (ed.), *Étienne Baluze (1630-1718): érudition et pouvoirs dans l'Europe Classique* (Limoges: PULIM, 2008).

Asa Briggs, *A History of Longmans and Their Books, 1724-1990* (London: Oak Knoll Press, 2008).

BIBLIOGRAPHY 369

Jan Broadway, 'No historie so meete': Gentry Culture and the Development of Local History in Elizabethan and Early Stuart England (Manchester: Manchester UP, 2006).

Barbara Burman and Ariane Fennetaux, The Pocket: A Hidden History of Women's Lives (New Haven: Yale UP, 2019).

Arthur Burns and Joanna Innes (eds), Rethinking the Age of Reform: Britain 1780–1850 (Cambridge: Cambridge UP, 2003).

Germain Butaud and Valérie Piétri, Les enjeux de la généalogie (XIIe–XVIIIe siècle): pouvoir et identité (Paris: Autrement, 2006).

Sandy Byrne, Jane Austen's Possessions and Dispossessions: The Significance of Objects (Basingstoke: Palgrave Macmillan, 2014).

Caroline Callard, Le temps des fantômes: spectralités de l'âge moderne (XVIe–XVIIe siècle) (Paris: Fayard, 2019).

David Cannadine, The Decline and Fall of the British Aristocracy (New Haven: Yale UP, 1990).

David Cannadine, Aspects of Aristocracy: Grandeur and Decline in Modern Britain (New Haven: Yale UP, 1994).

John Cannon, Aristocratic Century: The Peerage of Eighteenth-Century England (Cambridge: Cambridge UP, 1984).

Nicholas Canny, Imagining Ireland's Pasts: Early Modern Ireland through the Centuries (Oxford: Oxford UP, 2021).

Bernard S. Capp, The Ties That Bind: Siblings, Family, and Society in Early Modern England (Oxford: Oxford UP, 2018).

Jean-Luc Chappey, Ordres et désordres biographiques: dictionnaires, listes de noms, réputation des Lumières à Wikipédia (Seyssel: Champ Vallon, 2013).

John Charlton, Hidden Chains: The Slavery Business and North East England, 1600–1865 (Newcastle upon Tyne: Tyne Bridge, 2008).

Roger Chartier, L'ordre des livres: lecteurs, auteurs, bibliothèques en Europe entre XIVe et XVIIIe siècle (Aix-en-Provence: Alinéa, 1992).

Christopher Christie, The British Country House in the Eighteenth Century (Manchester: Manchester UP, 2000).

Jonathan Clark, English Society, 1688–1832: Ideology, Social Structure and Political. Practice during the Ancien Regime (Cambridge, Cambridge UP, 1985).

Deborah Cohen, Family Secrets: The Things We Tried to Hide (London: Penguin, 2013).

Stephen Colclough, Consuming Texts: Readers and Reading Communities, 1695–1870 (Basingstoke: Palgrave Macmillan, 2007).

Linda Colley, Britons: Forging the Nation (New Haven: Yale UP, 1992).

Sean J. Connolly, Religion, Law, and Power: The Making of Protestant Ireland 1660–1760 (Oxford: Clarendon Press, 1992).

Edward Copeland, The Silver Fork Novel: Fashionable Fiction in the Age of Reform (Cambridge: Cambridge UP, 2012).

Liesbeth Corens, Confessional Mobility and English Catholics in Counter-Reformation Europe (Oxford: Oxford UP, 2019).

Barbara Crosbie, Age Relations and Cultural Change in Eighteenth-Century England (Woodbridge: Boydell Press, 2020).

Laurent Curelly and Nigel Smith (eds), Radical Voices, Radical Ways: Articulating and Disseminating Radicalism in Seventeenth- and Eighteenth-Century Britain (Manchester: Manchester UP, 2016).

Martin J. Daunton, Progress and Poverty: An Economic and Social History of Britain (Oxford: Oxford UP, 1995).

370 BIBLIOGRAPHY

Leonore Davidoff and Catherine Hall, *Family Fortunes: Men and Women of the English Middle Class, 1780–1850* (London: Routledge, 3rd edn, 2018).

Richard Beale Davis, *A Colonial Southern Bookshelf: Reading in the Eighteenth Century* (Athens, Ga: University of Georgia Press, 1979).

Robert Descimon and Élie Haddad (eds), *Épreuves de noblesse: les expériences nobiliaires de la haute robe parisienne (XVIᵉ–XVIIIᵉ siècle)* (Paris: Les Belles Lettres, 2010).

Jonathan Dewald, *Status, Power, and Identity in Early Modern France: The Rohan Family, 1550–1715* (University Park, Pa: Penn State UP, 2015)

Claude-Olivier Doron, *L'homme altéré: race et dégénérescence* (Seyssel: Champ Vallon, 2016).

Stephanie Downes, Sally Holloway, and Sarah Randles (eds), *Feeling Things: Objects and Emotions Through History* (Oxford: Oxford UP, 2018).

William Doyle, *Aristocracy and its Enemies in the Age of Revolution* (Oxford: Oxford UP, 2009).

Jean-François Dunyach, *The Enlightenments of William Playfair: Invention, Politics and Patronage in the Time of the French Revolution* (Princeton: Princeton UP, forthcoming 2024).

Jost Eickmeyer, Markus Friedrich, and Volker Bauer (eds), *Genealogical Knowledge in the Making: Tools, Practices, and Evidence in Early Modern Europe* (Oldenburg: De Gruyter, 2019).

A. L. Erikson, *Women and Property in Early Modern England* (London: Routledge, 1993).

John Feather, *The Provincial Book Trade in Eighteenth-Century England* (Cambridge: Cambridge UP, 1985).

Margot C. Finn, Michael Lobban, and Jenny Bourne Taylor (eds), *Legitimacy and Illegitimacy in Nineteenth-Century Law, Literature and History* (Basingstoke: Palgrave Macmillan, 2010).

Christopher Flint, *Family Fictions: Narrative and Domestic Relations in Britain, 1688–1798* (Stanford, Calif.: Stanford UP, 1998).

Henry French, *Man's Estate: Landed Gentry Masculinities, c.1660–c.1900* (Oxford: Oxford UP, 2012).

Markus Friedrich, *Die Geburt des Archivs: Eine Wissensgeschichte* (Munich: Oldenburg Verlag, 2013).

Peter Garside, James Raven, and Rainer Schöwerling (eds), *The English Novel 1770–1829: A Bibliographical Survey of Prose Fiction Published in the British Isles*, vol. 2 (Oxford: Oxford UP, 2000).

John Gascoigne, *Joseph Banks and the English Enlightenment* (Cambridge: Cambridge UP, 1994).

Perry Gauci, *The Politics of Trade: The Overseas Merchant in State and Society, 1660–1720* (Oxford: Oxford UP, 2003).

Perry Gauci, *William Beckford: First Prime Minister of the London Empire* (New Haven: Yale UP, 2015).

Christine Gerrard, *The Patriot Opposition to Walpole: Politics, Poetry, and National Myth, 1725–1742* (Oxford: Oxford UP, 1994).

Claire Gheeraert-Graffeuille, *Lucy Hutchinson and the English Revolution: Gender, Genre and History-Writing* (Oxford: Oxford UP, 2022)

Sophie Gilmartin, *Ancestry and Narrative in Nineteenth-Century British Literature: Blood Relations from Edgeworth to Hardy* (Cambridge: Cambridge UP, 1998).

Mark Girouard, *Life in the English Country House: A Social and Architectural History* (New Haven and London: Yale UP, 1978).

BIBLIOGRAPHY 371

Gabriel Glickman, *The English Catholic Community 1688–1745: Politics, Culture and Ideology* (Cambridge: Cambridge UP, 2009).

Sarah Goldsmith, *Masculinity and Danger on the Eighteenth-Century Grand Tour* (London: London Press, 2020).

Dena Goodman, *The Republic of Letters: A Cultural History of the French Enlightenment* (Ithaca, NY, and London: Cornell UP, 1994).

Anthony Grafton, *The Footnote: A Curious History* (London: Faber and Faber, 1997).

Anthony Grafton and Daniel Rosenberg, *Cartographies of Times: A Visual History of the Timeline* (Princeton: Princeton UP, 2010).

Cyril Grange, *Gens du bottin mondain, 1903–1987: y être, c'est en être* (Paris: Fayard, 1996).

Chantal Grell, *L'histoire entre érudition et philosophie: étude sur la connaissance historique au siècle des Lumières* (Paris: PUF, 1993).

Dustin Griffin, *Literary Patronage in England, 1650–1800* (Cambridge: Cambridge UP, 1996.

Devin Griffiths, *The Age of Analogy: Science and Literature between the Darwins* (Baltimore: Johns Hopkins UP, 2016).

Tara Hamling, *Decorating the 'Godly' Household: Religious Art in Post-Reformation Britain* (New Haven: Yale UP, 2010).

Tara Hamling and Catherine Richardson, *A Day at Home in Early Modern England: Material Culture and Domestic Life, 1500–1700* (New Haven: Yale UP, 2017).

Brean S. Hammond, *Professional Imaginative Writing in England, 1670–1740: 'Hackney for bread'* (Oxford: Clarendon Press, 1997).

Sasha Handley, *Visions of an Unseen World: Ghost Beliefs and Ghost Stories in Eighteenth-Century England* (London: Routledge, 2015).

Amy Harris, *Sibling and Social Relations in Georgian England* (Manchester: Manchester UP, 2012).

Karen Harvey, *The Little Republic: Masculinity and Domestic Authority in Eighteenth-Century Britain* (Oxford: Oxford UP, 2012).

Boyd Hilton, *A Mad, Bad, and Dangerous People? England, 1783–1846* (Oxford: Oxford UP, 2006).

Melissa S. Jenkins, *Fatherhood, Authority, and British Reading Culture, 1831–1907* (London: Routledge, 2016).

Stéphane Jettot and Marie Lezowski (eds), *The Genealogical Enterprise: Social Practices and Collective Imagination in Europe (15th–20th Century)* (Brussels: Peter Lang, 2016).

Stéphane Jettot and J.-P. Zuniga (eds), *Genealogy and Social Status in the Enlightenment* (Liverpool: Liverpool UP, 2021).

Andrew Jones, *Memory and Material Culture* (Cambridge: Cambridge UP, 2007).

Colin Jones and Dror Wahrman (eds), *The Age of Cultural Revolution: Britain and France, 1750–1820* (Berkeley: University of California Press, 2002).

George L. Justice, *The Manufacturers of Literature: Writing and the Literary Marketplace in Eighteenth-Century England* (Newark, Del.: Delaware UP, 2002).

George L. Justice and Nathan Tinker (eds), *Women's Writing and the Circulation of Ideas: Manuscript Publication in England, 1550–1800* (Cambridge: Cambridge UP, 2002).

Colin Kidd, *British Identities before Nationalism: Ethnicity and Nationhood in the Atlantic World, 1600–1800* (Cambridge: Cambridge UP, 1999).

Colin Kidd, *Subverting Scotland's Past: Scottish Whig Historians and the Creation of an Anglo-British Identity 1689–1830* (Cambridge: Cambridge UP, 2003).

Matthew Kinservik, *Sex, Scandal, and Celebrity in Late Eighteenth-Century England* (Basingstoke: Palgrave Macmillan, 2007).

372 BIBLIOGRAPHY

Christiane Klapisch-Zuber, *La maison et le nom: stratégies et rituels dans l'Italie de la Renaissance* (Paris: EHESS, 1990).

Mark Knights, *Trust and Distrust: Corruption in Office in Britain and its Empire, 1600–1850* (Oxford: Oxford UP, 2021).

Paul Langford, *Public Life and the Propertied Englishman, 1689–1789* (Oxford: Clarendon Press, 1991).

Joseph M. Levine, *The Battle of the Books: History and Literature in the Augustan Age* (Ithaca, NY: Cornell UP, 1991).

Philippa Levine, *The Amateur and the Professional: Antiquarians, Historians and Archaeologists in Victorian England, 1838–1886* (Cambridge: Cambridge UP, 1986).

Antoine Lilti and Céline Spector (eds), *Penser l'Europe au XVIIIe siècle: commerce, civilisation, empire* (Oxford: Voltaire Foundation, 2014).

Andrew Lincoln, *Walter Scott and Modernity* (Edinburgh: Edinburgh UP, 2012).

Marie Loughlin, *Figures of Descent: Genealogy and the Early Modern Woman Writer, c.1580–1700* (London: Routledge, 2022).

Judith Lyon-Caen, *La griffe du temps: ce que l'histoire peut dire de la littérature* (Paris: Gallimard, 2019).

David McKitterick, *The Invention of Rare Books; Private Interest and Public Memory, 1600–1840* (Cambridge: Cambridge UP, 2018).

Christine MacLeod, *Heroes of Invention: Technology, Liberalism and British Identity 1750–1914* (Cambridge: Cambridge UP, 2007).

Emma Vincent MacLeod, *A War of Ideas: British Attitudes to the Wars Against Revolutionary France, 1792–1802* (Aldershot: Ashgate, 1998).

A. P. W. Malcomson, *The Pursuit of the Heiress: Aristocratic Marriage in Ireland, 1750–1820* (Belfast: Ulster Historical Foundation, 1982).

Sarah Mazah, *The Myth of the French Bourgeoisie: An Essay on the Social Imaginary, 1750–1850* (Cambridge, Mass.: Harvard UP, 2003).

Jane Moody (ed.), *The Cambridge Companion to British Theatre, 1730–1830* (Cambridge: Cambridge UP, 2007).

A. N. L. Munby, *The Formation of the Phillipps Library up to the Year 1840* (Cambridge: Cambridge UP, 1954).

Laird Okie, *Augustan Historical Writing: Histories of England in the Enlightenment* (Lanham, Md: University Press of America, 1991).

Graham Parry, *The Trophies of Time: English Antiquarianism of the Seventeenth Century* (Oxford: Oxford UP, 1995).

David Pearson, *Provenance Research in Book History* (Oxford: Bodleian Library, 1994).

Ruth Perry, *Novel Relations: The Transformation of Kinship in English Literature and Culture, 1748–1818* (Cambridge: Cambridge UP, 2004).

Christley Petley (ed.), *Rethinking the Fall of the Planter Class* (London: Routledge, 2018).

John Phillips, *The Great Reform Bill and the Boroughs: English Electoral Behaviour* (Oxford: Oxford UP, 1993).

Mark S. Phillips, *Society and Sentiment: Genres of Historical Writing in Britain 1740–1820* (Princeton: Princeton UP, 2010).

John V. Pickstone, *Ways of Knowing A New History of Science, Technology and Medicine* (Manchester: Manchester UP, 2000).

Judith Pollman, *Memory in Early Modern Europe, 1500–1800* (Oxford: Oxford UP, 2017).

Dominique Poulot, *Musée, nation, patrimoine, 1789–1815* (Paris: Gallimard, 1997).

Wilfrid Prest, *William Blackstone: Law and Letters in the Eighteenth Century* (Oxford: Oxford UP, 2008).

BIBLIOGRAPHY 373

Huw Pryce, *Writing Welsh History: From the Early Middle Ages to the Twenty-First Century* (Oxford: Oxford UP, 2022).

Dorit Raines, *L'invention du mythe aristocratique: l'image de soi du patriciat vénitien au temps de la Sérénissime* (Venice: Instituto Veneto, 2006).

Nigel Ramsey (ed.), *Heralds and Heraldry in Shakespeare's England* (Donington: Shaun Tyas, 2014).

James Raven, *Judging New Wealth: Popular Publishing and Responses to Commerce in England, 1750–1800* (Oxford: Oxford UP, 1992).

James Raven, *London Booksellers and American Customers: Transatlantic Literary Community and the Charleston Library Society 1758–1811* (Columbia, SC: University of South Carolina Press, 2002).

James Raven, *The Business of Books: Booksellers and the English Book Trade 1450–1850* (New Haven: Yale UP, 2011).

James Raven, *Publishing Business in Eighteenth-Century England* (Woodbridge: Boydell Press, 2014).

James Raven, Helen Small, and Naomi Tadmor (eds), *The Practice and Representation of Reading in England* (Cambridge: Cambridge UP, 1996).

Peter Roebuck, *Yorkshire Baronets 1640–1760* (Oxford: Oxford UP, 1980).

François-Joseph Ruggiu, *Les élites et les villes moyennes en France et en Angleterre (XVIIe–XVIIIe siècles)* (Paris: PUPS, 1997).

François-Joseph Ruggiu, *L'individu et la famille dans les sociétés urbaines anglaise et française (1720–1780)* (Paris: PUPS, 2007).

David Warren Sabean, Simon Teuscher, and Jon Mathieu (eds), *Kinship in Europe: Approaches to Long-Term Development (1300–1900)* (Oxford: Berghahn Books, 2007).

James J. Sack, *From Jacobite to Conservative: Reaction and Orthodoxy in Britain c.1760–1832* (Cambridge: Cambridge UP, 1993).

William St Clair, *The Reading Nation in the Romantic Period* (Cambridge: Cambridge UP, 2004).

Martine Segalen, *Historical Anthropology of the Family* (Cambridge: Cambridge UP, 1986).

Stuart Semmel, *Napoleon and the British* (New Haven: Yale UP, 2004).

Steven Shapin, *A Social History of Truth, Civility and Science in Seventeenth-Century England* (Chicago and London: University of Chicago Press, 1994).

Richard B. Sher, *The Enlightenment and the Book: Scottish Authors & Their Publishers in Eighteenth Century Britain, Ireland, & America* (Chicago: University of Chicago Press, 2006).

D. Brenton Simons and Peter Benes (eds), *The Art of Family: Genealogical Artifacts in New England* (Boston: Northeastern UP, 2002).

Will Slauter, *Who Owns the News? A History of Copyright* (Stanford, Calif.: Stanford UP, 2019).

Hannah Smith, *Georgian Monarchy: Politics and Culture 1714–1760* (Cambridge: Cambridge UP, 2006).

Jay M. Smith, *The French Nobility in the Eighteenth Century: Reassessments and New Approaches* (University Park, Pa: Penn State UP, 2006).

Jon Stobart and Mark Rothery, *Consumption and the Country House* (Oxford: Oxford UP, 2016).

Kristina Straub, *Sexual Suspects: Eighteenth-Century Players and Sexual Ideology* (Princeton: Princeton UP, 1992).

Rosemary Sweet, *The Writing of Urban Histories in Eighteenth-Century England* (Oxford: Oxford UP, 1997).

Rosemary Sweet, *Antiquaries: The Discovery of the Past in Eighteenth-Century Britain* (London: Hambledon and London, 2004).

374 BIBLIOGRAPHY

Naomi Tadmor, *Family and Friends in Eighteenth-Century England: Household, Kinship, and Patronage* (Cambridge: Cambridge UP, 2001).

Archer Taylor, *Book Catalogues: Their Varieties and Uses* (Winchester: St Paul's Bibliographies, 1986).

Mark Towsey, *Reading History in Britain and America, c.1750–c.1840* (Cambridge: Cambridge UP, 2019).

Mark Towsey and Kyle B. Roberts (eds), *Before the Public Library: Reading, Community, and Identity in the Atlantic World, 1650–1850* (Leiden: Brill, 2018).

Katie Trumpener, *Bardic Nationalism: The Romantic Novel and the British Empire* (Princeton: Princeton UP, 1997).

Edward Vallance, *Remembering Early Modern Revolutions: England, North America, France and Haiti* (London: Routledge, 2019).

Amanda Vickery, *The Gentleman's Daughter: Women's Lives in Georgian England* (New Haven: Yale UP, 2003).

Antony Wagner, *English Genealogy* (London: Clarendon Press, 1972).

Dror Wahrman, *Imagining the Middle Class: The Political Representation of Class in Britain, c.1780–1840* (Cambridge: Cambridge UP, 1995).

Alexandra Walsham, *The Reformation of the Landscape: Religion, Identity, and Memory in Early Modern Britain and Ireland* (Oxford: Oxford UP, 2011).

Alexandra Walsham, *Generations Age, Ancestry, and Memory in the English Reformations* (Oxford: Oxford UP, 2023).

Lyndan Warner (ed.), *Stepfamilies in Europe 1400–1800* (London: Routledge, 2018).

James Watt, *Contesting the Gothic: Fiction, Genre and Cultural Conflict, 1764–1832* (Cambridge: Cambridge UP 1999).

François Weil, *Family Trees: A History of Genealogy in America* (Cambridge, Mass.: Harvard UP, 2013).

Abigail Williams, *The Social Life of Books: Reading Together in the Eighteenth-Century Home* (New Haven: Yale UP, 2017).

Gillian Williamson, *British Masculinity in the 'Gentleman's Magazine', 1731–1815* (Basingstoke: Palgrave Macmillan, 2016).

R. G. Wilson, *Gentlemen Merchants: The Merchant Community in Leeds, 1700–1830* (Manchester: Manchester UP, 1971).

Susan Wiseman, *Conspiracy and Virtue: Women, Writing and Politics in Seventeenth-Century England* (Oxford: Oxford UP, 2006).

Daniel R. Woolf, *The Social Circulation of the Past: English Historical Culture, 1500–1730* (Oxford: Oxford UP, 2003).

Levent Yilmaz, *Le temps moderne: variations sur les Anciens et les contemporains* (Paris: Gallimard, 2004).

William Zachs, *The First John Murray and the Late Eighteenth-Century London Book Trade: With a Checklist of His Publications* (Oxford: Oxford UP, 1998).

Article and essays

Ilya Afanasyev and Milinda Banerjee, 'The Modern Invention of "Dynasty": An Introduction', *Global Intellectual History*, vol. 7, no. 3 (2022): 407–20.

Adrian Ailes, 'Can we Trust the Genealogical Record of the Heralds' Visitations? A Case Study (the 1665–66 Visitation of Berkshire)', in Stéphane Jettot and Marie Lezowski (eds), *The Genealogical Enterprise: Social Practices and Collective Imagination in Europe (15th–20th Century)* (Brussels: Peter Lang, 2016), 143–57.

BIBLIOGRAPHY 375

David Allan, '"What's in a Name?": Pedigree and Propaganda in Seventeenth-Century Scotland', in Edward J. Cowan and Richard J. Finlay (eds), *Scottish History: The Power of the Past* (Edinburgh: Edinburgh UP, 2002), 147–67.

David Allan, 'Circulation', in Peter Garside and Karen O'Brien (eds), *English and British Fiction, 1750–1820: The Oxford History of the Novel in English* (Oxford: Oxford UP, 2015), 53–73.

Susan D. Amussen, 'The Contradictions of Patriarchy in Early Modern England', *Gender & History*, vol. 30, no. 2 (2018): 343–53.

Ronda Arab, 'Sir George Sondes His plaine Narrative to the World: The Envious Younger Son and the Inequality of Inheritance in Seventeenth-Century England', *Journal of Medieval and Early Modern Studies*, vol. 49, no. 2 (2019): 403–26.

Paul Baines, '"Our Annius": Antiquaries and Fraud in the Eighteenth Century', *British Journal for Eighteenth-Century Studies*, vol. 20, no. 1 (1997): 33–51.

Jonathan Barry, 'Communicating with Authority: The Uses of Script, Print and Speech in Bristol, 1640–1714', in Alexandra Walsham and Julia Crick (eds), *The Uses of Script and Print, 1300–1700* (Cambridge: Cambridge UP, 2004), 191–208.

Jennie Batchelor, 'Fashion and Frugality: Eighteenth-Century Pocket Books for Women', *Studies in Eighteenth Century Culture*, vol. 32, no. 1 (2003): 1–18.

Volker Bauer, 'Herrschaftsordnung, Datenordnung, Suchoptionen: Recherchemöglichkeiten in Staatskalendern und Staatshandbüchern des 18. Jahrhunderts', in Thomas Brandstetter, Thomas Hübel, and Anton Tantner (eds), *Vor Google: Eine Mediengeschichte der Suchmaschine im analogen Zeitalter* (Bielefeld: Verlag, 2012), 85–108.

Volker Bauer, 'The Scope, Readership and Economy of Printed Genealogies in Early Modern Germany: "Special Genealogien" vs. "Universal Genealogien"', in Stéphane Jettot and Marie Lezowski (eds), *The Genealogical Enterprise: Social Practices and Collective Imagination in Europe (15th–20th Century)* (Brussels, 2016), 287–301.

Terry Belanger, 'Booksellers' Trade Sales, 1718–1768', *The Library*, vol. 30, no. 4 (1975): 281–303.

Lucien Bely, 'The New Monarchy in France, the Social Elite and the Society of Princes', in Robert von Friedeburg and John Morrill (eds), *Monarchy Transformed: Princes and Their Elites in Early Modern Western Europe* (Cambridge: Cambridge UP, 2017), 164–81.

Maxine Berg, 'New Commodities, Luxuries and Their Consumers in Eighteenth-Century England', in Maxine Berg and Helen Clifford (eds), *Consumers and Luxury: Consumer Culture in Europe, 1650–1850* (Manchester: Manchester UP, 1999), 63–73.

Stefan Berger, 'The Role of National Archives in Constructing National Master Narratives in Europe', *Archival Science*, vol. 13, no. 1 (2013): 1–22.

Helen Berry, 'Polite Consumption: Shopping in Eighteenth-Century England', *Transactions of the Royal Historical Society*, vol. 12 (2002): 375–94.

Ann Blair, 'Managing Information', in James Raven (ed.), *The Oxford Illustrated History of the Book* (Oxford: Oxford UP, 2020), 169–95.

Mary Bouquet, 'Family Trees and Their Affinities: The Visual Imperative of the Genealogical Diagram', *Journal of the Royal Anthropological Institute of London*, vol. 2, no. 1 (1996): 43–66.

Pierre Bourdieu, 'La noblesse: capital social et capital symbolique', in Didier Lancien, Monique de Saint Martin, and Pierre Bourdieu (eds), *Anciennes et nouvelles aristocraties de 1880 à nos jours* (Paris: Maison des sciences de l'homme, 2007), 385–97.

Rebecca Bowd, 'Useful Knowledge or Polite Learning', *Library & Information History*, vol. 29, no. 3 (2013): 182–95.

376 BIBLIOGRAPHY

Patrice Bret, 'Figures du savant, XVᵉ–XVIIIᵉ', in Liliane Hilaire-Pérez, Fabien Simon, and Marie Thébaud-Sorger (eds), *L'Europe des sciences et des techniques: un dialogue des savoirs, XVe–XVIIIe siècle* (Rennes: PUR, 2016), 95–103.

John Brewer, 'The Misfortunes of Lord Bute: A Case-Study in Eighteenth-Century Political Argument and Public Opinion', *The Historical Journal*, vol. 16, no. 1 (1973): 3–43.

Asa Briggs, 'The Background of the Parliamentary Reform movement in Three English Cities, 1830–1832', *The Historical Journal*, vol. 10 (1952): 293–317.

Trevor Burnard, 'Slave Naming Patterns: Onomastics and the Taxonomy of Race in Eighteenth-Century Jamaica', *The Journal of Interdisciplinary History*, vol. 31, no. 3 (2001): 325–46.

Toby Burrows, '"There never was such a collector since the world began": A New Look at Sir Thomas Phillipps', in Toby Burrows and Cynthia Johnston (eds), *Collecting the Past: British Collectors and Their Collections from the 18th to the 20th Centuries* (London: Routledge, 2019), 45–63.

Elaine Chalus, 'Shorter Notice. Secret Comment: The *Diaries* of *Gertrude Savile*', *The English Historical Review*, vol. 114, no. 456 (1999): 451–2.

Emmanuelle Chapron, Jean-Dominique Mellot, and Christine Benevent, 'Où va l'histoire du livre? Bilans et chantiers dans le sillage d'Henri-Jean Martin (1924–2007)', *Histoire et civilisation du livre: revue internationale*, no. 16 (2020): 9–247.

Emmanuelle Chapron, 'Les bibliothèques des séminaires et collèges britanniques à Paris, de l'Ancien Régime à l'Empire', *Bibliothèque de l'École des Chartes*, vol. 169 (2016): 567–96.

Peter Clark and R. A. Houston, 'Culture and Leisure, 1700–1840', in Peter Clark (ed.), *The Cambridge Urban History of Britain*, vol. 2: *1540–1840* (Cambridge: Cambridge UP, 2000), 575–615.

Stephen Colclough, 'Pocket Books and Portable Writing: The Pocket Memorandum Book in Eighteenth-Century England and Wales', *The Yearbook of English Studies*, vol. 45 (2015): 159–77.

Linda Colley, 'The Apotheosis of George III: Loyalty, Royalty and the British Nation 1760–1820', *Past and Present*, vol. 102 (1984): 94–129.

Penelope Corfield, '"Giving directions to the town": The Early Town Directories', *Urban History Yearbook*, vol. 11 (1984): 22–35.

Penelope Corfield, 'From Rank to Class: Innovation in Georgian England', *History Today*, vol. 37 (1987): 36–42.

M. R. S. Creese and T. M. Creese, 'British Women who Contributed to Research in Geological Sciences', *British Journal for the History of Science*, vol. 27 (1994): 23–54.

Richard Cust, 'The Material Culture of Lineage in Late Tudor and Early Stuart England', in Catherine Richardson, Tara Hamling, and David R. M. Gaimster (eds), *The Routledge Handbook of Material Culture in Early Modern Europe* (London: Routledge, 2017), 247–65.

Robert Darnton, 'Two Paths through the Social History of Ideas', in Haydn T. Mason (ed.), *The Darnton Debate: Books and Revolution in the Eighteenth Century* (Oxford: Voltaire edition, 1998), 251–95.

Natalie Zemon Davis, 'Ghosts, Kin and Progeny: Some Features of Family Life', *Daedalus*, vol. 106, no. 7 (1977): 87–114.

Robert Descimon, 'Élites parisiennes entre XVe et XVIIe siècle: du bon usage du Cabinet des titres', *Bibliothèque de l'École des Chartes*, vol. 155, no. 2 (1997): 607–44.

Gillian Dow and Katie Hasley, 'Jane Austen's Reading: The Chawton Years', *Jane Austen Society of North America*, vol. 30, no. 2 (2010). <http://www.jasna.org/persuasions/on-line/vol30no2/dow-halsey.html>.

John Dowling, 'Burros and Brays in Eighteenth-Century Spanish Literature and Art', *Hispanic Journal*, vol. 4, no. 1 (1982): 7–21.

Ian Duncan, 'Walter Scott and the Historical Novel', in Peter Garside and Karen O'Brien (eds), *English and British Fiction, 1750–1820: The Oxford History of the Novel in English*, vol. 2 (Oxford: Oxford UP, 2015), 312–32.

Jean-François Dunyach, 'Le British Family Antiquity de William Playfair (1809–1811), une entreprise généalogique', in Stéphane Jettot and Marie Lezowski (eds), *The Genealogical Enterprise: Social Practices and Collective Imagination in Europe (15th–20th Century)* (Brussels: Peter Lang, 2016), 303–39.

J. E. Elliot, 'The Cost of Reading in Eighteenth-Century Britain: Auction Sale Catalogues and the Cheap Literature Hypothesis', *English Literary History*, vol. 77, no. 2 (2010): 353–84.

Markman Ellis, 'Coffee-House Libraries in Mid-Eighteenth-Century London', *The Library*, vol. 10 (2009): 3–40.

Barbara English, 'Bateman Revisited: The Great Landowners of Great Britain', in Didier Lancien, Monique de Saint Martin, and Pierre Bourdieu (eds), *Anciennes et nouvelles aristocraties de 1880 à nos jours* (Paris: Maison des sciences de l'homme, 2007), 75–90.

Tanya Evans, 'Secrets and Lies: The Radical Potential of Family History', *History Workshop Journal*, vol. 71, no. 1 (2011): 49–73.

Margaret J. M. Ezell, 'Invisible Books', in Laura Runge and Pat Rogers (eds), *Producing the Eighteenth-Century Book: Writers and Publishers in England, 1650–1800* (Newark, Del.: University of Delaware Press, 2009), 53–71.

David Fallon, '"Stuffd up with books": The Bookshops and Business of Thomas Payne and Son, 1740–1831', *History of Retailing and Consumption*, vol. 5, no. 3 (2019): 228–45.

Jan Fergus and Ruth Portner, 'Provincial Bookselling in Eighteenth-Century England: The Case of John Clay Reconsidered', *Studies in Bibliography*, vol. 40 (1987): 147–63.

David Fielding and Shef Rogers, 'Copyright Payments in Eighteenth-Century Britain, 1701–1800', *Economics Discussion Papers*, no. 1506 (2015): 3–44.

Margot Finn, 'Anglo-Indian Lives in the Later Eighteenth and Early Nineteenth Centuries', *Journal for Eighteenth-Century Studies*, vol. 33, no. 1 (2010): 49–65.

Adam Fox, 'Printed Questionnaires, Research Networks and the Discovery of the British Isles, 1650–1800', *The Historical Journal*, vol. 53, no. 3 (2010): 593–621.

Henry R. French, 'The "Remembered Family" and Dynastic Senses of Identity Among the English Gentry c.1600–1800', *The Historical Research*, vol. 92, no. 257 (2019): 229–46.

Claire Gheeraert-Graffeuille, 'Lucy Hutchinson: bonne épouse ou femme rebelle?' in Marlène Bernos, Sandrine Parageau, and Laetitia Sansonetti (eds), *Les femmes et leurs représentations en Angleterre de la Renaissance aux Lumières* (Paris: Nouveau Monde Editions, 2009), 81–94.

Carlo Ginzburg, 'Family Resemblances and Family Trees: Two Cognitive Metaphors', *Critical Inquiry*, vol. 30, no. 3 (2004): 537–56.

Gabriel Glickman, 'Political Conflict and the Memory of the Revolution in England 1689–c.1750', in Stephen Taylor and Tim Harris (eds), *The Final Crisis of the Stuart Monarchy: The Revolutions of 1688–91 in Their British, Atlantic and European Contexts* (Woodbridge: Boydell Press, 2013), 243–71.

Amanda Goodrich, 'Understanding a Language of "Aristocracy", 1700–1850', *The Historical Journal*, vol. 56, no. 2 (2013): 369–98.

D. J. Greene, 'Jane Austen and the Peerage', *Modern Language Association*, vol. 68 (1953): 1017–31.

BIBLIOGRAPHY

Andrew Hanham, 'The Politics of Chivalry: Sir Robert Walpole, the Duke of Montagu and the Order of the Bath', *Parliamentary History*, vol. 35, no. 3 (2016): 262–97.

Sarah Hanley, 'Social Sites of Political Practices in France: Lawsuits, Civil Rights, and the Separation of Powers in Domestic and State Government, 1500–1800', *The American Historical Review*, vol. 102, no. 1 (1997): 27–52.

Tamara K. Haraven, 'What Difference Does it Make?', *Social Science History*, vol. 20, no. 3 (1996): 317–44.

Randolph C. Head, 'Documents, Archives, and Proof around 1700', *The Historical Journal*, vol. 56, no. 4 (2013): 909–30.

Derek Hirst, 'Remembering a Hero: Lucy Hutchinson's Memoirs of Her Husband', *EHR*, vol. 119 (2004): 682–91.

Tim Hitchcock, 'Confronting the Digital: Or How Academic History Writing Lost the Plot', *Cultural and Social History*, vol. 10, no. 1 (2013): 9–23.

Julian Hoppit, 'Sir Joseph Banks's Provincial Turn', *The Historical Journal*, vol. 61, no. 2 (2018): 403–29.

Thomas H. Hollingsworth, 'The Demography of the British Peerage', *Supplement to Population Studies*, vol. 18, no. 2 (1964): 73–6.

Winifred Hughes, 'Silver Fork Writers and Readers: Social Contexts of a Best Seller', *Novel*, vol. 25, no. 3 (1992): 328–47.

Ian Jackson, 'Approaches to the History of Readers and Reading in Eighteenth-Century Britain', *The Historical Journal*, vol. 47, no. 4 (2004): 1041–54.

E. H. Jacobs, 'Eighteenth-Century British Circulating Libraries and Cultural Book History', *Book History*, vol. 6 (2003): 1–22.

Stéphane Jettot, 'Les vaincus des guerres civiles: exil et réinvention de soi dans la gentry jacobite irlandaise (xviie–xviiie siècle)', in Emmanuel Dupraz and Claire Gheeraert-Graffeuille (dir.), *La Guerre Civile: représentations, idéalisations, identifications* (Rouen: PURH, 2014), 77–94.

Stéphane Jettot, 'Family Input in the Making of London Genealogical Directories in the 18th Century', in V. Bauer, F. Markus, and J. Eickmeyer (dir.), *Genealogical Knowledge in the Making: Tools, Practices, and Evidence in Early Modern Europe* (Oldenburg: De Gruyter, 2019), 169–98.

Stéphane Jettot and F.-J. Ruggiu, 'Cultures et pratiques généalogiques des élites anglaises (xvie–xixe siècle)', in Olivier Rouchon (dir.), *L'opération généalogique: cultures et pratiques européennes. XVe–XVIIIe siècle* (Rennes: PUR, 2014), 243–70.

Colin Jones, 'The Great Chain of Buying: Medical Advertisement, the Bourgeois Public Sphere, and the Origins of the French Revolution', *American Historical Review*, vol. 101, no. 1 (1996): 13–40.

Eric Ketelaar, 'The Genealogical Gaze: Family Identities and Family Archives in the Fourteenth to Seventeenth Centuries', *Libraries & the Cultural Record*, vol. 44, no. 1 (2009): 9–28.

Peter K. Klein, 'Insanity and the Sublime: Aesthetics and Theories of Mental Illness in Goya's Yard with Lunatics and Related Works', *Journal of the Warburg and Courtauld Institutes*, vol. 61 (1998): 198–252.

Mark Knights, 'The Tory Interpretation of History in the Rage of Parties', in Paulina Kewes (ed.), *The Uses of History in Early Modern England* (San Marino, Calif.: Huntington Library, 2006), 347–66.

Jennifer Kolpacoff Deane, Julie A. Eckerle, Michelle M. Dowd, and Megan Matchinske, 'Women's Kinship Networks: A Meditation on Creative Genealogies and Historical Labor', in Merry E. Wiesner-Hanks (ed.), *Mapping Gendered Routes and Spaces in the Early Modern World* (London: Routledge, 2015), 229–50.

BIBLIOGRAPHY 379

Paul Korshin, 'Types of Eighteenth-Century Literary Patronage', *Eighteenth-Century Studies*, vol. 7, no. 4 (1974): 453–73.

James M. Kuist, 'A Collaboration in Learning: "The Gentleman's Magazine" and Its Ingenious Contributors', *Studies in Bibliography*, vol. 44 (1991): 302–17.

Judith S. Lewis, 'When a House Is Not a Home: Elite English Women and the Eighteenth-Century Country House', *Journal of British Studies*, vol. 48, no. 2 (2009): 336–63.

Foteini Lika, 'Fact and Fancy in Nineteenth-Century Historiography and Fiction: The Case of Macaulay and Roidis', in Rens Bod, Jaa Maat, and Thijs Weststeijn (eds), *The Making of the Humanities*, vol. 2 (Amsterdam: Amsterdam UP, 2012), 149–67.

Michael Lobban, 'Henry Brougham and Law Reform', *EHR*, vol. 115 (2000): 1184–215.

William C. Lowe, 'George III, Peerage Creations and Politics, 1760–1784', *The Historical Journal*, vol. 35, no. 3 (1992): 587–609.

William. C. Lowe, 'Peers and Printers: The Beginning of Sustained Press Coverage of the House of Lords in the 1770s', *Parliamentary History*, vol. 7 (1988): 241–56.

Nicolas Lyon-Caen and Mathieu Marraud, 'Multiplicité et unité communautaire à Paris: appartenances professionnelles et carrières civiques, xviie–xviiie siècle', *Histoire urbaine*, vol. 40, no. 2 (2014), 19–35.

M. McCahill and E. Wasson, 'The New Peerage: Recruitment to the House of Lords, 1704–1847', *The Historical Journal*, vol. 46, no. 1 (2003): 1–38.

A. Malcomson, 'The Irish Peerage and the Act of Union 1800–1971', *Transactions of the Royal Historical Society*, vol. 10 (2000): 289–327.

Peter Mandler, '"In the olden time": Romantic History and English National Identity, 1820–1850', in L. Brockliss and D. Eastwood (eds), *A Union of Multiple Identities* (Manchester: Manchester UP, 1997), 78–92.

K. Maslen, 'Three Eighteenth-Century Reprints of the Castrated Sheets in Holinshed's Chronicles', *The Library*, 5th series, vol. 13 (1958): 120–4.

Frank Melton, 'Robert and Sir Francis Gosling: Eighteenth-Century Bankers and Stationers', in Robin Myers and Michael Harris (eds), *Economics of the British Book Trade 1605–1939* (Cambridge: Chadwyck-Healey, 1985), 60–77.

J. R. Milton, 'Benjamin Martyn, the Shaftesbury Family, and the Reputation of the First Earl of Shaftesbury', *The Historical Journal*, vol. 51, no. 2 (2008): 315–35.

Francesca Morgan, 'A Noble Pursuit? Bourgeois America's Uses of Lineage', in Sven Beckert and Julia B. Rosenbaum (eds), *The American Bourgeoisie: Distinction and Identity in the Nineteenth Century* (New York: Palgrave Macmillan, 2010), 135–51.

R. J. Morris, 'Voluntary Societies and the British Urban Elite, 1780–1850', *The Historical Journal*, vol. 26, no. 1 (1983): 95–118.

William Noblett, 'The Sale of James West Library in 1773', in John Hinks and Matthew Day (eds), *Compositor to Collector; Essays on Book Trade History* (London and New Castle, Del.: Oak Noll Press, 2012), 267–82.

David Norbrook, 'Memoirs and Oblivion: Lucy Hutchinson and the Restoration', *Huntington Library Quarterly*, vol. 75 (2012): 233–82.

Imogen Peck, "Of no sort of use"?: Manuscripts, Memory, and the Family Archive in Eighteenth Century England', *Cultural and Social History*, vol. 20, no. 2 (2023): 183–204.

Ruth Perry, '"All in the Family": Consanguinity, Marriage, and Property', in Peter Garside and Karen O'Brien (eds), *English and British Fiction. 1750–1820: The Oxford History of the Novel in English*, vol. 2 (Oxford: Oxford UP, 2015), 407–23.

Mark Salber Phillips, 'Reconsiderations on History and Antiquarianism: Arnaldo Momigliano and the Historiography of Eighteenth-Century Britain', *Journal of the History of Ideas*, vol. 57, no. 2 (1996): 297–316.

380 BIBLIOGRAPHY

Valérie Piétri, 'Les nobiliaires provinciaux et l'enjeu des généalogies collectives en France', in Olivier Rouchon (ed.), *L'opération généalogique: cultures et pratiques européennes, XVe–XVIIIe siècles* (Rennes: PUR, 2014), 213–43.

Linda Pollock, 'Rethinking Patriarchy and the Family in Seventeenth-Century England', *Journal of Family History*, vol. 23, no. 1 (1998): 3–27.

Olivier Poncet, 'Cercles savants et pratiques généalogiques en France (fin XVIe siècle-milieu du XVIIe siècle)', in Olivier Rouchon (ed.), *L'opération généalogique: cultures et pratiques européennes.* (Rennes: PUR, 2014), 101–40.

Olivier Poncet, 'The Genealogist at Work', in Jost Eickmeyer, Markus Friedrich, and Volker Bauer (eds), *Genealogical Knowledge in the Making: Tools, Practices, and Evidence in Early Modern Europe* (Oldenburg: De Gruyter, 2019), 199–221.

Julian Pooley, '"A Laborious and Truly Useful Gentleman": Mapping the Networks of John Nichols (1745–1826), Printer, Antiquary and Biographer', *Journal for Eighteenth-Century Studies*, vol. 38 no. 4 (2015): 497–509.

Kate Retford, 'Sensibility and Genealogy in the Eighteenth Century Family Portrait: The Collection at Kedleston Hall', *The Historical Journal*, vol. 46, no. 3 (2003): 533–60

Stephen K. Roberts, '"Ordering and Methodizing": *William Dugdale* in Restoration England', in Christopher Dyer and Catherine Richardson (eds), *William Dugdale, Historian, 1605–1686: His Life, His Writings and His County* (Woodbridge: Boydell Press, 2007), 66–88.

Nicholas Rogers, 'Money, Land and Lineage: The Big Bourgeoisie of Hanoverian London', *Social History*, vol. 4, no. 3 (1979): 437–54.

François-Joseph Ruggiu, 'The Urban Gentry in England, 1660–1780: A French Approach', *Historical Research,* vol. 74, no. 185 (2001): 249–70.

François-Joseph Ruggiu, 'Extraction, Wealth and Industry: The Ideas of Noblesse and of Gentility in the English and French Atlantics (17th–18th Centuries)', *History of European Ideas*, vol. 34, no. 4 (2008): 444–55.

François-Joseph Ruggiu, 'Histoire de la parenté ou anthropologie historique de la parenté? Autour de *Kinship in Europe*', *Annales de démographie historique*, vol. 119, no. 1 (2010), 223–56.

François-Joseph Ruggiu, Vincent Gourdon, and Cécile Alexandre, 'Les cultures familiales dans la France de la fin du XVIIe siècle au début du XIXe siècle', *Ohm: Obradoiro de Historia Moderna*, vol. 31 (2022): 1–34.

Michael John Sayer, 'English Nobility: The Gentry, the Heralds, and the Continental Context', *Norfolk Heraldry Society* (1979): 1–32.

Nicolas Schapira, 'Les sécrétaires particuliers sous l'Ancien Régime: les usages d'une dépendance', *Les Cahiers du Centre de Recherches Historiques*, vol. 40 (2007): 111–25.

Thomas P. Schofield, 'Conservative Political Thought in Britain in Response to the French Revolution', *The Historical Journal*, vol. 29, no. 3 (1986): 601–22.

Norbert Schürer, 'Four Catalogues of the Lowndes Circulating Library, 1755–66', *The Papers of the Bibliographical Society of America*, vol. 101, no. 3 (2007): 329–57.

Alexandra Shepard, 'From Anxious Patriarchs to Refined Gentlemen? Manhood in Britain, circa 1500–1700', *The Journal of British Studies*, vol. 44, no. 2 (2005): 281–95.

Ashley Sims, '"Selling Consumption": An Examination of Eighteenth-Century English Trade Cards', *Shift*, vol. 5 (2012): 1–22.

Max Skjönsberg, 'Lord Bolingbroke's Theory of Party and Opposition', *The Historical journal*, vol. 59, no. 4 (2016): 947–73.

Mark Stoyle, 'Remembering the English Civil Wars', in Peter Gray and Oliver Kendrick (eds), *The Memory of Catastrophe* (Manchester: Manchester University Press, 2014), 19–30.

Jon Stobart, 'Housekeeper, Correspondent and Confidante: The Under-Told Story of Mrs Hayes of Charlecote Park, 1744–73', *Family & Community History*, vol. 21, no. 2 (2018): 96–111.

Rosemary Sweet, 'Antiquaries and Antiquities in Eighteenth-Century England', *Eighteenth-Century Studies*, vol. 34, no. 2 (2001): 181–206.

Rosemary Sweet, 'Antiquarian Transformations in Historical Scholarship', in Elaine Chalus and Perry Gauci (eds), *Revisiting the Polite and Commercial People: Essays in Georgian Politics, Society and Culture in Honour of Professor Paul Langford* (Oxford: Oxford UP, 2019), 153–73.

Simon Targett, 'Government and |Ideology during the Age of Whig Supremacy: The Political Argument of Sir Robert Walpole's Newspaper Propagandists', *The Historical Journal*, vol. 37, no. 2 (1994): 289–317.

Michael Taylor, 'The British West India Interest and Its Allies, 1823–1833', *The English Historical Review*, vol. 133, no. 565 (2018): 1478–511.

Nigel Temple, 'Humphry Repton, Illustrator, and William Peacock's "Polite Repository," 1790–1811', *Garden History*, vol. 16, no. 2 (1988): 161–73.

Mark Towsey, '"I can't resist sending you the book": Private Libraries, Elite Women, and Shared Reading Practices in Georgian Britain', *Library & Information History*, vol. 29, no. 3 (2013): 210–22.

Federico Del Tredici, '"My desire would be to list them all": Lists of Nobility in the Cities of Central and Northern Italy (Late Middle Ages–Early Modern Period)', *Quaderni storici, Rivista quadrimestrale*, vol. 1 (2020): 139–58

Stéphane Van Damme, 'La grandeur d'Édimbourg: savoirs et mobilisation identitaire au XVIIIe siècle', *Revue d'histoire moderne & contemporaine*, vol. 55, no. 2 (2008): 152–81.

Denis Vincent and Milliot Vincent, 'Police et identification dans la France des Lumières', *Genèses*, vol. 54, no. 1 (2004): 4–27.

Dror Wahrman, 'National Society, Communal Culture: An Argument about the Recent Historiography of Eighteenth-Century Britain', *Social History*, vol. 17, no. 1 (1992): 43–72.

Dror Wahrman, 'The English Problem of Identity in the American Revolution', *The American Historical Review*, vol. 106, no. 4 (2001): 1236–62.

Alexandra Walsham, 'The Social History of the Archive: Record-Keeping in Early Modern Europe', *Past & Present*, vol. 230, no. 1 (2016): 9–48.

Ellis Archer Wasson, 'The House of Commons, 1660–1945: Parliamentary Families and the Political Elite', *The English Historical Review*, vol. 106, no. 420 (1991): 635–51.

Heather Wolfe and Peter Stallybrass, 'The Material Culture of Record-Keeping in Early Modern England', *Proceedings of the British Academy*, vol. 212 (2018): 179–208.

Daniel R. Woolf. 'A Feminine Past? Gender, Genre, and Historical Knowledge in England, 1500–1800', *American Historical Review*, vol. 102 (1997): 645–79.

Martin Wrede, 'De la haute noblesse à la semi-noblesse: formes d'existence nobiliaires en Europe au XVIIIe siècle', in Nicolas Le Roux and Martin Wrede (eds), *Noblesse oblige: identités et engagements aristocratiques à l'époque moderne* (Rennes: PUR, 2017), 47–71.

Karin Wulf, 'Bible, King and Common Law: Genealogical Literacies and Family History Practices in British America', *Early American Studies: An Interdisciplinary Journal*, vol. 10, no. 3 (2012): 467–502.

Natalie Zacek, 'West Indian Echoes: Dodington House, the Codrington Family and the Caribbean Heritage', in Madge Dresser and Andrew Hann (eds), *Slavery and the British Country House* (Swindon: English Heritage, 2013), 106–13.

Index

For the benefit of digital users, indexed terms that span two pages (e.g., 52–53) may, on occasion, appear on only one of those pages.

Abneys of Mesham Hal 293–5, 309–10
Act of Settlement 46–9
Acts of Union (1800) 138, 145
Addison, Joseph 23, 46, 155, 193–4
almanacs 73–4, 78–9, 83, 88, 90–1, 236–7
Almon, John 65–7, 69–70, 72–3, 88, 94, 236–8, 297
All Souls College 61–2, 217
Allan, William 149, 156–7
Allan, George 156–7, 252–4
Ancients and the Moderns 45–6, 259
Anstis, John 245
antiquarianism and antiquarians 44, 50–1, 78–9, 230, 243–5, 266–70, 272–3, 303
Archdall, Mervyn 200–2, 257–8
Ashmole, Elias 243–5, 263
Ashe, Sir James 121–2, 205
Assheton, Sir Ralph 186–7
Austen, Jane 72–4
Authority 16–17, 30, 62, 145, 214, 220, 238–41, 257–9, 261–2, 267–8, 270–1, 278–9, 282–3, 285–6
Authorship 16, 23, 78–9, 90–1, 108, 220–1, 230, 233–9, 242–3, 248–50, 255–6, 262–3, 270–1, 275–7, 279, 292

Bacon, Sir Francis 115, 155, 274–5
Banks, Sir Joseph 266–7, 270, 288–9
Banks, Thomas Christopher 266–7
Barlow, Frederic 105–9
Beckwith, Sir Roger 81–2, 99, 122, 129–31, 182
Bedford, duke of 1–2, 191–2, 246–7
Beltz, George Frederick 260–5
Bennetts of Pythouse 155–6, 189–90, 268–9
Berry, William 257–61
Betham, William 90–1, 98–9, 131–48, 167–8, 174–6, 182, 198–9, 214–16, 267, 272, 299–301
Betham Mathilda 133–7, 196–8
Betham, William Jr 137–8, 146–7, 193–4, 282–3
Blackstone, Sir William 216–17, 257–8
Blome, Richard 57–8, 82, 234–5
Blounts of Soddington 205–7

Bolingbroke, Viscount 62, 246–7, 249–50
Bond, Thomas 120–4, 128–9, 177–8, 187–8
Bradshaigh, Sir Roger 121–3, 125
British Museum 53, 176, 182, 253, 259, 271, 276–7
Brooke, Arthur 273–5
Brougham, Henry 149, 153–4, 258–9
Broun family 80–1, 177–8
Brydges, Sir Egerton 3–4, 24–5, 44, 50, 89, 149, 157–8, 257–8, 261–5, 303
Burke, Edmund 1, 51–2, 279–80
Burke, John 3–4, 7–8, 19–20, 80, 115–16, 150–66, 186, 220–4, 280–7, 291–3
Burke, Sir John Bernard 161, 228, 291–3
Bute, earl of 61–7, 144–5, 249–50

Camden's Britannia 57–8, 136–7, 157, 176, 182–4, 234–5, 268–9
Catholic Emancipation 154–5, 165–6, 280–5
Cavendish, William 65–8, 108
Chamberlain, Edward 37, 119–20, 122
Chandos, duke of 107, 251, 261–3
Charles I 58–9, 99, 126–8, 187–8, 223–4, 280
Charles II 125–8, 177–8, 243–5, 289–91, 297–8, 302–3
Charlton, Edmund Lechmere 178–9, 227–8
catalogue 69–70, 78, 85–6, 92–6, 108, 119–20, 178–9, 252–3, 274–5, 277–8
Catton, Charles 55–6, 60
Civil War 69, 120–1, 125–6, 128–9, 177–8, 280–1
Class 3–6, 15, 38–40, 67, 75, 91–2, 94–5, 104, 109–10, 148, 153, 259, 280
coats of arms 39–40, 56, 60, 68, 88–9, 115, 131–3, 178–9, 195–6, 234–5, 257–8, 273–4, 297–8
Codringtons of Barbados 220–4
Colburn, Henry 72–3, 149–51, 280, 285, 297–9
College of Arms 7–8, 38, 60–2, 64–5, 68, 131, 172–3, 199–200, 203, 210, 217, 220–1, 238–9, 243–5, 252–3, 256–8, 260, 263, 269–70, 273–4, 296, 303
Collins, Arthur 1, 3–4, 6, 11–12, 44–9, 81–2, 120–1, 218, 235–6, 243–8, 262, 273, 275–80, 288–91

384 INDEX

colonial families 96–7, 122–3, 126–8, 140–3, 154–5, 157–9, 179–80, 219–21
copyrights 1–2, 19–20, 27–8, 85–90, 236–7
Cotton Collection 277–9
Courthope, William 182–4, 207–9, 213–14, 219–20
Court of Chancery 217, 219–20, 223–4
Craftsman 115–16, 186–7, 242–3, 246, 276–7
Crawfurd, George 58–60
Crowley, Aaron 60, 257–8

Dallaway, James 14–15, 69, 268–9
Dillon, Frances 133, 174
Disraeli, Benjamin 150–1, 280
Domesday Book 148, 251–2
Drury, George Vandeput 214–17
Debrett, John 3, 72–3, 75, 80, 93–4, 111–12, 151, 223–4, 236–7, 297, 310–11
Douglas, Robert 28, 61, 69–70, 95–6, 285–6
Duchesne, André 14, 287–8
Dugdale, Sir William 14, 42–3, 45, 57–8, 69–70, 76–9, 176–7, 234–5, 243–5, 253, 266–7, 269–70, 272, 277–9, 303

East India Company 3, 41, 126–8, 144–8, 212–13, 215–16, 263
Edmondson, Joseph 61–2, 65, 83–4, 251, 253
Elizabeth Ist 148–9, 161–3, 178–9, 256–7, 259–60
emotions 4–5, 9–10, 71–4, 76–8, 97–8, 100–1, 119–20, 203–22, 259, 285, 291–3, 308
Enlightenment 12–13, 24, 42–3, 53–4, 230, 250–1, 268–9
Etherington, Henry Sir 140–4
Evelyn, Sir John 39–40, 175–6, 302–3

fiction 42–3, 58, 72, 75, 83, 188, 193, 224–5, 228–9, 246, 261, 280, 285
forgery 256–7, 263, 267, 296
Freeman, Edward Augustus 5–6, 228–30, 233
French Revolution 6, 14–15, 51–2, 68, 89, 111, 132–3, 193–4, 240–1, 279–80, 303
Fuller, Thomas 23, 274–5

gentility 15, 39–40, 46, 124–5, 152, 199–200, 233, 236–7, 258–9, 287–8
Gentleman's Magazine 61, 85–6, 90–1, 111–12, 115, 149, 193, 237, 239–40, 258–61, 264–5, 270–1, 275–7, 279–80, 288–9, 303
George I 53, 106–7, 122, 132–3
George II 247–9, 298–9
George III 61–2, 65, 105, 108–9, 132, 249–50, 257–8
Gibbon, Edward 42–4, 234–5

Glorious Revolution 46–7, 120–1, 124, 126–8, 166, 278–9
Godwin, William 236–7, 240–1
Gosling, Robert 87–8, 277–8
gossip 73, 97–9, 101, 104–6, 212–13, 274–5
Great Reform Act 152–4, 265, 280, 295–6, 303
Guillim, John 1, 40, 178–9
Guises of Rendcomb Hall 205–7
Guthrie, William 61–2, 65, 90, 105–6, 248–51

hacks 49, 112, 233, 237–8, 240–1, 267–8
Harley, earl of 46, 53, 78, 96–7, 243–5, 252–3, 266, 279
Henniker, Sir John 138–40, 143–4, 147
Heylin, Peter 87–8, 176
Hippisley, Sir John Coxe 136–7, 141–3, 184
Holinshed's Chronicles 60, 274–5
Holman, William 273, 297–8, 303
honour 3–5, 14–15, 17, 27–8, 30, 39–40, 45–6, 50–2, 55, 58–9, 61–2, 65, 67, 72–4, 81–2, 84, 87–8, 105–6, 108–12, 132–3, 138, 148–9, 152–5, 173, 186, 199, 208–9, 237–8, 242, 246–7, 250, 259–60, 276, 296
Hume, David 44, 235–8, 275–6, 278–9, 283–4
heraldry 1, 13–14, 39–41, 69, 80–1, 234–5, 257–60, 268–9, 282

Innes Anna, Eliza, and Maria 11–12, 75–6, 196–8
Inglis, Sir Robert Harry 133–6, 143–5, 175–6, 282

Jacob, Alexander 61, 251–2
James, Duke of York (later James II) 126–8, 207–8
Jenner, Charles 75–6, 81
Jerningham, Sir William 133, 143–4, 147
Johnson, Richard 237–9, 271–2
Johnson, Samuel 65, 146–7, 155, 235–6, 250
Jacobites 12–13, 137–8, 251–2, 283–4

Kearsley George and Catherine 19–20, 30–2, 236–7
Kimber, Edward 19–20, 28, 69–70, 88–9, 95–6, 105, 237–9
Kingdom, William 32–3, 41

Le Neve, Peter 80, 87–8, 100, 272–3
ledger book 24, 88, 237–8
library 39–40, 55–9, 78–9, 94, 175–6, 184–5, 277
Lhuyd, Edward 78, 234–5
lineage 6–7, 12–13, 16–17, 43–5, 54, 56, 70, 75–8, 96, 105, 148–9, 155–6, 184–5, 190–1, 195–6, 204–5, 208–9, 218, 242, 245–6, 266, 268–9

Lister, Thomas-Henry 157–8, 176–7
Lloyd, Gamaliel 98, 147–8, 165–6, 168, 174
Lloyd, William, Horton 168, 170–1
Lodge, John 14, 53, 77–8, 96, 200–1, 237, 257–8
Lombe, Sir Edward 140–1, 174
London Season 78, 83–4, 88–9, 150, 280–1
Longmate, Barak 42–3, 61, 89, 108–9, 240–1, 276–8
Louis XIV 138–40, 158–9, 199–200
Lowndes, Thomas 69–70, 72–3, 86, 88–9, 94, 235–41
Lygon, William Sir 143–5, 174

Maclellan, Sholto Henry 207–9
marginalia 77–80, 101–4
Marlborough, duke of 63–7, 195–6
masculinity 47–9, 173–4, 192, 203, 264–5
middling sort 1–2, 12–13, 25, 76–7, 83–5, 90–1, 97–8, 215–16, 230, 234–5, 239–40, 306
Millar, Andrew 58–9, 94, 235–6

natural history 12–13, 59–60, 189–90, 266, 268–9, 286–7
network 7, 10–11, 14–15, 24, 37–9, 57–8, 85–6, 90–6, 128–31, 144–7, 150–1, 167, 171, 187–8, 200–3, 251, 269–70, 273, 301–3
Newcastle 247–8
Nichols, Francis 26–8, 38–40, 72–3, 83, 235–7, 257–8
Nichols, John 85–6, 90–2, 106, 111–12, 136–7, 159–60, 236–8, 252–3, 270–1, 275, 298–9, 303
Nichols, John Gough 238–9, 286–7
Nicolas, Nicholas Harris 91–2, 193–4, 219, 228
Noble, Mark 52, 218, 240–1, 253, 259, 271–2, 276–7
Norman Conquest 14–15, 45–6, 106–7, 141–3, 146, 153–6, 165–7, 177–8, 182, 207, 216, 228, 241–2, 266, 278–9, 294–5, 303

Paine, Thomas 111–12, 240–1, 292–3
partisanship 46–7, 63–4, 107
patriarchy 17, 75, 103–5, 172–3, 195–6, 206–7, 308
patronage 61–2, 68, 88, 110–11, 133–6, 144–5, 147–8, 152, 242–54, 290–1, 300–1
Payne, Thomas 92–3, 261–2
Paynes of St Kitt 219–20
Peck, Francis 273–5
pedigree 16–17, 40–1, 50–1, 60, 65, 71, 140–4, 160–3, 173–8, 182–5, 228–30, 233–4, 238–40, 242, 257–9, 284, 291
Peel, Sir Robert 138–43, 152
Peerage Bill 2–3, 45–6, 245

Perrott, Sir Richard 237–40
Pitt, William, the Younger 51, 138, 144–5, 263
Phillipps, Sir Thomas 30, 158–9, 193–4, 280–1
Playfair, William 6, 14–15, 24–5, 68, 255–6
pocketbooks 21, 24, 57, 61, 70, 73–4, 83, 90, 240–1, 306
Pope, Alexander 106–7, 206–7, 210, 230, 233–4, 250

race 42–3, 46, 51–2, 177–81, 205–6, 229–30, 238–9, 294–5, 303
Restoration 25, 51–4, 57–8, 77–8, 120–4, 290, 302–3
Rickards-Mynors, Peter 209
Rivington, John 88–9, 240–1, 261–2
Robinson, George 237–8, 240–1
Roper, Abel 45, 87–8, 243–5
Royal Society 51–2, 72, 87–8, 168, 179–80, 247–8, 266, 269–70, 272–3, 280–2

Salmon, Nathaniel 27–8, 30
Salmon, Thomas 41, 47–9
Savile, Gertrude 71–2
satire 104–5, 108–11, 114, 280
Saxons 228, 272–3, 281–2
Scott, Sir Walter 159–60, 281–6
Segar, Sir William 30, 198–9, 243–5
Seymour, Sir Edward 47–9, 63–4
Sidney papers 218, 242, 247–8, 278–9
Sloane, Hans 252–3, 273
Smith, Adam 110–11, 157–8, 173
Smollett, Tobias 65–7, 235–8, 283–4
Smith, William 19–20, 30
Smyth, Robert 100–4, 272
Society of Antiquaries 91–2, 133–7, 164–5, 175–6, 228, 253, 261, 266, 269–73, 276–7, 300, 303
Staatskalender 8–9, 26–7
Stockdale, John 30–2, 93–4, 236, 297
Strahan, William 63–4, 87–9, 94, 235–6
subscriptions 57–8, 60, 95–6, 132–3, 167, 242–3, 252–3
Sullivan, Richard Joseph 133–7, 139, 146–7, 201–2

tables 25–7, 41, 132–3, 136–7, 140–1, 252–3
Terry, James 199–200
The Times 258–9, 292–3
Thackeray, William M. 72–4, 77–8
Thorpe, John 273–5
Tower of London 121, 125, 246–7, 271–2, 278–9
Treaty of Union (1707) 46–7, 58–9, 63–4, 306

386 INDEX

trust 12–13, 37–8, 62, 98–9, 104–5, 115, 131, 166, 202, 228, 230, 234–5, 237–8, 256–61, 273, 275, 289, 297–9, 304, 310
Twisleton, Thomas-James 211–12
Twisleton, Julia Eliza 211–12, 217

Walpole, Robert 62, 65–7, 81–2, 128, 242, 245–8, 251–2

Walpole, Horace 78–9, 242–3, 247–8
Walrond, Bethell 158–60, 222–4
Walrond, Henry 220–4
Wilkes, John 52, 104–5, 238–9, 249–50
Wotton, Thomas 37, 81–2, 88, 112, 115–16, 119–31, 173–4, 186, 188–9, 204–5, 218, 271–5, 293–9, 301–2